ERASMUS DARWIN

Desmond King-Hele is the leading authority on Erasmus Darwin, having studied his life and work for three decades. Dr King-Hele has had a distinguished career as a space scientist at the Royal Aircraft Establishment at Farnborough, where his mathematical analyses of satellite orbits led to many discoveries about the Earth's gravity field and upper atmosphere. He was elected a Fellow of the Royal Society in 1966. More recently he has served for nine years as Chairman of the British National Committee for the History of Science, and for seven years as editor of *Notes and Records of the Royal Society*, the Society's journal on the history of science. He has written fifteen books, including a literary study *Shelley: his Thought and Work*, two books of poems, and five books on satellites. His previous books on Darwin include *Erasmus Darwin and the Romantic Poets* and the standard edition of *The Letters of Erasmus Darwin*.

Also by Desmond King-Hele

Shelley: his Thought and Work
Satellites and Scientific Research
Essential Writings of Erasmus Darwin (ed.)
The End of the Twentieth Century?
Poems and Trixies
Doctor of Revolution
The Letters of Erasmus Darwin (ed.)
Observing Earth Satellites
Animal Spirits
The R.A.E. Table of Earth Satellites, 1957–1990 (ed.)
Erasmus Darwin and the Romantic Poets
Satellite Orbits in an Atmosphere
John Herschel, 1792–1871 (ed.)
A Tapestry of Orbits

Erasmus Darwin

A LIFE OF UNEQUALLED ACHIEVEMENT

by

DESMOND KING-HELE

dlm

for Rosemary

———————

First published in 1999
by Giles de la Mare Publishers Limited
3 Queen Square, London WC1N 3AU

Typeset by Tom Knott
Printed in Great Britain by
Hillman Printers (Frome) Limited
All rights reserved

A CIP record of this book is available
from the British Library

ISBN 1-900357-08-9

Contents

Illustrations

FIGURES

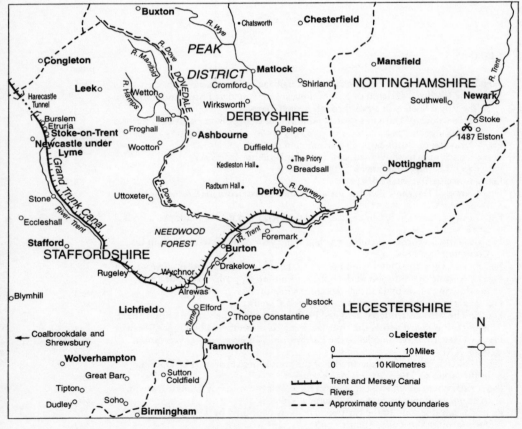

Sketch map showing the locations of places figuring in Darwin's life

Preface

Erasmus Darwin lived from 1731 until 1802. My interest in him began in the 1960s, and I soon became convinced that no one from his time to ours has rivalled him in achieving so much in subjects so widely varied: hence the subtitle of this book.

Darwin was a physician by profession, the foremost practitioner of the English Midlands. In the 1790s he became the most famous of medical men after the publication of his treatise *Zoonomia*. At this time he was already recognized as the leading English poet of the day, having been extravagantly praised for his long poem *The Botanic Garden*. Though his pre-eminence as a poet soon passed, he had a surprising influence over Blake, Wordsworth, Coleridge and Shelley – a theme discussed in my book *Erasmus Darwin and the Romantic Poets* (1986).

In person Darwin was friendly, sociable and full of teasing humour. He had two wives, an in-between mistress, fourteen children and dozens of lifelong friends, including Franklin, Wedgwood, Boulton and Watt. His gift for friendship enabled him to recruit the members of the Lunar Society of Birmingham, which is often seen as the main intellectual powerhouse of the Industrial Revolution in England. Darwin himself had a passion for machines: he was an obsessive inventor of mechanical devices, among them a speaking machine, a copying machine and the steering technique used in modern cars.

The most profound of his talents, in my view, was scientific insight, in physics, chemistry, geology, meteorology and all of biology. It was Darwin who first explained how clouds form and described the full process of photosynthesis in plants. While in his thirties he came to believe in biological evolution, as we now call it, and after twenty years of silence he publicized these ideas. He failed to convince the world. Instead he was condemned for denying God's role as creator of species, and he lost his popularity as a poet too. Undaunted, he wrote a long poem tracing the progress of life from microscopic specks in primeval seas through fishes and amphibians to humankind, as he calls us.

Much of Darwin's life was poorly documented when I wrote a biography of him in the mid 1970s, entitled *Doctor of Revolution*. More letters emerged soon afterwards, and my edition of *The Letters of Erasmus Darwin* in 1981 included 272 letters, mostly from his later years.

Then, in 1990, George Pember Darwin made a further large donation of family papers to Cambridge University Library. Among these were 174 lengthy 'new' letters written by Erasmus Darwin and hundreds of other manuscripts relevant to his life.

In my previous biography I was usually looking in from the outside. In this new book, with quotations from more than two hundred of the newly-available manuscripts, Erasmus Darwin can often speak for himself, and the result is far more illuminating. Of course the main facts of his life are unchanged, and the quotations from previously known letters are much the same as before. Also, when describing Darwin's books and inventions, I often reuse my previous wording in shortened form. But most of this book is new, with much more about his wives, his children, his mistress, his home life and his friends. The new manuscripts have led to a number of new interpretations, some speculative, although I have been wary of imputing motives.

Throughout the book I refer to Darwin as 'Erasmus' in his home life, and as 'Darwin' in more formal situations. In transcribing manuscripts I have followed the code of practice in *The Letters of Erasmus Darwin*. In the index I have added the dates of birth and death (if known) for Darwin's contemporaries.

CHAPTER ONE

Upbringing
1731–1756

If you ask where the Darwins come from, you can find an answer four miles south-west of Newark, inside Elston village church, where eighteen memorial slabs for Darwins from 1654 to 1990 occupy most of the wall area.

Elston is set among flat and fertile fields in the extensive valley of the river Trent, about two miles east of the river. The village appears in the Domesday Book as 'Elveston' and kept its coherence through the medieval period. With its ancient history, a church dating from before 1300, a rectory and a big house – Elston Hall – this is an archetypal English flatland village where nothing much seems to happen.

But 500 years ago the peaceful-looking fields west of Elston saw a scene of carnage never since exceeded on English soil. Seven thousand men died there on 16 June 1487 during the crucial battle of Stoke Field[1] that decided the future course of English history by establishing Henry VII and the Tudor dynasty on the throne. The boy impostor Lambert Simnel had been crowned as 'Edward VI' in Ireland a month before, and an army supporting him roamed unopposed in northern England. The army was led by John de la Pole, Earl of Lincoln, who was the nephew and designated successor of Richard III, killed two years earlier in the relatively bloodless battle of Bosworth Field. The battle of Stoke Field was desperate: neither side gave way in three hours of heavy fighting. Lincoln, all his main commanders and 4000 of his men were killed. Simnel was captured and became a menial in the household of Henry VII. But if Henry had gone down with the 3000 of his men who were killed, we would not have had Henry VIII or Queen Elizabeth. After the battle many of the bodies remained in the fields between Elston and the even smaller village of Stoke, a mile north-west. For centuries people digging there ran the risk of unearthing human bones.

At the time of this battle the Darwins had not arrived at Elston: they were yeomen of Marton, Lincolnshire, in the Trent valley fifteen miles north of Newark. During the sixteenth and seventeenth centuries the Darwins continued to live chiefly in Lincolnshire;[2] they grew more prosperous and professional, William Darwin (1620–75) being a bencher of Lincoln's Inn and Recorder of Lincoln. His son William Darwin (1655–82) was married in 1680 to Ann (1662–1722), daughter of Robert Waring, and this marriage brought Elston Hall into the family. William and Ann were Erasmus's grandparents: their second son, born two weeks before his father's death, was Erasmus's father Robert Darwin (1682–1754). Robert became a barrister of Lincoln's Inn in 1709 and inherited Elston Hall in 1722 on his mother's death. Two years later, at the age of forty-two, he retired from his profession, married Elizabeth Hill (1702–97) and settled at Elston Hall. Robert and Elizabeth Darwin had seven children in as many years, Erasmus being the youngest – born on 12 December 1731.

[2]

Little is known of Robert Darwin (Plate 2A) but that little is of great interest. Robert had a taste for science, and it was thanks to him that the first known fossilized skeleton of a Jurassic reptile was brought to the attention of the scientific world, in 1718. The fossil, embedded in a stone slab about three feet long and two feet broad, was a substantial portion of a plesiosaur, comprising sixteen vertebrae, nine ribs and other bones (Fig. 1). Plesiosaurs were the marine counterparts of dinosaurs and, in competition with ichthyosaurs, ruled the waters two hundred million years ago. Robert Darwin's fossil, from a plesiosaur about ten feet long, was found in a slab used face-down as a 'landing-place' beside the well at Elston Rectory, just across the road from the Hall. People at Elston thought the skeleton was human – another grisly relic of the battle. Robert showed the stone to Dr William Stukeley, the antiquary and friend of Sir Isaac Newton, and persuaded the rector, Mr South, to offer it to the Royal Society. At its meeting on 11 December 1718 the Royal Society accepted the stone as a gift for their 'Repository', or museum.

Stukeley rewarded Robert Darwin by introducing him as one of two guests at the Royal Society's next meeting, a week later, presided over as usual by Newton. The Fellows of the Society inspected the fossil on 12 February 1719 and concluded that it was probably not a known terrestrial animal but 'some Sea fish or amphibious creature'.[3] Not a bad guess! Stukeley himself wrote a paper about the fossil, published in the *Philosophical Transactions*: he calls it 'a rarity, the like whereof has not been observ'd before in this Island', and says 'it cannot be reckon'd Human, but seems to be a *Crocodile* or *Porpoise*'.[4] Later, after speculations about the Flood, he remarks that such fossils are usually 'amphibious or marine animals'. All this was surprisingly perceptive at a time when Jurassic rep-

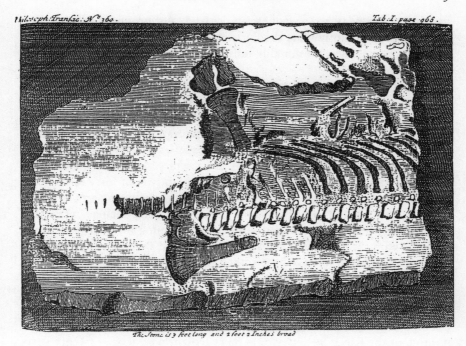

Philosoph. Transac. N° 360.   *Tab. I. page 965.*

The Stone is 3 feet long and 2 foot 2 Inches broad

FIG. 1 The fossilized skeleton of part of a plesiosaur found at Elston and presented to the Royal Society in 1718 through Robert Darwin. It was nearly a century before a more complete specimen was unearthed. This fossil is now on display at the Natural History Museum in London. From *Philosophical Transactions* (1719)

tiles were quite unknown to science. More such bones were found later in the century,[5] but systematic classification of plesiosaurs only began after Mary Anning discovered a complete skeleton at Lyme Regis in 1823.

Robert Darwin's fossil still exists and is on display among the plesiosaur skeletons in the Natural History Museum in London: it is classified as *Plesiosaurus dolichodeirus*, and its age is estimated as 194–208 million years. Robert has never received any credit for his scientific coup, which is a most appropriate preface to the theories of biological evolution later to be propounded by Erasmus and his grandson Charles.

Soon after his moment of glory as an honoured guest at the Royal Society, Robert was involved in a much less creditable incident at Lincoln's Inn, when he took his dog into the Hall. This was against the rules, but when the porter tried to turn the dog out, 'the said Mr Darwin did offer to fling a pot at the Porter's head, and threatened to knock him downe; whereby the said Porter was intimidated'.[6] Summoned to attend a Council meeting on 11 May 1719, Robert apologized 'and promised to offend no more'. If he could intimidate the Porter (and it was the Head Porter, James Jackson), Robert was presumably tall and sturdy like so many of the male Darwins.

A little later Robert Darwin became a member of the Gentleman's Society of Spalding,[7] founded in 1712 by Maurice Johnson, a friend of Stukeley (who came from Holbeach, not far away). This was one of the earliest and most enduring of literary-antiquarian societies, and seems to have been a model for the Society of Antiquaries in London, which was formally set up in 1717, with Stukeley as Secretary. Although Spalding is a small town in a sparsely populated area of fen-land about forty miles north of Cambridge, its Society achieved national eminence in the 1720s. There were twelve 'regular members' and numerous 'extra-regular members', including Robert Darwin. He was probably recruited in the 1720s, along with Newton, Stukeley, Sir Hans Sloane, Richard Bentley and Alexander Pope. They all seem to have been rather inactive members. But perhaps the idea filtered through to Erasmus: the Lunar Society of Birmingham, of which he was co-founder, had about twelve regular members and unwritten rules somewhat resembling the rules of the Spalding Society.

For Robert the memory of being presented to Sir Isaac Newton at a meeting of the Royal Society would have grown sweeter after twenty years of rural retirement at Elston. If he talked about it to his family he may have given Erasmus the idea of becoming a Fellow of the Royal Society at the earliest opportunity.

After these glimpses of Robert as 'a person of curiosity' (Stukeley's phrase) and as a person of passion, we can see him in another role, as a fairly dutiful son. In 1745, twenty years after his mother's death, he fulfilled the terms of her will by asking for permission to build four cottages as 'Ann Darwin's hospital' for 'four poor impotent widows'.[8]

Robert himself was never wealthy, but Elston Hall (Plate 2C) provided a substantial roof over his head, and his children grew up in modest affluence. After his father's death, Erasmus characterized Robert as a man

> of more sense than learning; of very great industry in the law, even after he had no business, nor expectation of any. He was frugal, but not covetous; very tender to his children, but still kept them at an awful kind of distance. He passed through this life with honesty and industry, and brought up seven healthy children to follow his example.[9]

The seven healthy children defied the current infant mortality rate (forty per cent in Nottingham) and lived to ages between fifty-seven and ninety-two. If Erasmus is to be believed, all the boys took their father as a role-model. Certainly none of them revolted against him: all pursued respectable careers, as he would have wished, with the eldest (Robert Waring) as squire of Elston, William a lawyer of Gray's Inn, John a clergyman and Erasmus a physician.

If little is known of Robert, still less is known of Erasmus's mother Elizabeth (Plate 2B). She must have contributed to his robust good health, for she not only survived the hard labour of bearing seven children in seven years but even thrived on it: she lived to the ripe age of ninety-four, and 'to the last day of her life got up to feed her pigeons'. Erasmus usually visited her at Christmas or Easter in later years and was with her a few weeks before she died. The only judgment on her in Erasmus's letters is decisive: 'a better mother never existed', he wrote when she was ninety-three. Elizabeth's reputation in the family was as a woman of strong character, capable, practical and scholarly. She may have been more than her husband could cope with, to judge from 'a sort of litany' he wrote, that was handed down in the family:

> From a morning that doth shine,
> From a boy that drinketh wine,
> From a wife that talketh Latine,
>   Good Lord deliver me.[10]

So Robert may have fretted at his marriage[11] and distanced himself by working in his study over-assiduously. If he did withdraw, keeping 'an awful kind of distance', his wife presumably influenced all her children quite powerfully.

There is no sign in her children's letters of any open reaction against Elizabeth, but she may have rather smothered two of her sons, who stayed at Elston and remained bachelors. The eldest, Robert Waring, a lawyer by profession, seems to have lived with her at Elston Hall as head of the family and lord of the manor. He was seventy-two when she died: if he had ever wished to escape, it was too late by then. Her third son, John, became rector of Elston in 1766 in succession to Mr South, and lived across the road. Her three daughters moved away from Elston: Elizabeth, the eldest, married the Revd Thomas Hall, rector of a parish seven miles away; the other two, Ann and Susannah, both lived unmarried at Sleaford, twenty miles off.

Dates and details of Erasmus's brothers and sisters, children and grand-children may be found in the family tree on pages 374–5. The best collection of family portraits is in Karl Pearson's *Life of Francis Galton*[12]. The name Erasmus came into the family from Erasmus Earle, serjeant at law to Oliver Cromwell: Earle's daughter Anne married Robert Darwin's grand-father, the lawyer William Darwin; and one of Robert's uncles was named Erasmus.

[3]

As a child, Erasmus was called 'Mus' or 'Rasee'. With three elder brothers and three elder sisters to bait him, he had an unsheltered childhood. According to his son Robert, he was 'of a bold disposition', but 'a series of bad accidents made a deep impression on his mind' and he became very cautious:

> When he was about five years old he received an accidental blow on the middle of his head from a maid-servant and ever afterwards a white lock of hair grew there. Later on, when fishing with his brothers, they put him into a bag with only his feet out, and being thus blinded he walked into the river and was very nearly drowned.[13]

His eldest brother Robert said that Erasmus 'had always a dislike to much exercise and rural diversions, and it was with great difficulty that we could ever persuade him to accompany us'.[14] If their idea of 'rural diversions' was putting him in a bag, his reluctance is not surprising. But he did sometimes indulge in country pursuits, and once, when he was eight, he went hunting with his brother John, who was a year older. The event was recorded by Robert in 'A new song in praise of two young hunters':

> One morning this winter from school J.D. came
> And him and his brother Erasmus went out to kill game
> And as it happened which was very rare
> With hounds and 2 spaniels kil'd a fine hair.

The young author's grammar and scansion collapse completely in the second verse, so we may pass to the third:

> One of the dogs catched her by the head,
> Which made Erasmus Darwin cry 'war dead war dead'.
> But John Darwin the dogs he could not hear
> Because he only cried out 'war, war, war'.[15]

In later life Robert Darwin was a meticulous writer, and he would have been shocked to know that this nearly illegible farrago has survived for us to read.

As a boy Erasmus was 'always fond of mechanicks'. Robert remembered him 'when very young making an ingenious alarum for his watch; he used also to show little experiments in electricity with a rude apparatus he then invented with a bottle'.[16] This early interest in mechanics and electricity seems to have been innate rather than taught, and stayed with him throughout his life.

In 1741, when Erasmus was nearly ten, the two young hunters were packed off to Chesterfield School, where Robert, now seventeen, was one of the senior boys. Between 1722 and 1752 the headmaster of Chesterfield

School was the Revd William Burrow, 'a very good and understanding teacher', and under his guidance 'the school became the leading establishment in the north of England',[17] with about three boys per year going on to Cambridge. After Burrow retired, the school's reputation declined. Erasmus was fortunate to have sampled Chesterfield School at its best.

At school as at home Erasmus was much influenced by his eldest brother Robert. Two of Robert's likings, for botany and for poetry, seem to have been passed on to Erasmus. The influence was strongest with poetry, and the two wrote to each other in verse. When towards the end of his life Erasmus put together a volume of manuscript poems, some of them juvenile, he dedicated it 'To my brother Robert Waring Darwin Esquire, by whose example and encouragement my mind was directed to the study of Poetry in my very early years'.[18] Robert modestly remarked that Erasmus 'was always fond of poetry', without mentioning his own role as a teacher.

Most of the poems written by Erasmus as a teenager are school exercises on set subjects. Some of them already reveal independence of thought as well as skill in verse. 'The Poetic Bridle'[19] probably written when he was fifteen, takes seventy-two lines to tell us about a learned young poet called Hal, who 'met with an equestrian muse' and mounted her for a 'journey to Parnassus'. Stung by a 'Critic gadfly', she tossed her head, broke the bridle and threw him. The doctor was called, and bled him:

Cup after cup in foamy rills
The only stream of life distills.

After this ritual blood-letting, the doctor ('looking sad') says 'I fear your case is somewhat bad'. This is a sharp critique of Erasmus's future profession. Later, after years of medical training, he had to go along with the idea that bleeding might be an appropriate treatment, especially if patients expected it. The poem is also critical of the profession of poetry, implying that clever literary types are jumped-up gents riding for a fall.

Another curious 'school exercise' is a recipe for writing sublime verse, and takes the form of a dialogue between a bookseller and a poet.[20] The bookseller proposes violent methods for waking 'the leaden-pinioned muse' and offers to whip the poet, who complains that your 'flagellating rules' would 'scare the muses'. So the bookseller changes tack: a glass of punch, he says, can make the poet sing, just as it makes 'physicians meditate their fees', lawyers ponder their pleas and priests dream 'of fatter livings'. Schoolboy irreverence is here developing into a precocious maturity critical of all the professions. The format of the poem is arresting because it seems to be the model for the discussion on the nature of poetry between bookseller and poet in the Interludes of *The Loves of the Plants* forty years later. The Beaux and Belles of that poem can also be found here, as well as

Darwin's habit of coining new words, such as the verb flagellate[21] and the inventive 'leaden-pinioned'.

Being inventive in science proved more dangerous for Erasmus and for his school friend Lord George Cavendish, second son of the Duke of Devonshire. One day they were playing with gunpowder together: it exploded, and Erasmus was quite badly hurt. This was another of the accidents that made the bold and active boy more cautious. His friendship with Cavendish remained undamaged by the explosion, and was probably useful later in bringing Darwin two important patients – Cavendish's nephew the fifth Duke of Devonshire and Georgiana, his Duchess.

Another very nasty accident suffered by Erasmus, presumably in his schooldays, was an attack of smallpox; in later life his face was said to bear 'the traces of a severe smallpox'.

The Darwins were a close-knit family, numerous enough to be socially self-sufficient. Erasmus's only recorded friend at Elston outside the family was Richard Dixon. Erasmus, with his brothers William and John, signed Dixon's apprenticeship indentures in 1747, and Dixon was to be a lifelong friend.[22]

Within the family, Susannah was his favourite sister, and the subject of one of his earliest poems:

My dearest Sue
of lovely hue
No sugar can be sweeter;
You do as far
Excel Su-gar
As sugar does saltpetre.[23]

The young poet would have been familiar with saltpetre as the active agent in gunpowder.

The sharpest picture of Erasmus as a schoolboy emerges from an exchange of letters with Susannah in 1749 when she was nineteen. She writes about her abstinence at Lent:

I come now to the chief design of my Letter, and that is to acquaint you with my Abstinence this Lent, which you will find on the other side.... As soon as we kill our hog I intend to take part thereof with the Family, for I'm informed by a learned Divine that Hogs Flesh is fish, and has been so ever since the Devil entered into them and they ran into the Sea ...

A typical day of her 'Diary in Lent' is Wednesday 8 February:

A little before seven I got up; said my Prayers; worked till eight; then took a walk, came in again and eate a farthing Loaf, then dress'd me, red a Chapter in the Bible, and spun till One, then dined temperately viz: on Puddin, Bread and Cheese; spun again till Fore ...[24]

The seventeen-year-old Erasmus replied at length to this ill-spelt but well-spun yarn, and his letter is salted with the banter characteristic of his later years:

... having had a convenient oppertunity to consult a Synod of my learned friends about your ingenious conscience ... I must inform you we unanimously agree in the Opinion of the Learned Divine you mention, that Swine may indeed be fish but then they are a devillish sort of fish; and we can prove from the same Authority that all fish is flesh whence we affirm Porck not only to be flesh but a devillish Sort of flesh; and I would advise you for Conscience sake altogether to abstain from tasting it; as I can assure you I have done, tho' roast Pork has come to Table several Times; and for my own part have lived upon Puding, milk, and vegetables all this Lent; but don't mistake me, I don't mean I have not touch'd roast beef, mutton, veal, goose, fowl, etc for what are all these? All flesh is grass!

His leaning towards temperance is also beginning to emerge:

For the temperate enjoy an ever-blooming Health free from all the Infections and disorders luxurious mortals are subject to, the whimsical Tribe of Phisitians cheated of their fees may sit down in penury and Want, they may curse mankind and imprecate the Gods and call down that parent of all Deseases, luxury, to infest Mankind.... [With] fever banished from our Streets, limping Gout would fly the land, and Sedentary Stone would vanish into oblivion and death himself be slain.[25]

After this flourish, he comes down to earth at the end: 'Excuse Hast, supper being called, very Hungry'. Bad spelling was common at the time and Erasmus even mis-spells his future profession, which again he treats with some suspicion.

Erasmus's brother John was still at Chesterfield School, and in April he suddenly changed his image: 'Bro Jack had his Hair cut off last Week, and I must say I like him much better in a Wigg', Erasmus wrote to his eldest brother Robert. 'As for myself', he says, 'Cuthbert Scullscraper has not been so expeditious with my Wigg'.[26] Even if Erasmus's teasing tone was spontaneous, Robert must have encouraged it.

Erasmus seems to have enjoyed his nine years at Chesterfield School: there are no derogatory comments about his schooldays in later letters. At Christmas in 1749 he wrote a long letter in verse to a school friend, Samuel Pegge, who was later well known as a musical composer and antiquary. 'Eras: D'Arwin', as the versifier calls himself, unlooses a barrage of puddings, Mince-Pyes and other Christmas cheer, which he pretends to be sending his friend, along with a book, 'at once to glut / His Head extensive, and extensive Gut'. This mini-quotation is enough to reveal the rumbustious style – and the trick of word-repetition, later used so successfully in *The Botanic Garden*.

Unlike most schoolboys, Erasmus seems to have appreciated the good

teaching at the school and always spoke of Mr Burrow with great respect.
A few months after leaving he wrote Burrow a thank-you letter, possibly a
semi-compulsory ritual. His letter was more than that, however, because he
offers as a bonus 130 lines of verse in imitation of the 5th Satire of Persius.
(Persius Flaccus, AD 34–62, little known now, was familiar enough to
Erasmus after his thorough classical education.) He obviously stood in awe
of Burrow, and the poem is rather restrained. At the end he compares
Burrow with a 'stately Pine' round which 'young Scions' sprout, 'Pupil-
plants' who will grow into 'the Burrows of the rising Age'.[27] So he was
already playing with the idea of humanizing plants.

[4]

Mr Burrow and many other headmasters in the north of England regarded
St John's College, Cambridge, as the natural next step for talented pupils.
Erasmus's eldest brother Robert took this step in 1743; John and Erasmus
followed, travelling to St John's to matriculate in June 1750.

On their way to Cambridge they stopped at a house near Peterborough,
with a letter of introduction from their father to two old gentlemen who
lived there. They arrived in the dark, and at first were rather coldly received, though afterwards more cordially. One of their hosts, who seemed
pleased with 'the animated Vivacity of the young Companions', was heard
to say to his brother with a sigh, 'What a Pity that one of us did not marry',
a remark that impressed Erasmus 'and perhaps confirmed his Aversion for
a Life of Celibacy'. This anecdote is from a short manuscript 'Memoir of
Dr Darwin' written by his second son Erasmus junior,[28] who attributes the
story to his father.

John and Erasmus matriculated on 30 June 1750[29] and would have
started residence in October. Their tutor was the Revd William Powell, 'a
sensible cautious Man, who never said one word too much'[30] and was later
Master of St John's College. Erasmus won an Exeter scholarship at the
college, and the £16 per annum that it brought in was welcome, because the
upkeep of two sons at Cambridge was a strain on their father's finances.
They lived frugally and mended their own clothes: 'Many years afterwards,
Erasmus boasted to his second wife that, if she cut the heel out of a stocking, he would put a new one in without missing a stitch'.[31]

Erasmus Darwin went to Cambridge at a time when the reputation of the
universities was low, and heavy drinking was rife among students and dons.
Intellectually, the universities were almost moribund, and seen as 'salutary
bulwarks against the precipitate and desolating spirit of innovation'.[32]
Darwin made the best of this unpromising environment and emerged

accomplished and knowledgeable, particularly in classics. It was a culture he cherished throughout his life, as we can see from the casual ease of the classical references in his poems many years later.

Darwin's verse also came of age at Cambridge as he began to write about real life. His first published poem was a ninety-two-line elegy for Frederick, Prince of Wales, who died in March 1751. Darwin's poem appears in the multilingual memorial miscellany rapidly compiled at Cambridge and published in May 1751 with the title *Academiae Cantabrigiensis Luctus in obitum Frederici celsissimi Walliae Principis*. A memorial volume was appropriate because Frederick, although much maligned, was a generous patron of the arts, who had tried his hand at writing poetry, songs and a play.[33] His death may even have been a historic event, because he might have treated the American colonies more prudently than his son George III did. Frederick deserves a better epitaph than the scurrilous rhyme beginning 'Here lies Fred, who was alive and is dead', and ending 'there's no more to be said'.

Darwin certainly had more to say. He was keen to exercise his Muse, and she proves to be in good fettle:

> Ye Meads enamel'd, and ye waving Woods,
>   With dismal yews and solemn cypress mourn;
> Ye rising Mountains, and ensilver'd Floods,
>   Repeat my sighs, and weep upon his urn.

After an elaborate simile comparing Frederick with a mighty cedar tree brought down by a storm, the young poet sighs over the vanities of life and deftly exploits an image of the aurora:

> Oft at the fall of Kings, th' astonish'd eye
>   Views fancy'd tumults in the mid-night gleams,
> Sees glittering crests, and darting lances fly,
>   Till one thick cloud absorbs the sportive beams.[34]

Then Neptune appears, and tells us to cease mourning because the Prince may still smile on 'Albion's sea-beat realms' from a brighter throne on high.

It was a smooth performance and won Darwin an immediate reputation as a man of letters.

Another of Darwin's enthusiasms in his first year at Cambridge was learning shorthand so as to be able to record lectures verbatim. He learnt the system of 'brachygraphy' devised by Thomas Gurney, who was appointed official shorthand writer at the Old Bailey in 1748. Gurney wrote a manual on his technique in 1750, and Darwin had become proficient in the art by the summer of 1751. He sent a specimen of his shorthand to Gurney, who printed it in the third edition of his *Brachygraphy* in 1752: it was the tenth chapter of *Revelation*.

If Prince Frederick was being celebrated in verse, why not the admirable Mr Gurney too? Darwin wrote a poem of three ten-line stanzas 'To Mr Gurney, on his book of short-writing'. This was published anonymously in the *London Magazine* in July 1751 and again the next year (without Darwin's knowledge) in the third edition of Gurney's book, where the author is given as 'E.D., Cambridge, St. John's'. The first stanza is severely practical, but the second is much more imaginative:

> Tale-licens'd Travellers are wont to boast
> Amazing Converse in the Realms of Frost;
> Lips move unheard, each Sound in Ice entomb'd,
> Stagnate his Current, and his Wing benumb'd,
> Slumbers inactive, till a warmer Sky
> Unbinds the Glebe, and bids the Accents fly –
> Thus *Gurney's* Arts the fleeting Word congeal,
> And stay the Wanderer to repeat his Tale,
> When the quick Eye-ball thaws the letter'd Plain,
> Calls out the Sound, and wakes the dormant Strain.[35]

Tongue in cheek, Darwin revives the hoary traveller's tale of words freezing as spoken (distancing himself via the traveller, like Shelley in 'Ozymandias'). Then, as our credulity is about to snap, he shows how well the story fits shorthand, which does 'congeal' spoken words.

Gurney reprinted Darwin's poem and his shorthand specimen in some of the subsequent editions of *Brachygraphy*. (It reached its fifteenth edition in 1825, and the Gurney system was used in Parliament until 1914 and beyond.)[36] Darwin filled several notebooks with shorthand while at Cambridge. He also wrote further letters to Gurney and another poem, which is of some merit. 'The pale-eye'd scribes' of old, he says, would not have needed to burn 'their midnight oil'

> If pages then beneath thy dash had sprung,
> Th' unfinished sounds still trembling on the tongue.[37]

The point is well made, though not everyone would applaud the idea of medieval manuscripts being written in shorthand. Darwin continued writing shorthand for a few years after leaving university, but eventually found that he had forgotten it.

The poems about Prince Frederick and Mr Gurney are detached and mannered. Erasmus came nearer to red-blooded life in his 'Epithalamium' for the marriage of his sister Elizabeth to the Revd Thomas Hall on 3 October 1751:

> Through all our frames the kindling pleasures dart,
> Beat in the pulse, and tremble at the heart,
> With quenchless heats in every bosom rage,
> Boil the young blood, and warm the frost of age.[38]

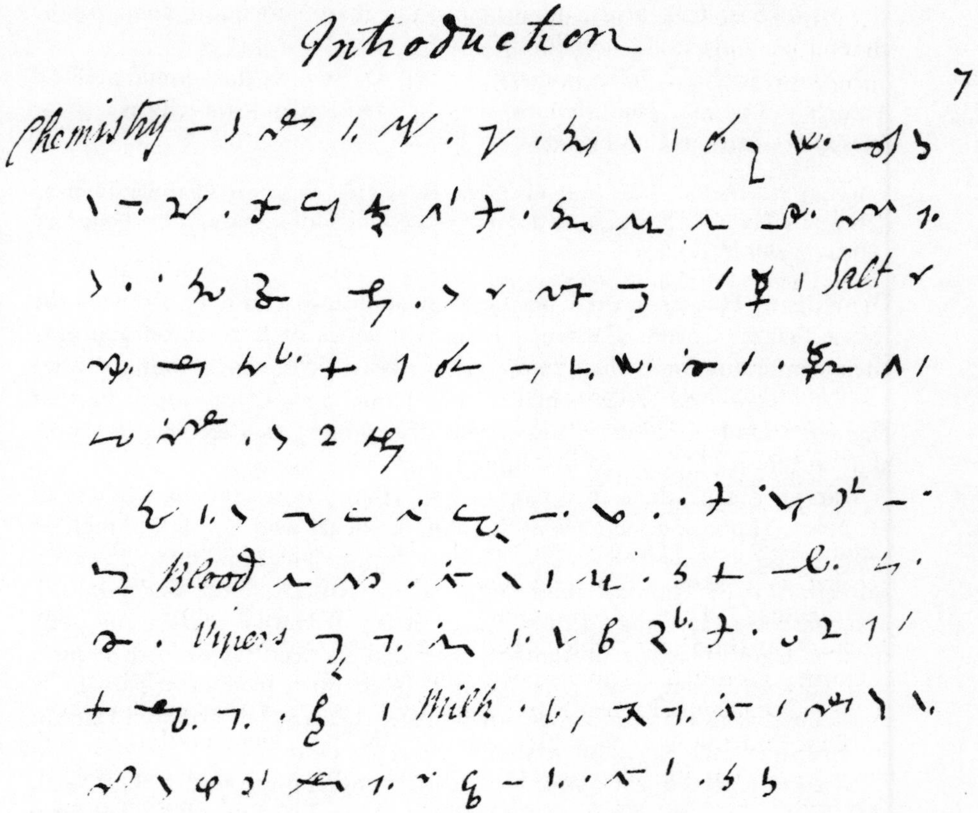

Introduction

7

[shorthand notes beginning with the word "Chemistry" and including the words "Salt", "Blood", "Ulcers", "Milk"]

FIG. 2 A specimen of Darwin's shorthand notes on George Baker's medical lectures at Cambridge in 1752

This can be seen as a foretaste of the sexual imagery in *The Botanic Garden*: but that poem nowhere recaptures the realism of these early verses.

The classic verse and shorthand that occupied Darwin in his first year at Cambridge had to give way to medicine in the next two years. He was able to attend lectures by three eminent doctors, two of them in London, and some of his neat shorthand notes on these lectures have survived.

The first series of lectures was given in 1752 at King's College, Cambridge, by Dr George Baker, who later became a baronet and a royal physician; he is best known medically for discovering that 'Devonshire colic' was due to lead poisoning, which he traced to leaden cider vats. Darwin's shorthand notes on his lectures (Fig. 2) extend to more than 170 pages, and cover 'the fossil and animal kingdoms': waters, earths, metals, stones; insects, fish, birds, quadrupeds and man – to quote some of the chapter headings in his notebooks.[39]

In 1753, probably from January to April, Darwin went to attend medical lectures in London. The 'Memoir' written by his second son tells us that he missed one term at Cambridge,

> having received an offer from his friend Kilvington, if he would go with him to hear Dr Hunter's Lectures, to accommodate him with a share of his Lodgings. This he did.[40]

Dr William Hunter started his London anatomy school in 1746 at the 'Little Piazza, Covent Garden', giving two series of lectures on anatomy each winter for more than thirty years (though the venue changed after 1755). The second series began in mid January. It is not surprising that Darwin attended, because Hunter was pre-eminent as a lecturer in scope, skill and thoroughness. No shorthand notes have survived.

Darwin did produce fifty pages of shorthand notes on the lectures of Dr Noah Thomas, a member of St John's College, who was later knighted after acting as royal physician. Thomas lectured in London in 1753 on salivation at St Thomas's Hospital, and on poisons, both 'acrimonious' and 'narcotic', at Cook's Court, Carey Street. If Darwin missed only one term at Cambridge, he presumably attended the lectures of both Hunter and Thomas during that term. Noah Thomas must have been personally acquainted with Darwin, either now or later, because he proposed Darwin for election to the Royal Society eight years afterwards.

Medical teaching at Cambridge had been much improved in the 1740s, mainly through the efforts of Dr William Heberden (1710–1801),[41] later a London physician of high repute, who was the first to describe angina pectoris and to distinguish chickenpox. Heberden had worked his way up from humble beginnings to become a Fellow of St John's in 1731. He then decided to make medicine his career, and each year between 1740 and 1748 (when he left for London) he gave twenty-six or more lectures on medicine. Seeing the need for an introductory course, Heberden also wrote a manuscript 'Introduction to the Study of Physic', and urged students to make their own copies of it. Another of Darwin's medical notebooks, fifty-four pages written neatly in longhand, is just such a copy, one of a few surviving today. The text copied into Darwin's notebook covers pharmacy, anatomy, diseases, etc, and lists 114 recommended books. The notebook also has a further twenty-five pages on 'The Doctrine of the Pulse', of which Heberden later published a revised version. Four of Darwin's fellow students apparently borrowed the notes and recorded their ungrateful thanks on the cover: 'damn you Darwin you have spelt a thousand words wrong, you son of a whore.'[42]

Medicinal herbs were very important in Darwin's day: so did his later love of botany originate at Cambridge? It seems not, because the Professor of Botany, John Martyn, was a real disgrace. Appointed in 1732, he lectured for three years and then left Cambridge for twenty-seven years, when he at last resigned in favour of his son Thomas. Thus there was no specialized teaching of botany, and no sign that Darwin was particularly interested in the subject.

Darwin's medical studies did not stop him writing verse: 'he had such a facility of practical Composition that he wrote the exercise burden for several of his friends'. Some of his own 'College exercises' have survived. In one of them 'The Fifth of November', he curses the inventor of gunpowder, no doubt remembering his own accident. Another, 'The Folly of Atheism', needs to be mentioned because it was fallaciously cited as evidence of his religious orthodoxy.

The only other Cambridge poem of interest was written at Christmas 1752, when he remained at St John's instead of going home. It is a frivolous letter in verse entitled 'A day in College at Christmas'.[43] Darwin pretends to bewail his fate –

> A ragged Soph, condemned to College,
> I haunt th' unpeopled walls of knowledge –

but then admits spending most of his day eating, or playing whist. If anyone tired of eating, there was music to help: fiddlers play

> While knives and forks and under-jaws
> Keep time, and move to musick's laws.

The whist addicts are mostly Fellows of the College, clergymen who

> move at five with step demure
> To chappel – if the rubber's o'er.

Strip off the satire and we have glimpses of what College life was really like in the 1750s.

Darwin became friendly with a few senior members of the University. The most important of these was John Michell (1724–93), tutor of Queen's College. He was already well known as a man of science, and helped Darwin in later years.

Darwin also had many 'college cronies' among the undergraduates. Only a few of their names have filtered down. The letter on college life was addressed to 'Mr Johnson'. This was Thomas Johnson who for nearly fifty years was rector of Wickham Market, Suffolk.[44] Darwin probably lost touch with Johnson, but he kept in contact with William Sayle, a school and university friend, to whom he wrote a rather ponderous ode in 1753. Sayle also became a clergyman, being vicar of Stowey, Somerset, from 1772 until his death in 1799. The medical student who shared lodgings with Darwin in London was Thomas Kilvington, who for much of his long life practised as a physician at Ripon in Yorkshire. Darwin's old school friend Samuel Pegge was another of his companions at St John's. Not much is heard of these college friends subsequently.

[5]

On 1 October 1753 Erasmus and his eldest brother Robert set out on horseback for Edinburgh, where Erasmus was to enter the Medical School to complete his training as a doctor. On the first day of the journey Erasmus's horse kicked Robert's on the forehead, and 'dinted in his Skull to a considerable depth'. The horse recovered, and they arrived at Edinburgh on 10 October. Having visited the Castle, they found lodgings for Erasmus 'at Miss Ogston's in Goldielocks Land, Head of the Luckenbooths', the rent being £20 per annum, 'fire and candles included'. Robert wrote a diary of the journey[45] with details of the expenditure, £10 2s 4½d on the outward leg and only half that on the return to Elston without Erasmus.

The Edinburgh Medical School, founded in 1726, was pre-eminent in Britain at this time. Most of the professors had been to Leyden as pupils of the great physician Boerhaave, a mechanist who tried to find physical and chemical explanations for all the bodily functions. Erasmus was twenty-one when he started attending lectures, and there is a record[46] of his paying three guineas for anatomy classes in October 1753.

One of his fellow-students at Edinburgh, James Keir (1735–1820), became a lifelong friend and later played a prominent role in the Lunar Society of Birmingham. The two complemented each other: 'Darwin was the brilliant creative thinker, Keir the cautious, self-disciplined, balanced personality'.[47] Keir tells us in his dry Scottish style that Darwin was quite conspicuous at Edinburgh: 'The classical and literary attainments which he had acquired at Cambridge gave him, when he came to Edinburgh, together with his poetical talents and ready wit, a distinguished superiority among the students there.'[48]

Keir came from a wealthy Scottish family, of Muirton near Edinburgh. His father died when he was very young and he was brought up by his mother with help from her brother George Lind, Lord Provost of Edinburgh, whose son Dr James Lind was a close friend of James Watt, and later royal physician at Windsor and the mentor of Shelley at Eton. Keir left Edinburgh without taking a degree and served in the Army for eleven years before retiring as a captain and settling near Birmingham, to become a pioneer of industrial chemistry.

Many years later, in a letter to Erasmus's son Robert in 1802, Keir remembered how mechanistic the medical teaching at Edinburgh had been, with only Dr Cullen beginning 'to throw off the Boerhaavian yoke', and he wondered how Erasmus had escaped indoctrination:

It would be curious to know (but he alone could have told us) the progress of your father's mind from the narrow Boerhaavian system, in which man was considered as an hydraulic machine whose pipes were filled with fluids susceptible of chemical fermentations, while the pipes themselves were liable to stoppages or obstructions (to which obstructions and fermentations all diseases were imputed), to the more enlarged consideration of man as a *living being*, which affects the phenomena of health and disease more than his merely mechanical and chemical properties.[49]

While at Edinburgh, Erasmus received news of his father's death on 20 November 1754. The event led him to reflect on life when he wrote to Dr Thomas Okes, another Cambridge friend, who later practised as a physician in Exeter. Erasmus was already something of a sceptic, it seems, and he starts by referring to an 'Ens Entium' or 'Being of Beings', so as to avoid the word 'God' (which, however, sneaks back later):

That there exists a superior Ens Entium, which formed these wonderful creatures [i.e. human beings], is mathematical demonstration. That HE influences things by a particular providence, is not so evident. The probability, according to my notion, is against it, since general laws seem sufficient for that end. Shall we say no particular providence is necessary to roll this Planet round the Sun, and yet affirm it necessary in turning up *cinque* and *quatorze*, while shaking a box of dies? or giving each his daily bread? – The light of Nature affords us not a single argument for a future state; this is the only one – that it is possible with God; since he who made us out of nothing can surely re-create us ...[50]

Such philosophizing was rare: Darwin's day-to-day life centred on the steady grind of lectures. Keir tells us that Darwin heard lectures from Dr Monro on anatomy, Dr Rutherford on the practice of medicine, Dr Whytt on the theory of medicine, Dr Plummer on chemistry and Dr Alston on botany. The only shorthand notes that have survived are of Alston's lectures, which also cover materia medica.

One new friend at Edinburgh was Albert Reimarus, son of the well-known German philosopher Hermann Reimarus, who was a deist sceptical of Christianity and a proponent of 'natural' rather than 'revealed' religion.[51] Darwin and Keir were both influenced by the ideas of Reimarus, and fourteen years later Darwin wrote to Albert Reimarus: 'Mr Keir and myself continue in the Religion you taught us, we hold you to be a great Reformer of the Church.'[52]

While at Edinburgh, Darwin wrote for Reimarus a spirited poem entitled 'A Medical Courtship'[53] in which he imagines Reimarus asking the 'Powers celestial' for a wife. As a result Reimarus finds himself wooed by Botany, who offers flowers, by Chemia with gold and gems, and by Anatomy, who 'unweaves the fibre-woof of Life'. But in the end he chooses the graceful Hygeia, goddess of health.

Little is known of Darwin's private life in Edinburgh. Only one anecdote has come down to us, from an anonymous friend (or enemy) who reports that 'in his youth Dr Darwin was fond of sacrificing to both Bacchus and Venus; but he soon discovered that he could not continue his devotions to both these deities without destroying his health and constitution. He there-fore resolved to relinquish Bacchus, but his affection for Venus was retained to the last period of life'.[54] This seems to be a roundabout way of saying that he suffered an attack of gout when quite young and decided to cut down on his drinking. His 'affection for Venus' is not in doubt. He was evidently attractive to women even after he had become fat and lame in middle life, and he probably enjoyed himself greatly at Edinburgh, en-dowed as he was with energy, wit, a strong heterosexual drive and the social ease acquired during his years at Cambridge. Presumably he spoke with a stammer, as in later years, but he never let it inhibit him. Darwin's sensuousness is neatly encapsulated in his genial translation of an epigram of Martial:

> Wine, women, warmth, against our lives combine;
> But what is life without warmth, women, wine![55]

Darwin himself rarely referred to his life at Edinburgh. There is one illuminating vignette hidden away in his discussion of phosphorescence many years later: 'In the streets of Edinburgh, where the heads of fish called whitings or haddies are frequently thrown out by the people, I have on a dark night easily seen the hour by holding one of them to my watch'.[56] Had he been 'sacrificing to Venus' on this dark night when he was so absorbed that he had no idea of the time?

Our ideas of the total time he spent at Edinburgh are a little fuzzy, too. His brother John took a BA degree when he left Cambridge in the summer of 1754 – he was head of the 'Junior Optimes'. But Erasmus did not take this degree. Instead he returned to Cambridge for a further term (or two?) to take his MB (Bachelor of Medicine) in June 1755. Keir says that Darwin stayed two winters at Edinburgh; presumably he returned there in October 1755 until the early summer of 1756. There is no record of his taking an MD degree at Edinburgh, but he is said to have defended the thesis 'that the movements of the heart and arteries are immediately produced by the stimulus of the blood'.[57] Darwin styled himself MD in later years, but he was rather casual about paper qualifications. No one would have dared to ask him for a certificate.

[6]

With or without a formal MD, Darwin was ready to let himself loose on the unsuspecting public in the summer of 1756. Where better to start his practice than in his home county-town, Nottingham? And so, after spending time at Elston in the midsummer months, he moved to Nottingham in early August. His closest friend was Albert Reimarus, who spent much of the summer in London, and was a guest at the meeting of the Royal Society on 27 May. Five letters from Darwin to Reimarus have survived, up to the time when Reimarus returned to Germany, in October.

Darwin arrived at Nottingham in a relaxed mood. In a letter to Reimarus started at Elston, he gives the address of his lodgings as 'Mrs Burden, Upholsterer, in the Long Row, Nottingham'. A little later he writes 'adieu in hast. I go to Nottingham just now'. This is immediately followed by: 'I am now at Nottingham and going to the Races this Minute'.[58] So, for once, he is writing his own biography without my help.

The euphoria did not last: his attempt to start a practice in Nottingham proved an abject failure. 'He had no introduction, and was not acquainted with one Individual'.[59] It seems that he did not attract any genteel patients.

He was left with plenty of time to continue his correspondence with Reimarus. During the summer they had arranged for a young Nottingham labourer called Marlow to be 'cut for the Hydrocele' by a London doctor called Douglas. Unfortunately Douglas charged six guineas, and Darwin was cross with Reimarus:

> Here my friend either you decieved me, or Douglass decieved you: but I re-member I was affraid you had not told Him in plain English that He was to do it for nothing. This young Man who has nothing but what hard Labour gives Him, is much distress'd by this Thing costing him near £30 in all, since the House where He lay cheated him much ... I shall send this young Man two Guineas.[60]

Darwin probably also sent an anonymous letter to Douglas and, when challenged by Reimarus, wrote, 'I will not say whether I am the Author or not'. At the end of this later letter, rather surprisingly, he asks Reimarus to show it to Douglas. Soon after that, Douglas paid back two-thirds of the fee. Darwin seems to have got himself into a real tangle here, with good intentions spoilt by bad tactics.

Apart from medical chit-chat, the other main topic of these letters to Reimarus is science and invention, for Darwin had at last found a mechanically-minded friend. The agenda include Egyptian mummies, furnaces with fermenting liquor ('if it succeeds I shall send it to the royal Society'), and coaches having wheels with spring rims as shock absorbers. This idea of spring spokes he later pursued further, and it is continually being re-invented. Darwin also declares himself a believer in electrical Franklinism: if two non-conducting globes approach, 'unum erit electricum minus, alterum plus'. Parts of the letters are written in this Darwinian latin, with bad grammar, bad spelling, mistakes and invented words, but possibly easier than English for Reimarus.

Darwin did have at least one patient at Nottingham: he regales Reimarus with two pages of details about the case,[61] so this was probably his first patient. 'A and B were both drunk. Shoemakers by Trade. A stab'd B with a conical Knife. A was taller than B. Sept.12.1756. The wound was just under the Cartilages of the Ribs on the left side.' Darwin was not called in until 16 September. He examined the wound and was pleased that there was 'No Vomitting or Nausea', though 'Pulse very quick and very weak'. After some medication, the swelling was less on 17 September, but diarrhoea had set in. A heroic mixture of medicines was prescribed. 'Sept.18. Diarrhoea stop'd, slept well, is more cheerful'. More medicine (Peruvian bark the favourite). 'At Night. Pulse imperceptible'. Then 'Convulsions of muscles of the Face. Death. Dissection'. The dissection showed that 'the Stomach was pierced'. The young doctor was dismayed: 'That there was no Vomitting or Nausea decieved me, and I think is surprizing'. Conscious of his failure, he tries to involve Reimarus in supportive tele-diagnosis: 'But what evidence had we, except the Pulse?'

If 'B' was Darwin's first patient, it was not a good start: he needed patients who recovered and would recommend him. Those who died and paid no fees were a dead loss. During October, still with no patients of substance, or possibly with no surviving patients at all, he decided to try his luck elsewhere. In November he migrated to Lichfield.

[7]

Before we follow Darwin to Lichfield, this early hiatus in his career is a good moment for a quick look at the state of medicine in the eighteenth century, against which Darwin's achievements must be judged. The yawning gap in medical science was the failure to realize that microbes caused diseases. Fracastoro expounded the germ theory in 1543 and specified the modes of infection – by direct contact, indirectly in clothes, and through airborne germs. Sydenham, in the seventeenth century, specified sound measures for public health which half-implied a germ theory of disease. There were many pointers to the germ theory: for centuries lepers had been kept isolated; quarantine laws existed against 'contagious' diseases; and in 1721 Lady Mary Wortley Montagu introduced the Turkish custom of smallpox inoculation with live virus. But we fail to see the obvious if the obvious does not fit in with our prejudices, and people couldn't really believe in the power of microbes they couldn't see. Microbes had been observed by Leeuwenhoek in 1683, but his famous microscopic researches came to be regarded as mere curiosities, fascinating but medically irrelevant. Microscopy was neglected during the eighteenth century, and its few practitioners, such as Henry Baker, made little progress. So the cause of many infectious diseases, of septicaemia in surgery and 'puerperal fever' in childbirth, remained obscure. The consequences were often fatal. In fairness to the eighteenth century, however, we should remember that high resistance overcomes most germs: otherwise all the doctors would have died young, and few did – George Baker lived to eighty-seven and Heberden to ninety.

In the first half of the century the most influential physician was Hermann Boerhaave, who (as already mentioned) concentrated on the hydraulics of the body; he also emphasized that patients deserved to be treated individually and not mass-medicated.

Sorting out the nervous system and showing that the nerves converge on the brain was in large measure the work of the Swiss biologist Albrecht von Haller. He had no idea that nerve impulses were electrical, a discovery that did not come till after 1850, though we can now see how it was foreshadowed in the 1790s by Galvani, who made frogs' legs twitch when touched by different metals, and by Volta, who showed how muscles could be kept excited by electrical impulses. Even before this, however, Darwin concluded that nerve impulses were electrical, through seeing how paralytic limbs were stimulated by electric shocks.

Surgery remained a painful and risky procedure throughout the eighteenth century. The failure to utilize anaesthetics in surgery now seems puzzling – surely someone could have thought of it to relieve the patients' agony? After all, opium and laudanum were often prescribed by physicians, and other anaesthetics were known in China during the second century AD and in medieval Italy. The surgeons' neglect of anaesthetics and hygiene does not mean they were butchers. Many were most humane, and some were immensely skilful. The 'lightning lithotomist' William Cheselden could complete an operation for a bladder stone in less than two minutes, thus minimizing the patient's suffering; and it is said that more than ninety per cent of his patients survived. The great surgeon John Hunter pioneered new operations and amassed the specimens for his famous museum. His brother William Hunter, whose lectures Darwin attended, did much to raise the status of surgery, and he became the leading midwifery doctor of London, as well as being a successful general physician and playing a major role in discovering the lymphatic system.

Ignorance of hygiene hampered the success of surgery, but was perhaps even worse in childbirth. Babies were delivered by midwives who were often unwashed and carried the germs of 'puerperal fever' from one bedside to the next. Hygiene was improved during the century, but only by chance, for aesthetic reasons. Many of England's open sewers were covered, because they were thought offensive. Army camps were fairly hygienic because of regulations imposed by Sir John Pringle, and the prisons were improved after the efforts of John Howard. Thanks chiefly to these measures and the building of hospitals, English people were slightly healthier in 1800 than in 1700.

A few diseases lost some of their horror. The dreaded maritime disease of scurvy was conquered, thanks to the work of James Lind (1716–94), not to be confused with his cousin James Lind (1736–1812), the friend of Watt and Shelley. Lind proved that plentiful fruit juices could prevent scurvy, and so saved the lives of more seamen than were killed in battle. Jenner's technique of vaccination against smallpox came at the very end of the century, too late to be of service in Darwin's medical career.

The treatment of mental illness by the 'mad doctors' was generally deplorable. Lunatics were often chained and treated brutally in the hope of driving out the devils that possessed them. There were some kinder doctors, Darwin among them, and in 1794 the first humane lunatic asylum, the Retreat at York, was founded by the Quaker William Tuke. But milder measures did not become common until later: even King George III was cruelly restrained.

There were some chemical insights, particularly the recognition that gastric juices help to digest food – that digestion is not merely mechanical. But chemistry was imprisoned by the phlogiston theory, which held that a burning substance gave off 'phlogiston'. Priestley's experiments in the 1770s revealed, as we now see, that the burning substance combined with oxygen. But Priestley himself clung to the phlogiston theory, as did most of the Lunar Society members, apart from Darwin, who adopted the French oxygen theory in the 1780s, publicized the word 'oxygen', and led the way in explaining the oxygenation of blood in the lungs.

The methods used by the gentlemanly physicians were far removed from those in vogue today. A physician 'examined' a patient by listening to the patient's story of the illness, observing the patient's face minutely and taking the pulse. Except in cases of injury it was not normal for patients to remove any clothes: physicians did not see – and, still less, touch – covered areas of the skin.[62] Thus it is not surprising that chest-tapping, begun in the 1760s, did not catch on: the stethoscope was not invented until after 1800. Blood pressure and circulation rate had been studied and measured by Stephen Hales in the 1730s, but the use of blood pressure in diagnosing disease came much later: Darwin never mentions it.

Also, strange as it now seems, the idea of body temperature being a guide to good health was not accepted, partly because the thermometers were difficult to use – the clinical thermometer dates from 1866. Physicians thus had to rely unduly on the speed and strength of the pulse. Even so, they rarely used the one-minute pulse-watch invented by the Lichfield physician Sir John Floyer in 1707. Pulse-taking was a subjective art based on experience, but it did at least have a rationale – in that weak or undetectable pulses did often indicate that the patient was dying or dead!

These crude techniques of diagnosis led to treatments that were mostly useless. Patients were usually subjected to purgatives, emetics, a cornucopia of herbs, from opium to cinchona bark, taken either singly or in groups, and of course to blood-letting. This pernicious practice derived from the idea of expelling humours, which were supposed to reside in the blood: the blood was taken by lancing a vein, by leeches or by 'cupping'. If patients recovered, it was usually because their body defences overcame both the disease and the treatment. No wonder there was a popular proverb, 'a physician is more dangerous than the disease'.

As diseases were often fatal, rich patients would pay doctors high fees to match the high stakes, and many fashionable physicians in London made fortunes from rich patients with strong constitutions, whose recovery would be wrongly attributed to the medication they received. There was credit to be gained even from patients who succumbed, if the physician had correctly pronounced a death sentence: as Belloc put it,

> They answered as they took their fees,
> 'There is no Cure for this Disease'.

Still, this is not to say that the physicians were useless. In the absence of medical science, common sense was paramount, and some of the doctors were among the most perceptive and intelligent men of the day. Their advice often helped to keep patients in good health. For example, Dr John Armstrong, in his popular poem *The Art of Preserving Health* (1744), advises his readers to avoid polluted air, to eat varied food in moderate quantities, to take adequate exercise and to avoid lowering resistance by excess. No one would quarrel with that.

A humane task for energetic doctors was the creation of a local infirmary for poor patients. The doctor would first have to raise the money by asking for subscriptions from the moneyed gentry. If that succeeded, the design and construction of the building had to be organized and supervised. Once the infirmary was open, the doctor would give his services free. The founding of the Birmingham General Hospital, on the initiative of Dr John Ash, followed this pattern. The hospital opened in 1779, after thirteen years of gestation. Stafford had an Infirmary from 1768, and Darwin tried to start one at Derby in the 1780s.

Infirmaries are social-medical phenomena, and lead on to the wider social history of the era, which I shall not stray into.[63]

Erasmus Darwin always resisted the idea of becoming a fashionable London physician. He stayed in the Midlands and tried to help all who called on his services. He treated the poorest free, and for the others scaled his fees to the patients' wealth, as expressed by their way of life – the number of their servants and the size or splendour of their home, furniture or equipage. In practice, because of the difficulties of travel, he tended to give free treatment to the poor near his house and charged for distant calls and affluent local people. Rich or poor, Darwin knew he had a challenging future – fighting with puny weapons a deadly enemy whose army was invisible.

CHAPTER TWO

A young doctor of Lichfield
1756–1760

There had been a cathedral at Lichfield for more than a thousand years when Erasmus Darwin arrived in November 1756. The list of bishops begins in 656, and the first cathedral was consecrated in 700. The building of the present cathedral began in 1195, though its three splendid spires were not completed until 1330. Ever since then, these three 'ladies of the vale' have beckoned travellers from afar. For Darwin their call proved compulsive: he was to live in their shadow for nearly twenty-five years.

The slow and ancient Lichfield, 'mother of the Midlands', was being overtaken by a brash new upstart, the manufacturing town of Birmingham fifteen miles to the south. Lichfield was still the better known of the two, partly for its cathedral and partly because it stood at a cross-roads where the road from London to Chester crossed that from Bristol to Derby and Yorkshire. Lichfield was a major staging-point for coaches and, thanks to a Turnpike Trust set up in 1729, had rather better roads than most other parts of the Midlands.[1]

In the seventeenth century Lichfield had been the birthplace of Elias Ashmole the scholar, and in the early eighteenth of Samuel Johnson and David Garrick, who set off together to seek fame and fortune in London twenty years before Darwin arrived. Another previous resident was the eminent doctor Sir John Floyer[2] (1649–1734), who investigated asthma and emphysema, and made careful studies of the pulse. He was also an enthusiast for cold baths and built a bath-house fed by springs at Maple Hayes west of the town. Darwin later bought the bath-house, which was within the grounds of his botanic garden.

Darwin arrived at Lichfield on 12 November 1756. He had made the mistake of riding naked into town at Nottingham, but he did not repeat the error. He entered Lichfield armed with two letters of introduction. One was from his brother-in-law the Revd Thomas Hall to Lady Gresley, stepmother of the sixth baronet Sir Nigel Gresley of Drakelow near Burton. The second, probably from a Cambridge friend, was to the Revd Thomas Seward[3] (1708–90), Canon Residentiary of Lichfield Cathedral and a graduate of St John's College, Cambridge.

The Seward family resided in some splendour at the Bishop's Palace in the Cathedral Close: the bishops preferred to live at Eccleshall Castle, twenty miles away, untroubled by day-to-day problems at the Cathedral. Canon Seward was an enterprising clergyman of literary tastes, well known for his edition of Beaumont and Fletcher, and he made the palace a meeting-place for a literary coterie. Seward had married Elizabeth Hunter, the daughter of Samuel Johnson's headmaster, the Revd John Hunter. The Sewards had two daughters, Anna, who was nearly fourteen when Darwin arrived, and Sarah, two years younger. Anna was already a precocious poet and must have been amazed and excited when this energetic doctor-poet burst into her small world. He may have come in like a tornado, or as an ultra-polite visitor: either way, he brought a breath of fresh air into the Cathedral Close. Darwin may have thought the Close too inward-looking, but he had cause to be grateful to the Sewards, and to Lady Gresley, for giving him access to the upper strata of local society – the *sine qua non* of success as a physician.

Anna was observing Darwin closely from the start of his career in Lichfield, and nearly fifty years later she wrote her *Memoirs of the Life of Dr Darwin*. The book is prolix in style and sometimes unreliable. It swings between extravagant praise and calumnies which she had to retract with printed apologies in magazines. But it is still essential to later biographers.

A few weeks after his arrival, Darwin achieved a brilliant medical coup. One of his first patients, Anna tells us, was Mr Inge, 'a young gentleman of family, fortune and consequence' who 'lay sick of a dangerous fever'. His doctor, 'the justly celebrated Dr Wilks of Willenhal', having treated him without success, eventually 'pronounced ... that speedy death must ensue, and took his leave'. Mr Inge's mother, 'wild with terror for the life of an only son', sent for the novice physician at Lichfield.

> By a reverse and entirely novel course of treatment, Dr Darwin gave his dying patient back to existence, to health, prosperity, and all that high reputation, which Mr Inge afterwards possessed as a public magistrate.[4]

Anna's circumlocutions are often puzzling: what was this 'reverse and entirely novel course of treatment'? Can it be that Inge was being poisoned by the drugs prescribed, and that Darwin just withdrew them?

Whatever the treatment, it succeeded, and Anna's story can be confirmed. The patient was William Inge (1737–85) of Thorpe Constantine, nine miles east of Lichfield. He later had four children and served as a Justice of the Peace and Chairman of the Sessions until his death.[5] The doctor was Richard Wilkes (1691–1760) and he was 'justly celebrated' as a doctor and antiquary.[6] He wrote *A Treatise on Dropsy* and collected materials for a history of Staffordshire that was completed by Stebbing Shaw.

'The far-spreading report of this judiciously daring and fortunate exertion', Anna tells us, 'brought Dr Darwin into immediate and extensive employment'. This is very believable, as is her report of 'an ingenious rival, who resigned the contest'. Then she flies off into a medical never-never land. 'Equal success, as in the case of Mr Inge, continued to result from the powers of Dr Darwin's genius ...' And she even acclaims 'his perpetual success'. This is unbelievable and is part of Anna's mythmaking, as she contrasts the perfect doctor with the imperfect man.

The smoke-screen of Anna's hype does not obscure the fact that Darwin had begun very well at Lichfield. A memorandum in his own hand[7] shows that his 'profits' for the seven weeks from 12 November to 31 December – that is, moneys already received – were £18 7s 6d. This is meaningless today without a suitable conversion factor, the choice of which can provoke endless argument. My own choice is to multiply by one hundred to give comparable values 'today' – that is, in the late 1990s. I believe this is realistic[8] for the years 1750–80, though rather too large for 1780–1803 when there was erosion of the value of money by about forty per cent. If my choice is accepted, the profits from Darwin's first seven weeks in Lichfield were equivalent to about £1800 today.

We don't know where Darwin lived after arriving in Lichfield. At first he 'lodged at Mr Bernards [in the] Close'.[9] But within the next few months his favourite sister Susannah, now twenty-eight, came to Lichfield as his house-keeper. So it seems that he quite soon rented a house, to consolidate his image as a successful doctor.

[2]

Darwin's clinical success with Mr Inge was soon followed by a notable scientific success: a paper he sent to the Royal Society in March 1757 was read at their meeting of 5 May and published in the *Philosophical Transactions* later in the year. The paper was entitled 'Remarks on the Opinion of Henry Eeles, Esq., concerning the Ascent of Vapour'. It fully deserved publication, for Darwin refuted a widely believed fallacy by making a decisive experiment; and he writes in an easy style that spares the dignity of Mr Eeles while gently destroying his hypothesis.

The paper begins with a flourish:

Gentlemen, There is ever such a charm attendant upon novelty, that be it in philosophy, medicine, or religion, the gazing world are too often led to adore, what they ought only to admire: whilst this vehemence of enthusiasm has generally soon rendered that object contemptible, that would otherwise have long laid claim to a more sober esteem. This was once the fate of chemistry ... and I should be sorry, if her sister electricity should share the same misfortunes ...

Eeles had argued that vapours rise only if they are electrically charged. Darwin points to various phenomena connected with clouds and steam that cast doubt on this idea, and then proceeds to his *pièce de résistance*, a conclusive experiment:

A glass tube, open at one end, and with a bulb at the other, had its bulb, and half way from thence to the aperture of the tube, coated on the inside with gilt paper. The tube was then inverted in a glass of oil of turpentine, which was placed on a cake of wax, and the tube kept in that perpendicular situation by a silk line from the ceiling of the room. The bulb was then warmed, so that, when it became cold, the turpentine rose about half-way up the tube. A bent wire then being introduced thro' the oil into the air above, high electricity was given. The oil did not appear at all to subside: whence I conclude, the electric atmosphere flowing round the wire and coating of the tube above the oil, did not displace the air, but existed in its pores.[10]

Darwin says he performed the experiment in the hope that electricity might make the air expand and so provide a means of improving the steam engine. But he found that electricity did not affect the mechanical properties of air, thus simultaneously dashing his own hopes and demolishing Eeles's idea.

This cogent early paper shows Darwin as a keen and skilful experimenter, and reveals his interest in steam and steam engines. It also foreshadows his classic work on the formation of clouds, for he refutes Eeles's idea that clouds only stay up if they are electrically charged. Darwin asserts that clouds stay up whether they are charged or not, and suggests that the decrease in air pressure as height increases is more important than the electrical state of the clouds.

Most scientific papers remain on the library shelf without creating any stir. Their authors fear they are unread. This is a common fate for a new author's first paper. But not for Darwin's: a hornet's nest of protest erupted in Lisburn, near Belfast, where Henry Eeles seethed with fury when he eventually read Darwin's paper, three years after it was published. Eeles had sent his paper to the Royal Society in 1754 and its publication in 1756 provoked Darwin's response, sent in March 1757. Unaware of this, Eeles sent a second paper to the Royal Society in August 1757 and a third in February 1758. In February 1760 he wrote complaining that these had not been acknowledged: presumably the Society decided to treat him as a crank.

Early in 1761 Eeles at last saw a copy of the *Philosophical Transactions* for 1757 and was appalled to find his paper rubbished by Darwin: 'with the liberties he has taken, he may confute or rather confound any author that ever wrote'.[11] He tries sarcasm, accuses Darwin of making 'a rhetorical flourish' and ends bluntly: 'I can tell Mr *Darwin* that the business of the steam engine is mostly carried on by the electric powers'. Even this thirty-six-page diatribe produced no response from the Royal Society; so the exasperated Eeles sent the President, Lord Macclesfield, an eighteen-page letter detailing his grievances. When that too was ignored, Eeles gathered together all his letters and published them, in 1771, as a book of 189 pages, called *Philosophical Essays*.

This could be the most voluminous response ever provoked by a virgin scientific author. Ironically, however, Darwin may never have known of the furore he created. It seems unlikely that the Royal Society told him about Eeles's complaint because there is no mention of it in his letters, and because he would have replied with a further paper. So he probably knew nothing about the hoo-ha until Eeles's book appeared fourteen years later. And, by a further irony, Darwin may not have known about the book: it was published in Dublin and was apparently not reviewed. Whether or not he was aware of it, Darwin's first scientific paper had a vigorous afterlife.

[3]

Erasmus enjoyed a very good year in 1757: in the spring or summer he fell in love with a girl whose home was in the Cathedral Close. Her name was Mary Howard, and she was seventeen. She was a friend and neighbour of Anna Seward, who was nearly three years younger. According to Anna, Mary was 'a blooming and lovely young lady' with a mind of 'native strength; an awakened taste for the works of imagination; ingenuous sweetness; delicacy animated by sprightliness, and sustained by fortitude'. These qualities 'made her a capable, as well as fascinating companion, even to a man of talents so illustrious'.[12]

Erasmus courted Mary in verse, as we might expect, and one of his courtship poems has survived. Its title is self-explanatory, 'To Miss Howard with Dodsley's miscellaneous Collection of Poems',[13] and Erasmus pretends he is merely offering a résumé of the volumes he is giving her. After a stilted start, sense soon melts into sensibility:

> From these mix'd Lines, my studious Fair shall know
> On human Breasts what chequer'd Passions glow:
> What trivial Deeds can serious Pains impart,
> Or pour soft-eddying Pleasures round the Heart.

'Eddying' was a favourite adjective of Darwin's, later taken over by Shelley, and 'soft-eddying' is a pleasing compound.

In subsequent verses Darwin works through his résumé: war-poems that may alarm Mary; smooth moral poems; comic verses; and of course she will find the 'Love-taught Lute ... Soft-warbling forth her sad-impassion'd Strains'. This is the nub of the poem and the cue for its real message:

> Then, peerless Fair! whom all my Soul approves,
> Esteems with Reason, and with Rapture loves,
> Indulgent hear thy Poet's honest Plea,
> And sometimes give one tender Thought on Me.

This suggests that Erasmus was still uncertain of her feelings; so the poem, for which he gives the date '1757', was probably written in the spring or summer.

It was not long before his ardent wooing impressed Mary, and she agreed to marry him. Keen to enjoy the pleasures of life, he saw no advantage in waiting; and his medical and scientific exploits were, it seems, enough to overcome her father's natural caution. So Erasmus and Polly, as he called her, were married at St Mary's Church, Lichfield,[14] on 30 December 1757. He was just twenty-six; her eighteenth birthday was six weeks ahead. Erasmus, with his wide experience of the world, was the dominant partner initially.

A long letter he wrote to her six days before the marriage catches the essence of Erasmus as a young man, bantering yet tender, exuberant, unconventional and confident of vaulting all obstacles. He was staying with the Jervis family at Darlaston Manor, near Stone, where he came across some musty recipes:

> Dear Polly,
> As I was turning over some old mouldy volumes, that were laid upon a Shelf in a Closet of my Bed-chamber; one I found, after blowing the Dust from it with a Pair of Bellows, to be a Receipt Book, formerly, no doubt, belonging to some good old Lady of the Family. The Title Page (so much of it as the Rats had left) told us it was 'a Bouk off verry monny muckle vallyed Receipts bouth in Kookery and Physicks'. Upon one Page was 'To make Pye-Crust', and in another 'To make Wall-Crust', – 'To make Tarts', – and at length 'To make Love'. 'This Receipt', says I, 'must be curious, I'll send it to Miss Howard next Post, let the way of making love be what it will.'[15]

(It was a long herbal recipe.) Next he found another prescription for making love, incomplete because 'Time with his long Teeth had gnattered away the remainder of this Leaf'.

> Then follow'd 'To make a good Wife'. 'Pshaw', continued I, 'an acquaintance of mine, a young Lady of Lichfield, knows how to make this Dish better than any other Person in the World, and she has promised to treat me with it sometime', and thus in a Pett I threw down the Book....

Erasmus is casual about the wedding arrangements and scornful of both bureaucracy and gossip:

> I will certainly be with Thee on Wednesday evening, the Writings are at my House, and may be dispatched that night, and if a License takes up any Time (for I know nothing at all about these things) I should be glad if Mr Howard would order one, and by this means, dear Polly, we may have the Ceremony over next morning at eight o'clock, before any Body in Lichfield can know almost of my being come Home.... I think this is much the best scheme, for to stay a few Days after my Return could serve no Purpose, it would only make us more watch'd and teazed by the Eye and Tongue of Impertinence.

He was ready to take marriage in his stride:

> Matrimony, my dear Girl, is undoubtedly a serious affair, (if any Thing be such) because it is an affair for Life. But, as we have deliberately determin'd, do not let us be *frighted* about this Change of Life; or however, not let any breathing Creature perceive that we have either Fears or Pleasures upon this Occasion: as I am certainly convinced, that the best of Confidants (tho' experienced on a thousand other Occasions) could as easily hold a burning cinder in their Mouth as anything the least ridiculous about a new married Couple!...

The 'Mr Howard' mentioned in the letter is Polly's father, the lawyer Charles Howard (1707–71), who was a proctor in the Ecclesiastical Court at Lichfield. His house was on the south side of the Close, on the site of the present No. 19, with a garden extending down to the Minster Pool. Born in Lichfield, Howard had been a schoolfellow and friend of Samuel Johnson, and he stood as surety at Johnson's marriage to Mrs Porter. Johnson thought him 'a cool and wise man', and Dr Thomas Newton, later Bishop of Bristol, called him 'a most facetious and pleasant companion' who with a better education 'would have been at the head of his profession'.[16]

Almost all we know of Howard confirms that he was cool, wise and capable: the one surprise is that he agreed so readily to the rapid marriage of his only daughter before she was eighteen. Presumably Erasmus was very persuasive. This is characteristic of him: he nearly always succeeded in what he wished to do, whether it was getting married, inventing a machine that spoke, or discovering how clouds form. There is no hint of coercion or haste about the marriage. The arrangements for settlements began a few months before: Mr Howard made a settlement of £1000 (equivalent to about £100,000 today) and this was matched on the Darwin side by 'a farm at Lincoln'[17] later valued at £1600. Though the first child of Erasmus and Polly was born just over eight months after their marriage, a slightly short pregnancy seems much more likely than a pre-marital one.

Mr Howard was a single parent, because his wife Penelope had died after childbirth when Polly was eight years old. Born Penelope Foley, she had married Charles Howard in 1734, and died at the age of forty in 1748.

Little is known of Penelope's father or mother; but her grandfather Philip Foley was the brother of Paul Foley, Speaker of the House of Commons; and her grandmother was born Penelope Paget, daughter of Lord Paget and Lady Frances Rich. Through her grandmother, Penelope Howard was descended via the Pagets from Anne Boleyn's sister Mary and (via the Rich family) from Lady Penelope Devereux, who was Sir Philip Sidney's 'Stella' and sister of Queen Elizabeth's favourite Earl of Essex.[18] This lineage was aristocratic but not very healthy. Only two of Penelope Howard's six children survived infancy. Of the two, Polly was to die at thirty, after much pain and illness in her last few years, while her brother Charles had a serious drink problem, but lived to forty-eight. These health details are of more than morbid interest, because of the prevalence of illness, apparently inherited, in later generations of Darwins, including the *cause célèbre* of Polly's grandson Charles Darwin.

[4]

Soon after their marriage Erasmus and Polly moved to a large house on the western boundary of the Cathedral Close, looking across Beacon Street to the open fields west of the town. Anna says they moved there in 1758, and I am inclined to accept this date because Erasmus would have been expected to take a substantial house in keeping with his status as a well-married and successful doctor – his earnings were £192 10s 6d in 1757, and £305 2s 6d in 1758 (about £30,000 today). Lady Gresley may have helped: she took a lease on Darwin's house and adjoining buildings[19] on 3 June 1758, perhaps on his behalf.

Anna says that the house was originally half-timbered and that Darwin added 'a handsome new front' facing Beacon Street, with 'venetian windows, and commodious apartments'. At first the Darwins lived in the old house, which faced the Cathedral. The new front was probably built in 1760, and can be seen in Plate 3A. As I write, the house is being renovated and converted into an Erasmus Darwin museum scheduled to open in 1999. The house has four large high-ceilinged rooms downstairs, an elegant staircase, and four rooms on the first floor, with another floor above of attic rooms. There is a cellar under the full area of the house, with several storerooms and with windows just above the present level of the ground outside, which is about eight feet below the ground-floor level. The present steps up to the front door were built after Darwin left. South of the house, on the right in the photograph, stands a separate brick-built block comprising coach-house, stables and saddling-room.

When Erasmus and Polly moved in, the front garden was 'merely a narrow, deep dingle ... overgrown with tangled briars and knot grass', Anna tells us.[20] This was part of 'the Dimble', the moat that surrounded the Close, and it can be seen today in front of the adjacent house. Across this dell 'Dr Darwin flung a broad bridge of shallow steps with chinese paling, descending from his hall-door to the pavement'. He cleared the dell 'into lawny smoothness' and 'planted it with lilacs and rose-bushes' and taller 'bushy shrubs'. Then he built a terrace along the front of the house, level with the ground floor. The taller shrubs, and perhaps a few ornamental trees, shielded the terrace in summer from passers-by on the road, but were probably cut low enough to let some afternoon sunshine reach the terrace. Plate 3B shows what the house and garden may have looked like when Erasmus and Polly were living there. The garden extended over the present footpath and probably to the edge of the present road.

In the summer of 1758 Polly went to stay with Erasmus's mother at Elston Hall, and he wrote to her there on 18 May. This letter, the only one from 1758, is chatty and of no consequence, but rich in snapshots of eighteenth-century life. Erasmus starts cheerfully enough: 'Dear Polly, I recieved and read your Letters with very great Pleasure, and hope you will weekly Write to me'.[21] Then the sad realities of daily life darken the scene. 'Fevers are very rife here', he says. 'I forgot to tell you that young Field-house dyed the next Day. Mrs Cobb's Hearse is this Moment going past our Door.' Moving away from 'all this Tragedy', he mentions that 'My Sister forgot that She had left some Cloths behind her'. Presumably Susannah took Polly to Elston, and may have been living with them at Lichfield earlier in the year, to help Polly gain confidence in housekeeping.

Erasmus then jumps to a different topic: 'I like the Mare my Brother has bought me, wonderfully'. This was his eldest brother Robert, who was called to the Bar in 1751 but succumbed to the call of Elston when he inherited the Hall on the death of his father in 1754. He lived there for sixty-two years.

Despite the alarming mortality at Lichfield, Erasmus himself is thriving:

> I am in good Health, have a baked Pudden every Day, and Milk and Bread to Breakfast ... a hot Toast and cold Milk is quite the Thing, taken in the Morning fasting.

He signs off 'from, dear Pollakin, thy very affect^t. Husband E.D.' Later he adds some more idle chit-chat: 'Lady Greasly [Gresley] has given me two queer colour'd Rabbits, so that I have now four: the Bantam Hen sits ... Mr Lamb pays close Addresses to Miss Robinson, so that Sudal is quite turn'd off.... Patty Fletcher has an Eruption all over her, which some suspect to be the Itch, caught from Ireland. O rare Food for Scandal!' The wrong spelling of Lady Gresley may be deliberate: she was known to gossips as

'Lady Blackwig'. The other names mean nothing to us today, but we can sniff something of the aroma of Lichfield life by reading between the lines.

Polly returned from Elston in time for the birth of her first child, a boy, on 3 September 1758. He was named Charles after Polly's father and brother, and was the first Charles in the Darwin family tree. Unlike his more famous nephew of the same name, he turned out to be a brilliant boy, and there is no mention of ill-health. In his short life he won the friendship and admiration of several men in the Lunar group.

All the available evidence confirms Anna Seward's judgment that Polly was an admirable partner for Erasmus. The marriage seems to have been very happy, marred only by Polly's illnesses in the last few years of her life. There is every reason to suppose that Charles was loved and cherished. In these early years Erasmus was out on his medical rounds more often and for longer than Polly would have wished. But he had to build up his practice by cultivating rich families living on distant country estates. In later years he covered about 10,000 miles a year by carriage, or thirty miles a day, and there is no reason why he should have travelled much less in the early years.

Polly was pregnant again by the spring of 1759, and in the summer she stayed at Elston for a time, as in the previous year. Presumably she enjoyed life there in the extended family.

One letter written to her at Elston in 1759 has survived: it is dated 'June 12 or 13'. Erasmus tells her that Mr and Mrs Peak of Birmingham were pressing so earnestly for her to stay some days with them that 'I almost promised for you'. After this serious start he reverts to the bantering tone so frequent in his letters:

> Tell Jack the Rabits please me and every Body wonderously: I tell People they are Bear's Cubbs, and that the Czarina sent me them as a present; and that I intend to breed them for Bacon, as is done in those Countrys.[22]

He also has a good gossipy story to tell. 'Jeff Gresley is run away from Bristol to Scotland with a young Girl, who He is going there to marry, to the great Concern of my Lady: She sent me Notice of it very early this Morning.' Lady Gresley was hoping that Erasmus might somehow intercept her errant son, who was eighteen. But 'how could I divine what Rout he had taken, or what Cloths he had on? Otherwise I would have despatched an express in search of him.' As he writes, 'it is now 4 o'Clock in the Afternoon', and 'Noboddy in this Town yet knows of this but me'. Jeff, he says, 'is a weak Boy, and has been spoilt in his Education, by being always treated like a Child. And, being always govern'd, never was taught to govern himself.' Then Erasmus signs off jokily with 'My Duty and Love and Service/from dear Poll/your faithful Friend E. Darwin', to which he adds, 'I hope the Cub's well'.

These two letters I have quoted so extensively are the only ones we have from Erasmus to Polly after their marriage. It is because neither has anything of real substance that both are so illuminating.

Polly was back in Lichfield when her second child, another son, was born on 11 October 1759. He was named Erasmus, and I shall call him Erasmus junior. As it turned out, this choice of name was unfortunate. He grew up introspective and retiring, unlike his exuberant father. He must have felt like a failure by comparison, and his father did not always behave well towards him when he was a boy, sometimes comparing him unfavourably with his brother Charles.

Erasmus and Polly were on good terms with the Sewards in these early years, and exchanged visits quite often, it seems. Erasmus was helping Anna with her poetry-writing. He must have been impressed because he began to doubt whether she was writing the verse unaided. One day in 1759 when she was sixteen, he gave her the beginning of a poem and asked her to complete it in the absence of her father. She passed the test and quashed his suspicions.[23]

This small episode had a serious outcome for Anna. When her father returned, Darwin praised her efforts and 'unluckily told him that his daughter's verses were better than his'.[24] This light-hearted remark was no joke for Seward. Eleven years before, Dodsley's *Collection of Poems* had included several by Seward, in particular 'The Female Right to Literature', written 'to a young Lady'. It is a feminist tract. Seward castigates 'that tyrant, man', who 'looks on slavery as the female dower', and urges the young lady to

> let thy growing mind
> Take ev'ry knowledge in of ev'ry kind.[25]

So Anna was given a full literary education. At the age of five she would stop playing and recite poetry. When she began writing poems, however, her mother did not approve: 'my father encouraged it, but my mother threw cold water on the rising fires'. It must have been a nagging source of marital discord. Darwin's comment was unfortunate because it changed her father's stance. Now both parents were against her, and Anna had to renounce authorship. Instead she became skilled in needlework and music. She still wrote a few poems in secret, but published nothing until after her mother's death in 1780. This parental ban on poetry will come to seem rather monstrous if, as is possible with help from feminists, Anna again becomes well known as a poet.

Anna might easily have turned against Darwin for his tactless remark to her father. To her credit she did not do so, because she was genuinely grateful to him for continuing to support her poetry writing, despite the ban imposed by her parents. Thirty years after the 'test' she wrote:

> He became a sort of poetic preceptor to me in my early youth. If I have critical knowledge in my favourite science, I hold myself chiefly indebted for it to him.... He had always very great poetic talents.[26]

Life in the Close was well insulated from the outer world, and Darwin did not take much notice of international events. But he was not immune to the spirit of the times, which was expansive and confident. His early years in Lichfield coincided with the Seven Years' War, which officially lasted from 1756 to 1763. The French were the main enemy, and William Pitt the elder became the war leader. Clive's victory at Plassey in 1757 led to British rule in India, and Wolfe's victory at Quebec in 1759 led to dominion over Canada. There are no surviving comments by Darwin on this expansion of empire, apart from a feeble poem in praise of Wolfe; local, domestic and scientific matters were of prime concern to him.

We leave Erasmus and Polly at the end of 1760 with two small sons to rear, and no more children to come for another three years. They were settled into their new home and, if there is such a thing as married bliss, they seem to have been close to it. Erasmus increased his earnings by more than fifty per cent in 1759: they totalled £469 4s; and in 1760 they were £544. He had lived at Lichfield for four years and was just twenty-nine. It was a success story by every criterion.

[5]

During his first five years at Lichfield Darwin found his most congenial new friends elsewhere, chiefly among men of science and men of business from Birmingham. In the late 1760s more were added, and the 'Lunar circle' came into being.

The first of these friends was Matthew Boulton (1728–1809) (Plate 4B), later 'the first manufacturer of England' but at this time a modest buckle-maker in Birmingham, a business he had taken over from his father. Darwin met Boulton quite soon after arriving at Lichfield, possibly through his Cambridge friend John Michell, who knew Boulton before 1758, or possibly through Boulton's brother-in-law Luke Robinson, who was one of Darwin's patients.

The friendship of Boulton and Darwin was to be strong and lifelong. Boulton was a business man with none of Darwin's cultural attainments in medicine, science and literature. But Boulton was eager to improve himself and his business, and not to go on for ever making buckles. Meeting Darwin gave him entrée into a new and more intellectual world. Darwin for his part did not want to spend all his time driving around dispensing good advice and dubious potions to rich patients: an enlightened manufacturer was a good friend for an inventor. As is obvious from all that followed, both Boulton and Darwin possessed superb social skills, for it was their combined bonhomie and persuasiveness that kept together the men of very diverse personalities who made up the Lunar Society.

There is not much written evidence about Darwin's meetings with his earliest scientific friend John Michell,[27] who continued to teach at Cambridge. 'A little short man, of a black complexion and fat', Michell was seven years older than Darwin and something of a mentor. He is now seen as the most distinguished man of science from Cambridge University in the second half of the eighteenth century. In 1750 he had written a treatise on 'Artificial Magnets', and he was called 'the father of seismology' as a result of his *Observations on Earthquakes* (1760). He helped to found modern geology through his studies of the strata of southern England. He was also influential in astronomy: he envisaged black holes, and had the idea of detecting the dark companions of stars from gravitational wobbles. He invented the torsion balance, which Henry Cavendish used to find the density of the Earth. He lectured on Hebrew and theology. Little wonder that Darwin referred to Michell seven years after his death as 'a man of such accurate and universal knowledge ... whose friendship I long possessed, and whose loss I have long lamented'.[28]

Michell rarely travelled to Birmingham after 1767, when he became rector of Thornhill near Leeds. But he was a major force in these early years. He certainly visited Darwin often enough to impress Anna Seward: 'To this *rus in urbe* of Darwinian creation [she means his house and garden] resorted, from its early rising, a knot of philosophic friends, in frequent visitation. The Rev. Mr Michell, many years deceased. He was skilled in astronomic science, modest and wise.' She mentions Boulton and others later, but Michell was first, in her memory at least.

Benjamin Franklin (Plate 4C) was the next of Darwin's scientific friends, and it was Michell who introduced him: 'I am sure you will readily excuse the Liberty I take', Michell wrote to Boulton on 5 July 1758, 'in sending this to introduce to your acquaintance the best Philosopher of America'.

After his invention of the lightning conductor and many researches in electricity, Franklin was the best-known man of science of the day. He was in England from 1757 to 1775, apart from a two-year return to Philadelphia in 1762–4. Franklin was touring the Midlands in 1758 and first visited Cambridge, where Michell gave him the letter of introduction. Boulton introduced Franklin to several of his friends, and would surely not have omitted Darwin, who had written about atmospheric electricity, Franklin's speciality. However, there is no written record of Darwin and Franklin meeting in 1758: if they did not, they would have met in 1760. I shall assume the earlier date, especially as Darwin was more inclined to travel that summer, with Polly away at Elston.

In the summer of 1758 Darwin was twenty-six and Franklin fifty-two. It is safe to say that Darwin was influenced and inspired by him. Darwin grew keener on experimental science after 1758, and the enthusiasm was lasting. Franklin may also have triggered the idea of the Lunar Society by talking about the American Philosophical Society which he founded at Philadelphia in 1743. His plan for this Society specified that the members should include 'a physician, a botanist, a mathematician, a chemist, a mechanician, a geographer and a natural philosopher'.[29] This could be seen as a model for the Lunar Society of Birmingham too: in both, variety was of the essence. Darwin usually treated Franklin as a friend rather than a mentor, but there is an occasional hint of deference that is absent from his bantering letters to other friends.

To complete Darwin's group of early scientific friends we have John Whitehurst (1713–88) of Derby (Plate 5A). Tall and quite thin, with long hair and no wig, he was 'easy and obliging' with a serious manner that sometimes covered a playful intent.[30] Immensely skilful as a maker of clocks and scientific instruments, he probably invented the 'clocking-in' time clock that ruled the lives of millions of factory workers for two centuries. Boulton was meeting Whitehurst by 1757 and, as Lichfield was on the road from Derby to Birmingham, Whitehurst was probably among Darwin's visitors in 1758–9. He may have re-aroused Darwin's interest in mechanical invention. We shall meet Whitehurst again as a member of the Lunar Society and a pioneer of geology.

Not all Darwin's friends were scientific and, in the absence of any written records, I shall mention three others who seem likely to have met him in these early years at Lichfield.

The first is the pioneering manufacturer Samuel Garbett (1717–1803).[31] About 1746, in Steelhouse Lane, Birmingham, he and Dr John Roebuck began constructing and operating the earliest sulphuric acid factory. They produced the acid far more cheaply than ever before and opened the way for the chemical industry. Garbett was also Roebuck's partner in a similar factory at Prestonpans and in the Carron Ironworks in Scotland. Boulton, Darwin and Wedgwood all sought advice from Garbett on business projects and Boulton later wrote, 'I have known him intimately three score years'; Darwin knew him well by 1763, and collaborated with him in one venture. Garbett would boldly promote new projects with loans 'secured' by promissory bills. This rashness, or enterprise, was a beguiling example to other entrepreneurs, including Boulton, who felt confident in following Garbett's lead, though with greater caution. Garbett remained outside the Lunar group, being a man fully committed to business and not intellectually inclined.

The second probable early friend is Robert Bage (1728–1801), the paper-maker and novelist. His paper mill at Elford, near Lichfield, was said to produce the finest paper in the country, and his radical-feminist novel *Hermsprong* (1796) is a classic text today. The historian William Hutton, who knew Bage for nearly sixty years, called him 'one of the most amiable of men'; William Godwin considered him 'a very memorable instance ... of great intellectual refinement, attained in the bosom of rusticity'; and Sir Walter Scott said, 'His integrity, his honour, his devotion to truth, were undeviating and incorruptible'.[32] This admirable man remained friendly with Darwin for more than forty years; but he was self-reliant rather than a joiner of societies.

The last of my trio is another remarkable Birmingham businessman, John Baskerville (1706–75), a friend of Bage and Garbett as well as of Boulton and Franklin. He made enough money as a japanner in the 1740s to allow him to pursue a passion for printing fine books, sometimes on Bage's paper. His first venture was the 'Virgil' of 1757, with Boulton, Darwin and Franklin among the subscribers. As well as admiring Basker-ville's books, Darwin may have been intrigued by his unconventional behaviour – he dressed in bright colours and was notorious for being an outspoken atheist. Baskerville was much praised in the 1760s for his beautiful Bibles, and he has often been called the finest printer of modern times.[33] Darwin would surely have met him, but probably in Birmingham rather than Lichfield, where he might have been allergic to the Cathedral.

Another possible early acquaintance of Darwin's, at Lichfield if at all, was the canal engineer James Brindley (1716–72), who was about to begin creating a new transport system for England.[34] In 1758 Brindley was com-missioned, by Lord Gower and others, to survey for a twenty-mile canal starting at the Minster Pool, adjacent to Lichfield Cathedral, and ending at King's Mills, near Derby. This was part of a greater plan for a canal to link Liverpool with Hull, which Brindley called the Grand Trunk Canal because he envisaged many branches, such as that to Lichfield. Brindley's estimate[35] for the section from Lichfield to King's Mills was £10,195. This may seem a remarkably low figure, equivalent to about £1 million today; but human diggers were cheaper than mechanical excavators. Nevertheless the project was judged to be too expensive. This 1758 survey was afterwards reviewed and extended by John Smeaton and Brindley jointly, and in 1760 they pub-lished the route from Burslem in the Potteries to Wilden near Derby, to-gether with the branch to Lichfield.[36]

Darwin could hardly have avoided knowing about the project because the Minster Pool is only a hundred yards from his house. The proposal may have sparked off the enthusiasm evident in his later campaigning for the Grand Trunk Canal, of which Brindley was chief engineer.

Brindley was a workman-genius, not someone who would have had intellectual conversations with Darwin. But Darwin always ignored class distinctions: in his poem *The Botanic Garden* Brindley is the only Englishman to be called 'immortal', and the epithet is justified because his canals live on today. (Darwin's only other 'immortal' is Franklin, for his role in founding the USA – which also lives on, despite its debts.)

Erasmus should not be blamed for the gender bias among his friends. As we shall see later, he was very much in favour of women learning science and technology, but he could not remove the existing barriers. Scientific women were rare in the eighteenth century: the best known are probably Voltaire's friend Emilie Du Châtelet, the Italian mathematician Maria Agnesi and the astronomer Caroline Herschel. There were a good number of women botanists, however, later in the century: Anna Blackburne and Maria Jacson were two known to Darwin. Female physicians and industrialists were very rare, being fewer than female soldiers and boxers. Businesswomen were not numerous, but it was fairly common for a widow to go on running her late husband's business. And the women skilled in domestic science far outnumbered the men skilled in academic science.

There is no indication that Erasmus tried to persuade Polly to learn science. Possibly she would have resisted the idea as unladylike. She would probably have seen her role as keeping up bright conversation with his visitors if they arrived when he was still out on his journeys, and she did this very well. She would join in general talk, too, but would expect 'the gentlemen' to have time on their own, in the conventional eighteenth-century manner.

The first of Darwin's friends, Matthew Boulton, remained the closest, but changes in his life left him less time for meeting Darwin. In 1749 Boulton had married the daughter of a rich mercer, Mary Robinson. They had three daughters who all died very young, and Mary herself died in 1759 at the age of thirty-two. The Robinson family, including Mary's sister Anne, lived at Lichfield, and Darwin was their physician. After Mary's death Boulton asked Anne to be his wife: but this was not strictly legal and, having consulted Darwin, Boulton married Anne away at Rotherhithe in 1760. Boulton's second marriage and the death of his father in 1759 made him quite rich, so he soon began planning a new and very large manufactory at Handsworth Heath on the outskirts of Birmingham. His abundant energy was almost absorbed by this ambitious project and the problems of its financing. He was often too busy to respond to Darwin's bright ideas. Their friendship had no chance of expanding into a society just yet.

CHAPTER THREE

Prospering
1761–1764

Now that Darwin was well established as a Lichfield doctor, what did others think of him in the early 1760s?

Our first witness has to be Anna Seward:*

> He was somewhat above the middle size, his form athletic, and inclined to corpulence; his limbs too heavy for exact proportion. The traces of a severe small-pox; features, and countenance, which, when they were not animated by social pleasure, were rather saturnine than sprightly; a stoop in the shoulders, and the then professional appendage, a large full-bottomed wig, gave, at that early period of life, an appearance of nearly twice the years he bore. Florid health, and the earnest of good humour, a sunny smile, on entering a room, and on first accosting his friends, rendered, in his youth, that exterior agreeable, to which beauty and symmetry had not been propitious.[1]

This is well written, and much less wordy than is usual with Anna. But she was a poet not a scholar, a woman of feeling rather than of accuracy. Erasmus's grandson Charles believed that, after Polly's illness and death, Anna had expected the grieving widower to turn to her for solace, and that she never overcame her resentment when this did not happen. Certainly she was sometimes waspish, sometimes generous, and nearly always ambivalent about her famous neighbour, whom she admired and yet at times detested.

The physical presence of Erasmus as described by Anna accords quite well with the general impression from others that he was tall and burly, like many male Darwins. My guess is that he was about six feet tall. His son Robert said 'his person was large and active', and R. L. Edgeworth called him 'a large man, fat and rather clumsy'. The 'sunny smile' mentioned by Anna is confirmed by all reports, though not recorded in his portraits. His son Robert wrote:

> When he parted from a person he regarded, his countenance was always cheerful with an expression that was pleasing as it conveyed that he had been pleased with his companion and not that he was glad to leave them.[2]

---

* All new paragraphs within quotations are inset, as in the originals.

Robert also confirms Anna by remarking that he 'was marked with the smallpox'.

Anna is critical about Darwin's demeanour towards others, both individually and in company, and this seems rather puzzling, if true. Dozens of his friends praised him for being kind and sympathetic to friends and patients; he had a great talent for friendship, and his friends were usually lifelong. His benevolence and his observant eye are said to have been the key to his great success as a doctor. However, Anna and a few others accused him of being domineering, irreligious and sarcastic.

I am not too surprised at these seeming inconsistencies: like many of us, Darwin was something of a chameleon in adapting to his environment. In congenial surroundings, with one friend or a group, he was charming, tolerant, kindly, thoughtful and also usually the life and soul of the party: his continuous talent for friendship was so strong that this judgment must be valid. But he could quickly be annoyed by cruelty or injustice, or by a casual acquaintance who contradicted him boorishly. His son Robert, again referring to a later period, wrote: 'He was sometimes violent in his anger, but ... if what he said was resented, he suspected he might have said too much, and his sympathy and benevolence made him try to sooth or soften matters.'[3]

The most important character-witness is his judicious friend James Keir, writing after Darwin's death:

> I think all those who knew him will allow that sympathy and benevolence were the most striking features. He felt very sensibly for others, and, from his knowledge of human nature, he entered into their feelings and sufferings in the different circumstances of their constitution, character, health, sickness, and prejudice. In benevolence, he thought that almost all virtue consisted. He despised the monkish abstinences and the hypocritical pretensions which so often impose on the world. The communication of happiness and the relief of misery were by him held as the only standard of moral merit. Though he extended his humanity to every sentient being, it was not like that of some philosophers, so diffused as to be of no effect; but his affection was there warmest where it could be of most service to his family and his friends, who will long remember the constancy of his attachment and his zeal for their welfare.[4]

Keir was always admired for his honesty and his grasp of human nature. He was the Lunar Society's favoured chairman, able to ensure that everyone had their say and adept at reconciling their varied views. His characterization of Darwin should be far more reliable than Anna's, and I see it as definitive.

On one subject, his benevolence as a doctor, all reports agree. Even Anna is quite specific, and less verbose than usual:

> Professional generosity distinguished Dr Darwin's medical practice. While resi-

dent in Lichfield, to the priests and lay-vicars of its cathedral, and their families, he always cheerfully gave his advice, but never took fees from any of them. Diligently, also, did he attend to the health of the poor in that city, and afterwards at Derby, and supplied their necessities by food, and all sort of charitable assistance. In each of those towns, *his* was the cheerful board of almost open-housed hospitality, without extravagance or parade.'[5]

Another point on which all his listeners agreed was his bad stammer. 'He stammered extremely', Anna tells us, 'but whatever he said, whether gravely or in jest, was always well worth waiting for, though the inevitable impression it made might not always be pleasant to individual self-love.' An example is given by his son Robert:

> A young man once asked him in, as he thought, an offensive manner, whether he did not find stammering very inconvenient. He answered, 'No, Sir, it gives me time for reflection, and saves me from asking impertinent questions.'[6]

If the question was asked less offensively, he often replied that stammering helped a young doctor by drawing attention to him. In *Zoonomia* Darwin says stammering arises from 'awe, bashfulness, ambition of shining, or fear of not succeeding'. He advocates long practice in speaking each difficult word, and 'much commerce with mankind, in order to acquire a carelessness about the opinions of others'.[7]

Despite his stammer Darwin was generally reckoned a splendid talker. His son Robert thought his greatest talent lay in his conversational powers and his skill in explaining abstruse topics intelligibly. Maria Edgeworth referred to 'those powers of wit, satire and peculiar humour, which never appeared fully to the public in his works, but which gained him strong ascendancy in private society.'[8] Lady Charleville, 'who had been accustomed to the most brilliant society in London', told Robert 'that Dr Darwin was one of the most agreeable men whom she had ever met'. That renowned conversationalist S. T. Coleridge called Darwin 'wonderfully entertaining and instructive'[9] as a talker: no one else received such praise from Coleridge.

In contrast stands Anna Seward's rebuke: 'he became, early in life, sore upon opposition, whether in argument or conduct, and always revenged it by sarcasm of very keen edge'.[10] As ever Anna is expressing personal feelings, and the phrase 'early in life' suggests she may have been taking a revenge forty years deferred: in Darwin's early years at Lichfield, Anna was an uppish teenager, and he may have been too vigorous in putting her down when she said silly things. Charles Darwin rebutted her accusation: 'Miss Seward speaks of him as being extremely sarcastic, but of this I can find no evidence in his letters or elsewhere'.[11] This is true: he was never sarcastic in writing. However, he could be wounding as well as charming in conversation. Charles Darwin himself gives an example:

When he wished to make himself disagreeable for any good cause, he was well able to do so. Lady *** married a widower, and became so jealous of his former wife that she cut and spoiled her picture, which hung up in one of the rooms. The husband, fearing that his young wife was becoming insane, was greatly alarmed, and sent for Dr Darwin. When he arrived he told her in the plainest manner many unpleasant truths, amongst others that the former wife was infinitely her superior in every respect, including beauty. The poor lady was astonished at being thus treated, and could never afterwards endure his name. He told the husband if she again behaved oddly, to hint that he would be sent for. The plan succeeded perfectly, and she ever afterwards restrained herself.[12]

What should we make of Darwin, after hearing these varied stories? I would emphasize something not mentioned so far, his sunny disposition and optimistic view of the world. It was his lifelong daily lot to visit dying patients while knowing he could do nothing for them, except to be cheerful. And that cheerfulness never crumpled, except after bereavement.

I also see Darwin as a supremely good communicator. He was uncannily perceptive and extremely knowledgeable: Coleridge thought that 'Dr Darwin possesses, perhaps, a greater range of knowledge than any other man in Europe'.[13] But, unlike most people stuffed with knowledge, Darwin could remember it and call up relevant items from the data-bank in his head – instantly, apart from the slight pause for the stammer. Armed with this potent weapon and his sunny smile, he seems to have been able to persuade almost anyone to do almost anything. He was very rarely thwarted, even being able to divine the workings of Nature as no one before him did – when he saw biological evolution as the key to the living world. He was also very sensitive, despite his bluff exterior. For the last word I call on Keir again: 'sympathy and benevolence were the most striking features. He felt very sensibly for others ...'

[2]

In 1760 Darwin's second paper in the *Philosophical Transactions* of the Royal Society was published. Entitled 'An uncommon case of an Haemoptysis', it describes a patient who was wakened nightly at 2 a.m. by the spitting of blood. Darwin argues that the lungs were 'not sufficiently sensible to push forwards the whole circulation' and that the blood accumulated and ruptured some small blood vessels. He advised the patient 'to be awakened, and rise out of his bed, at one in the morning, and remain awake till three, omitting all medicines'.[14] The case seems trivial, but at least the treatment was simple and, it seems, successful.

Throughout his life Darwin took little notice of what was going on in London. He was always fully involved with the local community, as a doctor, as a member of a social group, or just within his family. The Royal Society of London is the one exception to this rule, and the best explanation is his father's pride, handed down by word of mouth, at having been an invited guest of the Society in 1718. When Sir Isaac Newton died in 1727, the old order changed at the Royal Society. The emphasis moved away from the search for universal laws, such as the law of gravitation, towards more practical pursuits such as natural history, medicine, better measurements in astronomy and meteorology, and mathematics usefully applied – to geography and navigation, for example.[15] The Society was weak in chemistry and in physics, apart from experiments with electricity, in which Franklin was pre-eminent.

On 9 April 1761 Darwin was elected a Fellow of the Royal Society. His certificate of candidature had conventional wording. His proposers said he 'appears to us on our personal knowledge to be a Gentleman well qualified to be an usefull member of the Society'.[16] His certificate was first 'suspended' on 8 January 1761 and, as was customary, at ten subsequent meetings, before he was 'Ballotted and Elected' on 9 April.

Darwin had five Fellows as sponsors: Noah Thomas, John Hadley, John Lewis Petit, John Ross and Charlton Wollaston. We have already met Dr Noah Thomas, whose lectures Darwin attended. The other names are all new. This does not mean that Darwin had a separate group of friends in London: all four were acquaintances from his Cambridge years, and most of them are unlikely to have met him subsequently. John Hadley was Professor of Chemistry at Cambridge and, like Michell, a Fellow of Queen's College. John Ross was a Fellow of St John's College in the 1750s and became Bishop of Exeter in 1778.[17] Charlton Wollaston had been a medical student at Sidney Sussex College in Darwin's time, and was doing well as a physician until a fever carried him off.[18] These three, having given Darwin a helping hand, do not figure again in his life story.

That leaves one further signatory, J. L. Petit, a young live-wire member of Queen's College who became a physician. He was already familiar enough with Darwin to write in a letter to Boulton in 1762: 'I enclose this letter to Darwin who will convey it to you I hope, if he does not put it in his pockett, and forget it.'[19] Darwin did send it on, and told Boulton: 'Dr Petit desires you'll write a Paper and become a Member of the R.S.' So it was probably Petit who did most to propel Darwin into the Fellowship, no doubt with a nod from Michell, though Michell himself did not sign the certificate. Darwin would not have needed to push himself forward in any way. Nor did he make much use of his Fellowship. Every Fellow should sign the Charter Book, but he never did so, because his next visit to London was not until 1781, and by then he would have forgotten about signing the book. He was not alone in this neglect: about a quarter of all the eighteenth-century Fellows failed to sign (chiefly because of travel problems or premature death).

Erasmus may have been rather casual about his Fellowship of the Royal Society; but for the Society it turned out to be historic, the start of an overlapping succession of Fellows which has so far lasted for nearly 240 years through six generations of Darwins. Erasmus was a Fellow from 1761 to 1802, his son Robert from 1788 to 1848, Robert's son Charles from 1839 to 1881, Charles's son George Darwin from 1879 to 1912, George's brothers Francis from 1882 to 1925 and Horace from 1903 to 1928; and George's son Sir Charles Galton Darwin was a Fellow from 1922 to 1962. That is 201 years in the male succession. Abandoning such an outdated sexist concept extends the line of Fellows to the present day and to the sixth generation, with George's grandson Richard Keynes (elected 1959) and Horace's grandson Horace Barlow (elected 1969). This is a record unlikely ever to be equalled – the Everest of its genre.

[3]

We now return from the far future to Erasmus and Polly at Lichfield in the years 1761–4. Their house had been adequate at first; but with the two boys and, at a guess, two servants living in – a housemaid and a nursery maid – it did not seem so spacious. As Anna remarked, Erasmus liked to keep open house. His sister Susannah, or 'Sukey' as she was known, may have stayed quite often to keep Polly company, and he wished to be able to offer good overnight accommodation to any visiting friends who might arrive unexpectedly. Also he sometimes had to find room for a patient who was too ill to travel home or needed treatment over several days.

Darwin solved the space problem by using part of the building next door, known as the Vicars' Hall (on the left in Plate 3B). The legal arrangements seem to have been made[20] in August and September 1760, Lady Gresley again being involved. Within the next few years he joined the two houses by making a hole through the dividing wall – evidence of it remains today. He thus created an annexe for friends or patients, cut off from most of the house-noise. This larger house, which sometimes served as a mini-hotel or private hospital, was in line with his larger income: during 1761 he earned £669 18s.

As these figures suggest, Erasmus was 'very zealous in his profession', and it would be no surprise to Polly if he was away travelling for most of the daylight hours. But he would often have been at home on winter evenings to play his part in the social life of the Close. In the early 1760s these social comings and goings were frequent, largely because Mr Seward and his wife liked to host evening gatherings of their Close friends, and were egged on by their lively daughters Anna and Sarah, who were aged twenty and eighteen at the end of 1762. Many of Anna's stories about Darwin's conversation came from listening to him on these occasions.

Darwin's zeal for science and medicine would sometimes lure him into social activities that Anna would have found repulsive. In the eighteenth century it was difficult to acquire bodies for dissection, and the dastardly crime of body-snatching was rife. When the opportunity came legally, Darwin seized it:

> October 23rd, 1762 – The body of the Malefactor, who is order'd to be executed at Lichfield on Monday the 25th instant, will be afterwards conveyed to the House of Dr Darwin, who will begin a Course of Anatomical Lectures, at Four o'clock on Tuesday evening, and continue them every Day as long as the Body can be preserved; and shall be glad to be favoured with the Company of any who profess Medicine or Surgery, or whom the Love of Science may induce.[21]

We do not know how many were induced to attend; nor whether Polly welcomed such a macabre lodger in her house, or possibly in the new extension. His name was Thomas Williams,[22] and his fate qualifies him for a place among the men more famous after death than in life. Darwin's decision to dissect would not have been an impromptu whim but the fulfilment of a promise to do so if a body became available. He would have received requests to demonstrate human anatomy from local surgeons, apothecaries or medical students, or even from clergymen wishing to inspect God's handiwork – six years later the Revd Richard Gifford and the Revd Robert Clive made just such a request.[23]

A puzzling feature of Darwin's early medical practice is his attitude to alcohol. Anna tells us 'he avowed a conviction of the pernicious effects of all vinous fluid on the youthful and healthy constitution; an absolute horror of spirits of all sorts and however diluted.... From strong malt liquor he totally abstained, and if he drank a glass or two of English wine, he mixed it with water.'[24] Anna may be confusing his early and later attitudes, but she was probably right in saying that he abstained from strong spirits. If so, his alleged decision to 'relinquish Bacchus' at Edinburgh would only apply to spirits.

He seems to have been quite friendly to wine in the early years. The house at Lichfield has a large wine cellar, and in 1763 he wrote to Boulton: 'Now if you like Florence Wine, I begg leave to make you a present of one Bottle, or two, if the first does not answer, to drink success to Philosophy and Trade'.[25] He was still stocking up with wine six years later when he put in an order via Boulton: 'If you see Mr Baumgartner I shall be glad of a Chest of white Florence Wine'.[26] Later in his career Darwin condemned alcohol more vigorously, having concluded that it caused much of the illness he saw among the rich, from gout and liver disease to what he called the 'insanity' of alcoholism.

During the early 1760s, it seems, Erasmus and Polly continued to live happily in their enlarged house, receiving a fair number of visitors, either family (like Susannah) or scientific (like Michell). On 19 November 1763 Polly gave birth to a daughter, who was named Elizabeth after Erasmus's mother and eldest sister, and was christened in the Cathedral on 23 December. But the baby died after four months, on 29 March 1764, and was buried in the Cathedral Close on 1 April.

Untimely death also struck the Sewards in 1764. Anna's younger sister Sarah, now twenty, was engaged to marry Joseph Porter, Samuel Johnson's stepson. But Sarah fell ill, apparently of typhus fever, and Darwin could do nothing to save her. Anna sadly notes how 'Dr D. says when the fever returned it was with a fatal change in its nature from inflammatory to putrid, and that he has very little hope of saving her.'[27]

At the end of 1764 Erasmus was thirty-three and Polly was nearly twenty-five: their son Charles was six and Erasmus five. Darwin had been at Lichfield for eight years, and his income had now stabilized at about £700 per annum (about £70,000 today). The exact figures for 1762–4 were £726 7s, £639 13s and £750 13s. Settled in his medical career and with less need to seek new patients, he could relax a little.

Anna has a story difficult to believe but too circumstantial to ignore which certainly shows him relaxing, and confirms her belief that if he drank wine he mixed it with water:

> Mr Sneyd, then of Bishton, and a few more gentlemen of Staffordshire, prevailed upon the Doctor to join them in an expedition by water, from Burton to Nottingham, and on to Newark. They had cold provision on board, and plenty of wine. It was midsummer; the day ardent and sultry. The noontide meal had been made, and the glass gone gayly round. It was one of those *few* instances, in which the medical votary of the Naiads transgressed his general and strict sobriety. If not absolutely intoxicated, his spirits were in a high state of vinous exhilaration. On the boat approaching Nottingham, within the distance of a few fields, he surprised his companions by stepping, without any previous notice, from the boat into the middle of the river, and swimming to shore. They saw him get upon the bank, and walk coolly over the meadows toward the town: they called to him in vain, he did not once turn his head.[28]

Nonplussed at his behaviour, Mr Sneyd and his party pursued the Doctor, Anna says, and found him in the market place standing on a tub addressing a crowd, without a trace of his usual stammer. He was lecturing his audience on the benefits of fresh air, and telling them to keep their windows open at night. Then he calmly rejoined the party, slightly damp but otherwise normal. Anna has the temerity to give Darwin's speech verbatim, as if she had tape-recorded it, though she candidly admits she only heard the story after Darwin's death – perhaps forty years after he made the speech! When asked, Mr Sneyd said something 'similar' did happen: possibly one of the party tricked Darwin into drinking wine laced with stronger liquor.

[4]

The early 1760s can be seen as the years when the Industrial Revolution in Britain gained the momentum to make it unstoppable. There had been important isolated achievements earlier. The Lombes' six-floor silk mill on the Derwent at Derby, completed in the 1720s, was the first real factory, with 300 employees. (According to Defoe,[29] who called it 'a Curiosity of a very extraordinary Nature', the Mill worked 318 million yards of silk per day.) John Kay invented the flying shuttle in 1733; Abraham Darby II produced cast iron with coke at Coalbrookdale in the early 1740s; and in 1746, as we have seen, Roebuck and Garbett began making sulphuric acid by the lead-chamber process.[30]

The early 1760s, however, brought advances of wider significance. Roebuck introduced new processes at the Carron Ironworks. The Duke of Bridgewater's canal near Manchester pointed the way to a nationwide network – an idea keenly advocated by Darwin in 1765. James Hargreaves invented the 'spinning jenny' and James Watt the improved steam engine. Boulton was building his grand new manufactory, the Soho works, completed in 1766 and sometimes called the eighth wonder of the world. There Watt's engine was to be developed in the 1770s.

In the early 1760s Boulton was being infected with Darwin's enthusiasm for experiments on air, heat and electricity, and soon he became known for producing accurate scientific instruments, particularly thermometers. In 1762 Dr Petit wrote to Boulton 'to desire a few thermometers of you. I was greatly at a loss for some ... as I had only your Pocket one and another which I bought which I had not any great opinion of, as it did not correspond with yours.'[31] This was in the letter sent on by Darwin, who added, 'Why won't you sell these Thermometers, for I want one also myself.'[32] And it was not only Darwin: the lack of accurate thermometers was impeding research on heat.

Having acquired a Boulton thermometer, Darwin was preparing to make some bold advances in the theory of heat, as he explained to Boulton on 1 July 1763:

As you are now become a sober plodding Man of Business, I scarcely dare trouble you to do me a Favour in the nicknachatory, alias philosophical way:

I have got a most exquisitely fine Balance, and a very neat Glass Box, and have all this day been employ'd in twisting the necks of Florence-Flasks – in vain!

Then comes the offer of two bottles of Florence Wine, already quoted,

upon condition that you will procure me one of their Necks to be twisted into a little Hook according to the copper Plate on the reverse of this Paper. It must be truly hermetically seal'd, air tight, otherwise it will not answer my End at all ...

I am extreemly impatient for this new Play-Thing! as I intend to fortell every Shower by it, and make great medical Discovery as far as relates to the specific Gravity of air: and from the Quantity of Vapor. Thus the specific gravity of the air should be as the Absolute Gravity (shew'd by the Barometer), and as the Heat (shew'd by Boulton's Thermometer). Now if it is not always found as these two (that is as one and inversely as the other) then the Deviations at different Times must be as the Quantity of dissolved Vapour in the air.[33]

These last two sentences are astonishing: Darwin states what is now usually known as the ideal gas law, that density is proportional to pressure divided by absolute temperature; and he also has a clear premonition of the law of partial pressures. Of these two fundamental gas laws, the first is usually credited to J. A. C. Charles (1787) and the second to John Dalton (1801).

Darwin seems to have been particularly inventive in 1763. Besides casually enunciating these gas laws, he was keen to put the water vapour to good practical use by improving existing steam engines, and he was busy with new designs of carriages, to make his daily rounds as a doctor more comfortable.

Darwin's interests in steam and carriages combined to give birth (at least on paper) to a steam carriage. Boulton received the full flood of his enthusiasm in a long letter written in 1763 or 1764:

Dear Boulton,

As I was riding Home yesterday, I concider'd the Scheme of the fiery Chariot, and the longer I contemplated this favourite Idea, the [more] practicable it appear'd to me. I shall lay my Thoughts before you, crude and indigested as they occur'd to me ... as by those Hints you may be led into various Trains of thinking upon this Subject.... And as I am quite mad of this Scheme, I begg you will not mention it, or shew this Paper to ... any Body ...

He goes on to discuss whether the carriage should have three or four wheels, and comes down in favour of four. He suggests a design with two cylinders operating from one boiler: 'By the management of the steam Cocks the motion may be accelerated, retarded, destroy'd, revived, instantly and easyly. And if this answers in Practice as it does in theory, the Machine can not fail of Success! Eureka!'[34]

This is all very well, but what did Darwin propose for the transmission system? His design was for a beam engine, with cords from the ends of the beam winding and unwinding round a split rear axle. As his diagram

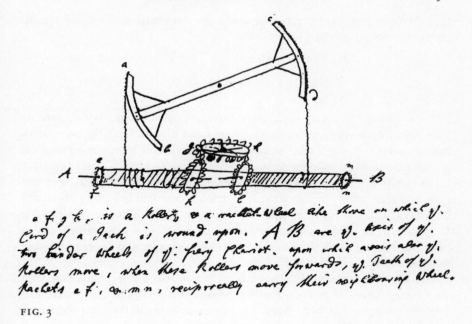

a f g k e, is a Roller, & a ratchet wheel like those on which y.
Cord of a Jack is wound upon. A B are y. axis of y.
two hinder wheels of y. fiery Chariot. upon which axis also y.
Rollers move, when these Rollers move forwards, y. Teeth of y.
rackets e f, & mn, reciprocally carry their neighbouring wheel.

FIG. 3

shows, Fig. 3, the semi-axles would be counter-rotating through the universal gear at the centre: each semi-axle would drive its wheel when the cord was being (forcibly) unwound by the motion of the beam, and would 'free-wheel' during the other half of the cycle, when the cord would be rewound through the forced counter-rotation of the axle. This method would propel the carriage smoothly, Darwin thought, 'without any loss of power or cumbersome weight of machinery'. A similar idea led to the design of the highly successful Daf cars, with belts for transmission, so Darwin's design does not deserve to be dismissed as impracticable. It might have been rather jerky, and disastrously so if the timing became inaccurate, but the same criticism applies to the modern internal combustion engine.

Darwin was keen for Boulton to build the vehicle:

> If you could learn the Expence of Coals of a common fire-engine, and the Weight of water it draws, some certain Estimate may be made if such a Scheme as this would answer.... If you think it feasible and will send me a Critique upon it, I will certainly ... endeavour to build a Fiery Chariot; and if that answers get a Patent. If you chuse to be Partner with me in the Profit, and Expense and Trouble, let me know: as I am determined to execute it, if you approve of it.[35]

Boulton, already in debt, was not prepared to chance his arm on such a futuristic project, and the inventor himself was too busy with his medical practice to do more than prod Boulton. So the scheme fizzled out, and the Frenchman N. J. Cugnot made the first working steam carriage,[36] in 1769.

Still, Darwin has rightly received credit for first stating the correct principles for making steam cars.[37]

[5]

For Darwin the years 1761–4 were the least eventful of his life, and he
may have felt he was getting into a rut. He was pleased with his inventions,
but he could not 'come out' as an inventor for fear of harming his medical
practice. So what should he do?

To him the Industrial Revolution seemed a glorious enterprise, with science and technology bringing great benefits to humankind. Why shouldn't
he himself become an industrial entrepreneur, like Boulton or Garbett? If
Boulton was being coy about the steam car, what about something not so
'way out', though still quite advanced technologically, and likely to prosper
as the Revolution burgeoned?

For Darwin this seems to have been the *raison d'être* of his role in a
surprising industrial project, the Wychnor Ironworks. The Ironworks had
four proprietors: Garbett, Bage, Darwin and John Barker, a prosperous
Lichfield businessman, variously described in documents as a draper, a
merchant, a banker and a gentleman.[38] Little is known about the enterprise, and most of that little has been discovered by Jim Gould,[39] whose
findings I shall summarize.

In the early 1760s Garbett was concerned about the poor quality of the
iron being produced in the Midlands: he feared disastrous failures of nails,
hoops, etc. He proposed that high-quality iron bars should be imported,
and then made into rods, hoops, sheets and nails in English rolling and slit-
ting mills, of which there were not enough.

A good site for such a mill would be where the river Trent crossed
the Lichfield-Derby turnpike, at Wychnor, six miles north-east of Lichfield.
The river might provide the power; the turnpike would give road access. By
a fortunate chance, Brindley's route for the Grand Trunk Canal merged
with the Trent near Wychnor for a few hundred yards. So someone, most
likely Darwin, had the bright idea of preparing a stretch of the canal in
advance, by making a cut fourteen feet wide from the Trent along the projected line of the canal for about 600 yards, and then for a further 400
yards into a basin adjacent to the proposed ironworks (Fig. 4). From the
basin there would be a fall of seven feet to the Trent, enough to power a
mill. When the canal came to be constructed, the 600-yard cut could be
(and was) sold 'advantageously' to the canal company. The ironworks
would also have the benefit of direct access to the future canal via the 400-
yard cut. The supply of water to the basin from the future canal would be

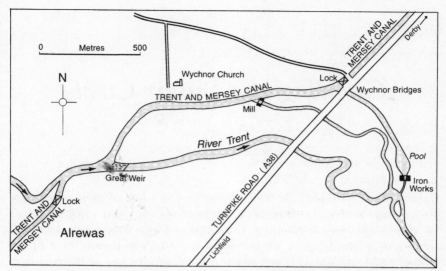

FIG. 4 Sketch map to show the location of the Wychnor Ironworks, with today's geography, which is much the same as in the 1770s – except that scarcely any trace of the Ironworks now remains, and the A38 is wider than the turnpike road

no problem because the canal would here be topped up by the river Trent. But there was a problem over the immediate water supply, which the miller at Wychnor corn-mill could control. So he had to be bought out.

This ambitious project called for much negotiation, with landowners, their lawyers and the Wychnor miller, Mr Woodhouse, who proved obstinate. There are ten letters from Darwin to Barker between December 1763 and March 1764, some setting out draft agreements and some frantically trying to direct agents who were dashing around in all directions.[40] (Mobile phones would have been a godsend.) In May 1764 the proprietors asked permission to build a bridge for 'a canal or ditch 14 feet wide' under the Turnpike road.[41] Barker, Darwin and his father-in-law Mr Howard were all Commissioners of the Turnpike Trust, so it is no surprise that permission was given. To satisfy Mr Woodhouse was not so easy. They had to buy him an empty mill at Alrewas where the eel-fishery was more valuable (being worth £15 a year). This buying-off was expensive, and in one letter Darwin speaks of £2000 being spent 'before we can begin to work at all'. Maybe it was even more, because Erasmus borrowed £1000 from his brother Robert[42] in 1765, presumably for this purpose.

Darwin expended much effort as well as money on this project in 1764. It seems that he was the energizer, Garbett the business adviser and metallurgist, Bage the expert in mill technology, and Barker the local link-man and manager of the mill once it was built. The Wychnor Ironworks was probably operating by 1765, but proved rather disappointing to its owners, as we shall see later.

CHAPTER FOUR

Creating the Lunar Circle
1765–1768

Darwin made friends easily but lost touch with some of them when they moved away to live at a distance. Then, between 1765 and 1768, his talent for friendship seems suddenly to have flowered into what might be called creative genius as he drew in, one by one and independently, most of the group of lifelong friends later known as the Lunar Society of Birmingham. At the beginning of 1765, he knew only Boulton and Whitehurst; by the end of 1768 nearly all of the group had met each other. They never were a formal 'Society', and I shall often use the words 'group' or 'circle' to signal this informality.

[2]

During 1765 much of Darwin's energy went into promoting the Grand Trunk Canal, in close collaboration with its chief activator, Josiah Wedgwood of Burslem (1730–95) (Plate 5B).[1] Humbly born, Wedgwood had by thrift, skill and hard work acquired a pottery of his own by 1759, and soon he began the experimental improvements that were to make him world-famous. But he was hampered by the problems of carrying the goods along the rutted tracks that masqueraded as roads. The pottery was often smashed as the bone-shaking vehicles bounced over the bumps and into the pot-holes or (at worst) overturned. Loading the goods on pack-horses was not much better.

In 1762, while travelling to Liverpool on horseback, Josiah himself was forced off the road by a passing carriage and injured his leg. In Liverpool he was most fortunate to be treated by Matthew Turner, a good doctor and a man of many talents.[2] During Wedgwood's slow convalescence Turner brought along as company a friend of his, Thomas Bentley, a cultured and affluent merchant,[3] whose wife had died in childbirth three years before. The outcome was extraordinary, because Wedgwood and Bentley liked each other so well and in business complemented each other so perfectly. Five years later they became business partners in the famous firm of Wedgwood and Bentley.

Wedgwood was familiar with the route for the canal from Burslem to Wilden Ferry as planned by Smeaton and Brindley. If only it could be constructed, and extended to Liverpool, he would be able to build a new factory beside it and send his goods safely to Hull or Liverpool. It was an idea whose time had come. All it needed was a superman to promote it. In 1764 Wedgwood discussed the idea with Bentley and also with Brindley, who was already known to Wedgwood as a local millwright of great ingenuity.

The first written sign of extra activity by Wedgwood is in his letter to Bentley of 2 January 1765.[4] He reports having travelled with Brindley to meet Lord Gower, Mr Garbett, Mr Gilbert and others to decide between two rival schemes of operation for the canal. Lord Gower was the leading landowner of the region and had commissioned Brindley's survey in 1758. He was a man of national influence who had already held several Government posts and later declined the Prime Ministership. 'Mr Gilbert' was Thomas Gilbert, MP for Newcastle-under-Lyme, who had proposed a scheme of operation that Wedgwood disliked and now successfully opposed.

For the next two years Wedgwood devoted much of his time and effort to the project. He began by seeking support from landowners and other influential residents along the route. He selected Darwin as a likely supporter from Lichfield, probably on Garbett's advice.

Darwin was enthusiastic about the proposed canal, perhaps even more so than Wedgwood at that time.[5] Wedgwood was delighted, and seems to have hoped at first that Darwin would lead the campaign. In a long letter on 3 April 1765, Wedgwood tells Darwin 'you … have public spirit enough to be Generalissimo in this affair'.[6] This is probably Wedgwood's first letter to Darwin, because it has the formal ending, 'I am very respectfully / Dear Sir / Your most obedt hble servt'. Wedgwood mentions that he has prevailed upon the Mayor of Newcastle-under-Lyme to call a meeting 'to petition Lord Gower to take this Navigation under his patronage' and to compose 'a Letter of approbation' that might be sent to the Mayor of Liverpool. 'But in this as well as every other step, we shall be govern'd by your advice.' Darwin wrote back on 5 April, probably saying he had not the time to be Generalissimo, and wrote again on 12 April, though both letters are lost.

In his next letter, on 13 April, Wedgwood tells Darwin that the Mayor's petition to Lord Gower 'will be presented today', and that he himself will present another tomorrow, from 'the Manufacturers of Earthenware'. Lord Gower lived within easy distance, at Trentham, five miles south of Burslem.

Two days later, on 15 April, Wedgwood writes again, having received Darwin's letter of the 12th, which included short articles intended for publication in the *St James's Chronicle* and other journals. He tells Darwin that on the way to Trentham, he met John Gilbert, the Duke of Bridgewater's agent, and showed him the plans for the canal. Gilbert wanted it to 'join the Duke's canal', and Wedgwood said he would 'do everything to make it agreeable to his Grace'. Thomas Gilbert the MP (and brother of John) 'was at Trentham and was highly pleased with the Plan'.[7] Mr Sparrow, clerk-designate to the embryonic canal company, reported that Lord Gower also favoured it.

For the next few days Darwin is busy writing, and soon sends Wedgwood two essays about inland navigation. 'They please me prodigiously', wrote Wedgwood, 'I am quite charm'd with your zeal in this Public spirited scheme'.[8] He assures Darwin that 'you shall be nameless', promises some facts for Darwin to add, and says 'your Inland Navigation paper is excellent … You never pleas'd me better … Yours most Cordialy'.

While Darwin writes a longer paper, the promotion fever continues. On 4 May Wedgwood sends him a progress report showing that Garbett is now committed to the cause. A few days later Wedgwood tells Darwin at great length about a public meeting at Newcastle on 6 May, when the Mayor and Corporation backed the scheme. On 16 May Wedgwood reports a meeting with 'Mr Brindley *the great*' and a few others. They agree to seek out the best route for a canal from Harecastle Hill, just north of Burslem, to the Duke of Bridgewater's canal, near Manchester. They also resolve 'that the money wanted be divided into lots of £250 each', with the subscribers receiving five per cent annual interest. In his next letter, in late May, Wedgwood tells Darwin he has been to Liverpool to meet the Mayor and various merchants who were offering their support. He signs off as 'Your obliged and affectionate friend'. In the twelfth known letter of this two-month outburst Wedgwood asks Darwin's advice on management details.[9]

Wedgwood's next letter, on 30 June, opens up a new topic. He thanks Darwin for sending the first two parts of a three-part paper on inland navigation, of which the complete manuscript[10] runs to sixty-seven pages:

> Thanks to my worthy friend for his very ingenious and most acceptable pacquet, which I doubt not when it is made public will answer our most sanguine expectations…. The arguments are strong, conclusive and easy to be understood, and the Dedication in my humble opinion is exceedingly clever.[11]

Darwin asked Wedgwood and Bentley to alter the paper as they felt necessary, but Wedgwood himself was diffident over literary niceties and left the editing to Bentley. Wedgwood's long letter ends: 'Unless you dare break forth from behind the cloud, what shall we do for a name to our Pamphlet?' But Darwin was determined to remain anonymous and continued to do so (except in scientific papers) for the next twenty-five years, because he feared damage to his medical practice if he was seen to be dabbling in other fields.

In editing the pamphlet Bentley removed Darwin's sonorous Dedication, which read as follows:

To the Queen

From your Majesty's known attachment to the Arts of Peace, and the general Welfare of these your Kingdoms, we humbly beg leave to lay this Plan of inland Navigation at your Majesty's Feet, and intreat your royal Permission to call the new Canal 'The River Charlotte', that our latest Progeny may know the source of their Prosperity and to the End of Time repeat the Name of their illustrious Patronness.[12]

Bentley was a no-nonsense northern businessman, and he probably thought this too sycophantic and too flowery.

This was not the only deletion. Darwin had given permission for changes, but he was rather upset by Bentley's heavy editing when he saw a printed version of the pamphlet in late September. Like most authors, he thought the changes made by the editor were for the worse, and he told the editor so, not very politely: 'this whole Sentence is formal and parsonic'; 'a very garrulous Sentence'; 'sad Language'; 'is not this Hobbyhorseycal'.[13] Wedgwood, off-stage for once and amused at this war of words, teased Bentley about Darwin's 'long, Critical Epistle ... which I doubt not ... hath afforded you entertainment and shook your diaphragm for you'.[14] Bentley's composure was shaken more than his diaphragm by Darwin's blunt words, and in replying to Darwin on 11 October he half excuses himself by saying that 'Mr Sparrow sent me the MS about a Month ago, desiring I would get it printed immediately'. He explains to Darwin that he believed the language of such a pamphlet 'should be plain and concise' and 'free from rhetorical Expressions'. He thinks readers would be 'looking out for Deceit and Artifice', and hopes to 'disappoint them with the manly Simplicity of Truth'.[15]

So it is no surprise that the edited version is more humdrum and less forceful than the original. On 22 October Bentley says he is always ready to accept criticisms of his own writings. 'But this work is not mine. There are hardly two Paragraphs together of my writing in the whole.'[16] There is a great difference, Bentley says, 'between *writing a piece* and endeavouring to *mend* one'. Despite these clear denials by Bentley himself, Wedgwood's biographer Eliza Meteyard asserted that Bentley not Darwin was the author, and several generations of scholars have followed her in this error.

The verbal duelling between Bentley and Darwin was soon resolved, with good humour on both sides. Wedgwood wrote to Bentley on 18 November: 'The Dr acknowledged he had wrote you two or three very rude letters, and said you had drub'd him genteely in return, which he seem'd to take very cordially and to be very well pleased with his treatment'.[17]

Edited or unedited, the pamphlet gives the arguments in favour of the canal in simple and cogent terms. To Wedgwood the pamphlet seemed extremely important: it was a tangible weapon capable of subduing opponents. That is why he was so grateful to Darwin. Its potency may have been less than he thought, but it saved the promoters from having to walk defenceless into the lion's den of Parliament, and may have been useful in convincing the unprejudiced and the waverers. It received glowing praise in the *Monthly Review*: 'there has not, for many years, been a more interesting publication than this little treatise ...'[18] This is not as impressive as it seems, because the editor of the *Monthly Review* was Ralph Griffiths, a friend of Wedgwood and Bentley.

In the autumn of 1765 there was still much to be done. The landowners en route (some would be Darwin's patients) had to be judiciously canvassed. The route and the termini had to be decided, after assessing the relative merits of locks, tunnels and detours. The system of charging for freight had to be settled, and the rates fixed at an optimum level. The Act of Parliament had to be discussed and drafted: 'we shall want all the advice you can give us', Wedgwood told Darwin. There would be opposition from turnpike trusts, rival canal promoters, landowners who refused to sell and conservatives who wanted to preserve the status quo. Darwin and Wedgwood met by chance at Uttoxeter on 27 September and by design in November, when Darwin went to treat Wedgwood, who was ill. But they lived thirty miles apart, and communicated mainly by letter.

Wedgwood, Darwin and their co-promoters were in effect inaugurating a new and potentially better transport system for Britain. It was rather like proposing in the early twentieth century a hundred-mile motorway (fume-free and landscape-friendly) with tolls for freight.

By the end of 1765 the project was well on its way, but Wedgwood was overstretched. 'Indeed my dear friend', he writes to Darwin on 6 January 1766, 'I am so hurryed up and down and allmost off my life with this Navigation that I have not time to write, speak or think out of that Magic circle.'[19]

Darwin replies on 12 January. The Mayor of Derby, he says, has complained to Lord Vernon that 'the Navigation would injure the Trade of Derby' and 'begged his Lordship to advise them what to do'. Unfortunately for the Mayor, 'his Lordship shewd me the Letter. I said the Mayor was drunk, and my Lord advised them to do nothing.' Darwin may have been bending the truth here, very persuasively it seems. 'The Wigg-interest at Lichfield are for the Navigation', Darwin goes on, but only because Lord Gower supports it. They are mere pawns: 'ye venerable enstalled Clergy, ye wise and demure Aldermen, ye Burgesses sodden with Ale, what are ye but Tools! mere Tools in the Hands of your Lord'. Free of the grind of pamphlet-writing, Darwin lets his fancy run amok:

I am determined to have the Mountain of Hare-castle cut into a Colossal Statue, bestriding the Navigation, and an inscription in honour of The Wedgewood, who by propagating a few holy Lies persuaded his Countrymen (like Orpheus of old) that those Things were easy, that they had thought impossible: and by incredible address united so many and so great Personages to undertake and compleat a work that will be the astonishment of all ages.[20]

The Grand Trunk Canal made rapid progress. The Parliamentary petition came to the Commons in January 1766 and a committee was appointed to consider it, with Thomas Gilbert as chairman. Wedgwood, Bentley and Brindley gave evidence in April, and the Bill was passed on 21 April in the Commons, and on 1 May in the Lords. King George III, who approved of the project, gave Royal Assent on 14 May. The Committee of Proprietors, including Boulton and Garbett, was set up in June, with Brindley as Surveyor-General at £200 per annum, and Wedgwood as Treasurer 'at £000 per annum'. On 26 July, on land near Burslem owned by his family, Wedgwood cut the first turf, which Brindley then wheeled away in a barrow. Thus began the most formidable engineering project of its kind that had been attempted in England. The canal would run south-east from the Mersey near Runcorn through Cheshire to its summit at the 2900-yard Harecastle Tunnel, and then south-east through the Potteries to just north of Lichfield, where it would turn north-east to join the Trent south of Derby.

The bond between Darwin and Wedgwood, forged in the furore of the canal promotion, endured at full strength until Wedgwood's death thirty years later. More than 120 letters from Darwin to Wedgwood have survived in manuscript and many others are lost. Although Wedgwood rarely attended Lunar meetings because Burslem is forty miles from Birmingham, he was undeniably one of the Lunar group. He already shared their aim of improving technology for the benefit of humankind, and he soon came to know all the other members.

[3]

The shape of the Lunar circle began to emerge when Dr William Small arrived in Birmingham, in May 1765. He was to be the calm centre towards which the more dynamic members would be attracted. Small is one of the talented group of Scottish men of science born around 1730 that included Black, Hutton, Keir, Lind and Watt. Small matched them in his abilities, but he is little known because he pursued a policy of self-denial, refusing to join societies or write papers. Edgeworth referred to Small as 'a man esteemed by all who knew him, and by all who were admitted to his friendship beloved with no common enthusiasm. Dr Small formed a link which combined Mr Boulton, Mr Watt, Dr Darwin, Mr Wedgwood, Mr Day, and myself, together.'[21]

William Small was born in 1734 and educated at Marischal College, Aberdeen. In 1758 he became Professor of Natural Philosophy at the College of William and Mary at Williamsburg in Virginia, where he was a great success with his pupils, especially Thomas Jefferson. Few teachers have ever had so fine a tribute from so illustrious a pupil as Small received from Jefferson:

> It was my great good fortune, and what probably fixed the destinies of my life, that Dr. Wm. Small of Scotland was then professor of Mathematics, a man profound in most of the useful branches of science, with a happy talent of communication, correct and gentlemanly manners, and an enlarged and Liberal mind. He, most happily for me, became soon attached to me and made me his daily companion when not engaged in the school; and from his conversation I got my first views of the expansion of science and of the system of things in which we are placed.[22]

Small left Virginia in 1764 after some friction at the College, and in January 1765 attended a Royal Society meeting as a guest of Franklin, who had also returned to England. Small heard of an opening for a physician in Birmingham, where he arrived with a letter of introduction to Boulton from Franklin. Boulton took to Small immediately, and in the next ten years did little without Small's help and advice. Small displaced Darwin as Boulton's chief friend and adviser, and also became Boulton's doctor. Darwin was not at all put out, however, for Small was soon his 'favourite friend'. Anna Seward, after naming Michell, Keir, Boulton and Watt, refers to 'the accomplished Dr Small' as 'above all others in Dr Darwin's personal regard'. On 11 March 1766 Darwin in writing to Boulton referred to 'our ingenious friend Dr Small, from whom and from you, when I was last at Birmingham, I received Ideas that for many days occurred to me at the Intervals of the common Business of Life, with inexpressible Pleasure'.[23] So the Boulton-Darwin duo grew painlessly into the Boulton-Small-Darwin trio, with Small as the willing link between them.

Small was the right man in the right place at the right time. He was not too keen on his new profession as a physician, but was fortunate to find a congenial partner in the admirable Dr John Ash.[24] Together they opened a clinic, and Ash began his long crusade for a General Hospital in Birmingham. Small was no crusader, and outside his practice he was happy to spend time talking or writing to Boulton, Darwin and later Watt. They were too busy to organize even an informal Lunar meeting. Small had the time and the inclination. Accomplished, attractive and self-effacing, he was ideal as an invisible secretary; and the invisible Lunar college was to flourish under his nurturing hand.

[4]

Darwin's next acquaintance was not at all like the affable Small. On 11 January 1766 Jean-Jacques Rousseau landed in England after being hounded out of several European states. He was the guest of David Hume, but Rousseau's persecution mania made it difficult to find a house that would suit him. Eventually Richard Davenport offered Wootton Hall, deep in rural Staffordshire, set in a steep-sided wooded valley with lakes, on the south slope of the Weaver Hills, which are 1200 feet high just north of the house. In the valley to the south the river Churnet flows swiftly to join the Dove. The nearest town is Ashbourne, five miles to the east.

Rousseau and Thérèse le Vasseur seem to have been happy at Wootton Hall, and lived there for more than a year. Their host Richard Davenport was an easy-going man of great wealth, who suffered much from gout. The deaths of his younger daughter and her husband had left him with two grandchildren to care for. One of these, Phoebe, was nearly ten years old and soon became Rousseau's 'pet'. He is said to have taught her the harpsichord, and he gave her a manuscript book, the *livre vert*. Rousseau was very famous in England, particularly for his love of nature and for his book *Emile* advocating education by kindness. Rousseau wrote the first five books of his *Confessions* at Wootton Hall and also occupied himself in silent yet ostentatious rapport with nature. He would walk the seven miles to Dovedale and also to the Manifold valley. His other favourite haunts were a grotto on the terrace at Wootton Hall and a group of twenty oaks[25] on high ground near Stanton.

Darwin met this legendary figure in the summer of 1766 when he was called to Wootton Hall to treat either Davenport or one of his grandchildren. Charles Darwin tells his family's story of how it happened:

> Rousseau ... used to spend much of his time 'in the well-known cave upon the terrace in melancholy contemplation'. He disliked being interrupted, so Dr Darwin, who was then a stranger to him, sauntered by the cave, and minutely examined a plant growing in front of it. This drew forth Rousseau, who was interested in botany, and they conversed together, and afterwards corresponded during several years.[26]

I have not traced any such letters, and their existence remains in doubt. However, Rousseau strongly influenced several of Darwin's friends, four of whom later visited him in Paris. Although Rousseau realized that Darwin's meeting with him had been contrived, they apparently remained on good terms; and Darwin did later take notice of Rousseau's ideas on education.

Rousseau's visit ended abruptly in May 1767. Davenport was away in London longer than he expected, because of his gout. Rousseau took fright, left Wootton Hall, and returned to France. Darwin never saw him again.

[5]

A genuine new friend arrived in 1766, Richard Lovell Edgeworth (Plate 6C). He was twelve years younger than Darwin, and began almost as a disciple. But the friendship soon equalized, and it strengthened as the years passed, even though Edgeworth was then living mostly in Ireland. When Darwin died, thirty-six years later, he was in the middle of writing a letter to Edgeworth. Young, rich, good-looking, cheerful and friendly, with a keenly inventive mind, Edgeworth was to have an exhilarating effect on Lichfield Close, especially since he also had 'a passion for the other sex, which brought upon him four marriages and twenty-two children'.[27]

Carriages rather than marriages drew Edgeworth towards Darwin. In the previous year, when Edgeworth was twenty-one and not long embarked on the first of his marriages, he was fascinated to hear that Darwin had designed a carriage 'able to turn in a small compass, without danger of oversetting'. Having money in hand and nothing particular to do in his house at Hare Hatch near Reading, Edgeworth constructed a 'very handsome Phaeton' on the Darwinian principle. Edgeworth then told the Society for the Encouragement of Arts (now the Royal Society of Arts) about the carriage, saying that it was Darwin's idea.

The Secretary of the Society, Dr Templeman, wrote to Darwin, who replied on 8 March 1766 describing some of his improvements in the design of four-wheel carriages:

> About seven or eight years ago, I observed that among other lesser defects in the common light Carriages that there were two principle ones, *First* that the foremost Wheels were for the conveniency of turning made too low, by which means the forepart of the Carriage was obliged to rise too suddenly over Stones or other Obstacles in the way; and thence continual Shocks produced, that injured both the Horses and the Carriage, and incommoded the Travellers ... *Secondly* That in the Time of turning, the Basis on which the Carriage rests was changed from a Parallelogram to a Triangle.
> Thus in Fig.[5A] the Carriage is a four-footed Stool, in Fig.[5B] a three-leg'd

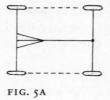

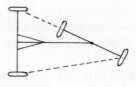

FIG. 5A   FIG. 5B

Stool. That from this Cause Carriages were most frequently overturn'd, viz at the Time of turning....

I contrived a Method of turning, which gets free of both these inconvenience, viz, it admits the foremost Wheels to be as high as you please, those I made were four feet diameter; and the Carriage stands on the same Basis (that is, is as safe from overturning) in the Act of turning as at other times.

I made a model about 7 or 8 years ago which is perished long since, three years ago I made a Phaeton on this principle, and have rode in it, I dare conjecture, above 10,000 miles and it is yet a good one, and weighs but 500 wgt. [250 kg]

About two years ago I made a Post Chaise on this principle, and have rode in that I dare say 10,000 miles and found no inconvenience from the new manner of turning in either of them.

Each of the foremost Wheels turns not from a Center between them but each on a Center of its own near the Knave. I can not give any drawing or Description that can be at all intelligible, as the parts tho' very simple, lie in different Planes.[28]

A year or so later Darwin produced a sketch[29] of the principle (Fig. 6). The two front wheels C and D are not parallel when turned; instead they have turning circles with the same centre, the point marked as E, which lies on the (extended) line of the back axle AB. This ensures that the front wheels move tangential to their track instead of dragging, and on a reasonably smooth road there would be no tendency to overturn.

Darwin's improved method of steering was reinvented by 'Mr Lankensperger of Munich' about 1818, and the British patent was held by Rudolph Ackermann. He tried to promote it[30] but failed to persuade the carriage builders. However, the technique was adopted for most modern cars until the 1940s, and was known as Ackermann steering: there is really no excuse for this misnomer when Darwin's priority is well documented and he road-tested the method over more than 20,000 miles. (Also Ackermann did not invent it!)

This was an impressive engineering achievement by Darwin. He proceeded in one imaginative leap from the standard design of the front wheels of eighteenth-century carriages to the standard design of the front wheels of twentieth-century cars, and proved his design by personally road-testing it

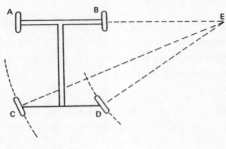

FIG. 6

on two carriages for three years. Of course he did not put it into production: he was a doctor not an industrialist (*pace* the ironworks). But he
did make his results available to the Society of Arts and did not even patent
his mechanism, as he explained to Dr Templeman:

> I had once thoughts of applying for a Patent for making the Axletrees for this
> new way of turning, which are uncommon shaped Cranks, and require a little
> Accuracy in making – but I defer'd this till much experience should ascertain their
> being really useful.

He also offers to show the Phaeton to the Society, or make a model at their
expense, and mentions other advantages in his designs, such as:

> ... a double cross Perch much *lighter* and more *springing* than the common.
> And one Shaft instead of two, by which both Horses can back the Carriage.
> And Swingle-Tree Bars to draw by, which prevents the Horses from galling on
> their Shoulders.
> I believe my Carriage has fewer pieces of wood, is lighter, and will last longer
> than any other Carriage of the Size and Conveniences, besides its being safer
> from overturning, and easier to draw.[31]

The improved steering was the main advantage of Darwin's design, but
these other innovations were useful too. Until the invention of pneumatic
tyres, larger front wheels provided greater comfort and easier traction, as
he pointed out. His idea of a single shaft above the horses, terminating in a
pivot on which the draw-bar hung, was scarcely new, because it was used
by the ancient Greeks.[32] With a single shaft the horses can back the carriage
and turn more freely.

Darwin's letter also gives some idea of the distances he covered on his
rounds. Since he drove more than 10,000 miles in three years in the
phaeton, about 10,000 miles in the post-chaise in two of the same three
years, and probably several thousand miles in other carriages, he probably
travelled about 10,000 miles a year or thirty miles a day.

Edgeworth showed his own phaeton to the Society of Arts, and told
Darwin about it: 'The Doctor wrote me a very civil answer, and ... invited
me to his house'.

So Edgeworth came to Lichfield in the summer of 1766. The doctor was
out, but Polly welcomed Edgeworth, who had 'the pleasure of passing the
evening with this most agreeable woman'. Erasmus was late returning, but
when he did so his entry was dramatic:

> When supper was nearly finished, a loud rapping at the door announced the
> Doctor. There was a bustle in the hall, which made Mrs Darwin get up and go
> to the door. Upon her exclaiming that they were bringing in a dead man, I went
> to the hall: I saw some persons, directed by one whom I guessed to be Doctor
> Darwin, carrying a man who appeared motionless.

'He is not dead', said Doctor Darwin. 'He is only dead drunk. I found him', continued the Doctor, 'nearly suffocated in a ditch; I had him lifted into my carriage, and brought hither, that we might take care of him to-night.'

Candles came, and what was the surprise of the Doctor, and of Mrs Darwin, to find that the person whom he had saved was Mrs Darwin's brother! who, for the first time in his life, as I was assured, had been intoxicated in this manner, and who would undoubtedly have perished, had it not been for Doctor Darwin's humanity.

Edgeworth gives his first impressions of Erasmus, 'my new friend':

He was a large man, fat, and rather clumsy; but intelligence and benevolence were painted in his countenance: he had a considerable impediment in his speech, a defect which is in general painful to others; but the Doctor repaid his auditors so well for making them wait for his wit or his knowledge, that he seldom found them impatient.[33]

The next day Erasmus introduced Edgeworth to Anna Seward (Plate 6A), now twenty-three, and 'in the height of youth and beauty, of an enthusiastic temper, a votary of the muses, and of the most eloquent and brilliant conversation'. In the evening Polly invited Anna and some of her friends to dinner. Edgeworth found that Polly 'had a little pique against Miss Seward', presumably because she was inclined to flirt with Erasmus, and, after Edgeworth had embarked on a few compliments to Anna, 'the watchful Mrs Darwin' confounded them both by 'drinking *Mrs Edgeworth's health*. Miss Seward's surprise was manifest. But [she] turned the laugh in her favor.'[34] Edgeworth was impressed: 'How much of my future life has depended upon this visit to Lichfield!' And Anna was impressed by Edgeworth: 'His address was gracefully spirited, and his conversation eloquent. He danced, he fenced, and winged his arrows with more than philosophic skill.'[35]

Darwin liked his lively visitor too, and wrote to Boulton:

I have got with me a mechanical Friend, Mr Edgeworth from Oxfordshire – The greatest Conjurer I ever saw – G-d send fair Weather, and pray come to my assistance, and prevail on Dr Small and Mrs Boulton to attend you, tomorrow Morning, and we will reconvoy you to Birmingham on Monday, if the D---l permit ...

He has the principles of Nature in his Palm, and moulds them as He pleases. Can take away polarity or give it to the Needle by rubbing it thrice on the Palm of his Hand.

And can see through two solid Oak Boards without Glasses, wonderful! astonishing! diabolical!!! Pray tell Dr Small He must come to see these Miracles.[36]

Boulton and Small came to Lichfield and they liked both the conjuror and his tricks. Boulton took him to see some factories and Edgeworth responded with enthusiasm. Soon he invented a robot wooden horse rather like a modern tank, a carriage with sails, the first semaphore telegraph system, an umbrella for covering hay-stacks, a turnip-cutter, and many other ingenious devices.

Edgeworth's inventions won him a silver medal from the Society of Arts in 1768. On 2 March 1769 he wrote to tell the Society about an improved four-wheel carriage, with Darwinian steering and independent springing of the wheels – possibly another idea of Darwin's. Edgeworth gives diagrams of the steering technique, and these are copied from a set of rough sketches that are probably drawn by Darwin. (Fig. 6 is from this paper.) The Society's Committee for Mechanics recommended an award for 'the application of the chains to the forepart of Mr Edgeworth's four-wheel carriage, whereby the wheels are turned on two centres'.[37] Edgeworth received a gold medal.

Darwin was not at all resentful that his idea had borne golden fruit for his friend. He did not seek mechanical fame himself, and was pleased at Edgeworth's award. In return Edgeworth thanked him with typical exuberance: 'To be engaged in any thing with you would give me the greatest pleasure as I find a congeniality of disposition in us which makes me think we should agree and succeed in any scheme we should be joined in'.[38]

Edgeworth's success must have boosted Darwin's self-confidence. His design was obviously a great improvement, and the Society's medal confirmed this. Yet, although he made his invention freely available to the Society of Arts, no one had the nous to exploit it commercially. Since nearly everyone wanted to travel more safely, this neglect is rather a mystery. What was lacking was a Peer of the Realm, like Bridgewater and Gower with the canals, to push the invention into public notice. The Society of Arts gave a clear signal by awarding its Gold Medal to Edgeworth, but apparently no one saw the signal. Perhaps the Society itself was inhibited by Dr Templeman's death in 1769; or perhaps we are seeing an early example of the British disease of failing to exploit good inventions.

Darwin's proposed steam carriage had already put him among the pioneers of the motor car. Inventing the method of steering cars makes him a doubly unsung pioneer.

[6]

After canals and carriages come steam engines, for Darwin lured James Watt (Plate 5C) into the nascent Lunar circle in 1767.

Darwin had tried in vain to improve the steam engine himself in 1757, and in 1763 he had failed to persuade Boulton to make a steam carriage, as we have seen. In 1765 Boulton himself urgently needed a steam engine; he had intended to rely on a water-wheel to power his new manufactory at Soho, until he realized (rather late) that he would be at the mercy of drought, and of anyone upstream who took too much water. Now he wanted a steam engine to pump water back into the reservoir pool that fed the water-wheel. He made his own engine and sent it to Franklin for comment. Darwin was impatient and wrote to Boulton on 12 December 1765:

> I am undone to know what Observations Dr Franklin supply'd you with about your Steam-Engine, besides giving you his approbation, and particularly to hear your final Opinion, and Dr Small's on the important Question, whether Evaporation is at the Surface of boiling Water, or not? – or if it be at the Surface of the Vessel, exposed to the Fire, which I rather suspect...[39]

In this letter Darwin calls Boulton and Small 'you Birmingham philosophers': he had conceived the Lunar Society without knowing it.

Darwin had still not seen the engine when he wrote again on 11 March 1766:

> Your Model of a Steam Engine I am told gain'd so much Approbation in London that I can not but congratulate you on the mechanical Fame you have acquired by it: which, assure yourself, is as great a Pleasure to me, as it could possibly be to yourself.[40]

He was so keen to see the model that he would travel on 'the first vacant day' and 'trust to the Stars for meeting with you at Home'. So the Lunar circle was already steam-minded in 1766.

In 1765 James Watt, instrument-maker to the University of Glasgow, twenty-nine years old, made his invention of the separate condenser to improve the efficiency of the steam engine: 'I can think of nothing else but this machine',[41] he wrote to his friend James Lind in April. But Watt had a deep-seated streak of self-doubt, and needed propping up by optimistic friends. One of these was Joseph Black the chemist, who saw the advantages of Watt's design, lent him money and introduced him to John Roebuck, the leading Scottish industrialist. With Garbett as partner, Roebuck was operating the Carron Ironworks, a thriving business in the early 1760s. Garbett decided to withdraw when Roebuck began expanding his activities by taking over the coal mines and salt workings at nearby Bo'ness.

In 1765 the mines were flooded, and the existing Newcomen steam engine could not cope. Roebuck urgently needed a better engine: he agreed to repay Watt's debt to Black and to develop Watt's engine, taking two thirds of the profits, if any. Meanwhile Watt found employment as a canal surveyor and engineer in Scotland.

In April 1767 Watt travelled to London with the difficult task of petitioning Parliament to sanction a Forth–Clyde canal. The petition failed, and Watt blamed the House of Commons: 'I never saw so many wrong-headed people on all sides gathered together ... I believe *the Deevil* has possession of them.'[42] Roebuck had asked Watt to visit Garbett at Birmingham. He did so, and met two of Garbett's friends, Darwin and Small. It was the turning point of Watt's life: they took an immediate liking to him, and he to them. Though Boulton was away, Watt looked over the Soho works.

Watt stayed overnight at Darwin's house and told Darwin the secret of his new engine. From this moment Watt was fixed in the Lunar circle. The optimistic Darwin and the patient Small kept his spirits up and urged him to move to Birmingham and work with Boulton. Darwin first wrote to Watt on 18 August 1767, and Small's first recorded letter to him was in January 1768. Small wrote almost fortnightly for the next six years and eventually persuaded Watt to make the move.

Darwin's first letter to Watt takes us back to carriages and carts, because Darwin had told Watt about his technique for improved steering. The letter begins:

> I have been so continually engaged in travelling about the Country from sick People to sick People, that it was not till this Afternoon in my Power to measure the Iron-work of my Chaise. There is an iron Crank in this Shape, and the Arm of the Axle is on the same Crank, and stands out at (W).

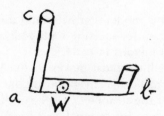

> Perhaps it would be better at the angle (a)? But in this place it admits of the Wheels being larger in the act of Turning.[43]

Then he gives the measurements: ab is 13 inches long, ac is 12 inches and aW is 1½ inches. He also mentions Edgeworth's phaeton, which is on the same principles.

As well as these four-wheel carriages, Darwin is now trying out a two-wheel cart drawn by two horses:

> My Cart is to draw a Ton, by Two Horses, a-breast. The wheels are seven feet Hight. The Body swings under the Axis. Now I think the Body should be fix'd to the Axis, and the Arms of the Axis should be cylindrical, and not the frustrum of a Cone. And 3rd the Axis should, as near as may be, pass through the Center of the Load....

With this vehicle he avoids the problem of turning the front wheels – by abolishing them. The design is not clear from this description, as Darwin acknowledges: 'NB I have not well digested this'.

The rest of Darwin's letter is in the bubbly style so prevalent in his correspondence and shows his high regard for Watt:

> Enough of Carts and Chaises! Now my dear new Friend, I first hope you are well, and less hypochondriacal; and that Mrs Watt and your Child are well. The Plan of your Steam-Improvements I have religiously kept secret, but begin myself to see some difficulties in the Execution that did not strike me when you was here. I have got another and another new Hobby-Horse since I saw you. I wish the Lord would send you to pass a Week with me, and Mrs Watt along with you – a Week! – a Month, a Year.[44]

Before Watt came to Lichfield again, his friend John Robison made a visit and stayed with Darwin. Robison wrote to Watt on 8 July 1768:

> I write this principally to thank you for the favour you have done me in introducing me to the acquaintance of Dr darwin and Dr Small. I can't tell how much I think myself obliged to you. I was quite charmed with the unaffected ease and Civility of darwin.... I met with no less kindness ... from Mrs darwin. You are happy in the Esteem of such worthy people ... I spent one day (Tuesday) at Lichfield and was lucky enough to meet with Dr Small at Mr Darwin's, and along with him another most agreeable Man and your very warm friend, Mr Boulton.[45]

Watt had to go to London again in August 1768 to apply for a patent, and he stopped off in the Midlands on his way back. Probably he took a coach to Lichfield and stayed overnight with Darwin, meeting Small and Boulton the next day. Watt liked Boulton, stayed at Soho House for a fortnight and concluded that here if anywhere was the place where his engine would be successfully manufactured.

Darwin's thirty-five years of friendship with Watt seem to have been quite unclouded. Watt was ever grateful to Darwin for his cheerfulness, medical advice and enthusiasm for steam; Darwin admired Watt's engineering skills and wide knowledge.[46]

When Robison chanced to meet Small and Boulton at Darwin's house, he saw the beginnings of the Lunar circle. Boulton and his wife Anne often visited friends and relatives in Lichfield, her home town. They sometimes took Small and dropped him at Darwin's house. At other times Boulton and Small would go together to see Darwin and would stay the night. These meetings started about 1766. The three of them would also meet occasionally at Boulton's house, when Darwin was visiting a patient in Birmingham. But it was Darwin's house at Lichfield that was the birthplace of the Lunar circle, which grew into the Lunar Society.[47]

[7]

Another Lunar recruit in 1767 was James Keir (Plate 5D), the fellow-student of Darwin at Edinburgh. Keir had joined the Army and served throughout the Seven Years' War. However, his only fighting was against disease. The worst moment came as he lay ill with a fever in his cabin on a ship in the West Indies and could see sharks tearing to pieces the bodies of his fellow-soldiers who had died of the same fever. He grew worse and, while he could neither speak nor move, the doctor came in and said, 'He is gone too'. But when a man came to throw him overboard, Keir managed to move and so saved himself.[48]

By 1766 he was a Captain and stationed in Ireland. He had already visited Erasmus and Polly at Lichfield, and he wrote a social letter from Ireland to Polly and a scientific one to Erasmus.

By 1767 he decided to leave the Army and to settle somewhere near Lichfield. In the autumn he was travelling around before making a choice: he stayed first with Edgeworth, then with Darwin. After that he went on to see Wedgwood, carrying a letter from Darwin: 'I have the Pleasure to introduce to your acquaintance Captain James Keir, an old Friend of mine, a successful cultivator of both Arts and Arms. He begs the Favour of seeing your elegant manufactory and hopes to meet our common Friend, the Philosopher, Mr Whitehurst at your House.'[49] Keir thought Wedgwood's house 'fit for a Prince'. Keir also met Boulton and Small, and within a month or two he was confiding to Small his plans for manufacturing alkali.

Keir resigned his commission in 1768, and in that year met Watt, who thought him 'a mighty chemist before the Lord, and a very agreeable man'.[50] Keir was working on his translation of Macquer's *Dictionnaire de Chymie*, the standard work on chemistry at that time. The translation was published in 1771.

Everyone agreed that Keir was a very agreeable man: friendly now with all the early Lunar group, he was to become the most popular choice for chairman of the Lunar meetings in later years. Though not so well known as Boulton or Wedgwood, Keir rivals them in originality and success through his achievements as a pioneer of the chemical industry.

Keir saw the Soho manufactory just after it was completed, and he was most impressed. So was Darwin, who in 1768 took the trouble to write a short description for a history of Staffordshire:

> Soho is the name of a hill in the county of Stafford, about two miles from Birmingham; which a very few years ago was a barren heath, on the bleak summit of which stood a naked hut, the habitation of a warrener.
> The transformation of this place is a recent monument to the effects of trade

on population. A beautiful garden, with wood, lawn, and water, now covers one side of this hill; five spacious squares of building, erected on the other side, supply workshops, or houses, for above six hundred people. The extensive pool at the approach to this building is conveyed to a large water-wheel in one of the courts, and communicates motion to a prodigious number of different tools. And the mechanic inventions for this purpose are superior in multitude, variety, and simplicity, to those of any manufactory (I suppose) in the known world.[51]

And this was six years before Boulton began to manufacture Watt's engine.

All the known world acknowledged Soho's pre-eminence, well expressed thirty years later in the naive verse of James Bisset:

Soho! – where GENIUS and the ARTS preside,
Europa's wonder and Britannia's pride.
Thy matchless works have raised old England's fame
And future ages will recall thy name.[52]

When Keir started to build his own factory in later years, he had experience of managing Soho in Boulton's absence, and it was a model for him in its organization.

[8]

These new friends and old ones like Michell would come to stay with the Darwins from time to time, and Polly seems to have welcomed and liked them all. She was certainly at ease with the flirtatious Edgeworth, and with Keir, to whom she sent on a billet-doux delivered to her house, to be told by him that it was 'the very quintessence of love-letter writing'.[53] There were visits too from Josiah Wedgwood and his wife Sally, the beginnings of a close intertwining of the families in later years. Most frequent of all were the visits of the affable duo Boulton and Small. Polly could have objected that the annexe was being turned into a hotel, but the evidence points the other way: being well supported by servants, she would probably have liked more rather than fewer visitors.

Polly also remained on good terms with the Sewards, although Erasmus was increasingly irritated by Mr Seward's literary pretensions and his double standards in discouraging Anna from writing poetry. Darwin's irritation would have been enhanced by his uneasy feeling that he ought to be grateful to Seward for having launched him as a doctor at Lichfield: debts of gratitude can rarely be repaid and, when they are not, the beneficiary often bites the benefactor. So we need not be surprised that the publication of Samuel Johnson's edition of Shakespeare in 1765, paralleling Seward's edition of Beaumont, provoked Darwin to bite them both in verse:

From Lichfield famed two giant critics come,
Tremble, ye Poets! hear them! 'Fe, Fo, Fum!'
By Seward's arm the mangled Beaumont bled,
And Johnson grinds poor Shakespear's bones for bread.[54]

Though little concerned to preserve his friendship with Seward, Darwin did help to preserve the fabric of the Cathedral. A lightning conductor was installed 'by the advice of some philosophic Gentlemen'[55] in September 1766. This was three years ahead of St Paul's Cathedral in London.

Darwin's satirical verses did not bode well for his first meeting with Johnson, probably in 1767 when Johnson stayed in Lichfield from July to October. Johnson looked on his birthplace with affection: its inhabitants were, he said, 'the most sober, decent people in England, the genteelest in proportion to their wealth, and spoke the purest English'.[56] The Bishop's Palace held special memories for him, because his benefactor Gilbert Walmsley had lived there, and he did not much relish the sight of Sewards in residence. They were no strangers to him, because Sarah Seward, who had died so tragically three years before, was to have married his stepson. But Johnson despised Canon Seward as a provincial dilettante: 'Sir, his ambition is to be a fine talker; so he goes to Buxton, and such places, where he may find companies to listen to him ...'[57]

Meeting the Sewards was bad enough for Johnson: meeting Darwin was worse. Here, installed in his home town, was a sage more wide-ranging and knowledgeable than himself and as little inclined to yield in argument. 'Mutual and strong dislike subsisted between them', Anna tells us. 'Johnson liked only *worshippers*', and neither Darwin nor the Sewards were among those who 'sunk, in servile silence, under the force of his dogmas'. Opposing him was hazardous, Anna says, no doubt from bitter experience. She refers to his 'stentor lungs; that combination of wit, humour and eloquence, which "could make the *worse* appear the *better* reason"; that sarcastic contempt of his antagonist, never suppressed or even softened by the due restraints of good-breeding'.[58] Darwin, with 'his impeded utterance', had 'no chance of being heard', and he shunned Johnson. There was no room for two such weighty and opinionated sages in the small goldfish-bowl of Lichfield society.

So Darwin, Johnson and Seward form an unusual grouping – a mutually repellent triumvirate. However, they did still speak to each other, even if only with icy civility.

[9]

For Polly and Erasmus their growing children were of more concern than

these social attractions and repulsions. At the beginning of 1766 Charles
was seven years old and Erasmus six.

On 30 May 1766 Polly's third son was born and was named Robert
Waring after Erasmus's eldest brother, who seems to have been enjoying his
role as squire at Elston and his interests as a naturalist and gardener. The
choice of name was a happy one: for fifty years uncle Robert took a fatherly
interest in nephew Robert. The baby Robert proved to be the healthiest of
Polly's children. He survived an experimental inoculation against measles
and lived to be eighty-two, long enough to see some of the successes of his
famous son Charles in the 1840s.

In the 1760s, however, the relevant Charles is Polly's eldest son, who was
showing brilliant promise. Even as an infant, his father tells us, Charles
examined natural objects with unusual attention, 'first by his senses simply;
then by tools, which were his playthings'.[59] Soon 'the invention and
improvement of machines' occupied and amused him. When he was old
enough he (and his father) 'descended the mines, and climbed the precipices
of Derbyshire, and of some other counties, with uncommon pleasure and
observation'.[60] Charles collected fossils and minerals and, as he was
familiar with actual substances, 'the complicate science of chemistry became not only easy, but delightful to him'.

This paragon of virtue had one flaw: he stammered. In the hope of a
cure, Erasmus and Polly decided to take the drastic step of sending Charles
to live in France for up to a year. This decision strongly suggests that
Erasmus himself had suffered at school because he stammered; and he
wanted Charles to avoid the same fate. Forcible exile may seem a strange
method of treatment, but it was quite successful. If not, it would at least
have been useful in improving Charles's knowledge of French.

Fortunately Erasmus knew of a reliable tutor to take care of Charles:
the Revd Samuel Dickenson, a contemporary of his at St John's College,
Cambridge.[61] Dickenson was highly regarded both as a teacher and as a
botanist, and the visit to France confirmed that he was a good and trust-
worthy tutor. He had another well-known pupil a few years later: Thomas
Beddoes. Then in 1777 he became Rector of Blymhill in west Staffordshire,
and remained so for forty-six years.

Polly kept in touch with Dickenson and Charles by letter. Fortunately
two of these letters have survived, giving us some more glimpses of her
character.

The travellers left in October 1766 and stopped in London for nearly
two months. Polly's first letter to Dickenson is written on 1 November and
begins:

> I fancy my veracity will not be question'd when I assure you I received great
> pleasure from the letter you was so kind to favour me with; yours will always

meet with a very sincere welcome and add if possible to the gratitude and friendship I already entertain for you.[62]

The wording is slightly defensive but elegantly polite ('you was' being quite a common variant at this time). She then suggests that 'it might not be unuseful for Charley to claim relationship to Mr Foley who was first cousin to my mother'. This was Robert Foley, a banker in Paris, and Polly persuaded her father to provide a letter of introduction. Written on the reverse of Polly's, this letter from Mr Howard is lucid and appealing.

Polly continues: 'The Doctor is unfortunately from home, or might perhaps have had something to say to you; but I am too uncertain how long your stay in London will be to risk neglecting this post'. She hopes that 'you and your little friend' will call on 'Mr Darwin Attorney' at Gray's Inn, 'as I daresay he would be glad to see his nephew'. This is Erasmus's elder brother William Alvey Darwin: he lived in London for most of his life, and did not have much contact with Erasmus, who was the younger by five years. She also suggests calling on the Revd Mr Jauncey, 'Miss Nelly White's husband elect': Nelly White was one of Polly's friends in the Close; known as 'the Belle of Lichfield', she was the daughter of the Revd John White.

Polly did not feel at ease in writing – life not literature was her forte. She finishes the letter by warning Dickenson of her limitations as a letter-writer:

> I must now, once for all, desire you will excuse the frequent mistakes you will meet with, for I never did, and I now begin to fear I never shall write as I ought to do; however if my pen mistakes, and puts in, and leaves out letters, it generally conveys my ideas, and is a faithfull index to my heart[;] as a proof give me leave to assure you and your Dear little companion that, wherever you go, my most ardent wishes for your healths, happiness, and pleasure will ever attend you.

Rarely has a confession of incompetent writing been more competently written.

Dickenson left for Paris with his 'little friend' on 18 December, and soon afterwards wrote to Polly, though the letter is lost. She replied on 14 January 1767. She hopes he will write often, because of 'the strong desire of a mother to hear frequently of her little boy, the most trifling incidents about whom, are beheld by her, as things of consequence':

> How beneficently has nature given that partiality to mothers, that those little observations unattended too, by others, should engage her admiration, more than the eloquence of a Ciciro, to counterballance those anxietys she often feels, when to an uninterested beholder there appears no cause of alarm.[63]

She begs his pardon for harping on this topic, and turns to something more factual: Nelly White has just married Mr Jauncey.

Polly adds a special letter for Charles, with news of Robert, now aged seven months, and the seven-year-old Erasmus:

> Bob has got two teeth. Rassy has done nothing but throw snow these last two or three days. Your papa is very well ... I hope you will write a little letter ... we shall be very glad to hear from you.
> I am my Dear Charles your most affectionate mama
> Mary Darwin

She also tells him that 'Miss Michell and your aunt Sukey' are staying at the house.

The reply from Dickenson, on 5 February 1767, has also survived. 'My little Companion and I thank God continue well', he writes. There is a good French master in the house, and Charles divides his time 'pretty equally' between 'these Lectures, Writing and walking about to see the City'.[64] Dickenson guesses that a further sum of £200 will be needed 'during our Stay in this Country', in addition to £160 already spent or placed in accounts. So the expected cost of the visit was £360, equivalent to about £36,000 today and nearly half Erasmus's earnings for the year. A continental tour with a tutor was a luxury usually reserved for the landed gentry. It was quite dangerous as well as expensive: Polly would have known that Mr Seward had made one journey in Europe as a tutor, and his pupil had died en route.

Charles did add a 'little letter', as his mother asked. He says that 'The People here behave very civil to us', and 'tho' the Frosts have been very severe, I have not had a Cold since I left England'.[65]

Charles and his tutor probably travelled to the south of France in the summer and returned in the autumn. It is not clear whether the Tour de France cured the stammer. Anna Seward gives the theory behind the treatment: it was (in brief) 'to break the force of habit, formed on the contagion of daily example',[66] and Dickenson was to ensure that Charles spoke only French while in France. The result of the therapy, according to family tradition, was that 'when speaking French he never stammered',[67] rather implying that he did in English. However, Anna Seward asserts that Charles was 'completely cured of stammering ... but his utterance was, from that time, somewhat thick and hurried'. Anna often met Charles in the years after his return, and I am inclined to accept her report.

The stay in France seems to have been a great success in most respects. Charles learnt much from his 'scientific, learned, modest and worthy' tutor – to quote the adjectives bestowed on him by Anna Seward. Charles also acquired a taste for botany, a command of French, and experience of French people and customs.

Although Charles fared well, 1767 was not a good year for Erasmus and Polly. Their fifth child, baptized William Alvey after Erasmus's elder brother, was born on 27 July; but he died on 15 August and was buried at the Cathedral on 18 August.

Worse still in the long term was Polly's declining health. The first hint of illness is in a postscript to her letter of 1 November 1766: 'I did not design to have said any thing about my health, but as Mr Jauncey will perhaps inform you, I have been ill. I am now not well again'.[68] From then onwards her health gradually deteriorated.

Drafts of four unsigned letters written by Polly about this time have survived in manuscript: they are to four different people. The earliest, probably in the spring of either 1766 or 1767, was a letter of condolence to Matthew Turner at Liverpool, apparently after the death of his wife. The wording is quite stylish at times:

> Grief demands a tribute from the heart, whilst it disdains the unfeeling arguments of the head. Time is alone the true consoler of disunited friends and with a humanity peculiar to himself changes imperceptibly the unutterable anguish, into the gloomy but pleasing remembrance.[69]

Polly reveals some decided views on the development of children when she foresees 'an inexhaustable fund of happiness' for Turner as he watches his two daughters grow up: for 'all children will unbidden repay' affection that 'comes unattended with austerity and restraint'. In case he wishes the girls to go to a boarding school, Polly mentions one that recently moved from Reading to Lichfield, run by 'sensible active people with adress and good nature'. This was the Latuffières' school, which came to the Close in 1766 and moved to Derby in 1775.

The second manuscript is a fragment from the draft of a letter from Polly to the elder daughter, Miss Turner, with some playful examples of role-playing:

> I can promise you I can play with dolls ... as well almost as any of your little friends.... My boys like me as well at ... blindsmans bluf as any of their playfellows, but you must know I am not Mrs Darwin then but Miss Polly.[70]

Her only comment on Erasmus is that 'the Dr' and Mr Turner 'are so full of employment they have no time I see to write to each other'.

The third manuscript is the draft of a letter to Boulton's wife Anne, thanking her for 'the happy days I passed lately at Soho and ... the many civilities I then received'.[71] Polly's two little boys were 'made so very happy'. The letter is unduly deferential in tone: Polly apologizes for giving Anne the trouble of reading it. As Anne was expecting a baby in a few months and her daughter Anne was born early in 1768, the letter probably dates from the autumn of 1767, when Polly was still cast down by the death of her baby son in August. The letter gives the impression that Polly had not visited Anne before: perhaps the family visit was delayed until the Boultons moved into Soho House.

The fourth manuscript, on the same sheet, is the draft of a letter to Samuel Garbett, congratulating him on the marriage of his son. Polly also says she enjoyed having Garbett's granddaughter to stay; 'as soon as Mrs D gets free from her present indisposition, she will be glad to prove her sincerity, by desiring a repetition of her visit'.[72] Her illness may explain the over-defensive style of both these letters.

Apart from his inability to help Polly, Erasmus's medical career was going smoothly – or perhaps 'roughly' would be a better word, for neither his carriage designs nor his efforts as a trustee of the Lichfield Turnpike could smooth the bumps and ruts in the public roads and the tracks leading to country houses. He took with him on his journeys a horse called Doctor, trained to follow his carriage. When the road became impassable, Darwin would get out and complete his journey on Doctor's back. In his carriage were a hamper of food, in case he was stuck in mud out in the country; and pen and paper, for jotting down thoughts shaken out of him on the road. Darwin's income was steadier than his carriage: the figures for 1765–7 were £800, £748 and £847, equivalent to about £80,000 today.

In February 1767 Erasmus received a letter from a friend about an illegitimate child apparently drowned by its mother. He replied at some length with helpful details of forensic anatomy, and also with these characteristic comments:

> I am sorry you should think it necessary to make any excuse for the Letter I this morning recieved from you. The Cause of Humanity needs no Apology to me....
>
> The Women that have committed this most unnatural Crime, are real Objects of our greatest Pity; their education has produced in them so much Modesty, or Sense of Shame, that this artificial Passion overturns the very Instincts of Nature! – what Struggles must there be in their Minds, what agonies! – and at a Time when, after the Pains of Parturition, Nature has designed them the sweet Consolation of giving Suck to a little helpless Babe, that depends on them for its hourly Existence! – Hence the Cause of this most horrid Crime is an excess of what is really a Virtue, of the Sense of Shame, or Modesty. Such is the Condition of human Nature![73]

[10]

For Darwin the intellectual flavour of the year for 1767 was geology: he caught the infection from his old friend John Whitehurst of Derby, who was now studying geology keenly.[74] Whitehurst was a quiet and unassuming man of little formal education but great natural talent, and he was eighteen years older than Darwin. He was an original member of the Lunar group through his friendships with Boulton and Darwin when they were in their twenties and could profit from his wider experience in the world of science and technology. For many years Whitehurst had travelled among the caves and mines in the Peak District of Derbyshire. These expeditions inspired him to seek a theory of the Earth's formation and also enabled him to help Wedgwood by supplying suitable minerals for his experiments on new materials for his pottery.

By now Darwin had an almost religious faith in the virtue of experiment, and he spurred Wedgwood on to try to find better ingredients for his ceramics. Wedgwood received minerals from Bentley and Brindley as well as Whitehurst and Darwin, while Turner sent varnishes and other chemical concoctions.

Wedgwood was now planning his new works to be built alongside the Grand Trunk Canal near Burslem. Darwin probably suggested the name 'Etruria', because Etruscan art was at that time rated the finest in all antiquity, and also possibly because Wedgwood was experimenting with encaustic painting in the Etruscan style.[75]

Not all Darwin's suggestions were accepted so readily. In 1766 he told Wedgwood about a 'French Nobleman' at Birmingham, Count Lauraguais, who offered to sell for £2000 'the Secret of making the finest old China, as cheap as your Pots'.[76] Wedgwood was not tempted.

Wedgwood played on Darwin's liking for fossils and geology in another way, by bombarding him with bones dug out during the excavations for the Harecastle Tunnel. Who better than a doctor to identify bones? Darwin was embarrassed that he couldn't do so, and on 2 July 1767 he wrote a jokey letter to cover up his failure. Wedgwood was not deceived, and placed it among 'humorous letters' in his Commonplace Book:

> The bone seems the third vertebra of the back of a camel. The horn is larger than any modern horn I have measured, and must have been that of a Patagonian ox I believe.... If at your leisure you will be at the trouble to tell me the strata they shall penetrate ... I will in return send you some mineral observations of exactly the same value (weighed nicely).[77]

The outsize bones were found on the south side of Harecastle 'under a bed of clay, at the depth of about five yards from the surface'.[78] They were probably embedded in drift deposits brought down by glaciers, and may have been bones from extinct varieties of elephant (the 'horn' mentioned by Darwin being a tusk). Much older fossils, with impressions of ferns, were found at the north end of the tunnel in strata underlying a bed of coal.

The frivolity of Darwin's letter was only skin-deep. These fossil remains of extinct creatures fascinated and disturbed him. Within three years he was to accept the idea of biological evolution, as we shall see.

For the moment, however, he was enjoying himself as an explorer of the Derbyshire caverns. The jokey letter continues:

> I have lately travel'd two days journey into the bowels of the earth, with three most able philosophers, and have seen the Goddess of Minerals naked, as she lay in her inmost bowers.

Probably he had explored some of the Blue John caverns near Castleton, in company with John Whitehurst and the brothers Anthony and George Tissington, who were Derbyshire mine agents. Darwin was still exuberant about his exploration when he wrote to Boulton on 29 July: 'I have been into the Bowels of old Mother Earth, and seen Wonders and learnt much curious Knowlege in the Regions of Darkness ... I have seen the two Tissingtons, subterranean Genii!'[79]

[11]

In 1768 the Lunar group acquired its youngest, wealthiest, most eccentric, most literary and least scientific member, the twenty-year-old Thomas Day (Plate 6D).[80] Day's family estate at Bear Hill in Berkshire was within two miles of Edgeworth's house at Hare Hatch, and on returning from Lichfield in 1766 Edgeworth became friendly with Day, who had enjoyed an income of £1200 a year ever since he was one year old. During 1767 Day became a frequent visitor at Hare Hatch, where he met Keir.

In the spring of 1768 Edgeworth decided to visit his father in Ireland with his young son Richard; Day came too. The long journey needed enlivening, so they agreed that Edgeworth should pose as Day's servant, while Day pretended to be an odd and boorish gentleman. (The pretence was scarcely needed, as Day was notorious for his bad manners and unkempt appearance.) They stopped at an inn at Eccleshall, where Edgeworth played the buffoon – he ordered the entire larder of the inn for dinner, and loudly told everyone about the oddities of his 'master'. These antics ended when a traveller arrived at the inn and asked him what he was playing at.

It was Darwin, and Whitehurst was with him. They talked about mechanics, leaving Day speechless. When they turned to other subjects, Day 'displayed so much knowledge, feeling, and eloquence, as to captivate the Doctor entirely. He invited Mr Day to Lichfield.'[81] Although so different from Darwin, and much younger, Day was to become a good friend in the 1770s.

Day was the odd man out in the Lunar circle, because he was unscientific. But he fitted in with curious ease, becoming friendly with Keir, Boulton and Wedgwood, and above all of course with Dr Small. The others probably admired him because he was such an 'original', and so fluent a speaker – Edgeworth said he never knew anyone 'who in conversation reasoned so profoundly and so logically, or who stated his arguments with so much eloquence'.[82]

So by the spring of 1768 the early Lunar circle can be regarded as fully formed (though Day had not yet met everyone). For seven years there were no changes among the nine members. With Small sitting at the centre, Darwin, Boulton, Whitehurst, Wedgwood, Watt, Keir, Edgeworth and Day revolved in interlinked orbits at various distances about him. The most distant orbit was Watt's, for he was still in Scotland: but he kept in touch through Small's frequent letters. There were others on the fringe of the group. There was Michell, who would have been within it had he not moved to Thornhill near Leeds in 1767. And of course there was Benjamin Franklin, who can be seen as the founding father of the group, but who rarely visited the Birmingham area.

The most important future Lunar member, Joseph Priestley (1733–1804),[83] was already on the fringe too. In 1761 he became lecturer in 'languages and belles lettres' at the Warrington Academy, not far from Liverpool, and he soon got to know Bentley, who was one of the founders of the Academy. At Bentley's house he met the convalescent Wedgwood in 1762 and also Matthew Turner. Priestley persuaded Turner to lecture on chemistry at Warrington Academy. His lectures, in 1764–5, were a great success, and the star pupil was Priestley himself, who learnt his chemistry from Turner.[84] At Warrington, Priestley was too far away to qualify for the Lunar group; and in 1767 he moved even further away when he became Unitarian minister at Leeds. Michell was a great help to him; but Birmingham was ninety miles off.

During the early years of the Lunar group, their meetings were usually in threes or fours at most. Later there were semi-formal meetings at the time of full moon, but not until the mid-1770s.

By the spring of 1768 one typically Lunar project was already under way, and it was to involve at least five members in the next ten years. This was Darwin's 'horizontal windmill'; the axis was vertical and the sails rotated in a horizontal plane. This invention was for the benefit of Wedgwood, who needed a source of power to operate a flint mill for grinding colours. 'I think it is peculiarly adapted to your kind of Business, where the Motion is slow and horizontal', he told Wedgwood about December 1767. Though slightly worried that the mixture might set solid if the wind dropped for a few hours, Darwin was still confident:

> I will make you the Model if you require it immediately, which I can do for the expense of 3 or 4 guineas, so as to evince its Effects. The advantages are, 1. Its Power may be extended much further than the common Wind-Mill. 2. It has

fewer moving Parts. 3. In your Business no Tooth and Pinion-Work will be necessary.[85]

Darwin soon made the model, which was about three feet in diameter; Wedgwood came to Lichfield and inspected it on 10 March 1768. He wrote to Bentley: 'I think [the Windmill] a very ingenious invention and have some hopes that it will answer our expectations'.[86] Darwin estimated that the full-sized windmill would need '68,000 Bricks, and 4800 ft of inch deal Boards, besides one upright shaft 30 ft long and about one foot thick, and a Sail ... on the top'.[87] On 9 April Darwin wrote: 'The windmill turns out much better than Expectation and will probably be the best possible Windmill ... I will send it to the Society of Arts.'[88]

Despite his breezy optimism, the windmill developed into a long-running saga.

The spring of 1768 proved to be a difficult time for Wedgwood. For many years his right leg had given him pain: it was the aftermath of smallpox when he was a boy. His injury on the way to Liverpool in 1762 made matters worse, and by 1768 he regarded the leg as useless. With Darwin's agreement, Wedgwood's right leg was amputated above the knee on 28 May by the surgeon James Bent. As far as is known, Darwin was not present at the operation, presumably to avoid making the surgeon nervous. But he visited Wedgwood several times in the next month, and on 14 June there is a letter from Darwin regretting he could not come that day and giving some news 'in the philosophical arts': Edgeworth 'has nearly completed a Waggon drawn by Fire and a walking Table which will carry 40 men'.[89]

Wedgwood's abounding energy was unaffected by the operation. He recovered within a month, and soon, when he inspected pottery in the factory, he would use his wooden leg to smash any pieces he thought were substandard. Wedgwood was particularly busy in 1768 because his new factory at Etruria was being built, and he was planning further ventures, including the mating of metal with clay, in collaboration with Boulton. 'This ... is a field, to the farther end of which we shall never be able to travel',[90] he told Bentley.

The artificial leg was less trouble than the real one had been, and the next ten years were to be the glory days of the new business partnership of Wedgwood and Bentley.

CHAPTER FIVE

A great change
1768–1771

———

So far, Erasmus had been going from one success to another, prospering as a physician, giving free rein to his inventiveness, creating a charismatic circle of new friends, enjoying a happy marriage, seeing three of his children thrive, and living in a fine house well suited to his needs.

The summer of 1768 saw a change in his fortunes, for Erasmus suffered a serious road accident at Rugeley, probably on 11 July.[1] He was thrown from his carriage and broke the patella of his right knee, 'an accident of irretrievable injury in the human frame', as Anna Seward put it – from bitter experience, since she suffered a similar injury in the same year. Afterwards Erasmus always walked with a limp, and was much less active.

According to the Revd R. G. Robinson, Chancellor's Vicar of Lichfield Cathedral, the accident occurred when Darwin was using a light two-wheeled carriage: 'It was in the form of a garden chair, fix'd upon the axle-tree; the footboard terminated in an elastic pole, which ... went through a ring fix'd on the saddle'.[2] Two days before the accident, Robinson dined with Sir John Every at Egginton, near Burton. The next day,

> the Doctor call'd there to see Lady Every, who was under his care in the inoculated smallpox. He took me with him to Burton in this carriage, and the horse took fright on the road at a barrow of gravel, thrown down by a labourer, employed in making the canal, called the grand trunk; and ran one of the wheels on the top of a hedge, a yard or two. The carriage received a violent shock, which I really believe injured the axle-tree; for it broke the next day in one of the streets of Rugeley when the knee pan of the doctor was broken. He never used the carriage afterwards.[3]

This flimsy open carriage was a sporty design, which Anna Seward says needed constant attention from the driver to control the horse. Presumably Erasmus was using it because the weather was warm in the first two weeks of July.[4]

In his travels of 10,000 miles a year on his medical rounds such an accident was all too likely. This was an era when people often made their wills before going on a long journey, and the wonder is that he remained so long unscathed.

A further cause for much concern in 1768 was Polly's deteriorating health. The only written comment about her is in a letter to Boulton on 31 July, when Erasmus says: 'Mrs Darwin continues to get better'.[5] As it turned out, the bright days were over, and, through no fault of theirs, the marriage of Erasmus and Polly was heading for the darkness.

In 1769 Erasmus made no new friends and took no new initiatives. His anxiety over Polly was beginning to take its toll. '[I] was seldom for an Hour together in my absence from Home free of Tears on her Account',[6] he wrote in 1770, looking back on the previous year. Yet he had to keep up his professional front of being cheerful when visiting patients, while also feeling the cruel irony of being unable to treat Polly effectively. This was probably his most difficult time as a physician: having to be out on the road prevented him from brooding at home, but his long journeys must have seemed quite futile.

[2]

I shall brighten the gloom by introducing a new patient of Darwin's, a master of light who soon became a lifelong friend: this was Joseph Wright of Derby,[7] the artist who captured the Lunar spirit with his superb paintings *The Air Pump* and *The Orrery*. Wright was friendly with Whitehurst in Derby and could have known Darwin by the early 1760s. But Wright's ill health began in 1767, and it was probably then that he first consulted Darwin. At any time after that Wright may have stayed in the annexe of Darwin's house while receiving medical treatment, perhaps for as long as a week. For the next three years Wright travelled widely in the Midlands seeking or fulfilling commissions, though his base was at Liverpool, where he knew Thomas Bentley and Matthew Turner.

Wright's famous picture *An Experiment with a Bird in the Air Pump* was exhibited in April 1768, having been painted in the previous winter. The figure seen in profile sitting at the table in the left foreground appears to be Erasmus, as suggested in the 1980s by Eric Evans,[8] who was encouraged by a tradition in the Darwin family that Erasmus appears in the picture.[9] Plate 6B shows the left half of the painting. The Erasmus-figure is holding a watch: he will tell the lecturer when to let air into the flask to revive the bird. Thus he is currently in charge of the proceedings; and the lecturer would not have deferred to him at such a critical moment unless he had been a man of science of some repute.

A travelling lecturer who came to Lichfield would probably be invited to give his demonstration in Darwin's house, and if so his two sons Charles and Erasmus would be present. They are probably the two boys in the painting: Charles, aged nine, on the right, holds the cage; Erasmus, aged eight, stays behind his father. Wright may have been at Darwin's house on such an occasion, though not necessarily for an air pump experiment. Wright probably attended a lecture with air pump experiments by James Ferguson at Derby several years earlier.[10]

I am not suggesting that Wright painted an actual gathering. His candle-light pictures are imaginative scenarios. But the figures are usually real people. In *The Air Pump* the two lovers on the left are Thomas Coltman and Mary Barlow, who were married in 1769 and are the subjects of one of Wright's best double-portraits, now in the National Gallery. The Coltmans are unlikely ever to have visited Darwin's house: Wright just put them in. In such a scientific painting Wright might well have included the two scientific men he knew best, Whitehurst (aged fifty-four) and Darwin (aged thirty-six). The thoughtful figure seated on the right could be the unassuming Whitehurst, though the shape of his nose may not be quite right. The moon peering through the window is one of Wright's favourite devices and has no 'Lunar' resonance. The use of a valuable cockatoo in the experiment is most unlikely in practice. Nor does it mean that Erasmus would have approved of such an animal experiment: he did not know that Wright would 'frame' him in this way. Most lecturers used a 'lungs-glass' of air instead of a bird.[11]

There is no indication that Darwin ever saw Wright's picture: it was purchased by an acquaintance of Darwin and Wright, Dr Benjamin Bates of Missenden,[12] who paid £130 for it, though Wright's official price[13] was £200, equivalent to about £20,000 today.

When Wright stayed at the Darwins' house in the years 1767–70, did he ever paint a portrait of the beautiful Polly? This would have been a gift, in lieu of medical fees, and would not appear in Wright's account book. A portrait of Polly did exist at the time of her death, and Wright was the only portrait painter Darwin knew. Is there any suitable candidate among Wright's unnamed portraits of 1768–70?

After examining all known portraits by Wright, I would choose as the most likely one a painting of unknown provenance first exhibited in 1990 at the Tate Gallery's Wright exhibition[14] and there entitled *Portrait of a Lady with her Lacework, c.1770*. The age of the sitter seems about right, and this is one of Wright's rare half-smiling portraits, which fits what we know of Polly. The main objection to this or any other attribution is that Robert Darwin would have treasured any portrait of his mother, but apparently he never had one. Thus it is necessary to assume that the portrait was lost, or put away out of sight after Erasmus's second marriage. A further objection is that the lady of the lace looks like Mary Barlow. So my suggestion remains merely speculative.

[3]

Darwin acted on his intention of telling the Society of Arts about the wind-mill. On 4 February 1769 he wrote to Dr Templeman, explaining the virtues of his windmill and asking whether the Society might grant a premium for making a full-size version:

> I have lately constructed the Model of an horizontal Windmill, which appears to have a third more Power than any vertical Windmill, whose Sail is of the same diameter, and is in other respects more manageable and less liable to Repair, as it has less wheel-work, having only an upright Shaft on the top of which the Sail is fix'd, and will move three pairs of Stones.[15]

Unless there was a chance of financial help, he says, 'I should not chuse the Expense of sending it up'. He asks Dr Templeman's opinion, 'and must beg of you, *and in this Confidence I write to you,* not to mention my Name, as I do not court this kind of Reputation, as I believe it might injure me.' In a postscript to his letter Darwin says: 'The Mill consists much of Brick-Work and could not be executed in its greatest size for less than 300 £'.

The Society of Arts was unable to give Darwin financial help, because its method was to offer a premium for particular subjects, and windmills were not among them, though the Society did offer a prize for a horizontal wind-mill seventeen years later (when Darwin's mill was already in operation).

In 1769 Darwin's windmill was not developed beyond the model Wedg-wood saw and admired. Wedgwood was keen to have it at once, but on 15 March Darwin advised him to wait:

> I should long ago have wrote to you, but waited to learn in what forwardness Mr Watt's Fire-Engine was in. He has taken a Partner [Dr Roebuck], and I can make no Conjecture how soon you may be accommodated by Him with a Power so much more convenient than that of Wind. I will make packing Boxes and send you my Model, that you may consult the Ingenious. I am of opinion it will be a powerful and a convenient Windmill, but would recommend Steam to you if you can wait awhile.[16]

As Roebuck was a well-known and respected entrepreneur, Darwin expected rapid progress on Watt's engine and did not send the model. In fact the engine was to remain almost at a standstill until Watt moved to Birmingham five years later. And it was nearly ten years before Darwin re-suscitated the windmill: in 1769 his heart was not really in it, and it was in part a displacement activity during Polly's decline.

His letter to Templeman shows how heavily shackled Darwin was as an inventor. He believed his medical career would be damaged if his patients got to know that he was busy designing and constructing carriages and windmills. With several of his inventions he let others take the credit for executing them, as happened with Edgeworth and the carriages. It was not because Darwin couldn't be bothered to bring the design to fruition, but because he feared for his livelihood. His timidity was basically reasonable, but perhaps rather overdone: fearing to publicize the diversity of his talents was Darwin's nearest approach to a neurosis. He was bashful not only as an inventor but also as an author: the canal pamphlet was the first of several anonymities.

In retrospect Darwin's medical career seems to have been a triumphant success, undamaged by his diversity. But in early 1769 he had cause for concern. His practice depended very largely on travelling, and his knee injury made him realize that he would lose his income if he lost his mobility; there would be no pay-out from an insurance company to cushion the loss. In 1768 his income dropped to £775, but there were no further accidents in 1769 and his earnings increased to £959.

Not included in these earnings was free advice given to Wedgwood, who began to see spots before his eyes. The doctors consulted took a serious view (to match their serious fees), and Wedgwood thought he was going blind.[17] But Darwin said everybody at some time in life had such 'appearances before their eyes, but everybody *did not look at them*'.[18] Whitehurst had suffered similarly, and Darwin told both of them that they would soon be well again: he proved to be right.

[4]

Although there were no new friends in 1769, Darwin was able to communicate with his friend from Edinburgh days, Albert Reimarus. In April Darwin received a visit from J. J. Ferber, a well-known scientific traveller interested chiefly in mineralogy. During his two-day visit Ferber revealed that he knew Reimarus, who was in practice as a doctor in Hamburg.

Darwin wrote a hasty letter: 'I received very great pleasure in hearing ... that my old friend Dr Reimarus is alive and succeeds in the World.' After mentioning that Keir has left the Army 'to study Chemistry and Philosophy more at Leizure', Darwin goes on:

> For my own part I practise Medecine in Lichfield, Staffordshire, where I shall hope to hear from you. I have a good House, a pleasant Situation, a sensible Wife, and three healthful Children, and as much medical Business as I can do with Ease, and rather more. Mechanics, and Chemistry are my Hobby-horses, but a Comparison of the Laws of the Mind with those of the Body, has of late been my favorite Study.[19]

Darwin offers an exchange of medical observations, and of children: he

PLATE 1 Erasmus Darwin, cast in bronze in 1967 from a bust by William Coffee (1804)

PLATE 2A Robert Darwin (1682–1754), Erasmus's father

PLATE 2B Elizabeth Darwin, née Hill (1702–97), Erasmus's mother

PLATE 2C Elston Hall in the village of Elston, near Newark: Erasmus's birthplace and his home until 1756

PLATE 3A Erasmus Darwin's house at the edge of the Cathedral Close in Lichfield, where he lived from 1758 to 1781. The house is being restored and is due to open as an Erasmus Darwin museum and study centre in 1999

PLATE 3B A sketch of Darwin's house as it probably appeared in the 1760s, with a wide terrace in front and a sloping wooden bridge down from the front door to the road, over a sunken garden planted with shrubs

PLATE 4A Erasmus Darwin at the age of thirty-eight, painted by his friend and patient Joseph Wright of Derby in 1770

PLATE 4B Matthew Boulton (1728–1809), Darwin's earliest friend in Birmingham

PLATE 4C Benjamin Franklin (1706–90), a probable role-model for Darwin and a friend for thirty years

PLATE 5A John Whitehurst of Derby (1713–88), painted by his friend Joseph Wright in 1783

PLATE 5B Josiah Wedgwood (1730–95), from the portrait by Sir Joshua Reynolds

PLATE 5C James Watt (1736–1819), from a portrait by C. F. von Breda

PLATE 5D James Keir (1735–1820) with his granddaughter Amelia Moilliet

PLATE 6A Anna Seward (1742–1809), painted by George Romney in 1786

PLATE 6B Detail (*left half*) from Joseph Wright's *An Experiment with a Bird in the Air Pump*. Erasmus Darwin is the likely model for the man with the watch, and the boy is probably his son Erasmus

PLATE 6C Richard Lovell Edgeworth (1744–1817) from an engraving by A. Cardon in 1812

PLATE 6D Thomas Day (1748–89), engraved by H. Meyer from the 1770 portrait by Joseph Wright

PLATE 7A The memorial inscription for Charles Darwin (1758–78) at the chapel of St Cuthbert in Edinburgh

PLATE 7B
The Wedgwood medallion of Erasmus Darwin, 1780, based on Wright's portrait of 1770

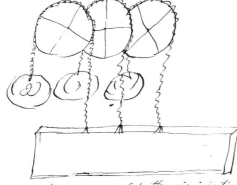

PLATE 7C Some of Darwin's sketches for a canal lift, from his Commonplace Book, 1777

PLATE 8A Elizabeth Pole and her son Sacheverel, painted by Joseph Wright, 1770–1. She married Erasmus Darwin in 1781

PLATE 8B Elizabeth Pole with a frisky dog, supposed in family tradition to be Erasmus, being led a dance

asks Reimarus to send a child to learn English, 'and I will send you a Son in exchange ... if such a Trafic be agreable to you'.

In this letter Darwin discards the veil of conventional reserve because Reimarus is far away, without contacts in England. Today the idea of child-exchange will seem ruthless to some, beneficial to others. The victim, or beneficiary, would have been Erasmus junior, now nine years old. It is typical of Darwin that when he decided something was good, he would try to bring it about. He thought Erasmus junior, like Charles, should have the advantage of foreign experience, but by a cheaper method than travel with a tutor. On this occasion Darwin was unsuccessful, and there is no record of any reply from Reimarus.

An unexpected feature of the letter is Darwin's new interest in comparing 'the Laws of the Mind with those of the Body'. This is his first foray into the thickets of metaphysics, an interest that continued as a sideline for many years and probably began while he was recovering from his accident. He was lured into metaphysics by his two lively clerical friends the Revd Robert Clive of Moreton in Shropshire,[20] cousin and brother-in-law of Lord Clive, and the Revd Richard Gifford, vicar of Duffield near Derby.[21] Darwin wrote them a letter discussing the ideas of Locke and 'the modern sceptics', but said he would not publish the paper he had written.[22]

Another unguarded remark to Reimarus, already quoted in chapter 1, is that 'Mr Keir and myself continue in the Religion you taught us', which might be called sceptical Deism.

By this time Albert Reimarus himself had become more sceptical and was busy campaigning in favour of the ultimate insult to God – the installation of lightning conductors on churches, to save congregations from God's wrath. (Of course, Reimarus did not give that reason: his stance was philanthropic.) He fitted a lightning conductor to his own house in 1768, apparently the first in mainland Europe, and within twelve years more than 200 buildings in Hamburg were protected, though he argued wrongly (and dangerously) that the rods did not need to be well earthed.[23]

[5]

For Erasmus 1769 was a year of thinking rather than doing. The carriage accident reduced his activity and may have bred a mood of contemplation. Polly's illness made him more reluctant to accept social engagements and even to visit his Lunar friends. This semi-withdrawal may have given rise to his writings on the relations between mind and body; but a far more important idea was gradually unfolding itself. It was an idea that came to dominate his views about the development of life, and it is the very idea that biologists adopt today.

On thinking about the fossil bones found in the Harecastle Tunnel, and the bones he came across in the Derbyshire caves, Darwin arrived at what is now called the theory of common descent, the belief that all life as we see it today is descended from one microscopic ancestor – a 'single living filament' as Darwin was to express it in *Zoonomia* twenty-five years later.

It is an obvious consequence of this idea that species have undergone change down the ages, as shown by the fossils of unknown species. Endowed with this strong belief in biological evolution, as we now call it, Darwin could see into the workings of nature more successfully than any of his contemporaries. Many aspects of vegetable and animal life fell into place for him.

He may have felt he should shout the news of his revelation all round Lichfield like a town crier, but he immediately realized that he must not do so. The current orthodoxy was that God created species, and a doctor who dared to propose a different mode of species-creation would be crucified by the religious establishment and would offend many of his rich patients. Darwin's biological revelation was not inconsistent with his previous re-

FIG. 7 Erasmus Darwin's bookplate. To the family arms, of three scallop shells, he added the motto *E conchis omnia* ('Everything from shells') to express his belief that all life has developed from a single microscopic ancestor – 'the theory of common descent', as it is now called

ligious attitude as a sceptical deist. For some years to come he was at ease
with the ideas that God created the original living filament, and that life
then developed free of intervention from God.

But did he have to suppress his brilliant insight completely? He thought
of a neat way of publicizing it without anyone noticing. His family coat of
arms consisted of three scallop shells. What a good idea to add the motto
E conchis omnia, or 'everything from shells'. It was not exactly right,
because 'shells' should have been 'small shelly sea-creatures' or, better still,
'microscopic filaments'; but it expressed the essence of evolutionary development. He could well have been chuckling to himself as he had the
motto painted on his carriage in 1770 and printed on his bookplate in 1771
(Fig. 7).

But he reckoned without the watchful Canon Seward, who was sharper
than Darwin imagined. Already alert to Darwin's unorthodoxy in religion,
Seward wanted revenge for those satirical verses. This was his chance, and
he took it. Seward begins obliquely by attacking Epicurus for having taught
that the world is accidental and not designed by God. Now Epicurus has a
modern disciple, Darwin:

> He too renounces his Creator,
> And forms all sense from senseless matter.
> Great wizard he! by magic spells
> Can all things raise from cockle shells....
> O Doctor, change thy foolish motto,
> Or keep it for some lady's grotto.
> Else thy poor patients well may quake
> If thou no more canst *mend* than *make*.[24]

Pierced in a sensitive spot – his fundamental belief about life – by his own
rapier of satirical verse, Darwin had to submit. Now that the truth was out,
he could not openly insult the Church on his medical rounds, so he had to
paint out the motto on his carriage (though he kept it on the bookplate).
It was a humiliating climb-down, and he must have been seething with
rage: Anna says he was never again friendly with her father.[25] This episode
reinforced his decision to keep quiet about his idea. He kept it under wraps
for twenty-four years.

[6]

Erasmus found the key to the secrets of life on Earth just when he was failing to find a way of fending off the disease that was threatening Polly's life.
It was a tragic paradox.

There are just a few current glimpses of her illness. On 22 January 1769,

Edgeworth wrote: 'I feel a real pleasure to hear that Mrs Darwin re-
covers.'[26] Another glimpse is provided by Miss M. Newton, possibly a
niece of Thomas Newton, once the favourite friend of Polly's father. The
Newton and Howard families remained close, and Polly was a special
friend of Miss Newton, who, in an undated letter to her, says 'it was very
kind in Mr Howard to let me know how you did in every letter, but his not
nameing you in his last gives me a fear that you was not so well'.[27] A more
professional opinion comes from Dr Small on 7 February, 'Mrs Darwin has
long been ill', a stark sentence that says it all.

As the four seasons of 1769 passed and 1770 began, Polly was suffering
spasms of pain more often and more violently, and she took longer to recover. The medication offered by Erasmus was of no avail, apart from the
opium to relieve the pain, and Polly died on 30 June 1770, aged thirty.

During the last few weeks of Polly's life, Anna Seward sat with her
several times. Anna offers a two-page report of what Polly said, allegedly
verbatim but translated into stilted Sewardese:

> In the short term of my life, a great deal of happiness has been comprised. The
> maladies of my frame were peculiar; the pains in my head and stomach, which no
> medicine could eradicate, were spasmodic and violent; and required stronger
> measures to render them supportable while they lasted, than my constitution
> could sustain without injury.[28]

The 'stronger measures' consisted of the opium prescribed by Erasmus,
supplemented by the brandy and other alcoholic spirits favoured by Polly
herself. Anna/Polly continues:

> Pain taught me the value of ease, and I enjoyed it with a glow of spirit, seldom,
> perhaps, felt by the habitually healthy. While Dr Darwin combated and assuaged
> my disease from time to time, his indulgence to all my wishes, his active desire to
> see me amused and happy, proved incessant....
> Married to any other man, I do not suppose I could have lived a third part of
> those years which I have passed with Dr Darwin; he has prolonged my days, and
> he has blessed them.

We can see how much Erasmus loved her from an eight-page account of
her death, dated 2 July 1770, two days after the event. On 8 July he sent
this to Polly's friend Miss Newton with a letter:

> Your poor Friend Mrs Darwin after a very painful Disease of many Months,
> I may say, of many year's Continuance, on the thirtyth of last Month ceased to be
> ill! –
> She had so long lost all Hopes of regaining her Health, that her Life was
> only valuable to Herself, as She most tenderly loved her Family and her Friends,
> and should be regretted by Me, and by You, for our own Sakes; rather than for
> Hers.
> I can not however yet cease feelingly to lament her Loss; and send you this

Account, as I well know, from the long and tender Friendship that existed between you, that you will *in Truth* sympathize with Me.[29]

At the end of the letter he adds: 'To Miss Newton, Mrs Darwin's Hair and
Ring'.

The copy of 'this Account' of Polly's death sent to Miss Newton has
survived with the letter, and I am confident that it is a faithful copy because
it has several of Erasmus's characteristic mis-spellings, such as 'Sollicitude'
and 'Dilirium'.

Throughout his life Erasmus was reluctant to write about emotional
events, unless they could be sublimated into verse. His son Robert said
'he never would allow any common acquaintance to converse with him
upon any subject that he felt poignantly'.[30] This is quoted from the *Life*
of Erasmus by Robert's son Charles, who adds his own comment that
Erasmus 'wished to conceal his own feelings'.

But Polly's death was so great a shock that it swept away his inhibitions:

On Saturday night about six – that hour shall ever be remember'd – the dear
Partner of all the Cares and Pleasures of my Life ceased to be ill – and I felt myself
alone in the World! Early on Sunday Morning after long having wept over her
pale Corse, I forced myself from Home into the labour of my Profession; this I
believed was my Duty as a Man, and I hoped it would abstract my mind from
those Ideas, that were so painful to me whilst alone.

This morning [Monday] I return'd to take a last farewel, and after gazing for
an Hour on the poor Remains of what was once most dear to me; and indulging
my grief quite to excess by reading her Letters, and comparing the vermil Tints of
her Picture with the palid Hue of her dead Features.[31]

This is the unknown portrait of Polly, possibly by Wright, already mentioned.
Erasmus goes on to say that 'I am now so composed as to write this
Account to you', that is, to Miss Newton, 'to whom the Flow of the Heart
is more agreeable than all the Eloquence of labour'd Wit'. He felt he needed
to send the 'Account' to someone, and Miss Newton seemed to him to be
the most sympathetic of the possible recipients. It is unlikely that he sent it
to anyone else.

Next, Erasmus looks back over Polly's last years:

She had many years labour'd under a most painful Disease, for which no other
Remedy, but the temporary one of Opium, was of any Service. Many hundred
Nights have I watched to console and assist her, and was seldom for an Hour
together in my Absence from Home free from Tears on her Account – Yet her Life
was valuable to Her for She loved her Family most tenderly! and to me, as her
Approbation stampt the Pleasures on all the Conveniences and Amusements of
my Situation! The shady walk in my Garden, the Harbour, and the wild Woodbine and Primroses, that she planted and admired seem to have lost their Beauty
and their Odour!...

When She felt the Iron-Hand of Death cold at her Heart, She said 'it was hard

so early in Life to leave her Children and her Husband whom she loved so much
– pray take Care of yourself and them!' – 'Yes, my poor dear Polly, I will take
Care of your Children, you know I will, with all a Mother's Tenderness, and all a
Father's Sollicitude!'

This is already quite harrowing, but there is worse to follow, because
Polly was overwhelmed by delusions in her last days:

> In her succeeding Dilirium She was most violently agitated for many hours with
> Fears that some one was about to kill the objects of her Love – 'Take Care (said
> She a hundred Times over) He is going to strike a Dagger to your Heart', and
> with the greatest Energy put her feeble Hands to defend me, with such wild and
> vehement Expressions of Fear in her Countenance as nothing can represent – but
> my Memory!
>
> To this succeeded weaker Efforts, 'don't kill my Children, sais She, pray don't'
> – with such a beseeching Countenance – 'don't kill them all, leave me one, pray
> leave me one!' – Oh Heavens! –

Echoes from *King Lear* and *Macbeth* can perhaps be heard here; but is
there any scene in drama to outdo the real-life horror of this description?
The aftermath was quieter, but still hard to bear:

> On the next day, her Passions subsided, as her Reason had done the preceeding
> one, and a calm unmeaning Dilirium took Place, which was chiefly employ'd
> about visible objects. 'Is not that a pretty silk, those Candlesticks are elegant',
> and innumerable half Sentences, that seem'd rather customary modes of Ex-
> pression, than Words fraught with Ideas: But not a Word that shew'd the least
> Fear of Death, or a Passion that was not dictated by Virtue and Benevolence.

In the final section of the manuscript, headed 'Consolation', Erasmus
tries to argue himself out of his grief:

> Had she continued to live, such was the unconquerable Nature of her Disease,
> that Life would have been twisted with many threads of black.
>
> Thousands have sunk before her.... Cities have perished.... Life I must con-
> tinue for the Care of her children, and her Desire.
>
> A few Months will soften these Ideas and smooth the Remembrance of her
> down to Pleasure, and turn my Tears to Rapture.[32]

This account of Polly's last days and death is a poignant and deeply
personal document. When Erasmus's grandson Charles wrote his *Life* in
1879, he never mentioned this manuscript, though it was probably available to him. Presumably he would have found it too painful to quote, not
just because Polly was his grandmother, but also because her death left his
revered father Robert motherless at the age of four, a tragedy all the more
distressing to Charles because he himself was left motherless at the age of
seven.

Now that two centuries have passed, publication is more justifiable, and
the manuscript is significant in offering new insight into the characters of

both Erasmus and Polly. Also I believe it generates its own *imprimatur* through the high quality of its elegiac prose, rich in imagery.

Erasmus was famous for his outward cheerfulness and geniality. He told Robert that 'in order to feel cheerful you must appear to be so'.[33] Even Anna Seward admitted that he always had 'a sunny smile'. This smiling image contributed to his great sucess as a doctor and his genius for making and keeping friends. The manuscript lets us see behind the smiling mask and reveals his sensitivity to human suffering – another quality that helped to earn him the gratitude of his patients.

Polly was buried in the Lady Choir at Lichfield Cathedral on 4 July, the funeral expenses being £2 12s 6d. Erasmus kept the poignant scrap of paper recording the details.[34]

[7]

Post mortem, and with two centuries of hindsight, we can see that Polly had more influence on future events than she or anyone else could have known. Of course she passed on many genes to her grandson Charles, but her main influence was cultural rather than physical. The children were brought up by her rather than by Erasmus, who was usually out all day. After her death Erasmus hid his feelings and might never have recorded her role in educating the children. Only the tragic death of his eldest son Charles induced him to describe her cultural upbringing of the boy:

> Nor ... was his taste for morality neglected; for his ingenious mother, even to her latest hour! instilled into his breast a sympathy with the pains and with the pleasures of others, by sympathizing herself with their distress or exultation: she flattered him into a sense of honour by commending his integrity, and scorn of falsehood, before her friends: and taught him prudence by pointing out to him the ill consequences of the bad conduct of others ... and as she had wisely sown no seeds of superstition in his mind, there was nothing to overshade the virtues she had implanted.[35]

This is a secular morality: Polly's children were brought up free of religious imperatives, with 'no seeds of superstition' as Erasmus delicately phrased it. And he made sure that her principles were followed after her death with her youngest son Robert. So, when Erasmus eventually 'went public' with his belief in biological evolution (as we now call it), in *Zoonomia* in 1794, Robert had no difficulty in accepting it, because he had no 'religious block'. Robert in turn created a family environment that was evolution-friendly and free of religious prohibitions, and his son Charles may have been infected with the idea of evolution even before reading *Zoonomia*.

Erasmus may seem a little starry-eyed in reporting Polly's system of child care, but she herself spoke in a similar vein, it seems. 'My three boys have ever been docile, and affectionate', Anna reports her as saying, 'children as they are, I could trust them with important secrets, so sacred do they hold every promise they make. They scorn deceit, and falsehood of every kind, and have less selfishness than generally belongs to childhood.'[36]

Polly's preference for secular morality was quite unusual in the eighteenth century for a married woman who was no radical, no bluestocking, and whose father was part of the cathedral hierarchy. Her independence of religion during her illness is even more remarkable. Her house was only 120 yards from the ornate west front of Lichfield Cathedral, and most of her friends lived in the Close. She could easily have opted for the solace of the rich cathedral rituals; but she held aloof and faced death calmly without supernatural assistance. Erasmus was deeply moved at her strength of mind, and may have wondered whether he would have been so sure and dignified.

Post mortem, too, Polly's illness can be diagnosed. Erasmus said nothing about it at the time, because the subject was too painful. It was not until twenty-one years later, when his son Robert asked whether the illness might be hereditary, that Erasmus sketched her medical history:

> In respect to your mother, the following is the true history, which I shall neither aggravate nor diminish any thing. Her mind was truly amiable and her person hansome, which you may perhaps in some measure remember.
>
> She was siezed with pain on the right side about the lower edge of the liver, this pain was follow'd in about an hour by violent convulsions, and these sometimes relieved by great doses of opium, and some wine, which induced intoxication. At other times a tempor[ar]y dilirium, or what by some might be term'd insanity, came on for half an hour, and then she became herself again, and the paroxism was terminated. This disease is called hysteric by some people, I think it allied to Epilepsy.
>
> This kind of disease had several returns in the course of 4 or 6 years and she then took to drinking spirit and water to relieve the pain, and I found (when it was too late) that she had done this in great quantity, the liver became swelled and she gradually sunk. A few days before her death, she bled at the mouth, and wherever she had a scratch, as some hepatic patients do.[37]

The impersonal tone is an attempt to keep the lid on the volcano of re-aroused emotions. But Erasmus allows one suppressed memory to surface: 'I well remember when your mother fainted away in these hysteric fits (which she often did) that she told me, you, who was not 2 or 2½ years old, [would] run into the kitchen to call the maid-servant to her assistance'.

One immediate comment has to be made about Erasmus's medical report on Polly: in the first printed transcript of this letter,[38] published by Nora Barlow in 1958, the words 'right side' in the first line of the second paragraph were printed as 'left side', and this wording was carried through into my books in 1963 and 1977. In editing the *Letters* (1981) I adopted the wording of an independent transcript by Sir Geoffrey Keynes, which had 'right side'. The latter reading proved to be correct when the manuscript became available in the early 1990s. The change makes quite a difference to the diagnosis.

The retrospective diagnosis by Dr Gordon C. Cook, published in 1996, is widely accepted. Erasmus, he says, describes first an organic illness and then subsequent problems related to the therapeutic measures used. The original organic illness Cook diagnoses as 'biliary-tract disease', which is 'probably secondary to gall-stone formation'. He adds, 'The intermittent nature of the acute attacks of severe pain in the right hypochondrium – followed by transient bouts of "delirium" (organic psychoses) – leave one in little doubt of this diagnosis.' Later the 'alcohol taken "in great quantity" to relieve the biliary colic' would in itself lead to alcoholic cirrhosis. The swelling of the liver 'could have occurred as a result of biliary cirrhosis; it would also be likely if alcohol was involved *per se*; overall the two factors probably operated simultaneously.'[39]

Darwin himself recognized biliary-tract disease and gall-stones. In *Zoonomia* (1794) he writes:

> This disease is attended with much pain, which at first is felt at the pit of the stomach, exactly in the centre of the body, where the bile-duct enters the duodenum; afterwards, when the size of the bile-stones increase, it is also felt on the right side, where the gall-bladder is situated. The former pain at the pit of the stomach recurs by intervals, as the bile-stone is pushed against the neck of the duct; ... the other is a more dull and constant pain.
>
> Where these bile-stones are too large to pass, and the bile-ducts possess their sensibility, this becomes a very painful and hopeless disease.[40]

So he made some experiments and found that bile-stones were quickly dissolved by being 'put into vitriolic aether'. 'Might not aether mixed with yolk of egg or with honey be given advantageously in bilious concretions?'

Despite this knowledge, he did not recognize the disease in Polly. Perhaps his knowledge came after 1770. But I cannot understand why he never mentions it in 1792 when writing to Robert, who was himself a doctor.

Gall-bladder disease was not properly described until late in the nineteenth century; gall-bladder surgery began in the twentieth century.[41]

The tenor of the letter to Robert shows that he and his father did not discuss Polly. Robert felt it was a forbidden subject; Erasmus said in the letter that he would willingly answer such questions, thus implying that he had never previously done so. Also he does not know how much Robert can remember of his mother, a sure sign that they had never talked about her.

[8]

So Erasmus was left a widower at the age of thirty-eight with three young sons to bring up, Charles, Erasmus and Robert, then aged eleven, ten and four respectively. In the eighteenth century it was not unusual for a wife to die at thirty, childbirth being the most assiduous executioner. But that did not make it any easier for Erasmus. He needed, preferably from the family, someone who could look after the large house, supervise the servants and guide the boys in his absence; he also needed a well-brought-up girl to take care of the four-year-old Robert.

He was fortunate that his favourite sister Susannah, unmarried and now forty, was willing to move in and to act as housekeeper and indulgent aunt to the three boys, who already knew her well. Robert became very fond of her and spoke of her in later years 'as the very pattern of an old lady, so nice looking, so gentle, kind, and charitable, and passionately fond of flowers'.[42]

Erasmus was also fortunate in finding a girl to look after Robert. She arrived within a month, on 26 July 1770.[43] She was seventeen, her name was Mary Parker and she came from Elston, presumably being recommended by Erasmus's mother, who at the age of sixty-seven was still active, well and perhaps domineering – could she even have said, 'I know just the girl for you'? Be that as it may, Mary Parker's appointment was to prove unexpectedly fruitful.

We know that Robert was in Mary Parker's care, but there is no information about Charles and Erasmus junior at this time, apart from a cryptic entry years later in a notebook of Robert's,[44] which reads: 'C and E left London School 25 May 1770'. So they had both been at a boarding school in London, and presumably returned at Polly's request so that she could see them again before she died. The name of the school; how long they had been there; whether they returned in the autumn – all these are unknown.

Among the many changes in Erasmus's life at this time was his decision to become an author. This was to be most significant in the long term, not immediately. So far he had written nothing more solid than his two papers for the Royal Society and the anonymous canal pamphlet. Now he began work on a medical book, which during the next twenty years grew into his two-volume treatise on animal life and medical practice, *Zoonomia*.

Writing more implies going out less, and in 1770 Erasmus seems to have lost his appetite for travel. Apart from his medical journeys, he rarely left Lichfield.

[9]

In the summer of 1770 Joseph Wright stayed in Lichfield for some time. While he was there he painted the best known – and in my opinion the best – portrait of Erasmus (Plate 4A). Anna Seward vouches for its accuracy: she calls it 'a simply contemplative portrait, of the most perfect resemblance'.[45] Judy Egerton, nearly two centuries later, has this to say about it:

> The pose, with the patient spread of the arms on the table and the attentive tilt of the head, expresses that faculty for listening which made Darwin such an incomparably good doctor; but while there is kindness in the face, there is also large sagacity, and little doubt that the sitter is potentially formidable.[46]

Wright never painted a fully smiling portrait, and so we are denied a view of Darwin's famous smile. Although there is no flattery in the portrait, it may seem that Wright improved on reality a little by using a table-top to hide Darwin's rotundity. But this reflective table may be as real as it looks: it could be the same as the one in *The Air Pump*.

Wright's account book does not record any payment by Darwin for his portrait, so it is probable that Wright stayed with Darwin as a patient for perhaps a week or two, and painted his portrait in gratitude. Wright's normal charge for such a portrait would have been ten guineas. Darwin might have sat for it in his house at his reflective table, as in *The Air Pump* but full face instead of profile.

There are three versions of the portrait. The first and best is at Darwin College, Cambridge. The second is privately owned. The third, at the National Portrait Gallery, is a copy, probably but not certainly by Wright.[47]

That Darwin and Wright were now on friendly terms is confirmed by an incongruous page in Wright's private account book, where Darwin has written a rhetorical 'caption' for Wright's emotive picture *Miravan robbing the Tomb of his Ancestors*. Darwin's caption was printed in the catalogue when the painting was exhibited. Wright was not familiar with Persian/Syrian mythology and, as the story of Miravan is most obscure,[48] Darwin probably suggested the theme to him.

In the autumn of 1770 Wright left Lichfield, having received his most important commission so far, the decoration of Radburn Hall near Derby.

Before he left, however, there was a new face at Lichfield for him to paint – Thomas Day's. The arrival of the loquacious Day may have helped to divert Darwin from his grief during the summer; while Wright took the chance to create another fine portrait, as well as earning himself £42, for two copies.

[10]

The arrival of Day electrified the Seward circle because he was conducting a curious human experiment. In the previous year he had reached the age of twenty-one and decided he ought to marry. But who would suit him? He detested fashionable ladies, and wanted a wife 'simple as a mountain girl, in her dress, her diet and her manners; fearless and intrepid'. As Anna Seward admitted, 'there was no finding such a creature ready made'. Day was a keen disciple of Rousseau, and his faith in education was unbounded; so he decided to mould a girl to his own design.

Armed with testimonials of moral probity, and with the lawyer John Bicknell to vouch for him, he visited two orphanages: from each he was allowed to select a twelve-year-old girl to educate. He promised to apprentice one within a year and support her, and to groom the other as his wife; and if she didn't suit him, he promised to maintain her until she married. Both were beautiful, Anna tells us: 'one fair, with flaxen locks, and light eyes; her he called Lucretia. The other, a clear, auburn brunette, with darker eyes, more glowing bloom, and chestnut tresses, he named Sabrina.'[49] Day took them away to France to mould. But instead they moulded him, or at least played him up. Lucretia, the more fractious of the two, he apprenticed to a milliner; Sabrina he persevered with.

In his task of unique difficulty, who better than Darwin to help him? So Day came to Lichfield and rented Stowe House, only ten minutes' walk from Darwin. Sabrina favourably impressed nearly everyone she met, but she disappointed Day because she was averse to books and science, and was not stoical enough: when he fired a pistol at her petticoats, she screamed, because she had neither the intelligence to realize the shots were blanks nor the courage that might redeem her stupidity. Darwin probably restrained him from even more outrageous acts. Anyone today who behaved as he did would fall foul of the law. But Day was known to be virtuous, and was therefore accepted as merely eccentric by the clergymen of the Close. As for Sabrina, she enjoyed being the focus of attention and gossip in the Seward circle and a privileged visitor at the palace.

Day gave up his experiment after a year and sent Sabrina to a boarding school. Later in the 1770s she came back several times to Lichfield, where she was always welcomed as a local celebrity. She was 'often the guest of Dr Darwin, and other of her friends in Lichfield', Anna tells us. Later Sabrina married Day's friend John Bicknell and after his death became housekeeper to Fanny Burney's brother Charles.

In December 1770 Edgeworth arrived in Lichfield, probably seated in a 'superb one-wheeled one-horsed carriage'.[50] This elongated wheelbarrow expressed his exuberance and impressed the natives. Not long after climbing out of his weird vehicle, Edgeworth became captivated by Anna's beautiful companion Honora Sneyd, who had been living with the Sewards for ten years since the death of her mother, and was now nineteen. Edgeworth was so smitten that after a Lunar meeting at Darwin's house, he insisted that his friends should come to see her at the palace. Small, Keir, Darwin and others, we are told, duly trooped along to admire her. Edgeworth then remembered he was married, and went home to Hare Hatch early in 1771.

But he was soon back at Lichfield with his wife and three children, having taken over the lease of Stowe House, though Day remained as a guest. Now that Sabrina had gone, Day himself fell in love with Honora. Edgeworth offered to press Day's suit for him and took her Day's proposal for marriage (of several thousand words). She rejected him, not wishing to retire from the world as required in his proposal. Day fell ill after this rebuff: Darwin bled him and then talked him out of his imagined malady.

Everyone – even the sedate churchmen of the Close – became infected by Edgeworth's exuberance, and during the summer of 1771 there was dancing, vaulting, leaping and archery. In the evenings the terrace of the Close rang with laughter, Anna says, 'Mr Edgeworth enlivening us by a wit, extensive as the light of the sun and active as its heat, Dr Darwin laughing with us, while we have felt the fine edge of elegant, ingenious, and what is most rare, good-humor'd irony ... Mr Day *improving* our minds, while he delights our imaginations.'[51]

So ended the first act of the tragic-romantic comedy of the Two Gentlemen of Lichfield. Act 2 starts with the entry of Mr Sneyd, alarmed that two such lively gentlemen of leisure had designs on his daughter. He came to live at Lichfield, bringing with him four more daughters, one of whom, Elizabeth, was very like Honora. Day promptly fell in love with Elizabeth, while Edgeworth remained faithful to Honora. But Day's hopes were quickly dashed: Elizabeth rejected him, telling him he was lacking in social graces. Edgeworth and Day were now both rather desperate.

Impulsive as ever, Edgeworth decided to go to France. Day went with him, to learn those graces. They set off in August 1771, taking with them Edgeworth's seven-year-old son Richard, a wild boy educated à la Rousseau. In Paris they called on Rousseau himself, who took Richard out for a walk and was favourably impressed by him. Then Edgeworth and Day went on to Lyons, beyond Darwin's ken.

[11]

For some months Darwin's enthusiasm for mechanics and inventions seems to have been buried with Polly. But by the end of 1770 these interests were beginning to resurface, as shown by several letters to Wedgwood.

The elusive Wychnor Ironworks appears for the first time in five years, in a letter of 9 December 1770. 'The Company concern'd in the Wichnor Iron-Works', Darwin says, 'have been advised by Mr Brindley to set up a Mill for grinding Flints at that Place'.[52]

The next topic in this letter is the windmill. 'Mr Watt's Fire-Engine I believe goes on, but I don't know at what rate. I have not sent you your Model of a Windmill, but it may be sent you at any Time ... but the Fire-Engine will be more convenient to you I should think.' When the inventor was so bashful, it is not surprising that Wedgwood did nothing. Nearly a year later Darwin says 'your Windmill sleeps at my House'; but he still advises Wedgwood to wait for the 'Wheel Fire-engine, which goes on slowly'.[53] The windmill stayed asleep for a further seven years.

Darwin was briefly involved in another project, this time with Boulton and Wedgwood, at the beginning of 1771. On New Year's Day, Boulton, Wedgwood and Darwin were due to meet Thomas Anson, the local MP and grandee, at Shugborough Hall. (He was the elder brother of Admiral Lord Anson, who had died in 1762.) The meeting was to discuss 'an immense large tripod for Mr Anson', with iron legs weighing 'about 5 cwt', made by Boulton, supporting a pottery bowl to be made by Wedgwood.[54] Anson had to go to London, so the meeting was postponed until 21 January. Darwin was quite keen, and told Boulton, 'I shall be glad to see you Birmingham Philosophers-and-Navigators',[55] a wording that hints at a revived interest in canals. The tripod project did not go ahead because Anson fell ill.

The renaissance of science and technology in Darwin's life was given a further fillip in May 1771 when Benjamin Franklin came to stay, probably for two nights, during a tour of the industrial north and midlands. They talked about mechanical methods for producing sound, theories of phonetics and possible designs for a speaking machine. Canals and iron manufacturing may also have been discussed, but Darwin did not tell Franklin (or anyone else) about his belief in biological evolution.

While at Lichfield, Franklin met Day, no doubt a novel experience even for him, and apparently a pleasant one. Writing from London a year later, Franklin said 'I shall be glad to see Mr Day here, for whom I have much esteem'.

There is more news about the Wychnor Ironworks, where nails were now being manufactured, in a letter from Darwin to Wedgwood during October 1771:

> Our Mills at Whichnor begin to prosper much since we began the Nail-Trade, and now our down-Freights will be nearly as great as our up-Freights. That we shall (we believe) be enabled to increase our Works soon.[56]

This rather implies that the enterprise had not hitherto been a great success, and explains why Darwin said so little about it. Now that things were looking up, he was quite proud of being an entrepreneur and manufacturer, even if output was puny beside that of Boulton or Wedgwood.

Darwin's passionate faith in the power of technology to improve the quality of life is well shown by a new enthusiasm of his, for narrow canals. This idea is developed in five long letters to Wedgwood during October–November 1771. In the first he sets out a plan for constructing a narrow canal from the Grand Trunk Canal to the centre of Lichfield. A full-width canal would cost about £7000 and only bring an annual profit of about £100.

> My plan is therefore to make a narrow Canal about 7 ft wide from Fradley Heath to Lichfield, which is three miles and ½, to carry Boats of only 4 or 5 Tons burthern, to be drawn by one Man, to draw but one foot Water, to be about 4 ft wide and about 30 ft long.[57]

He believes that such a canal would cost less than £300 per mile with no fencing, and no bridges but footbridges. He hopes 'to gain the Consent of the Landholders' and writes to Wedgwood 'to know if I could have the Permission to join such a Canal to the Trunk at Fradley Heath'. The narrow canal would serve Lichfield 'with Coal and Lime and with Small-Beer from Burton', and thus add to the traffic and profits of the Trunk Canal company. Also, 'from this Example many other small Canals' might follow, 'from Collieries, etc'. He asks Wedgwood to keep the plan secret and to discuss it only with 'Mr Gilbert and Mr Brindley, and whom else you think proper'. If they do not approve, 'I shall drop the Plan'. He ends by asking Wedgwood to 'give me your plain and undisguised opinion … in this Affair, in which I have already much interrested my Passions, and am, dear Wedgewood, your affect. Friend/E. Darwin'.

His passions are so strongly engaged that he very soon dashes off another letter, plunging without preamble into a rationale of narrow canals:

> The more I think about narrow Canals the more I am persuaded it is the Interest of the Trunk Company to encourage them. Indeed I think this the only means of rendering Water-Carriage so universal as to make the great Trunk pay Interest.
>
> Those great Trunks are like the large Veins in animal Bodies and must be indebted to numerous Ramifications of smaller Vessels, to be supply'd with vital Fluid for the purposes of Circulation.[58]

The next letter, on 21 October, is more specific about details, and he now suggests that the boats might carry up to 7½ tons. He still insists on secrecy because Lichfield people all favour a navigation, 'but if one Party proposes it, the other will oppose'.

Wedgwood replied a few days later, and Darwin wrote again on 27 October, saying that the scheme might be 'a profitable one to me' if 'I could supply Lichfield with Coal and Lime'.[59] Again it is interesting that Darwin felt he ought to be an entrepreneur: it was the trendy thing to do. In this letter Darwin defends his belief that one man could draw a boat, and it 'need have no Helm' if the man hauled it with two cords. The idea of a very strong man hauling and steering a seven-ton boat seems a weakness in Darwin's plan. An average man might be tempted to bring along a horse to do the donkey work.

The last letter, on 4 November, opens with a well-deserved tribute to Wedgwood: 'I shall always esteem myself most strongly bound to you for the Trouble you take and the Affection you shew me in this Affair'.[60]

Evidently Wedgwood had told Darwin that the canal kingpins – Brindley, or Gilbert, or both – favoured a full-width canal to Lichfield. Darwin gives the reasons against this: not enough water available; not enough goods to carry; and too much expense.

No more is heard of the project, and no canal to Lichfield was ever constructed. Presumably the wide-canal 'establishment' did not want any competition, and they succeeded in marginalizing the narrow-canal upstart from Lichfield.

In retrospect Darwin's idea seems reasonable. Just as motorways are fed by narrower roads, so trunk canals might be fed by narrower canals. But it was not to be: turnpike roads, despite their defects, met the need. This was just as well for Darwin. A narrow-canal company would have involved him in much work, probably for little reward, either intellectually or financially.

[12]

Darwin's inventive talents were much better suited to the creation of a speaking machine. For this he needed both a theory of phonetics and a mechanism for producing the required sound. The theory in its mature form was published thirty years later in the fourteen-page 'Analysis of Articulate Sounds', printed as Note XV in *The Temple of Nature*.

Darwin divides the sounds of speech into four classes: (1) clear continued sounds, vowels; (2) hissing sounds, sibilants; (3) semi-vocals, a mixture of (1) and (2); and (4) interrupted sounds, or consonants. He analyses the vibrations of the air which give rise to each. The vowels, for example,

are produced by the streams of air passing from the lungs in respiration through the larynx; which is furnished with many small muscles, which by their action give a proper tension to the extremity of this tube; and the sounds, I suppose, are produced by the opening and closing of its aperture; something like the trumpet stop of an organ, as may be observed by blowing through the wind-pipe of a dead goose ...

and similarly for sibilants, semi-vocals and consonants, with much detail. He then describes the exact formation of each sound:

P. If the lips be pressed close together and some air be condensed in the mouth behind them, on opening the lips the mute consonant P begins a syllable....

And similarly for every other sound. He found most difficulty, he says, with the vowels, especially in deciding where exactly in the mouth they were modulated.

Guided by an earlier version of this theory, he began to construct his speaking machine, which he describes as follows:

I contrived a wooden mouth with lips of soft leather, and with a valve over the back part of it for nostrils, both which could be quickly opened or closed by the pressure of the fingers; the vocality was given by a silk ribbon about an inch long and a quarter of an inch wide stretched between two bits of smooth wood a little hollowed; so that when a gentle current of air from bellows was blown on the edge of the ribbon, it gave an agreeable tone, as it vibrated between the wooden sides, much like a human voice. This head pronounced the *p*, *b*, *m*, and the vowel *a*, with so great nicety as to deceive all who heard it unseen, when it pronounced the words *mama*, *papa*, *map*, and *pam*; and had a most plaintive tone, when the lips were gradually closed.[61]

The machine was never completed because 'my other occupations prevented me', but might 'have required but thirteen movements'. He believed it could have been linked with a pianoforte to perform a song with accompaniment. He also believed, over-optimistically perhaps, that 'if built in a gigantic form', the machine 'might speak so loud as to command an army or instruct a crowd'.

Even the incomplete version of the speaking machine created a sensation whenever it spoke. There had been nothing like it before, though Vaucanson in 1736 had built a machine to play musical tunes.[62] Darwin's Lunar friends were greatly impressed: after this *tour de force* his reputation as an inventor was secure. Unfortunately neither the speaking machine nor any drawing of it has survived.

The only remaining relic is a document dated 3 September 1771, witnessed by Keir and Small, in which Boulton promises to pay Darwin £1000 for 'an Instrument called an Organ that is capable of pronouncing the Lord's Prayer, the Creed and Ten Commandments in the Vulgar Tongue'.[63] In return Boulton would receive the rights to the machine. This contract was largely a joke, not only because Boulton's finances were precarious but also because Darwin the deist would not have wished to create a robot priest whose novelty value would benefit the Established Church.

Though Darwin never completed the machine in its speak-all form, he was still worrying over the theory in 1772. When he wrote to Franklin on 18 July, he included some detailed questions about vowels:

I think there are but four Vowels, their successive Compounds, and their synchronous Compounds. For as they are made by apertures of different parts of the mouth, they may have synchronous, as well as successive Combinations. *Aw* is made like H or Ch spanish by opening that part of the Fauces a little further ...[64]

and so on for other sounds, with much detail.

Franklin replied with a long letter on 1 August saying that the vowels are 'as you observe Compositions, as *aui* or *i*, *ieu* for *u*; the latter is a barbarous and abominable one: We have however many Words in which each of these Vowels has its natural simple Sound, as *inimitable*, *peruse*, etc'.[65] Franklin's reply is not particularly helpful, and it may be that doubts about the theory deterred Darwin from completing the machine.

After these technical minutiae it is a relief to hear that Darwin had a much simpler speaking machine in his house – a speaking-tube from his study to the kitchen, useful when he grew hungry. One day a local yokel, who had arrived with a message for Darwin, was left alone in the kitchen. He was terrified when a sepulchral and authoritative voice from nowhere demanded 'I want some coals'. Such a request could only come from the Devil, he thought, wishing to stoke up hell's fires. The man fled and would not come near the house again.

[13]

Erasmus's domestic life seemed to have settled down by 1771. Aunt Sukey pleased her three nephews and there were no complaints about Mary Parker.

The two clergymen keen on metaphysics, Robert Clive and Richard Gifford, resumed their visits. Writing to Gifford on 10 January 1771, Clive mentioned 'the cheerfulness and benevolence of disposition with which you and I and all who know the good Doctor are so much charmed'.[66] So Erasmus had recovered his spirits by then.

In another respect 1771 was the end of an era, for Polly's father Charles Howard died in May, aged sixty-four. To judge from his will,[67] he and Darwin were not on the best of terms. Howard left to his son Charles, in trust for Darwin's sons at twenty-one, £1000 'and money owing me from Dr Darwin to be added to same'. This was something of an insult, and the damage was not repaired when Howard left ten guineas to Erasmus and ten pounds to his servant Mary Thompson. As there is no other sign of coolness, it seems likely that Howard was irritated because he knew that the money Erasmus had borrowed was financing the Ironworks, new carriage designs or other madcap schemes unpalatable to a cool and careful lawyer. Mr Howard seems to have been the only relative to sit in moral judgment on Erasmus. After his death the high moral ground was left unoccupied, and Erasmus must have felt a sense of liberation.

[14]

I have a puzzling tailpiece for this chapter – an event of 1771 that may conceivably be linked with Erasmus, or may not.

The story begins in 1864, in one of Charles Darwin's letters. He says he suspects that Mary Boott, the widow of Francis Boott, is an illegitimate granddaughter of Erasmus.[68] If so, Mary's mother, the botanist Mrs Lucy Hardcastle of Derby, would have been Erasmus's daughter. When Lucy was married to John Hardcastle, in 1792 at All Saints, Derby, her name was given as Lucy Swift. She had been christened on 29 July 1771 at Shirland, twelve miles north of Derby, her parents being stated to be William and Lucy Swift. The marriage of William Swift to Lucy Turner is recorded in 1755 at Shirland.[69]

At first sight it seems unlikely that Erasmus was Lucy Hardcastle's father, but four unrelated pieces of circumstantial evidence hint at the opposite. The date of Lucy's birth is suspicious: in September 1770, three months after Polly's death, Erasmus could well have been a sexually active roaming male, frustrated at celibacy. Thirty years later, Lucy Hardcastle was running a school in Derby; Erasmus's two acknowledged natural daughters were also running a school, at Ashbourne. Later still, after Erasmus's death, Lucy became well known as a botanist. In 1830 she published an admirable book entitled *An Introduction to the Elements of the Linnaean System of Botany*,[70] as if inspired by Erasmus's books on Linnaean botany. The Linnaean link is more than coincidence, because Mary Boott told Joseph Hooker in 1864 that Erasmus supervised her mother's education.[71]

However, such suspicions do not add up to proof. Perhaps Lucy was not christened until she was a year old. Perhaps Mary Boott's hearsay about her mother's education was exaggerated. Also I have not seen the names of Swift or Hardcastle in any of Erasmus's books or manuscripts.

So I leave the question tantalizingly open, and shall not be mentioning Lucy again.

CHAPTER SIX

Interregnum
1772–1774

For Erasmus, his smooth and well-organized home life still left much to be desired. His 'affection for Venus' grew with the years, and a celibate bachelor's life was not for him. Most sexual relationships depend on chance proximity, and so it was here. Before long there was a change in the household. Susannah was still mistress of the house but Mary Parker was the mistress of its master. Little is known of Mary Parker, but we can assume that she was a nifty number rather than a po-faced puritan. It was a male-dominated era; Erasmus was forty, Mary was eighteen; Erasmus was the employer, Mary the employee. Was it the old story of the servant seduced by the master? Many people, and especially feminists, would say 'not necessarily'. It may be that Erasmus offered verbal compliments on her beauty and that Mary chose to encourage him. By all accounts he was attractive to women, and an encounter with him may have seemed more appealing than just being nursemaid to Robert. He was prosperous and could give a good home to any children who might appear on the scene. He might even marry her.

All this is conjecture. The facts are that Mary Parker bore Erasmus two daughters: Susan born on 16 May 1772, and Mary born on 20 May 1774; they were known as the Miss Parkers and were brought up in his home for nearly twenty years[1]. Their dates of birth show that the liaison lasted for at least two years, and probably three or four; evidently Erasmus found Mary pleasing as a person, not just as a sex-object. She was well brought up, and he was ready to defer to women in women's matters. So she may have influenced him considerably on subjects such as child care. Many friends of the family remarked that Erasmus was particularly kind to his daughters Susan and Mary, indeed kinder than he was to his sons. This may be because he thought boys needed more discipline than girls. Or it may be that he was guided by his current partner, and that Mary Parker was more permissive than Polly in her attitude to children, as well as sexually.

What did Susannah think of her brother's liaison? She did *not* walk out in high dudgeon; she remained as aunt and housekeeper, and she welcomed visitors. Otherwise, facts are scarce and guesswork rules. It seems unlikely

that Susannah entirely approved of such goings-on. If they had to be, however, Mary was much better than a woman of the town. Indeed Mary had
probably won her good opinion for helping in the house during the year or
so before the sexual relationship developed. Perhaps Susannah, now forty-
two and childless, enjoyed two babies growing up in the house. Perhaps
Erasmus mollified his sister by naming the baby Susan after her.

Equally doubtful is Anna Seward's reaction. Anna was twenty-nine in
1772 and, although beyond the usual age for attracting suitors, she was a
talented and beautiful woman. Walter Scott, who knew her in her fifties, said
'Miss Seward when young must have been exquisitely beautiful'. Robert
Southey agreed: 'More beautiful eyes I never saw in any human countenance'.[2] She was tall and elegant in her mid-twenties. But after the accident
in 1768 when she broke the patella of her knee she developed a serious
limp. And later she became quite fat. It has often been suggested that Anna
hoped and expected Erasmus to ask her to be the second Mrs Darwin.
Those pleasant evenings in the Close with Edgeworth, Day and Darwin
during the summer of 1771 would have kept such a hope alive. Perhaps
Anna was not physical enough for him: like many women at the time, she
tried to cultivate sensibility and repress physicality. Perhaps she was too
verbose. And, as the most telling 'perhaps' of all, he would probably have
regarded her as already committed to another man.

The other man was John Saville, a vicar-choral of the Cathedral from
1755, widely admired for his fine voice.[3] His friendship with Anna began
before 1770 and lasted until his death in 1803. Although never carnal, it
caused some scandal in the Close. Saville had married early, and Anna
called his wife 'a vulgar abusive Shrew'. Saville began giving Anna music
lessons in the 1760s, and in 1770 Mrs Saville complained about their
association. Anna was told of 'her railing at me violently, and calling me by
the most contemptuous names, cursing and swearing at her husband'. Un-
deterred by 'this torrent of billinsgate abuse', Anna kept up her friendship
with Saville, which was 'a very great source of happiness to me'.

These quotations come from a letter dated Monday 16 March 1772, in
which Anna scolds Erasmus for not being supportive of John Saville at a
social gathering on the previous Saturday evening. She accuses Erasmus of

> saying that Mr Baskerville had sold his wife, and that you fancied Saville would
> be glad to do the same. Now, tho' you did justice in allowing Saville to be a
> worthy man, yet you proceeded to declare you thought he deserv'd to be *horse-
> whipt* as much as his wife, from what you said, deserv'd.[4]

Whether or not these contradictory remarks were what Darwin intended,
their effect was to destroy 'the domestic peace of our family', Anna says.
So her rebuke of Erasmus seems just, though even Anna admits her letter

is excessively long: 'subjects deeply interesting to ourselves run us into prolixity'. After more than 3000 words, she concludes: 'Because I have long lov'd and esteemed *you*, I take this method of remonstrating to you upon prejudices which ... I ... must *lament* in Doctor Darwin'. This is Anna with a human face at last, and her use of 'loved' is tantalizing. Darwin must have thought this extraordinary letter worth keeping; and it has survived. His reply is not known.

At the time she wrote the letter, Anna was probably unaware of Mary Parker's pregnancy. When she did hear of it, she would no doubt have shared her parents' horror at such hanky-panky in the outer reaches of the Close. She may have been mortified that Erasmus preferred Mary Parker. However, she may also have been encouraged to continue her pursuit of Saville. If Erasmus could go so far beyond convention and get away with it, surely her innocent friendship would be tolerated in the Close?

[2]

Another lucky survival from 1772 is a portion of Darwin's account book for the years 1772–3 – fifteen out of thirty-five pages. The most interesting page is a list of his capital assets in 1772, as follows:[5]

A Farm at Lincoln, let for £53 a year ...	[£]1600
Capital in Wichnor Mills	2000
Farm at Bushberry	3100
House at Lichfield	1000
Reversion of an Estate	1000
	8700

The total is equivalent to about £800,000 today. Darwin adds a note that 'all the above estimates are beneath their value', and he also mentions that 'Mr Howard left 1000£ with Interest to be equally divided amongst my three Children when they come of age'.

All the items in this list need some explanation. The farm at Lincoln was made over to Erasmus on his marriage in 1757, under the terms of his father's will.[6] The 'Capital in Wichnor Mills' would be the money he put in: its real value would be determined by market forces some ten years later. Bushbury was a village just north of Wolverhampton. Darwin bought the farm in 1772 for £3050 from 'Mr Mansfield'[7] (there was a local farming family of that name).[8] The account book also records a loan of £1050 at 4½% from Mr Mansfield, as well as a loan of £1000 at 4% from 'Mr Garrick', no doubt David Garrick's elder brother Peter, who was a near neighbour of Darwin. The estimate of £1000 for the house at Lichfield seems rather low, but it would have been on a lease: the Dean and Chapter of Lichfield Cathedral, then as now, would have been the ultimate owners. The 'Reversion of an Estate' may refer to the £1000 in Mr Howard's will. It looks as though Darwin persuaded Charles Howard junior to hand over the money and was including it among his own assets. Meanwhile he used it to help buy the farm at Bushbury, which would bring in rent income.

Opposite the list of assets is a list of money borrowed, which amounts to £3260. The two recent loans of £1050 and £1000 are the largest. The others, all long-standing, include £450 from his mother, £200 from Miss Newton and £410 from Mr Howard. It was this last loan that upset Mr Howard, for it dates from 26 December 1763, just when the Wychnor Iron-works began to eat up capital.

The pages of the account book devoted to current payments and receipts are less illuminating. Mr Barker receives various payments for the running of the Wychnor Mills, including the corn-mill: the amounts are quite large, with £412 being recorded for the last quarter of 1772. The rent received for Bushbury Farm (or part of it?) was £32 a year, and with the £53 from the farm at Lincoln gave Erasmus an annual rent-income of £85, which was not enough to cover the interest on the loans.

[3]

Darwin's medical practice was his main source of income, and in 1772 some of his hard labour as a doctor is well documented.

Wedgwood's wife Sally was seriously ill several times during the year, and Darwin often had to make the sixty-mile out-and-back journey to Etruria. Wedgwood's letters to Bentley give many glimpses of Darwin at work:

> When do I bring Mrs Wedgwood? – God knows. We had Dr Derwin with her yesterday. He says he is afraid her disorder will be stubborn ... she is as complete a Cripple as you can easily imagine (30 March). Mrs W is not yet able to dress herself (12 May).[9]

But she made a rapid recovery during May, and Josiah went to Bath with her before the end of the month. They offered to take the thirteen-year-old Charles with them to Bath and London, but Darwin was doubtful about 'the Effect a Scene of Pleasurable Dissipation might produce on a Mind so young, and at present so well disposed'.[10] Whatever his doubts about the established Church, Darwin was still locked into the Protestant work ethic: Charles was hard-working, and his father wanted him to remain so.

The visit to Bath may have improved Sally's health, but it also produced another pregnancy, which led to more trouble:

Mrs Wedgwood has had an extreme bad night, and miscarried this morning. Her situation is attended with much danger (7 September). My Dear Sally ... does not seem to have a drop of blood in her body ... Doctor Derwin has left me to act as Physician in his absense (10 September).[11]

On 30 September Darwin wrote three pages of advice, suggesting a visit to Buxton or Matlock to drink the waters, and prescribing a course of steel, in the form of ten grains of fresh iron filings mixed with quince marmalade taken twice a day (with four drops of laudanum added to each dose if necessary). By giving iron for anaemia Darwin shows that he is sometimes on the right track with his potions.

Josiah himself was worn down by the worry. On 12 October he told Bentley: 'Shewing Dr Darwin by one of my Wastcoats how much I was sunk in 9 or 10 months, he said it was wrong, and I must be very carefull of my health.'[12] On 15 October Darwin wrote, 'I would advise you to live as high as your Constitution will admit of, in respect to both eating and drinking. – This Advice could be given to very few People!'[13] There are more instructions for Sally too in the letter. If her fever continues, she must omit the Steel and also the Bark (cinchona bark) for a few days.

Soon Sally took another turn for the worse: 'My poor Girl is in a very dangerous situation ... I have sent for Dr Derwin' (2 November). 'Dr Darwin has been here and invited her to come and stay with him a few weeks, and we are to go on Sunday' (5 November). 'I brought her to [Lichfield] yesterday and we were lucky enough to find the good Doctor at home.... I shall ... leave Mrs W with her Doctor for a week or ten days' (9 November). But Darwin had other calls to honour, and Wedgwood was not always lucky: 'He is gone to Wolverhampton ... so I must go back solo as I came, which mortifies me not a little' (1 December).[14]

At Christmas Sally was seized with 'a sudden sickness and giddiness ... we thought every moment would be her last'. So Darwin spent much of Christmas Day travelling to Etruria: 'I sent for her favorite Esculapius, who came here last night and he is just now left us. He says if we can preserve her thro' the cold weather to april, she will do very well, and make a perfect recovery in the summer' (26 December).[15] Fortunately Darwin's favourable diagnosis proved right: Sally lived for another forty-two years, longer than either her husband or her doctor.

This tedious detail brings out, as nothing else can, the grind of day-to-day doctoring which dominated Darwin's life. We have heard about just one patient, Sally Wedgwood, in one year. Multiply that by about 4000 – for a hundred patients rather than one, over forty years rather than one – and add in all the mud and discomfort en route. That was the reality of Darwin's life. Often, too, he never got home at night. Robert Clive reported on 25 October 1772 that 'he has lain at home but one night these five weeks, so great is his fame and usefulness'.[16] Presumably Susannah would send a messenger to intercept her brother and divert him to a new patient.

Darwin was able to round off the saga of Sally's illness with a letter on 1 January 1773: 'I am very happy to hear Mrs Wedgewood continues to recover ...'[17] Then he prescribes 'a Decoction of the Bark', thanks Wedgwood for 'a Couple of Woodcocks yesterday' and in the name of his sister invites Sally to visit them whenever she wishes.

Not all the illnesses of 1772 were as amenable as Sally's: James Brindley, worn down by the labour of canal surveying and construction in all weathers, became seriously ill at Froghall, where he had been thoroughly drenched by rain while surveying the Caldon canal. Darwin was called to see him and diagnosed diabetes in an advanced stage, with occasional discharge of blood: he had suffered great thirst for several years. There was no cure, and Wedgwood's letters chronicle another sad story:

> Poor Mr Brindley has nearly finish'd his course in this world ... His disorder ... is a Diabetes ... though I believe no one of his Doctors found it out till Dr Derwin discover'd it in the present illness, which I fear will deprive us of a valuable friend, and the world of one of those great Genius's who seldom live to see justice done to their singular abilities, but must trust to future ages for that tribute of praise and fair fame they so greatly merit from their fellow Mortals.[18]

Brindley died on 27 September 1772, aged fifty-six, and was buried at Newchapel, on the high ground adjoining Harecastle Hill.

Wedgwood wrote to tell Darwin, who replied on 30 September:

> Your letter ... gave me most sincere Grief about Mr Brindley, whom I have always esteem'd to be a great Genius, and whose Loss is truly a public one. I don't believe He has left his equal. I think the various Navigations should erect him a Monument in Westminster Abbey, and hope you will at a proper Time give them this Hint.[19]

Darwin was not kept informed about the progress of Brindley's illness, 'tho' I so much desired it, since if I had understood that He got worse nothing should have hinder'd me from seeing Him again'. Darwin asks Wedgwood to write down any details of Brindley's life that he knows, 'and I will some time digest them into an Eulogium. These Men should not die: this Nature denys, but their Memories are above her Malice.'

Darwin kept his promise to write 'an Eulogium'. In *The Economy of Vegetation* twenty years later he praises several men of science or industry, such as Franklin, Herschel, Priestley, and Wedgwood. But it is Brindley who receives the longest tribute:

> So with strong arm immortal BRINDLEY leads
> His long canals, and parts the velvet meads;
> Winding in lucid lines, the watery mass

Mines the firm rock, or loads the deep morass,
With rising locks a thousand hills alarms,
Flings o'er a thousand streams its silver arms,
Feeds the long vale, the nodding woodland laves;
And Plenty, Arts, and Commerce freight the waves.   [III 329-36]

Darwin suggests a monument which shows Brindley 'balancing the lands', a nice phrase for Brindley's unrivalled skill in choosing routes and levels so as to equalize the volumes of earth extracted from cuttings with those needed for embankments.

It would be wrong to think that for Darwin the year was dominated by illness and death. These were the commonplaces of his medical life, and 1772 was no worse than other years; it just happens to be better documented.

[4]

A new enthusiasm for chemistry gripped Darwin in 1772. The spark came from Keir, whose translation of Macquer had just been published as *A Dictionary of Chemistry*. This was an important encyclopedia, being better than the original because Keir added notes on recent discoveries. The book influenced Watt as well as Darwin, and generally stimulated chemical research in Britain. 'I rejoice exceedingly that you study chemistry so eagerly',[20] Keir wrote to Darwin, giving him a list of fourteen books to read. Keir himself found scope for his chemical talents when he became partner and manager in a glass manufactory at Stourbridge at the end of 1772. Darwin's new interest in chemistry also pleased Wedgwood, who wanted to know more about the minerals he used in his wares, and was beginning his experiments with jasper.

It was the right time for Darwin to embark on a chemical voyage. In 1772 Lavoisier made his first experiments on combustion; and Priestley published the results of his experiments on gases, thereby doubling previous knowledge and reawakening the spirit of experimental science in Britain. Darwin had probably not yet met Priestley, who was now living at Leeds. But they had friends in common, including Franklin, who communicated Priestley's papers to the Royal Society and sent Darwin a copy of Priestley's pamphlet on aerated water.

Franklin visited the Birmingham area again in July 1772, and again stayed with Darwin for a day or two at least. Afterwards, on 18 July, Darwin wrote him a long letter:

I was unfortunate in not being able to go to Birmingham, till a Day after you left it. The apparatus you constructed with the Bladder and Funnel I took into my

Pond the next Day, whilst I was bathing, and fill'd the Bladder well with unmix'd Air, that rose from the muddy Bottom, and tying it up, brought it Home.[21]

But Darwin could not ignite the gas, so the experiment failed. The letter then switches to the queries about phonetics mentioned earlier.

In this letter Darwin tells us he was in the habit of bathing in 'my Pond'. There was no room for a deep pool in his garden, and it was probably on a separate piece of rented land. The account book records payment of two guineas for 'rent of a garden' in April.[22] The garden may well have had a pond as it was probably in the Dimble,[23] which was once the moat round the Cathedral Close.

Though Franklin approved of bathing, and also of 'bathing in air' to let the body breathe, he was not so pleased with one outcome of his visit. In his reply on 1 August he complains that he has suffered from gout, fever and headache for sixteen days, for which he blames 'the Amount of Dabbling in and over your Ponds and Ditches, and those of Mr Bolton, after Sunset, and snuffing up too much of their Effluvia'.[24] Yet he was still appreciative of Darwin's hospitality: 'A 1000 Thanks for your Civilities while I had the Pleasure of being with you'. Even gout and fever could not silence Franklin's unfailing courtesy.

Besides seeking out smelly gases, Darwin was still riding his hobby-horse of carriage design. The spring spokes for the wheels, proposed by Darwin in a letter to Reimarus sixteen years before, were now being tried out on a real carriage, built by Mr Butler, a Lichfield coachmaker. In December 1772 Wedgwood told Bentley he had intended to travel to London in this new carriage with

> Patent spring wheels, every spoke being a spring, by which means the Vis inertia of all sudden obstructions it meets with upon the road are overcome without any Jolt to the rider, or what is more with perfect ease to the poor Horses. Another advantage these carriages have over the common ones is their stillness, and as every spoke in the wheel is in the form of the line of beauty, I am told they have a most elegant appearance.[25]

Butler patented the invention, in British Patent No 1026, authorized on 17 February 1773. According to the patent, 'the springs which serve instead of spokes are made of steel' and are in the form of a gently curved S. The spokes are made 'with square feet' which 'are strongly screwed into the nave'. The feet of the other ends are made lengthways and with two holes to receive the ends of the bolts that come through the iron hoop confining the rim. Such S-shaped spring-spokes are continually being reinvented. British Patent 1292928, filed in 1973, is remarkably similar to Butler's patent of 1773. The main defect is that the rim becomes non-circular, which does not make for a comfortable ride. So this was one of Darwin's innovations that did not survive its 10,000-mile road test.

[5]

It is time for the next act in the tragi-comedy of Edgeworth and Day. During their first months in France Day tortured himself for up to eight hours a day with exercises and dancing lessons, to earn Elizabeth Sneyd's approval. The ever-active Edgeworth was trying to divert the course of the river Rhone so that the city of Lyons could be enlarged. For eighteen months he continued his Herculean task, supervising armies of workmen laden with baskets of rubble.

Day's task proved no easier. When he presented himself at Lichfield early in 1772, Elizabeth decided he was no better as a fop than as a boor. Rejected again, he went away disconsolate. He expressed his feelings in 'an ode supposed to be written on an Inn Window' at Sutton Coldfield – more likely written on paper stuck on the window. The second stanza is the best:

> Away! – Ye disenchanted scenes adieu!
>   Lichfield no more my tranquil bosom fires;
> Farewell, ye walks where perjured lovers woo,
>   Ye fading trees, and dull diminished spires![26]

Edgeworth's wife Anna joined him in Lyons for the summer of 1772, returning to England in the autumn. In March 1773 she gave birth to a daughter, but died ten days later.[27] She left four children: her bold and unruly son Richard, aged eight; a studious daughter Maria, five; Emmeline, three; and the baby Anna, who was later to marry Thomas Beddoes.

Edgeworth came back to England and, probably in May, called at Darwin's house. He was out, but Susannah welcomed Edgeworth. She was about to go to tea with the Sneyds, so he went with her and, to cut a short story shorter, Edgeworth was married to Honora Sneyd in Lichfield Cathedral by Canon Seward in July. Anna Seward was devastated at losing Honora, her substitute sister – or perhaps at losing Edgeworth to Honora? The happy newly-weds went off to Edgeworth's estate in Ireland for the next three years. Anna did not forgive Edgeworth.

Day was left unhappy, deprived of his intended wife and his best friend. He visited Birmingham several times in 1773 and 1774, probably to see Dr Small. His visits were providential for the industrialists. There had been a general collapse of credit in Britain in 1772, and Boulton was in serious financial trouble. Day made a generous loan of £2200, later increased to £3000,[28] and probably saved Boulton from the bankruptcy that engulfed many entrepreneurs. As a result Boulton was able to take over Watt's engine from Roebuck. The least technological member of the Lunar group was thus instrumental in ensuring the success of the engine that created so much of the impetus of the Industrial Revolution. Day also lent money to

Small and Keir; but he kept away from Lichfield to avoid meeting Elizabeth Sneyd, and Darwin rarely saw him from now onwards.

Day helped the Lunar group, without thought of advantage to himself; and the Lunar group, in the person of Dr Small, helped Day. To everyone's amazement, Small succeeded in sorting out Day's personal affairs: Miss Esther Milnes from Wakefield would, he thought, tolerate Day's eccentricities and make an excellent wife for him. At first Day objected that Esther was too wealthy, to which Small replied, 'My friend, what prevents you from despising the fortune and taking the lady?' A few years later Esther married Day and became quite devoted to him.

Darwin's enthusiasm was often diverted into new paths by the interests of his Lunar friends, and Day inspired one of those changes. When Day read the story of a Negro slave who escaped, married a white servant and then shot himself, all his Rousseauistic ideas of the Noble Savage were aroused. With his friend John Bicknell, he wrote a poem, *The Dying Negro*, which was published in 1773. It proved popular, going through four editions and identifying Day with the nascent anti-slavery campaign. Its effect on Darwin was probably subconscious: he and Day were often linked as the most literary of the Lunar circle; so the idea of writing a popular poem himself was injected into Darwin's mind. And when *The Loves of the Plants* was published sixteen years later, attacks on slavery were its strongest 'political' feature.

Day was the most political of the Lunar group, and the others expected him to become a leading Parliamentary orator. Darwin had so far kept clear of all politics, knowing that his patients had differing views. Not that there was much to be keen about. The Ministers shuffling in and out of power, such as Grenville, Rockingham, Grafton and North, were uninspiring and inward-looking intriguers.

Now the American Revolution was beginning, with the Boston Tea Party in December 1773 and the first Congress of the colonies in September 1774. Benjamin Franklin, the Lunar group's father-figure, was still in England, acting virtually as American ambassador: King George III was to call him the evil genius behind the Revolution, and Lord North branded him as 'the great fomenter of the opposition in America'. Darwin had to take a stance: it was strongly on the side of Franklin and the American colonists. From this time onwards he can safely be labelled a radical in politics, though he did not publicize the fact to his patients. Most of the Lunar circle supported the Americans, Darwin and Day being the most fervent; but Boulton, as a conservative and captain of industry, deplored the trade embargo imposed by the colonists. Franklin's friendship with Boulton seems to have ended, but his correspondence with Darwin and Whitehurst continued.

Darwin's next letter to Franklin is however entirely scientific, being written in January 1774, probably just before the events at Boston were known in England. He sends Franklin

a medico-philosophical Paper which I should take it as a Favour if you will communicate to the royal Society, if you think it worthy a place in their Volum; otherwise must desire you to return it to the Writer.[29]

Its title was 'Experiments on Animal Fluids in the exhausted Receiver'. The experiments consisted mainly in taking blood, or fluids from the gall bladder and urinary bladder, from sheep and swine at slaughter, and placing the fluids in a vacuum pump, or 'exhausted receiver'. The aim was to discover whether 'elastic vapours' are dissolved in blood. But Darwin did not do the experiments himself: he is reporting on measurements by 'Mr Young ... Mr Warltire ... and Mr Webster'. Unfortunately their results conflicted; so Darwin was left at a loss, and covered up his embarrassment by adding irrelevant comments about deafness.

It is his worst scientific paper. He tried to get others to do the work, though he must have regretted this when the results conflicted; and after their efforts he felt bound to 'write it up'. Unlike his earlier papers, the manuscript is not in his writing. No wonder he was diffident in offering the paper. Perhaps he hoped Franklin would send it back. If so, he was out of luck. It was read on 24 March and printed in the *Philosophical Transactions* later in the year.[30]

[6]

Domestically, the years 1773–4 produced no new perturbations, apart from the birth of Mary Parker's second daughter Mary in 1774. Erasmus's two elder sons were now old enough to be developing their own personalities: at the end of 1773 Charles was fifteen and Erasmus junior was fourteen, both presumably at school but it is not known where. The youngest son Robert was seven years old, in the care of Mary Parker or Aunt Susannah, or both of them.

Even at fifteen, Charles was all that his father could have wished: intelligent, knowledgeable in science and keen to learn it, serious, industrious, polite, unselfish – the very opposite of most modern teenagers. He seems to have struck up friendships with several of his father's Lunar friends, though they may have been over-indulgent to please Erasmus.

An interesting relic from 1773 is Charles's autograph book, presented to him by his father with the following injunction:

The names of our ingenious friends collected in a book, with a sentiment, the picture of their minds, resembles a room hung round with the paintings of our eminent ancestors. Take care, young man, that you behave well, so as not to disgrace the company you are with![31]

This is so unlike Erasmus's normal relaxed and jokey style that I would doubt whether he had written it if it were not in his writing. It seems he felt he must be didactic and deadly serious in his dealings with his eldest son. There is no sign that Erasmus ever stood in awe of the capabilities of anyone he met, except possibly Charles. The reason is, I think, that Erasmus compared himself at each age of his life with Charles at that age, and decided that Charles was the easy winner in every aspect of knowledge and behaviour. Erasmus took great interest – probably too much – in the boy's upbringing, and Charles may have felt oppressed by the high standards expected of him.

The signatures in the autograph book are a fair cross-section of Darwin's friends, and the book is of rarity interest as being the only place where their names all appear together. The names are mostly as would be expected: Thomas Day, Anna Seward, Susannah Darwin, William Small, Robert Waring Darwin, Matthew Boulton, Thomas Seward. There are two new names, whom we shall meet later: 'William Jackson of Lichfield Close, 13 March 1774' and 'J. Hutton Edinburgh, Lichfield 3 June 1774'.

Darwin's second son, Erasmus junior, was overshadowed by his brilliant elder brother. Being one year younger, he was always second-best to Charles. Innately, too, he was more diffident and certainly less energetic than his brother, though he was ingenious and intelligent. It is easy to criticize his father for not bringing out his virtues; but the boy would probably have reacted against any jollying along, and the 'softly-softly' approach was not natural to Erasmus senior as a father, though he would sometimes use it as a doctor.

Erasmus junior showed a literary bias from an early age, and his father responded by forming what is sometimes called the Lichfield literary circle. Another motive for this move may have been to challenge Canon Seward's coterie of old fogeys by encouraging younger talent. So Darwin's informal group might be called the 'young literary circle of Lichfield'. It was a foretaste of Darwin's growing tendency to set up societies, though this one was never more than a handful of people meeting from time to time at his house to read, discuss and sometimes write poetry, and to a lesser extent prose and drama.

Anna Seward was of course one of the circle. In 1773 she was thirty, and still stifled as a writer by the disapproval of her parents. Darwin was giving her a partial escape route: group readings and discussions of poetry were deemed fairly harmless. The group also included Edgeworth, who was twenty-nine, or Day, who was twenty-five, when they were in Lichfield. Erasmus junior was by far the youngest member.

The most important recruit to Darwin's literary circle, who later became a close friend, was Brooke Boothby. As a young man of twenty-two, Boothby had become friendly with Rousseau at Wootton Hall, and from then on was a staunch disciple of Rousseau. He lived at Lichfield for some time in the 1770s.

Boothby was the very model of a literary young man, learned, humane and enlightened, but completely lacking the energy of Darwin, Boulton and Wedgwood, who were all motivated by having to earn their living. Boothby was a man of ease rather than a man of industry, inclined towards gentle melancholy, a mood captured in Joseph Wright's reclining portrait,[32] which shows him reading one of Rousseau's books.

Boothby admired Darwin most for his kindness to patients, and in a poem he urges us to be taught by Darwin,

> whose ever-open door
> Draws, like Bethesda's pool, the suffering poor;
> Where some fit cure the wretched all obtain,
> Relieved at once from poverty and pain.[33]

The literary circle was not as solemn as it sounds. Darwin could not stand dreary sermonizing. He listened to the first sermon of the new Bishop (Richard Hurd) in 1774 and, when asked what he thought of it, stuttered: 'Why – it c-contained some very good words indeed'.[34] This is a fair example of his social skill: the sarcasm is indirect.

In the literary circle he would pep up the proceedings with some of his jokey verses. One squib that seems to date from about 1773 is:

> O mortal man that liv'st by bread,
> What makes thy nose to look so red?
> 'Tis Burton Ale, so strong and stale,
> That keeps my nose from growing pale.[35]

The literary circle was very much Darwin's baby and met in his house: he seems to have kept it going for about five years.

He received another literary visitor at his house in 1774, Samuel Johnson on his journey to North Wales with Mr and Mrs Thrale. The visit was on 8 July and Mrs Thrale was astonished at a huge rose tree growing up the south side of Darwin's house.

[7]

The major missing link in the Lunar circle was forged during 1774: James Watt settled in Birmingham to work with Matthew Boulton.

At the beginning of the year Watt was still in Scotland, employed as a canal surveyor and engineer. Developing his steam engine in Roebuck's workshop at Kinneil had proved frustrating, chiefly because the moving parts could not be machined accurately enough. Boulton had tried to take over the engine in 1769, but without success. In 1773 Roebuck was caught in the general collapse of credit and became bankrupt. He owed £1200 to Boulton and his partner Fothergill, and, since the trustees of Roebuck's estate attached no value to Watt's rusting steam engine, Boulton was able to acquire it in August. Watt was still reluctant to move south, despite continued pleas from Small and his own dislike of the Scottish weather, which made his canal surveys so arduous. Then, in September 1773, Watt's wife Margaret died in childbirth: he was the fourth of the seven married Lunar members to lose his first wife. 'I am heartsick of this country', he wrote to Small.

At last, to the delight of Boulton, Small and Darwin, Watt arrived in Birmingham on 31 May 1774 with his friend James Hutton (1726–97), the geologist.[36] Hutton met Boulton and Small, and very soon went on to Lichfield to see Darwin – he signed Charles's autograph book on 3 June. Hutton stayed at Darwin's house for some time, using it as a base for geological expeditions to the Peak District of Derbyshire. While at Lichfield he helped Darwin in experiments with an air gun to show how air was cooled by expansion. Hutton left the Midlands in July for an arduous geological journey to central and southern Wales and much of western England. He returned home to Edinburgh in late autumn.[37] Although Hutton never visited the Birmingham area again, Darwin had acquired another enduring friend of Lunar mould. And who better than 'the founder of modern geology' to guide Darwin in explaining geology to a wider public in the 1790s?

Small, Boulton and Darwin all did their best to keep Watt happy in Birmingham, hoping he would stay. They succeeded. So began one of the most illustrious partnerships in the history of technology. The genial optimist Matthew Boulton, owner of the finest metal works in the world and the indulgent employer of nearly a thousand workmen, was the perfect foil for the gloomy self-doubting James Watt, one of the greatest of engineers, who hated dealing with workmen and accounts. After two years of work, and the essential assistance of the ironfounder John Wilkinson, the Boulton-and-Watt engine was to begin its career in the world, and do more than any other single invention to bring about the modern technological era. But it was more than ten years before the engine brought any profit to Boulton.

Darwin had never lost faith in Watt's engine and now, with Boulton's energy to push it on, he was confident of early success. Darwin liked to help his friends with their scientific interests, and on Watt's arrival he took up again his studies of the mechanical and chemical properties of steam and water vapour.

With Watt in place, the centre of gravity of the Lunar group shifted from Lichfield to Birmingham. At the end of 1774 Boulton, Small and Watt were settled in Birmingham, Edgeworth was out of the picture in Ireland and Day was of no fixed address. That left as outliers, in order of distance, Darwin at Lichfield and Keir at Stourbridge, both about twelve miles away, Wedgwood at Etruria and Whitehurst at Derby, both about forty miles away. The name 'Lunar Society of Birmingham', previously quite erroneous, becomes one-third defensible, though it was still not yet really a Society and did not yet meet at the time of the Full Moon.

CHAPTER SEVEN

Fresh starts
1775–1777

Darwin was now entering a short period of outward calm in his personal life, with the trauma of Polly's death softened by five years of living, and with no more offspring via Mary Parker. His liaison with her was on the wane, and possibly finished, by 1775: certainly by then he had decided not to marry her. As far as the world could see, he was cruising smoothly through the years 1775–7. His own perspective, however, was rather different. For him it was cruising in another sense, on the lookout for a new wife. A touch of spice was added to his medical journeys. Whatever medical ethics may prescribe, every female patient and every mother of a child-patient became a possible candidate. And, as we shall see, it was not long before he found a woman who attracted him.

[2]

In contrast, the Lunar circle suffered a disastrous loss, for Dr Small died at the age of forty on 25 February 1775, after weeks of 'assiduous and affectionate' care from Darwin. Poor health had pursued Small for several years: he may have suffered from malaria contracted in Williamsburg.

The only known details about Small's last illness are in a letter written by the fifteen-year-old Erasmus junior. Small wrote several letters to the boy, whom he calls 'Peter', and would give him messages to pass on to his father, such as an invitation to come to see Watt's engine, now 'at last in a condition that satisfies even me'.[1] The letter here quoted is the only one that has survived, and in it Small advises his young protégé about microscopes and books, signing off as 'Your affectionate friend'. The loss of this benevolent uncle was a blow to the young Erasmus, and he describes Small's illness in a letter to a friend on 9 March 1775. About three weeks before his death, when already 'poorly', Small had to travel ten miles to Tamworth when called by 'a Patient for whom he had a great Regard'. He 'vomited most of the Way in the Chaise' and 'when he arrived there he was so feeble that he was obliged to lye down as he prescribed'. On his return he went to bed and 'was delirious above half his Illness, which was a nervous Fever attended with great Feebleness'. Much of this information must have come from Erasmus senior. Erasmus junior goes on to say that Small 'is universally lamented here. I don't think there ever was a Man who had more friends or fewer Enemies.... I am sure the more intimately any one knew him the more they must love him.'[2]

The buoyant Boulton was thoroughly depressed by Small's death and, in a strange reversal of roles, Watt had to cheer Boulton: 'Come, my dear Sir, and immerse yourself in this sea of business as soon as possible, and do not add to the griefs of your friends by giving way to the tide of sorrow.'[3]

Small, the hub of the Lunar wheel, was unobtrusive but essential, and the tributes to him were many and sincere. Boulton wrote: 'His virtues were more and his foibles fewer (for vices he had none) than in any man I ever knew.'[4] Keir said that 'he had, I think, the greatest variety, as well as the greatest accuracy of knowledge, that I have ever met in any man'.[5] Day wrote an elegy full of fine feeling:

O gentle bosom! O unsullied mind!
O friend to truth, to virtue, and mankind!...[6]

For Darwin he was 'my ever to be lamented friend Doctor Small of Birmingham, whose strength of reasoning, quickness of Invention, patience of investigation, and, what is above them all, whose benevolence of Heart, have scarcely left an equal, not a superior, in these sub-lunary realms!'[7] Darwin also wrote an elegy for engraving on a vase in Boulton's garden. But it lacks the human touch and ends bleakly, with 'cold Contemplation' mourning 'for Science, Virtue, and for SMALL'.[8]

Later in the year Small received a different kind of tribute, from Thomas Jefferson, who did not know of his death. In May, a year before he wrote the Declaration of Independence, Jefferson honoured the teacher who had shaped the destinies of his life by sending a present of six dozen bottles of Madeira: 'I hope you will find it as fine as it came to me genuine from the island and has been kept in my own cellar eight years'.[9]

Without Small, the Lunar circle he had shaped was in danger of falling apart. As a tribute to his memory, the other members agreed to make semi-formal arrangements for meeting on a day set in advance. So the death of Small had the effect of converting the circle into a Society, though an informal one without any written records. Schofield in his history of the Lunar Society suggests that their gathering on Sunday 31 December 1775 should be regarded as the first meeting. This seems a logical choice because the first reference to the full moon is in a letter from Boulton to Keir two months later: 'Pray, where were you the last full moon? ... I saw Darwin yesterday at Lichfield. He desires to know if you will come to Soho on

Sunday 3rd March.'[10] So the title 'Lunar Society of Birmingham' is now at last fully appropriate.

The group was shaky in 1775 because two other members seemed about to vanish from the scene. The first was James Watt, who was offered a post in Russia at £1000 a year. On 29 March Darwin tried to restrain him:

> Lord, how frighten'd I was, when I heard a Russian Bear had laid hold of you with his great Paw, and was dragging you to Russia. – Pray don't go, if you can help it: Russia is like the Den of Cacus, you see the Footsteps of many Beasts going thither but of few returning. I hope your Fire-Machines will keep you here.[11]

Fortunately the Fire-Machines proved stronger than the Bear, and Watt stayed in Birmingham.

The second potential defector was John Whitehurst, who accepted the new government post of 'Stamper of the Money Weights' in London. But he kept his house in Derby and was usually addressed there until 1779, when he went to live in London.[12] Even after that he made visits to the Midlands from time to time and kept in touch with the Lunar group.

[3]

The death of Dr Small left an opening for a physician who might take over his practice, preferably a man of Lunar mind. Again Darwin took the initiative. His chosen recruit was Dr William Withering, a young doctor with interests in chemistry and botany as well as medicine. When Withering was a medical student, he spent his summers in Lichfield, and Darwin got to know him. Now he saw the chance to help Withering and wrote to him at once. 'If you should choose that situation', Darwin says, 'your philosophical taste would gain you the Friendship of Mr Boulton, which would operate all that for you which it did for Dr Small', who had been earning 'above £600' a year, 'chiefly in the town, without the Expense and Fatigue of Travelling and Horsekeeping, and without being troubled with visiting the people, for he lived quite a recluse studious Life'. Darwin sees it as 'a very eligible situation'.[13] This letter shows Darwin at his most resilient. Though grieved at the death of Small, he got on quickly with what needed to be done, before a rival doctor moved in.

Within a few weeks Withering had agreed to leave his post as physician to the Infirmary at Stafford, and to take on Small's practice. But he did not fit well into the Lunar group, being rather prickly and reserved.

Withering had nearly completed a book on British botany, and Darwin wrote to him in May suggesting possible titles – 'The scientific Herbal',

'Linnean Herbal' or 'English Botany'. Darwin unwisely added, 'We'll settle all this at Mr Boulton's with the assistance of Mr Keir and Mr Watt.'[14] Alarmed at losing control of his book to the heavy brigade, Withering ignored their advice and chose a title running to twenty-four lines that begins *A Botanical Arrangement of all the Vegetables naturally growing in Great Britain....*Withering bowdlerized some of the sexual terms, so that they would not give offence to ladies: he changed 'stamen' to 'chive' and 'pistil' to 'pointal'. Such mealy-mouthedness irritated Darwin, and he may have been sarcastic enough to germinate the seeds of animosity already sown between Withering and himself.

Most eighteenth-century doctors relied on herbal remedies and were knowledgeable in botany. Darwin was no exception. So far, however, botany had been only a fringe interest for him. From now onwards it was to be a major theme in his life. Withering's book was one source of Darwin's new enthusiasm. Another was the increasing public interest in botany from about 1760 onwards, created by Linnaeus (Carl von Linné, 1707–78), whose encyclopedic works classifying plants, such as the *Genera Plantarum*, went through many editions and brought order out of chaos in the vegetable world.[15]

Botany began to flourish in Britain for an unusual reason.[16] King George III's mother, the Princess Augusta (widow of Prince Frederick), was a passionate gardener and developed her garden at Kew under the expert advice of the fanatical botanist Lord Bute, who spent some of his time being Prime Minister and more of it writing a nine-volume treatise on botanical classification. Another boost for botany came in 1771 when Joseph Banks returned from his round-the-world voyage with Captain James Cook, having discovered 1300 hitherto unknown species. When Princess Augusta died in 1772, Banks became the King's adviser on her garden at Kew, which soon became famous. With this royal lead, many books on botany appeared, many natural history societies were formed and enthusiasts like Gilbert White (1720–93) found themselves in tune with the times, instead of being regarded as eccentrics.

[4]

Strangely enough, gardening also figures in Darwin's quest for a wife. In November 1775 a patient, Joseph Cradock, sent a copy of his sententious book *Village Memoirs*. Darwin replied with an unusually confidential letter:

> What shall I send you in return for these? I who have for twenty years neglected the Muses, and cultivated medicine alone with all my industry! Medical

Dissertations I have several finished for the press, but dare not publish them, well knowing the reception a living writer in medicine is sure to meet with from those who wish to raise their own reputation on the ruin of their antagonists. Faults may be found or invented; or at least ridicule may cast blots on a book were it written with a pen from the wings of the angel Gabriel.[17]

This is why Darwin waited until he was sixty-three before publishing his book on medicine, *Zoonomia*.

Darwin's regret about neglecting poetry leads on to some revealing remarks:

I lately interceded with a Derbyshire lady to desist from lopping a grove of trees, which has occasioned me ... to try again the long-neglected art of verse-making, which I shall inclose to amuse you, promising, at the same time, never to write another verse as long as I live, but to apply my time to finishing a work on some branches of medicine, which I intend for a posthumous publication.

He confesses to poetry-writing almost as if he were a penitent confessing to murder – 'I will never do it again, father'. Why such a fuss about a short poem? The answer is: because of the Derbyshire lady.

By good fortune the poem has survived, and, as it announces the second half of Darwin's adult life, I quote three of the four stanzas:

> *Speech of a Wood-nymph*
> Hear, bright Eliza! ere thy dread commands
> Lop my green arms, my leafy tresses tear,
> Relent, sweet Belle, nor with unpitying hands
> Wound the sad Nymphs, who dwell and tremble here.
>
> Know, in this Grove there sleeps in every tree
> A Nymph, embalmed by some poetic spell,
> Who once had beauty, wit and life like thee.
> Oh, spare the mansions, where thy sisters dwell!...
>
> The love-struck swain, when summer's heat invades,
> Or winter's blasts perplex the billowy sky,
> With folded arms shall walk beneath our shades,
> And think on bright Eliza – think, and sigh![18]

The poem is from a typescript collection of Erasmus's verse edited by his son Francis (1786–1859), who adds a note: 'Addressed to a Lady (Mrs Pole) who had given instructions to cut down some branches of trees in Dr Darwin's garden at Lichfield'.[19] This information could only have come from the 'Lady' herself, his mother.

For most of the poem Erasmus is decently disguised as a wood nymph, who obediently expresses for him his admiration of Eliza. The last stanza is more subtle: the 'love-struck swain' seems to be a third person; it is really Erasmus himself, for the trees are in his garden.

This is the first of more than twenty poems written by Erasmus during the next six years in praise of Elizabeth Pole. Their son Francis gathered these together, with others, into a ninety-four-page collection entitled 'A Poetical Courtship'.

Before Elizabeth floats away as a fully-fledged fantasy figure, it may be as well to drag her back to earth with the story of her real life, as far as it is known. Born in 1747, she was the illegitimate daughter of Charles Colyear, second Earl of Portmore (1700–85), known as 'Beau Colyear' and noted for 'the magnificence of his equipages'. His father, Sir David Colyear, created Earl of Portmore in 1703, had in 1696 married Catharine Sedley, mistress of King James II, who is said to have scourged himself for creating her Countess of Dorchester in 1686. Her wit and unflappable joyous temperament seem to have reappeared in Elizabeth Pole.

But who was Elizabeth's mother? There are two plausible stories. Elizabeth's granddaughter Elizabeth Wheler (née Galton) wrote: 'The Duke of Leeds, Sir Nathaniel Curzon and Lord Portmore were racing men, and used to be much at the house of a trainer [at Newmarket] – Collier by name – one of whose daughters, Elizabeth, was really the child of Lord Portmore'.[20] So Elizabeth's mother was Mrs Collier in this story. To understand the second story it is necessary to know that Lord Portmore was married in 1732 to the Duchess of Leeds, widow of the third Duke, and they had two daughters, Caroline (born 1733) and Juliana (born 1735). In the second story, by Karl Pearson,[21] Elizabeth's mother was born Elizabeth Collier in 1713 and was governess to Caroline and Juliana. With either of these two scenarios, Elizabeth Pole would have been known before her marriage as Elizabeth Collier, which is the name in the marriage register. A third possibility is that the name Collier was fictional, chosen because it sounds the same as the Portmore family name Colyear.

Elizabeth was brought up at Farnham in Surrey by a foster-mother, Mrs Susan Mainwaring, who remained a close friend in later life. Meanwhile Elizabeth's half-sister Lady Caroline Colyear married Sir Nathaniel Curzon (later Lord Scarsdale). They built themselves a new house: it was Kedleston Hall in Derbyshire, and was largely completed by 1765. On a visit there Elizabeth met the owner of the nearby Radburn Hall. He was Colonel Edward Sacheverel Pole, recently retired from arduous military service. He married her in 1769 when he was fifty-one and she was twenty-one (and already pregnant).

Colonel Pole was from an old Derbyshire family[22] of military tradition – a relative of John de la Pole who died at the battle of Stoke Field. The Colonel had a valorous military career in the Seven Years' War. According to Whitehurst, he fought in eleven battles and was left for dead in the field in three of them. At the battle of Minden he was shot through the head, the ball going in at his left eye and coming out at the back of his head. So intrepid a military hero would soon chase off an obese doctor from Lichfield with designs on his wife.

Colonel Pole was a patient of Darwin in November 1771, when Darwin wrote a prescription for him;[23] but he soon changed his doctor. Elizabeth presumably insisted on the best medical care for her children, and they were being treated by Darwin in the autumn of 1775, and possibly earlier. Elizabeth had three children living then (one had died in 1774): Sacheverel, aged six; Elizabeth, aged five; and Millicent, aged one. They may have come to Lichfield so that Darwin could monitor progress with inoculations.

Darwin had good reason to be more than grateful to the person who recommended him to the Poles as a doctor and made possible the new phase of his life. That benefactor was almost certainly Joseph Wright, who spent much time in 1771 decorating the main rooms at Radburn Hall with portraits and group pictures. The portrait of Colonel Pole is impressively severe, but the best portrait is that of Elizabeth with her baby son Sacheverel (Plate 8A): Benedict Nicolson calls it 'astonishing'.[24]

It may seem surprising that Elizabeth Pole was bold enough in 1775 to order the lopping of trees in Erasmus's garden. But she was never predictable, and her anarchic streak was attractive to Erasmus. It was also in her nature to be flirtatious without ever compromising herself. This is the theme of a 'Hunting Song' that may be one of the earliest of the courtship poems, though the dating is conjectural. The first stanza praises Eliza for her graceful riding – watching her, the hunters ignore the fox. The second stanza celebrates her dancing:

> When the gay Belle her light step leads,
>   With such sweet grace she dances,
> Each Female heart with envy bleeds
>   And Beaux are fixed in trances.

The third and fourth stanzas round off the conceit with passion and a touch of wit:

> Grace still attends on Pole's fair wife
>   Or riding, dancing, walking;
> Gods! and her smile is light and life!
>   And Heaven to hear her talking!

> Ye love-struck swains, one thing I'll tell
>   I fear may discontent you:
> There is one fault attends this Belle,
>   You'll hate her for her Virtue.[25]

Did Erasmus show these verses to Elizabeth, or was he just privately sublimating his frustration? He certainly gave her the poem about the wood nymphs, and I believe that he showed her most of his 'courtship poems'. Otherwise it would scarcely have been a courtship at all.

[5]

In 1775, tickled by Cupid's arrows, Darwin had embarked on his long courtship of Elizabeth Pole. In 1776 a whole quiverful of fresh starts opened up several new prospects.

As far as is known, arrangements at home remained the same through the years 1775–7. Erasmus's sister Susannah continued to supervise the household, and Mary Parker remained there, looking after her own children and perhaps also Robert. He was nine in 1775 and apparently thriving.

His elder brother Erasmus, or 'Rassy', as his school friends still called him, was a quiet and retiring boy with scholarly ingenuity beyond his years. Now fifteen, he wrote poetry, constructed genealogical tables, collected coins and dabbled in statistics. At about this time he made a census of Lichfield by counting all the houses and finding out or estimating the number of inhabitants in each. When a real census was first made, 'his estimate was found to be nearly accurate.'[26] This information comes from Erasmus junior's nephew Charles, who adds, 'My father [Robert] had a very high opinion of his abilities'.

This opinion seems to have been well founded: Erasmus was already capable and reliable. He kept up a correspondence with Keir as well as Small, and Keir trusted him to pass on messages to his father, who in turn often relied on his son to write letters to his friends if too busy to do so himself.

The young Erasmus was specializing in law, with the idea of becoming a solicitor. In November 1776 he left Lichfield for London to begin legal studies under the wing of his uncle William Alvey Darwin[27] at Gray's Inn. However, his uncle decided to retire during the summer of 1777, to live in Sleaford, and Erasmus may have stayed in London for only one year, though he says in a letter in February that 'I am to continue in Town for two or three years'.[28] In the same letter he says that he has been on a visit to Edgeworth, who was then living near London, and that Day has offered him accommodation 'after Uncle leaves'. He also reports Bentley as saying that Whitehurst's book, like everything else of his, 'would perhaps be finished at the day of Judgement'. Erasmus did not dare to ask Whitehurst when it would appear (actually 1778). By the age of sixteen, therefore, it seems that Erasmus had independent relationships with Keir, Edgeworth, Day, Bentley and Whitehurst. He must have been remarkably mature.

The oldest of the three brothers, the brilliant Charles, was sixteen at the beginning of 1775. It is not known where, nor for how long, he went to school. His father's idealized account of Charles's life suggests that he did not go to one of the conventional 'classic schools', which, he says, divert attention from careful scientific study of real things to 'the vain verbal allusions which constitute the ornaments of poetry and of oratory'.[29] Instead, he says, Charles 'acquired a competent knowledge of the latin and greek languages, chiefly by reading books of useful knowledge'. These were 'more agreeable' to him than 'the monstrous and immoral tales of heathen mythology'. The tirade thunders on for more than a page and comes strangely from a future poet who exploited Greek mythology. Not wishing to 'waste the first twenty years of life in learning the metaphors of language', Charles spent his time studying science, mathematics and anatomy, and also 'sought the society of ingenious men', to learn from them. So perhaps he did not go to school, and had private tutors?

All this changed on 30 March 1775, when Charles entered Christ Church, Oxford, as an undergraduate. Erasmus obviously did not approve, and says 'he was induced by the advice of his friends to admit himself of Christ Church College in Oxford'. Perhaps this was Charles's teenage revolt – refusing to follow father to Cambridge. However, if Erasmus is to be believed, Charles soon realized his mistake. 'He thought the vigour of the mind languished in the pursuit of classical elegance', and, having 'passed a year rather against his inclination' at Oxford, he 'sigh'd to be removed to the robuster exercises of the medical schools of Edinburgh'.[30]

Charles left Christ Church on 10 February 1776 and transferred to the Edinburgh Medical School; his official start-date was 16 October,[31] but he may have been there during the summer.[32] Erasmus was delighted at this fresh start: 'His genius breathed its natural element, sprung aloft, and soared on strong and glittering wing'. The wording is over the top, but Charles did extremely well in his first eighteen months at Edinburgh and won golden opinions from everyone who knew him.

The 'ingenious men' whom Charles sought as mentors were presumably members of the Lunar group. Like his brother he was on terms of friendship with several of them and he may have attended some Lunar meetings, to judge from a casual reference by Boulton, who told Watt that 'Keir, Darwin, Charles and Withering' would be at the meeting on 28 July 1776.

In 1777, with Charles studying medicine in Edinburgh and Erasmus learning law in London, their father could regard them as well settled in progress towards careers they were happy to adopt.

[6]

Outside the family 1776 was a busy year, with fairly regular Lunar meetings and a variety of other events.

In March James Boswell came with Samuel Johnson to Birmingham, and was shown round Soho by Boulton: 'I shall never forget Mr Boulton's expression to me: "I sell here, Sir, what all the world desires to have – POWER". He had about seven hundred people at work. I contemplated him as an *iron chieftain*, and he seemed to be a father to his tribe.'[33] Johnson and Boswell then made for Lichfield and admired the museum of fossils and minerals created by the apothecary Richard Greene,[34] with help from Darwin and others.

Boulton was all agog about power in March 1776 because the first of Watt's engines had just begun work. It was a notable date in the history of technology and indeed in the history of civilization: from now onwards human muscle was destined to be superseded gradually as a source of power.

Watt's engine had a cylinder of diameter fifty inches and stroke seven feet. Aris's *Birmingham Gazette* records that on 8 March 1776 'a Steam Engine constructed upon Mr Watt's new Principles was set to work at Bloomfield Colliery, near Dudley, in the presence of … a Number of Scientific Gentlemen whose Curiosity was excited to see the first Movements of so singular and so powerful a Machine; and whose Expectations were fully gratified by the Excellence of its performance.' (It emptied the engine pit, which stood fifty-seven-feet deep in water, in less than an hour.) It seems likely that Darwin was among the 'Scientific Gentlemen' there. As the *Gazette* notes, 'the Iron Foundry parts (which are unparalleled for truth) were executed by Mr Wilkinson'; and a second engine was erected for Wilkinson's blast furnace at Broseley, near Coalbrookdale.

This was the most impressive British new start of 1776 – perhaps even outdoing the American Declaration of Independence? – and Boulton was delighted at Soho's growing fame, which attracted visitors from all over the world. The Lunar members were riding high in international esteem: the Empress Catherine the Great of Russia had recently received the 952-piece Frog dinner-and-dessert service from Wedgwood and Bentley.

Darwin grew closer to Wedgwood in 1776 because both were concerned about the education of their sons. Schools in England were for turning out gentlemen with classical attainments, not doctors and men of science, nor future captains of industry, as Wedgwood hoped his sons would be. The Warrington Academy now seemed to be in decline and the idea of starting their own school was in the air.

They had a similar problem with religion. They wanted their children to be imbued with strong moral principles, but they were not keen on the Church of England, Wedgwood probably being more anti-clerical than Darwin.[35]

So they were both interested in David Williams's Chapel, just opened in Margaret Street near Cavendish Square in London. The chapel was based on a proposal of Franklin's for teaching morality without any mention of religious faith: Wedgwood, Bentley and Joseph Banks were among the sponsors. Wedgwood wished to publicize the chapel more widely, and in May 1776 he told Bentley of Darwin's suggestions on how to do so: 'to hire some Parsons to abuse it in the Papers – To call upon the Government for immediate help, and advise the burning of them (Parson and Congregation) altogether. – To lay the disturbances in America, and any other public Disasters which may happen at their Door – and he offers his service if you should be at a loss for an abuser of this new Sect.'[36] Darwin's advice seems to have been accepted. A letter signed 'Clericus' appeared in the *Morning Chronicle* on 30 May, attacking Williams, referring to the deluded rebels in America, etc. A long correspondence followed, between Clericus, 'Erasmus', and 'Palemon'. It is not clear whether Darwin was really involved or whether his name was used fictitiously.

Bentley, who lived in London, was more directly concerned with the chapel, and when he visited Paris in August he called on Rousseau to give him a copy of the prospectus. Rousseau was supportive of the project.[37] He was not so pleased when Bentley gave him a copy of Thomas Day's poem *The Dying Negro*, because Day criticized the Americans for owning slaves, and Rousseau was pro-American.

Another of Rousseau's disciples, Richard Edgeworth, visited Lichfield several times in 1776. He had enjoyed three years of wedded bliss with Honora in Ireland, and now they had decided to spend a few years in England. Darwin welcomed them, but when they called on Anna Seward, she took it very badly: 'I had not the least expectation of such an event. Good God! I exclaimed, and sunk back in my chair more dead than alive ... A violent flood of tears relieved me ... It was an hour before my aunt could prevail upon me to go down.'[38] Anna could not bear to describe the 'heart-rending scene' when she and Honora actually met. It is all long ago now, and we may scoff at such overdone feeling; but this was the penalty for over-cultivating sensibility as a shelter against the roughness of the age.

[7]

Darwin's literary circle seems to have taken on new life in 1776. Its revival was triggered by a pleasant poem about the Needwood Forest, not far from

Lichfield. The author was Francis Mundy, a country gentleman known to Darwin, and he probably read his poem at a meeting of the circle. Mundy leads his readers into the woods quite seductively:

> What green-rob'd Nymph, all loose her hair,
> With buskin'd leg, and bosom bare,
> Steps lightly down the turfy glades,
> And beckons tow'rd yon opening shades?[39]

Darwin accepts Mundy's invitation into the forest but rather surprisingly ignores the Nymph. Instead he focuses on the ancient Swilcar Oak:

> Hail, stately oak, whose wrinkled trunk hath stood
> Age after age, the Sov'reign of this wood;
> You, who have seen a thousand springs unfold
> Their ravell'd buds, and dip their flowers in gold;
> Ten thousand times yon moon relight her horn,
> And that bright eye of evening gild the morn.[40]

There are three further verses in Darwin's poem, called 'Address to the Swilcar Oak'. It was published in 1776 as a tailpiece to Mundy's poem, and signed E.D.

Is the mask of anonymity beginning to slip? Not really, because Darwin was playing tricks. Three other short poems were added at the end of *Needwood Forest*, signed A.S., B.B. and E.D.Jun. The literary circle in full cry? Not so, it would seem. Anna says that Darwin wrote three of the four poems himself: 'To the best he put his son's initials; to the second best his own; and to the worst mine. Not a syllable of any of the three did I see, or hear of, till I saw them in print ... I did not like this manoeuvre, and reproached him with it. He laught it off in a manner peculiar to himself.'[41]

Darwin revised the 'Swilcar Oak' about twenty years later, and the revised version was printed in 1800 in the *European Magazine* and in *Phytologia*. It next appeared in *Sylva Britannica* (1822), and then, with a few changes, in 1873 in the *Quarterly Review*, where it is said to have referred to a tree at Holland House and to have been written by Samuel Rogers.[42] Perhaps some Victorian was punishing Darwin: he had thrown away the authorship of two of his poems, so wouldn't it be poetic justice to deprive him of the third as well?

The presumed author of the fourth Needwood poem, Brooke Boothby, achieved the one high spot of his literary career in 1776 when his friendship with Rousseau unexpectedly burst into flower. Rousseau was looking for someone to whom he could entrust the manuscript of his autobiographical *Dialogues*. While in Paris, Boothby called to see him, and Rousseau decided that Boothby was the person chosen by Providence. Boothby took the manuscript away with him; Rousseau died in 1778; and Boothby published the book at Lichfield in 1780 as *Rousseau: juge de Jean-Jacques* (he gave the manuscript to the British Museum).

A literary project of a quite different kind occupied Darwin in 1776: a system of shorthand. He was returning to the art he learnt while at Cambridge, and he wrote a twenty-five-page manuscript guide.[43]

[8]

Another fresh start for Darwin in 1776 was to begin writing down his ideas, mainly on medicine, inventions and science, in a 'Commonplace Book'. It might better be called an uncommonplace book, for among the hundreds of medical case histories and sketches of inventions there are many ideas too unconventional to appear in any of his printed books.

The Commonplace Book is preserved in the Darwin Museum at Down House. It is a massive volume of 300 outsize pages, and about 200 are filled with his untidy but legible writing. The early pages are mostly medical: probably he wanted to record unusual cases that might be quoted in the medical treatise he was writing.

In 1776 the Commonplace Book has fourteen pages of case notes on scarlet fever, gangrenous sore throat, drunkenness, headache from diseased teeth, dropsy, carbuncles of the eyelid, polypus of the nose, worms, small-pox and lockjaw, the last two of which he treated with opium. Most of these narratives are of little interest now, but some of Darwin's incidental remarks are arresting. For example, he notes that witches often floated when subjected to trial by ordeal. He attributes this to the fact that hypo-chondriacs and hysterics have bad digestion, so that 'the stomach and bowels become distended with air'.

There is one startling case history that was certainly not intended for publication: 'Mrs --- was asthmatic and dropsical, but did not appear near her end. She took four draughts of the decoction of Foxglove ... She vomit-ted two or three times, and then purged twice and died upon the close-stool.'[44] This looks rather like murder from an overdose of drugs, but such accidents were inevitable when doses were a matter of trial and error. The question was, 'Did the doctor learn from his mistakes?', and with Darwin the answer was usually 'yes'.

Much more successful was Darwin's treatment in 1777 of Mr Saville, probably Anna Seward's inamorato. Here Darwin uses electrotherapy to good effect, and the case history is reproduced with a few additions in *Zoonomia*.

Mr S., a gentleman between 40 and 50 years of age, had had the jaundice about six weeks, without pain, sickness, or fever; and had taken emetics, cathartics, mercurials, bitters, chalybeates, essential oil, and ether, without apparent advantage. On a supposition that the obstruction of the bile might be owing to the paralysis or torpid action of the common bile-duct, and the stimulants taken into the stomach seeming to have no effect, I directed half a score smart electric shocks from a coated bottle, which held about a quart, to be passed through the liver, and along the course of the common gall-duct, as near as could be guessed, and on that very day the stools became yellow; he continued the electric shocks a few days more, and his skin gradually became clear.[45]

The medical use of electricity was not unknown in the eighteenth century,[46] but it was rare. So Darwin's treatment was decidedly experimental, and on this occasion most successful.

Some of the medical entries are short notes rather than case histories. For example: 'In diabetes the quantity of sugar to be obtained from the urine is quite astonishing'. 'Dilute an acquired taste and it ceases to be agreeable, hence a test of acquired taste.'[47] Darwin was already wondering about the role of sugar in plants: 'the farinaceous matter in the grain of barley or peas is converted into sugar during germination'.[48]

Other medical entries, running to about fifteen pages, dwell on asthma, consumption, epilepsy, menstruation, sleep, tears, pain, hydrophobia, vertigo and angina. Mumps is another of the topics and it provokes some curious queries: 'Mr S died of a sore throat, which retreated and fell on the brain. Mr P had a sore throat ceased suddenly and he became stupid but recover'd. I suppose both these might be a Mumps originally?'[49]

[9]

The most important of Darwin's fresh starts in 1776 was his purchase of land a mile west of his house: here in the next three years he created a botanic garden. Anna describes the site quite accurately as

a little, wild, umbrageous valley, a mile from Lichfield, amongst the only rocks which neighbour that city so nearly. It was irriguous from various springs, and swampy from their plenitude. A mossy fountain, of the purest and coldest water imaginable, had, near a century back, induced the inhabitants of Lichfield to build a cold bath in the bosom of the vale. *That*, till the doctor took it into his possession, was the only mark of human industry which could be found in the tangled and sequestered scene.[50]

Today the bath still exists and is still the only mark of human industry in the little valley. The bath is about fifteen feet square, and the water is still perfectly clear and cold, as Anna says, and about three feet deep. An inscription nearby reads: 'This stone marks the site of the Ancient Bathhouse purchased by Dr ERASMUS DARWIN of Lichfield and his son ERASMUS

DARWIN the younger from Thomas Weld of Lulworth Castle, Dorset, Esq. in the 20th year of the reign of KING GEORGE III ...' So, two or three years after buying the land, Erasmus and his son also acquired the bath-house, built in the previous century by Sir John Floyer, the Lichfield physician who was so keen on cold baths.

The little valley bought by Darwin runs down from west to east about a hundred yards south of Abnalls Lane. It is still pasture-land today: in 1998 it was part of a deer park. Darwin's first move was to dam the stream to form a chain of lakes: three are visible today, but there may have been more. Anna says that 'in some parts he widened the brook into small lakes, that mirrored the valley; in others, he taught it to wind between shrubby margins.'[51] The whole site, including the area round the bath-house at the upper end, is about 200 yards long; the width can only be guessed, but was probably not more than 100 yards. If so, the total area would not have been more than four acres.

This was enough for Darwin to create an attractive botanic garden centred on the steep-sided little valley with its streams and lakes. As Anna remarks: 'Not only with trees of various growth did he adorn the borders of the fountain, the brook, and the lakes, but with various classes of plants, uniting the Linnean science with the charm of landscape.'[52] He also took advantage of a perpetually-dripping rock in the valley. The drops fell three times a minute, unaffected by summer drought, autumn rain or winter frost. 'Aquatic plants border its top and branch from its fissures', Anna tells us.

In the rural peace of this valley Darwin found a refuge from the busy world he had so far always seemed to relish. This major change in his attitude to life is quite brutally expressed in a short poem supposed to be spoken by a water nymph of the valley:

> If the meek flower of bashful dye
> Delights not thy incurious eye;
> If the soft murmuring rills to rest
> Compose not thy tumultuous breast;
> Oh do not on my grott intrude,
> Nor haunt my banks with footstep rude;
> Go where Ambition lures the vain,
> Or Avarice barters peace for gain![53]

This pointed insult to the busy commercial world reveals an anti-Lunar trend. No longer would Darwin yearn to be an entrepreneur. Instead he was entering a rural and Romantic phase. This new mind-set bore fruit in the 1780s with his translations from Linnaeus and above all with his poem *The Botanic Garden*, which so greatly influenced the Romantic poets, especially Wordsworth and Coleridge.

Gardens take time to mature, and it was about three years before Darwin's little valley was transformed into a proper botanic garden. We shall return to it then.

Darwin's new enthusiasm for gardening was obviously inspired by Elizabeth Pole. She was an almost obsessive gardener: fifty years later, when she was eighty, she would spend all day outside working, and supervising improvements to her extensive gardens. Darwin could not meet her unless she or her children were ill; so he tried to impress her in other ways, by plying her with poems and offering her a beautiful and intriguing garden to visit and admire.

[10]

The Lunar Society seems to have lost momentum during 1777, perhaps as a result of Darwin's rural pursuits. But he was still busy inventing, as the Commonplace Book reveals.

The most massive of these inventions, elaborating a sketch made four years earlier, is the canal lift. If a canal has to climb a hill, a flight of locks is needed; this delays traffic, may be difficult to build, and allows water to escape from the upper stretches of the canal whenever a boat passes. Darwin saw the merits of a lift, which avoids these troubles and is especially good for linking a canal with a river passing beneath it. He describes his design (Plate 7C) as follows:

> Let a wooden box be constructed so large as to receive a loaded boat. Let the box be join'd [to] the end of the upper canal and then the boat is admitted, and the doors of admission secured again. Then the box with the boat in it, being balanced on wheels, or levers, is let down, and becomes part of the inferior lock.

His idea is that the box should hang from chains which run over pulleys and have counterweights to balance the weight of the box. The key to success is, as he notes, the fact that

> nothing is to be overcome but the vis inertiae and friction, as the water box is always the same weight, whether the boat is in it or not, since the boat whether full or empty will detrude [displace] just as much water as its own weight.[54]

Darwin at first proposed a metal counterweight, but then he saw the advantages of having a second box identical with the first. This doubles the possible capacity of the lift; and when repairs are needed, both caissons can be emptied of water simultaneously without upsetting the balance.

The first actual canal lift was built about ten years later, in Saxony, and was counterbalanced by weights. In 1792 a lock with a submerged caisson was patented by Robert Weldon of Lichfield, and one of these began

operating at Combe Hay in Somerset in 1798. In 1800 James Fussell's
'patent balance lock', very like Darwin's lift, was installed on the Dorset
and Somerset canal. The large Anderton lift near Northwich in Cheshire,
opened in 1875, was similar in design to Darwin's. This lift, which still
operated until recently, raised boats some fifty feet from the Weaver Navigation Canal to the Grand Trunk Canal – the very canal Darwin had been
associated with. Many large lifts have since been built in other European
countries and the USA.[55]

Another far-seeing invention of 1777, at the opposite extreme to the
heavy engineering of the canal lift, is the fascinating 'artificial bird' or
'artificial goose', shown in Fig. 8, with flapping wings driven by a watch-
spring. Darwin describes it as follows:

> Let a watch-spring be fix[ed] with one end to a frame and the other wrap'd
> round an axis; at each end of the axis let a wheel be put with teeth of such form
> and situation that they shall move a wing, like a bat's wing, or like a ladies fan,
> one tooth carrying it downwards, another carrying it towards the body, another
> carrying it upwards, and a fourth outwards again from the body. N.B. One edge
> of the wing is to be fasten'd to the body and the other to a kind of fan-stick made
> of a porcupine quill. The tail of feathers spread out and lying obliquely to the
> action of the wings, or rather to its intended track in the air.[56]

In the main diagram as drawn, the porcupine quill is replaced by a fine steel
wire.

Darwin's design has been carefully analysed by Clive Hart, who follows
the action of the notches and teeth in detail. Hart shows that Darwin
changed his mind and improved the movement-cycle of the wings.

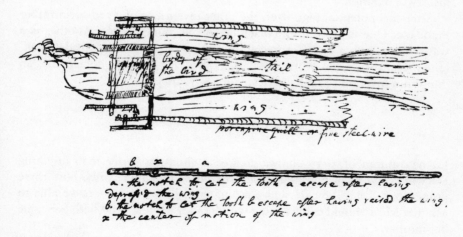

FIG. 8 Some of Darwin's sketches for an 'artificial bird' from his Commonplace
Book, 1778

Before flight begins, the wing lies folded back against the body. The cycle is then
(1) out from the body, the leading edge moving radially forward about point x,
like an opening fan; (2) down, while fully open; (3) back and in towards the body
to fold the wind; (4) up, in closed position.[57]

Hart calls this an 'interestingly original' sequence: 'no one before him, as
far as I know, suggested anything similar either for artificial wings or in
explanation of bird flight'. Darwin is 'very much closer to the truth of bird
flight' than any of his numerous predecessors.[58]

A few pages later in the Commonplace Book Darwin improves his
watch-spring power plant. He first suggests an in-flight rewinding by means
of a gunpowder motor (a doughnut-shaped ring of nine small charges set
off in turn by a slow fuse). His second idea is more attractive: 'But the
simpler way, and better, would be to have a copper globe fill'd with condensed air'.[59] He shows the globe with a long tube attached. In the tube
there slides a piston on a stiff wire attached to the watch-spring. When the
spring unwinds, the wire trips a valve that lets out a pulse of air to rewind
the spring. This power source is quite practicable, and has been used for
actuating the control surfaces of many modern guided missiles.

Thus Darwin specified methods for overcoming two of the three main
obstacles to artificial flight, namely the generation of lift and forward thrust,
and the provision of adequate power. He did not address the third obstacle,
the problems of aerodynamic stability. As Hart concludes, however, Darwin's bird is 'the first, after two thousand years of speculation, to have been
described with a complete, if summary, account of a power plant and the
intended flight cycle for the wings. As such it deserves a special place in the
history of aviation.'[60]

After this potential high-flyer, the other inventions of 1777 seem rather
mundane. One is a lever-type machine for weighing people. Another is a
water pump with a constant stream, with two cogged wheels inside a con-
tainer. He also began work on a 'bigrapher' for copying documents, an
important invention that he perfected a few years later.

[11]

In the autumn of 1777 chance created a situation better than anything
Darwin could have invented. Elizabeth Pole's daughter Milly, now three
years old, fell ill. The case was puzzling enough for Darwin to be able to
ask that Milly should come to stay with him for a while. And with her came
her mother.

Darwin records the case in his Commonplace Book: 'Miss Milly Pole
about 3 years old from a very healthy lively beautiful child lost her spirits

and flesh, without fever, or tumid belly, or any apparent cause ... Her hands and feet are almost always cold, and what is strange they appear of a florid red'.[61] During October he notes that 'She take opium $^2/_3$ of a grain thrice a day'. Apparently this was not enough, because the next entry is 'Nov. 16: She has now taken a grain of opium thrice a day for a month and seems nearly perfectly recovered'. Darwin handed out opium with nonchalance that may seem rather shocking, especially as he was aware that it could produce hallucinations.[62] However, as it was one of the few medicines that did have some effect, he would often give it a try, and here it may have been beneficial (or maybe she would have recovered anyway).

According to Anna Seward, the Pole children became ill in the spring of 1778. 'Mrs Pole brought them to the house of Dr Darwin, in Lichfield, remaining with them there a few weeks, till, by his art, the poison was expelled from their constitutions, and their health restored.'[63] This could be a second bout of illness, but seems more likely to be late dating by Anna of Milly's treatment (and multiplication to include the other children). Anna was probably right in saying that Elizabeth Pole stayed in Darwin's house – Lady Northesk stayed for two weeks some months later.

Elizabeth Pole was now thirty and, Anna Seward tells us, 'in the full bloom of her youth and beauty'. In a surprisingly generous pen-portrait, Anna also admits that Elizabeth was witty, 'benevolent' and a good mother. These qualities, she says, 'contributed to inspire Dr Darwin's admiration, and to secure his esteem.'[64]

Erasmus must have been tantalized by the proximity of Elizabeth, protected by a nursemaid, no doubt, as well as the shield of 'Virtue'. And he would have been cast down when she eventually left 'with her renovated little ones', in Anna's memorable phrase. Her visit (or her departure) inspired further verses, some gloomy and some buoyant.

His worst moments were probably when leaving Radburn Hall after treating one of the children. Presumably he was not asked to lunch by Colonel Pole, but was sent off without ceremony. He could only look back and sigh:

Dim, distant towers! whose ample roof protects
  All that my beating bosom holds so dear,
Far shining lake! whose silver wave reflects
  Of Nature's fairest forms, the form most fair....

He also invokes the groves she visits and the lawns that feel 'her graceful footsteps': lake, groves, lawns, all hear 'my secret sighs', he says, and see 'the tear of hopeless love'. He wished her to know that a passionate and sentimental heart was thumping away within that bluff exterior. On such departures from Radburn he would sometimes come near to giving up entirely:

Farewell! a long farewell! – your shades among
  No more these eyes shall drink Eliza's charms;
No more these ears the music of her tongue! –
  O! doom'd for ever to another's arms![65]

At the opposite extreme is a confident poem instructing Boulton to make a tea-vase for Elizabeth. This was written soon after she left Lichfield, so Anna tells us – perhaps about Christmas 1777.

Friend Boulton! take these ingots fine
From rich Potosi's sparkling mine;
With your nice art a Tea-vase mould,
Your art, more valu'd than the gold!
With orient pearl, in letters white,
Around it, 'To the Fairest', write;
And where proud Radburn's turrets rise,
To bright Eliza send the prize.

There follow detailed directions. He wants no dragons, naiads, sphinxes or dolphins, but myrtle and rose buds, woodbine stalks, a Cupid at the base and a turtle dove on the lid.

Vase! when Eliza deigns to pour
With snowy hand thy boiling shower,
And sweetly talks, and smiles, and sips
The fragrant steam with ruby lips,
More charms thy polish'd orb shall shew
Than Titian's glowing pencil drew...[66]

Apparently Boulton accepted this exuberant order-in-verse and Elizabeth eventually received a very fine teapot.

CHAPTER EIGHT

Deaths, devices and desires
1778–1780

The outward calm of Darwin's personal life came to an end in 1778, when death stepped in again to destroy his plans and hopes for the future.

The year began positively with Darwin agitating for Lunar meetings to be resumed, and Keir wrote to Boulton: 'I had a letter yesterday from Dr Darwin in which he says he longs for a little philosophical laughing – Therefore when you are at leisure some full Moon Sunday, I hope you will indulge the Dr ...'[1] Darwin wrote himself to rouse Boulton on 4 February:

> Not having heard of you for so many moons has induced me to think you are dead – pray send me word that I may begin your epitaph – if you are still alive I design to visit you next Sunday but one.[2]

It was only in a Lunar sense that Darwin had not heard of Boulton: three weeks earlier he had sent Boulton a long letter, returning some verses of Miss Rogers which he had 'polish'd, japan'd, and handed up'.[3]

Soon, on 5 April, Darwin himself had to send apologies:

> I am sorry the infernal Divinities, who visit mankind with diseases, and are therefore at perpetual war with Doctors, should have prevented my seeing all you great Men at Soho today – Lord! what inventions, what wit, what rhetoric, metaphysical, mechanical, and pyrotecnical, will be on the wing, bandy'd like a shuttlecock from one to another of your troop of philosophers! While poor I, I by myself I, imprizon'd in a post chaise, am joggled, and jostled, and bump'd, and bruised along the King's high road, to make war upon a pox or a fever![4]

After this flowing flight of fancy Darwin descends to earth with a reminder about some prints by Angelica Kauffmann that Boulton had promised to buy and frame for him. Selling power to the world was now Boulton's aim, and his role as general factotum for Darwin household goods was ending. Erasmus had to write again about the prints.

Within the family, all seemed well. Susannah continued to act as an indulgent aunt to Robert, who was now eleven. The young Erasmus, now eighteen, was probably working with a Lichfield attorney. Charles was in his second year at the Edinburgh Medical School.

[2]

Charles was enjoying a brilliant undergraduate career. In March 1778 he won the first gold medal of the newly established Aesculapian Society of Edinburgh for his essay on the best ways of distinguishing between pus and mucus. He was fortunate in his teacher Dr Andrew Duncan, a man of great kindness and energy, who was already well on the way to becoming one of the leading figures in Scottish medicine.[5] Duncan was much impressed by his pupil's abilities and gladly accepted Charles's help in his public dispensary, where Charles 'undertook the care, and attended with diligence all the sick poor of the parish of Waterleith, and supplied them with the necessary medicines'.[6] Charles had nearly completed a thesis on 'Retrograde motions of the lymphatic vessels', and on 24 April 1778 he wrote a letter to his father[7] about a case of diabetes where his results were relevant.

At the end of April, Charles cut his finger while dissecting the brain of a child who had died of 'hydrocephalus internus', and on the same evening was seized with a severe headache, followed the next day by 'delirium, petechiae, haemorrhage, paralysis of the bladder and other circumstances of extreme debility'.[8] Charles had the benefit of being treated by three of Scotland's most eminent doctors, Dr William Cullen, Dr Joseph Black and Dr Duncan himself; but their efforts seemed of no avail.

Erasmus was summoned to Edinburgh, though he is unlikely to have arrived before about 8 May because of the slowness of travel. On 12 May he wrote to his son Erasmus:

> I was flatter'd into a belief, when I arrived here, that your brother, as ill as he appear'd to me, was considerably better than he had been – alass in 12 hours I saw he was declining fast, and that the case as far as I could judge was nearly hopeless. – I fear in two or three days he will cease to live. Perhaps you may see me in a day or two after you recieve this letter.[9]

He sent a similar letter to Wedgwood, ending 'may your children succeed better'.

The prognosis was accurate: Charles died on 15 May, four months before his twentieth birthday. He was buried in Dr Duncan's family vault in the churchyard of the chapel of St Cuthbert (at the junction of Chapel Street and Buccleuch Street), and the inscription composed by Erasmus can still be seen (Plate 7A).

Erasmus probably stayed with James Hutton in Edinburgh, and it was Hutton who supervised the cutting of the inscription. Darwin wrote to him on 3 July: 'I esteem myself highly obliged to you on many accounts. I have inclosed an inscription, which I wish to be put on marble, ornamented so as to cost between five and ten pounds, in such manner as shall be most agreable to Dr Duncan, whom you will please to consult on this matter.'[10]

Darwin also asks Hutton to let him know 'the name of the place he is buried in, that I may some years hence direct his brother to find his tomb!' This last remark reveals that Erasmus had already decided that his son Robert, now twelve years old, should step into Charles's shoes as a doctor.

Later in the letter Erasmus tells Hutton that 'I intend shortly to publish my poor Charles's treatise on pus and mucus', and he did so two years later.

A quicker response to Charles's death came within a few months in a poem of 360 lines, *An Elegy on the much-lamented Death of a most ingenious young Gentleman, who lately died in the College at Edinburgh where he was a Student*. Most library catalogues attribute the poem to Andrew Duncan. This is plausible, because it was published by Duncan's regular publisher (G. Robinson of London), and because Duncan himself had some reputation as a poet. Certainly Duncan was involved in the process of publication. However, as Janet Browne[11] has remarked, the poem is in Erasmus's 'inimitable style': the technique is similar to that of his *Botanic Garden*. This is true, and Duncan's published verse is in a different style. So the likelihood is that Erasmus wrote much of the poem, while preserving his customary anonymity.

But there is another puzzle to be solved. The title page of the poem says that it is sold (for one shilling) by three booksellers outside London, including 'M. Morgan in Lichfield'. Anna Seward took an obsessive interest in all Erasmus's verse, and more than 200 pages of her *Memoirs* of him are devoted to detailed criticism of his poems. Yet she says nothing about the *Elegy*; so she did not know about it. Why not? The answer may be that Erasmus realized rather late that the gossipy literati of Lichfield Close would soon see through the mask of anonymity. To avoid this embarrassment, perhaps he bought up all the copies and told Morgan that no more were available.

The *Elegy*, if Erasmus did write most of it, is his longest and most important poem so far, and it includes some uncensored autobiography. The two-page preface quotes an obituary in *Medical Commentaries* which says that Charles possessed 'great natural acuteness' and 'the most unremitting industry'. His 'genius and industry' gave 'well-grounded expectations that the art of medicine would have been improved' had he lived. (Maybe he would also have developed his father's ideas of evolution with 'genius and industry', thus pre-empting the work of his nephew and namesake?) The preface ends with a personal paragraph:

> The Author of the following lines looks back upon the hours he spent in the company of the deceased, as the most instructing and happy of his life; he had for him the most sincere attachment and perfect esteem; whence his unfeigned sorrow.[12]

In the poem he has 'almost extempore', he says, 'poured forth ... the feelings of his wounded heart; and wept over scenes which never can return'.
No wonder he wished to suppress sales in Lichfield.

The first twenty-six lines of the *Elegy* are a generalized expression of
grief, and line 25 says 'he was my friend'. These lines may be by Duncan.

In line 27 a new narrator appears who can only be Erasmus himself:

> From birth I knew him; ev'n his infant plays
> Created love, awak'd the voice of praise;
> And as he grew, attracted by her charms,
> He woo'd fair Science, won her to his arms.

Under her tutelage he learnt nature's laws:

> And daily as his passion stronger grew,
> She gradual gave her beauties to his view;
> Till all her world of charms he saw, possess'd.

In later poems Erasmus sexualized science discreetly for genteel readers:
here it is explicit.

The goddess of Science (Erasmus's puppet) then tells Charles how the
world works its wicked wiles:

> How states by virtue rise, by vice decay,
> What foul injustice marks ambition's way!
> How her train-bearers War and Rapine joy
> In fields of blood, all order to destroy;
> What blessings wait around the throne of Peace,
> Where free industry gives her rich increase;
> Where pers'nal merit wins the public smile;
> And commerce pours her treasures without guile.[13]

This is a rare declaration of Erasmus's real opinions in spontaneous verse.

Erasmus continues in autobiographical mode via a stark image of dark
and light:

> As raven-night with wing recedent flies
> When off his perch the eagle-day doth rise;
> So Ignorance to Reason yields her reign,
> And Genius sweeps grim Terror from the plain.

Erasmus passionately felt the optimism of the Enlightenment, and had faith
that Ignorance would yield to Reason.

After hearing about chemistry and electricity, Charles samples the delights of spring by walking through the fields with his father and Ceres,
while Ceres explains the processes of 'germination, growth, decline'. This
leads on to a hundred lines of sentimentality about Erasmus's close and harmonious relationship with his son; there is no mention of those ten months
away at Oxford University.

Then we follow Charles to Edinburgh,

> that Aesculapian school,
> Where worth is cherish'd, excellence bears rule.[14]

Here Charles dives deep in 'the Epidauric stream' (Aesculapius lived at Epidaurus) and 'culls the choicest of its pearly stores'. The Genius of the stream warns him that 'adown my stream putrescent matter glides', and advises caution, in vain. The medical faculty 'with grateful joy hail'd his ascending light', and wished to see him rise in 'honoured glory'.

In the last twenty-two lines, which are spattered with seventeen exclamation marks, there is another change of style. I would judge that most of these lines were not written by Erasmus.

With hindsight it is easy to see that the *Elegy* discloses a new voice in English poetry: fifteen years later the *Elegy*'s author was to be acclaimed as the leading poet of the day. All the essential skills are in place here, but the poem is sentimental, hastily written and overburdened with grief not 'recollected in tranquillity' but pouring out in pain.

Erasmus insists that he had a special relationship with Charles, and in the poem he speaks of them going swimming naked together with delight. He seems almost to be encouraging the idea that he was sexually attracted by his son in the years when he had no female partner. I do not accept this idea because all his other writings and the events of his life point to strong heterosexuality. Also the poem is very far from being realistic: he never walked in the fields with Charles and Ceres. However, he and Charles did have an unusually harmonious friendship, which explains the violence of his grief.

This was the worst event in his life. Polly's death had been expected, and she enjoyed a fulfilled life by eighteenth-century standards, in that she had a happy marriage and left three healthy sons. With Charles there was immense potential but no achievement. The *Elegy* confirms that Charles was the one person of whom Erasmus stood in awe. If, as he says, his hours with Charles were 'the most instructing and happy' he had known, all his Lunar friends were on a lower plane.

The memory of Charles's energy and talents remained strong for many years. His namesake and nephew said that 'the venerable professor [Duncan] spoke to me about him with the warmest affection forty-seven years after his death, when I was a young medical student in Edinburgh'.[15]

[3]

Darwin's visit to Edinburgh would have taken about two weeks, and on his return he would have buried his grief in the busyness of his practice. Even

in his letter to Erasmus junior on 12 May he added a postscript: 'I shall return by Newcastle [under-Lyme], write to me there if any medical business
on that side of the country wants me'. If so, his son would presumably have
written to Wedgwood.

One case in the summer of 1778, that of Lady Northesk, is fully chron-
icled by Anna Seward.[16] Lady Northesk stopped at a Lichfield inn on her
way home to Scotland to die, after the most eminent physicians of London
and Bath had decided there was no hope for her. The innkeeper advised her
to 'send for *our* Doctor, he is so famous'. Darwin invited her to stay at his
house and asked Anna to visit her frequently. Anna found her lying on a
couch in the parlour 'drawing with difficulty that breath which seemed
often on the point of final evaporation'.

Darwin first suggested a blood transfusion. Lady Northesk agreed, and
Anna bravely offered herself as a donor; but after 'consulting his pillow'
Darwin told them he had decided it was too dangerous. Instead he put Lady
Northesk on a diet of milk, vegetables and fruit. Within three weeks she
was cured and went back to Scotland with a feeling of 'grateful veneration
towards her physician, whose rescuing skill had saved her from the grave'.
In a letter of thanks a few months later she refers to 'your Humanity and
Goodness, accompanied by your usual Humor and Spirit'.[17] She remained
well, but died a year later through setting her clothes alight.

Some of the cases recorded in the Commonplace Book during 1778 are
less impressive, for example that of Mr Jauncey, presumably the clergyman
who had married Nelly White in 1767. He was suffering from pleurisy:

> Mr Jauncey was blooded nine times, he then became feeble, with obscure hic-
> cup for a day and twitching of the corners of his mouth into a kind of risus
> sardonicus.[18]

After such treatment his laugh might well be sardonic: but he did recover in
about ten days.

Though Jauncey may seem badly done to, Darwin makes up for it with
many touches of kindness: 'I have this day (Dec.25 –78) seen Mrs Riley of
Stafford, who has a diseased digestion, and perpetual sickness.'[19] Few doctors today would care to drive forty miles on Christmas Day over muddy
rutted 'roads' in an unheated bone-shaking carriage, to see a patient with
bad digestion.

A more formal medical case-report of 1778 was the paper 'A new Case
in Squinting' published in the *Philosophical Transactions* of the Royal
Society.[20] The subject is a five-year-old boy, Master D. Sandford, who
looked at every object with only one eye (the one furthest from the object)
by turning his head so that the image fell on the blind spot in the retina of
the nearer eye. Darwin believed the habit was caused by his wearing, as

a baby, a nightcap which had appendages at each side visible only to the opposite eye. Darwin's proposed cure was to fit a large false nose like the gnomon of a sundial, which would force the boy to view with the near eye. This unsightly treatment was not persevered with, and when Darwin saw the boy again six years later he found the habit more fixed. He made experiments which revealed that Master Sandford had blind spots four times larger than normal. The experiments were simple but show how Darwin would take trouble to resolve a puzzling case, even though here he thought the gnomon would cure the habit.

Optical experimentation is followed by dental extermination. The victim was 'Mrs Stubs', probably the partner of George Stubbs the painter, a close associate of Wedgwood (who habitually spelt him 'Stubs'). In his Commonplace Book Darwin notes that Mrs Stubs had a sore throat and 'the greatest number of rotten teeth in the highest degree of decay, that I ever saw in one mouth.... I have advised her teeth to be drawn and 10 or 20 electric shocks from a pint or quart phial to be passed through the sore part twice a day for a month.'[21] Though well meant, this electrical torture sounds more like a punishment than a cure.

[4]

Some of Darwin's inventions sprang from his medical needs, and when he prescribed electrotherapy he needed an electrical machine. He devised an 'electrical doubler' that was well known in its day and is the subject of a rather rough sketch in the Commonplace Book, shown (slightly touched up) in Fig. 9. The central disc, apparently of glass with a metal sheet embedded

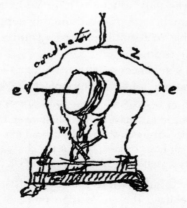

FIG. 9 Darwin's sketch for an electrostatic doubler, from his Commonplace Book, 1778

in it, was given an initial charge. The two outer discs are 'movable brass plates which being mounted on cranked levers, could be made to approach or recede from the central plate by turning a winch'.[22] As the plates approach the central one, charges are induced on them which apparently pass to a Leyden jar via the conductor *w*. Then the plates are withdrawn and earthed via *e* and *s*. The mechanism is not clear in the sketch.

Afterwards Darwin made several improvements in his electrical doubler and then handed it over to his friend Abraham Bennet, curate of Wirksworth and inventor of the gold-leaf electroscope. Bennet tells us: 'Dr Darwin ... made the first attempt with two plates moving between two others by a lever, so as to bring them exactly to the same position in each operation. This contrivance he soon improved by another instrument in which the plates stood vertically and moved by rack work in a direction exactly parallel to each other.'[23] Bennet also says that he kept a diary of atmospheric electricity 'at the request of my friend Dr Darwin, who hoped some important atmospheric discoveries might be made thereby'.

The mention of 'atmospheric discoveries' is a reminder of the most persistent of Darwin's scientific interests – the weather and the atmosphere. Like carriage design, it affected him daily in his travels through the muddy Midlands, over vile roads which were impassable to carriages after heavy rain. He had to decide whether to take his horse Doctor with him or not, and to weigh the chance of being stranded, stuck in the mud miles from anywhere, against the chance of a patient dying if he didn't try to make the journey.

To help with his personal weather forecasting service, he had a weathercock with an extended spindle which came through to the ceiling of his study, where it operated a pointer. He could then monitor the changes in wind from the comfort of his armchair. John Whitehurst installed several such weathervanes elsewhere,[24] and presumably supplied Darwin's. With its aid Darwin was able to formulate three advances in meteorology not rediscovered until after 1920.

The first of Darwin's advances was to recognize the importance of cold and warm fronts. He wrote in his Commonplace Book:

> Certain it is that in change of the wind from N.E. to S.W. the air becomes instantly warm, before it can have moved half over this island: and on the contrary when it changes from S.W. to N.E. it becomes instantly cold before it has blown more than an hour or two, so that the change of the direction of the wind evidently changes its tendency to absorb or to give out heat.[25]

This early hint remained unknown to meteorologists, and it was not until the 1920s that they realized the great importance of fronts, which today tend to dominate the weather charts.

Darwin's second insight was to see that these sudden changes of wind required an instrument with a sharp time-resolution to detect them. In contrast meteorologists tended to be satisfied, until quite recently, with intermittent data, often six-hourly. Even today, the computer models operate primarily with data at fixed time intervals, whereas the exact times of changes in wind direction at a multitude of places would be a stronger determinant of the movement of fronts, and hence would improve forecasts.

Darwin's third achievement was to seize on the virtues of continuous telemetry – observing from a distance in comfort. In contrast, subsequent meteorologists made rather a fetish of on-the-spot observation, as if, perhaps by some puritan mystique, a weather-beaten and possibly frozen observer (virtually always male) made better observations because he endured hardship. Telemetry began to triumph only in the 1970s, and now forecasters sit in comfort like Darwin, receiving continuous telemetry greater in quantity and better in quality than he ever dreamt of.

Among other meteorological gadgets in the Commonplace Book is a north-south airflow meter. This is an open tube fixed horizontally and north-south on a chimney, with a windmill sail inside it. The number of revolutions of the rotor is recorded, with a series of cogged wheels to cope with hundreds of thousands of revolutions.[26] The machine is interesting because it reveals Darwin's intuitive grasp of what mathematicians now call the continuity equation, one of the fundamental equations on which computer weather forecasting rests.

[5]

We can stay out in the fresh air by revisiting Darwin's botanic garden. It was probably still being planted in 1778: the *Medical Register* for 1779, based on questionnaires sent to doctors in the previous year, states that 'Dr Darwin is now planting an extensive botanic garden'; in the 1780 edition the wording is, 'he has an extensive botanic garden'.

Darwin kept Anna away from the garden until the landscaping and planting were completed. Then, after inviting her to see it, he was called to an urgent case. So she came alone, 'took her tablets and pencil, and, seated on a flower-bank in the midst of that luxuriant retreat', she began writing. Her theme was the same as Darwin's, warning off the worldly:

O, come not here, ye Proud, whose breasts infold
Th' insatiate wish of glory, or of gold.

She welcomes instead the tasteful and virtuous visitor:

For thee my borders nurse the glowing wreath,
My fountains murmur, and my zephyrs breathe.[27]

And so on, with forty-six lines of description of 'the steep slopes', the 'vagrant rill', etc.

Darwin liked her poem and later arranged for it to be published in the *Gentleman's Magazine*[28] with her name. Also, according to Anna, he told her that her poem

> ought to form the exordium of a great work. The Linnean System is unexplored poetic ground, and an happy subject for the muse. It affords fine scope for poetic landscape; it suggests metamorphoses of the Ovidian kind, though reversed. Ovid made men and women into flowers, plants, and trees. You should make flowers, plants, and trees, into men and women. I ... will write the notes, which must be scientific; and you shall write the verse.[29]

Anna replied that the plan was 'not strictly proper for a female pen': she feared that a humanized version of the Linnaean sexual system would be unbecoming. But 'she felt how eminently it was adapted to the efflorescence of his own fancy'.

Anna tries to imply that she gave Darwin the idea of *The Botanic Garden*. But Edgeworth said that Darwin had already written some of the verses;[30] and even in Anna's own narrative the idea of the poem comes from him. It also figures in the Commonplace Book, where he wrote in 1778:

> Linneus might certainly be translated into English without losing his sexual terms, or other metaphors, and yet avoiding any indecent idea. Thus, Classes: 1, One male (beau); 2, two males, etc.; 13 many males; 14, two masters (lords); 15, four masters ... 20, male-coquetts ['male ladies' and 'viragoes' crossed out] ... 23, polygamies ['cuckoldoms' and 'many marriages' crossed out]; 24, clandestine marriages.[31]

Many of these names appear in *The Botanic Garden* eleven years later.

Unfortunately there is no list of the plants in Darwin's botanic garden and no sketch of its appearance. This is an occasion when one photograph would have been worth more than a thousand words of Anna's verses.

However, there is a word-picture of the garden in its finished state from another eye-witness, the Lichfield historian C. E. Stringer:

> Dr Darwin ... formed a botanic garden which under his skilful hands, assumed a form of the greatest beauty; after leaving the baths, the stream was conducted by several falls of highly picturesque appearance to a small pool surrounded by a shrubbery, through whose thickets were wound a mazy path, having, to the stranger, all the effect of an extensive wilderness.[32]

His gardening led Darwin to decide that some of the works of Linnaeus urgently needed to be translated from Latin into English. It was a daunting task for one person. Hoping that many hands might make lighter work, Darwin set up the Botanical Society of Lichfield. The three founder members were Darwin himself, Brooke Boothby and William Jackson, a proctor in the Cathedral Court. Anna looked on amused: 'no recruits flocked to his botanical standard ... the original triumvirate received no augmentation', she tells us.

There are both good and bad reports about the third man in the Botanical Society, William Jackson. Darwin seems to have liked him and worked with him for eight years. But Jackson provoked Anna's most venomous pen-portrait:

> Sprung from the lowest possible origin, and wholly uneducated, that man had, by the force of literary ambition and unwearied industry, obtained admittance into the courts of the spiritual law.... He passed through [life] a would-be philosopher, a turgid and solemn coxcomb, whose morals were not the best, and who was vain of lancing his pointless sneers at Revealed Religion.[33]

She also says that Jackson admired Boothby, 'worshipped and *aped* Dr Darwin' and was a 'useful drudge' in the translations. The obituary of Jackson in the *Gentleman's Magazine* calls him 'a man of literature, and a useful assistant to Dr Darwin' in the translations. If he was really 'a man of literature', he could well be the 'William Jackson of Lichfield Close' who wrote the book *Beauties of Nature* (1769), superbly printed by Baskerville and enlivened by some ribald poems that may have offended Anna. Jackson did rise by his own efforts, as Anna says. He was described as a yeoman when he married in 1759, but as a 'notary public' in 1776 on his appointment as proctor. The character of this self-made man remains enigmatic.

With or without Jackson's help, there was little progress with the translations until after 1780.

[6]

One of Darwin's inventions that would have been useful for the Linnaean translations was his copying machine. In the eighteenth century all copies were normally made by hand, and there was an obvious need for a mechanical copier to duplicate any document as it was being written. Darwin's first attempts appear in the Commonplace Book in 1777 and one of these is shown in Fig. 10. The writing is done with the quill on the extreme right and the copy is produced by the tube near the middle. Darwin called this device a 'bigrapher': the name is logical, but not recognized in the OED (which does have 'polygrapher'). Darwin's bigrapher has the disadvantages that it is rather large, about four feet long, and produces a copy that is a quarter narrower than in the original, so that it might be called a slenderizer.

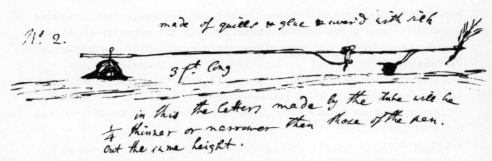

FIG. 10 Darwin's earliest sketch for a 'bigrapher', for copying writing. Words written by the quill on the right are reproduced by the quill in the middle. From his Commonplace Book, 1777. He abandoned this technique in favour of the pantograph principle in the final version of the machine (1779)

Darwin abandoned this first design and during the next two years he perfected a model working on the pantograph principle. He called this a polygrapher, and it could make reduced-size copies, and copies of drawings and facial profiles, as well as of documents.

Darwin persevered with the design at the request of one of his few London friends, Charles Greville (1749–1809), a politician with scientific interests. 'I can assure you at my few vacant hours I have incessantly labour'd at the completion of the Polygrapher in its triple capacity',[34] Darwin wrote to Greville on 12 December 1778. Greville, the second son of the Earl of Warwick and nephew of Sir William Hamilton, was MP for Warwick from 1774 to 1790, and in 1779 held government office as Lord of Trade. Greville had a taste for science and was already amassing his famous collection of about 15,000 geological specimens, widely regarded (when complete) as the finest in the world, because of 'the beauty of the specimens and their immense variety', and bought for the British Museum after his death.

Greville often found himself in debt, not only through buying minerals but also because of 'his liberality to unfortunates', as one obituary nicely phrases it. He is best known for his 'rescue' of Emma Hart: he met her in 1781 at Uppark in Sussex when she was sixteen, and took her under his protection when he found she was bearing his child. He taught her social graces, and she became quite devoted to him. After a few years, however, he handed her over to his uncle Sir William Hamilton, who paid the debts that had plagued Greville. Emma married Hamilton in 1791 and they became friendly with Nelson in 1798.

Darwin used the polygrapher to write his letter to Greville of 12 December 1778, and this is probably the earliest manuscript of which a perfect mechanical copy exists.[35] Plate 9 shows the original and the copy, but it is not certain which is which. Darwin's writing is not noticeably worse than usual in this letter, so the machine cannot much have restricted the free movement of the pen; as he remarks in the letter, 'I have quite the free use of one pen'. However, he does make more mistakes than usual in grammar and spelling, probably because some of his attention was occupied in watching the operation of the machine.

This letter, as well as being unique because it is the first non-unique document, is also unique among Darwin's known letters because it is partly about politics. As Greville was about to become Lord of Trade, it was a good moment for some philosophical lobbying. 'I am sorry to see by the papers that we are lik[e]ly to have a violent french war – I hate war!' is Darwin's first shot, leaving no doubt about his attitude. He goes on to say that seamen 'cannot be *made*, but must be *educated*', because hanging by the hands is a capability that 'adult men can not well acquire'. He concludes that 'the strength of any nation' depends directly on 'the number of seamen they can employ in time of peace'.

> What an empire would this have been if Lord Chatham's idea had been followed? England to have supply'd America with all manufactured commodities, and America have supplied England with the raw products of the soil. The number of Seamen thus employ'd in times of Peace might at the time of war have been put into Ships of war, and have conquer'd the world![36]

Having produced this imperialistic argument in favour of maximizing trade, Darwin shoots it down: 'But the Lord and King George thought otherwise! perhaps it is for better – Britain would have enslaved mankind, as ancient Room [Rome], and have been at length enslaved themselves, adieu'. This sudden and subtle condemnation of imperialism 200 years early must have bemused Greville, who would also have wondered whether Darwin was referring to the good Lord or one of the bad Lords who advised the King. After the 'adieu', Darwin adds 'I never talk'd so much politicks in my life before'.

To return from politics to polygraphers, Darwin finally pronounced himself satisfied with his machine on 16 May 1779. 'It is now as much finish'd as I intend to finish it', he wrote to Greville. 'This machine I would much wish to shew you here, as it can not well be pack'd up without being taken in pieces; and till you have actually seen it, you would find some trouble in putting it together for all its uses.'[37] But unfortunately Greville was not able to visit Lichfield that summer, despite Darwin's offer of a 'well-air'd and quiet bed for you'.

So, rashly as it now seems, Darwin dismantled his machine and sent it to Greville in pieces in a packing-case on 7 June. Presumably Greville encouraged him to do this, and he thought it the best hope. Darwin also sent eighteen pages of instructions on how to re-assemble and use the polygrapher.[38] Darwin wanted Greville to reconstruct the machine and then find 'one in the trade', who would purchase the machine, patent it and make money by selling it. Darwin would not himself risk the cost of a patent, 'suppose £80', and 'the expense of making 100 of the machines, suppose for £200'. He had himself entered a *Caveat* in September 1777 'to prevent any person from gaining a patent for a machine for the purpose of connecting two pens' so that 'when one is used in writing ... the other shall not only perform the same horizontal motions, but *shall rise or descend* more or less, correspondent with the former'.

There are no signs that Greville ever put the machine together in London. He was a dilettante not an engineer, and fixing mechanisms was not in his life-style. Darwin made the mistake of assuming that Greville's interest in the machine implied the ability to reconstruct it. Darwin's idea that the Lord of Trade would hawk the machine around for sale to 'one of the Trade' also seems bizarre.

In short, Darwin's splendid invention was heading for oblivion, and will remain there until someone resurrects it by interpreting the instructions. Darwin's copier was probably rather like the 'writing and drawing machine' devised in 1796 by M. I. Brunel.[39]

Darwin's polygrapher may have failed to excite Greville, but it had an electrifying effect on James Watt, who borrowed it for several months early in 1779. Presumably Darwin hoped that Boulton and Watt might be induced to manufacture and market the machine. But the opposite result occurred. Watt suddenly realized the great advantages of such a copier, and he was nettled that Darwin had outdone him by making such a superb mechanical copier. After all, Watt was the mechanical genius, so why didn't he think of it first? To manufacture Darwin's machine, or even use it, was unthinkable for Watt: he would have to produce something better; but how could he, when this was virtually perfect?

Watt's answer was to seek a chemical method for copying writing. This was a most unusual activity for him: he was an engineer not a chemist. But within two months, perhaps with help from Keir, he achieved success by pressing down a thin sheet of unsized paper on a letter after it was written, in special ink. He obtained a mirror-image copy which could be read from the back. He then rapidly designed a copying press, obtained a patent (his first since the steam engine ten years before), and in 1780 set up a new company, James Watt and Co., to make and market his copier, with Boulton and Keir as partners. Financially this was Watt's most successful invention: 630 of the copiers were sold in the first year, for £4630. The steam engines only brought in royalties and ran at a loss until the mid-1780s. Without the income from the copier, Boulton's financial problems in the early 1780s might have led to bankruptcy. Watt's copier became standard office equipment for more than a century before being displaced by typewriters with carbon paper.[40]

It was to outdo Darwin that Watt made this unexpected invention, and the rapid formation of his company was to forestall any attempts by Darwin to market his machine. When Watt succeeded he was uncharacteristically triumphant, writing on 12 May 1779:

> I have fallen on a way of copying writing *chemically* which beats your bigrapher hollow. I can copy a whole-sheet letter in 5 minutes. I send a copy of the other page inclosed for your conviction, and I tell you farther that I can do still better than that copy.[41]

The copied page has not survived. Nor has Darwin's reply, but it was probably Watt's letter that prompted him to write to Greville four days later and then vainly to pin his hopes on Greville as a marketing manager.

In replying to Watt, Darwin might justifiably have said that he preferred his own machine, which gave an instantaneous copy without having to waste five minutes and cope with messy chemicals. Also Darwin's copies were perfect, not smudged like Watt's, and were on high-quality paper, not fiddly flimsies. If Darwin's machine had been marketed as vigorously as Watt's, it might well have been the winner. Its only important defect seems to have been its large size: it was twenty inches high and possibly forty inches long and thirty inches wide. Still, such a monster might have been acceptable in a large Victorian office with many clerks. It is significant that the most fanatical early user of copying machines, Thomas Jefferson, had a Watt machine for twenty years and then decided to abandon it in favour of a newly invented polygrapher rather like Darwin's, saying 'I only lament it had not been invented 30 years sooner'.[42] In the absence of any marketing agent, however, Darwin was merely the sower of the seed and Watt the reaper of the harvest.

A pantograph double-writing machine had been devised about 1650 by Sir William Petty. It was much inferior to Darwin's, because writing with it took more than twice as long as normal. Petty told Samuel Hartlib about it, and Hartlib devised a chemical method which would give a dozen copies.[43] The parallel with Darwin and Watt is extraordinary, except that Hartlib's technique was not developed commercially.

[7]

Elizabeth Pole has not yet appeared in this chapter: had Erasmus given her up in favour of copying machines? Not at all: his desire was unabated. (However, he may have used the polygrapher to make copies of his poems – one for her and one for him.)

The circumstances of his courtship were still most unsatisfactory. Elizabeth lived twenty miles away. Her husband was nearly always at home, and she was a model of virtue. Erasmus could only visit her if she or her children were ill. He would have been tempted to exaggerate their ailments, so as to justify another visit.

In the autumn of 1778, according to Anna Seward, Elizabeth was taken ill of a violent fever. Darwin was called to Radburn to treat her, but was pointedly not invited to stay the night, which he expected would be critical in the disease. Anna says he spent the night beneath a tree outside Elizabeth's room, 'watching the passing and repassing lights'. This romantic vigil inspired an elegy based on Petrarch's sonnet:

> Dread Dream that, hovering in the midnight air,
>   Clasp'd with thy dusky wing my aching head,
> While, to Imagination's startled ear,
>   Toll'd the slow bell, for bright Eliza dead ...[44]

The rest of the poem is quite morbid and sentimental, as if he had really scribbled the first draft under the tree.

Fortunately Elizabeth survived the crisis and Darwin celebrated her recovery with an 'Ode to the River Derwent', a cheerful landscape-poem of eight quatrains. The first four follow the Derwent from its source deep in the Peak country past the lawns of Chatsworth and the gorge of Matlock to its full strength at Derby, where perhaps Elizabeth may be strolling along its banks:

> But when proud Derby's glittering vanes you view,
>   And her gay meads your sparkling currents drink,
> Should bright Eliza press the morning dew,
>   And bend her graceful footsteps to your brink,
>
> Stop, gentle waves, in circling eddies play,
>   And as your scaly squadrons gaze around,
> Quick let your Nymphs with pencil fine pourtray
>   Her radiant form upon your silver ground.

With all these verses the first requirement was that Elizabeth should find them appealing. Confronted by this imperative, Erasmus successfully nurtured within himself a new delicacy of touch. Heavy and clumsy as a person, he was deft and charming in his persona as poet. He learnt from Anna's sensibility too, and used it playfully in the final verse:

> And tell her, Derwent, as you murmur by,
>   How in these wilds with hopeless Love I burn;
> Teach your soft gales and echoing caves to sigh,
>   And mix my briny sorrows in your Urn.[45]

The longest and most accomplished of Erasmus's courtship verses is the

'Platonic Epistle to a married Lady', a poem of ninety-six lines in rhyming couplets, possibly also written late in 1778. As it has been published in full in my edition of Erasmus's letters, I shall not quote much of it here.

In this poem Erasmus offers compliments to Elizabeth and also at times poses as a detached observer reporting her virtues:

> Ah, who unmoved that radiant brow descrys,
> Sweet pouting lips, and blue voluptuous eyes? ...
> Charms such as thine, which all my soul possess,
> Who views unloved, is more than man – or less.[46]

Yes, everyone is enchanted by her:

> Thrill'd at her touch, where'er Eliza treads,
> To circling crowds the electric passion spreads.

Towards the end the mask slips, and Erasmus sees himself as a pilgrim leaving a shrine:

> So, step by step, with oft reverted eyes,
> Tears unobserved, and unavailing sighs,
> To Radbourne's towery groves I bad adieu,
> And tore my heart, my bleeding heart, from you.

Elizabeth may have thought he was exaggerating his emotions; but taking the trouble to express them with such seeming sincerity was as impressive as the sentiments. As a doctor Erasmus had to cover up his feelings; as a suitor he revealed some of his hidden thoughts in the poems, and they are a significant feature of his total biography.

When his grandson Charles wrote a biography of Erasmus in 1879, he was amazed by these poems so far beyond his own experience or ability. But he made a good comment: 'The love of woman is a very different affair from friendship, and my grandfather seems to have been capable of the most ardent love of this kind. This is seen in his many MS verses addressed to her before their marriage.'[47] But in 1778 that marriage seemed unlikely.

[8]

Erasmus could switch rapidly from writing romantic verses to designing unromantic machines: the horizontal windmill was resuscitated in 1779 after ten years asleep in his cellar. Although the copier had triggered Lunar competition, cooperation was the norm, and never more so than with the windmill.

The first sign of new life is in a letter from Darwin to Wedgwood on 7 April:

I have seen Mr Whitehurst, who approves much of the windmil, and proposes some improvements in the execution of it. I have some *hopes*, not assurances of seeing Mr Wat and the philosophers of Birmingham next Sunday, to criticise all the parts of the model, as he also approves generally, both of the novelty and advantage of this method of applying the wind.[48]

So there was to be a Lunar meeting at Darwin's house when the model would be on display for criticism. It was Watt's opinion that Darwin really wanted, and he tells Wedgwood that 'the uncertainty and hypochondriacism of Mr Watt makes me fear he may disappoint me, and this prevents me from pressing you to meet them'.

Watt probably did come to the meeting and on 12 May he wrote a long technical letter about the windmill – this is the letter that Watt copied to convince Darwin of the excellence of his copier. Darwin summarized the information from Watt in a letter to Wedgwood on 16 May: 'I have recieved a letter from Mr Watt, who calculates that a sail 18 feet diameter will give a force equal to one horse working constantly at his maximum'.[49] This one-horse-power output would be achieved at a wind speed of $12^2/_3$ feet per second, according to Watt's calculation. Darwin thought the power might be increased by adding 'wings' to the sail.

'If you continue to be in earnest about this mill', Darwin tells Wedgwood, 'I will make some experiments on the wings … and take all other steps to perfect the idea, and execution of it'. Wedgwood replied on 18 May confirming that he was 'as much in earnest as ever' and thanking Darwin for his efforts.

Darwin's chief problem, how to find time for the experiments, was solved by the arrival of Edgeworth. Early in the year Edgeworth had to go to Ireland to settle a lawsuit. This was his first separation from Honora and on his return he found her 'weak, flushed, feverish'. They quickly made for Lichfield, where 'I consulted my friend Doctor Darwin, from whose manner I soon perceived that he thought Honora's illness more serious than I had in the least suspected'.[50] Darwin had known Honora as a child, and had always thought she had a tendency to consumption.

In June the Edgeworths moved into Mr Sneyd's house at Lichfield for the summer. Soon Edgeworth was busy making the experiments on the windmill. Darwin wrote to Wedgwood on 4 July saying that Edgeworth 'has made very numerous and decisive experiments with me about your windmil'. Darwin has received 'the mill-stones etc from Derby from Mr Whitehurst', and stresses that Edgeworth 'has indeed been at great labour and patience in trying numerous experiments which my leizure would not admit of'.[51] He promises to write again soon, and does so on 23 July with the news that Edgeworth is making an accurate model, with Darwin looking on: 'I write this at the joiner's shop, with the machine whirling before me'.[52] He suggests that Wedgwood should come to see the final version in mid-August.

Edgeworth was away in early August, and Darwin himself made experiments, recorded in his Commonplace Book under the date 6 August 1779. First he tried a naked windmill sail six inches in diameter with the axis horizontal (as in a normal windmill); this turned 875 times in eighty-four seconds. Then he put it in a square box with the axis vertical, 'an aperture 6 inches high and two sides taken off so as to present one corner to the wind'. Two tries gave 820 revolutions only. He then added wings 'above and below so as to stand diagonally from the corners'. This is not very clear, but the number of rotations increased to '1044–1035'. Then 'a board was added under the arm to represent the friction of the Earth', and 1053 turns were obtained. Finally a cover, six inches square, was put on top: this gave 970–965 turns. Darwin concludes 'N.B. I made all these experiments with great accuracy, such as was quite satisfactory to myself'.[53]

Darwin was willing to do tedious experimental work in physical science if need be. Here he showed foresight in investigating ground effects, later exploited in the hovercraft. But he did not allow for scale effects. This is not surprising because the Reynolds number now so important in wind-tunnel experiments was not defined until the 1890s.

Edgeworth helped Darwin to finalize the design, and wrote to Wedgwood on 20 August 1779: 'by several ingeneous contrivances which the Dr proposed and which I subjected to the test of Experience this species of Machinery may be made to exceed any other horizontal wind-mill in the proportion of four to one or perhaps in a yet higher ratio.'[54]

Darwin's windmill was apparently soon installed at Etruria and used in grinding colours for thirteen years, when it was displaced by steam. No detailed drawing survives of the windmill as built for Wedgwood, but it was probably similar to the horizontal windmill Darwin describes in *Phytologia*, though this design (Fig. 11) was for use as a pump to drain morasses or irrigate land a few feet above the water table:

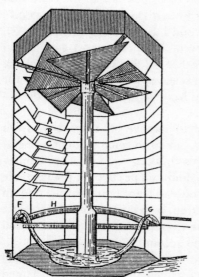

FIG. 11 Darwin's horizontal windmill, 1779. Based on the drawing in *Phytologia*

It consists of a windmill sail placed horizontally like that of a smoak-jack, surrounded by an octagon tower ... [The pillars at the eight corners] are connected together by oblique horizontal boards A, B, C ... at an angle of about 45° ...; the wind as it strikes against any of them, from whatever quarter it comes, is bent upwards and then strikes against the horizontal wind-sail...

At the bottom of the shaft of the wind-sail is placed a centrifugal pump with two arms at F, G ...

H is a circular trough to receive the streams of water from F and G, to convey them where required. (*Phytologia*, Plate VII)

In the mill at Etruria there would have been grindstones rather than a centrifugal pump.

The horizontal windmill is a good example of Lunar cooperation. Wedgwood was in need of the machine, Darwin was the inventor, Whitehurst and Watt gave Darwin confidence by their expert advice, and Edgeworth did much of the experimental work under Darwin's guidance.

[9]

It may seem that 1779 was dominated by inventions, with the copier and the windmill both being finalized: but there were also innovations of a quite different kind, in education.

Wedgwood and Darwin began to act on their ideas about the education of their sons. At the beginning of the year Robert Darwin and Wedgwood's eldest son John were both twelve. Wedgwood's second son, Josiah II (Joss), was nine and his youngest, Tom, was seven. The first sign of action is in February when Wedgwood engaged a teacher – John Warltire, one of the most famous of the itinerant lecturers on science, who partly made up for the absence of science teaching by giving lectures. The boys 'took the infection very kindly'.

Later in the year Wedgwood decided to remove his three boys from school at Bolton, where they had become ill, and to teach them at home. 'I had some talk with Dr Darwin upon my plan', Wedgwood wrote to Bentley on 8 November. 'He approv'd of the idea, and said he thought it a very idle waste of time for any boys intended for trade to learn latin, as they seldom learnt it to any tolerable degree of perfection, or retain'd what they learnt. Besides they did not want it, and the time would be much better bestowed in making themselves perfect in french and accounts.'[55]

The course began at Etruria and then, near the end of November, the boys all came to Lichfield, where Darwin engaged a French prisoner named Potet to teach the language, and wrote to Wedgwood early in December: 'Your little boys are very good, and learn french and drawing with avidity, and I hope you will let them stay, till we write you word we are tired of them.'[56] The French that Joss learnt in three weeks at Lichfield so impressed Wedgwood that he engaged Potet for a year. On 19 December he wrote telling Bentley of his Etruscan school, and the curriculum – drawing, riding, gardening, fossiling or experimenting, Latin, French, accounts.

While the boys were being brought up well, other Wedgwoods were going down ill. Not Sally this time, but her father, quickly followed by the youngest daughter of Josiah and Sally, the one-year-old Mary Anne. She suffered alarming convulsions and paralysis, apparently from the pain of teething. Darwin 'order'd our little girl to be electrified two or three times a day on the side affected, and to be continued for some weeks. We are willing to flatter our selves that she has received some benefit from electricity already, as she begins to move her arm and leg a little.'[57] But the improvement was limited, and Darwin next advised lancing her gums. When that did not work, he wrote on 22 November recommending a series of measures, including up to seven drops of laudanum twice a day – 'such as abates the pain'. But the results were not good: 'I am truly sorry that your little girl again experiences such a violent return of convulsion', he wrote two weeks later.

Darwin was growing desperate about Mary Anne: 'I am clear of opinion that, whenever these fits recur, the exhibition of opium, *so as to induce intoxication*, is the only method, which can prevent (if any can) the sensibility of her mind from being impaired'. Knowing that his advice went beyond conventional wisdom, Darwin justified himself with a denunciation of the normal practice of his profession:

> Opium is the only drug to be rely'd on – all the boasted nostrums only take up time, and as the disease [is] often of short duration, or of small quantity, they have gain'd credit which they do not deserve. If they contain an opiate they will often relieve – but the common ones are only *animal charcoal* ...[58]

This peep behind the professional façade was definitely not for publication. Wedgwood was sufficiently impressed to copy it all out in his next letter to Bentley. As for the victim, Mary Anne, she was on the mend by the end of December, though she remained rather sickly.

As always there were plenty of other patients, and one was very unusual: Erasmus himself.

> Aug.10 1779 ... this morning about three I waked with much pain, and tumour, and redness about the joint of the toe. I bled immediately to about 10 or 12 ounces, my pulse was not much quicken'd nor much hard. about 4 I took calomel gr. vi. at six this operated, at seven I was very faint, and had a slight chillness and 3 or 4 more stools. At 8 I put aether repeatedly on the tumid and red part, and kept it from evaporating by a piece of oil'd silk, the pain became less. At 9 set out for Burton, with difficulty got into the chaise. At 11 was easier, went on to Aston ... About Mar 10 1780 I had a similar fit of less violence ... and then totally left

off all spirituous potation. In April 27 1780, having abstained about six weeks from all spirituous potation, I had another slight attack of the gout.[59]

So Darwin did not give up alcohol completely until 1780. Before that he still indulged in table wines, though he had renounced hard liquor in his early twenties. Abstaining kept him free of gout for the next seven years.

A patient of 1779 not so easy to cure was the consumptive Honora Edgeworth. 'Doctor Darwin showed the most earnest attention to his patient', her husband reports. 'At times he thought the disease, which came on slowly, might be averted before it had taken root in her constitution, and at others he spoke with so much reserve as to alarm her most sanguine friends.'

Edgeworth also offers a general view of Darwin as a doctor:

I had the utmost reliance on the skill and attention of Doctor Darwin. His enemies, for merit must excite envy, always hinted that he was inclined to try experiments upon such patients as were disposed to any chronic disease. I had frequent opportunity of knowing this to be false; and, in the treatment of Mrs Edgeworth, he never, without the entire concurrence of her friends, followed any suggestion, even of his own comprehensive and sagacious mind, that was out of the usual line of practice; on the contrary, it was always in the most cautious, I may almost say the most timid manner, that he proposed anything, which he thought beyond the established limits.[60]

[10]

To judge the past by the standards of the present is taboo for historians of science, so they will have to avert their gaze from three inventions sketched by Darwin in his Commonplace Book during 1779 which remained unmanufactured for up to 200 years.

The first sketch shows high-pressure steam directed towards the blades of a multi-bladed turbine wheel, very like the Parsons steam turbine which came into use about a century later. This is elaborated in another drawing with a boiler added.[61]

Even more advanced is a very rough sketch,[62] without explanation, of what appears to be a rocket motor with compressed hydrogen and oxygen as propellants. (Of course he calls them 'inflammable air' and 'dephlogisticated air'.) He shows the hydrogen and oxygen stored in separate containers and being fed into a cylindrical combustion chamber with an exit nozzle at one end, rather like the propellant feed and combustion chamber of a modern rocket. However, he also has a small inflow of 'common air' from the atmosphere; it presumably enters as the engine moves, though no movement is marked in the drawing. Tsiolkovsky (1903) is usually credited with the idea of the hydrogen-oxygen rocket, and it came into operational use in the late 1960s, in the upper stages of the Saturn rockets that propelled the Apollo spacecraft on their journeys to the Moon. The Space Shuttle also uses a hydrogen-oxygen engine.

Another idea in the Commonplace Book is the multi-lens or multi-mirror telescope: 'Suppose twenty glasses, either lenses or concave specula, are so placed as to throw all their images of a certain object on to one focus – there will then be one image with 20 times the brightness that one lens or speculum would produce.'[63] That is true, and the idea began to become relevant in the mid-twentieth century, when the largest telescope was the 200-inch at Mount Palomar. Any new telescope of larger diameter would be much more costly and difficult to make: multi-mirror telescopes became an attractive option. The first successful multi-mirror model, with six mirrors each seventy-two inches in diameter, began operating at Mount Hopkins observatory in Arizona in 1977. Since then, designers of many of the world's largest new telescopes have chosen the Darwinian multi-mirror arrangement.

Many people will find Darwin's futuristic designs more impressive than his workaday copier and windmill. In several respects Darwin is modern-minded and can leap across the centuries to speak directly to us today.

[11]

During 1780 the Lunar Society took on a new look, and great changes occurred in the lives of several members.

In January Darwin gave up hope for Honora Edgeworth: 'Mrs Edgeworth sinks fast', he wrote to Wedgwood.[64] Honora died on 1 May, having enjoyed seven happy years married to Edgeworth. He called her 'the most beloved as a wife, a sister, and a friend, of any person I have ever known'. Before she died, Honora advised her husband to marry her sister Elizabeth, but at first she and Edgeworth thought they were unsuited to each other. Since Elizabeth was beginning to show symptoms suspiciously like Honora's, Darwin recommended sea-bathing, and in the summer the Sneyds went to Scarborough, taking Edgeworth with them. At Scarborough, Edgeworth and Elizabeth Sneyd changed their minds. Acting with his usual rapidity, Edgeworth tried to get married. But he became involved in an acrimonious newspaper controversy with the Bishop of Lichfield, who thwarted him on the day of his wedding by forbidding clergymen in his diocese to marry a man to his deceased wife's sister. Nothing daunted, Edgeworth and his deceased wife's sister went to Holborn to be married, with Day as a witness. This third marriage proved as successful as the second: Edgeworth was a family man par excellence.

For Boulton, Watt and Keir, 1780 was an improvement on the previous year, when Boulton and Watt had been away in Cornwall a great deal, arranging for their engines to be installed at various tin mines. Keir acted as manager at Soho in their absence, though he was uneasy about their finances. In 1780 the three of them began the profitable company marketing Watt's copier. Boulton did have to travel to Cornwall again in the autumn, for quite a long stay, and Erasmus junior joined him there, presumably to give secretarial and legal help.

Keir also made a fresh start of his own when he set up the Tipton Chemical Works, where he began by producing lead oxide for sale to glass makers and was soon to develop his ingenious process for making soda from salt. The factory at Tipton stood on a twenty-acre site, and was to grow and prosper.

The Lunar Society's new look was produced by the arrival in Birmingham of one of the greatest experimental chemists of all time, Joseph Priestley. As Humphry Davy remarked, 'no single person ever discovered so many new and curious substances', including the gases now known as oxygen, ammonia, sulphur dioxide, carbon monoxide, and many more. Priestley was a fervent Unitarian who thought theology more important than science: he was continually engaged in religious controversy and published about a hundred theological books and pamphlets. Despite a stammer almost as bad as Darwin's, Priestley had been appointed minister of the New Meeting in Birmingham, and he came to live there in October. Darwin was among the contributors to a fund that would enable Priestley to start a chemical laboratory, and his subsequent chemical researches were to dominate the proceedings of the Lunar Society for the next decade. The day of meeting was changed to Monday because he was occupied on Sundays with his religious (some said irreligious) duties.

But 1780 was also the year of the first Lunar quarrel, between Withering and Darwin. It arose when Darwin published the prize essay and medical dissertation of his son Charles, with the biographical memoir I have already quoted. The dissertation includes an account of five cases treated with digitalis (foxglove): these may have been written by Charles, but seem more likely to have been added by Erasmus. Whoever wrote it, this was the first published account of the therapeutic use of digitalis. Withering was furious, because he regarded the discovery as his, and Darwin was furious that Withering should attack his dead son, who could not answer back. Also he was annoyed that the controversy was obscuring the merits of Charles's work, which was impressive and ingenious.

Foxglove was a traditional 'country remedy' known even in antiquity and mentioned by Pliny, so neither Darwin nor Withering deserves credit for 'discovering' it. Darwin probably used it unscientifically when Withering was still a student; but Withering rightly receives credit for scientifically assessing the proper doses, and his *Account of the Foxglove* (1785) remains a classic. After this dispute Withering and Darwin were never friendly again.

There were two other Lunar members, Whitehurst and Day, who now lived in or near London. Whitehurst seems to have enjoyed his official post there, and he was pleased to welcome Boulton and Wedgwood on their visits to London. His most famous book *The Formation of the Earth* was published in 1778, and Darwin was to find it useful in his own studies of geology. Whitehurst did make visits to the Midlands, but Day now rarely if ever came to a Lunar meeting. He had eventually married Esther Milnes in 1778. 'They are good people and I hope will not sacrifice real solid happiness to whim and caprice', Wedgwood remarked.[65] His hope was at least partially fulfilled, for Esther was content to live as Day wished, secluded and far from the taint of society.

For Wedgwood himself, 1780 began positively. He was pleased with the 'Etruscan education' of his sons: 'they make great progress in their french', he reports on 27 February. In his letters to Bentley during the summer he mentions that Darwin spent two days with him (in May), he deplores the Gordon riots (in June) and he discusses the alterations to his house. Wedgwood was also continuing to innovate, with portrait medallions now being added to his repertoire.[66] He made more than a thousand of these, including one of Erasmus Darwin (Plate 7B), based on the Wright portrait.

[12]

Anna Seward came out as a poet in 1780, and Darwin was deeply involved. In deference to her parents' wishes, Anna had not yet attempted to publish any poems herself. But in 1780 her mother died and her father suffered a stroke, so the restraints dissolved.

Captain James Cook had been killed at Hawaii in 1779, and Anna's *Elegy on Captain Cook* was written in 1780. The passive verb is needed because Darwin seems to have been co-author, or perhaps the main author. After Anna's death Edgeworth described the poem's origins in a letter to Walter Scott:

Miss Seward's ode to Captain Cook stands deservedly high in the public opinion. Now, to my certain knowledge, most of the passages, which have been selected in the various reviews of that work, were written by Dr Darwin. Indeed they bear such strong internal marks of the Doctor's style of composition that they may easily be distinguished by any reader who will take the trouble to select them. I remember them distinctly to have been his, and to have read them aloud before Miss Seward and Doctor Darwin, in presence of Sir Brooke Boothby, who will corroborate my assertion.[67]

Boothby is reported to have done so.[68]

My own assessment of the poem supports Edgeworth. The *Concordance to The Botanic Garden*[69] shows that dozens of Darwin's favourite words or phrases appear in the *Elegy*. Also there are many scientific notes, and scientific words that Anna would scarcely have known and are not found elsewhere in her verse. The poem is in rhyming couplets and reads like a rehearsal for *The Botanic Garden*. One example of Darwin's style and scientific wording is:

> Now the warm solstice o'er the shining bay,
> Darts from the north its mild meridian ray.[70]

As Edgeworth says, it was Darwin's lines that were singled out for praise. For example Samuel Johnson told Anna: 'Madam, there is not any thing equal to your description of the sea around the North Pole'.[71] One couplet in the description is:

> Barb'd with the sleeted snow, the driving hail,
> Rush the fierce arrows of the polar gale.[72]

This has a sharpness typical of Darwin.

Anna's *Elegy* looks like another instance of Darwin allowing someone else to receive the kudos for his work. So it is, but this time his motives were not just altruistic. He was using the poem as a stalking horse to see whether a poem of his own, in a similar style, would be well received. The critical success of the *Elegy* gave him confidence to proceed with *The Botanic Garden*.

Apart from helping to write Anna's poem, Darwin also did his best to ensure that the reviewers were kind to her. Bentley was a close friend of Ralph Griffiths, the editor of the *Monthly Review*, and at Darwin's request Wedgwood wrote a diplomatic letter to Bentley asking him to put in 'a word spoken in due season' to 'prevent the catastrophe' of a harsh review from 'the very awfull tribunal in your neighbourhood'.[73] It was quite Machiavellian of Darwin to write much of the poem, allow Anna to masquerade as the author and then, like a kind uncle, pretend to be protecting her.

The *Elegy on Captain Cook* was published by Dodsley in the autumn of 1780 and won Anna much praise. She consolidated her reputation with two very different poems, the *Monody on Major André* in 1781 and the 'poetic novel' *Louisa* in 1784. By then she was known as 'the Swan of Lichfield' and, after two centuries of neglect she may fly again, if feminist critics decide to canonize her as the first Romantic poet.

But what will feminist critics say about the *Elegy on Captain Cook*? It is the reverse of the standard scenario of a man stealing the work of a woman and, with her submissive consent, publishing it as his own. Will Anna be applauded for ruthlessly appropriating Darwin's work? And will Darwin be condemned for having manipulated her? Yet without his manipulation Anna might never have won fame as a poet. Saint Erasmus, the first male feminist? I doubt it.

After these literary dilemmas we meet Lichfield's literary cats – real ones too, not gossips. In November Darwin wrote a letter on behalf of his Persian cat, Snow Grimalkin, to Anna's tabby, Miss Po Felina:

Dear Miss Pussy,

As I sat the other day carelessly basking myself in the sun in my parlour window, and saw you in the opposite window washing your beautiful round face, and elegant brinded ears with your velvet paw; and whisking about with graceful sinuosity your meandring tail; the treacherous porcupine, Cupid, concealing himself behind your tabby beauties, shot one of his too well-aim'd quills, and pierced, O cruel fate! my fluttering heart....[74]

As she has so far ignored his many serenades, he asks her to join in a boisterous chorus:

> Cats I scorn who, sleek and fat,
> Shiver at a Norway-rat ...
> Rough and hardy, bold and free,
> Be the cat that's made for me....

Deign, most adorable heart, to pur your assent to this request, and believe me with most profound respect your true admirer / Snow Grimalkin.

Anna responds to the innuendo with a reply that runs to eight pages.[75] The tenor of it is that Po Felina could never marry so ferocious a creature: how could a 'cat of Darwin' be so brutal when it 'listens day by day' to 'mercy's mild and honied lay'?

[13]

This frivolous courtship of Anna's cat did not deflect Erasmus from his serious courtship of Elizabeth Pole, and there are several poems that may date from 1779 or 1780.

Erasmus ingeniously varies the theme between one poem and another. In 'The Sleeping Nymph' he imagines Elizabeth falling asleep in the grove at Radburn, and asks all the wildlife to help, by providing a pillow of 'softest moss', by guarding her from the 'scaly earwig', and so on. He hopes she will dream of him and his 'ceaseless love'.[76]

In another poem he tells the story of Edward, a military hero, and Eleonora his bride. She goes with him into battle and holds up a shield to protect him, but fails to ward off a fatal dart. Erasmus, pierced by Eliza's 'shining shafts of beauty', pretends to see a parallel with the other E & E. He pictures Eliza as she 'bounds along' in 'gay health',

> And every passing swain alarms
> With all her panoply of charms.[77]

In sad contrast is Erasmus, 'with moping step and slow', writing poems far away.

In 'The Car of Beauty' Eliza rides in a magic car as it floats over 'sunny hills and daisy'd meads', with 'attendant Loves on fluttering wings'. Erasmus is dragged along 'in triumph bound to Beauty's Car'.[78]

In 'Advice to a Friend' – really himself – he warns against her 'tempting wiles':

> Smiles round her mouth in bright succession beam,
>   With whisper'd sighs her polish'd bosom heaves,
> Down her white neck her shadowy tresses stream,
>   Who sees, adores her, and who hears, believes.[79]

But it is all an illusion: when he follows, she vanishes.

In a little poem called 'The Bait' he imagines her standing by a river. The fish offer themselves to be caught, just for the pleasure of seeing her close up:

> And each enamour'd fish, delay'd
> Shall gaze, and beg to be betray'd.[80]

There are also a few riddles, where he can be saucier:

> Eliza now my folding arms are pressed
> Round your fine waist, and clasp your snowy breast.

The solution is 'whalebone stays'. Another is more subtle:

> Courted by millions, millions I deceive,
> Yet still I promise, and they still believe ...
> If yet in vain my name you would discover,
> Eliza! search the bosom of your Lover![81]

Here the solution is 'hope'.

And hope was the life-blood of Erasmus's courtship. His verses, romantic or ingenious, kept his hopes alive while achieving nothing of practical significance. But near the end of November 1780 death struck twice on successive days; and life was to change for Erasmus.

[14]

On 26 November Thomas Bentley died in London, aged forty-nine. It was a shattering blow for Wedgwood, for they had achieved a rare rapport. Wedgwood entirely relied on his great friend to handle the business in London, and they had written to each other about once a week for fifteen years.

Wedgwood set off for London on 28 November, but when he passed through Lichfield Darwin was nowhere to be found. Wedgwood left a letter, to which Darwin replied on 29 November:

> Your letter communicating to me the death of your friend, and I beg I may call him mine, Mr Bently, gives me very great concern; and a train of very melancholy ideas succeeds in my mind, unconnected indeed with your loss, but which still at times casts a shadow over me, which nothing but exertion in business or in acquiring knowlege can remove. This exertion I must recommend to you, as it for a time dispossesses the disagreable ideas of our loss; and gradually their impression or effect upon us becomes thus weaken'd, till the traces are scarcely perceptible; and a scar only is left, which reminds us of the past pain of the united wound.[82]

Darwin invites Wedgwood to 'pass a day or two with me at Lichfield' and commends the letter of Sulpicius to Cicero on the loss of his daughter:[83] 'I think it contains every thing which could be said upon the subject'. He concludes glumly by saying, 'I am rather in a situation to demand than to administer consolation.'

This is the gloomiest of Darwin's letters, and the reason is clear: on 27 November Colonel Pole died, aged sixty-three. Probably Darwin went to Radburn on the 28th when Wedgwood found him away. His visit would have been depressing because of fear that his long courtship in verse of this wealthy and beautiful widow might be in vain. How could a portly and pock-marked forty-nine-year-old compete with handsome young bachelors? As it turned out, however, the death of Colonel Pole was to open a new chapter in Darwin's life.

CHAPTER NINE

Newly wed at Radburn
1781–1783

The news of Colonel Pole's death was soon the gossip of Lichfield. Elizabeth was thirty-three and her husband had left her £600 a year. Her eleven-year-old son Sacheverel would in due course inherit Radburn Hall, and her two daughters were 'amply portioned'.

Anna followed the state of play with keen interest:

> Mrs Pole ... had much vivacity and sportive humor, with very engaging frankness of temper and manners. Early in her widowhood she was rallied in a large company upon Dr Darwin's passion for her, and was asked what she would do with her captive philosopher. 'He is not very fond of churches, I believe, and if he would go there for my sake, I shall scarcely follow him. He is too old for me.' – 'Nay, madam, what are fifteen years on the right side?' She replied, with an arch smile, 'I have had so *much* of that right side!'[1]

What chance would Erasmus have against the 'young fox-hunting esquires' and 'dashing militaries' who crowded round her? People thought she was playing with the 'old dog' (Plate 8B). But, against all the odds,

> she took Dr Darwin for her husband. Darwin, never handsome or personally graceful, with extremely impeded utterance; with hard features on a rough surface; older much in appearance than in reality; lame and clumsy! – and this, when half the wealthy youth of Derbyshire were said to have disputed the prize with him.[2]

Elizabeth imposed one condition: she refused to live at Lichfield. Possibly she disliked the religious ambience; more probably she could not stand Anna and her clique. Whatever the reason, it was a hard condition for Erasmus. He was bound to Lichfield by many ties – his house, his medical practice, his botanic garden, his Lunar Society friends and twenty-four years of living there. 'But the philosopher was too much in love to hesitate one moment',[3] and he agreed to live at Radburn Hall after the marriage in March 1781. Susannah remained in charge of the house at Lichfield for a short while and then went to live with her sister Ann at Sleaford. Now fifty-one, Susannah may have been glad to shed the responsibility; or she may have regretted the change. Her nephew Robert was fourteen and soon to begin his medical education.

Mary Parker was still living at the house in 1778, and probably until the time of the marriage, with her two daughters Susan and Mary, by then eight and six years old. The girls went with Erasmus to Radburn Hall: Elizabeth's daughters were of a similar age and she was apparently happy to add Susan and Mary to the family. For their mother Mary Parker it was the parting of the ways: she was married in 1782 to Joseph Day, a Birmingham merchant, and she kept in touch with her Darwinian children and with Erasmus himself.

Erasmus no longer needed to woo Elizabeth in verse now that he could approach her in person, but there are a few poems probably written in the early months of 1781. One of these is ostensibly about a painting of Cupid and Psyche, with Cupid complaining that the fashionable Belles are not attractive enough and then finding an answer:

> Deck them with Beauty's artless blaze,
> Such as round Eliza plays,
> And, tho' their Beaux were bullet-proof,
> They'll find my arrows sharp enough.[4]

Quite different in tone is a poem called 'Despair', apparently written when Erasmus feared she was about to be 'plighted to a happier swain'. If so, he would not sadden her with vain protests:

> Throb on, my heart! availless passion, burn!
>   While with lone step o'er distant realms I rove,
> Unseen, unheard, and unremember'd mourn,
>   Nor give one shade of sorrow to my Love.[5]

In complete contrast to this pathetic plaint is a triumphant 'Song' written on the day before the wedding in March 1781:

> On, on, gay dance and jocund song,
> And lead the lazy hours along!...
> Thou, beamy star of morning shine!
> Tomorrow makes Eliza mine.[6]

As a finale there is a serious poem called 'Oath', with Erasmus facing up to his marriage vows. He swears by the sun, the moon, the stars, the flowers, the fruits, by life and love and 'by Thyself', that he will be true.

> If false to thee my perjured bosom prove,
> To thee, my sweet Eliza, and to love;
> That hour – oh Heaven, that guilty hour avert! –
> Shall plunge a dagger in my worthless Heart.[7]

Whatever sexual diversions tempted him in the past, he was promising to be a monogamic saint from now onwards. All the indications are that he did live up to this ideal of faithfulness.

[2]

Elizabeth and Erasmus were married on 6 March 1781 at Radburn church.[8] The witnesses were Francis Mundy, author of the poem *Needwood Forest*, and Richard French, Mundy's brother-in-law, who became a good friend of Erasmus later in the 1780s. As arranged, Erasmus moved in with Elizabeth at Radburn Hall. This new home deep in the country was a complete contrast to his Lichfield house, where the coaches between London and Liverpool rumbled up and down Beacon Street.[9] The Hall (Plate 10A) is still remote and peaceful today, though Derby is only four miles to the east and a huge Toyota factory has been built three miles to the south.

Today Radburne Hall (as it is now spelt) is almost unaltered and is considered 'the most perfect of all the Georgian seats in Derbyshire ... grand, yet intimate, delightfully compact, beautifully proportioned and contains craftsmanship of the highest order',[10] including Wright's portraits and candlelight pictures.[11] The Pole family has been associated with the village of Radbourne (in modern spelling) for more than 700 years. The present house was built about 1740 by Colonel Pole's uncle German Pole and stands in a park of 600 acres, with the village and church at its northern edge, just as in Erasmus's time.

About three weeks after their marriage Elizabeth and Erasmus travelled to London, and stayed for six weeks. It was Erasmus's first visit to the capital for nearly thirty years.

There Elizabeth met several of his friends. They included Whitehurst, who had lived in London for six years, and Greville, who was starting his visits to Uppark. Wedgwood had to travel to London more often now that he was deprived of Bentley's help. Elizabeth and Erasmus may have stayed at Wedgwood's London house: Erasmus later apologized to him because 'I forgot to pay you my share of the expenses at London – which shocks me much'.[12] Another friend living in London was Edgeworth, his marriage to Elizabeth Sneyd still only three months old. Edgeworth had previously belonged to one of the coffee-house clubs, presided over by the surgeon John Hunter and with Joseph Banks, John Smeaton and others as members.[13] Edgeworth renewed his links with this circle. Banks, who was created a baronet in March, had been President of the Royal Society for three years, and at his suggestion Edgeworth was proposed and elected a Fellow of the Society, twenty years after Darwin and two years after Whitehurst.

Whilst in London the Darwins made several new acquaintances, the most important being Sir Joseph and Lady Banks. This introduction is no surprise, as Greville was a close friend of Banks and may have been trying to atone for his failure to promote Darwin's copying machine. Banks had the best botanical library in the country and was to prove most helpful over Darwin's translations from Linnaeus.

Another new acquaintance was Henry Fuseli the painter. This was the year of his picture *The Nightmare*, and when an engraving was published two years later, it carried verses written by Darwin which later appeared in *The Loves of the Plants*. It is not known who brought Darwin and Fuseli together, but again this was a link that helped Darwin, because Fuseli was a close friend of Joseph Johnson the publisher. Fuseli encouraged Darwin to publish and encouraged Johnson to publish him.

One old friend whom Erasmus did not see because of mix-ups in timing was Thomas Day. He wrote to Day on 16 May, after returning to Radburn Hall, and told him about Elizabeth:

> Mrs Darwin and I had long been acquainted with each other; she is possessed of much inoffensive vivacity, with a clear and distinct understanding, and great active benevolence; like myself, she loves the country and retirement, and makes me as happy as my nature is capable of.[14]

He showed Elizabeth what he had written, and she added: 'Mrs Darwin ... thinks the Doctor has done her great injustice, as he has left out a principal part of her character, that is, that she loves and esteems her husband'.

[3]

This seems an appropriate moment for attempting a rounded portrait of Elizabeth. As the illegitimate daughter of an Earl, her upbringing was unusual. At the time of her birth, her father Lord Portmore had been married for fifteen years to the Duchess of Leeds, as she was always called, and their daughters Caroline and Juliana were aged fourteen and twelve. The Duchess did not wish to have her husband's love-child at home with her own children. She looked for a good foster-mother for Elizabeth, and chose Mrs Susan Mainwaring who lived at Sandford House in Farnham, Surrey. The Portmores were very rich, and no doubt Mrs Mainwaring was well paid. There is every sign that Elizabeth had a happy childhood at Farnham: Mrs Mainwaring became a lifelong friend who often visited the Darwins and was staying with them when Erasmus died many years later.

By 1765 Elizabeth was eighteen and her half-sister, formerly Lady Caroline Colyear, was living at Kedleston Hall with her husband Lord Scarsdale. They invited Elizabeth to visit Kedleston or possibly to live there. Whether as visitor or resident, she must have been deeply impressed by Kedleston Hall after being brought up in a town house. Here was a virtual palace, with art treasures, a large park, a marble hall and saloon that are among the most splendid in any stately home, and the imposing north front now regarded as the finest Palladian façade in Britain.

Radburn Hall is four miles from Kedleston: so Colonel Pole, who inherited Radburn in 1765, was next-door neighbour of the Scarsdales. He would have been invited to social gatherings, though it would not have been polite to mention that he had an illegitimate son, born in 1757. Unmarried and nearly fifty, the Colonel was now looking for a wife. He fell in love with Elizabeth. She responded to his advances and became pregnant in the autumn of 1768 when she was twenty-one. They married in April 1769, and their son Sacheverel was born in June. This pregnancy and the long delay over the marriage must have been crucial experiences for Elizabeth. After marriage she was determined to be a faithful wife, and fended off the ardent Erasmus, as we have seen.

The idea of asking Joseph Wright to decorate Radburn Hall in 1770 probably came from Elizabeth rather than her husband, who was a soldier and not familiar with art and artists. Radburn would have seemed rather bare after Kedleston, and her sister Caroline would have recommended Wright, whose first commission was to paint Caroline's children[15] though he never painted Caroline herself. Elizabeth outdid her here, and has left an appealing image of herself via Wright (Plate 8A). However, Elizabeth smiled a great deal, whereas Wright never painted his sitters smiling; so perhaps she deserves an even more attractive image. A word of praise is due to Colonel Pole too: he was a generous patron to Wright, whose charges for the six Radburn pictures totalled £210.

Another of Elizabeth's qualities was maternal affection, made obvious to Erasmus when she stayed at Lichfield with her ailing daughter in 1777. Elizabeth's first two pregnancies had produced healthy babies; the third resulted in twins, German and Milly, and German died after ten weeks. When she married Erasmus, she had not had a baby for six years, and she wanted more, as well as hoping for a happy marriage with a man she might love and admire. These wishes were fulfilled: she was pregnant in the summer of 1781 and in the next nine years she had seven children. And everyone said the marriage was happy.

The best snapshot of Elizabeth is Anna Seward's: 'Agreeable features; the glow of health; a fascinating smile; a fine form, tall and graceful; playful sprightliness of manners; a benevolent heart, and maternal affection ...'.[16] To this could be added her taste for art and a love of nature and gardening, the confidence underlying her vivacity, and her own insistence that 'she loves and esteems' Erasmus. The love and esteem proved enduring, and a few years later Anna Seward remarked that 'she makes her ponderous spouse a very attached, and indeed devoted wife'.[17] Though capable, self-confident and often unconventional, Elizabeth was no revolutionary. She was keen to be a good wife and mother, and seems to have had no ambitions outside marriage.

By marrying Erasmus, Elizabeth had doubled the number of children in her care. To her own Sacheverel, Elizabeth and Milly (aged eleven, ten and six) were added Susan and Mary Parker (aged eight and six) and Robert Darwin, who was fourteen. The idea of taking on her husband's illegitimate children was not new to her: when she married Colonel Pole, his illegitimate son Edward was twelve.

She did not have to concern herself with Erasmus's elder son Erasmus junior, who was now twenty-one. He stayed at Lichfield until early in 1782, when he 'got the receivership of the Pole-Estate'.[18] This was just the start he needed for his independent career as a solicitor. He moved to Derby and began a law practice there which soon became very successful.

Darwin's second marriage drastically altered his way of life. His social activities in the Lichfield and Lunar circles ceased almost completely, and he had as yet no friends in Derby apart from Joseph Wright, who had returned there in 1779 after two years in Italy and two years at Bath.

His new happiness more than made up for the decline in his social life. For five years he had lived on a knife-edge, wondering whether he would ever fulfil his passion for Elizabeth. Now he could be with her whenever he wished, unless a messenger arrived with an urgent medical call. For the first time in twelve years he really wanted to be at home. The new home-loving Erasmus also grew more studious and he was feeling a stronger impulsion to distil the experience of his life into books. His friends were becoming middle-aged and even he saw advantages in a more restful life, though mentally he remained a supremely free thinker and his years of fame were yet to come.

So he enjoyed the open rural life at Radburn, free from Close scrutiny. In 1781 he passed his happiest summer for many a year, perhaps his happiest ever. But happiness rarely leaves written records of its presence.

[4]

And what of those he left behind? The Lunar Society felt his absence, because he often provided the fireworks at their meetings by floating new ideas or tearing old ones to pieces. It was fortunate for the Lunaticks that Priestley had arrived to fascinate them with his explosive experiments on gases. Darwin had a hand in suggesting some of these.

The Lunar meeting in January 1781 was hosted by Watt, who wrote: 'I beg that you would impress on your memory the idea that you promised to dine with sundry men of learning at my house on Monday next'.[19] Darwin replied on 6 January:

> You know there is a perpetual war carried on between the Devil and all holy men.... This said Devil has play'd me a slippery trick, and I fear prevented me from coming to join the holy men at your house, by sending the measles with peripneumony amongst nine beautiful children of Lord Paget's. For I must suppose it is a work of the Devil? Surely the Lord could never think of amusing himself by setting nine innocent little animals to cough their hearts up? Pray ask your learned society if this partial evil contributes to any public good?... Pray enquire of your Philosophs, and rescue me from Manichaeism.[20]

These were tricky questions for the 'Philosophs', wrapped in Lunar banter to disguise their venom.

Under cover of his flippancy Darwin slips in a serious scientific idea that marks the birth of the celebrated 'water controversy' soon to convulse the scientific world. This is what Darwin wrote: 'As to material philosophy, I can tell you some secrets in return for yours, viz, that ... water is composed of aqueous gas, which is displaced from its earth by oil of vitriol.'

In 1781 nearly everyone interested in chemistry believed in the phlogiston theory. When a substance burns, it combines with oxygen and becomes heavier; but the phlogistians believed that a burning substance gave off an elusive effluvium called phlogiston, and they explained the weight increase by supposing that 'fire' had weight. In England most of the chemists, including Priestley and his Lunar friends Watt and Keir, continued as phlogistians throughout the 1780s, rejecting Lavoisier's 'French heresy' of oxygen.

Water was a mystery to both groups and in 1781 was generally thought to be a 'simple element' which could not be decomposed. Darwin's letter was the spark that changed the situation.

The 'secret' which Darwin told Watt now looks like three secrets in one. First, he was saying that water is not an element, but can be decomposed; second, that one of its components is a gas; third, that the gas is hydrogen, generated when sulphuric acid (oil of vitriol) acts on a metal (though 'earth' is more often a mineral). Hydrogen ('inflammable air') had been discovered by Henry Cavendish fifteen years before.

At the time neither Darwin nor anyone else knew that his speculations were correct. Probably spurred on by Darwin's letter, Priestley soon started using an electric spark to explode a mixture of hydrogen and air in a glass vessel. After this hazardous operation the glass 'became dewy': he had synthesized water, though he didn't realize it. His experiments provoked a complex tangle of hypothesizing over several years, involving Cavendish, Watt, Priestley, Lavoisier and others.[21] In the end water was recognized as H_2O. Darwin's letter to Watt started the chain of events, and Muirhead[22] believed he deserved credit for the discovery, though Darwin never made any such claim himself.

[5]

To return to Radburn in 1781, we can see in retrospect that such rural living was a further step towards nature for Erasmus. During the 1760s he did not show much interest in plants and gardens; promoting canals, designing carriages, or starting up an ironworks seemed more to his taste. Then about 1775 he felt Elizabeth's influence and soon created the botanic garden to please her. From the garden grew the idea of the Linnaean translations and of the light-hearted poem *The Loves of the Plants*. This formed Part II of the longer poem *The Botanic Garden*, the very title of which made readers see him as a nature-poet.

However, the rurality of Radburn was no defence against a ghost from the industrial past that came clanking to haunt him. The name of the ghost was John Barker: after managing the Wychnor Ironworks for fifteen years, Barker died in 1781. None of the other three proprietors (Garbett, Bage and Darwin) wished to be closely involved, and Barker's widow was pressing for a sale.[23] That proved difficult and, when the Ironworks was eventually sold, the proprietors lost money on the deal, chiefly because water-powered iron-mills did not seem a good investment in view of the growing competition from steam power.

According to a notebook of Darwin's son Robert,[24] his father lost £1500 (equivalent to about £120,000 today) on the Ironworks. If he put in £2000 capital, as indicated in the 1772 account book, he received only £500 from the sale. Fortunately for him, he had married a wealthy widow with a large house, and did not urgently need the sale money.

Bage also lost £1500 and felt the blow severely because he had mortgaged his mill to raise the original capital. His loss 'filled him with melancholy thoughts', and as therapy he started writing novels full of 'gay and cheerful ideas', he later told William Godwin.[25] By unexpectedly breaking his professional mould and producing light literature at the age of fifty-three, Bage probably helped to point the way for Darwin, who was to do the same at the age of fifty-seven.

For Garbett, the situation was more disastrous. In the early 1770s he had been in serious financial trouble[26] through signing bills totalling about £150,000 (about £12 million today). He fought for years to clear his debts, but was declared bankrupt on 1 March 1782. His impending loss on the Wychnor Ironworks, though small by his standards, might have been the last straw. Garbett, now sixty-four, was one of the most respected and experienced of Birmingham businessmen, and his bankruptcy must have shocked his 'disciple' Boulton.

Though this industrial venture of Darwin's was not profitable, no one can really be blamed. It seemed a good idea in 1764: who could have known that Watt would invent his improved steam engine a year later? Nor should the Ironworks be called a failure: it remained in operation for eighty years. The problem was that its low selling price and modest profits were not enough to cover the initial outlay. Darwin never again involved himself in an industrial enterprise.

Instead he was doing the opposite: he was at Radburn enjoying the hottest summer on record,[27] until 1947. It was almost as if for a month or two he had decided to observe Thomas Day's eccentric rules of life.

With his wife Esther, Day had now returned to nature and was trying to make a barren plot of land bring forth fruit. Having reached the advanced age of thirty-two, he had thought of standing for Parliament in the election at the end of 1780, but would not compromise his integrity by angling for a seat, or buying one. Darwin wrote jestingly to him on 16 May 1781:

> Pray, my good friend, why did not you contribute to the *benevolent* designs of Providence by *buying* a seat in Parliament? Mankind will not be *served* without being first *pleased* or tickled. They take the present pleasure of *getting drunk* with their candidate, as an *earnest* or proof, that he will contribute to their *future good*; as some men think the goodness of the Lord to us mortals in this world, his temporary goodness, is a proof of his future and eternal goodness to us.
>
> Now you wrap up your talent in a *napkin*, and instead of speaking in the assembly of the nation, and pleading the cause of America and Africa, you are sowing turnips, in which every farmer can equal or excel you.[28]

Darwin's last remark was truer than he knew, for Day had bought Anningsley House at Ottershaw, with 200 unproductive acres on the edge of the Surrey heathland near Woking, and settled there in 1782. 'The soil I have taken in hand, I am convinced, is one of the most completely barren in England', he said. Day did not write many letters and was in danger of being forgotten by some of his busy Lunar friends. Darwin kept in touch because his son Erasmus was a close friend of Day and often visited him.

The danger of isolation also threatened Darwin in his hidy-hole at Radburn. But his first autumn there convinced him that such a remote house was not suitable for a busy doctor. He had a long journey to nearly every patient, and travelling to and from Radburn was difficult in bad weather, both for him and for the messengers who came to summon him. So he began to think of looking for a house in Derby as a base for his practice.

[6]

The rural peace of Radburn seems to have inspired Darwin to go ahead with translating Linnaeus, the project scheduled for the Lichfield Botanical Society. The three members of the Society were now scattered: Boothby was at Ashbourne, nine miles north-west of Radburn; William Jackson was still at Lichfield, where he was looking after Darwin's botanic garden. Boothby and Jackson might help with checking and proof-reading, but Darwin knew he would have to do the translating himself. He could have conveniently forgotten this daunting task. But he was determined to go ahead with it and to do it as well as he possibly could.

'Operation Linnaeus' was in full swing by the autumn of 1781, as Darwin set about enlisting the advice and interest of as many British botanists as possible. He began by preparing some specimen pages of the translation, and in September he sent these to forty leading botanists, including Carl Linnaeus the younger, seeking their opinions.

Darwin also wrote six letters to Sir Joseph Banks. In the first, on 13 September, he asks permission to dedicate the work to Banks and solicits comments: 'your opinion will much encourage or retard the progress of the work'.

This was followed by a very long letter to Banks on 29 September. Darwin is keen to discuss the niceties of the language in the translation. He tells Banks that he thinks the English words can be more precise and expressive than the Latin, for example, 'bristle pointed' is better than *cuspidatum*, and 'scollop'd' is better than *repandum*. In the next paragraph Darwin discusses at length whether 'eggshape' should be changed to 'eggshaped', and mentions other similar minutiae on which he says he will consult Dr Johnson.[29] This is a new Darwin – serious, unbantering, all intent on scholarly detail.

Banks made a helpful reply and offered to lend books. On 24 October Darwin takes up this offer and says he hopes to publish the translation in monthly parts. On 1 November he writes again, sending Banks a translation of Elmgren's *Termini*, a list of botanical terms which is to preface the main translation. Then on 2 December Darwin approaches the bookseller Thomas Cadell: 'Our design is to publish it in monthly numbers, 112 pages in a number, at 2/- each with a few prints'. The whole work will run to about 2500 pages, Darwin estimates. On 23 February 1782 he asks Banks for the loan of more botanical books: 'Your known liberality of sentiment, and desire of encouraging every kind of science, is my excuse for asking these favours'. Darwin writes to Banks again on 17 March, returning one of the books and regretting the difficulty of obtaining others.[30]

These letters to Banks, deadly dull after the Lunar banter, are revealing for that very reason. They show Darwin working hard on the translation and being sensibly practical in canvassing botanical opinion before starting work. They also show Banks generously lending valuable and often irreplaceable books from his private library to help Darwin.

In the event, the first instalment of the translation ran to 176 pages and was published in 1782 at a price of five shillings.[31] There were four instalments, issued at intervals of about six months.

The translation was then published (probably in 1785) as a two-volume book (with the date 1783) under a lengthy title which may be abbreviated to: *A System of Vegetables, according to their classes, orders* ... translated from the *Systema Vegetabilium* of Linneus by a Botanical Society at Lichfield. Darwin was still shy of being an author, as with the canal pamphlet and the elegy on Captain Cook. So he modestly credits the book to 'a Botanical Society at Lichfield' rather than 'a hard-working doctor at Radburn'. Deprived of the society of his Lunar friends, he became a Society in himself.

The translation might not have been possible without the Banksian lending library, and Darwin was pleased to dedicate the book to Banks, and to praise his round-the-world voyage with Cook:

> The rare and excellent example you have given, so honourable to science, by forgoing the more brilliant advantages of birth and fortune, to seek for knowledge through difficulties and dangers, at a period of life when the allurements of pleasure are least resistable ... justly entitles you to the pre-eminence you enjoy in the philosophical world.

Darwin politely thanks thirty-three other botanists for their suggestions, but Withering is rudely dismissed:

> Dr Withering has given a *Flora Anglica* under the title of *Botanical Arrangements* ... but has intirely omitted the sexual distinctions, which are essential to the philosophy of the system; and has ... rendered many parts of his work unintelligible to the latin Botanist.[32]

Having thus felled his rival, Darwin states his own plan: 'We propose to give a literal and accurate translation of the *Systema Vegetabilium* of LINNEUS, which unfolds and describes the whole of his ingenious and elaborate system of vegetation'. Darwin's main problem was to decide whether to translate the Latin names or merely anglicize them. 'We hope we have steered between these extremes',[33] he says, and his compromises seem reasonable. 'We have retained the word *calyx* for flower cup; ... *pericarp* for fruit vessel'. However, 'corolla is translated *Corol*, petalum *Petal*, anthera *Anther* ...'. This choice was largely governed by the need for compound words like *five-petal'd* (as he spells it). He also constructed diminutives such as *leaflet, stalklet, valvelet*.

Darwin emphasizes 'the general difficulty of the undertaking, in which almost a new language was to be formed'[34] and he calls this 'the Gorgon-feature that has hitherto frozen the designs, or blasted the progress of all who looked upon this giant Naturalist'. Here probably he was referring obliquely to Hugh Rose's *Elements of Botany* (1775), which is a semi-translation of Linnaeus's *Philosophia Botanica*, with many of the Latin words retained. Darwin had to be willing to endure the drudgery and to act as a philologist as well as a botanist: in his preface he thanks 'that great Master of the English tongue Dr Samuel Johnson, for his advice in the formation of the botanic language'.[35]

The *System of Vegetables* begins with a table defining 674 botanic terms; then, after two alphabetical catalogues of plants, one of English and one of Latin names, come eleven plates by the Lichfield artist Edward Stringer. Plate I shows sixty-six forms of leaf, from orbicular, roundish, and egg'd to scollop'd, tooth'd, saw'd – to name but six. The other plates deal in equal detail with the forms of stems, roots, flowers, foliation and the twenty-four classes of the Linnaean system.

After about a hundred pages of these preliminaries we reach page 1, and the catalogue of plants, 1444 of them in all, divided among the twenty-four classes. The detailed descriptions begin on page 51, with

1. CANNA. *Corol* 6-parted, erect; lip 2-parted, revolute. *Style* lanced, growing to the corol. *Calyx* 3-leaved....

The varieties are then listed. And so it goes on, through the rest of Volume I and up to page 838 in Volume II, the final entry being *Mucor*, or mould, of which the last variety is *septicus*, unctuous yellow and putrescent. Two more indexes, of genuine and trivial names, bring us to page 897.

A thousand pages with the preliminary material, the *System of Vegetables* is the complete answer to anyone who accuses Darwin of dabbling in too many fields without much depth. This is a massive work of scientific scholarship.

The translation pleased the reviewers: the twenty-two-page notice in the *Monthly Review* says its publication 'is a matter of too much consequence in the annals of natural history to be passed over in silence. We therefore congratulate the Lichfield Society, upon the completion of this first part of their labours – labours, arduous, as they appear to be successful.'[36] In its day the translation was much admired, and was extensively plagiarized by Thomas Martyn in his *Language of Botany* (1793).

Today historians rarely mention the *System of Vegetables*, but this neglect has not affected its power to inject new words into the English language. Their place of birth has been forgotten because the book was not among those selected for citation in the *Oxford English Dictionary*. In pages xv–xl of the translation, I found fifty words which are earlier than any of the usages cited in the *OED* and have the same definition as in the dictionary.[37] Of course, some of the words may have been used still earlier, but most of them are likely to have been coined by Darwin.

Some of the new botanical words are now in general use, for example, *bract, floret, leaflet, stemless* and *vernation*. Also the plurals *anthers* and *stamens* are the first recorded uses; they were previously written as *antherae* and *stamina*. Non-botanists may dismiss many of the fifty words as obscure, but half of them are well enough known to appear in the *Concise Oxford Dictionary*. On the other hand, dozens of the words coined by Darwin were stillborn and never 'made it' into a dictionary, for example, *egg'd* (egg-shaped) and *two'd* (two-lobed).

It is not surprising that this first detailed translation of Linnaeus yielded such a harvest of words. With its obsessive demands for exact description, botany is a hotbed for the generation of words.

[7]

The first child of Elizabeth and Erasmus was a son Edward, born on 31 January 1782. The event was recorded in the Commonplace Book: 'Mrs Darwin was brought to bed in the morning – the child had a violent purging all the next night'.[38] The purging was brought on through the baby being suckled by a woman of the parish, a practice Darwin normally opposed; but on this occasion he no doubt gave way to Elizabeth's wishes, especially as she was also ill. However, both soon recovered.

By this time Erasmus had been successful with his house-hunting in Derby, as emerges from a torrent of Lunar banter in a letter to Boulton on 27 January:

> Whether you are dead, and breathing inflammable air below, or dephogisti-
> cated air above; or whether you continue to crawl upon this miry globe, measur-
> ing its surface with your legs instead of compasses, and boring long galleries, as
> you pass along, through its dense heterogeneous atmosphere ...

He never finishes the sentence, and continues:

> Now a second purport of this letter is to tell you, that I have bought a large
> house at Derby, and if it be not inconvenient to you, should be glad if you could
> repay me the £200 you have of mine. As I shall want money to compleat this
> purchase.[39]

The Ironworks was still unsold, and it was clear by now that the price would be low.

The Lunar banter was in lieu of Darwin's presence; Birmingham was a long way from Radburn, and he rarely attended a meeting unless he was already there to see a patient.

Inevitably there was some loss of togetherness, although Darwin remained on the best of terms with Watt and Keir, and saw them individually from time to time. Priestley he never knew well, because he left Lichfield a few months after Priestley arrived in Birmingham. However, he made a generous contribution towards the expenses of Priestley's experiments and offered a friendly welcome to Priestley in a letter to Wedgwood: 'Pray give my best compl. to Dr Priestly, and say, if he should come near Derby I shall be happy to see him'.[40] Darwin was also happy to see Whitehurst whenever he revisited his home town of Derby. Their long friendship was kept in flower by their shared enthusiasm for geology and invention.

There was of course one member of the Lunar Society whom Darwin would rather not meet – Withering. The prospect of encountering him may sometimes have deterred Darwin from making the journey to Birmingham.

Two other members, Day and Edgeworth, dropped out in 1782, Day by retiring to Anningsley House, and Edgeworth by settling at Edgeworthstown in Ireland. There he looked after his estates, making few visits to England and possibly none to the Lunar Society. However, distance did not diminish the friendship between Darwin and Edgeworth, and they cooked up several inventive new schemes by correspondence: the nineteen letters from Edgeworth to Darwin between 1785 and 1800 that have survived in manuscript are probably less than half the total.

Nor did distance weaken his ties with Wedgwood. Indeed the link strengthened, because Darwin became Wedgwood's closest friend after the death of Bentley. One of the routes from Etruria to London was through Derby: 'Mrs Darwin charges me not to forget to press you to make our house a resting place in your descent into this country',[41] Erasmus wrote in April 1782. The Wedgwoods had begun their visits in May 1781, soon after Erasmus and Elizabeth returned from London, and the visiting continued through the 1780s.

Erasmus's letters to Josiah Wedgwood – more than fifty have survived from the 1780s – reveal some of his successive 'hobby-horses'.

By the summer of 1782 he has taken up mechanical invention again:

> It is so long that I had existed here without seeing a mechanical philosopher, that I had almost forgot there were such beings; till last week Mr Michel, a comet of the first magnitude, journey'd through this part of space, or rather of vacuity.[42]

For twelve months Darwin had been toying with the idea of a 'fire-engine' or 'great steam wheel in oil', as he also calls it, and he discussed the design with Michell. It was like old times, twenty years ago on the terrace of the house at Lichfield, and Darwin became keen to pursue his invention. He wrote to Wedgwood: 'Now if you would join me in this machine, and take with me half the profit or loss, I shall be encouraged to compleat my idea'. Wedgwood replied ten days later: 'I sigh that I am becoming an old man [he was fifty-two], that age and infirmities overtake me, and more than wisper in my ear that it is time to diminish rather than increase the objects of my attention'.[43] So he politely declined 'the very flattering offer you have made me'.

This is not surprising, for Wedgwood's own enthusiasms were now increasingly in art. He had for some years been concerned with producing large earthenware plaques for George Stubbs's paintings in enamel. Only a few of these were completed, and one is supposed to be of Darwin: if so, it is not a good likeness. (Another, *Labourers*, for which Wedgwood paid 350 guineas, is said to have been owned by Darwin.[44]) Wedgwood also became Joseph Wright's chief patron in the 1780s. Wright extended his range with classical subjects commissioned by Wedgwood.

Without Wedgwood's support the 'great steam wheel' languished. After his experience with the Ironworks Darwin was not prepared to go it alone. 'The steam wheel must stand still', he wrote in September 1782. Its design is uncertain: the two sketches in the Commonplace Book are both early attempts, dated 'July 1781'. One shows a steam-turbine format, with steam impinging on a bladed wheel; the other is quite different, a waterwheel with the water being continuously raised by steam pressure. The final design may have been different from both these.

By the autumn of 1782 Darwin was diverting himself with more homely engineering at the new house. 'At present I am repairing a house at Derby where we intend to pass the winters',[45] he wrote to Wedgwood in August. In a letter written at a short stop on a medical journey in September he remarks that 'we have great convenience of spontaneous water at our new house', and asks Wedgwood for 'any decided opinions about water closets'. Darwin then embarks on a mock rhapsody to the goddess Cloacina:

> Pray say if the Goddess delights most in porcelain, in lead, or in marble – Goddess august! whose provident care collects the refuse of animation, again to reanimate it! whose transmuting wand changes the heads of philosophers into cabages, and cabages into philosophers!....[46]

This overflow of natural ebullience – and there is half a page more – is the quality in Darwin that the Lunar Society missed most in his absence: no one else was capable of such playfulness.

Darwin soon produced his own design for an automated water closet. The sketch of it in his Commonplace Book[47] shows a high cistern that is normally kept filled, the water level being regulated by a cork 'floating valve'. The pipe from the cistern down to the basin is normally full of water held in by a valve at the lower end. The valve is opened, thus flushing the basin, by closing the cover of the basin, and 'when the person leaves the room, the opening of the door' makes the valve close again, so that the pipe and cistern fill up. At the bottom of the basin is another valve, a pivoted plate held in place by a counterweight, and this valve swings open under the weight of the flushing water. Darwin thus fails to include the modern water-trap, but as if to anticipate this omission, he writes across the drawing: 'There should be no valve at bottom but a stink trap'. Darwin's model is technologically more advanced than designs with manual operation, but would be less reliable.

While setting his house in order, Darwin did not forget his old friends far away. The American war was still dragging on in 1782, and a letter to Wedgwood in October reveals Darwin's continuing sympathy for the Americans:

> I hope Dr Franklin will live to see Peace, to see *America* reclined under her own Vine and Figtree, turning her swords into Ploughshares and her Spears into pruning hooks.[48]

Franklin had been in France for five years as American ambassador, and during this time the French had given growing support to the American cause.

Another far-off friend of Darwin, James Hutton at Edinburgh, kept up a correspondence of Lunar tone, to judge from a letter in the early 1780s. Hutton quizzically discusses the absolute zero of temperature, the connection between light and heat, the temperature of hell and whether the soul can feel it without sense organs.[49] Unfortunately no other letters have survived from this skittish Scottish Lunatick-at-a-distance.

There was a new member of the Lunar Society to help fill the 'Darwin gap': this was Samuel Galton, a Quaker gun-maker with a taste for science. Darwin became friendly with the Galton family in the 1780s, not because of the Lunar connection but because Galton's wife Lucy demanded frequent medical aid and the wealthy Galton was not deterred by Darwin's high fees for driving to Birmingham.

On his way to Birmingham, Darwin would pass Lichfield, but he did little to keep up his old friendships there. Anna felt the slight, and in a letter she retaliated by calling him 'that large mass of genius and sarcasm'.[50]

Though Darwin was content to forgo the wisecracks of the Lichfield canons, he did miss the stimulus of Lunar meetings, as he told Boulton on 26 December 1782:

> I am here cut off from the milk of science, which flows in such redundant streams from your learned lunations; which, I can assure you, is a very great regret to me.... Pray if you think of it, make my devoirs to the learned Insane of your society.[51]

The same letter shows that Boulton was still unable to repay the £200 he owed Darwin. Business confidence was in decline during 1782, the year of Garbett's bankruptcy, because the American war was going badly. Unaware of Boulton's problem, Darwin repeated his request: 'I have purchased a house here and furnished it, which has rather distressed me for money; that if you could repay me the 200£, it would be a great convenience to me, and I hope not a great inconvenience to you'.[52] Boulton paid £30 interest on the loan in March 1783, and Darwin apologized for having asked for the full repayment: 'I should not have written to you for it, but that I supposed the income from your Engins would have render'd it not inconvenient to you to return it'.[53] Boulton's image of easy affluence was good for promoting business but quickly shattered by an actual demand for money.

Darwin's old Lunar friendships needed renewing to avoid being weakened by distance, but he was already making new friends in Derby. One of the earliest was the physician Dr John Beridge (1745-88). He had practised in Derby for ten years and might have resented Darwin's arrival on his territory. In fact they seem to have been friendly from the outset. Presumably Darwin already had enough patients and would not have been poaching.

Beridge was a close friend of William Hayley (1745-1821), who was by now well known for his poem *The Triumphs of Temper*. Hayley visited Beridge in December 1781, and Beridge introduced him to Darwin. Hayley went on to Lichfield, to meet Anna Seward: soon they were praising each other in verse. Joseph Wright was also a friend of Hayley, who often advised him over his paintings for Wedgwood in the next few years.

Darwin could scarcely complain that Derby was uncultured when he met there both Wright, whom some regard as the greatest English painter of the time, and Hayley, who thought himself the leading poet of the day and declined the Poet Laureateship nine years later.

[8]

Darwin's passion for mechanical gadgets was not much dampened by living at Radburn, far removed from skilled workmen capable of producing the hardware. Besides the steam wheel and the water closet, there are several other sketches in the Commonplace Book,[54] mostly for house and garden.

The indoor inventions are little more than party tricks. There is a 'factitious spider', designed to startle the innocent by moving around on a salver under the influence of hidden rotating magnets. Far more complicated is a machine for moving chessmen, which occupies two full pages in the Commonplace Book. More practical, though trivial mechanically, is a telescopic candlestick.

There are two bright ideas for automation in the garden. The first is a mini-plough to make trenches for potato planting. The second is more interesting, more ingenious and more useful. This is a 'melonometer, or brazen gardener', to open the windows of a hotbed frame or greenhouse when the sun shines. The design is basically a see-saw, with two four-inch copper globes joined underneath by a long pivoted horizontal tube. One globe is filled with hydrogen gas and the other with mercury (with a vacuum above the mercury in the top half of the globe). The tube is pivoted near the mercury sphere, so that the hydrogen sphere wins the see-saw when the weather is cold, and the window is held closed. When the sun shines on the hydrogen globe, the gas expands and pushes the mercury along the tube and up into its globe, thereby overbalancing the see-saw and providing by its weight enough force to open the window. As the hydrogen cools, the process reverses. It is a pity that this invention never caught on, for the financial losses due to lack of automation in horticulture have been huge over the centuries, and could have been greatly reduced by simple devices like the melonometer.

The invention that fired Darwin's imagination in 1783 was ballooning, with either hydrogen or hot-air balloons. It is curious that he never thought of it himself despite his leading role in defining the laws of heated gases. His non-invention of balloons is on a par with Watt's failure to produce a mechanical copying machine.

The Montgolfier brothers in France were the first to release large hot-air balloons on successful flights, in April and June 1783. The first hydrogen balloon was sent up by J. A. C. Charles in August from Paris. In September a Montgolfier hot-air balloon flew from Versailles with living passengers – a sheep, a cock and a duck (they all survived). In November came the first manned flight, with Pilâtre de Rozier as pilot in a hot-air balloon about fifty feet in diameter. Eleven days later, Charles made the first manned flight in a hydrogen balloon.[55]

Darwin was immediately gripped by the idea of human aerial flight. In *The Loves of the Plants*, which he had now begun to write, he hails the 'intrepid' aeronauts:

> So on the shoreless air the intrepid Gaul
> Launch'd the vast concave of his buoyant ball. –
> Journeying on high, the silken castle glides
> Bright as a meteor through the azure tides....

Then Darwin lets his enthusiasm run away with him, foreseeing the interplanetary flights of the 1970s and after:

Rise, great MONTGOLFIER! urge thy venturous flight
High o'er the Moon's pale ice-reflected light;
High o'er the pearly Star, whose beamy horn
Hangs in the east, gay harbinger of morn;
Leave the red eye of Mars on rapid wing,
Jove's silver guards, and Saturn's crystal ring;
Leave the fair beams, which, issuing from afar,
Play with new lustres round the Georgian star....[56]

The 'Georgian star' is the planet Uranus, discovered by William Herschel in 1781 and first visited by the space probe Voyager 2 in 1986.

At the other extreme to these interplanetary fantasies is Darwin's earthy suggestion that Edgeworth should use balloons to carry manure up the hills on his muddy estate.

Darwin's enthusiasm for balloons alerted him to the idea of air travel and led to the most famous lines in *The Botanic Garden*, about mechanically-propelled cars and aircraft:

Soon shall thy arm UNCONQUER'D STEAM! afar
Drag the slow barge, or drive the rapid car;
Or on wide-waving wings expanded bear
The flying-chariot through the fields of air.
Fair crews triumphant, leaning from above,
Shall wave their fluttering kerchiefs as they move;
Or warrior bands alarm the gaping crowd,
And armies shrink beneath the shadowy cloud.[57]

To this he adds a note saying that 'there seems no probable method of flying conveniently but by the power of steam, or some other explosive material, which another half century may probably discover'. And in less than a century the explosive petrol-vapour engine made air travel practicable.[58]

[9]

Erasmus began running his medical practice from the new house in Derby towards the end of 1782. His son Robert records[59] that he 'went to live in Derby Dec.17 1782'. But the house was still being renovated, and Elizabeth stayed with the children at Radburn Hall. I would guess that Erasmus commuted between Derby and Radburn according to the needs of his practice. The five-mile journey over flat ground from Radburn to Derby was quite easy by Darwin's standards. In good weather it might have been made in about half an hour.

Derby had no scientific discussion-society like the Lunar Society, and

Erasmus was soon using some of his still superabundant energy to create the Philosophical Society of Derby, as he told Boulton on 4 March 1783:

> We have establish'd an infant philosophical Society at Derby, but do not presume to compare it to you well-grown gigantic philosophers at Birmingham.... I wish you would bring a party of your Society and hold one Moon at our house. N.B. our Society intend to eclipse the Moon on the 18 of this month, pray don't you counteract our conjurations. I beg to be remember'd to all the Insane at your next meeting.[60]

Susannah Wedgwood wrote to her father on 13 March that 'the Philosophical Club goes on with great spirit, all the ingenious gentlemen in the town belong to it, they meet every saturday night at each others houses'. At a meeting when non-scientific ladies were present, 'Doctor D----- with his usual politeness made it very agreeable to them by shewing several entertaining experiments adapted to the capacities of young women; one was roasting a tube, which turned round itself'.[61] At this stage the Society had seven members.

As spring approached, Darwin returned to Radburn more often and the Society seems to have lapsed until sixteen months later, when Darwin gave his inaugural address as president.

At Radburn Elizabeth was expecting the birth of their second child, and on 18 April they had to cancel a visit from the Wedgwoods, 'as Mrs is confined to her room, though not yet brought to bed, and expects every hour, and the Dr is obliged to go to Ipstoc in Leicestershire early tomorrow morning unless prevented by Mrs Darwin'.[62] The child, Violetta, was born on 23 April 1783 at Radburn Hall. She was the most talented of their children and also the healthiest, 'a joyous and unconventional girl'[63] who married Galton's son Tertius and lived to be ninety.

Erasmus and Elizabeth spent another happy summer at Radburn in 1783. Elizabeth's son Sacheverel was now fourteen, her elder daughter Elizabeth thirteen and Milly nine. Robert Darwin was seventeen and now a medical student. Susan Parker was eleven and Mary Parker nine. They were probably all at Radburn, together with the toddler Edward and the baby Violetta – a total of eight children.

There was at least one visit from the Wedgwood family, and on 18 July Erasmus wrote to Josiah:

> Our young ladies are made very happy with the presents your young gentlemen sent them: I told Miss Pole, that Love had hid his arrows in the pocket book, and apprized her of the danger of opening it.[64]

Erasmus also mentions that 'Mr Whitehurst has been with me, and says he can make nothing of the present dry-misty weather'. With a mean temperature of 18.8°C, July 1783 was the hottest month ever recorded in central England,[65] until 1976. Erasmus notes the red look of the sun and says it 'is owing to the red rays penetrating bodies more forceably than the other colours'. Although he could not have known until later, the redness of the sun was caused by the dust cloud from the violent eruption of the volcano Laki in Iceland, which began on 8 June and continued during July and August with further explosions, ash clouds and three cubic miles of lava. It was Iceland's worst disaster: 10,000 people, one-fifth of the popu- lation, died directly or indirectly. The dust cloud may have trapped heat and contributed to the hot July. The next two winters were very severe all over Europe, and Franklin astutely suggested that the 'vast quantity of smoke' from the Icelandic volcano might be to blame.[66]

The red sun was curious, but a more spectacular sight was to be seen on 18 August at 9.30 pm, when one of the brightest fireballs of the decade sped across the sky. Shining more brightly than the full moon, it streaked along a line from Edinburgh to Lincoln to Margate, and was observed from the Shetlands in the north to Paris in the south. The many observations sent to the Royal Society were put together by Charles Blagden,[67] who established the track of the fireball and deduced that its height was about fifty-eight miles over England and its speed about twenty miles per second.

Darwin was lucky enough to see it, and later sent a letter to the Royal Society:

> At Radbourn-Hall about four miles west from Derby I ... observed the meteor pass from north-west to north-east, and give out numerous large sparks just before it was conceal'd by the cornice of the corner of the house. This part of the cornice I accurately attended to, and also to the height of my eye against the window-frame: and on the next morning found a line drawn from these two points lay, as nearly as could be easily measured, at an angle of forty-five degrees.
>
> As the four corners of this house lie within a few degrees to the four cardinal points of the compass, the line, along which I look'd, would intersect the course of the meteor, as described by Dr Blagden, nearly as it pass'd over Lincoln; where it was probably vertical.... Lincoln is ... from Radbourn ... about 58 miles in a straight line; which must have been nearly the height of the meteor in that part of its course; which well coincides with the other estimations mention'd in Dr Blagden's ingenious paper on this subject.[68]

As would be expected, Darwin had the presence of mind to make an accurate observation, which independently validates Blagden's findings.

Darwin was still working hard on the translation from Linnaeus in the early summer, though it was nearly finished. With the publication in four parts, each of about 200 pages, at about six-month intervals, he had found himself on a treadmill. As one part went through the probably painful pro- cess of proof-reading and production, the next part had to be written, re- vised and prepared for the printers. Since John Jackson of Lichfield was the printer, the proof-reading may well have been done locally by William

Jackson; it is not clear how Brooke Boothby contributed, if at all. With Darwin himself doing nearly all the work, the summer at Radburn in 1783 was no picnic but hard labour interspersed with pleasures.

Darwin still had to meet the demands of his practice too, as shown by the remark about 'being obliged to go to Ipstoc'. People tended to be healthier in the summer, but there were more of them around because landed families usually returned from London to their country estates. The medical treatise Darwin had been writing for twelve years was now at a standstill. At this stage it was entitled 'Nosonomia', that is, the laws of diseases, though eventually published as Zoonomia; or the laws of organic life. He lent part of it to Wedgwood – 'MS books in parchment covers' – and in July 1783 he told Wedgwood he had lost two of these books. Probably he put them away too safely until he could start work again.

Darwin sometimes had to act as a vet as well as a doctor, and in September 1783 he gave advice on combating an infectious and deadly cattle disease that was rife in the Derby area. His careful account of the mortality traces the chain of infection from the first dead cow to all the others. This tale of detection is a reminder of the portrait of Darwin as a Sherlock Holmes manqué in Charles Sheffield's book of short stories, Erasmus Magister.[69] These stories are much more entertaining than Darwin's own real-life saga of the cows, which was nevertheless published in the Derby Weekly Entertainer for 29 September. Darwin's advice was to kill and bury any infected cattle when they began to be ill. It is a preview of the twentieth-century 'slaughter policy' for foot-and-mouth disease and bovine spongiform encephalopathy.

The usual procedure in Darwin's day was for uninfected cows to be 'blooded and purged'. He opposed this:

Blood-letting and purging are of the worst consequence; and, on the contrary, whatever contributes to encrease their strength makes them less liable to the infection.[70]

Good advice: yet, despite this insight into what now seems the obvious, Darwin did not condemn the universal practice of bleeding, purging and weakening human patients. With cattle, reason ruled; with humans, tradition over-ruled reason.

After the 'mortality of horned cattle' came intimations of mortality within the family. Erasmus's elder brother William Alvey Darwin died on 7 October 1783, aged fifty-seven. This must have seemed too close for comfort.

In his letter to Boulton in March 1783 Darwin wrote, 'We intend to pass this Summer at Radburn ... in the Autumn we design to return to Derby to reside for good (I hope) as they say'.[71] The move was made as planned.

CHAPTER TEN

Settled at Derby
1784–1787

The new home at Derby was near the centre of town, in Full Street, a three-storey terrace house[1] built in 1722, facing south-west with a frontage of about forty feet on Full Street. At the back was a large walled garden sloping down to the river Derwent, here about fifty yards wide. Across the river was an extensive orchard, which Darwin soon acquired.

As the renovations had taken more than a year, Elizabeth presumably insisted that the interior be remoulded closer to her heart's desire, and Fig. 12 (though depicting later events) shows the elegantly curved stairs. The photograph of the house just before it was demolished in 1933 (Plate 10B) does not do it justice. However, even when freshly decorated, it could not rival Radburn Hall, and Elizabeth must have been sad to leave her country home after nearly fifteen years there. It was some solace to her that they intended to return during the summer each year.

Their move into town was timely because the approaching winter proved to be severe, and so was the next one: the average temperature for these two winters is the lowest two-year average ever recorded in central England.[2] The front of their house would have been relatively warm because Full Street was fully built up on both sides. That was not the reason for its name. Full Street was so called because it had been the home of fullers – the textile workers who scoured and cleansed cloth and removed grease, and therefore needed plenty of water. Today there are fewer buildings in Full Street; the Darwins' house was opposite the present Assembly Rooms Car Park.

In Darwin's day there were several historic buildings nearby. Its neighbour to the south was Exeter House, where Prince Charles Edward set up his headquarters on 4 December 1745 on his march from Scotland towards London with 7000 men. He was welcomed to Derby by German Pole of Radburn Hall (Colonel Pole's uncle), who rode with the Prince to seek support from other landed gentry on 5 December.[3] This delay was fatal: if he had pushed on, the Pretender could have reached London, because the road was open. But a false report from a captured government spy, Eliezer Birch, persuaded the Jacobites that the Duke of Cumberland's army was lying in wait. The next morning, Black Friday as they called it, the Jacobites

FIG. 12 A scene of confusion in the house at Full Street, probably about 1790.
Francis Darwin, then about four years old and confined to bed after being bitten
by a dog, barks and growls like a dog to frighten his mother and the surgeon Mr
Hadley, who both fall down the stairs. Higher up the stairs are Susan and Mary
Parker (*left*), and Violetta and Emma Darwin. Erasmus comes from his study to
see what is happening. The drawing was made about forty years later by Francis's
daughter Violetta, based on the memories of her father and possibly also of some
of those on the stairs

marched back to Ashbourne – and eventually to Culloden. Just before they
left, Birch escaped from Exeter House and climbed over the wall into what
was later Darwin's garden. A desperate man, he jumped into the river,
swam downstream a little way and then ran naked for three miles to elude
the Jacobites, unaware of their departure in the opposite direction.[4]

To the north-west of the Darwins' house was All Saints' Church, which
became Derby Cathedral in 1927. At Lichfield he had been a hundred yards
from an ancient cathedral; here he was little further from a future one. No
one could say that he was not attracted to cathedrals.

He was just as close to the Cathedral of Technology, the Lombes' huge
silk mill, which stood on an island in the river a hundred yards from the
end of his garden. This, the first large mechanized factory, built in the
1720s, was driven by a water-wheel twenty-three feet in diameter which

worked 73,000 yards of silk thread every time it went round.[5] The Coal-brookdale iron foundries and the Derby silk mill are the joint birthplaces of the Industrial Revolution. It is fitting that the poet laureate of the Industrial Revolution should have lived so near, but strange that he never mentioned the silk mill in his poems.

There were other factories upstream. At Belper, seven miles north, was the textile mill of Jedediah Strutt,[6] based on patents for a stocking frame. At Cromford, seven miles further north, was the famous cotton mill of Richard Arkwright,[7] built with help from Strutt in 1771. Darwin soon got to know these two enterprising manufacturers: like Boulton and Keir, they were at the cutting edge of industrial advance, but they never became so friendly with Darwin. Still, they showed him that Derby, with only about 9000 people, could rival Birmingham in industrial innovation.

Derby was also well known for the manufacture of porcelain. William Duesbury was the owner of the porcelain factory – the Wedgwood of Derby, as it were.[8] But Darwin was never a close friend of either Duesbury or his son of the same name, who took over in 1786.

It is curious that Darwin should have come to live beside the river Derwent, which is marked as 'Darwen Flu.' in old maps,[9] the *e* and *a* being interchangeable. He had shown a liking for the river in his Ode five years before, when he had imagined that Eliza might 'bend her graceful footsteps to your brink'. Now she would really do so.

[2]

The abundant water flowing by in the Derwent would not have been good to drink because of the effluents from the silk mill upstream, and Darwin's most brilliant innovation at the house was to drill a new type of well, an 'artesian well' as it is now known. He explains its origin in a paper sent to the Royal Society in July 1784 and published in the *Philosophical Transactions*:

> I send you an account of an artificial spring of water, which I produced last summer near the side of the river Darwent in Derby.
>   Near my house was an old well ... about four yards deep, which had been many years disused on account of the badness of the water.... At the bottom was found a bed of red marl ...

About half a mile up river was a 'very copious spring', called St Alkmund's well,

> and having observed that the higher lands, at the distance of a mile or two behind these wells, consisted of red marl like that in the well; I concluded that, if I should

bore through this stratum of marl, I might probably gain a water similar to that of St. Alkmund's well, and hoped that at the same time it might rise above the surface of my old well to the level of St. Alkmunds's.

With this intent a pump was first put down for the purpose of more easily keeping dry the bottom of the old well, and a hole about two and a half inches diameter was then bored about thirteen yards below the bottom of the well, till some sand was brought up by the auger. A wooden pipe, which was previously cut in a conical form at one end, and armed with an iron ring at the other, was driven into the top of this hole, and stood up about two yards from the bottom of the well, and being surrounded with well-rammed clay, the new water ascended in a small stream through the wooden pipe.[10]

He then stopped up the old well, and the new water flowed up 'over the edges of the well'.

Here we see Darwin at his best, solving a practical problem by a bold idea and decisive engineering work to test the idea.

He then fixed a lead pipe from the well into the house 'for the agreeable purpose of procuring the water at all times quite cold and fresh'. This stream of water, which 'has now flowed about twelve months', was as pure as that in St Alkmund's well.

He next explains the principle of the artesian well. 'Many mountains bear incontestable marks of their having been forcibly raised by some power beneath them'. If the mountain is of 'conical form with the apex cut off',

the strata which compose the central parts of it, and which are found nearly horizontal in the plain, are raised almost perpendicularly, and placed upon their edges, while those on each side decline like the surface of the hill; so that this mountain may well be represented by a bur made by forcing a bodkin through several parallel sheets of paper.

If this model applies, the highest strata on the mountain are likely to be the lowest in the plains nearby (Fig. 13). The waters of springs in the mountain will then slide between two strata and

descend till they find or make themselves an outlet, and will in consequence rise to a level with the part of the mountain where they originated. And hence, if by piercing the earth you gain a spring between the second and third, or third and fourth stratum, it must generally happen that the water from the lowest stratum will rise the highest, if confined in pipes, because it comes originally from a higher part of the country in its vicinity.[11]

Such springs should grow stronger as they make themselves a wider channel through soluble materials, and these older stronger springs should also be purer, since at first they would be loaded with the 'soluble impurities'.

Darwin ends with a plea for the wider use of artesian wells for supplying water to houses, and for irrigation. He does not use the name 'artesian', which was not coined until the 1830s when a well in the Artois region of

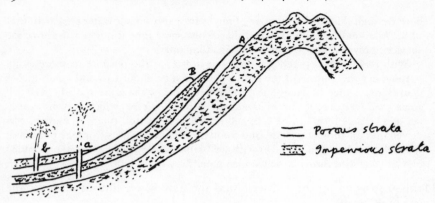

FIG. 13 Darwin's model for explaining 'artesian' wells. The wells marked 'a' and 'b' tap water originating at A and B respectively

France gave its name to the breed. It would be more logical to refer to 'darwinian wells'; but long usage generally prevails over logic.

Darwin's explanation of the artesian well is among the cleanest and clearest-cut of scientific discoveries – and one of the few to spring directly from a household problem. His idea has been of great practical value: half of southern England relies on artesian wells for its water supply. Many older wells were artesian, of course, but by chance rather than design.

His own well was commemorated by an iron plaque fixed to the garden wall[12] – and now in the Derby Museum.

[3]

The artesian well was among several fresh starts Darwin made on moving to Derby, and most of them succeeded.

One might better be called a restart: the Derby Philosophical Society. During the long summer at Radburn he had left the Society unfed, and it had nearly died. Now he rushed in to revive it. And how better to lift the spirits of the stodgier members than by flying a balloon? The first balloon flight in Britain was organized by Count Francesco Zambeccari, who sent up a hydrogen balloon five feet in diameter on 4 November 1783; three weeks later he released a larger hydrogen balloon, which flew forty miles from London into West Sussex.[13]

Darwin was not far behind, and may have been the first Englishman to fly a hydrogen balloon. He gives details in a letter to Wedgwood on 9 January 1784: 'Our air-balloon was at first a sphere of 4 ft. I then proposed to cut it in two at the equator, and add a torrid zone of nine inches breadth'.[14]

This was because he feared it might not be large enough to lift itself. The balloon was made of silk 'all cover'd with oil boil'd with red lead in it'. The hydrogen gas was generated by treating iron filings with dilute sulphuric acid (one part of 'oil of vitriol' to six parts of water). The gas was fed into two barrels filled with water under pressure, and it bubbled through into a pipe leading up to the balloon.

Darwin was disappointed that the balloon only flew for thirty miles before coming down: presumably the silk was rather heavy and the gas leaked through it. He makes a joke of the flight in a letter to Boulton on 17 January: 'We sent your society an air-balloon, which was calculated to have fallen in your garden at Soho; but the wicked wind carried to Sir Edward Littleton's'[15] – about fifteen miles north-west of Soho. The flight was probably on 26 December 1783, the only day for four weeks when the wind at Derby was a strong east-north-easter.[16]

Later in January Darwin wrote to Wedgwood again: 'I admire your idea of making an air-balloon of Gold-beater skin' – a thin animal membrane. 'If yours is made of skin it will I suppose hold the air well, and will be so light that one of 2 ft diameter will fly.'[17] Even these small balloons caused problems, so it is not surprising that Darwin never tried the more expensive and dangerous experiment of flying in a hot-air balloon.

The Derby Philosophical Society needed to be more formal than the Lunar Society because its members were not all friends of each other like the Lunaticks.

On 18 July 1784 the members gathered at Darwin's house to hear his presidential address. He spoke about the avenues by which science advances, citing the senses of touch and of vision as leading to arithmetic, geometry and the science of motion. The invention of the alphabet was a crucial advance because it allowed discoveries to be transmitted; and the invention of printing, 'like the Giant with a hundred hands', greatly accelerated the diffusion of knowledge. The printed scientific word has, he says,

> strangled the monstrous births of superstitious ignorance; and scatter'd among the great mass of mankind the happy contagion of science and of truth.[18]

Today this last phrase sounds wildly over-optimistic, a relic from a more innocent and hopeful age. But it is very Darwinian, shining like a good deed in a naughty world. Darwin passionately believed in the power 'of science and of truth' and in the idea of progress, exemplified in the Industrial Revolution, which he saw as machines to improve the lot of humankind.

Darwin urged the Derby Philosophical Society to help in the enlightenment by building up a library, 'which may hold our Society together'. Perhaps, too, 'by our own publications we may add something to the common Heap of knowledge; which I prophesy will never cease to accumulate, so long as the human footstep is seen upon the Earth.' That prophecy at least is still valid, even if the knowledge is not used well.

The idea of starting a library was a good one, because scholarly libraries were scandalously few at the time, and their rarity was a real bar to progress. Not everyone could borrow books from Sir Joseph Banks. Darwin did not have the power to choose the books himself; the Society was quite democratic, and he had no formal privileges as President.

The 'Laws and Regulations' of the Society[19] were adopted at its first full meeting on 7 August 1784. They were to meet at the King's Head Inn on the first Saturday of every month at 6 pm, a president and secretary being chosen by majority vote at the two 'annual meetings' in April and October. The entry fee was one guinea and the subscription one guinea a year, with a fine of one shilling for missing a meeting ('half-a-crown' for annual meetings). These fees and fines were quite steep: the subscription is equivalent to about £80 a year today and the fine to about £4 per meeting missed. The Society was for moneyed gentlemen, not the deserving poor.

This income was for purchasing 'books of natural history and philosophy' to be suggested by members and ordered by the president at every meeting, if approved by the members present. The books were to be circulated to members, each being allowed a fortnight's loan (for an octavo volume) and being fined at a rate of 'Two-pence a Day' on overdue books. This is again draconian, 'two pence' being equivalent to nearly £1 today. The system worked well. A 200-page 'Catalogue and Charging Ledger' for 1786–9 shows the dates of receipt and return by the members of more than a hundred books,[20] while a cash book records the fines for overdue books and absence. In 1786, for example, Darwin was absent on 4 August and 1 September, for which he was fined two shillings, and his fines for overdue books totalled nine shillings.[21]

These rules served the Society well for more than fifty years. A set of its rules in 1835 is almost identical,[22] and there is a catalogue of books which shows that by then the library had nearly 1200 volumes.

The Derby Philosophical Society was not a one-man band, like the Lichfield Botanical. The most helpful member and Darwin's deputy was William Strutt (1756–1830), who was a fanatical inventor[23] and became Darwin's closest friend in Derby. During its first few years the Society had about twelve local members and about fifteen non-residents. The locals include familiar names, such as Erasmus junior ('Mr Darwin'), Richard French, and Dr Beridge, and others whom we shall meet later: Samuel Fox, Dr John Pigot, the Revd Charles Hope, Dr W. B. Johnson and the surgeon Henry Hadley. The non-residents include Brooke Boothby and William Jackson, and Robert Bage joined in 1788. There was also a Secretary, Richard Roe, a schoolmaster, who was paid twelve guineas a year.[24]

The Derby Society never became as important as the Manchester Literary and Philosophical Society, of which Darwin was made an honorary member in 1784. Nonetheless, the Derby Society endured for over seventy years, organizing lectures and meetings until 1857, when it was merged with the Derby Museum and Library.[25]

[4]

Darwin's medical practice in Derby was already two years old, but he began one new project in 1784, a dispensary for the sick poor of the town. There was no infirmary or general hospital in Derbyshire to match those in Stafford or Birmingham. Darwin himself continued to give free advice to the local poor, but he felt that a central dispensary or clinic needed to be organized in the town. In his appeal for funds he decided to play on the fears of smallpox, which could easily spread from the poor to the moneyed classes:

> As the smallpox has already made great ravages in Derby, showing much malignity even at its commencement; and as it is now three years since it was last epidemic in this town, there is great reason to fear that it will become very fatal in the approaching spring, particularly amongst the poor, who want both the knowledge and the assistance necessary for the preservation of their children.[26]

Darwin proposed forming a society – yes, another one, the Derby medical aid society perhaps? – to be financed by subscriptions of one guinea a year. A room would be hired as a dispensary, and the doctors of the town would give their services free. To disarm criticism, he suggested the prescriptions should be taken in turn to each apothecary in the town. His hope was that this dispensary 'may prove to be the foundation stone of a future infirmary'. The dispensary, with Darwin's 'Derby Health Service', apparently did come into being, but I have not found any details about it. The infirmary was eventually built on the initiative of William Strutt[27] in 1810.

The move to Derby made Darwin even more famous medically, by extending his catchment area for patients. Among his new patients in these years was the fifth Duke of Devonshire at Chatsworth, the foremost public figure in the county, and the nephew of Darwin's school friend Lord George Cavendish.

The Duke suffered from inflammation of the liver and 'the rosy eruption of the face'. It was the demon drink at work, and Darwin was quite severe with the Duke. In a long letter he explains that alcohol damages the liver and that the injury is sometimes 'removed upon the joints, and causes the gout', or sometimes affects the face. After mentioning some palliatives Darwin comes to the crunch, saying that the problem will only be eased by obstinately persevering in drinking daily but a certain quantity of spirituous or fermented liquor, and this quantity should be about half that which you have been generally accustomed to.[28]

This was bad news for the Duke, and worse was to follow: 'I express myself strongly on this head, as I know in this kind of disease Health is not to be bought at any other price'.

Darwin also tells the Duke that inebriate drinking is much worse than gluttonous eating. Starch and sugar are natural foods,

but when this sugar is converted into spirit by fermentation ... our food is converted into poison; and becomes the greatest curse of the christian world, destroying more than the sword, and wisely interdicted by the disciples of Mahomet and Confucius.

This is perhaps the most strident outburst in any of Darwin's 450 surviving letters, and it is ironic that the victim of his tirade was not some drunken nobody but the Duke of Devonshire.

Reforming heavy drinkers by force of personality is no easy task, and Darwin's apparent success helped to build his 'legendary reputation'. Anna Seward tells us, 'It is well known that Dr Darwin's influence and example have sobered the county of Derby; that intemperance in fermented fluid of every species is almost unknown amongst its gentlemen'.[29] Maria Edgeworth says he thought 'vinous potation' caused most 'distempers of the higher classes of people'. She says 'he almost banished wine from the tables of the rich of his acquaintance; and persuaded most of the gentry in his own and the neighbouring counties to become water-drinkers'.[30] All this is difficult to believe: but even if the gentry did still drink in secret, the fact that people accepted such reports is proof of Darwin's high prestige.

Kindness to poor patients is another aspect of the legend, illustrated by a story that Charles Darwin quoted because he had traced it back 'through four distinct channels to my grandfather, whose veracity has never been doubted by anyone who knew him':

As the doctor was riding at night on the road to Nottingham a man on horseback passed him, to whom he said good night. As the man soon slackened his pace, Dr. Darwin was forced to pass him, and again spoke, but neither time did the man give any answer. A few nights afterwards a traveller was robbed at nearly the same spot by a man who, from the description, appeared to be the same.[31]

Apparently Darwin later visited the robber in prison, and he admitted that he was bent on robbery, but added: 'I thought it was you, and when you spoke I was sure of it. You saved my life many years ago, and nothing could make me rob you.'

The highwayman and the Duke of Devonshire illustrate Darwin's complete lack of class consciousness. He seems to have been more polite to the highwayman than to the Duke. They also show how Darwin's patients were spread right across the social scale. He tried to help everyone – not always successfully, but he did his best.

[5]

The most important of Darwin's fresh starts in 1784, and the basis of his future national fame, was the decision to publish his poem *The Loves of the Plants*. He had written the first draft at various times over the previous five or six years, much of it probably at Radburn during the late summer of 1783, when he had almost finished his work on the *System of Vegetables*. The poem is a versified romp through the Linnaean system, a frivolous follow-up of the translation. Although the poem was almost complete in 1784, five more years passed before it was published, anonymously.

Darwin's reluctance to publish in his own name seems almost neurotic. But we have the benefit of hindsight, and he would have argued that he had good reason for caution. Several earlier physicians who had ventured into verse, such as John Armstrong and Mark Akenside, had suffered setbacks in their careers.

It could only have been Elizabeth who persuaded him to publish, even if he would not use his own name. From his courtship poems she well knew his great talents as a writer of verse and she probably regretted the hundreds of hours he spent on the Linnaean translations. She would have been delighted to read *The Loves of the Plants*. Here was something worthy of his talents and something she could take a real interest in. She had an aristocratic attitude to money: it just flowed in; you didn't have to worry about it. Erasmus, like his Lunar friends Boulton, Keir, Watt and Wedgwood, felt he had to continue working hard to earn the money that would preserve his family from penury in the future. Elizabeth would have been in favour of publication and unconcerned about fears of damage to his medical practice.

Darwin followed Fuseli's advice and sent his poem to Joseph Johnson, soon to become the leading radical publisher of the time.[32] Johnson's reply, through Fuseli, provoked an unusually cautious letter from Darwin to Johnson on 23 May 1784. After expressing confidence in Johnson, he states his conditions:

> 1. I would not have my name affix'd to this work on any account, as I think it would be injurious to me in my medical practise, as it has been to all other physicians who have published poetry.
> 2. I would not wish to part with the intire coppy-right....
> I would propose ... that we publish one edition consisting of 500 copies, at our

joint equal expense, and equal profits, and afterwards, if you think proper, to publish another edition of 500 copies....

The above refers to the work only, which you have seen, call'd the *second part* of the botanical garden; for I would not yet bind myself to publish the first part, which I believe will consist of but 400 lines, but which will have 3 or 4 times the quantity of notes, and those of more learned, and newer matter, but half of which are not yet done.[33]

This 'first part' grew into *The Economy of Vegetation*: it was probably not yet started apart from the notes, because the final version ran to 2448 lines rather than the 400 he predicted. With *The Loves of the Plants*, however, the published version was probably the 1784 draft with minor additions and some revisions.

Later in his letter, Darwin asks Johnson for criticisms of the poem, 'as I am unacquainted with what is like to make a book sell'. He says that Fuseli has kindly promised 'some ornament for the work', and also offers to have the book printed at Lichfield, so that he could correct the press himself. This suggestion was eventually adopted. But it was three years before Darwin finally brought himself to agree that the poem should be published.

[6]

Darwin's old Lunar friends were not forgotten among the fresh starts. The letters surviving from 1784 include one to Boulton and seven to Wedgwood. I would guess that he also wrote to Edgeworth, Keir and Watt during the year. I can only quote excerpts from letters that still exist, and the accident of survival does create a bias. However, the main bias does reflect reality because Wedgwood was now the closest of his Lunar friends.

The delicate question of Darwin's loan to Boulton was settled early in 1784. Darwin wrote on 17 January: 'If it be not very inconvenient to you to pay me the 200£ (as you seem'd to say when I had the pleasure of seeing you), it would be very acceptable to me at this time'.[34] Boulton was unable to repay Thomas Day's larger loan, and Day was eventually driven to sarcasm: 'I have been employed in the unentertaining ceremonial of soliciting for near three years what it appears to me I have so good a right to'.[35] Boulton treated the money borrowed from his friends as part of his working capital, rather than a loan to be repaid. In the end Day got the money, at the expense of his friendship with Boulton.

Darwin's letters to Wedgwood became much more scientific in 1784. Three years earlier Wedgwood had begun experiments on a pyrometer, to measure very high temperatures, and he devised a method depending on the contraction of pieces of clay. Wedgwood's pyrometer was described in the *Philosophical Transactions* in 1782, and he became a Fellow of the Royal Society in 1783. Darwin's first letter in January 1784 offers some ideas for improving the pyrometer, and then shoots off to the other extreme of temperature, boldly announcing: 'I am endeavouring to produce greater cold than has been done, if I succeed I will acquaint you'.[36] Perhaps he was inspired by the very cold weather that month, but evidently he did not succeed.

In March Wedgwood wrote to Darwin with the erroneous idea that water vapour freezes more easily than liquid water, citing 'hoar frost, etc' in support. Darwin wrote a very long and diplomatic scientific letter on 11 March: 'Now this same et caetera, my dear friend, seems to be to be a gentleman of such consequence ... that I wish he would unfold himself a little more'.[37] Darwin then discusses the melting of ice or snow and the freezing of water, and states the principle of latent heat of fusion, discovered by Joseph Black in the 1760s: 'Thus ice in freezing gives out heat suddenly, and in thawing gives out cold suddenly'.

Having mollified Wedgwood with this lengthy letter, Darwin wrote again two days later. Probably ashamed of his previous double-speak, he refers to 'the error of your proposition' and explains the reasons. Wedgwood replied with a new question, why ice-cold water expands when it freezes into ice. No one knew. But Darwin did his best to answer, saying it may be due to some gas trapped 'in small moleculae in the ice'[38] – an ingenious though erroneous guess.

In the next letter, on 1 April, Darwin suggests that all metallic bodies crystallize on cooling. He also says that explosions in icy mountains are caused by 'water from thawing ice in the daytime filling valleys in the remaining ice' and then 'cracking the old ice by its expansion at freezing'.[39]

At the end of each letter Darwin flips over from the scientific to the social and personal. On 11 March 'our little boy [Edward] has got the ague, and will not take the bark'. On 13 March

> Mrs Darwin says she hears your whole family are going to town in a body, like a caravan going to Mecca; and we therefore hope you will make Derby a resting place, and recruit yourselves and your Camels for a few days, after having travel'd over the burning sands of Cheadle and Uttoxeter.[40]

He adds, 'You will find three spare beds in our Caravansery'. On 1 April he mentions that 'Mrs and Miss Manwaring are come to make some stay with us ... but we can make ample room for you'. Elizabeth is uneasy, he says, because 'Miss Pole is ill of a rheumatic fever at Cambden house': she was now thirteen and at school in London, and Erasmus hoped Sally Wedgwood would call to see her there. Both the children recovered as spring advanced.

The domestic event of the summer was the birth of their second daughter, Emma, on 24 August 1784. As a child she suffered measles and scarlet fever at the same time, and afterwards she never enjoyed really good health. But she was remembered by one of her nieces as 'very beautiful and agreeable'.

And what of her beautiful and agreeable mother, who had now given birth for three years in succession? Elizabeth was far from being exhausted by 'the frequency of her maternal situation': she cruised through life with an unruffled exuberance, and no one criticized her, not even Anna Seward. She seems to have enjoyed the love and affection of all her children and grandchildren. She was probably too lax in disciplining them, but Erasmus regarded this as her domain and he welcomed her smiling optimism, which made life so pleasant at the house in Full Street.

Erasmus rarely saw his old house at Lichfield now, but he still had patients in the town and would sometimes make a social call. Anna Seward told Hayley on 23 December 1784 that he had recently visited her. They walked to Mr Saville's garden, and Darwin told her about Kalmia, 'a flower of such exquisite beauty, that would make you waste the summer's day in examining it: – you would forget the hour of dinner; all your senses would be absorbed in *one*; you would be all *eye*'. She asked its colour. 'Precisely that of a seraph's plume', he replied, and later admitted he had never seen it.[41]

Anna was happy. On the strength of *Louisa, a Poetic Novel*, published earlier in the year, she completed her ascent to the heights of national literary fame. Not only was she now the Swan of Lichfield but also ruler of the roost locally, because Samuel Johnson had died in London on 13 December after spending the autumn at Lichfield.

[7]

It was full steam ahead in 1784 for Darwin as an inventor, and he set off down some new tracks. He filled thirty-one pages in the Commonplace Book, probably more than in any other year. Thirteen of those pages are devoted to a new interest, spinning machines for use in textile manufacture, with many detailed drawings of what he thought were better designs. His was no cloistered talent: he was driven by what went on in the world around. His interest in spinning machines had arisen through meeting Arkwright and the Strutts, the leading local spinners of cotton – and money.

It was fifteen years since Richard Arkwright had patented a 'water-frame' for spinning cotton with rollers powered by water. Joining forces with two other manufacturers, Jedediah Strutt of Derby and Samuel Need of Nottingham, Arkwright had built a mill at Cromford employing 300 workers, and seen by historians as one of the important take-off points of the Industrial Revolution; it is now being preserved and restored.

Darwin was fascinated by Arkwright's machinery and made himself the master of all the recent improvements, as well as trying to devise more.[42] He explains the mechanism clearly in The Loves of the Plants, first in a note and then in twelve lines of verse. The last four lines will show the style:

With quicken'd pace *successive rollers* move,
And these retain, and those extend the *rove*;
Then fly the spoles, the rapid axles glow,
And slowly circumvolves the labouring wheel below.[43]

The slow rotation of the waterwheel producing via gears the quick rotation of the spinning machinery is in itself a source of wonder and inspiration to Darwin.

As F. D. Klingender pointed out, Darwin's burning faith in the new technology validates the verse. Such lines were an easy target for parody, 'for where the faith is lacking the form becomes ridiculous'.[44] When Darwin was later satirized by George Canning and his co-authors in The Loves of the Triangles, they chose to pervert these lines into a picture of a roasting-spit:

The spiral *grooves* in smooth meanders flow,
Drags the long *chain*, the polish'd axles glow,
While slowly circumvolves the piece of beef below.[45]

Though Darwin's verse is open to parody, his prose description of the cotton spinning is not, and he foresees the development of industrial Lancashire in the nineteenth century when he predicts that 'the clothing of this small seed [cotton] will become the principal clothing of mankind. Though animal wool and silk may be preferable in colder climates, as they are more imperfect conductors of heat, and are thence a warmer clothing.'[46]

Darwin's interest in Cromford mill was heightened by what he thought was an injustice to Arkwright. He wrote to Boulton on 26 January 1785:

I was desired lately to look at the specification of Mr Arkwright's patent, about which He had a trial last year; and it was in my opinion unjustly given against him.... The essential parts of the machine are described in the specification in my opinion.[47]

He tries to rouse Boulton's sympathy by pointing out how the Boulton-and-Watt patents might be subverted because they had failed to mention that the piston was worked in oil.

Darwin knew that Boulton and Watt disliked Arkwright: only three months earlier Watt had written, 'as to Mr Arkwright, he is to say no worse one of the most self sufficient Ignorant men I have ever met with'.[48] But as Darwin had agreed to help Arkwright, he now approached Boulton with diplomatic language:

> I believe some shyness has existed between you and Mr Arkwright, but is it not your interest to assist him with your evidence on his trial? Which also may make good humour between you, and you make fire-engines for cotton-works in future.

Darwin suggests that 'you should defend each other from the ingratitude of mankind'. And since 'his case comes on the 14th of February', the matter is urgent.

With this letter Darwin achieved a near-miracle: Boulton and Watt accepted his argument and did an immediate U-turn. Only Darwin could have persuaded them; but he had done himself no favour, for he could not now back out. So it was that Darwin and Watt found themselves travelling to London a fortnight later, in the middle of the coldest February since the great freeze of 1740 (and it was followed by the coldest-ever March). They appeared as witnesses for Arkwright at the Court of Common Pleas on 17 February 1785. Thanks to their help, Arkwright won the case.

But that was not the end of the trials. Because of a conflict with an earlier decision, there was another hearing before the King's Bench in June. This time, with warmer weather, Erasmus combined business with pleasure, because Elizabeth seized the chance of a visit to London and travelled with him.[49] (She was not yet pregnant again.) They arrived on 15 June, with no servant, stayed at Wedgwood's house in Great George Street, and started their journey back to Derby on 21 June. Watt and Darwin again testified that the specifications in the patent were adequate to reconstruct the water-frame. The verdict went against Arkwright, probably because of doubts about the originality of the patent. Arkwright was furious, and there was a good deal of further lobbying for new parliamentary bills on cotton and wool-spinning: Wedgwood, Arkwright, Watt and Banks were all involved, but there is no mention of Darwin, who had probably had more than enough of this contentious and irrelevant business.

[8]

Arkwright's patent was not the only controversy of 1785: there was a further skirmish with Withering. Although five years had passed, his attack on Darwin's dead son still rankled as deeply as ever. Unwilling to cede the rights in foxglove to his rival, Darwin wrote a paper entitled 'An Account of the Successful Use of Foxglove in some Dropsies …' which he sent to the

College of Physicians in London on 14 January. It was read on 16 March, and published in the *Medical Transactions* later in the year.[50] Darwin claims success in most of the cases he cites.

Darwin's paper carries an appendix by the eminent physician Sir George Baker, who describes an unsuccessful treatment by digitalis and says that its use may have been known to Pliny. The paper ends with a plaintive footnote: 'While the last pages of this volume were in the press Dr Withering published a large number of cases'. This was Withering's *Account of the Foxglove*, which superseded Darwin's paper.

Withering was a quarrelsome man. Probably nettled by Darwin's paper, he launched a venomous counter-attack. The favourable review of the Lichfield Society's translation of Linnaeus in the *Monthly Review* included a comment on Withering's 'overstrained notions of delicacy'. Withering immediately sent in a libellous six-page letter beginning: 'I either must suppose the reviewer to be in the secret counsels of the Lich Society, or that the Article was written by the Society itself'.[51] Withering also complains that the Society stole his system of accentuation, upset a friend of his who was about to translate the *Systema Vegetabilium*, and used his advice without acknowledgment – though in fact Darwin rejected his terminology. The editor, Wedgwood's friend Ralph Griffiths, politely refuted Withering and assured him that the reviewer was 'indeed a most respectable man'[52] (actually Dr Samuel Goodenough).

Encouraged by this review, Darwin started to translate Linnaeus's *Genera Plantarum*, presumably from an outdated edition because on 17 August he wrote to Charles Blagden, Secretary of the Royal Society, asking his help in procuring the latest edition.[53]

[9]

Domestically, 1785 was uneventful, apart from the two journeys to London. Joseph Wright had nearly completed his paintings for Josiah Wedgwood, so the Wedgwoods probably stayed at the Darwins' house while on the way to or from London. Wright was also finishing the *View of Gibraltar*, his largest and most expensive painting (£420), now lost. Darwin saw the picture, which showed the destruction of the Spanish fleet: 'The Giberalter is indeed sublime', Darwin says, and mentions it (as Calpè) as part of his tribute to Wright in *The Loves of the Plants*:

> So Wright's bold pencil from Vesuvio's height
> Hurls his red lavas to the troubled night;
> From Calpè starts the intolerable flash,
> Skies burst in flames, and blazing oceans dash ...[54]

Wright lived 500 yards from Darwin and needed quite frequent medical or psychological treatment; so Darwin had the privilege of seeing Wright's later paintings in his house, sometimes finished, sometimes in progress. However, Darwin probably never saw *The Orrery* or *The Air Pump*, which were in private hands.

In 1785 Wright was one of the painters derided in the popular series of satires by 'Peter Pindar' (John Wolcot). In reply, it seems, Darwin wrote a 358-line manuscript poem 'To Peter Pindar', a rough and hurried satire on satires. In the course of his poem Darwin warmly defends Wright, 'for whom no verse of mine / Can e'er ascend to merits such as thine'.[55]

There is another artistic judgment in Darwin's letter to Wedgwood of 14 January: 'I have seen two of Fuseli's paintings. He is certainly great in subjects of imagination – fairies, witches, daemons &c are all his own.'[56] Fuseli later drew seven of the illustrations for Darwin's poems.

This letter also has some medical news. Wedgwood had asked him about the illness of Mr Inge, his first patient. In reply Darwin says that Dr Trevor Jones, his successor at Lichfield, has told him that Inge was better, and was being treated by Dr Withering. That was enough to keep Darwin away. Inge died within a month – another black mark for Withering. 'Saved by Darwin, 1756; lost by Withering, 1785' may have suggested itself to Darwin as an epitaph for Inge.

Another voice from the past was that of Darwin's boyhood friend Richard Dixon. Darwin still kept in touch and had advised Dixon to slim. The outcome inspires a jokey letter on 18 March:

> I am glad you find yourself better by losing 7£ – you may say with the Irishman 'you have gained a loss' – but I should not advise you to sink yourself any further.[57]

Darwin recommends Dixon to get false teeth, preferably 'made of *ivory* instead of the bone of the *seahorse*'. He says he gave the same advice to his brother at Elston (Robert?), 'but I believe he thought it a sin and would not at all listen to me about it'. He also tells Dixon about Mary Parker, who had married Joseph Day in 1782: 'She is got into her new house at No. 21 Prospect Row, Birmingham, and has a good-tempered man for her husband and is very happy I believe'. Presumably Dixon knew her at Elston. Dixon seems to have been a radical and an unbeliever. Darwin addresses his letter 'Richard Dixon, Citizen', and ends it with: 'Adieu. God bless you if it be possible.' Three months later, when he was in London during June, Darwin wrote to Dixon suggesting they should meet.[58]

The year 1786 was no warmer than 1785, and the three-year average for 1784–6 is the lowest on record, a mini ice-age created by the volcano in Iceland. The severe weather must have made Darwin's medical journeys difficult, and as late as 22 March he comments on the snow being 'so much more than I expected'. The cold would also have made home life less pleasant; but they were better off in Derby than out at Radburn.

The house in Full Street seems to have met their needs well, but they had a problem with a pernickety neighbour, Mr Upton, a lawyer. The trouble had begun four years earlier, when Upton complained about Darwin enlarging a cellar window. Darwin wrote a very polite letter saying that he had stopped up five of the old windows looking into Upton's property and had a legal right to enlarge the cellar window. Upton was determined to cause trouble, and in 1785 deliberately obstructed one of Darwin's windows. Darwin took him to court, and won. Upton fumed and fulminated but could find no legal redress. So in 1786 he let off steam by writing a pamphlet stating his case.[59]

Elizabeth would have laughed at such male fussing: she had weightier matters to deal with, for her next child, a son Francis, was born on 17 June 1786. On the previous day Elizabeth had fainted when a murderer's bone fell nearby as she was passing a gibbet. The shock may have speeded the birth, but the gibbet cast no shadow over the long and adventurous life of the new baby. He was as a boy the most unruly of Elizabeth's sons, and in later years the best known – Sir Francis Sacheverel Darwin, a doctor and an intrepid traveller.

Time was not standing still for the growing brood of Darwins and Poles. In 1786 Erasmus's daughter Susan Parker was fourteen and Mary was twelve, while Elizabeth's daughters Elizabeth and Milly Pole were sixteen and twelve respectively. Her son Sacheverel, seventeen, was in his last year at Harrow. Then there were the four young Darwins, Edward (four), Violetta (three), Emma (two) and the baby Francis. All in all, there can scarcely have been a dull moment, and at times chaos probably reigned supreme in that full house in Full Street.

The bustle in the house did not disturb Erasmus in his study, unless it escalated unbearably as in Fig. 12. He was well used to concentrating in noisy environments, and people said he wrote his poems while on his medical journeys, the verses being shaken out of him. This appealing myth seems to be a mere fiction: none of his letters bear the marks of having been written on the road.

Some letters of 1786 do look different from any others because they are blotched copies on flimsy paper, taken with a Watt copying press. The letters[60] are nearly all of medical advice. Darwin probably decided he ought to keep full copies rather than notes, and, having no news from Greville about his own copying machine, decided to buy one of Watt's. He used it for about two years.

He did not see much of his Lunar friends in 1786, apart from Wedgwood, who seems to have made several visits to Derby. It was a sad time for the Wedgwoods because their eight-year-old daughter Mary Anne, whom Darwin had treated with opium as a baby, was still chronically ill. He seemed to have given up hope by now; and on 4 April said she should have 'no medicine at all':[61] she died on 21 April.

Darwin continued to exchange letters with Edgeworth, who was as full of ideas as ever. He was laying down light railways, with a number of small carriages linked together, to take lime and marl across his Irish estates. Edgeworth was unwell in 1786 and told Darwin 'I never took any drug except of your prescription'. Darwin treated him by post, successfully it seems. Later in the year Darwin wrote a humorous letter against alcohol, because he suspected Edgeworth had fallen in with Irish customs and had been drinking too freely. The letter was burnt, but Maria Edgeworth remembered that he ended it: 'Farewell, my dear friend. God keep you from whiskey – if he can.'[62] The suspicion was groundless, because Edgeworth was famous in Ireland for his temperance. Edgeworth turned the tables by asking Darwin to explain why the Irish, nearly all of whom 'drink intemperately of whiskey-punch', usually live to a ripe age. His reply is not known.

Darwin's substitute for the Lunar Society, the Derby Philosophical Society, met throughout 1786 at the King's-Head Inn. Was 'vinous potation' permitted, I wonder? Darwin presided at nearly every meeting, though Erasmus junior seems to have given up attending towards the end of the year.

Despite this truancy, the young Erasmus pleased his father by making such a success of his legal career. Though nominally independent, he lived quite close and seems not to have wished to escape from his father's influence. Now twenty-six, he was keen on travelling and quick to make friends. A few years earlier the Devonshire poet Richard Polwhele became friendly with him on a coach journey from Truro to Bristol, after Erasmus had been with Boulton in Cornwall. Polwhele called him 'an intelligent and enlightened companion. We parted at Bristol with tears reciprocally shed! So rapid in their growth are the friendships of the young!'[63]

We have already seen how the young Erasmus had become friendly with Boulton, Keir, Small, Whitehurst, Bentley and Edgeworth. He was also well acquainted with the Wedgwood family, whom he met on their visits to Derby. His closest friend and the nearest in age among the Lunar group was Thomas Day, whom he often visited and travelled with. Cultivating and keeping such a distinguished group of friends calls for continuous effort. I suspect that the young Erasmus built on the role he played in his teens of writing to Lunar friends on behalf of his father, and began to see himself in the guise of a seventeenth-century 'communicator' like Samuel Hartlib, keeping the philosophers in touch with each other. As part of this perceived role, he was keen to help his father by acting as courier on visits to London: for example, he probably took the manuscript of *The Loves of the Plants* to Fuseli or Johnson.

The young Erasmus seems to have been satisfied with his life as one of the many bachelor-Darwins, like his uncles Robert and John, and later two of his half-brothers. Like most male Darwins he was tall, about six feet two inches. He was very intelligent but, to judge from his letters, tended to fuss about trivialities. He lacked the energy to be a great doer like his father and had none of his father's genius for seeing into the heart of things.

For Darwin's son Robert the years 1784–7 were crucial, and his experiences are a story in themselves.

[10]

Robert Darwin's early life was not easy, though he had many advantages to compensate for his problems. His first and worst blow was the death of his mother when he was just four years old. The shock must have been severe, for he was Polly's youngest and favourite child. However, the early arrival of Aunt Sukey and Mary Parker, who looked after him well, helped to soften the trauma. He would have been too young to know about his father's liaison with Mary Parker, but when he was nearly twelve another trauma came upon him with the death of his brother Charles, who may well have been a role model for him.

Soon after Charles's death, his father decided Robert should become a doctor. Today this may seem a high-handed action, but in the eighteenth century it was normal. The sons of the middling gentry like the Darwins had the choice of the Law, the Army or Navy, the Church or Medicine (the eldest son sometimes had extra options, as squire or Member of Parliament). Two of Erasmus's brothers entered the legal profession and one the Church. Of the sons of his second marriage, one went into the Army, one became a doctor and one a clergyman (though this was after Erasmus's death). Robert's elder brother was already training to be a lawyer; his father was hostile to the armed forces – 'I hate war' – and did not have much respect for the religious fraternity at Lichfield because he thought too many did too little. But he wanted one son to follow him as a doctor. Thus it was more inevitable than inequitable that Robert began to tread a medical path from 1778 onwards.

The process began in the spring of 1779, when Robert went to the Wedgwood-Darwin school. He liked it: 'I think every day of the happyniss I enjoyed at Etruria',[64] the twelve-year-old wrote to Josiah. After that he may have had a tutor or gone to boarding school, though not in London because he says in his notebook that he 'first went to London January 22 1781, second time in autumn of the year'.[65] Elsewhere, in 'extracts from old pocket books', he says, 'I left Lichfield on 30 March 1781....Went to London 21 Jan 1782'.[66] Probably he went to London in both years to attend William Hunter's lectures on anatomy, like his father before him. From 1746 to 1782 Hunter gave two sessions each winter: one in the autumn, ending about Christmas; the second beginning 'about January the 20th'.[67] This fits the dates when Robert 'went to London'.

After these lecture courses Robert entered the Edinburgh Medical School. He was there in the autumn of 1783 when he was seventeen, and it may be that he started in the previous autumn. At Edinburgh the memory of Charles had bound Dr Andrew Duncan to the Darwin family. Duncan was now a leading academic, and six times president of the Royal Medical Society.[68] He looked after Robert with much kindness, soon introducing him to several of the professors, including Joseph Black. Robert was not brilliant like Charles, but he had a very good memory. Everyone spoke well of him and he seems to have handled his eminent acquaintances with good judgment.

Robert left Edinburgh in 1784 for two terms at the other great medical school of Europe, Leyden in Holland. He set sail from England on 11 October 1784, probably with Peter Crompton of Derby, and arrived in Leyden on 14 October[69]. He took examinations there on 9-11 December and was awarded his doctor's degree on 2 February 1785 after presenting a thesis on ocular spectra – the colours seen in the eye as after-images. He was still three months short of his nineteenth birthday.

After this apparently effortless progress (or was it forced growth?), Robert travelled into France at quite a leisurely pace. He left Leyden on 4 February and arrived in Paris on 14 March, remaining there for about three months, presumably to study medicine further. His was an education with no expense spared: his father was keen to give him the best possible chance to succeed as a doctor.

Two pages have survived of a letter written by Erasmus to Robert at 'L'Hotel de Luxembourg' in Paris during the spring of 1785. One page is largely devoted to a theory of how winds blowing towards mountains create huge eddies. Erasmus asks Robert to 'mention this theory with my best respects to Dr Franklin if you have the pleasure of seeing him'.[70] Once again Robert was meeting all the best people, and he was kindly received by Franklin. Erasmus ends the letter: 'I hope you are not quite so thin as you wer – adieu from dear Robt / your affect. friend and father / E. Darwin'. He adds as a postscript, 'I shall do nothing about your thesis, you will do what you please, when you return'.

Robert arrived at Derby on 23 July, seemingly in high spirits. When he visited Lichfield, Anna Seward said he was 'grown to an uncommon height, gay and blooming as a morn of summer'.[71] Like his brother Erasmus, he was about six feet two inches tall, and quite slender at this age, though later he expanded into 'the largest man whom I ever saw', in the words of his son Charles.[72]

In the autumn of 1785 Robert returned for a further year at Edinburgh, and in the summer of 1786 he was ready to practise medicine. On hearing of a vacancy in Shrewsbury, after the death of Dr Owen there, Robert set off for Shropshire on 28 August with his brother Erasmus. They stayed overnight with Robert Clive near Market Drayton, and he went with them to Shrewsbury: 'Young Dr Darwin ... is a very clever worthy young man', Clive wrote, 'and I should have great pleasure in being of service to him'.[73]

Robert was pleased with what he found at Shrewsbury and decided to start a practice there. His father had given him £20 and said, 'Let me know when you want more, and I will send it to you'.[74] His uncle at Elston also sent him £20. After this initial funding of £40, equivalent to about £3300 today, Robert never needed to ask for more, so successful was he. He had fifty patients within six months, and his son Charles wrote: 'I have heard him say that his practice during the first year allowed him to keep two horses and a man-servant'. It was helpful to be the son of the legendary Dr Darwin, but Robert himself deserves all credit for his great success. His earnings in the first ten months (31 August 1786 to 30 June 1787) were £55, increasing in the next year to £259. In the year after that, when he was twenty-two, his income was £520, equivalent to about £40,000 today. Soon he was earning more than his father, and in 1813 he received £3610 in fees.[75]

Robert's splendid start as a doctor was matched by a scientific success. His doctoral thesis at Leyden, with some alterations, was published as a thirty-page paper, 'New experiments on the Ocular Spectra of Light' by Robert W. Darwin, in the *Philosophical Transactions* of the Royal Society.[76] The subject of the paper is the image left on the retina after gazing intently at a coloured pattern. For example, if you stare at a circular yellow patch for about a minute, and then cover your eyes, you will see a violet after-image of the same size and shape; if the original is red, the after-image is green; if the original is blue, the after-image is orange.

Robert's paper describes a series of experiments on ocular spectra. It is dated '1 November 1785', but his thesis was examined nine months earlier, when he was eighteen. It is well written, in a mature style. Was Erasmus at work under a filial pseudonym? The suspicion deepens when we find that Robert never wrote another scientific paper: his son Charles, who revered him, says that his father did not have a scientific mind. Of the paper on ocular spectra Charles says: 'I believe he was largely aided in writing it by his father'.[77] Twelve years earlier Erasmus had told Benjamin Franklin, 'I have another very curious Paper containing Experiments on the Colours seen in the closed Eye after having gazed some Time on luminous Objects'.[78] Presumably Erasmus kept this paper and then, when Robert had to write a thesis, took the paper out of the cupboard, helped him with further experiments and the writing up, and set him up as the author. Erasmus was ready to bend the rules in a good cause, and what better cause than the career of his son? Moralists may condemn him, much as they might condemn the millions of middle-class parents who have helped with their children's homework in the belief that doing well at school improves a child's prospects in life. It often does, and did with Robert.

His paper was the first scientific study of after-images, and it impressed later researchers such as Goethe, Helmholtz and Thomas Young.

The paper also describes the colour-top, a disc painted with different colours in different sectors. When spun rapidly, it appears to be of one colour, determined by the colours of the individual sectors and their proportions. If the red sector is removed, the spinning disc looks green, the paper tells us. There is a mystery of timing here, because Thomas Young is usually credited with the invention of the colour-top, in 1801. Yet Samuel Galton wrote a paper about it[79] in 1782 (not published until 1799), and this may have been used by the Darwins. However, Galton never wrote another scientific paper, so it may be that Erasmus had the idea of the top during his experiments in 1774, and later told Galton, who then developed it further.

Robert was not as keen on science as Erasmus would have liked. How could he be roused? Why not have him elected a Fellow of the Royal Society? Boulton, Keir and Watt had become Fellows in 1785; Whitehurst, Edgeworth and Wedgwood were already Fellows. So there was a Lunar quorum of signatories available. Erasmus wrote to Wedgwood on 8 May 1787, saying that he wished Robert 'to be a Member of the Royal Society, as it would be a feather in his cap, and might encourage him in philosophical pursuits; and I flatter myself He will make an useful member of that ingenious society'.[80] The paper on ocular spectra would have justified Robert's election, if he had done the work himself.

As usual, Erasmus's efforts were successful. Robert was proposed for election on 15 November 1787, and his certificate has eleven signatures, the first four being 'Charles Greville, Josiah Wedgwood, James Watt, Matthew Boulton'. Erasmus himself was tactful enough not to sign. Robert was elected F.R.S. three months later at the age of twenty-one, but he did nothing for the Royal Society during his sixty years of Fellowship – except for nurturing his son Charles.

Robert's early career in medicine and science sounds like a triumphant success story. So it was in most respects, but there was a down-side to it: although probably the highest-earning provincial physician in England, Robert hated being a doctor and could not stand the sight of blood. For that reason Robert always felt some resentment against his father for making him take up medicine.

Robert had another source of complaint, according to his son Charles:

> from my father's conversation, I infer that Dr Darwin had acted towards him in his youth rather harshly and imperiously, and not always justly; and though in after years he felt the greatest interest in his son's success, and frequently wrote to him with affection, in my opinion the early impression on my father's mind was never quite obliterated.[81]

There is no sign of any harsh words in the fifty-seven long letters from Erasmus to Robert that have survived. Just the opposite: they are written with affection, as Charles says and as is also shown by their being so numerous and lengthy. Again, after Erasmus's death, Robert was active and assiduous in defending him against slanders in journals.

Any 'imperious' action by Erasmus must have occurred much earlier. Could it have been in 1781 when Erasmus was busy getting married and might have neglected Robert? This seems unlikely: Elizabeth was a professional mother and she would have been careful to avoid the 'wicked stepmother' label by treating him kindly. She was always on good terms with Robert. Perhaps Robert resented being sent off to Hunter's lectures at an early age (he was not yet fifteen) and felt he was being pushed too far and too fast? Possibly, but the opposite seems more likely: Robert may have felt everything was made too easy. He just walked into Edinburgh, Leyden and the Royal Society without having to do anything. He was not allowed any choices. His road was not only signposted beforehand but also made smooth for him. He could not take credit for any of it; he probably felt no sense of achievement; even his thesis may have been provided ready-made. His complete lack of interest in scientific matters after he graduated could have been a reaction against this overplanning of his student years.

[11]

During 1786, the year when Robert settled at Shrewsbury, Erasmus was much occupied in designing oil lamps, which he hoped Wedgwood would make and market. He wrote nine long letters about lamps to Wedgwood between March and December, and three more the next year, illustrated with drawings of several different basic designs.[82]

The Lunar group took a keen interest in the oil lamp invented in 1782 by

Aimé Argand. This had a tubular wick and a glass chimney, which induced an upward current of air on both the inside and outside of the wick and produced a continuous bright light almost free of smoke and smell. Boulton and Small had designed a similar lamp in the 1770s, and Boulton obtained rights to manufacture the metal parts of the Argand lamp.

Darwin thought he could do better, and Wedgwood encouraged him. Darwin's first design, in the Commonplace Book with the date 30 November 1785, has a doughnut-shaped lump of lead to compress the oil bladder. A different design is in favour by the time of his first letter to Wedgwood on 22 March 1786. Darwin wrote five more letters in April and May:[83] he was bubbling over with ideas and changed the design in response to comments from Wedgwood, who still seemed keen to cooperate. There is another letter from Darwin in December about the best size for the lamp, with a drawing.[84] Wedgwood again replied positively: 'we will find means to make it ornamental of any dimensions'. Darwin's final letter is in September 1787, and he speaks of an 'ultimate trial'. By then the lamp was well tested and may have been better than any rival. But Wedgwood rather let him down by doing nothing about it. This was because Wedgwood acquired the Portland Vase on loan in June 1786 and began to devote his energy to producing a perfect copy, rather than starting up in business with oil lamps.

Darwin seems to have been just as inventive in 1784–6 as in previous years, and the Commonplace Book touches on several other topics besides spinning machines and oil lamps. There are many pages on meteorology. These reveal some of the ideas about vapours, heat and cold that led to Darwin's classic paper on cloud formation. Seven years before he had written: 'Now if air be suddenly rarefy'd without the addition of heat, as in going into an exhausted receiver, or by being pump'd out of it, cold is produced'.[85] And there is a marginal note: 'Rarefy'd air attracts heat, condensed air gives it out'. Now he was making some careful experiments on measuring the drop in temperature when air is allowed to rush into a vacuum, and Plate 15 shows his apparatus, which is a primitive refrigerator.

The other notes on weather are varied. Darwin suggests that hot air rises above the tropics and comes down again at higher latitudes, a model of atmospheric circulation previously proposed by George Hadley. Three pages on winds and weather control later served as the basis for notes to *The Botanic Garden*. He expands on his ideas about eddies near mountains, as outlined (for Franklin's eye) in his letter to Robert at Paris. He believes that north-east winds blowing towards the Appalachian mountains may, instead of creeping up the slopes, create an eddy like a great wheel, and turn into north-west winds.

In December 1784 Darwin began an 'occasional journal' in the Commonplace Book, a weather diary with speculations added. Unaware of the complexity of the British weather, Darwin thought he might comprehend it by intelligent analysis of his own observations. The daily entries in his weather diary, like his stocking-frame designs and plant dictionaries, show him once again working with the fine detail of the subject he is studying.

Normal entries in the Commonplace Book seem to cease about 1786, but their variety remains undiminished to the end. The medical entries cover melancholia, gastric juices and jaundice. As a rousing medical finale, he tries electrocuting intestinal worms: 'Now he had 20 smart electric shocks passed from the region of the stomach ...'[86] The mechanical designs include a machine to convert circular to reciprocating motion, three drawings of wooden bridges, another water pump, a machine for sewing silk and a clock governed by dripping mercury.

He goes out with a bang, mechanically, with the idea that hydrogen could be exploded with air or oxygen to provide propulsion. Yes, he has thought of the internal combustion engine. Although up to now the engine has been developed to burn hydrocarbons rather than hydrogen, the hydrogen engine is almost pollution-free, and may quite soon come into use in eco-friendly cars.[87]

[12]

The demise of the Commonplace Book in 1786 came when Darwin was working on the second Linnaean translation. This was published in two thick volumes in the summer of 1787, as *The Families of Plants, with their natural characters* ... translated from the last edition of the *Genera Plantarum*. As before, the book is said to be 'By a Botanical Society at Lichfield', but Darwin's two sleeping helpers are unlikely to have done more than comment on the text and check the proofs.

This translation was easier than the first because he had already decided on the principles of the anglicization. But the work was more boring because it lacked intellectual content now that the language was sorted out. I am surprised that Darwin completed it so quickly. Perhaps he felt a sense of duty to the many botanists who praised the earlier translation. Whatever the reason, the work was done just as carefully as before.

He expresses his own views only in the preface. Here he admits a weakness in the Linnaean system: 'The Classes and Orders are in general artificial, like the streets and squares of a populous city'. In the real world the resemblances between species are more significant than the artificial divisions. 'Birds are connected to Quadrupeds by the Bat', and quadrupeds 'to Fish by Seals and Crocodiles; and by the Monkey-kind to Man'. After this muffled hint of his evolutionary biology, he unmuffles himself, and emerges red in tooth and claw with some Withering criticism. He accuses his arch-enemy of coining 'uncouth' English botanical names and writes him off as a 'pseudo-botanist'. Darwin would be pleased to know that his 'stamens and pistils' have prevailed over the 'chives and pointals' of Withering.

In *The Families of Plants* the main catalogue runs to 751 pages, with prefaces and indexes bringing the total to near 1000. The format of the main text is indicated by one of the shortest examples:

13. CALLITRICHE (Fine-Hair) ... Stargrass
      CAL.   none.
      COR.   *Petals* two, incurved, pointed, channel'd, opposite.
      STAM.   *Filament* one, long, recurved. *Anther* simple.
      PIST.   *Germ* roundish. *Styles* two, capillary, recurved. *Stigmas* acute.
      PER.   *Capsule* roundish, quadrangular, compressed, two-cell'd.
      SEEDS   solitary, oblong ...[88]

And so on, through another 1400 plants.

With *The Families of Plants* Darwin proved himself as a hard-working scholar. Reading through the book is hard work too, and would serve as a Mikado-like punishment for the superficial critics who have dared to call him superficial.

Other superficial critics have contrasted the 'speculative' Erasmus with his 'factual' grandson Charles. The fact is that they both had a passion for facts and for cataloguing them, like most genuine naturalists. Charles Darwin himself recognized this clearly: 'From my earliest days I had the strongest desire to collect objects of natural history, and this was certainly innate or spontaneous, being probably inherited from my grandfather.'[89]

Further proof of this family trait comes from an unexpected quarter, Elston Hall. In the same year, 1787, Erasmus's eldest brother Robert published an admirable textbook entitled *Principia Botanica*, 'a concise and easy introduction to the sexual botany of Linnaeus'. This was no cut-throat competition between two brothers, but a simultaneous flowering of similar seeds. Rarely if ever can two brothers have produced independently two substantial and similar botanical books in the same year. The family passion for scientific classification in biology is here publicly displayed.

The elder Robert deserves another brief minute on the stage. He was an assiduous naturalist and gardener, and his book has 'many curious notes on biology', as Charles Darwin remarked.[90] The book existed in manuscript for many years, and Erasmus may have used it to teach himself the Linnaean system. Robert's book proved more popular than his brother's translations: there was a second edition in 1793, and a third in 1810, dedicated to 'Robert Waring Darwin, M.D. & F.R.S.... one so eminent in his profession', by 'his truly affectionate Uncle, Robert Waring Darwin'.[91]

Dedicating a book to a person of the same name is cheeky; and so is publishing a book on the same subject as one by your brother, in the same year.
It also seems the height of impudence to publish a book called *Principia
Botanica* in the centenary year of Newton's *Principia Mathematica* of
1687, as if to put yourself on a par with Newton. Was it so that Robert
could say 'my father met Newton' if anyone commented? Or was it a joke?
Or was it by chance? I don't know the answer. Robert was conventional in
behaviour, and his only other formal writing, as far as is known, is an 800-
line manuscript poem called 'Providence, or the Unhappy Atheist',[92] which
has notes condemning most forms of frivolity. So it seems unlikely that he
was a secret joker.

After this unexpected hijacking by Robert, I can complete my original
journey with a helpful summary of Erasmus's translations in a letter to
Benjamin Franklin on 29 May 1787:

> Since I had the pleasure of seeing you, I have removed from Lichfield to Derby,
> and have superintended a publication of a translation of the botanical works of
> Linneus, viz. The System of Vegetables in two volumes octavo and the Genera or
> Families of Plants in 2 vol octavo also. I did this with design to propagate the
> knowlege of Botany. They are sold to the booksellers at 14/- the System of
> Vegetables – the Genera will be finished in a month, and will be sold to the book-
> sellers at 12/- I believe ... I think they would not be worth reprinting in America,
> and perhaps 20 sets would be as many as would find purchasers.[93]

[13]

For the Darwin family, 1787 seems to have been a quiet year: Robert the
younger was thriving at Shrewsbury; *The Families of Plants* came out; the
Derby Philosophical Society met monthly; and Erasmus was preparing his
best scientific paper, on the expansion of gases.

Elizabeth was pregnant again, and 'too unwieldy to travel this summer'.[94] The Darwins' third son, John, was born on 5 September. John was
one of the non-exuberant Darwins, like his half-brother Erasmus junior,
and he became a clergyman like his uncle John.

Elizabeth's eldest son Sacheverel Pole entered St John's College, Cambridge, in March. He was eighteen in June, a year older than William
Wordsworth, a fellow-student with the same tutor.

Darwin's letters to Wedgwood were fewer in 1787, but he kept up his
correspondence with Edgeworth in Ireland. When Edgeworth complains
about shortness of breath, Darwin teases him by saying it was partly 'owing
to disuse of juvenile exertions' and 'partly to old age – which gradually
comes upon us all after 35 – sometimes earlier'. More seriously, he says

'I am happy to hear Farming is your Hobbyhorse as gardening is mine – I am writing a theory of Gardening now, wonderful, and useful, and delightful'.[95]

He also wrote a friendly letter to his old colleague Dr John Ash, the partner of Dr Small. He hopes Ash may return to Birmingham, where he 'would be recieved with open arms, as I know the want of you has been much felt, and much lamented'.[96]

Erasmus may have visited Ironbridge gorge in 1787. A 'fountain of fossil tar' was found there in October 1786, and he wrote a paper about it soon afterwards, at first intended for the Royal Society but eventually published in the notes to The Botanic Garden.

This discovery was probably the trigger for a new friendship, with Dr Thomas Beddoes (1760–1808),[97] who was a fellow student of Robert at Edinburgh, and may also have been known to Erasmus through his tutor Samuel Dickenson. Beddoes lived near Ironbridge, at Shifnal, and seems to have met Darwin in the summer of 1787. In the autumn Beddoes became a lecturer in chemistry at the University of Oxford, where Darwin sent him a box of fossils. After a gap of a few years, Beddoes became Darwin's most ardent disciple and most frequent correspondent in the 1790s.

In 1787 Darwin continued hard at work as a general practitioner, always in touch with local medical problems through the dispensary, and un-impressed by his growing fame. In November he was elected to the Medical Society of London, an honour he politely acknowledged in a letter to Dr Lettsom. But he had no wish to live an easier life as a fashionable London physician.

Erasmus's reputation as a 'learned and excellent physician' was attract-ing visitors to Derby. The literary traveller John Nichols, who came in 1787, says 'he shewed me much kindness, and deferred until another time business which he thought to do, that he might teach me the things I had need to know'.[98]

Erasmus was nearly always well himself, but in November he had a touch of gout severe enough to earn a note in the Commonplace Book now so rarely opened:

> Nov.13 1787, after eating much salt ham, and drinking near a pint of beer, con-trary to my custome, having many years totally abstain'd from spirituous drink, I felt a debility at night, and next day had a little gout. The next more, still more on the third. Took 6 grains of calomel, and had but one restless night. The top of the foot, and right toe swell'd considerably.[99]

This small problem, soon overcome by abstinence, did little to disturb the even tenor of 1787.

The year was quiet too in the wider world – the calm before the storm of the French Revolution, the year of Mozart's Don Giovanni and Eine Kleine

Nachtmusik, that swansong of polite society in the eighteenth century. In England the young William Pitt was Prime Minister, but for Darwin the elderly Benjamin Franklin in America was the statesman most worthy of respect. Darwin wrote to Franklin on 29 May 1787, addressing his letter as usual to 'Doctor Franklin, America', and he begins with a flourish:

> Whilst I am writing to a Philosopher and a Friend, I can scarcely forget that I am also writing to the greatest Statesman of the present, or perhaps of any century, who spread the happy contagion of Liberty among his countrymen; and ... deliver'd them from the house of bondage, and the scourge of oppression.[100]

This was no flattery but Darwin's real opinion. His letter was written during the Philadelphia Convention that produced the Constitution of the United States. Although eighty-one, Franklin attended the exhausting debates through the scorching summer months. He did much to devise, and persuade the delegates to accept, the Constitution that has now stood the test of time for more than two hundred years.

'I can with difficulty descend to plain prose, after these sublime ideas', Darwin continues, 'to thank you for your kindness to my son Robert Darwin in France'. Then he tells Franklin about electrical experiments made by his friend Abraham Bennet, who 'has found out a method of doubling the smallest conceivable quantity of either plus, or minus electricity, till it becomes perceptible to a common electrometer, or increases to a spark'. Darwin explains how Bennet samples atmospheric electricity and doubles it up until it is detectable with the gold-leaf electroscope, Bennet's best-known invention.

Further 'philosophical news' for Franklin is Herschel's discovery of 'three Volcanoes in the Moon'. These bright spots in the dark part of the Moon, now often called 'transient lunar phenomena',[101] were the source of Coleridge's 'bright star within the nether tip' of the moon in the 'Ancient Mariner'.

The letter ends:

> A Line from you at your leizure, only to acquaint me that you continue to possess a tollerable share of health would be very acceptable to, dear Sir with true esteem your most obed. ser. E. Darwin.

It is a charming farewell to the man who 'snatched the lightning from the heavens and their sceptre from tyrants'. Franklin died three years later.

CHAPTER ELEVEN

Renaissance
1788–1790

This is not just a new chapter. It is also the story of a metamorphosis. In 1789 Darwin's image changed completely. He became known to far more people, and most of his many new admirers were unaware of his previous reputation in science and technology, or of his legendary fame as a doctor. For them he was a sexy poet, presenting a bizarre tale of gaudily dressed characters engrossed in various forms of polygamy.

Indeed there is some merit in pretending to forget all I have so far said about Darwin and to observe in this chapter the birth of a new man, the author of *The Loves of the Plants*. But he remained just the same person to his family and friends.

Three years after his tacit agreement with Joseph Johnson, Darwin was still reluctant to publish *The Loves of the Plants*. So he sent a copy of the manuscript to his most judicious friend James Keir, who replied in September 1787: 'I return with this your exquisite Poem … I am confirmed in the opinion I always had, that you would have been the first Poet of the kingdom if you had not suppressed your talent'.[1] Everyone Darwin had asked was in favour of publication, and Keir's advice finally convinced him. On 21 February 1788 he wrote to his son Robert: 'I am printing the Loves of the Plants, which I shall not put my name to, tho' it will be known to many: but the addition of my name would seem as if I thought it a work of consequence'.[2]

He felt that he was on to a certain loser: it *was* a frivolous poem, not a 'work of consequence'. He would gain nothing if it failed; and if it was a great success, he would be written off as a superficial versifier by readers ignorant of his scientific papers and scholarly translations.

His fears were well founded. The reading public seizes on a writer's most popular work to create a single image: multiple images are bewildering. Darwin's poem 'won instant and lasting popularity',[3] and he was typecast as an author of amusing didactic poems in rhyming couplets. Unfortunately for Darwin's long-term reputation as a poet, rhyming couplets were about to fall out of fashion, and the Darwinian style would soon be washed away by the new wave of 'Lake poets' – though not before Darwin had exerted a strong influence on the poets of the new Romantic era.[4]

[2]

Early in 1788, the year before the change in his image, Erasmus began writing to Robert more often. This is not as trivial as it seems, because many of the letters have survived and they are like an intermittent journal, revealing domestic events we should otherwise be quite unaware of. There are fifty-six of these letters, and most of them run to four pages somewhat larger than A4 size. Kindly in wording and intent, the letters are primarily medical: Erasmus hoped that candid accounts of his own cases would help Robert to improve his medical skills.

The first letter, written on 21 February, is rich in homely detail. Erasmus starts with Keir's new *Dictionary of Chemistry* and says he has arranged for the pages to be sent to him four at a time from the printer, so that 'I should read them like a newspaper as they came'. The aim is 'to improve myself by all methods'. If Robert has the same object, Erasmus says, he could also ask for this service. These well-meant attempts to push Robert into improving his professional knowledge were not wise. He had no self-generated thirst for knowledge and no wish to emulate his father. His favourite course of action was to do nothing.

Erasmus then moves on to Keir's soap: 'He sells white soap in boxes of not less than 100 in each.... I have this day order'd 400 for ourselves, 400 for Mr Strutt and 200 for Mr French'.[5] It conjures up a vision of an orgy of washing in Derby, and much foaming in the Derwent.

This letter was written on the day when Robert was elected a Fellow of the Royal Society in London, and Erasmus says, 'I have not heard a word about your fate at the Royal Society, have you?' A letter from Blagden[6] was on its way to Robert.

Robert's brother Erasmus had been looking a little yellow in the eyes and in need of exercise, according to his father. 'He has yesterday bought a horse' as the answer to that need, 'saying that a horse is the best Physician, and the best Apothecary an Ass'.

This little witticism is followed by a surprising revelation: Mary Parker suddenly reappears, with her former sexual partner satisfying his hunger at her expense. As Erasmus slyly says, 'I happen'd to call at Mrs Day at Birmingham and open'd the fine goose-pye you had sent, and eat a hearty meal out of it'. The miscellany of curious information continues with several medical cases, and a new method for writing: 'I have put a stuffed cushion upon the right arm of my cornerwise arm'd chair, exactly the height of my round table, and the edge of my slanting writing board upon it, which has enabled me to write you this long letter with much more ease'. Again this is not as trivial as it may seem because Darwin's future letters were generally longer – and so were his books.

The letter ends with a scandalous medical titbit:

I saw a patient at Birmingham of Dr Withering's, one Yates, whom he had a week
before pronounced to be out of danger, and ordered him to eat beef and porter. –
I found him in the last stages of a consumption![7]

Fortunately the other fifty-five letters do not invite such excessive quotation as this one. (Robert's side of the correspondence has not survived: it
was probably meagre.)

The second letter, written the next day, has details of medical cases.
Robert was still only twenty-one, and he might have found some of these
useful.

In the third letter, on 1 May, Erasmus says he is sending Robert a hamper
and a box filled with 'the Fossiles Erasmus collected in Cornwall', some
'elastic bitumen for Mr Reynolds' (the Coalbrookdale ironmaster), and
many other minerals.[8] Erasmus then refers to various geological ideas of
James Hutton, whom he mentions many times when writing to Robert.

The next letter, on 17 June 1788, announces another box of goodies for
Robert, with 'shirts and stockings according to your desire' and 'my second
volume of Botanic Garden', that is *The Loves of the Plants, 'which you
must not lend to anybody,* as it is not yet published, tho' printed'. Ten
months passed before publication, and this is the only indication that it was
available in print so early. Erasmus has further writing plans:

I intend next year to revise and correct, and enlarge, and perhaps print my
Zoonomia, and in this should be glad of your assistance ... I am writing notes to
the first part of the botanic garden, which I intend to print next spring.[9]

Like all authors, he was over-optimistic about publication dates. Part I of
The Botanic Garden did not come out for four years, and *Zoonomia* not
for six.

This letter, 'written on the hottest day I have felt' in 'my summer-house
over the water' carries more advice that Robert probably ignored. For
example, Erasmus kindly sends his manuscript notes on the lectures of Dr
Heberden and passes on Heberden's advice to a young physician, 'to write
prescriptions daily on all loose ends of letters etc'.

Erasmus was encouraging Robert to write a paper about the stratifi-
cation of coal, and offered for inclusion in it his comments on the bitumen
found at Coalbrookdale. Robert resisted the idea: he was averse to writing
scientific papers and to putting his name on papers written by his father.
Erasmus responded by trying to arrange for borings to be made in various
coal mines, which 'would add to the value of your paper'.[10] This is from
his letter of 19 July, which is full of ardour and detail about coal, fossils
and strata. In his next letter Erasmus is still banging on about coal and
petroleum, and (amazingly) he has obtained borings from five collieries. But

he almost admits defeat. He asks Robert to return the paper so that he can improve it, and says that 'if you do not like it' he will publish it in the notes to *The Botanic Garden*. Despairingly he adds, 'I think it would do you no discredit, but of this determine as you please'.[11] So inertia triumphed over enthusiasm.

In his next letter, on 8 October 1788, Erasmus announces his conversion: he has embraced the new French chemistry of Lavoisier, abandoning phlogiston and accepting oxygen. 'Pray read the preliminary discourse of Fourcroy – I am become an antiphlogistian from that discourse'.[12] He was the first of the Lunar group to be converted. The 'professional' chemists, Priestley, Keir and Watt, remained phlogistians for years.

A few days after this, Robert suffered a head-on collision with Dr Withering, who muscled in on one of Robert's patients, Mrs Houlston of Wellington. Withering reversed the treatment Robert had prescribed the previous evening and did not tell him, although knowing he was in the town. Robert wrote to protest at 'such ungenteel medical behaviour', and Withering replied that he had taken a different view of the case and had no 'time to spare, either for the purpose of idle ceremony or useless altercation'. This further insult was followed by an exchange of letters of increasing rudeness.

Erasmus was furious that Withering, not content with having attacked his dead son Charles, was now trying to wreck Robert's career. He encouraged Robert to retaliate by publicizing Withering's unfortunate habit of congratulating patients on their recovery just before they died. This happened in 1781 with Mrs Gresley of Tamworth,[13] in 1785 with Mr Inge of Thorpe, and in 1787 with Mr Francis of Birmingham. On 16 December 1788 Erasmus wrote to Dr Johnstone of Birmingham saying that Robert intended to ask Withering: 'Did not you by the solemn quackery of large serious promises of a cure get the management of this patient [Mr Francis] into your own hands, and did not you, Sir on the night before He died congratulate his son on his perfect recovery?'[14] Darwin was told of this blunder by Boulton, who was unwilling to confirm it in writing because he did not wish to make an enemy of Withering.

Dr Johnstone fuelled the quarrel further by giving Darwin's letter to Withering, who publicized it. Darwin was unabashed: on 12 March 1789 he told Boulton that 'Dr W by shewing it only published his own disgrace. I think Dr Robt Darwin has given him a dressing He will not soon forget'.[15]

This 'dressing' took the form of a forty-five-page pamphlet issued in February 1789 and entitled *Appeal to the Faculty Concerning the case of Mrs Houlston*, in which Robert printed the text of the seven letters between Withering and himself.[16] Some of the letters have phrases more redolent of Erasmus than of Robert: for example, 'Your pride dazzles your eyes and will not permit you to see your own ignorance'. Other sentences seem likely to be Robert's, for example when he says Withering mistook as a symptom what was really the effect of rhubarb. The letters were probably joint efforts, but Robert would have decided the final wording because he wrote the letters: Shrewsbury was sixty miles from Derby and there were no telephones. Reading the pamphlet leaves the impression that Robert won the argument.

In later years Robert tried to suppress the pamphlet: it was a blemish on his respectability. He probably also destroyed the relevant correspondence with his father: after the letter of 8 October there is a gap of six months.

[3]

In 1788 Darwin's image was still scholarly and scientific, and it is the year of his greatest achievement in physical science, with the publication of his classic paper defining the adiabatic expansion of gases and explaining the formation of clouds.

A gas expands 'adiabatically' when it is allowed to expand into a region of lower pressure in the absence of any external sources of heat. A familiar example is air let out of a tyre: under pressure inside the tyre the air is generally rather hotter than the ambient air, but it feels cool when it is allowed to escape. Examples of this cooling had often been noted before, but Darwin was the first to propound it as a principle.[17]

The paper was published in the *Philosophical Transactions* of the Royal Society, and with the first sentence Darwin plunges straight in:

> Having often revolved in my mind the great degree of cold producible by the well known experiments on evaporation; in which, by the expansion of a few drops of ether into vapour, a thermometer may be sunk much below the freezing point; and recollecting at the same time the great quantity of heat which is necessary to evaporate or convert into steam a few ounces of boiling water; I was led to suspect that elastic fluids, when they were mechanically expanded, would attract or absorb heat from the bodies in their vicinity.[18]

He tried several experiments. In the first (with Hutton and Edgeworth to help) he charged an air gun, left it for half an hour to take up room temperature, and then discharged it onto the bulb of a thermometer, which showed a decrease of 2°F. The experiment was repeated many times with the same result. Later, with the help of William Strutt and Samuel Fox, he repeatedly obtained a decrease of about 5° by placing the thermometer bulb in the exit jet. Then Darwin tapped the high-pressure air in the principal pipe of the waterworks that supplied Derby: a thermometer fell by 4° when held in the escaping air.

His next piece of evidence comes from a version of the fountain of Hiero at the Chemnic metal mines in Hungary:[19]

> In this machine the air, in a large vessel, is compressed by a column of water 260 feet high; a stop-cock is then opened, and as the air issues out with great vehemence, and, in consequence of its previous condensation [i.e. compression], becomes immediately much expanded, the moisture it contained is not only precipitated ... but falls down in a shower of snow, with icicles adhering to the nosel of the cock.

It is interesting that Darwin's terminology is better than that used now. Today 'condense' has two meanings: either to compress (as when we condense a verbose sentence); or to describe the formation of water droplets from vapour ('water was condensing on the walls'). This ambiguity is confusing, and Darwin avoids it by coining the word 'devaporate',[20] the opposite of 'evaporate', to take over our second meaning of 'condense'. By not using his word, we have befogged ourselves in ambiguity.

Having shown how air always cools when allowed to expand from a condition of higher pressure to lower, Darwin applies the principle to explain the coldness of the atmosphere several miles up:

> When large districts of air from the lower parts of the atmosphere are raised two or three miles high, they become so much expanded by the great diminution of the pressure over them, and thence become so cold, that hail or snow is produced from the precipitated vapour, if they contain any.

Darwin goes on to discuss 'The devaporation of aerial moisture' – that is, the formation of clouds:

> As heat appears to be the principal cause of evaporation ... the privation of heat may be esteemed the principal cause of devaporation.... When the barometer sinks (from whatever cause not yet understood this may happen), the lower stratum of air becomes expanded by its elasticity, being released from a part of the superincumbent pressure, and, in consequence of its expansion, robs the vapour which it contains of its heat; whence that vapour becomes condensed, and is precipitated in showers.

(Yes, he has nodded, and used 'condensed' to mean 'devaporated' in the last sentence.)

Darwin emphasizes that 'the deduction of a small quantity of heat' can devaporate a whole 'cloud or province of vapour', as happens at the start of thunderstorms, when 'a small black cloud at first appears', and 'in a few minutes the whole heaven is covered with condensing vapour'.

Forward-looking as ever, Darwin ends with some over-optimism about national warming:

> ... if it should ever be in the power of human ingenuity to govern the course of the winds ... by always keeping the under currents of air from the S.W. and the

upper currents from the N.E. I suppose the produce and comfort of this part of the world would be doubled at least to its inhabitants, and the discovery would thence be of greater utility than any that has yet occurred in the annals of mankind.

The propaganda in the 1990s for action *against* global warming would have puzzled him.

In this paper Darwin makes two separate discoveries in science. The principle of adiabatic expansion is an advance in fundamental physics; explaining how clouds usually form is an advance in meteorology. Darwin did not give a mathematical relation between pressure and temperature in adiabatic expansion, though his third experiment indicates that the temperature fell by at least 4° when pressure fell to half. The mathematical formulation of the adiabatic law[21] did not come until after the work of James Joule in the 1840s. Darwin's achievement was acknowledged by John Dalton, Thomas Young and Joule,[22] but has been largely ignored in most modern histories of science, despite its fundamental importance in all heat engines, including the atmosphere.

[4]

While Darwin sorted out the science of atmospheric humidity, Edgeworth exploited changes in humidity to power a robot caterpillar. This was an ingenious wooden device that crept along a shelf whenever the humidity changed. Darwin explains that it

> consisted of soft Fir-wood, about an inch square and four feet long, made of pieces cut the cross way in respect to the fibres of the wood, and glued together; it had two feet before, and two behind, which ... were armed with sharp points of iron, bending backwards. Hence in moist weather the back lengthened and the two foremost feet were pushed forwards; in dry weather the hinder feet were drawn after.... And thus in a month or two it walked across the room which it inhabited.[23]

Edgeworth often wrote to Darwin, and when Darwin replied on 20 February 1788, he accused Edgeworth of writing 'short scrawling letters full of questions' and expecting 'dissertations in return'. This mock complaint precedes a dissertation by Darwin about the hothouse on the northern side of his garden. It 'has a fire 4 months in a year only ... is about 82 ft long and 9 ft wide ... produces abundance of Kidney-beans, cucumbers, Melons, and Grapes'.[24] He then gives a diagram showing a lean-to design against a wall twelve feet high, with details of the positions of the hearths, chimneys and plants – while still protesting that he 'can not write a volume for you to light tapers with'.

Edgeworth's short questions receive short answers:

Mr [Sacheverel] Pole is at Cambrige. Miss Pole, at Derby, goes to London with Mrs and Miss Wedgewood for some weeks. Miss M. Pole at Cambden-House. Erasmus is indifferent well, and writes law-parchments.

On Keir's soap-works Darwin is more expansive: 'Mr Keir amuses his vacant hours by mixing oil and alcaline salts together, to preserve his Majesty's subjects clean and sweet – and pays 1000 Guineas every six weeks to an animal call'd an Exciseman'. Keir was doing well with his alkali manufactory at Tipton. Here he made large quantities of soap, soda, white and red lead, and other products. His factory was one of the show-places of the Midlands and the excise duties on his soap totalled £10,000 a year,[25] as Darwin says – equivalent to nearly £1 million today.

Of himself Darwin says, 'I drink water *only*, and am always well';[26] and of his family, 'We have five young creatures, 3 male, and two female, all tall (and hansome as Mrs Darwin thinks), the boys strong, the girls less so'.

When he wrote to Edgeworth, Darwin did not know that John White-hurst had died two days before, on 18 February, aged seventy-four. He was the oldest of the Lunar Society members, and Darwin had known and re-spected him for thirty years. Whitehurst has not figured prominently in my narrative, partly because he was an unassuming man and partly because no letters between Darwin and Whitehurst have survived. In his tastes he was closer to Darwin than to any other of the Lunaticks, and he may well have been an unseen hand during the 1760s, encouraging Darwin in his roles as inventor and geologist. Personally, Whitehurst was an entirely admirable man. Charles Hutton, the editor of his writings, calls him upright and punctual in all business dealings, 'a philanthropist in the truest sense of that word', a modest man who never made the least display of what he knew and would never stoop to flattery. All this is confirmed by other friends, including Darwin, who wrote that Whitehurst's 'ingenuity, integrity, and humanity, were rarely equalled in any station of life'.[27]

Whitehurst's was not the only unexpected death in 1788: Darwin's medical colleague Dr John Beridge died in October at the age of forty-five. Beridge had introduced him to Hayley and had been a fellow member of the Derby Philosophical Society. He had been at Derby before Darwin arrived, and acted as deputy when Darwin was too busy. That role now passed to a younger physician, Dr John Pigot (1756–94), also a member of the Society.

Erasmus was happy for Elizabeth to look after the younger children, but he now had to decide on the futures of Susan and Mary Parker, who were sixteen and fourteen respectively. Although they had so far been brought up like his other children, he accepted the convention that they should seek employment, perhaps as governesses, rather than leading genteel unemployed lives waiting for husbands, the future to be expected for Elizabeth's daughters Elizabeth and Milly.

None of Erasmus's own family wrote much about him, and a ten-year-old child in Birmingham had more influence on his future image. This child was Mary Anne Galton, later Mrs SchimmelPenninck, who was responsible for breaking off 'eleven marriages', according to her nephew Sir Francis Galton. This notorious mischief-maker wrote a caricature of Erasmus that has often been naively accepted as valid just because it is vivid. In his carriage, she says, he had

> a receptacle for writing-paper and pencils, likewise for a knife, fork and spoon; on one side was a pile of books reaching from the floor to nearly the front window of the carriage; on the other, a hamper containing fruit and sweetmeats, cream and sugar, the greater part of which, however, was demolished during the time the carriage traversed the forty miles which separated Derby from Barr.

The Galtons lived at Great Barr, near Birmingham. Mary Anne describes a visit in 1788 when she was ten. For dramatic effect she wrongly calls it his first visit.

> What then was my astonishment at beholding him as he slowly got out of the carriage! His figure was vast and massive, his head was almost buried on his shoulders, and he wore a scratch wig, as it was then called, tied up in a little bob-tail behind. A habit of stammering made the closest attention necessary, in order to understand what he said. Meanwhile, amidst all this, the doctor's eye was deeply sagacious, the most so I think of any eye I remember ever to have seen; and I can conceive that no patient consulted Dr Darwin who, so far as intelligence was concerned, was not inspired with confidence in beholding him: his observation was most keen; he constantly detected disease, from his sagacious observation of symptoms apparently so slight as to be unobserved by other doctors.

Such skill in assessing sagacious eyes is unusual in a ten-year-old.

She analyses his diet and conversation with equal aplomb:

> His horror of fermented liquors, and his belief in the advantages both of eating largely, and eating an almost immeasurable abundance of sweet things, was well known to all his friends; and we had on this occasion, as indeed was the custom whenever he came, a luncheon-table set out with hothouse fruits, and West India sweetmeats, clotted cream, Stilton cheese, etc.... I was astonished at his wit, his anecdotes, and most entertaining conversation.[28]

When he visited the Galtons, Darwin could catch up with the Lunar news, for he was rarely in Birmingham on the right day for a meeting. He did still try to keep his Lunar links. Writing to Watt on 18 November 1788, he says: 'I have some design, if not prevented, of coming to see the next Lunar Meeting – pray acquaint me, whether yourself and Mr Boulton and Dr Priestly are likely to attend it and likewise, what day it will be celebrated upon'.[29] Darwin was a close friend of Watt to the end of his life, and in this letter he shows a tender concern about Watt's health, prescribing Balsam of Canada for his stomach complaint and reminding him of Rabelais's 'philosophical experiment' for 'the good of the Public': this was 'to try how long an ingenious and agreable man might last, if taken good care of'. Watt took this advice and 'lasted' until well into his eighties, outliving Darwin by seventeen years and ever grateful for his help and support.

[5]

The Wedgwood and Darwin families grew closer as the 1780s advanced. Susannah Wedgwood was staying with the Darwins early in 1788, and on 29 January Erasmus expressed the 'pleasure and improvement we all had from her short visit'.[30] She had been teaching him music – virtually the only subject of which he was ignorant – and he was delighted to have such an attractive young lady as his musical mentor. In her absence 'I fear I shall lose the progress I made in music', he says. Susannah was now twenty-two, and the possibility that she might marry Robert would already have occurred to him. When the Wedgwoods went to London in March they took Elizabeth Pole with them, as expected. After a month Erasmus wrote 'I am affraid Miss Pole and Miss Wedgewood have forgot there are such places as Etruria and Derby'.[31]

Eight letters from Erasmus to Josiah or Susannah Wedgwood have survived from the first six months of 1788. Most of them are about Josiah's health. His 'no leg' was giving pain and he was troubled by his eyes, for which Darwin suggested taking the root of wild valerian. Wedgwood was willing to do so, not uninfluenced by the old wives' tale he tells of valerian's reputed 'tendence to render the animal fibre rigid, the very essence you know of old age'.[32]

Erasmus was trying to find a good gardener for Josiah, by asking his patients for recommendations. 'I have talked with Talkington', he tells Josiah, 'he asks 25 Guineas a year, and his board'; and with Mathers, who 'looks of stronger body but less energy of mind. He expects £20 a year and his board.'[33]

Only once does Erasmus refer to his own interests, when he says the mercurial oil lamp 'succeeds very well' and is 'I think ... worth a patent'. He has already entered a caveat. He is delayed because a spring ordered from Birmingham 'is iron instead of steel, the rascal thought I should not distinguish them'.[34]

Wedgwood and Darwin were drawn together in 1788 by an issue of international concern: slavery and the slave trade, the source of wealth for

so many British owners of West Indian sugar estates. William Wilberforce
and Thomas Clarkson were leading the campaign by the Society for the
Abolition of the Slave Trade, and Wedgwood was by now on their committee. (The campaign was to go on for twenty years because the planters'
lobby was so strong in the House of Commons.) Wedgwood produced the
famous medallion of a slave in chains, which was used as a seal by the
Society and as a hairpin ornament by society ladies. The cameo was further
publicized by Darwin when he reproduced it in *The Botanic Garden*, and
wrote of

> the poor fetter'd SLAVE on bended knee
> From Britain's sons imploring to be free.[35]

This is from Part I of *The Botanic Garden* – it was too late for *The Loves of
the Plants*.

Darwin was also eager to help with the propaganda. In February 1789
he suggested printing a résumé of a story in Defoe's *Colonel Jacque* which
shows 'the generous spirit of black slaves'.[36] On 13 April he wrote to
Wedgwood:

> I have just heard that there are muzzles or gags made at Birmingham for the
> slaves in our islands. If this be true, and such an instrument could be exhibited by
> a speaker in the house of commons, it might have great effect.[37]

Darwin felt so angry about slavery that he made a last-minute addition
to *The Loves of the Plants*:

> E'en now in Afric's groves with hideous yell
> Fierce SLAVERY stalks, and slips the dogs of hell;
> From vale to vale the gathering cries rebound,
> And sable nations tremble at the sound ...   [III 441-4]*

These lines are attached to his discussion of the plant Cassia, because its
seeds, like the slaves, cross the Atlantic Ocean (though in the opposite
direction, on the Gulf Stream) and also suffer quite heavy mortality on the
way.

[6]

That brings us to the great dividing line in Darwin's intellectual life, the
publication of *The Loves of the Plants* anonymously in April 1789, when
he was fifty-seven.

He began the poem as a versification of Linnaean botany, with the

---

* Canto and line numbers (in the third edition) are given in brackets after each quotation
from *The Loves of the Plants*.

obvious danger that it might be as boring as the repetitive catalogue of *The Families of Plants*. Darwin says his hope is to interest readers in botany, 'that delightful science', by enlisting 'Imagination under the banner of Science'. He explains in the preface that Linnaeus has divided plants into twenty-four Classes, according to the characteristics of the 'the males in each flower'. By using 'males' here instead of 'stamens', he is announcing that he will humanize the vegetable sexuality.

Darwin goes through the twenty-four classes, with English translations: Class 1, *Monandria*, one male, i.e., one stamen per flower; Class 2, *Diandria*, two males; and so on down to Class 13, *Polyandria*, many males; then through other more complex systems, such as Class 17, *Diadelphia*, two brotherhoods (with many stamens united into two companies), down to *Cryptogamia*, clandestine marriage (plants whose flowers are not discernible). These classes are divided into about 120 Orders, based on the number of females or pistils, and he gives two pages of drawings to show examples. In the poem the number of males or females is given in italics, for example, '*five* hapless swains' or '*four* sylvan youths'. This number-game is reminiscent of the counting rituals in children's rhymes: but here an added frisson comes from the multiple sexual situations.

The first edition of *The Loves of the Plants* has 1746 lines of verse and runs to 184 quarto pages. It was published by Joseph Johnson after being printed at Lichfield by John Jackson. Though plagued by misprints and mis-spellings, the book is beautifully printed and laid out, with the verses in very large type (fifteen point) and the footnotes much smaller.

The Loves of the Plants is a brilliant title: it breathes an air of sexual intrigue and signals the poem's mock-heroics by half-echoing *The Rape of the Lock*.

More playfulness shines through in the elegant Proem, where Darwin foresees and exploits the future popular appeal of cinema and television:

> Gentle reader!
> Lo, here a CAMERA OBSCURA is presented to thy view, in which are lights and shades dancing on a whited canvas, and magnified into apparent life! – if thou art perfectly at leisure for such trivial amusement, walk in, and view the wonders of my INCHANTED GARDEN.

He could assume that his readers would be familiar with Ovid's *Metamorphoses*, where 'by art poetic' men and women are transmuted into trees and flowers. 'I have undertaken by similar art to restore some of them to their original animality.' His exhibits should, he says, be looked on as 'diverse little pictures suspended over the chimney of a Lady's dressing-room, *connected only by a slight festoon of ribbons*'.

This female bias continues: the whole poem is 'spoken' by the Goddess of Botany. We may see her as Darwin in drag, but that does not detract from her overt status as the most powerful figure in the poem. Within the poem there are no dominant macho men, only a few minor heroes like Montgolfier. Men have subordinate roles, acting mainly as suitors.

The glittering pageant of vegetable sex-life begins with Darwin preparing to tell us

> What Beaux and Beauties crowd the gaudy groves,
> And woo and win their vegetable Loves.   [I 9–10]

This is the very essence of the poem. Darwin wallows in irony as he goes into the sex-life of the humanized vegetables and pokes fun at the humans, though some humourless literary critics of the early twentieth century were too thick to see it.

The Goddess begins with *Canna*, or Indian reed, which bears a crimson flower housing one male and one female; so the male virtuously 'plights his nuptial vow' to the solitary female. Next is *Callitriche*, Stargrass, in which one male enjoys two females:

> Thy love, CALLITRICHE, *two* Virgins share,
> Smit with thy starry eye and radiant hair.   [I 45–6]

In *Collinsonia* two males woo one female, who satisfies each in turn; while in *Meadia*, American cowslip, '*five* suppliant beaux' attend the 'laughing belle', who

> bows with wanton air,
> Rolls her dark eye, and waves her golden hair.   [I 63–4]

And so the catalogue goes on, accurate in its essentials and fanciful in its embellishments, and with footnotes of about the same length as the verses.

Darwin's personalization of the plants was no gimmick: he believed that plants feel, though much less keenly than animals. That is why he liked insectivorous, climbing and sensitive plants, which seem 'almost human'. He is particularly keen on two insectivorous plants, *Silene* (catchfly) and *Drosera* (sundew). In each flower of *Silene* three females lie in wait for the insects, which are advised to steer clear before 'the *three* dread Syrens' lure them to destruction. The tiny *Drosera* fascinated Erasmus's grandson Charles, who wrote in 1860: 'At this present moment I care more about Drosera than the origin of all the species in the world'.[38] Erasmus also rates it highly:

> Queen of the marsh, imperial DROSERA treads
> Rush-fringed banks, and moss-embroider'd beds;
> Redundant folds of glossy silk surround
> Her slender waist, and trail upon the ground.   [I 231–4]

Two of the five plates in *The Loves of the Plants* are of insectivorous plants: *Dionaea muscipula* (Venus flytrap), with leaves which close 'like the teeth of a spring rat-trap'; and *Apocynum androsoemifolium*, 'a kind of dog's bane'. Both plants are drawn in the act of catching insects, and Erasmus mentions that his brother Robert showed him *Apocynum* in flower, with a fly 'held fast by the end of its proboscis'.[39]

Just as interesting to him is the sensitive plant, mimosa:

> Weak with nice sense, the chaste MIMOSA stands,
> From each rude touch withdraws her timid hands ...   [I 301–2]

This was an inspiration for Shelley, who also humanized mimosa in rhyming couplets, in his poem 'The Sensitive Plant'.

The second canto of Darwin's poem is announced as 'wilder' in line 2, and the botany begins to be submerged in far-reaching digressions. The first plant, the Carline thistle, whose plumes drift far in the wind, leads on to the Montgolfiers' balloon; flax and cotton provide the cue for the verses about Arkwright's cotton mill; and Papyra provokes a digression about writing.

Menispermum, or Indian berry, which intoxicates fish, provokes the most ludicrous scenario, St Antony preaching to the fishes:

> 'To Man's dull ear', He cry'd, 'I call in vain,
> Hear me, ye scaly tenants of the main!'...
> The listening shoals the quick contagion feel,
> Pant on the floods, inebriate with their zeal,
> Ope their wide jaws, and bow their slimy heads,
> And dash with frantic fins their foamy beds.   [II 249–50, 263–6]

Darwin regarded the veneration of saints and their bones as superstition, so it is no surprise to come upon his burlesque of St Antony.

Darwin knew that opium was an addictive narcotic, and in his lines on the effects of *Papaver*, poppy, he mentions the 'feelings of intense cold'[40] on withdrawal:

> And now the Sorceress bares her shrivel'd hand,
> And circles thrice in air her ebon wand ...
> – She waves her wand again! – fresh horrors seize
> Their stiffening limbs, their vital currents freeze;
> By each cold nymph her marble lover lies,
> And iron slumbers seal their glassy eyes.   [II 277–8, 287–90]

The Romantic poets took these lines to heart, it seems, for there are verbal resemblances in Coleridge's 'Kubla Khan', Shelley's *Queen Mab*, Keats's *Eve of St Agnes* and Wordsworth's poem, 'A slumber did my spirit seal'.[41]

After poppy, Darwin's favourite herbal remedy was cinchona, the Peruvian bark, the source of quinine. From restoring health it is a short step to philanthropy, and hence to John Howard and his devoted work in the prisons:

> He treads, inemulous of fame or wealth,
> Profuse of toil, and prodigal of health ...   [II 453–4]

Darwin had a special empathy for Howard, who died a year later from 'fever' caught on his travels. Darwin also risked disease on his daily travels among the sick: idealizing himself as a philanthropist helped him through the drudgery of his medical practice. He was usually paid, of course, but not when the patients were poor.

Canto III strikes a darker note. First on the scene is *Circaea*, enchanter's nightshade, much used in witchcraft. Darwin is tempted into mock-Gothic imagery:

> Shrill scream the famish'd bats, and shivering owls,
> And loud and long the dog of midnight howls!   [III 13–14]

Two 'imps obscene' unbar the 'ponderous portals' of a church:

> As through the colour'd glass the moon-beam falls,
> Huge shapeless spectres quiver on the walls.   [III 23–4]

It is all designedly 'over the top', but seemingly memorable; for again echoes can be heard in the poems of Wordsworth, Coleridge, Shelley and Keats.[42]

The roll-call of unwholesome plants continues with Laurel, that 'most sudden poison', which gives Darwin the chance to reprint his verses about Fuseli's *Nightmare*. Another miscreant is the alleged poison-tree of Java, the Upas tree: Darwin's lines about it were much admired at the time but too long to quote (III 219–58).

A subtler villain is 'seductive Vitis', the vine, with her tempting alcoholic poison:

> 'Drink deep', she carols, as she waves in air
> The mantling goblet, 'and forget your care'...
> Fell Gout peeps grinning through the flimsy scene,
> And bloated Dropsy pants behind unseen.   [III 363–4, 367–8]

Darwin suggests in a note that the fire Prometheus stole was really fiery spirits, the 'vulture perpetually gnawing his liver' being 'so apt an allegory for the effects of drinking spirituous liquors'.

In Canto IV, with all poison spent, pleasantry takes over. This is the most graceful canto, embellished with many vivid pictures. There is music too, as the 'tuneful Goddess' moves in to play 'softer chords' and 'sweeter tones'. She celebrates the oat, in the form of the oaten reed, the first musical instrument. It sounds with such a 'silver tongue' that all nature listens:

From ozier bowers the brooding Halcyons peep,
The Swans pursuing cleave the glassy deep,
On hovering wings the wondering Reed-larks play,
And silent Bitterns listen to the lay.   [IV 95–8]

Shelley listened too, and echoed these lines in *Epipsychidion*.[43]

Most pleasant of all for many of Darwin's readers was their entry into a genuine world where sex was multiplex. In the mobile plant *Hedysarum gyrans* ten males eye one female:

Clasp'd round her ivory neck with studs of gold
Flows her thin vest in many a gauzy fold;
O'er her light limbs the dim transparence plays,
And the fair form, it seems to hide, betrays.   [IV 341–4]

The *Critical Review* called this 'exquisitely beautiful'.[44] In contrast 'the chaste Truffelia' relies on a showy underground palace:

High o'er her couch impending diamonds blaze,
And branching gold the crystal roof inlays; ...
Light piers of lazuli the dome surround,
And pictured mochoes tessellate the ground.   [IV 399–400, 403–4]

For his final fling Darwin chooses the plant *Adonis*, where many males and females live together in one flower. They move in 'bright procession' to the shrine of 'licentious Hymen', attended by 'light Joys on twinkling feet', while 'exulting Cupids' pepper them with 'promiscuous arrows'. They are like the Areoi on the island of Tahiti, 'about 100 males and females who form one promiscuous marriage':

Thus where pleased VENUS, in the southern main,
Sheds all her smiles on Otaheite's plain,
Wide o'er the isle her silken net she draws,
And the Loves laugh at all but Nature's laws.   [IV 487–90]

It is a happy finale, and subtly subversive too with its sudden change to a real human society.

[7]

The Loves of the Plants seems to have delighted all its readers, young and old, male and female. The elderly Horace Walpole, doyen of the literary world and a difficult man to please, was captivated: 'You will agree with me that the author is a great poet.... I send you the most delicious poem upon earth.... I can read this over and over again forever ... all, all is the most lovely poetry'.[45] Nowhere else in the forty-eight volumes of Walpole's correspondence does such enthusiasm erupt. The effect on Edgeworth was similar:

> I have felt such continued, such increasing admiration in reading the Loves of the Plants, that I dare not express any of my Enthusiasm, lest you should suspect me of that tendency to Exaggeration, which you used to charge me with.... It has silenced for ever the complaints of poets, who lament that Homer, Milton, Shakespeare and a few Classics had left nothing new to describe.[46]

The young were captivated too, if we may believe an anonymous writer in *The Gentleman* in 1818: 'When Dr Darwyn's Loves of the Plants first appeared, I heard many young men extol it above Pope and Milton'. Even the ever-critical Mrs SchimmelPenninck admitted that it gave great pleasure at Barr: its effect, 'though at the distance of sixty years, I shall never forget'.[47] The reviewers were united in approval. 'We have perused this volume with great pleasure' (*Critical Review*); 'we have received from it so much pleasure and instruction' (*Monthly Review*); 'it was with uncommon pleasure that we followed the author through the cantos of this agreeable poem' (*New Annual Register*).[48] If poetry is 'for the purpose of immediate pleasure', as Coleridge said, Darwin had succeeded.

There was no jealousy among the leading poets of the day, who generously recognized that Darwin's poem was beyond their own capabilities. William Cowper in his eight-page review says the poetry 'is of a very superior cast', and he commends the author for showing 'so much versatility of genius' in his descriptions, which 'are luminous as language selected with the finest taste can make them, and meet the eye with a boldness of projection unattainable by any hand but that of a master'.[49] William Hayley admired the poem too, as we shall see later. And what of that other leading poet, Anna Seward? Surely she would be critical?

Surprisingly, Anna praises the poem, and her one-hundred-page analysis is the most thorough critique of *The Loves of the Plants* that has yet appeared. She is not troubled by the sexiness because 'the sexual nature of plants' has been proved, and 'the female form is always attractive from the poetic pencil of Darwin'. She hands out bouquets, such as, 'Creative imagination, the high and peculiar province of the genuine Poet, has few more beautiful creations'. She has criticisms too, including the perceptive comment that 'Dr Darwin's poetry, while it delights the imagination, leaves the nerves at rest'.[50]

The Loves of the Plants also pleased the Revd William Stevens, a minor poet[51] and headmaster of Repton School, who had become friendly with Darwin. He wrote some verses of pastoral pleasantry which were prefixed to later editions of *The Botanic Garden*.

The up-and-coming poets showed their appreciation by accepting Darwin as a mentor. William Wordsworth was nineteen and a Cambridge under-graduate when *The Loves of the Plants* appeared. The idea of humanizing plants appealed to Wordsworth and inspired his credo:

> 'Tis my faith that every flower
> Enjoys the air it breathes.

His first poems *An Evening Walk* and *Descriptive Sketches* (1793) were in Darwinian couplets and with many verbal and stylistic similarities.[52] Coleridge was sixteen and soon knew the poem by heart, to judge from the dozens of verbal resemblances in his poems of the 1790s.[53]

Darwin knew and liked Wordsworth's early work, and later met Coleridge; but he probably never knew of his immediate impact on a third major poet, William Blake, whose poems were almost unknown in his lifetime. Blake was thirty-two when *The Loves of the Plants* appeared, and a few months later he engraved the first and most charming of his symbolic poems, *The Book of Thel*. Its title-page (Plate 11A) springs straight from *The Loves of the Plants*. As David Erdman noted,[54] Blake presents Thel as a shepherdess watching not sheep but the strange spectacle of two huge blossoms with a gowned maiden stepping out of one flower and a naked youth leaping out of the other to seize her with amorous intent. This is precisely Darwin's personified pistils and stamens. And Blake's poems, especially the *Songs of Experience*, have many verbal similarities to Darwin's.[55]

With the more substantial *Economy of Vegetation* quickly overshadowing it, *The Loves of the Plants* has not received much critical attention in its own right since Anna Seward's analysis. One substantial critique, from J. V. Logan in 1936, emphasizes Darwin's humour and 'visual legerdemain'.[56] Donald Hassler in his books on Darwin's writings in 1973 concentrates on his playfulness and comic 'double truth'.[57] There are two more recent socially-orientated approaches. Maureen McNeil[58] makes the point that Darwin celebrates the new machines and the brain-work of their inventors, while ignoring the plight of the workers toiling in the cotton mills. Janet Browne[59] analyses the images of women in the poem: 'there are no sexual victims, no rape or violence' in Darwin's 'rustic poetic paradise'. To these I might add my own view that *The Loves of the Plants* is a feminist poem because women are in charge throughout and their world-view prevails.

One early critical crux with the poem, the question 'can plants feel?', remains unresolved today. Darwin was ridiculed for believing that all life derived from 'a single living filament', so that ants, worms and plants were our distant cousins. That ridicule has now dissolved, and re-emerged as biological orthodoxy. But the idea of sentient plants still troubles their human cousins. Speeded-up films of insectivorous plants feeding, or of

Dodder and Convolvulus fighting, look horribly human; and Sir Jagadis Bose made experiments in the 1920s showing that plants such as mimosa have a central nervous system like animals.[60] The official verdict at present is against him, but he has had his disciples,[61] including even James Bond.[62] The idea of sentient plants, whatever its merits, seems unlikely to prevail. Otherwise agriculture, gardening and forestry would have to be condemned as cruel.

[8]

Life for the Darwins in 1789 went on unaffected by *The Loves of the Plants*, which is rarely mentioned in Erasmus's letters. He did send a copy to Wedgwood in February and suggested that he might like to read the pages on the slave trade and on John Howard. In his reply Wedgwood offers 'a thousand thanks for the pleasure and instruction I am receiving in the perusal of these beautiful and charming Cantos'.[63]

The poem's birth in April coincided with a real-life birth, for on 10 April the sixth child of Elizabeth and Erasmus was born, a son Henry. Erasmus mentions the event rather casually at the end of his letter to Wedgwood about muzzles and gags: 'Mrs D is in the straw, has a fine boy and very well'. He is even more casual on the third page of a letter to Robert: 'You never mention your new horse ... I have not yet seen Mr French about the dog. You have got a new Brother called Henry. He was born last friday, and himself and Mother are well'.[64] This leaves the impression that Erasmus did not altogether welcome the new arrival. Perhaps he felt the present houseful was expensive enough. Despite his good start, young Henry did not thrive, and he died when twelve months old.

Death began to loom larger for Erasmus himself when his sister Susannah died at Sleaford on 29 April 1789, aged sixty. They had always been close, and his life might have been very different without her. Susannah had helped Polly in the early years of marriage, and above all she had cared for the children and supervised the house after Polly's death. Without the stability she provided, Erasmus might have felt obliged to marry again quickly, perhaps Mary Parker or a Lichfield widow? His later life would then have been very different, and *The Botanic Garden* might never have been written.

Susannah was buried at Elston, and there is a memorial tablet in the church. Her death was disturbing for Erasmus: his brother William had died at fifty-seven, Susannah at sixty; he himself would be fifty-eight later in the year. A more hopeful example was his mother, eighty-seven and still well.

There is not much news of Erasmus junior in these years. He was doing good business as a lawyer and was reasonably well, apart from an intermittent 'bilious complaint'. He became quite friendly with Hayley's wife Eliza, who came to live with the widowed Maria Beridge in Derby. This was a 'friendly separation' between the Hayleys, though arranged to suit the husband, who could not stand his wife's obsessive laughing.

Robert Darwin's dispute with Withering was finished by April, but he still felt the world was against him. He told his father so, and received this advice:

> I am sorry to hear you say you have many enemies, and one enemy often does much harm. The best way, when any little slander is told one, is never to make any piquant or angry answer; as the person who tells you what another sais against you, always tells them in return what you say of them.... Dr Small always went and drank tea with those who he heard had spoken against him.[65]

Would Robert have taken notice of this? As no extra work was involved, he probably did.

By now there was a new toy at Full Street for visitors, such as the Wedgwoods, who came in June. After buying the orchard on the other side of the river, Erasmus designed a cable-controlled ferry boat for crossing the river. The ferry was constructed and Fig. 14 shows it in action in 1789, as remembered by Francis Darwin, the child in the boat. Though the winding mechanism is not clear, the ferry seems to have worked well and is another of Darwin's successful inventions. The wires presumably lay on the river bed when the ferry was not in use. The ferry would seem to have been dangerous if a wire had broken. But there are no reports of accidents, so perhaps Erasmus included extra wires for safety.

There was a tragic and unexpected accident far away in September 1789, which caused the death of Thomas Day. During the 1780s Day had remained in seclusion farming his land near Ottershaw in Surrey. Even so, he became famous as the author of the children's book *Sandford and Merton*, published in three volumes between 1783 and 1789. A precept in the book is that 'even the fiercest beasts are capable of being softened by gratitude and moved by humanity'. Fortified by this belief, Day rode a horse that was only half broken-in when he went to join his wife and mother at Bear Hill in Berkshire on 28 September. But the horse shied at a man winnowing corn. Day was thrown head-first onto the stony road and died immediately.

Day was only forty-one at the time of his death and he had not yet achieved the great things expected of him by his friends. Whether he would ever have made much of a mark in politics remains an open question. His great achievement was literary, and 'great' is the right word: in the century after his death *Sandford and Merton* probably had 'a larger number of readers

FIG. 14 The wire-drawn ferry designed by Darwin to link the garden at Full
Street with their orchard across the river Derwent, here about fifty yards wide.
As remembered by Francis Darwin, the child in the boat, with his mother and
Dewhurst Bilsborrow, 1789

than any other work of the period'.[66] Although Day and his book are now
forgotten, writing the most-read book of a century is a rare distinction.

Erasmus had probably not seen Day for ten years, but the bonds between
them remained strong. Erasmus wrote in one of his letters to Robert, 'I
much lament the death of Mr Day.... He was dear to me by many names ...
as friend, philosopher, scholar, honest man.'[67]

Day's wife Esther was shattered by his death. Erasmus junior, who
counted Day as his best friend outside Derby, worked hard to sort out the
legal problems of his estate. Keir tried to help Esther too and wrote a
circumspect *Life* of Day. But Esther was inconsolable and died within three
years.

[9]

With the death of Day, and earlier of Small and Whitehurst, the nine men
in the original Lunar circle of 1768 were reduced to six. Darwin was in

contact with all the other five in 1789–90 and also with that man of Lunar mould James Hutton, who is mentioned twelve times in *The Botanic Garden*.[68]

One of Wedgwood's current projects depended on some clay brought back from Botany Bay and given to him by Sir Joseph Banks. From this clay Wedgwood made medallions of Hope attended by Peace, Art and Labour at Sydney Cove, 'to show the inhabitants what their materials would do, and to encourage their industry',[69] as Darwin put it. An illustration of the medallion was to appear in a book about Botany Bay, and Darwin wrote some verses to go with it, prophetic in their vision of the future Sydney, including the bridge:

There shall broad streets their stately walls extend,
The circus widen, and the crescent bend....
There the proud arch, Colossus-like, bestride
Yon glittering streams, and bound the chafing tide....
There shall tall spires, and dome-capt towers ascend,
And piers and quays their massy structures blend ...[70]

Darwin says 'I have ... taken as much from Thomson as I could, to guard it from minor Critics': his lines are based on a passage in Thomson's *Liberty*, as L. Richard Smith has noted,[71] but Darwin greatly improves on the original.

Wedgwood admired the verses[72] and in return was helping Darwin to beautify *The Loves of the Plants* for the second edition. 'Nothing can be too good to accompany your charming poem', he wrote, and sent a much better engraving of Cupid for the end of the Proem.

Then Wedgwood jumps without warning to the events of 14 July:

I know you will rejoice with me in the glorious revolution which has taken place in France. The politicians tell me that as a manufacturer I shall be ruined if France has her liberty, but I am willing to take my chance in that respect, nor do I yet see that the happiness of one nation includes in it the misery of its next neighbour.[73]

Darwin shared his approval of the early phases of the French Revolution.

Wedgwood himself was still hard at work trying to make a perfect copy of the Portland Vase. In October 1789 he at last succeeded, and immediately sent it to Darwin, with instructions that he should show it to no one outside his family. But Darwin could not resist the temptation: 'I have disobeyed you, and shewn your Vase to two or three, but they were philosophers, not cogniscenti. How can I possess a jewel, and not communicate the pleasure to a few Derby Philosophes?'[74]

Darwin had his own explanation for the figures on the vase, and soon Wedgwood was thanking him 'for a page of charming poetry, and many pages of very ingenious and learned notes, which I have read over and over with great pleasure'.[75] Darwin believed the figures on the Vase represent a ritual of death and rebirth deriving from the Eleusinian mysteries, and he expounds this view persuasively in his note, printed in *The Economy of Vegetation*. Many explanations of the scenes on the vase have been suggested; Darwin's is well regarded by some commentators on the Vase.[76]

In November 1789 Darwin met Charles Greville, 'who has himself written an explanation of the figures – and possesses fine plates of it',[77] he told Wedgwood. This gave Darwin the idea of getting 'two or three common etchings' of Greville's plates 'to put into my book'.

Though Wedgwood was Darwin's closest friend, he did not forget Boulton during 1789, and he refers to 'the true spirit of our long and antient friendship; which I dare say will not cease on either side, till the earthy tenement of our minds becomes decomposed'.[78] Darwin asks for information on the Boulton and Watt engine, and also on Boulton's coining machine, to include in his poem. Boulton responded with a masterly 'catalogue of facts' and Darwin produced a long note about the 'magnificent apparatus for coining' that precludes 'clandestine imitation'. Boulton deserved the country's thanks, Darwin says, not only for providing Britain with a secure currency, but also for abolishing at a stroke the crime of counterfeiting and thereby saving 'many lives from the hand of the executioner'. It is characteristic of Darwin that he should seize on this humane by-product of Boulton's work.

Darwin also versified the operation of the coining machine, which 'gave me great pleasure for a week after I saw it':

> With iron lips his rapid rollers seize
> The lengthening bars, in thin expansion squeeze;
> Descending screws with ponderous fly-wheels wound
> The tawny plates, the new medallions round;
> Hard dyes of steel and cupreous circles cramp,
> And with quick fall his massy hammers stamp.
> The Harp, the Lily and the Lion join,
> And GEORGE and BRITAIN guard the sterling coin.[79]

The poetry of mechanisms is never dead, as long as you share Darwin's lifelong passion for machines.

Darwin wrote to Watt on a similar quest on 20 November 1789, saying he would include a note on steam engines in *The Economy of Vegetation* 'if you will at leisure hour tell me what the world may know about your *improvements* of the steam-engine'.[80] Watt replied on 24 November: 'I know not how steam-engines come among the plants; I cannot find them in the Systema Naturae, by which I should conclude that they are neither plants, animals, nor fossils.'[81] Despite these doubts, he sent an account of his work, which Darwin used in a long note on the history of steam engines.

[10]

Darwin was becoming increasingly involved with geology and chemistry in 1789. In geology he was fascinated by theories of the past history of the rocks, being most influenced by the ideas of James Hutton. But he was also very keen on collecting fossils and mineral specimens. Some of these he bought at Derby from Richard Brown, 'fossil-philosopher of this place'. He had several cabinets of minerals in his house and also took the trouble to send boxes and hampers of fossils and minerals to his son Robert, Thomas Beddoes, Edgeworth's son Henry, and perhaps others.

Darwin also wrote a twenty-page essay on the waters of Buxton and Matlock, for James Pilkington's *View of the Present State of Derbyshire*, published in 1789. Darwin believes that the warmth of the springs at Buxton and Matlock is due not to chemical action, as was often suggested, but to heat deep in the Earth. He gives several reasons for this correct opinion: the heat has been constant for centuries; when cold springs dry up, these hot ones do not and hence have deep sources; the limestone has many perpendicular clefts; volcanoes prove the existence of 'central fires'. He went with Edgeworth, he says, when two of the springs at Matlock were opened 'about 200 yards above their usual place of appearance. We found them both at these new openings about one degree of heat, or somewhat more, warmer than at the places of their usual exit.'[82]

Darwin discusses vapours condensing and sliding between strata, as in his paper on the artesian well, and says his own well has continued to flow for five years, increasing 'in quantity and perhaps in purity'. Darwin emphasizes that the Derbyshire caverns are very ancient, but he did not know that most of them were formed by water erosion: he thought they were caused by the Earth opening its jaws and failing to shut them exactly.

In geology Darwin was quite expert; in chemistry he was much less so, but his decisions proved surprisingly influential, and particularly his conversion to the 'French heresy' of oxygen in 1788. The old orthodoxy of phlogiston still gripped Priestley, Keir and Watt, who all knew more than he did about chemistry. They would regard him as a traitor defecting to the French. But Darwin did not hesitate: for him the pursuit of scientific truth was paramount. If his friends were upset, he would tease them with diplomatic banter.

He is quite direct when writing to Watt on 18 November 1788:

Pray read the 40 first pages of the Introduction to Fourcroy's Elements, and tell me if the facts are in general true – if they be, the theory holds them nicely together.

When steam is passed through red hot iron scrapings, if the water be not decomposed, whence comes the vital air, which unites to the iron? – does the water vanish, or is it annihilated? Pray explain this experiment.

He then becomes more diplomatic:

I shall wait with Patience to see this great dispute decided, which involves so great a part of the theory of chemistry – and thank the Lord, that chemical Faith is not propagated by fire and sword. At present I am inclined to the heterodox side of the question.[83]

Keir was a stronger phlogistian than Watt, and Darwin had to be more tactful. When he read the preface of Keir's dictionary of chemistry in 1789, he politely commented: 'You have successfully combated the new nomenclature, and strangled him in the cradle, before he has learnt to speak'.[84]

When Darwin invited Keir 'to be converted to the true faith in chemistry', he replied, on 15 March 1790: 'You are such an infidel in religion that you cannot believe in transubstantiation, yet you can believe that apples and pears, hay and oats, bread and wine, sugar, oil, and vinegar, are nothing but water and charcoal, and that it is a great improvement in language to call all these things by one word, oxyde hydro-carbonneux'.[85] Keir might easily have written that one word as 'carbohydrate' (first used in 1869); if he had, his ridicule would have jumped across the centuries as modern orthodoxy.

Darwin was not deterred, and presented the new chemistry in *The Economy of Vegetation*. This greatly enhances the appeal of the poem. Had it been written ten years earlier, reeking of phlogiston, it would today have seemed as remote from reality as *Paradise Lost*.

Because the poem was such a success, Darwin's presentation of chemistry was most influential. When he wrote the word 'oxygen' in *The Economy of Vegetation* it was the first positive use of the word in English, according to the *OED*, though Keir had used it disparagingly a year earlier. Darwin not only popularized the importance of oxygen, he also introduced the very word to the reading public. The first uses of the words 'hydrogen', 'azote' (nitrogen) and 'azotic' were also in *The Botanic Garden*. (There may be earlier examples in little-known books, but Darwin brought the words to public attention.) He was, as it were, the verbal father of oxygen and hydrogen. He dodged the implacable opposition of the leading chemists by speaking directly to the reading public, and so he made oxygen respectable in the early 1790s. For the chemists of the new generation, such as Humphry Davy, he changed the paradigm: he was the public champion of oxygen in England.

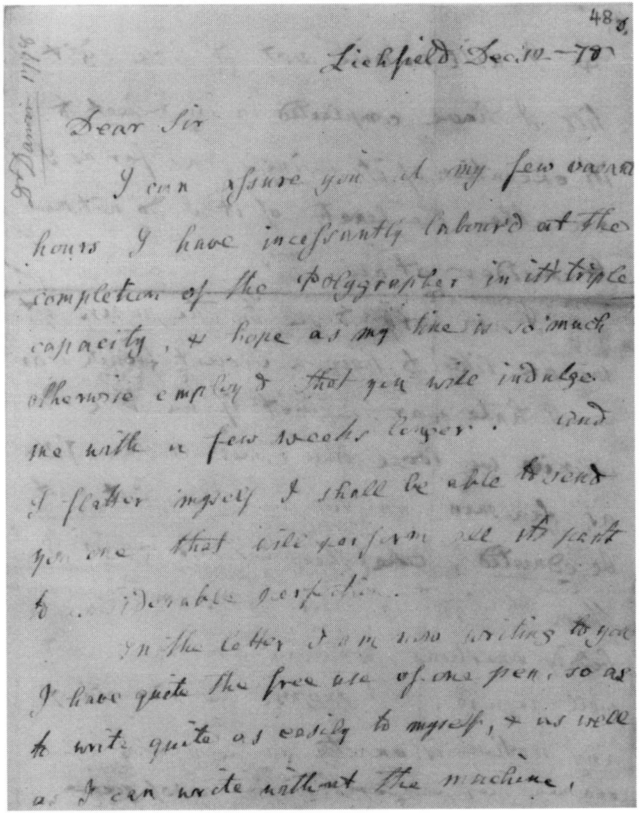

PLATE 9 The first page of Darwin's letter to Charles Greville of 12 December 1778, with the identical copy made by Darwin's mechanical copying machine (British Library Add MS 42071, folios 48 and 51). This is probably the earliest perfect mechanical copy of a document. The copy is so good that it is not certain which of the two is the original

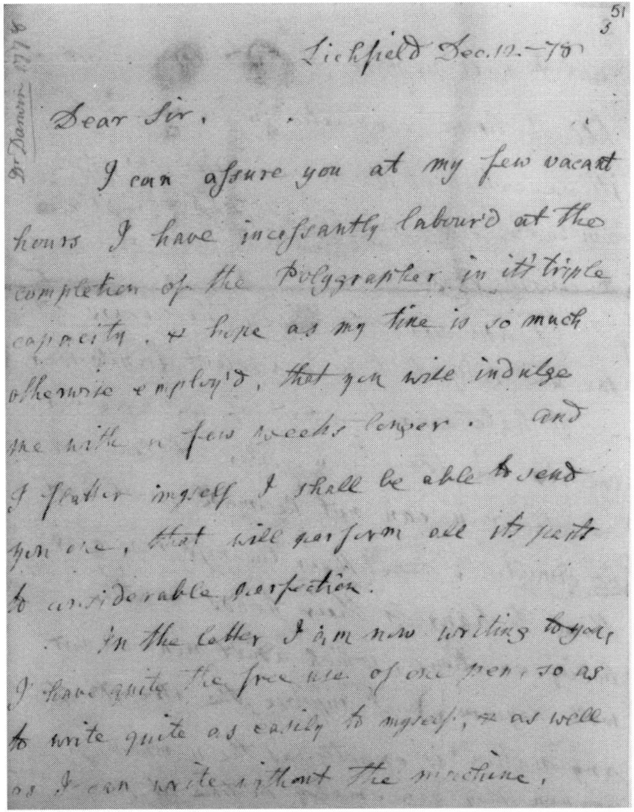

PLATE 10A Radburn Hall, near Derby. Elizabeth Pole lived here from 1769 until she married Erasmus Darwin in 1781. They were both living here from 1781 to 1783

PLATE 10B The Darwins' house in Full Street, Derby, where they lived from the autumn of 1783 until March 1802, as it appeared before its demolition in 1933

PLATE 10C Plaque on the house at St John Street, Ashbourne, where Susanna and Mary Parker began a girls' boarding school in 1794

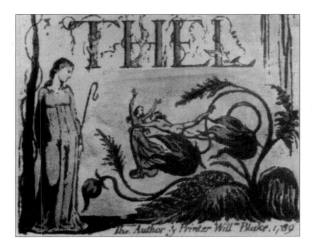

PLATE 11A Detail from the title page of William Blake's poem *The Book of Thel* (1789). A naked youth jumps out of one bloom to seize a girl emerging from the next bloom, just as in Darwin's *Loves of the Plants*

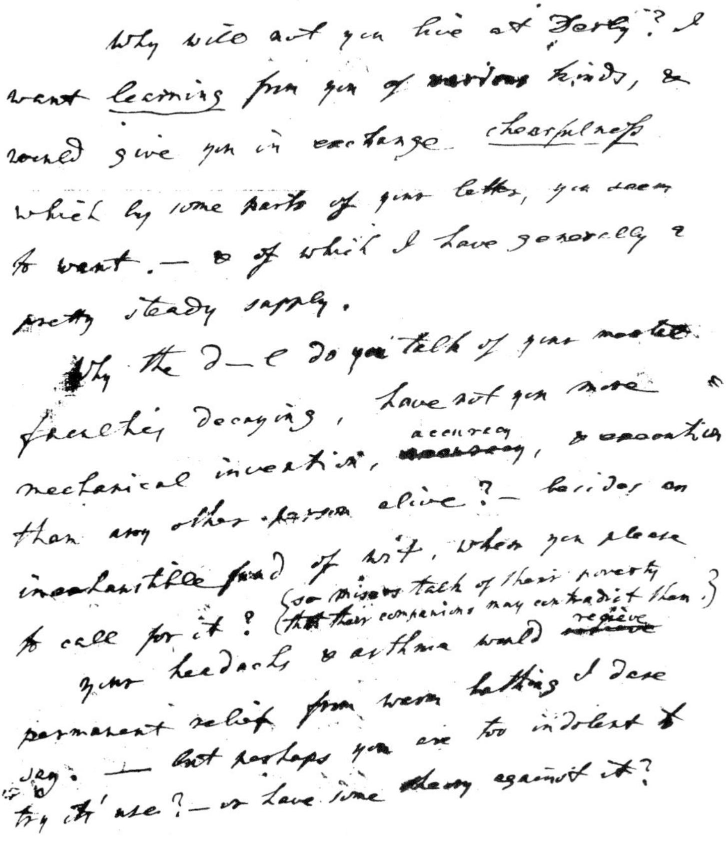

Why will not you live at Derby? I
want learning from you of various kinds, &
would give you in exchange cheerfulness
which by some parts of your letter, you seem
to want. — & of which I have generally a
pretty steady supply.
Why the D—l do you talk of your mental
faculties decaying, have not you more
mechanical invention, accuracy, & execution
than any other person alive? — besides an
inexhaustible fund of wit, when you please
to call for it? (so misers talk of their poverty that their companions may contradict them.)
Your headachs & asthma would relieve
permanent relief from warm bathing I dare
say. — but perhaps you are too indolent to
try its use? — or have some theory against it?

PLATE 11B Part of Darwin's letter of 19 January 1790 to James Watt. See page 248 for transcript

PLATE 12A Dr Erasmus Darwin (*right*) playing chess with his son Erasmus (1759–99), probably in the 1790s

PLATE 12B Erasmus's son Robert Darwin (1766–1848), probably about 1800

PLATE 12C Charles Robert Darwin (1809–82), grandson of Erasmus, in 1840, four years after returning from the voyage of the *Beagle*

PLATE 13A Breadsall Priory, where Erasmus Darwin died in April 1802, four weeks after the family moved there

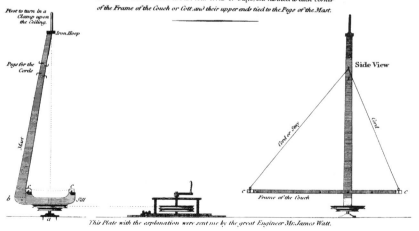

A MOVABLE ROTATIVE COUCH which may be put out of the way when not in use.

Vol.IV. p.456.

The length of the Mast must be suited to the height of the Ceiling.— The angle at b must be secured by a Plate of Iron screwed on the outside.—
The cast Iron Cup (a) for the bottom Pivot may have three spikes to fix it to the Floor.— The whole of the Wood-work may be made of Oak or
Elm.— The frame of the Couch (cc) is not fixed to the Sill, but the latter has two projecting Iron Pegs, which go into holes in the Frame, so
that the centre of motion may be changed at pleasure.—When not in use, the Frame may be lifted off the Sill, and set up paralel to the Mast, in
a corner of the room.. There are four Cords or Stays, one fastened to each corner
of the Frame of the Couch or Cott. and their upper ends tied to the Pegs of the Mast.

PLATE 13B Design by James Watt for a 'rotative couch' to try out Darwin's ideas on the benefits of centrifugation

The first Compartment.

2. *London. Published Decr 1.st 1792. by J. Johnson. St Pauls Church Yard.*

PLATE 14 One of William Blake's engravings of the Portland Vase in Part I of Darwin's *The Botanic Garden* (1792)

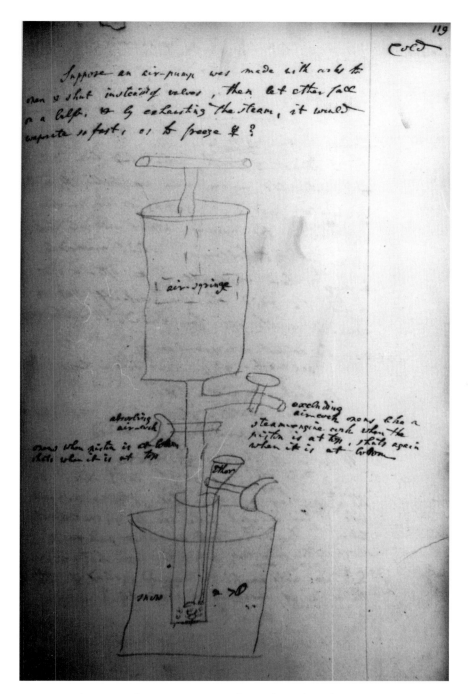

Cold

Suppose an air-pump was made with corks to open & shut instead of valves, then let ether fall on a bulb, & by exhausting the steam, it would evaporate so fast, as to freeze it?

air-syringe

absorbing air-cork

opens when piston is at bottom shuts when it is at top

expelling air-cork opens when a steam-engine cork when the piston is at top, shuts again when it is at bottom

ether

ether

PLATE 15 Apparatus for experiments on the cooling of air, from Darwin's Commonplace Book, 1784

PLATE 16 Erasmus Darwin at the age of sixty, painted in 1792 by Joseph Wright, his friend, patient and neighbour in Derby

[11]

As a postscript for 1789, I should mention that *The Loves of the Plants* includes a manifesto for the Darwinian school of poetry, as it came to be known. This appears as three prose 'Interludes' totalling thirty-one pages, sandwiched between the four cantos. Because of their influence these interludes deserve a little space on their own.

In each interlude the poet is questioned by a bookseller. Though only a stooge, he does ask the right questions. The first is: 'Pray tell me, what is the essential difference between Poetry and Prose?' Darwin replies:

> Next to the measure of the language, the principal distinction appears to me to consist in this: that Poetry admits of but few words expressive of very abstracted ideas, whereas Prose abounds with them. And as our ideas derived from visible objects are more distinct than those derived from the objects of our other senses, the words expressive of these ideas belonging to vision make up the principal part of poetic language. That is, the Poet writes principally to the eye, the Prose-writer uses more abstracted terms.[86]

When Wordsworth and Coleridge made their protest against Darwinian verse by publishing *Lyrical Ballads*, Wordsworth followed Darwin's example of manifesto-interludes by writing a manifesto-preface. The question Wordsworth asks is almost identical to the bookseller's: 'Is there then, it will be asked, no essential difference between the language of prose and metrical composition?'[87] Wordsworth's answer is of course quite different: 'all good poetry is the spontaneous overflow of powerful feeling' – not picture painting in words à la Darwin. This new Romantic paradigm was to displace Darwin's rubric just as completely as oxygen displaced phlogiston.

The bookseller also seeks Darwin's opinion on drama. In reply he defines 'theatric reverie', in which we suffer 'a similar kind of deception as in our dreams', when we are deceived because 'in sleep there is a total suspension of our voluntary power'.[88] Some years later Coleridge, after referring to 'sleep, which consists in a suspension of voluntary power',[89] regurgitated Darwin's 'theatric reverie' under the name 'dramatic illusion'.

In the second interlude the bookseller asks Darwin to distinguish the horrid from the tragic. The tragic, he says, 'consists in Distress attended with Pity, which is said to be allied to Love, the most agreeable of all our passions'. The horrid consists in 'Distress accompanied with Disgust, which is allied to Hate', a disagreeable sensation.

The third interlude treats the links between poetry, painting and music. Poetry can travel in time, whereas painting cannot, Darwin says. He dwells on the similarities between poetic metre and musical tempo, and dissects several couplets into crochets and quavers. To link painting and music, Darwin equates the seven colours of the spectrum with the seven notes of the octave. He suggests projecting 'luminous-music' movies on a screen by linking the keys of a harpsichord to movable blinds, and thus producing the Proem's 'lights and shades dancing on a whited canvas'.

[12]

During 1789 the change in Darwin's image was as radical as the changes in France; but 1790 proved much quieter. The second edition of *The Loves of the Plants* appeared in January, and Erasmus was expecting to see *The Economy of Vegetation* before long. He told Robert on 9 November 1789 that 'the first part of the Botanic Garden ... will blossom in June I hope, or May'.[90] But it was not to be so soon.

Towards the end of 1789 Erasmus received a gloomy letter from James Watt complaining that 'nothing now remains but the desire of money, which I cannot take much pains to get as I find it can neither bring health nor happiness'. Watt admits that he is sometimes 'tolerably well'. At other times he suffers 'troublesome headache or asthma and am as stupid as a bat and cannot add 3 figures together without error'. Now fifty-three, Watt regrets 'the loss of the few mental faculties one possessed in youth'.[91]

In his reply on 19 January 1790, Darwin begins with some financial banter: 'For my part I court not fame, I write for money; I am offer'd £600 for this work, but have not sold it'. Darwin often told his Lunar friends he was writing for money. He invented this myth partly because he felt ashamed of being a mere scribbler rather than a man of industry exploiting the newest technology. The pretence was also partly bravado, implying that his book was as valuable as a steam engine, and more easily produced. Had he really been writing for money, he would have started another poem instead of plodding on with *Zoonomia*, now twenty years in the making.

Darwin continues his letter to Watt (Plate 11B) more warmly:

Why will not you live at Derby? I want *learning* from you of various kinds, and would give you in exchange *chearfulness*, which by some parts of your letter, you seem to want – and of which I have generally a pretty steady supply.

Why the d---l do you talk of your mental faculties decaying, have not you more mechanical invention, accuracy, and execution than any other person alive? – besides an inexhaustible fund of wit, when you please to call for it? So Misers talk of their poverty that their companions may contradict them....

What I said about your steam-engine, I believed; I said it was the most in-genious of human inventions, can you tell me of one more ingenious? I can think of none unless you will except the Jew's harp, which is a combination of wind and wire instruments – or the partridge-call, which is a combination of the drum and fiddle.

Seriously, I do think the inventor of a wheel for a carriage had wonderful luck, or wonderful genius. The bow and arrow is also a curious invention, which the people of New South Wales, a continent of 2000 miles square, had not discover'd.

Do you not congratulate your grand-children on the dawn of universal liberty? I feel myself becoming all french both in chemistry and politics. Adieu ...[92]

Acting as both friend and psychiatrist, Darwin tries to lift Watt from the trough of depression and imagined debility by a mix of sympathy, praise and a little teasing.

Edgeworth was also in need of sympathy in 1790: his daughter Honora died of consumption, like her mother ten years before. Honora was just fifteen, a girl of outstanding talent and beauty, according to Maria and all who knew her. She had written a story called 'Rivuletta' not long before her death, and Edgeworth sent a copy to Darwin, who replied on 24 April:

> I much condole with you on your late loss, I know how to feel for your misfortune! The paper you sent me is a prodigy, written by so young a person with such elegance of imagination. Nil admirari may be a means to escape misery, but not to procure happyness – there is not much to be had in this world, we *expect* too much – I have had my loss also! – the letter of Sulpitius to Cicero ... is fine eloquence, but comes not to the heart, it tugs but does not draw the arrow – pains and diseases of the mind are only cured by Forgetfulness; Reason but skins the wound, which is perpetually liable to fester again.[93]

In a second letter Edgeworth gave his opinion of *The Loves of the Plants*. Darwin says this 'is very flattering to me indeed' and thanks Edgeworth for having encouraged him to go on with the poem ten years before.

Edgeworth also sent him a second walking hygrometer, called 'brazen-wheels' by Darwin. 'But I prefer *long-back* for a race; and would wager him against *brazen-wheels* for a cool hundred'. He says, 'I will sometime make a shelf for your animal to walk upon, but not till I repair my study, which wants a new roof'. Darwin's study was on the ground floor, if Fig. 12 is to be believed; if it also had a roof, it must have been at the back of the house projecting into the garden, away from the street noise and insulated a little from the bustle of the house.

On the day after Erasmus wrote to Edgeworth, 25 April, the baby Henry died, aged twelve months. He had been ill several times during his short life. In a letter during January Erasmus tells Robert how the baby was being treated for inflammation of the lungs. Even for his own son he prescribed bleeding, and, when that did no good, more bleeding. It seems like infanticide, or at best child abuse; but he was guilty only of following convention.

It was another bad year for deaths. Erasmus's old friend and mentor Benjamin Franklin died on 17 April 1790 aged eighty-four, and the House of Representatives voted to wear mourning for a month.

On 21 May the Poet Laureate Thomas Warton died, and six days later

Darwin wrote the strangest of his letters, to Dudley Ryder, a close friend of William Pitt. Darwin asks Ryder

> whether I might have any chance for the vacant Laureatship ... as I have a large and increasing family, and from my time of life am not likely to live long enough to provide well for them.[94]

The '£100 a year addition to my income' would be very welcome. Ryder knew Darwin and praised *The Loves of the Plants*, so the request was not unreasonable. But Darwin sabotaged his plea of poverty by telling Ryder that he had just received £800 from Johnson: if he had not long to live, he would never earn as much as that from the laureateship. Ryder made a lengthy and courteous reply, and told him that the appointment was already made. When Darwin wrote again, he knew (via Eliza Hayley and Erasmus junior) that Hayley had declined the laureateship. Darwin cannot imagine 'what reasons could induce him to refuse it': Hayley 'is not in very opulent circumstances', and 'I am conscious I should not have done so'.[95] (Henry Pye became Poet Laureate, and suffered much ridicule.)

These two letters from Erasmus are puzzling: was he really under financial stress? One possibility is loss of income when Sacheverel Pole reached the age of twenty-one, on 16 June 1790; under his father's will he then became owner of Radburn Hall. Erasmus tells Robert on 21 June that 'Erasmus [junior] and Mr Pole are in London',[96] no doubt on legal business. Perhaps the Darwins were receiving rent for Radburn Hall, or for the grounds, or both? Another possibility is that Erasmus thought he was developing a serious illness, and that his days were numbered. Or it may just have been the worry of running a large house with ten children and a wife who was extravagant rather than frugal. Her eldest daughter, always called 'Miss Pole', was often in London, an expensive place to visit. Also Erasmus may have begun to fret because Elizabeth was heavily pregnant again.

The child, their seventh and last, was a daughter Harriot (or Harriotte, as Erasmus first spelt it), born on 5 July. Like her sister Emma, she grew to be a beautiful girl. She started a school at Derby but gave it up when she married at the age of twenty-one.[97]

Elizabeth may have been glad to rest from her labours: she had given birth to eleven children, seven of them during her nine years married to Erasmus. Still only half way through her life, she was as vivacious as ever. Her fall downstairs (Fig. 12) was probably in 1790 but did her no harm.

Erasmus continued writing letters to Robert, mostly on medical matters. One letter in June is a discourse on insanity, instancing Sir Wolstan Dixie, who wrongly 'believed he had the itch'. He stripped 'three of his servants naked, with a pistol in his hand, that he might find out who had given him the itch'. More philosophically, Erasmus notes that 'In this age the fear of Hell, or of Death, or of Poverty are the most common topics of melancholy'.[98]

In the autumn Robert asked him to recommend a young man setting up as an apothecary in Lichfield. He replied: 'I cannot give any letters of recommendation to Lichfield; as I am, and have been from their infancy, acquainted with all the Apothecaries; and, as such letters must be directed to some of their patients, they would both feel and resent it'. To make up for this rebuff, Erasmus carefully explains how the apothecary might succeed: 'I should advise your friend to use at first all means to get acquainted with the people of all ranks. At first a parcel of blue and red glasses at the window might gain part of the retail business on market days, and thus get acquaintance with that class of people ...'[99] There follow several pages of painstaking advice, a good example of the patient 'benevolence' for which Erasmus was famous.

The Economy of Vegetation had still not come out. This was largely Erasmus's own fault, because he wished to include engravings of the Portland Vase as well as his interpretations of the scenes on it. At the end of 1790 he was predicting that publication would be in May 1791.

CHAPTER TWELVE

Eminence
1791–1793

The pre-publication problems of *The Economy of Vegetation* continued throughout 1791. Darwin had naively assumed that Joseph Johnson would provide engravings of the Portland Vase; but it was not so simple. The only engravings available were those by Bartolozzi, Johnson told him, and 'they cannot be copied without Hamilton's consent, being protected by act of parliament'.[1] Darwin might have obtained consent via Greville. But there was a further problem: Wedgwood was highly critical of Bartolozzi's work. As Wedgwood had spent years perfecting his copy of the Vase in black jasper, it would have been embarrassing for Darwin to have had sub-standard engraved copies in his poem. So it was back to square one, after a delay of six months. All was not lost, because Johnson was offering to have new engravings made. Darwin told Wedgwood on 9 July: 'The name of the engraver I don't know, but Johnson sais He is capable of doing any thing well'.[2]

This paragon among engravers was of course William Blake. On 23 July Johnson told Darwin that 'Blake is certainly capable of making an exact copy ... if the Vase were lent him for that purpose, and I see no other way of its being done'.[3] Evidently Blake did borrow the Vase (or perhaps a Wedgwood copy?), for he made the four superb engravings of the Vase that have ever since graced the pages of Darwin's poem – and boosted its auction price. Although Darwin was much indebted to Blake, and they had common friends in Fuseli, Johnson and Hayley, they never met. And Darwin never knew that Blake in *The Book of Thel* had produced such a suitable frontispiece for *The Loves of the Plants*. Blake engraved eleven plates for *The Economy of Vegetation*: for the quarto editions there were four of the Portland Vase and one of Fuseli's *Fertilization of Egypt*; and the same five were engraved again for the later octavo editions. The eleventh was Fuseli's *Typhoon* for the third edition.[4]

Johnson hoped to publish *The Economy of Vegetation* in 1791: that is the date given on the title page, and the engravings of the Vase are dated 1 December 1791. In reality the poem did not appear until June 1792: the reason for the delay may emerge if some of Johnson's correspondence in private hands becomes public.

There was no delay with the third edition of *The Loves of the Plants*, which did appear in 1791. Many of the misprints and misnumberings of the first edition are corrected, and more verses are added: there are 1938 lines in the third edition, compared with 1746 in the first. In Canto IV Darwin adds nearly a hundred lines and includes a potent newcomer, *Cannabis*. He notes that a cannabis plant grown in England from seed sown on 4 June reached a height of 14 feet 7 inches by October, with a stem seven inches in circumference. Darwin was ahead of his time (and of ours) in seizing on these extraordinary growth rates. Today growing cannabis to make paper could reduce the huge expense of British timber imports and help to preserve the world's forests.[5]

Johnson ensured that enough copies of *The Loves of the Plants* were available in 1792 for binding up with the first edition of *The Economy of Vegetation* to form the complete *Botanic Garden*. So the first edition of *The Botanic Garden* consists of the first edition of Part I, dated 1791 but published in June 1792, and the third edition of Part II, published in 1791. It is most confusing.

[2]

The real world of the family was less confusing but quite eventful.

Elizabeth's son Sacheverel Pole seems to have been a fast mover. On 16 March 1791, when still only twenty-one, he married Mary Ware, the seventeen-year-old daughter of a clergyman; within three months the first of their six children was on the way. Also Sacheverel commissioned Joseph Wright to paint two portraits to hang at Radburn, of himself and of his stepfather Erasmus. These fine portraits were probably in place by 1793, when Sacheverel became Sheriff of Derbyshire.

A humbler station in life was being planned for Erasmus's daughters Susan and Mary Parker, now eighteen and sixteen respectively. Early in 1791 they went to stay with Erasmus's 'dear old friend' Richard Dixon, and on 30 March he wrote to Dixon:

> I have often experienced the readiness with which you serve your friends; as to these girls, they ought to esteem you as a Father ...
> Your goodness to them requires that I should tell you my whole design about them. I think to leave them when I die (NB, that is not till the next century) the value of 500£ a piece – part in money and part in annuities, which last I design to prevent their coming to absolute poverty in case of unhappy marriage. If they marry with my approbation I shall give them 2 or 300£ a piece at the marriage

and an annuity of the value of the remainder at my death. By this sum and some employment as Lady's Maid or teacher of work they may be happier than my other girls, who will have not much more than double or treble that sum and brought up in more genteel life – for I think happiness consists much in being *well* in one's situation in life, and not in that situation being higher or lower.[6]

In fact Erasmus did much more for the girls than he says here, as we shall see. So far they had lived at Full Street; now he was trying to let them see the world. He speaks of them as 'at Birmingham', presumably with their mother Mrs Mary Day, and also arranges for them to stay '3 or 4 weeks' as paying guests with Dixon's son Robert, probably in London.

Erasmus's younger daughters Violetta and Emma, aged seven and six, were playmates of Penelope, the five-year-old daughter of Sir Brooke Boothby (who had now succeeded to his father's title). Penelope fell ill in mid-February: 'she began to scream out with pain on the left side of her head, or ear, or eye and temple ... succeeded by vomitting ... about thrice in 24 hours'. Erasmus gives these details in a letter to Robert, written from Ashbourne on 9 March.[7] He says she 'has I think the hydrocephalus – or, if not so, an abscess ...'. After a blister, calomel and bark, 'she appeared quite well ... about a week ago', and then became torpid for two days, after which 'the pain and vomitting' recurred. The pain was relieved by filling her affected ear with laudanum. Erasmus did not know what to do next.

Penelope died four days later, a month short of her sixth birthday. She is commemorated in the painting *Simplicity* by Sir Joshua Reynolds and in the marble monument by Thomas Banks in Ashbourne Church, with the inscription:

> She was in form and intellect most exquisite. The unfortunate parents ventured their all on this frail bark, and the wreck was total.

It is said that Boothby's wife left him at the graveside, and never returned to Ashbourne. Boothby himself was diverted from suicide only by Darwin's counselling, as Boothby recalled:

> When the last efforts of thy art had fail'd,
> And all my thoughts were wedded to the tomb,
> Thy mild philosophy repell'd the gloom,
> And bade me bear the ills on life entail'd.[8]

After this tragedy the accomplished and elegant Boothby published three more books, including *Sonnets sacred to the Memory of Penelope* (1796), and then toured Europe in genteel poverty for many years.

The summer of 1791 was free of such tragedies, and stirred memories of Lichfield for Erasmus. Anna Seward called on the Darwins in June, possibly her only visit to them. In July or August Erasmus was invited to a lavish archery meeting at Drakelow near Burton, the seat of Sir Nigel Bowyer

Gresley. He is recorded as the occupant of Darwin's house at Lichfield[9] in 1784, before he succeeded to the title. (His father Sir Nigel Gresley, who died in 1787, was the stepson of Darwin's patron Lady Gresley, who died in January 1791.)

The winner of the archery was Miss Susan Sneyd, and Darwin applauded her skill:

> With careless eye she view'd the central ring,
> Stretched her white arms, and drew the silken string!
> Mute wonder gaz'd the brazen studs betwixt;
> Full in the boss the flying arrow fix'd!
> Admiring circles greet the victor fair,
> And shouts of triumph rend the breezy air ...[10]

Robert Darwin may not have uttered shouts of triumph, but he was doing well. There had been no more interference by Dr Withering, and Robert was now confident enough of himself to take advantage of his father's medical knowledge. On 4 September Erasmus writes, 'You say you want a letter on inoculation ...', and launches into a three-page essay about the techniques of smallpox inoculation.

As well as receiving this wealth of advice, Robert was beginning to grow quite rich, through bequests and through his own efforts. His uncle Charles Howard died in January, leaving £100 to each nephew, according to a letter from Erasmus junior, who also tells Robert, 'I will take care to let you have as much of the £1000 as you may want'.[11] This was presumably the money Robert inherited from his grandfather when he became twenty-one, not so far used because he did not need it. Add in his medical earnings for the year, £1180, and Robert had a total potential cash inflow in 1791 of £2280.

This letter also shows how Erasmus junior took care of the family money just as successfully as he had managed the Pole estate. He was a capable and trusted lawyer-accountant, a good man to have in the family. Robert admired his talents, and learnt from him.

[3]

The Lunar Society was fatally wounded by the Birmingham riots in July 1791. The late 1780s had seen the growth of the radical reform movement in England, and 'Revolution Societies' sprang up, to press for the liberties promised in the 'Glorious Revolution' of 1688. The exclusion of dissenters from all official posts was one obvious grievance, and dissenters were prominent in these societies. Joseph Priestley had long been known for his controversial books on religious issues, and he was a member of the

Revolution Society at Birmingham. However, he was not present at the Society's dinner held on 14 July to celebrate Bastille Day. James Keir agreed to be chairman at the dinner,

> never conceiving that a peaceable meeting for the purpose of rejoicing that 26 millions of our fellow-creatures were rescued from despotism, and made as free and happy as we Britons are, could be misinterpreted as being offensive to a government, whose greatest boast is liberty.[12]

The riots began that evening and went on for three days. Their origin has been much discussed but never clarified.[13] They were directed primarily at dissenters. After burning the Old and New Meeting Houses, the mob attacked Priestley's house and destroyed all his goods, scientific apparatus, books and papers. He and his family had to flee for their lives. The same fate befell William Hutton, another dissenter who had as a magistrate devoted two days a week (unpaid) to settling quarrels. At least fourteen houses were burnt and others ransacked. Withering was told a day in advance that his house would be attacked, and he managed to organize a defence force. Boulton and Watt armed their workmen, but Soho was not on the hit-list. The riots were directed by well-dressed strangers, whom the dissenters suspected were Government agents, and cries of 'No philosophers – Church and King forever' were heard. Three local magistrates, who refused to act against the rioters, can be regarded as accomplices.[14] After three days, detachments of Dragoons arrived and restored order. The Government refused an inquiry, but Hutton and Priestley did receive compensation after lengthy legal cases.

For the Lunar Society the wreck was total, or nearly so. Priestley was their most active member, and he was not only driven from Birmingham but also persecuted and vilified in London, especially when the excesses of the French Revolution fuelled 'Anti-Jacobin' fever. Three years later Priestley felt obliged to leave Britain and emigrate to America. He told his 'valued friends, the members of the Lunar Society of Birmingham', that 'I consider my settlement at Birmingham as the happiest event in my life'.[15]

Without Priestley the Lunar Society 'insensibly dissolved'. So informal a group needed a spark to keep it healthy. Looking back, it seems that Darwin was the sparkler in the 1770s and Priestley in the 1780s. Although sporadic meetings continued after 1791, Boulton lost his enthusiasm: the perceived link between the Society and the riots was a threat to his lucrative Government contracts for coining.

Needless to say, the savagery of the riots upset everyone. Darwin wrote to Wedgwood on 25 July: 'The Birmingham riots are a disgrace to Mankind'.[16] Joseph Johnson believed 'that if Dr P. had been found by the high church mob he would have been murdered'.[17] Robert Bage wrote to William Hutton: 'may my house be burned too, if I am not become sick of my species'.[18]

For Darwin the riots sent a clear smoke signal. Britain's brief flirtation with the French Revolution was over; soon it was to be 'Church and King for ever' and to hell with liberty. From now onwards Darwin grew more cautious in publishing radical opinions, though it was too late to tone down the enthusiasm for the French Revolution expressed in his poem.

At the meeting of the Derby Philosophical Society on 3 September the members agreed to send Priestley a message written by Darwin:

> We condole with yourself and with the scientific world on the loss of your valuable library, your experimental apparatus, and your more valuable manuscripts.... Almost all great minds in all ages of the world, who have endeavoured to benefit mankind, have been persecuted by them.... Your enemies, unable to conquer your arguments by reason, have had recourse to violence; they have halloo'd upon you the dogs of unfeeling ignorance, and of frantic fanaticism.[19]

He urges Priestley to avoid further danger by leaving 'the unfruitful fields of polemical theology' and concentrating on science, which will 'overturn the empire of superstition'. The only clergyman in the Derby Philosophical Society, the Revd Charles Hope, complained in the newspapers that not enough members were present at the meeting when this message was sent. Darwin had him thrown out: the Society, having heard Mr Hope's explanation, resolved that 'he be desired to withdraw his name from the list of the Society'.[20]

In reply, Priestley said he was resuming his chemical pursuits. 'Excuse me, however, if I still join theological to philosophical studies, and if I consider the former as greatly superior in importance to mankind to the latter'. Darwin and Priestley were poles apart in their valuations of theology.

[4]

The Economy of Vegetation eventually came out in June 1792, to a chorus of approval from its expectant readers. With 2440 lines of verse and about 80,000 words of Notes, it was a longer and stronger poem than *The Loves of the Plants*, and served as the basis of Darwin's pre-eminent reputation as a poet. Its title was unappealing and inaccurate; but no one seemed to mind, and most people referred to it as *The Botanic Garden*.

Again Darwin speaks through the Goddess of Botany, who addresses the Nymphs of Fire in Canto I, the Gnomes of Earth in Canto II, the Nymphs of Water in Canto III and the Sylphs of Air in Canto IV. This Rosicrucian machinery is also unappealing today. The exclamations 'Nymphs!', 'Gnomes!', or 'Sylphs!' at the beginnings of paragraphs are distracting, useless and best ignored.

It all sounds most unpromising, and even more so when the verse gets off to a bad start because thirty-four of the first fifty-eight lines consist largely of Anna's stilted poem about the botanic garden at Lichfield.[21] How many intending modern readers have been put off by these irrelevant lines, I wonder? This tactical blunder was made worse because Darwin failed to say that Anna had written them, though they had been published as hers years before.[22] She was annoyed to find her work reprinted in a mangled form without acknowledgment. Darwin said he included the verses as a compliment to her: this was true, because the lines were out of keeping with the rest of the poem and of no advantage whatever to him. She could not protest too strongly because she had used his verses unacknowledged in the *Elegy on Captain Cook*, and she graciously turned her complaint into a compliment: 'So great a work ought not to contain lines ... known to have been written by another'.[23]

After this bumbling start, can Darwin recover? He takes over at line 59, as the Goddess of Botany comes down in a flowery car to make a graceful landing. The nymphs, gnomes and sylphs fuss around. The sylphs beat the air with 'winnowing wings, and waft her golden hair'. The nymphs perfume her: 'Musked in the rose's lap fresh dews they shed'. The Goddess calls on the fiery forms nestling in 'each nice pore of ocean, earth, and air'. This is more promising: indeed all three phrases quoted have echoes in Keats and Shelley, in 'To Autumn', the 'Ode to a Nightingale' and 'The Cloud'.[24]

The action now begins, with the creation of the universe, which Darwin describes with supreme confidence and a teasing ambiguity as to who is really responsible for the event:

NYMPHS OF PRIMEVAL FIRE! your vestal train
Hung with gold-tresses o'er the vast inane,
Pierced with your silver shafts the throne of Night,
And charm'd young Nature's opening eyes with light;
When LOVE DIVINE, with brooding wings unfurl'd,
Call'd from the rude abyss the living world.
– 'LET THERE BE LIGHT!' proclaim'd the ALMIGHTY LORD,
Astonish'd Chaos heard the potent word; –
Through all his realms the kindling Ether runs,
And the mass starts into a million suns;
Earths round each sun with quick explosions burst,
And second planets issue from the first;
Bend, as they journey with projectile force,
In bright ellipses their reluctant course;

Orbs wheel in orbs, round centres centres roll,
And form, self-balanced, one revolving Whole.   [I 97–112]*

It was a concoction heady enough to intoxicate Horace Walpole: 'The twelve verses that by miracle describe and comprehend the creation of the Universe out of chaos, are in my opinion the most sublime passage in any author, or in any of the few languages with which I am acquainted'.[25] Anna Seward was no less impressed and thought the passage 'of excellence yet unequalled in its kind, and never to be excelled in the grandeur of its conceptions'.[26] Though there are a few echoes from *Paradise Lost*, Darwin's lines have a fine resonance.

There is more than mere rhetoric too, because Darwin speaks across the centuries to modern astronomers in his footnote, where he adopts the now fashionable 'big bang' theory of cosmogony:

It may be objected, that if the stars had been projected from a Chaos by explosions, that they must have returned again into it from the known laws of gravitation; this however would not happen, if the whole of Chaos, like grains of gunpowder, was exploded at the same time, and dispersed through infinite space at once, or in quick succession, in every possible direction. [I 105, note]

This is very similar to the description on page 5 of Steven Weinberg's book *The First Three Minutes*, published in 1977: 'In the beginning there was an explosion ... which occurred simultaneously everywhere, filling all space from the beginning, with every particle of matter rushing apart from every other particle'.

Darwin's flair for scientific prophecy is matched by his skill in evading ultimate questions by creating a myth of multiple responsibility. He has the 'Almighty Lord' making the world out of chaos, but the Lord acts only when told to do so by 'Love Divine'. Before and during creation, it is the Nymphs who rule. Yet they are subordinate to the Goddess, and she is only the spokesperson of Darwin himself, the ultimate creator of this fivefold hierarchy. It is surprising that no one condemned him for hubris. Rather, they thought it put him in a class of his own. And it did: no other author of the time would have dared to play such games with the creation.

Other episodes in the poem would repay analysis too, but here I shall limit myself to outlining the action.

After the expansive start Darwin focuses on the Earth, and particularly on its atmosphere alive with shooting-stars, lightning, rainbows, fireballs and auroral streamers:

ETHEREAL POWERS! you chase the shooting stars,
Or yoke the vollied lightnings to your cars,

* Canto and line numbers in the first edition of *The Economy of Vegetation* are given after quotations.

Cling round the aërial bow with prisms bright,
And pleased untwist the sevenfold threads of light....
Ride, with broad eye and scintillating hair,
The rapid Fire-ball through the midnight air;
Dart from the North on pale electric streams,
Fringing Night's sable robe with transient beams.   [I 115–18, 127–30]

In case anyone has forgotten, this is the canto of fire, and therefore of heat, light and electricity, and Darwin runs through volcanoes, glow-worms and gunpowder before arriving at fire's finest product (in his view): the steam engine. Its 'Giant-Power' has many uses. It drives Boulton's coining machine. It can pump water up into 'lead-lined towers' to provide each household with water flowing 'fresh through a thousand pipes' for 'thirsty cities'. Or it can operate a mill-stone,

Whose flinty teeth the golden harvests grind,
Feast without blood! and nourish human-kind.   [I 277–8]

Darwin liked the non-sexist word 'human-kind': he was already well attuned to a (future) feminist viewpoint. He also shows he is attuned to the vegetarian view by approving of bloodless food. Though he ate meat, he thought that to feed animals 'by the destruction of other animals' was a 'less perfect part of the economy of nature', and his own favourite lunch was meatless, if Mrs SchimmelPenninck can be believed.[27]

Steam engines also inspire the lines about the flying chariot already quoted in chapter 9, and the look forward to flying machines with engines fuelled by 'some other explosive material'.

Electricity is next on the list of friendly fiery forces. A 'fearless Beauty' touches 'the sparkling rod with graceful hand', and 'mimic lightnings' dart 'through her fine limbs'. Real lightning strikes when Franklin stretches up to the sky to 'seize the tiptoe lightnings ere they fly'. Darwin, no less elemental, wants to equalize the benefits of warmth: 'instead of exhausting their wealth in unnecessary wars', nations should cooperate by fixing sails to a thousand icebergs and then steering them into equatorial waters, to cool the tropics and warm our northern winters. This idea, possibly derived from Dr Small, was warmly welcomed by readers in frigid Britain.[28]

Canto II belongs to the Gnomes of Earth. Darwin suggests that the Earth was created

When high in ether, with explosion dire,
From the deep craters of his realms of fire,
The whirling Sun this ponderous planet hurl'd,
And gave the astonish'd void another world.   [II 13–16]

Today's science sees the Earth as having been formed in a different way, by accretion of a cloud of smaller objects in orbit round the Sun.

At first the Earth was mostly ocean, Darwin believes, thus giving himself a licence to uncover Venus as she rises from the sea:

> The bright drops, rolling from her lifted arms,
> In slow meanders wander o'er her charms,
> Seek round her snowy neck their lucid track,
> Pearl her white shoulders, gem her ivory back,
> Round her fine waist and swelling bosom swim,
> And star with glittering brine each crystal limb.   [II 59–64]

This new declaration of his 'affection for Venus' was much praised: Anna Seward calls it 'peerless', and William Cowper in his manuscript notes on the poem says the lines 'are exquisitely touch'd and with a delicacy suited to the subject'.[29] Another digression praised by Cowper is Darwin's spirited story of Mars and Venus netted by Vulcan while coupled. It is beautifully written but too long to quote (lines 151–82).

The next traumatic event presided over by the Gnomes is the birth of the Moon:

> When rose the continents, and sunk the main,
> And Earth's huge sphere exploding burst in twain. –
> GNOMES! how you gazed! when from her wounded side
> Where now the South-Sea heaves its waste of tide,
> Rose on swift wheels the MOON's refulgent car,
> Circling the solar orb, a sister-star,
> Dimpled with vales, with shining hills emboss'd,
> And roll'd round Earth her airless realms of frost.   [II 75–82]

The idea that the Moon was formed by fission of the Earth was put on a sound mathematical footing by Sir George Darwin,[30] Erasmus's great-grandson, and is for that reason known as the Darwinian theory. The Moon's origin remains controversial today.

Less controversial is Darwin's geology, which provokes digressions not on the amours of Greek goddesses but on current affairs. He explains how limestone forms from sea shells, and salt is deposited by evaporation. Iron ores, acids, precious stones and clay lure him to pottery and hence to Wedgwood, whom he salutes for his classical vases and modern medallions. Next Darwin dashes past coal, amber and electricity (again) to Franklin and the liberation of America, and then to France, where the 'Giant-form' of Liberty had long

> Inglorious slept, unconscious of his chains;
> Round his large limbs were wound a thousand strings
> By the weak hands of Confessors and Kings....
> Touch'd by the patriot-flame, he rent amazed
> The flimsy bonds, and round and round him gazed.   [II 378–80, 385–6]

These lines about the French Revolution became well known, and they
were to damage Darwin during the anti-Jacobin furore later in the 1790s.
His Giant-form of Liberty and Giant-Power of steam seem twin brothers:
one frees the people from tyranny, the other frees them from heavy labour,
or so he hopes.

The roll-call of metals and minerals continues with tin, copper, zinc and
lead, which receive only one line each. But the Spanish conquest of Mexico
and Peru for their mineral wealth rouses Darwin to fury:

> Heavens! on my sight what sanguine colours blaze!
> Spain's deathless shame! the crimes of modern days!
> When Avarice, shrouded in Religion's robe,
> Sail'd to the West, and slaughter'd half the globe.   [II 413–6]

This leads to a further onslaught on the British slave trade. He asks
Britannia to note

> How AFRIC'S coasts thy craftier sons invade
> With murder, rapine, theft, – and call it Trade!
> – The SLAVE, in chains, on supplicating knee,
> Spreads his wide arms, and lifts his eyes to Thee;
> With hunger pale, with wounds and toil oppress'd,
> 'ARE WE NOT BRETHREN? sorrow choaks the rest.   [II 423–8]

Nowhere else in the poem does Darwin become so emotional.

He tells the Gnomes to smite every 'blood-nursed Tyrant' they can find.
They oblige by burying the army of Cambyses in sand during a desert
march. The scene is 'described with great force and animation', as Cowper
says, with Darwin dealing out seven of his favourite 'double hammer
blows':[31]

> Onward resistless rolls the infuriate surge,
> Clouds follow clouds, and mountains mountains urge;
> Wave over wave the driving desert swims,
> Bursts o'er their heads, inhumes their struggling limbs;
> Man mounts on man, on camels camels rush,
> Hosts march o'er hosts, and nations nations crush, –
> Wheeling in air the wingèd islands fall,
> And one great earthy Ocean covers all!   [II 487–94]

In Canto III the treacherous sands give way to calm waters, the realm of
the 'aquatic Nymphs' who 'lead with viewless march / The wingèd vapours
up the aërial arch', and then lead them down again, as rivers, to the sea – an
endless cycle that Darwin likens to the circulation of the blood.

The nymphs have learnt the new chemistry and can combine 'pure air'
(oxygen) with 'flaming gas' (hydrogen) to create water. They control waters
of all kinds, rivers under Alpine snows, Icelandic geysers, the warm springs

of Buxton and the cascades of Chatsworth. These sportive nymphs beautify Britain with 'lucid cataracts', smile on Brindley's cradle and guide their 'liquid silver' through 'peopled vales'.

This third canto was the most admired of the four, as Cowper's manuscript notes confirm. The gems he selects are the 'beautiful description of the Alps and of the rivers that break out from beneath the snows' (lines 103–18), and two delicate landscape scenes – the 'charming lines' 427–60, and lines 509–26 ('the whole passage exquisite'). Best of all, he thinks, and better than in Homer,[32] is the wooing of Jupiter by Juno (lines 211–60): 'No description indeed in all our poetry has ever been more exquisitely finished'.[33] Walter Scott also picked on this episode as ensuring Darwin 'a ranking among British poets of the highest class'.[34] All these passages need to be read in full, and are too long to quote here.

Canto IV brings on the Sylphs of Air, who occupy themselves in making the plants exude oxygen and the sea breezes blow. In sourer mood they create fogs, the sirocco, simoom and tornado. They can measure 'the spring and pressure of the viewless air', and their barometers

> Weigh the long column of the incumbent skies,
> And with the changeful moment fall and rise.   [IV 133–4]

This triggers the thought of balloons, and Darwin promptly thinks also of 'Sea-Balloons', long-distance submarines supplied with pure air through the discoveries of Priestley, 'the Sage':

> Led by the Sage, Lo! Britain's sons shall guide
> Huge SEA-BALLOONS beneath the tossing tide;
> The diving castles, roof'd with spheric glass,
> Ribb'd with strong oak, and barr'd with bolts of brass,
> Buoy'd with pure air shall endless tracks pursue,
> And PRIESTLEY's hand the vital flood renew...   [IV 195–200]

Darwin envisages the submarines travelling 'beneath the shadowy ice-isles of the Pole', as eventually happened in 1958.

He also commends the great astronomer William Herschel, whose ideas on cosmology he outlines:

> Star after star from Heaven's high arch shall rush,
> Suns sink on suns, and systems systems crush,
> Headlong, extinct, to one dark centre fall,
> And Death and Night and Chaos mingle all!   [IV 373–6]

In the third line Darwin versifies the idea of a black hole, which his friend John Michell had envisaged nine years before.[35]

There are the usual digressions in Canto IV. A pestilential wind destroys the army of another tyrant (Senacherib) in another flurry of double hammer-blows ('Man falls on Man, on buckler buckler rings'). A saucier digression, with man falling on woman, tells the story of the plague victim Aegle and her lover Thyrsis.

The poem's title is not wholly misleading: Darwin does give the Sylphs a crash course on the economy of vegetation in the last 200 lines of the poem. (Presumably these lines were the earliest to be written.) He tells the Sylphs how seeds burst into life, buds unfold and disease threatens. As a digression from the plant physiology, he paints a pleasant picture of the new gardens at 'imperial Kew'. At the end, after asking the sylphs to load her car with flowers, the Botanic Goddess drives off again into the upper atmosphere.

[5]

For about six years after the publication of the complete *Botanic Garden*, Darwin was generally regarded as the leading English poet of the time. His array of brilliants dazzled his contemporaries. The comments by Cowper, Walpole and Scott are typical. Cowper's manuscript notes were the basis for his glowing seven-page notice in the *Analytical Review*, where he savours

> the splendour of his poem, which could not have been more highly finished, sweeter in the flow of its numbers, more exquisite in the expression, more diversified in the matter, or richer in every species of embellishment.[36]

Could praise be higher? Well, yes: at the suggestion of his friend William Hayley, Cowper wrote a poem 'To Dr Darwin',

> Two poets (poets by report
>   Not oft so well agree)
> Sweet Harmonist of Flora's court!
>   Conspire to honour thee ...

There are five more verses, just as friendly.

Hayley also composed a poem in Darwin's honour. It begins:

> As Nature lovely Science led
>   Through all her flowery maze,
> The volume she before her spread
>   Of Darwin's radiant lays.[37]

Further flattery follows. Hayley makes Nature talk to Science, and they are both grateful that their images have been much improved by Darwin, 'an artist so divine'.

Hayley sent the poems to Darwin in a letter dated 27 June 1792: 'you have two very ardent admirers', he says, and adds, 'I am in raptures with a thousand Beauties in your Poem'.[38] Darwin replied on 15 July, politely thanking them and saying he has studied their work 'with great delight and improvement'.[39]

Cowper and Hayley were arguably the leading poets of the 1780s, and their admiration of Darwin certified his pre-eminence. The mutual admiration of the three may seem laughable today. But it is no credit to our era that we expect discourtesy.

There was plenty more praise on offer. According to the *Critical Review*, 'its merits occur in every page and might give occasion for undistinguishing panegyric'.[40] For the *New Annual Register*, the poem 'afforded us greater pleasure and entertainment than its predecessor'.[41] The great engineer Thomas Telford called it 'a very wonderful and masterly performance'.[42] Horace Walpole said that 'Dr Darwin has destroyed my admiration for any poetry but his own'.[43] Anna Seward believed that 'not one great Poet of England is more original than Darwin', and that by bringing in science he had created a new class in poetry, 'so brilliantly that ... it will probably never have an equal in its particular class'.[44] That has so far been true: 'it was an achievement which was never repeated or even attempted',[45] as L. T. C. Rolt remarked in 1958.

The young poets were also captivated. Fifty years later Wordsworth admitted that 'my taste and natural tendencies were under an injurious influence from the dazzling manner of Darwin'.[46]

Coleridge was more generous. Although he had rejected the Darwinian style by 1796, when he wrote 'I absolutely nauseate Darwin's poem', Coleridge told John Thelwall in 1797:

> Dr Darwin will no doubt excite your respectful curiosity. On the whole, I think, he is the first *literary* character in Europe, and the most original-minded Man.[47]

This is a stunning tribute, considering that Coleridge detested his verse style and his evolutionary biology.

Darwin's poem seemed strikingly original in his day. And so it was. There had been nothing quite like it before. Yet he was influenced in his style by a whole shelf of eighteenth-century poems, led by Alexander Pope's *The Rape of the Lock*, with its mock-heroic tone and Rosicrucian figures. Teasing out Darwin's literary ancestors became quite a pastime in the 1790s, and about twenty poems have been fingered, then or later. I have looked at all these, without finding a winner. There are some similarities, but the differences are more striking. As might be expected, it seems that Darwin just absorbed the general idiom of the time. He was indebted more to Lucretius than to any modern poet.

Darwin's poem was the most highly praised book of 1792, and a second edition was printed as soon as possible; but it was too expensive to be the most popular book, and was not as much read as Part II of Thomas Paine's

Rights of Man, with its programme for democracy, state education and graduated income tax. The book of the year in retrospect is Mary Wollstonecraft's *Vindication of the Rights of Woman*, which has possibly had the most effect in changing society. In the realm of imaginative literature Darwin did not have much competition: among novels there was Robert Bage's *Man as He Is* and in poetry Samuel Rogers's lacklustre *Pleasures of Memory*.

Another mark of originality in Darwin's poem is his use of so many 'new' words. While compiling a concordance to *The Botanic Garden*,[48] I checked with the *OED*, and found 147 words in the poem that are either cited in the *OED* as the earliest example (65), or are earlier than the earliest citation in the *OED* (82). (It is of course possible that earlier examples exist.) Many of the words are adjectives, such as *blubbery, brineless, convoluted, eddying, freightless, frenzied, gauzy, inemulous, iridescent, pillowy, renovated, scintillating, susurrant, uncurtained, writhing.* Some are compound words, such as *snow-clad*; some are words with special meanings, like *airless* (devoid of air); some are nouns used as verbs, for example *car*. There are other 'new' words in the Notes, such as *geological*.

The concordance also shows how Darwin shuns the commonplace and the unpleasant. He never uses the adjectives *good, bad, evil* or *ugly*, whereas *bright* occurs 109 times, *fair* 104 times and *glittering* 26 times. *Beauty* appears 63 times, *ugliness* not at all.

[6]

In the Notes to *The Economy of Vegetation*, which are its scientific backbone, Darwin scampers around the frontiers of knowledge, looking at the unanswered questions and sometimes offering speculative answers himself. Today there are many popular science books probing the boundaries of the known. But in Darwin's day there was nothing comparable: the nearest were books by the itinerant lecturers, like Adam Walker's *Familiar Philosophy* (1799).

Darwin's portfolio of essays on selected topics of burning scientific interest was a new genre. An omnivorous reader like Coleridge absorbed the facts or theories and used them in his poems – for example, the luminosity of tropical seas, important in the 'Ancient Mariner'. Because the *Botanic Garden* was so popular and influential, the Notes were widely read. Even the three short sentences about Memnon's lyre had a visible effect on Wordsworth.[49] Though the topics of the Notes vary widely, most are concerned with the sciences of Earth in the widest sense. These 'Earth notes' can usefully be grouped under three headings: vegetation, geology and the atmosphere.

Darwin writes twenty pages about vegetation and 'the economy of nature'. All vegetables, he says, create sugar, and 'since animals are sustained by these vegetable productions, it would seem that the sugar-making process carried on in vegetable vessels was the great source of life to all organized beings'. To sum up:

It would seem that roots fixed in the earth, and leaves innumerable waving in the air were necessary for the decomposition of water, and the conversion of it into saccharine matter, which would have been not only cumbrous but totally incompatible with the locomotion of animal bodies.   [Notes, pp.111–12]

The individuality of buds impressed him: 'A tree is properly speaking a family or swarm of buds, each bud being an individual plant' (p.27). Charles Darwin gives credit to his grandfather for originating this idea, 'now universally adopted'.[50] The anthers and stigmas too, Erasmus believes, are 'separate beings, endued with the passion and power of reproduction' (p.112). There is no mention of his evolutionary ideas – reserved for *Zoonomia* two years later.

Thirty pages are devoted to geology, another of Darwin's passionate interests. Guided probably by his friend James Hutton, he steers between the extremes of the Neptunists, who saw the deposition of strata beneath the sea as all-important, and the Vulcanists, who believed in the supremacy of volcanic or plutonic events. Darwin believes both processes to be at work. Hot springs and volcanoes convince him that the Earth is very hot at great depths, and he believes that 'the central parts of the earth' – what is now called the 'core' – 'consist of a fluid mass and that part of this mass is iron', the remainder being molten lava. The iron in the core creates the Earth's magnetic field, he thinks. Coming nearer the surface, Darwin notes 'that many of the highest mountains of the world consist of limestone replete with shells' and 'bear the marks of having been lifted up by subterraneous fires'. The limestone strata, he says, 'consist of the accumulated exuviae of shell-fish, the animals perished age after age but their shells remained, and in progression of time produced the amazing quantities of limestone which almost cover the earth' (Notes, p.32).

Darwin continues with notes on morasses, iron, flint, clays, enamel and coal. The formation of coal from buried forests he regards as proved, as 'evinced from the vegetable matters frequently found' in the coal.

He can also be said to have begun the scientific study of the origins of oil.[51] He was fascinated by the 'fountain of fossil tar, or petroleum' found associated with a seam of coal in the gorge of the Severn at Coalbrookdale 'about a mile and a half below the celebrated iron-bridge' (Notes, p.60).

Section of the Earth

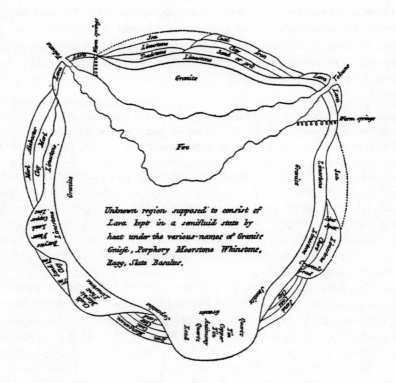

A sketch of a supposed Section of the Earth in respect to the disposition of the Strata over each other without regard to their proportions or number.

FIG. 15 Darwin's sketch model of the Earth. Note that it is diagrammatic rather than geographically realistic and shows possible dispositions of the strata. From *The Economy of Vegetation*, Note XXIV

'From ten to fifteen barrels a day' of this petroleum, 'each barrel containing 32 gallons, were at first collected'. But later the rate decreased. The petroleum is, he thinks, 'distilled' out of the coal by the effects of heat and pressure down the ages. Although this North Severn oilfield proved a dud by North Sea oil standards, Darwin was alert to the idea of extracting petroleum, more than sixty years before the first oil well was bored in the USA.

A detailed diagram, Fig. 15, illustrates his views on geology and Earth history. Briefly, he sees the 'masses of granite, porphery, basalt ...' as 'part of the original nucleus of the earth', or 'volcanic productions since formed'. On this nucleus, when covered by ocean, were formed

> the calcareous beds of limestone, marble, chalk, spar, from the exuviae of marine animals; with the flints, or chertz, which accompany them. And were stratified by their having been formed at different and very distant periods of time. [Notes, p.65]

Long ago, he thought, the central fires burst out, raising 'islands and continents' and ejecting the Moon, as already suggested in the poem.

Darwin's survey of geology, though not entirely correct by modern standards, was the best available at the time, or for many years to come. For twenty years he had been collecting minerals in the Peak District of Derbyshire and Staffordshire. Three of the century's leading geologists, Whitehurst, Michell and Hutton, were his friends. He learnt from them the best of their ideas, and added insights of his own. It was an impressive performance.

Even more impressive are the twenty-five pages on atmospheric science, for Darwin takes a space-age view of the complete atmosphere that was not really bettered until the 1950s.[52]

Darwin divides the atmosphere into three strata, as shown in Fig. 16. His first stratum, with clouds and lightning, is almost the same as the modern troposphere, though his upper boundary should be higher, at about six miles. His second and cloudless region is what is now called the stratosphere and lower mesosphere. This region ends, he says, 'where the air is 3000 times rarer than at the surface of the Earth', at a height of thirty-seven miles in the model he adopts. Models of the upper atmosphere were woefully

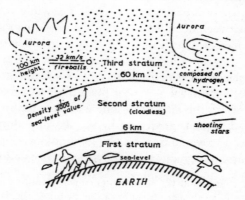

FIG. 16 Sketch of the three-tier model of the atmosphere proposed by Darwin in the Notes to *The Economy of Vegetation*

erroneous, even in the early twentieth century, but Darwin's value is almost correct – it should be thirty-six miles. This is because he used Halley's model from a century before, which was excellent.[53]

At greater heights, he says,

> it seems probable that the common air ends, and is surrounded by an atmosphere of inflammable gas [hydrogen] tenfold rarer than itself. In this region I believe fire-balls sometimes to pass, and at other times the northern lights to exist. [Notes, p.2]

Darwin was right in believing that the lighter gases would rise to greater heights, leading to an outermost atmosphere of hydrogen, though he placed the base of the 'hydrogen exosphere' too low – it should be at least 300 miles. However, his mistake with the height was a far less serious error than that of orthodox scientists in the early twentieth century, who thought there was no hydrogen at all.[54] It was not until the 1960s that Darwin was shown to be right.

Darwin was also right in believing that the aurora was electrical and appeared in the third stratum, above forty miles. This was confirmed by Dalton. But when the International Polar Year of 1882 was planned, Darwin's views on the atmosphere were unknown and unheeded. The stations for photographing the aurora were sited on the assumption that it was five miles high, and the results were almost useless – except to show that the height was more than sixty miles.[55]

Darwin thought that the presence of hydrogen was confirmed by the red colouring often seen in auroras. 'It was observed by Dr Priestley', he says, 'that the electric shock taken through inflammable air was red' (Notes, p.4). This was good thinking, but actually hydrogen produces only a small fraction of the red colour in the aurora.

Relying on the analysis of the 1783 fireball, Darwin gives the right height for fireballs, as 'between 60 and 70 miles'. But he thought they were caused by electrical discharges, which made hydrogen combine with oxygen. He had no idea that they were lumps of material from space: this hypothesis, familiar to the ancients, was revived in 1794 by Chladni.[56]

Another type of light in the sky is the night airglow, caused by the flashes of light from atoms in the high atmosphere as they return to normal after having been raised to an excited state by the sunshine during the day. The night airglow was discovered in 1909, the textbooks say. So why mention it now? Because Darwin correctly specified its existence and its mechanism:

> The light of the evening, at the same distance from noon, is much greater, as I have repeatedly observed, than the light of the morning; this is owing, I suppose, to the phosphorescent quality of almost all bodies, in a greater or less degree, which thus absorb light during the sun-shine, and continue to emit it again for

some time afterwards, though not in such quantity as to produce apparent scintillations.[57]

The night airglow often emits more light than all the stars combined, and is plainly visible to astronauts in orbit. Everyone on the ground can also 'see' it on a starry night, but the glow is very difficult to identify with the eye – most observers would say it is impossible. Did Darwin really observe it? He was a great observer and he lived at a time when artificial lighting was weak or non-existent. Possibly he did sense the airglow. If not, his correct analysis is even more astonishing.

The longest of the notes on the atmosphere discusses winds. Darwin formulates one useful concept, the idea that 'vertical spiral eddies', or 'great cylinders of air rolling on the surface of the earth', are created when air flows over a coast with a line of mountains behind (Notes, p.84). This process is now well-recognized as a source of gravity waves, which are important in generating weather systems. The rest of his essay is intelligent but nugatory, because he did not realize that winds are caused by pressure gradients.

Darwin's achievements in atmospheric science were many and fundamental: besides those just mentioned, he recognized weather fronts, suggested weather maps and explained how clouds form. These insights are all the more remarkable because they came 'out of the blue', with no one to help him. It was Darwin versus the air, and he won. The secrets of the atmosphere were not safe while he was around.

The remaining Notes to *The Economy of Vegetation* defy logical ordering. A long Note is devoted to the history of steam engines; another gives Darwin's interpretation of the Portland Vase, with Blake's engravings (Plate 14). In shorter Notes he discusses oil on water, luminous insects, shellfish, electricity and solar volcanoes – a real cornucopia of the curious.

[7]

Erasmus was unimpressed by his new-found literary fame and made no changes in his lifestyle. With six children aged between one and nine in the house, he could not expect scholarly calm. In his later years he usually woke early, and probably did much of his writing in the comparative peace of the early morning. His health remained good, but he was now sixty and sometimes felt it, to judge from his letter to Robert on 5 January 1792: 'I have lately taken to drink two glasses of made-wine with water at my dinner, instead of water alone, as I found myself growing weak about two months ago; but am recover'd and only now feel the approaches of old age'.[58] In turning from water to wine, Erasmus also miraculously made the deadly alcohol nutritious, it seems.

In February there was another wedding: Elizabeth's eldest daughter Elizabeth Pole, now twenty-one, was married to Captain Bromley on 6 February, and departed to London. There were other changes in the offing: 'Mary Parker has got a good place (I believe) in a boarding school at Chesterfield', and 'Susanna wants to get into a boarding school',[59] Erasmus told Robert on 7 February.

A few days later a welcome visitor arrived. It was Edgeworth, who had six months previously brought his son Lovell to Clifton, Bristol, to combat suspected consumption. Edgeworth stayed with the Darwins for three weeks and met William Strutt, whose inventiveness reminded Edgeworth of himself when young. Maria says the Darwins 'were extremely kind, and pressed him very much to take a house in or near Derby for the summer'.[60]

In his letter to Robert in February, Erasmus answered a question about finance: 'To live comfortably all one's life, is better than to make a very large fortune towards the end of it'. He also has news about his next book: 'I am studying my "Zoonomia", which I think I shall publish'.

On 13 April Erasmus subjected Robert to 'a long medical letter'. Sir Joshua Reynolds, he says, advised painters 'to study the works of all other artists'. Doctors should do the same. 'If they do not thus copy others, they will be liable to copy themselves', and then 'the apothecaries say the doctor has but 4 or 6 prescriptions to cure all diseases'. For this reason, 'I am determined to read all the new medical journals which come out'.[61] This letter showed Erasmus's 'continued zeal in his profession', as Charles Darwin aptly remarked. Robert's zeal was more doubtful. In this letter Erasmus takes the trouble to write out details of two puzzling cases for him to think over, but these further attempts to activate his son were useless. He was a doctor, not a thinker.

In April The Economy of Vegetation had still not appeared and, unknown to Darwin, was in danger of being pre-empted by a rival. This was a 562-line poem called Alexander's Expedition by Thomas Beddoes. After reading The Loves of the Plants Beddoes had said it was easy to write in the Darwinian style. Challenged to do so, the hyper-active Beddoes dashed off a poem about Alexander's progress on his expedition down the rivers Hydaspes and Indus to the Indian Ocean. Beddoes says he 'attempted to assume the style of the most elegant of modern poets'; and he succeeded, because he had 'a wild and active imagination, which was as poetical as Darwin's', in Humphry Davy's opinion.[62]

If Beddoes had publicized the poem widely, Darwin would have been damaged, because his uniqueness would have been thrown in doubt. But Beddoes did not wish to embarrass him, and had the poem printed at

Madeley near Coalbrookdale, the cost being borne by William Reynolds, who was a friend of Beddoes. The title page has 'London: sold by J. Murray' as a spoof. Perhaps Darwin's kindness in giving Beddoes geological specimens five years before induced him to become a disciple rather than a rival. Whatever the reason, it was fortunate for Darwin.

Another disciple declared himself in June, when Darwin received an appreciative sonnet by Richard Polwhele, a Devonshire poet who had met Erasmus junior twelve years before.

In his reply to Polwhele, Darwin writes:

> My son Erasmus, who remembers passing some days on a journey with you, speaks of you with great pleasure. He is settled as an attorney in Derby, and is in great business, built on the most lasting foundation of ingenuity and integrity.[63]

The young Erasmus, now thirty-two, had evidently won the whole-hearted approval of his father. Any doubts about his ability or forcefulness had vanished. Of the two sons, it was Robert rather than Erasmus who was a worry to his father, because of his lack of ardour in medical science.

The young Erasmus won himself great credit locally after an unusual incident in August 1792. The leading local gentry had been much upset for some months by being sent malicious anonymous letters with slanders against their friends, and they asked Erasmus for advice. He suspected 'old Mr Bateman' of writing the letters, and devised a clever and courageous scheme for testing his suspicion. He wrote a letter with slanders against himself, had his clerk copy it out and sent it anonymously to Bateman. His scheme seemed to have gone awry when Bateman called to tell him about the new slanders. But within half-an-hour a recipient of previous letters arrived, saying that he had been sent the slander about Erasmus in the same writing as the previous anonymous letters. A meeting of thirty Derbyshire gentlemen was arranged. Erasmus presented his case, and so did Bateman, who accused Erasmus of writing all the anonymous letters because he had admitted sending one. The proceedings took three hours. The gentlemen decided unanimously against Bateman, and asked Erasmus if he wished to prosecute. He said not, and they concluded that making Bateman a social outcast would be punishment enough.[64]

After this *coup de théâtre* Erasmus junior began to feel the victim of his own success: 'I find my Clients, my Wealth and my Cases increase',[65] he complained to Robert three months later. He was not a high-flier, and might have been happier with a less successful career. Probably he did not learn to say 'no' soon enough: here he would have had little help from either his father or his brother, who succeeded as doctors by not saying 'no' to new patients.

His father now also often said 'yes' to the requests of travellers attracted to Derby by his new fame as a poet. Among them was one of the heroes of the poem, William Herschel. When he called, in July, Darwin 'shewed me a curious specimen of lead confined like a nucleus in a shell of iron ore'.[66] Darwin's collection of minerals was a public sign of his deep interest in geology.

The Derby Philosophical Society was still thriving too, and sometimes Darwin would invite visitors to a meeting. One such guest in 1792, Marianne Sykes, remembered his 'wonderful sallies of imagination and wit, which kept us in perpetual laughter and astonishment'.[67] This was what the Lunar Society lost when he left Lichfield.

Although ready to entertain visitors, Darwin made no move to visit London, where he would have been lionized. Indeed he never went to London again, except possibly on medical journeys.

In July he was consulted about the illness of Sir Richard Arkwright, who had been knighted six years earlier. Darwin had no miracle treatment to offer and Arkwright died early in August. Darwin wrote a generous obituary in the *Derby Mercury*, praising Arkwright as a philanthropist for his enterprise in providing so many people with work and housing, and for contributing 'more to the general benefit of mankind ... than any other single effort of human ingenuity'.[68].

The idea of retiring did not appeal to Erasmus. He told Robert early in October:

It is a dangerous experiment, and generally ends either in drunkenness or hypochondriacism. Thus I reason, 'one must do something' (so country squires foxhunt), 'otherwise one grows weary of life, and becomes a prey to ennui'. And therefore one may as well do something advantageous to one's self or friends, or to mankind, as employ one's self in cards, or other things equally insignificant.[69]

As Robert owed a little money, Erasmus suggests he should buy a Christmas pie,

to be sent to Mrs Day, No 21 Prospect row, Coleshill-street, Birmingham (who you recollect was your nurse, which is the greatest obligation, if well perform'd, that can be recieved from an inferior) to be sent about Christmas time.

Despite her 'inferior' status under current conventions, Erasmus did not conveniently forget Mary Day. But he does seem to have forgotten that, four years before, he helped her to eat a goose-pie sent by Robert. Most of the passage quoted above appears in Charles Darwin's *Life* of Erasmus, but with Mrs Day's name and address altered to 'an old woman living in Birmingham'. This Victorian euphemism has the effect of making Erasmus seem supremely virtuous by being kind to unknown old ladies; in reality, Mary Day was not unknown and only thirty-nine.

In this letter Erasmus gives Robert the latest news about the Parker sisters. Susan, now promoted to 'Susanna', is going to be 'governess to Mrs Gladwin's children at Stubbing near Chesterfield', while Mary continues as a teacher at 'Miss Ton's school', at Chesterfield.

Another wedding was imminent in the Darwin household. Millicent Pole, now eighteen, was married on 13 October 1792 to John Gisborne, author of the poem *The Vales of Wever* and younger brother of Thomas Gisborne, Joseph Wright's close friend. John Gisborne was quite a saintly man, and his diary[70] is dominated by the deaths of friends, all seen as proofs of the goodness of God. Though Millicent was not always well, her marriage seems to have been a happy one for most of its fifty-nine years. Erasmus's letter offers a preview: 'Our two Lovers sit close together all day like two paraquets on a perch'. Eight years later Erasmus said Gisborne was 'an extraordinary good husband'.[71]

With this wedding, all three children in Elizabeth's first family had been married within less than two years. She was extremely indulgent to the children of her second family, allowing them to do as they wished, à la Rousseau. Erasmus followed her lead, but may have begun to regret it with the six-year-old Francis, a young tearaway.

Soon after the wedding he wrote to his 'dear old friend' Richard Dixon:

> I go on as usual to practice physic and to write books. I sold a work called The Botanic Garden for 900£ to Johnson the bookseller near St Paul's, it is a poem; perhaps you may borrow it from some circulating library – it is in two parts and sold for 1-13-0.

'I sold a work called The Botanic Garden … it is a poem': Horace Walpole would have been amazed to read this understatement of the year.

Darwin is as exuberant as ever in this letter. Dixon had suffered a slight stroke that left his mouth drawn down at one side. Dixon's cousin Elizabeth Sumner at Elston, Darwin says, expects an annual kiss from him: 'You must mind on which side you approach lest you should kiss her ear'. He starts talking of his own health but soon slides into banter:

> The worst thing I find now is this d—n'd old age, which creeps slily upon one like moss upon a tree, and wrinkles one all over like a baked pear. But I see by your letter that your juvenility will never fail you; you'l laugh on to the last, like Pope Alexander, who died laughing on seeing his tame monkey steal to his bedside and put on the holy Tiara, the triple crown, which denotes him 'King of Kings'. Now Mr Pain says that he thinks a monkey or a bear, or a goose, may govern a Kingdom as well, and at a much less expense than any King in Christendom, whether idiot or madman or in his royal senses.[72]

Darwin addresses the letter to 'Richard Dixon Citizen' and ends it with 'adieu dear Citizen from thy affectionate equal'. There is only one sentence about the French Revolution in the letter, but it shows where Darwin stands: 'The success of the French against a confederacy of Kings gives me great pleasure, and I hope they will preserve their liberty and spread the holy flame of freedom over Europe'.

[8]

To 'spread the holy flame of freedom' was the idea behind the new reform societies that sprang up all over England during 1792. Their members were inspired and inflamed by Part I of Paine's *Rights of Man*, which appeared in 1791. Their declared aim was gradual reform, not violent revolution. (Confusingly, some grew out of the existing 'Revolution Societies' celebrating the 1688 Revolution.) The most famous of the new societies was the London Corresponding Society founded in 1792; but the two earliest[73] seem to have been the Sheffield Constitutional Society and the Derby Society for Political Information, both formed in December 1791.

There are no prizes for guessing the name of one founding member of the Derby society: Erasmus himself. But the initiator seems to have been Joseph Strutt, William's younger brother, and the chairman was Samuel Fox, who had helped Erasmus with his air-gun experiments and was now a business man married to Joseph Strutt's sister Martha. After she died in 1793, he married Erasmus's niece Ann Darwin. (Their son William Darwin Fox was a close friend of Erasmus's grandson Charles.) An important member outside this incestuous circle was the young William Ward,[74] editor of the *Derby Mercury* and later a missionary, who wrote an 'Address to the Friends of Free Enquiry and the General Good'.[75] This was a manifesto for the Society, and was approved at a meeting in July 1792. It was quite radical, setting out a programme of social welfare benefits, and demanding reform of Parliament by giving the franchise to all adult males. The address was presented to the French National Assembly in November 1792 by Darwin's friend Dr W. B. Johnson.[76] It was also presented to the House of Commons, in May 1793, and rejected.

The 'Address' seems innocent enough now, but the government was in a panic after Part II of Paine's *Rights of Man* appeared in 1792. After all, Paine was said to have fomented the American Revolution with his pamphlet *Common Sense* and was a member of the French National Assembly. Paine's book was suppressed, and many men went to prison for the crime of reprinting it. In January 1793 Louis XVI was executed, and in February France declared war on Britain.

Soon repressive judges began to make martyrs of respectable reformers. At Edinburgh in August 1793 the brutal Lord Braxfield, sitting with a rigged jury, sentenced the lawyer Thomas Muir to be transported for four-

teen years. In September the Unitarian clergyman Thomas Palmer suffered
a sentence of transportation for seven years. Their crime was to have
advocated Parliamentary reform.[77] Both survived the degrading voyage to
Botany Bay: Muir was fairly soon rescued by an American warship, while
Palmer served out his sentence; but both died during their return journeys
to Britain.[78]

The Derby 'Address' also attracted the Government's attention and was
honoured with a show trial. The Address was printed as an advertisement
in the *Morning Chronicle* on 25 December 1792, and the unfortunate
editors of the paper were arraigned for seditious libel. The trial began on
9 December 1793, with the Attorney-General Sir John Scott (later Lord
Eldon) leading for the Crown and the famous Thomas Erskine defending.
Ominously for Darwin, Erskine told the jury that the Address

> is rumoured to come from the pen of a writer, whose productions justly entitle
> him to rank as the first poet of the age; – who has enlarged the circle of the
> pleasures of taste, and embellished with new flowers the regions of fancy.[79]

The judge was the Lord Chief Justice, Lord Kenyon, and in his summing-up
he said the Address was 'published with wicked, malicious intent ... I consider it a gross and seditious libel'. The jury sat for five hours and gave a
verdict 'guilty of publishing but with no malicious intent'. Lord Kenyon
refused to record it. The jury was out for a further ten hours, and at 5 am
gave the verdict 'Not guilty'. This was fortunate for Darwin, who might
otherwise have been prosecuted.

The idea of Darwin being transported to Botany Bay may seem bizarre.
But so was the transportation of Muir and Palmer; yet it happened.
Darwin's private letters in 1792, if publicized, would have been more than
enough to convict him in the repressive climate of 1793–4. He was in the
public eye now, and had to keep watch on public events. He would have
been pleased that there was no prosecution of William Godwin's radical
and high-principled *Political Justice*, the book of the year in 1793. The
Government thought it too expensive for the working classes to buy.
The same safeguard shielded *The Botanic Garden* from any chance of
prosecution. Darwin was perceived as at risk by William Stevens, who
wrote in his journal in February 1793: 'In the present ferment of men's
minds, were I to visit him frequently we should be supposed to be plotting
sedition'.[80]

[9]

As yet unworried by the dangers of the sedition trials later in the year,
Darwin immersed himself in the half-million words of *Zoonomia* in 1793.

He consulted James Keir and again received good advice: 'I have much availed myself of your observations', he wrote on 17 January, 'and have corrected my work accordingly'.[81] Darwin adopted Keir's suggestion of publishing the book in two volumes a year or two apart, and thus reduced the ocean of words needing immediate attention to less than a quarter of a million. Johnson had offered Darwin £1000 for *Zoonomia* without having seen it;[82] so there was a financial incentive to complete it.

Despite his heavy literary workload, Darwin was still active as a doctor. He successfully treated Anna Seward[83] in April 1793 and despatched her to Buxton to recuperate. Sometimes he would go on long journeys, although he charged high fees in protest at the discomfort of the journeys. In the summer he travelled to Margate in Kent to treat Mary Anne Galton (later Mrs SchimmelPenninck), and charged her father a hundred guineas, which he could well afford out of the profits of his arms manufacturing.

Another long medical journey at about this time was to Newmarket, to treat his old schoolfellow Lord George Cavendish, who was godfather to Erasmus's daughter Emma. This was the occasion of another of the stories vouched for by Charles Darwin. While asleep at his hotel, Darwin was woken by a man at his bedside, who said he had not dared to speak in the daytime: 'I have never forgotten your kindness to my mother in her bad illness, but have not been able to show you my gratitude before. I now tell you to bet largely on a certain horse (naming one), and not on the favourite whom I am to ride, and who we have settled is not to win.'[84] And that is just what happened the next day.

A much shorter and more frequent medical journey was to see Joseph Wright. After his wife died in 1790, Wright became anxious about high winds blowing chimneys down and he could not sleep.[85] In 1793 Wright moved to 27 Queen Street, only 300 yards from Darwin's house. Continual illness was 'the blight on Wright's life',[86] though some of it was hypochondria. There is no knowing how often Darwin called on Wright, because they lived so close and we have no written evidence. Joseph Farington reported in 1796 that Darwin 'has regulated the life of Wright in whatever relates to Health for some years past',[87] and I would guess that he rarely passed a month without a cheerful visit from Darwin.

The medical event of the greatest long-term importance for Darwin occurred far away. Thomas Beddoes was making himself unpopular in Oxford by his support for the French Revolution, and he was being watched by Government spies.[88] Early in 1793 he decided to start a medical practice. At the suggestion of Darwin, who gave him a letter of introduction to Edgeworth, Beddoes set up his practice in the Clifton area of Bristol. Edgeworth was soon impressed by his great energy. Beddoes's vast output of short books began with several in 1793, including the *History of Isaac*

Jenkins (which sold 40,000 copies) and *A Letter to Erasmus Darwin* about pulmonary consumption. The latter is quite short (seventy pages), and includes a seven-page letter *from* Darwin. Beddoes had the idea of breathing mixtures of airs, and thus launched himself into an obsession with pneumatic medicine that lasted ten years and drew in Watt, Darwin and Davy.

In his letter to Beddoes, dated 17 January, Darwin commends him for trying to combat consumption, 'this giant-malady', which, 'like war, cuts off the young in their prime of life, sparing old age and infirmity'.[89] He wishes Beddoes well in his experiments.

Erasmus mentions Beddoes's 'ingenious' pneumatic technique in a letter to Robert in July: 'but experiment alone can show whether it will succeed'. It seemed a good idea at the time, when existing medicines were mostly useless; but it was doomed to failure. Had Darwin known this, he might have saved himself a good deal of work in the next few years. Beddoes was not yet fully committed to pneumatic medicine, and had time for other activities. Erasmus tells Robert that Beddoes 'is going to marry Mr Edgeworth's daughter Anna', who was now twenty.

The weather was warm and settled in July 1793, and tempted the tribe of Darwins into the river:

> I bathe and swim every day, and all our children, and Mrs Darwin, this warm season: it is wonderful how this diminution of heat strengthens one. It is just the contrary to a flannel shirt, which may be of service in winter, but is death in summer.[90]

This unexpected glimpse of family life at Derby is rather appealing. The young Darwins were all taught to swim by the age of four, and presumably there was a barrier to save them from being swept away by the current.

Besides taking to the water and giving advice to young doctors, Erasmus was also now receiving recognition for his scientific work. In 1792 he had become one of the early Fellows of the Linnean Society. He subsequently wrote to the founder and president, J. E. Smith, mentioning two friends who would like to be admitted 'if it be agreable for you'.[91] They were Brooke Boothby and Dr W. B. Johnson, who was a keen botanist as well as a democrat.

In 1793 Erasmus was elected to the American Philosophical Society, of which Franklin had been President until his death. In a letter to Professor B. S. Barton on 3 July, Erasmus sent his 'thanks for the great honor the society has confer'd upon me'.[92]

Another sign of the times was the completion of Wright's second formal portrait of Darwin (Plate 16). His friend William Stevens called it 'a strong but severe likeness. His countenance is seldom without a Smile playing around it'. Smile or no, eight copies of the portrait were commissioned, two being by Wright himself.[93]

Darwin's pre-Lunar friend John Michell died in 1793, but his other old Lunar friends were all well. Boulton wrote a cheerful New Year letter, saying 'I want to come to see Mrs Darwin and your fine family' and ending, 'God bless and preserve your Body says your old and affect. friend Matthew Boulton'. 'Pray come and see us', Erasmus replied on 5 January. He told Boulton, 'I was lately at Mr Keir's to visit Miss Keir, who was ill': this was Amelia Keir, aged eleven. Erasmus had hoped to visit Soho, 'but Time and Fate, two great Despots, withstood my efforts'.[94] Boulton had mellowed now that he was free of financial worries, but he had only one son and one daughter, who was partially crippled. So he envied Darwin's 'fine family'.

The Darwins and Wedgwoods remained close during 1793. The Wedgwoods probably stayed at Derby two or three times, and Josiah liked to repay this hospitality by sending beautiful or useful presents. In October Erasmus wrote to thank him for a 'very excellent Bath', a gift for Elizabeth.[95] It was packed with straw, and 'the bowels of the proliferous animal' were stuffed with smaller presents, to the delight of the children.

Darwin wrote to Watt on 13 December about the health of his daughter Janet, or Jessie as she was known. After giving medical advice Darwin belies his age by ending with a skip and a jump:

> Ye days, which are past! – when I could have pursued the rolling Taw [a large marble] with spirits light as air; and limbs supple as the bending grass-blade; when I could have crept through an Alderman's thumb-ring! – where are ye! – Corpulency of body, hebitude of mind, or in one word old-age I feel your irresistable approach – but care little about it.[96]

Had Darwin been aware of the dangers posed by the trial for seditious libel in London that had begun four days before, his jollity might have been amputated. Repression was outside his experience. Not until the next year did he see how much his world of rational enlightenment was being damaged.

CHAPTER THIRTEEN

Leading man of medicine
1794–1796

Darwin's public image was about to change again. Having achieved eminence as a poet, he published no further poems of any substance in his lifetime, merely resting on his laurels, it would seem. But in fact he was still hard at work on *Zoonomia*. Volume I was published in 1794 and Volume II in 1796. These theories of medicine and of life made him the leading medical author of the day. His reputation as an author was on the surface higher in 1796 than it had been three years before, though rumblings of discontent could be heard underground.

[2]

At the beginning of 1794 Erasmus was otherwise occupied – in creating careers for his two daughters Susanna and Mary Parker, aged twenty-one and nineteen. So far they had served as assistant teachers, or governesses in polite households. Both the girls were enterprising, and he felt they would not find long-term job satisfaction in such posts. Instead, Erasmus had it in mind to set them up in a school of their own. He had long been critical of conventional education for women, and now his daughters might try out some of his own ideas in practice.

The chance came in the autumn of 1793 when he was able to buy quite cheaply a large house at Ashbourne, an ancient and attractive town fifteen miles north-west of Derby, and the gateway to the Peak District. The site of the house was ideal, on a south-facing sandy slope at the eastern edge of the town, with hills to the north and the open ground of Brooke Boothby's estate to the east. Darwin bought the house in December 1793, paying only £550. Previously it had been a pub, the Nag's Head, and he probably chuckled at the idea of converting it into a ladies' seminary. Darwin also bought an acre of grounds (for £100) and a pew in Ashbourne Church (for £5). In a codicil to his will in May 1795 Erasmus made over the property to the Misses Parker.[1]

The school opened in the summer term of 1794 with 'two of our own girls' and 'two other boarders', Erasmus told Josiah Wedgwood in June.[2] The two Darwin girls were Violetta, now eleven, and Emma, nearly ten. 'They are happy and healthy, and much improved', Erasmus said. In the autumn there were ten boarders, and next spring sixteen. Soon the full complement of thirty pupils was reached, and the school won a high reputation. Susanna was in charge for fifteen years, until her marriage. Mary then took over, retiring in the late 1820s. The building, 48 St John Street, still stands at the corner of Park Road, and is marked with a plaque (Plate 10c).

When the sisters set up school, they asked their father for guidance, and he wrote down his ideas for their benefit. His manuscript was much in demand and copies were circulated widely, to obtain comments from local parents and to publicize the school. Three years later, suitably amended after this early example of parent power, the manuscript was published as a book of 128 pages, *A Plan for the Conduct of Female Education in Boarding Schools*. As it was in effect 'published' locally in 1794, we may appropriately look at it now.

The book is the most appealing of Darwin's prose publications. The parents of prospective pupils must not be scared off, so he is on his best behaviour. He still manages to be quite radical, however, and his book has a distinctive place in the history of girls' education in England.[3] Darwin was totally opposed to the idea that girls were meant to be weak and emptyheaded, and he went a long way towards modern ideas on sexual equality.

He begins unconventionally, with priority for physical education:

> The advantages of a good education consist in uniting health and agility of body with cheerfulness and activity of mind ... and in the acquirement of the rudiments of such arts and sciences as may amuse ourselves, or gain us the esteem of others.   [p.10]

Generally, 'the female character should possess the mild and retiring virtues rather than the bold and dazzling ones'; but circumstances such as 'the inactivity, folly or death of a husband' may call for energy of mind.

> Hence if to softness of manners, complacency of countenance, gentle unhurried motion, with a voice clear and yet tender, the charms which enchant all hearts! can be superadded internal strength and activity of mind, capable to transact the business or combat the evils of life; with a due sense of moral and religious obligation; all is obtained which education can supply; the female character becomes complete, excites our love, and commands our admiration.   [p.11]

After these generalities comes the detail, in thirty-nine sections on specific topics. Music and dancing are overdone, he says; and modern languages, like French and Italian, are easier and more useful than Latin and Greek. He condemns the 'illiterate men' who ridicule well-informed women, and he wants young ladies to learn scientific subjects, especially botany, chemistry and mineralogy: they should also do practical work, and visit local factories.

He thinks girls should learn shorthand, but he has two criticisms of it from his own experience. First, those who master shorthand when young are 'liable not afterwards to spell our language correctly'; second, he finds his student notes in shorthand are now 'difficult to decypher'.

On the tricky question of morals, Darwin makes guarded references to religion and specifies a secular morality based on compassion:

> A sympathy with the pains and pleasures of others is the foundation of all our social virtues. 'Do as you would be done by' is a precept which descended from heaven.... The lady who possesses this christian virtue of compassion cannot but be a good daughter, a good wife, and a good mother, that is, an amiable character in every department of life.... This compassion, or sympathy with the pains of others, ought also to extend to the brute creation, as far as our necessities will admit.... To destroy even insects wantonly shows an unreflecting mind, or a depraved heart. [pp.46–8]

Darwin also commends fortitude: the girls should aim for a 'serene strength of mind, which faces unavoidable danger with open eyes'.

For their health he advises exercise. Most school pupils are too sedentary, he says, 'which impairs their strength, makes their countenances pale and bloated, and lays the foundation of many diseases'. Some hours each day should be devoted to bodily exercises, such as 'playing at ball, at shuttlecock, swinging as they sit on a cord or a cushion, and dancing'. He would also recommend 'skating on the ice in winter, swimming in summer, funambulation, or dancing on the straight rope'; but these are 'not allowed to ladies by the fashion of this age and country' (p.70).

The pupils also need to breathe pure air, Darwin says. Crowded rooms should be ventilated by sawing off an inch from the top of every door and fixing a two-inch tin plate at 45°. Bedrooms need fresh air too: 'during the summer months a window should be kept a few inches open during the night as well as the day' (p.72). This was quite radical: bedrooms were usually sealed, to keep out the 'noxious vapours of the night'.

Darwin has a chapter on 'Care of the shape', as 'delicate young ladies are very liable to become awry at many boarding schools'. He advises that their stays should be symmetrical or (preferably) done away with. The shape thus cared for should be clothed as gracefully as fashion permits. And grace is achieved by 'lines flowing in easy curves', such as 'a sash descending from one shoulder to the opposite hip, or a Grecian veil thrown back and winding carelessly down behind' (p.83).

As amusements, Darwin recommends the sports previously mentioned, plus embroidery, drawing, music and chess, but not card-playing. He is against harsh punishment. He thinks refractory children should be governed by the teacher's superiority of mind.

Darwin knows all about childish ailments. Stammering is 'a disease of the mind, and not of the organs of speech'. Nail-biting and face-twitching occur when children become fidgety through being confined too long in the schoolroom; once started, the habits are difficult to eradicate. Darwin discusses diet too, recommending fresh milk, ripe fruit, fruit pies, butter and sugar, but not too much salt or spice.

Darwin's *Female Education* is rich in uncommon common sense and well ahead of its time. Most of his ideas have now been adopted. In retrospect the most important feature of the book is his determined stand against the nearly universal belief that women ought to be feather-brained and feeble-bodied. He was taking the first crucial step along the path that has led to sexual equality and feminism. His ideas were influential because many of the leading families in the Midlands sent their daughters to the Ashbourne school. At the same time his own daughters enjoyed satisfying lives and won respect locally: in the 1821 Directory of Derbyshire, Miss Mary Parker appears in the highest category, 'Nobility, gentry and clergy', thus outdoing her father.

[3]

Darwin's busy life as a doctor is well documented in 1794. At the age of sixty-two he was still at full stretch, treating patients over a wide area round Derby.

Perhaps the most demanding patients were the Burdetts, of Foremark Hall seven miles south of Derby – Sir Robert Burdett, who was seventy-seven, and his son Francis, who was forty-nine. Darwin was at Foremark quite often in January. He usually stayed to supper, and William Stevens was also a regular supper-guest. Stevens implies that the Burdetts were troublesome: 'The Bart ill, and his Son no better. They know not how to fight disease but moan incessantly.'

Stevens gives glimpses of Darwin's conversation. On 13 January there was 'a little altercation ... after Supper. Darwin showed infinite address and temper.' On 19 January: 'His Conversation critical and interesting.... He had laid out Work, he said, for his Mind for years to come.'[4] After *Zoonomia* he would give a year to composing a poem, the subject of which he would not disclose (presumably it was *The Temple of Nature*). 'His last Work' would be 'an examination of Wit' (which was never written).

Francis Burdett's illness worsened during January, and he died on 3 February. His father lived for another three years, and the title then passed to his grandson Sir Francis Burdett, the leading advocate of Parliamentary reform.

A less demanding titled patient was the Duke of Devonshire, who wrote complaining about shortness of breath and pain in his stomach. Darwin knew the Duke's liver was dodgy, and in his lengthy reply he advised palliative measures: 'Your Grace should avoid all violent exercise; and should be cautious in the use of much supper, or much wine at night …'.[5]

In the first five months of 1794 Darwin watched with anguish the decline of Jessie Watt, another victim of the 'giant malady' of consumption. James Watt and his second wife Ann had a happy marriage with two promising children, the brilliant Gregory, who was now sixteen, and Jessie, who was fourteen. Darwin visited her several times in the early months of 1794 and wrote at least five times to James or Ann Watt. His first letter, on 1 January, suggests several possible treatments, from foxglove to swinging. On 12 March he recommends a blister and moderate exercise. On 25 April this has changed to bark and three grains of opium a day. On 29 May he returns to foxglove and swinging, plus blue vitriol (copper sulphate). On 6 June he confesses, 'I do not think I can suggest any thing further'.[6] This is equivalent to a death sentence; and Jessie died on that very day. Darwin again had to face the depressing truth that his treatments for consumption were useless.

On 11 June he wrote to Watt:

> My dear friend,
>   I have not felt so poignant a grief of some years, as I feel now for the very affecting loss, which Mrs Watt and yourself have experienced! – a young companion of such uncommon beauty, of such amiable character, and of such ingenious and active mind as are rarely equal'd, never perhaps exceeded! – Mrs Darwin has wept two or three times for the sufferings of Mrs Watt and yourself, tho' she only knew your daughter by my description.[7]

Watt responded to this letter on 30 June, saying 'I have long found that when an evil is irreparable, the best consolation is to turn the mind to another subject'.[8]

Impressed by the inadequacy of Jessie's treatment, Watt turned his mind towards pneumatic medicine, which might be more effective. The production of pure gases for medicinal use was proving a serious problem for Beddoes, and this sudden offer of help from the great engineer (and no mean chemist) was a godsend. In a few weeks of inspired chemical engineering Watt converted pneumatic medicine from an idea into reality by designing apparatus for producing the gases in good quantity and reasonably free of pollutants, a task that would have been beyond Beddoes.

Darwin was delighted: 'It gave me great satisfaction both on your account and on that of the public, that you are employing your mind on the subject of medicinal airs', he wrote to Watt on 3 July.[9] And on 17 August, after thanking Watt for sending his 'magnificent apparatus', Darwin adds: 'I hope you will proceed to supply the world with a new Materia Medica, to be drank in by the lungs.'[10] After a short holiday in Wales, Watt continued to improve the apparatus. He wrote three long letters to Darwin on 14, 19 and 27 August. In his reply on 1 September, Darwin notes a possible snag with pneumatic treatment: that gases may not reach the lungs. 'I think I remember, when I was a smoaker of tobacco, that I only drew the smoke into my mouth, as I could never puff it out at my nose, and therefore it did not pass into the lungs'.[11] Presumably he had smoked at university.

Darwin did not have time for experiments of his own on medicinal airs, nor even for answering Watt quickly: 'I have been so perpetually from home, that I could not answer sooner'. His overload of work was probably caused by the illness and death of his young friend and colleague Dr John Pigot, who died on 23 August aged only thirty-seven.[12] No details of his illness are known. His widow Margaret returned to her home town, Southwell (near Elston), with her four children. Her daughter Elizabeth may have been a pupil at the Miss Parkers' school.

Despite his workload, Darwin took the trouble to obtain subscriptions in Derby for Beddoes's proposed Pneumatic Institution,[13] raising thirty-two guineas by personal canvassing (including five guineas of his own and one guinea from Erasmus junior). For an unproven technique, this was a good haul. Watt organized a similar subscription at Birmingham, and Beddoes began to plan his Institution. The plan ripened into reality after a gift of £1000 from Tom Wedgwood two years later.

In 1794 Tom Wedgwood was one of Darwin's most difficult patients. Now twenty-two, he was the third and most unhealthy of Josiah's sons. Darwin had known and treated Tom from his earliest years and feared that his exceptional brilliance might be blighted by disease more imaginary than real. This is what happened: Tom never completed his projects and only half invented photography.

Tom Wedgwood received at least eleven long and diplomatic medical letters from Darwin. Tom had headaches and believed he was suffering from cataracts in his eyes, and worms (ascarides) in his intestines. Darwin makes light of the cataracts and offers various purges in case Tom is harbouring the ascarides. Two more letters and a visit followed, and then another letter on 6 January 1794 with diets, physical and mental:

> That lassitude or want of spirits, you complain of, may in some measure be owing to want of employment: you should find out something to teaze you a little – a wife – or a law-suit – or some such thing. I think Virgil sais that Jupiter found it necessary to send Care amongst mankind, to prevent them from feeling less evils ...[14]

This may have silenced Tom, for Darwin's next known letter to him is on 10 August. It was extremely long and probably disastrous. He recommends 'a grain of opium taken every night for many months, perhaps during the whole winter'.[15] Darwin knew of opium addiction but did not realize the dangers.[16] Tom evidently accepted this advice, for he soon became an addict.

Darwin's letter to Tom Wedgwood is addressed to 'Ottery St Mary, Devonshire'. He was staying at Tallaton, his brother's house there. By this time Tom had probably met S. T. Coleridge, who was to be his closest friend and whose family still lived at Ottery St Mary. It is quite likely that Coleridge and Southey visited Ottery on their walking tour during August 1794. Coleridge had symptoms of vague illness rather like Tom's, so he may have adopted the treatment Darwin prescribed for Tom. After all, this was a prescription specially sent by the leading doctor of his time.

Alternatively, Coleridge may have read *Zoonomia* (as Tom did), and noticed how often Darwin recommended opium. For example:

Anorexia. Want of appetite ... Opium half a grain twice a day ...
Impotency ... advised to take a grain of opium before he went to bed ...
Gallstones ... Opium a grain and a half ...
Painful epilepsy ... Opium a grain every half hour ...
Sleepwalking ... Opium in large doses ...
Tetanus trismus ... Opium in very large doses ...

These escalating doses of opium are all from pages 300–50 of Volume II. Another possible source of Coleridge's opium habit is by prescription from his mentor Dr Beddoes, who much admired *Zoonomia*. With any of these three sources, Coleridge might have come to regard Darwin as responsible for his opium addiction. Is that why Coleridge turned against Darwin in later years?

[4]

When he was not out on medical journeys, Erasmus was grappling with Volume II of *Zoonomia*, 'which absorbs all my leisure hours', he told Watt in November. Erasmus junior (Plate 12A) and Robert both continued to grow more wealthy. Robert's income from medical fees[17] in 1794 was £1430, probably more than his father's. Now twenty-eight, Robert was thinking of getting married, and there were signs that Susannah Wedgwood might become his wife. Josiah and Erasmus were both delighted at the prospect of their families being united in this way.

Erasmus wrote to Robert on 31 March asking his permission to make some changes in the paper on ocular spectra, which he was reprinting in

Zoonomia. Erasmus signs off the letter more effusively than usual 'with all our love / from yours affect^ly ...'[18]

On 18 August Erasmus tells Robert that 'we were at Elston last week – my mother is 92, very lame with rheumatism in one hip and thigh and leg. Otherwise well. Your unkles Robert and John both very well.'[19]

At home, besides contending with the six younger children, Erasmus and Elizabeth often received visitors, especially young admirers of Darwin's books. One such disciple and a frequent caller was Dewhurst Bilsborrow, a Cambridge undergraduate and later a doctor. At Cambridge Bilsborrow told Christopher Wordsworth that Darwin admired the poetry of Christopher's brother William. Later, Bilsborrow began writing a biography of Darwin, but it was never published and has been lost.

Another visitor during 1794 was Thomas Young, then twenty-one, who seven years later propounded the wave theory of light, and became as wide-ranging as Darwin in his talents and knowledge. Darwin and Young took to each other at once. Young wrote: 'I was highly gratified with the remainder of the day, which I spent almost entirely with Darwin. He gave me my choice of looking over three cabinets, of cameos, of minerals and of plants.' And Darwin wrote a letter of introduction which pleased Young: 'He unites the scholar with the philosopher, and the cultivation of modern arts with the simplicity of ancient manners'.[20]

Yet another young man of science who looked up to Darwin was Dr Thomas Garnett (1766–1802), who was Humphry Davy's predecessor as lecturer at the Royal Institution but died young of typhus. Garnett was much impressed by Darwin's note on the winds in *The Botanic Garden*, and wrote a 124-page essay on meteorology, which he sent to Darwin. In his reply Darwin suggested Europe-wide weather maps.[21]

Darwin kept in touch with old friends too. He asked Boulton for the name of the supplier of aerated alkaline water, and was told it was 'Mr J. Schweppe, 141 Drury Lane', who had come to London in 1792. Boulton then mentions his 'gravelly complaint', probably kidney stones, and says he is too busy to let himself grow old: 'I am kept up like a top, by constant whipping'. He ends in a friendly vein, 'by assuring you that there is no good, pleasant, or desireable, thing in this World but what I wish you Mrs Darwin and all your Olive Branches the full possession of'.[22]

Edgeworth's letters were as friendly as ever, too. On 7 September 1794 he thanked Erasmus for sending Volume I of *Zoonomia*, 'your immortal present'. He foresees that one 'of my Great Great grandchildren' will show everyone the inscription 'and exult in the friendship of his Ancestor'. He ends with flattering ambiguity by offering his 'best Services to Mrs D, whom I admire as much as a man ought to admire the wife of his friend'.[23]

[5]

Volume I of *Zoonomia; or, the Laws of Organic Life* was published in May or June of 1794. The volume runs to more than 200,000 words, has 586 quarto pages and weighs four pounds. As the subtitle implies, Darwin was hoping to classify animal life, and to bring its exuberant chaos into some kind of order; 'to reduce the facts belonging to ANIMAL LIFE into classes, orders, genera, and species; and, by comparing them with each other, to unravel the theory of diseases' (i 1).* This ambitious aim shows Darwin's unbounded confidence and wide-ranging mind. He felt that he might be able to grasp and analyse the complex operations of nature. In fact he was not destined to be the Linnaeus of medicine: nor was anyone else.

Historians of medicine see *Zoonomia* in the context of other contemporary medical literature, and from this viewpoint there is much virtue in it.[24] As I am writing for modern non-medical readers rather than for historians of science or medicine, I have to be more severe, because Darwin's classifications and treatments do not seem very impressive today.

This unkind judgment does not apply to the fifty-five-page chapter on 'Generation', where Darwin specifies what we now call biological evolution and declares his faith in it. This is chapter 39, starting on page 482, and it seems like an afterthought, though Darwin had been pondering it for more than twenty years. Chapter 39 was not much noticed at first: the fifty-page notice of *Zoonomia* in the *Analytical Review* ignored it. Not until 1795 did it come under fire for its subversiveness. So I shall treat the chapter on its own, as if it were published separately in 1795.

Darwin begins Volume I of *Zoonomia* by dividing all bodily action into four classes, called irritation, sensation, volition and association:

> The sensorium possesses four distinct powers, or faculties ... These are the faculties of producing fibrous motions in consequence of irritation, which is excited by external bodies; in consequence of sensation, which is excited by pleasure or pain; in consequence of volition, which is excited by desire or aversion; and in consequence of association, which is excited by other fibrous motions.[25]

This is none too clear and unlike his normal plain-speaking. Still he does later put each disease into its appropriate class with an air of certainty.

Some examples may help. 'Irritation' is response to external stimuli, such as the effect of drinking alcohol; and drunkenness would be a 'disease of irritation'. 'Sensation' is the most teasing class, because it seems to cover almost everything: the 'diseases of sensation' range from sneezing to cancer, and from smallpox to dreams. But Darwin's category of 'Volition' is a good

* Volume and page numbers refer to the 1796 edition of *Zoonomia* (2nd ed. of Vol.I, 1st ed. of Vol.II).

one, and the diseases of volition are what might be called mental aberrations, with Darwinian extras such as anger, sleep and credulity. The class of 'Association' has some validity, since it covers conditions which are basically side effects, for instance, vomiting or fever. However, Darwin postpones discussion of individual diseases until Volume II.

Volume I of *Zoonomia* comprises forty general essays on a wide range of biological subjects, including instinct, sleep, reverie, vertigo, circulation, saliva, the stomach, the liver, temperaments, and digestion, to quote the shortest. The essay on drunkenness shows what he said to his patients:

> Mark what happens to a man who drinks a quart of wine or of ale, if he has not been habituated to it. He loses the use both of his limbs and of his understanding! He becomes a temporary idiot, and has a temporary stroke of the palsy! And though he slowly recovers after some hours, is it not reasonable to conclude that a perpetual repetition of so powerful a poison must at length permanently affect him?   [i 251]

Darwin's theory of ideas was influential in psychology; and his chapters 'Of Sleep' and 'Of Reverie' had a profound effect on the concept of poetry developed by Wordsworth and Coleridge.[26] Some of his suggestions remain relevant today. For example, the daily periodicity of sleep alerts him to the 'periods of diseases', and connects with modern studies of 'circadian rhythms' arising from jet-lag problems. Also of interest is his idea that dreams are not 'a useless expenditure of sensorial power'; they allow us to let off steam and avoid a painful 'accumulation of sensorial power'.

One of Darwin's successes is his chapter on oxygenation of the blood, where he cuts through the fog of phlogiston to a correct picture:

> It appears that the basis of atmospherical air, called oxygene, is received by the blood through the membranes of the lungs; and that by this addition the colour of the blood is changed from a dark to a light red.   [i 476]

The same process occurs in the gills of fish, he says, and in the placenta.

Another of Darwin's successes is his prediction of the future importance of electricity, at a time when it was thought of only as a toy. The modern era in electricity began in 1800 with the invention of the Voltaic cell: Volta found that two different metals (such as lead and zinc), when dipped in a conducting solution, generate an electric current in a wire attached to the dry ends. Darwin was writing before 1800, but he sensed the importance of Volta's earlier experiments, remarking that if pieces of lead and silver, touching outside the mouth, are applied to different parts of the tongue, an 'acidulous taste is perceived, as of a fluid like a stream of electricity passing from one of them to the other' (i 120). Having tasted current electricity, he looks forward to its future uses: it 'deserves further investigation, as it may acquaint us with new properties of matter'.

The most controversial of Darwin's essays was his fifty-page chapter on Instinct. He was particularly criticized[27] for taking too much notice of Hogarth's *Analysis of Beauty* and suggesting that ideas of beauty come from the infant's perception of the form of the mother's breast:

> Hence at our maturer years, when any object of vision is presented to us, which by its waving or spiral lines bears any similitude to the form of the female bosom ... we feel a general glow of delight, which seems to influence all our senses.... This animal attraction is love ... the purest source of human felicity, the cordial drop in the otherwise vapid cup of life.   [i 146–7]

The writing is seductive, but people were uneasy because they felt that Darwin was playing God, as indeed he is throughout the book.

One innovation in it that aroused no hostility is Darwin's use of points: *Zoonomia* is apparently the first book to have the numbered paragraph subdivisions now so widely used in scientific textbooks and reports, for example, section 5.3.4. Darwin adopted this system as a result of his experience with Linnaean classification.

The worst flaw in Darwin's treatment of disease is his ignorance of bacteria and viruses. In his day microscopy was treated as a triviality, and he was one of the few who perceived its future potential: 'I hope that microscopic researches may again excite the attention of philosophers, as unforeseen advantages may probably be derived from them, like the discovery of a new world'.[28] How true that was: but Darwin himself did not discover this micro-world, the key to much disease. Still Darwin did come close to the germ theory, when writing about smallpox inoculation: 'One grain of variolous matter, inserted by inoculation, shall in about seven days stimulate the system into unnatural action; which in about seven days more produces ten thousand times the quantity of a similar material thrown out on the skin in pustules!'[29] Darwin himself had high resistance to disease and (apart from gout) was apparently never ill. This is one reason why he did not favour the idea that invisible germs cause many diseases.

Today the insights in *Zoonomia* have to be weighed against the fallacies, but in its own day the book enjoyed immense success. The *European Magazine* quoted the opinion that *Zoonomia* 'bids fair to do for Medicine what Sir Isaac Newton's *Principia* has done for Natural Philosophy'. The *Monthly Magazine* thought it 'one of the most important productions of the age'. A second edition was needed to go with Volume II in 1796, and a third in 1801, of four octavo volumes. There were at least five American and three Irish editions, together with multi-volume translations into German, Italian, French and Portuguese. The book was rightly 'honoured by the Pope by being placed in the Index Expurgatorius', as Charles Darwin phrased it.

Thomas Beddoes, who was not unbiased, said of *Zoonomia*: 'It is, as to materials and arrangement, perhaps the most original work ever composed by mortal man'.[30] This was too extreme, because Darwin may have borrowed some ideas and approaches from earlier books, such as those of William Cullen and John Brown,[31] and William Smellie's *Philosophy of Natural History* (Volume I). Beddoes knew this, but it did not deter him from announcing that *Zoonomia* 'will place the Author amongst the greatest of mankind, the founders of sciences'.[32]

[6]

In the wider world things were going from bad to worse during 1794, and Darwin was not untouched by the backwash. The problems had begun the previous November at Edinburgh during the 'British Convention of the Delegates of the People, associated to obtain Universal Suffrage and Annual Parliaments'. The phraseology seemed menacing to the government, and several leaders of the Convention were tried for sedition. Maurice Margarot and William Skirving were sentenced by Lord Braxfield to transportation for fourteen years, and later in the year Joseph Gerrald received a similar sentence.[33]

How many more among the moderate reformers would shortly be suffering transportation? No one knew; but the climate was repressive enough to persuade Joseph Priestley to transport himself and his family to America. They left in April and settled at Northumberland on the Susquehanna river in Pennsylvania. Later in the year Coleridge and Southey showed their distaste for British society by planning a Pantisocracy on the banks of the Susquehanna. They married the Fricker sisters in preparation, but then abandoned their emigration plans. They were not politically active and never in danger of prosecution; but Watt's son James Watt junior was at risk because he had been in France during 1792-3 and had become friendly with the leaders of the Revolution. He thought of emigrating to America but in the end came home and kept quiet.[34]

Pitt's government was thoroughly alarmed, and in May 1794 introduced a bill to suspend Habeas Corpus for eight months. Twelve reformers were arrested and most were imprisoned in the Tower of London, in conditions they thought worse than the Bastille.

In October they were brought to trial one by one. The charge was high treason and the penalty was death. In the *Morning Chronicle* for 20 October, William Godwin wrote, 'This is the most important crisis in the history of British liberty that the world ever saw'. The first defendant was Thomas Hardy, Secretary of the London Corresponding Society. The prosecutor was again Sir John Scott, and he began with a nine-hour speech. The court often sat from 8 am until 2 am the next day. After Erskine's six-hour speech for the defence, the jury acquitted Hardy. The next victim was Horne Tooke, the philologist and lawyer, and this time the jury was hand-picked. Thanks to Erskine's skill and Horne Tooke's own caustic wit and legal knowledge, he too escaped execution. The third victim was John Thel-wall, agitator and poet. But he too was acquitted, and no further charges were brought.[35] 'This timely check saved England from a reign of terror' in the opinion of Trevelyan.[36]

By comparison Darwin and Beddoes escaped very lightly, although the government and its supporters were irritated by the provocative language of Beddoes's pamphlets and the continued popularity of Darwin's *Botanic Garden* with its open sympathy for the French Revolution.

Why not deflate this disgusting duo with a parody, written in rhyming couplets, as if by Darwin? The outcome was a poem of 202 lines, *The Golden Age*, said to be 'a poetical epistle from Erasmus D---n M.D. to Thomas Beddoes M.D.'; the leading Tory publisher, Rivingtons, put it out and gave it good publicity. The anonymous author, probably from Oxford, damaged Beddoes's credibility by ridiculing his extreme ideas, and damaged Darwin by making him seem to praise these ideas. Darwin put a notice in the *Derby Mercury* to say he was not the author, but this was only a local anaesthetic for the wound he received.

The golden age of the poem's title is the time when vegetables are adapted to grow animal products, a wild idea floated by Beddoes. The author (taken as Darwin by the casual reader) begins with fulsome praise of Beddoes as the Bigot's Scourge and the Pride of Democrats, and then looks forward to picking beef off trees. This opens the way for a side-swipe at Darwin himself:

> See plants, susceptible of joy and woe,
> Feel all we feel, and know whate'er we know!   [73–4]

In this golden age, free of priests, of kings, and of the King of Kings, 'that Bugbear of the sky',

> Ranks and Distinctions cease, all reeking lie
> In the mean muck of low Equality.   [129–30]

In 1794 Beddoes was much occupied with medicinal airs, and he kept out of politics. It was probably just as well. By 1795 the show trials had ended, and Beddoes returned to sting the government like a gadfly with little books like *Where would be the Harm of a Speedy Peace?*

As for Darwin, he had only been dipping a finger in the river of radical-ism. Now the author of *The Golden Age* had stolen up unseen behind and pushed him right into the water. It gave him a nasty shock, and con-firmed that the spirit of the age had turned against him. Christianity and patriotism, not deism and democracy, were what was needed when Britain was fighting for survival against Napoleon in the next decade. In these years of repression the time was out of joint for Darwin, who was a prime example of an unrepressed mind, inquiring and free-thinking. It was not his ideas but Paley's *Evidences of Christianity*, also published in 1794, that provided the politically-correct attitude for the rest of the decade. Darwin's reputation was to suffer death by a thousand pin-pricks.

One of these came in 1794 from *The Pursuits of Literature* by T. J. Mathias. This is another versified parody, which attacks many poets. Darwin escapes with a rebuke for the unbridled sexuality of *The Loves of the Plants* and snide remarks about his style. Only a pin-prick, but a repeated one, because the *Pursuits* went through many editions.

It was the local effects of the repressive climate that dismayed Darwin most. John Reeves's 'Association for preserving Liberty and Property against Republicans and Levellers', founded in 1792, had been campaigning effectively against reformers by recruiting local spies. Unfortunately for Darwin, one of these was his cantankerous neighbour Mr Upton, who may also have been among the many attorneys asked by the government to report on local seditious literature. Upton was not only darkening Darwin's windows but also casting a shadow over his ideal of Enlightenment.

[7]

The year 1795 began badly with the death of Josiah Wedgwood on 3 January at the age of sixty-four. Josiah had been ill for part of the previous year with familiar symptoms of pain in the right jaw and in what Erasmus called his 'no leg'. But he had been much better after a visit to Buxton, and Erasmus wrote cheerfully on 9 December 1794: 'Your letter gives me great pleasure in assuring me ... that you have become free from your complaint.... As you are *so* well, I advise you to leave off the bark, and to take no medecine at present'.[37]

Unfortunately his optimism was misjudged: within a few days Josiah's face began to swell and there were signs of mortification. Erasmus hurried to Etruria and stayed there for some days. But nothing could be done. Josiah gradually sank, in pain and fever. It was a sad end for Darwin's closest friend, as famous then as now for advancing art, technology and industry.

This was a time of low ebb for Erasmus, with private grief adding to despair at national trends. He wrote to Edgeworth on 15 March:

> The death of Mr Wedgwood grieves me very much. He is a public as well as private loss – we all grow old, but you! – when I think of dying, it is always without pain or fear – this world was made for the demon you speak of, who

seems daily to gain ground upon the *other gentleman*, by the assistance of Mr Pitt and our gracious — I dare not mention his name for fear that high treason may be in the sound; and I have a profess'd spy shoulders us on the right, and another on the opposite side of the street, both attornies! and I hear every name supposed to think different from the minister is put ... in Mr Reeve's doomsday book, and that if the French should land, these recorded gentlemen are to be all imprison'd to prevent them from committing crimes of a deeper dye. Poor Wedgwood told me he heard his name stood high in the list.[38]

The repressive atmosphere in Britain made Erasmus think of following Priestley by emigrating to his favourite land across the sea, America, where George Washington was in his second term as President, and Dr Small's protégé Thomas Jefferson had until recently been Secretary of State. Darwin's letter to Edgeworth continues: 'America is the only place of safety – and what does a man past 50 (I don't mean you) want? Potatoes and milk – nothing else. These may be had in America, untax'd by Kings and Priests.'

The rest of this letter is more cheerful. Darwin commends Edgeworth's planned semaphore telegraph system for the defence of Ireland: 'it would be like a Giant wielding his long arms, and talking with his fingers'. It was not adopted, but a similar system was later set up between London and Portsmouth.

An innovation of a more homely kind was proving useful to Erasmus: false teeth. In a letter to Robert on 13 April he says old Mr Bott 'has just made me an intire new set of teeth, so that when you next see me, you will be amazed at my juvenility'.[39] Erasmus junior seemed to be doing well still; but he identified a growing cloud ahead when he wrote to Eliza Hayley on 7 March: 'you know I am apt to "put off a little"...'[40]

One friend of Darwin who never 'put off' at all was Thomas Beddoes, who continued his postal bombardment. Very few of the replies have survived because Beddoes's biographer (J. E. Stock) printed excerpts and then apparently burnt the originals. Darwin was pleased to have such an active doctor-disciple, but sometimes became tired of answering so many queries – Beddoes even inquired about the false teeth, which Darwin says are made from 'the bone of the Hippopotamos'. Having asked Beddoes to read the proofs of *Zoonomia*, he should not have been surprised at the flood of comments and questions.

Darwin usually admired Beddoes's publications. After reading *A Guide for Self Preservation*, he wrote 'You deserve a civic crown for saving the lives of your fellow citizens'.[41] When Beddoes asked him for medical experiences, he would produce a letter for publication, as when he explains how fine-ground charcoal can relieve dyspepsia. Darwin also welcomed the important book by Beddoes and Watt on the *Medicinal Use of Factitious Airs*, with detailed drawings of Watt's apparatus, published at the end of

1794. 'I shall wait for Dr Beddoes' next book, I think, before I carbonate, or hydrogenate, or azotate, or oxygenate anyone',[42] Darwin had told Watt in September.

In 1795 he often found himself writing to Watt for new sets of pneumatic apparatus and all the chemicals needed to make it function. Unfortunately for Darwin, patients liked the excitement of this new toy and insisted that it did them good. He then had to find the supplies: 'I have a Lady now, who consumes a pound or two of manganese every day'[43] – that is, she inhaled the oxygen from it. This relieved her headache, she said. So Darwin asks Watt to send urgently a further half-hundredweight of 'Exeter Manganese', which yielded the purest gas. The logistical problems and the expense were becoming excessive, and the real benefits were dubious, although patients might perk up because they became of special interest to their doctor. Darwin soon began to drop 'medicinal airs' from his array of treatments.

Writing to Watt in November, Erasmus describes the illness of his own daughter Emma. She is taking oxygen and '2 grains of opium a day' for her 'nervous cough'. She also takes 'bone ashes, soda phosphoreta and powder of bark' to combat 'softness of bones', the ribs being weak. 'But why do I tell you all this stuff? I do it, because you have been so good as to interest yourself about her health.' Erasmus is also more confiding than usual about his own life in this letter:

> Now I grow old and not so well amused in common society, I think writing books an amusement – I wish you would write books, instead of having those confounded headachs, which you complain of.[44]

Another patient with headaches, Tom Wedgwood, was less troubled by his health in 1795, presumably being helped by the regular opium. He was still interested in operations for cataract of the eye. Darwin advises him to procure calves' or sheep's eyes for experiments, perhaps fearing he might start on humans. Although Darwin was a physician rather than a surgeon, he takes much trouble to think out and sketch possible instruments for cutting through 'the external part of the opake cornea'. He also offers an innovative idea: 'Could not a bit of glass ground into a shape like a shirt-sleeve stud be put into the hole made in the center of the cornea, and left there, which would stay, and become a glass eye?' This is a big step towards the lens implantation so successfully used in recent years. Darwin foresaw its potential, and told Tom: 'if you can make these people see by such glass eyes, you will gain immortal honour, and serve the human animal'.[45]

A patient who was to gain more 'immortal honour' than Tom was Joseph Wright, whose health declined badly in 1795. He wrote in March that the severe winter 'has almost demolished me'. Darwin advised him 'to use a hot bath every night, from 94 to 96 degrees of heat, in which I stay half an hour. It has certainly braced me and removed some disagreeable sensations.'[46] But he was still not well enough 'to think of handling the pencil'.

Darwin was featured in the *European Magazine* in 1795. The article includes the poem on Prince Frederick, a summary of his life, and the remark that 'the annals of literature scarcely produce a single instance' of so high a poetical talent being hidden until the age of nearly sixty. (An exact parallel occurred later with Thomas Hardy, who was born 109 years after Darwin and published his first book of verse 109 years after Darwin's. Hardy was not so quickly acclaimed as Darwin.)

Darwin's talent for verse seemed to have gone back into hiding but re-emerged when he wrote a short poem about a debtors' prison, which was published in the *Monthly Magazine*.[47]

Darwin also wrote a letter to the *Staffordshire Advertiser* about an earthquake that shook a wide area round Lichfield and Burton on 18 November 1795, and was 'strongly felt' in neighbouring counties.[48] Darwin had little or no experience of earthquakes, yet he managed to arrive at a valid scientific conclusion: as it was so widespread, he says, it must have originated deep in the Earth.

[8]

'A deep intellectual earthquake' would be no bad description of Darwin's statement of biological evolution in chapter 39 of *Zoonomia*.

The ancient Greeks had the idea[49] that the species now seen on Earth evolved gradually from primitive forms, and the idea was revived from time to time. But it made little headway in eighteenth-century Europe, for two reasons. First and foremost, the Christian Church decreed that species were created by God and immutable. Second, the men of science also tended to accept the fixity of species because of the success of Linnaeus in classifying species of plants. Anyone wishing to propound evolutionary ideas had to leap over these two invisible psychological barriers, which Darwin was well able to do because he cared little for conventional wisdom.

We have seen how the bones found in the Harecastle Tunnel in 1767 persuaded him to adopt the evolutionary idea in 1770. By his defiant choice of the motto *E conchis omnia* for his coat of arms, he had declared his belief in the theory of common descent, that all living things are descended from a single microscopic ancestor. This implies that species have evolved down the ages. (A belief in, say, a dozen separate ancestors could still be compatible with evolution; but Darwin leapt at once to the most extreme belief, which is modern orthodoxy.[50])

Canon Seward's scathing verses had warned Darwin that the Church would not tolerate the theory of common descent, and he had kept quiet about it for twenty-four years.

Now, 'too old and hardened to fear a little abuse',[51] he was prepared to go public. He told Robert that 'when a boat is in danger from a whale, the wise sailors throw out a barrel' for the whale 'to amuse himself with'.[52] Chapter 39 is like such a barrel, he says, and may save the vessel from damage.

In that chapter Darwin presents the evidence that species can and do change, and suggests some of the forces that drive the changes. He starts perversely, implying male dominance of heredity. He soon corrects this aberration and asserts (i 501) that the female contributes almost equally to the make-up of the progeny. He believes that the embryo begins as a 'simple living filament' capable of being excited, perhaps by 'the surrounding fluid', to develop and grow.

Darwin then draws attention to the great changes which occur in animals. First, there are the changes during the life of an individual animal 'as in the production of the butterfly with painted wings from the crawling caterpillar; or of the respiring frog from the subnatant tadpole' (i 504). Second, he points to the great changes which have, down the centuries, been produced in animals 'by artifical or accidental cultivation, as in horses, which we have exercised for the different purposes of strength or swiftness, in carrying burthens or in running races' (i 504); or in the various breeds of dog, the bulldog for strength and courage, the greyhound for speed; and so on, with many further examples, including cattle, pigeons, sheep and camels. Third, he notes that monstrosities, or mutations as we should now say, may be inherited: 'Many of these enormities of shape are propagated, and continued as a variety at least, if not as a new species of animal. I have seen a breed of cats with an additional claw on every foot; of poultry also with an additional claw, and with wings to their feet' (i 505). In modern jargon, Darwin is aware of 'hard' heredity and dominant genes.

These anatomical changes and the similarity in structure of all warm-blooded animals lead him

> to conclude that they have alike been produced from a similar living filament. In some this filament in its advance to maturity has acquired hands and fingers, with a fine sense of touch, as in mankind. In others it has acquired claws or talons, as in tygers and eagles. In others, toes with an intervening web, or membrane, as in seals and geese ...   [i 506]

All animals therefore 'undergo perpetual transformations'.

If adequate air and water are available, he says, the three great objects of desire, which have changed the forms of many animals by their exertions to gratify them, are those of lust, hunger and security.

The first controlling force, lust, leads Darwin to define sexual selection. In some species the males desire 'exclusive possession of the females; and these have acquired weapons to combat each other for this purpose'.

So the horns of the stag are sharp to offend his adversary, but are branched for the purpose of parrying or receiving the thrusts of horns similar to his own, and have therefore been formed for the purpose of combating other stags for the exclusive possession of the females; who are observed, like the ladies in the times of chivalry, to attend the car of the victor. [i 507]

Other examples are boars and polygamous birds, such as the cock and the quail. The outcome of 'this contest among the males' is, Darwin says, 'that the strongest and most active animal should propagate the species, which should thence become improved' (i 507). This is the essence of sexual selection, and indeed of natural selection.

The second of the controlling forces is 'the means of procuring food, which has diversified the forms of all species of animals'. Darwin explains how each animal has become adapted to its method of acquiring food, citing the hard noses of swine, the elephant's trunk, the rough tongues of cattle, and the peculiarities of birds, which later impressed Charles Darwin in the Galapagos Islands.

Some birds have acquired harder beaks to crack nuts, as the parrot. Others have acquired beaks adapted to break the harder seeds, as sparrows. Others for the softer seeds of flowers, or the buds of trees, as the finches.... All which seem to have been gradually produced during many generations by the perpetual endeavour of the creatures to supply the want of food. [i 508]

The third of the controlling forces, the want of security, or the means of escaping other more powerful animals, 'seems much to have diversified the forms of their bodies and the colour of them'. Some animals, he says,

have acquired wings instead of legs, as the smaller birds, for the purpose of escape.... Others great swiftness of foot, as the hare. Others have acquired hard or armed shells, as the tortoise and the echinus marinus.... The colours of many animals seem adapted to their purposes of concealing themselves either to avoid danger, or to spring upon their prey. [i 508, 513]

He identifies the use of mimicry as well as camouflage, mentioning the

frog-fish, Lophius Histrio, which inhabits the large floating islands of sea-weed about the Cape of Good Hope, and has fulcra resembling leaves, that the fishes of prey may mistake it for the sea-weed, which it inhabits. [i 508]

After mulling over all these mechanisms, Darwin concludes:

Would it be too bold to imagine, that in the great length of time since the earth began to exist, perhaps millions of ages before the commencement of the history of mankind, would it be too bold to imagine, that all warm-blooded animals have arisen from one living filament, which THE GREAT FIRST CAUSE endued with animality, with the power of acquiring new parts, attended with new propensities, directed by irritations, sensations, volitions, and associations; and thus possessing the faculty of continuing to improve by its own inherent activity, and of delivering down those improvements by generation to its posterity, world without end!   [i 509]

This long sentence is more a declaration of faith in evolution than a question, and there is no question mark at the end. There is, however, some euphemism, which calls for comment.

Darwin is careful to be tender with religious susceptibilities. He salutes the 'GREAT FIRST CAUSE' as maker of the living filament: he probably accepted this as consistent with deism. But he also has to make it clear that he is depriving God of his traditional role as officer-in-charge of changing species, and Darwin devises euphemistic phrases to say that evolution proceeds naturally, without divine intervention. Thus the phrase 'directed by irritations, sensations, volitions and associations' is another way of saying 'directed by natural forces' (because everything is 'directed by irritations, etc' in his scheme). Similarly, his phrase 'by its own inherent activity' means 'by natural processes': he is not proposing the absurd idea that animals consciously control their own evolution, as some have suggested.

A notable feature of Darwin's summary is his insight into the time scale. In his day good Christians accepted that the world was formed in 4004 BC, but Darwin realized that this was most unlikely, and specified 'millions of ages', which, if we take an age as roughly a century, means 'hundreds of millions of years'. This has indeed proved to be the time scale of evolution. His new time scale was 100,000 times longer than the old: it was a new scientific paradigm (if I may lapse into twentieth-century jargon).

One vagueness in Darwin's summary, that all creatures arise from 'one living filament', is clarified a few years later in The Temple of Nature: 'all vegetables and animals now existing were originally derived from the smallest microscopic ones, formed by spontaneous vitality' in primeval oceans.[53] This is in general accord with orthodox modern views about the origins of life.

To use modern words rather than his own, Erasmus adopted the theory of common descent in 1770, after seeing the fossils of vanished species dug from the Harecastle Tunnel. Tadpoles changing to frogs, horses bred for different roles, and other transformations, convinced him that species did change: it was not just a theory. In Zoonomia he clearly described sexual selection and the importance of adaptation to environmental changes. He was very familiar with the struggle for existence and the 'survival of the fittest', of which he was to paint a vivid picture in The Temple of Nature. So he was well aware of the operation of natural selection. But if the environment was stable, he thought that natural selection was not a strong enough engine to drive evolution. Instead he looked to environmental pressures in times of change. He would have liked the 'punctuated equilibria' version of evolution proposed in 1972 by Eldredge and Gould,[54] in which periods of stasis are punctuated by spells of rapid evolution.

Darwin saw evolution as the key to the development of life and he propounded evolutionary theory and facts that are largely acceptable today. These are his greatest achievements in science. But he failed to convince his contemporaries: the whales of the Establishment not only tossed the barrel around but also sank the boat: Darwin's reputation as a poet foundered too because his evolutionism was obnoxious in time of war.

No one stepped forward to support him, not even Beddoes. He had one silent supporter, his son Robert, who looked on appalled at the mayhem and wisely resolved never to mention the subject himself. Like his father, however, Robert made a mute protest by using a bookplate with the magic words *E conchis omnia*.

[9]

In January 1796 Darwin received a visit from a loquacious young man with a slight Devonshire accent, a close friend of Tom Wedgwood: it was Samuel Taylor Coleridge. Now twenty-three and uncertain of his future, Coleridge was touring the Midlands to seek subscribers for his proposed periodical *The Watchman*. He arrived in Derby on 22 January with an introduction to Darwin from either Beddoes or Tom Wedgwood. Darwin made time for a long talk with him, probably on 24 January. This may have been a mere courtesy on Darwin's side, but it made an indelible impresion on Coleridge, giving him a model for depth and breadth of knowledge, and an ideal for him to try to rival and outdo.

On 27 January Coleridge told Josiah Wade:

> Derby is full of curiosities, the cotton, the silk mills, Wright, the painter, and Dr Darwin, the everything, except the Christian! Dr Darwin possesses, perhaps, a greater range of knowledge than any other man in Europe, and is the most inventive of philosophical men. He thinks in a *new* train on all subjects except religion.[55]

Two days later Coleridge wrote to John Edwards: 'Dr Darwin is an extraordinary man, and received me very courteously – He had heard that I was a Unitarian and bantered incessantly on the subject of Religion'.[56] It seems that Darwin called Unitarianism 'a feather-bed to catch a falling Christian'. Coleridge was able to answer the banter: 'He is an Atheist – but has no new arguments.... When he talks on any other subject he is a wonderfully entertaining and instructive old man'. Darwin also teased Coleridge by professing to be scornful of revealed religion and saying 'he had never read one book in defence of such stuff, but he had read all the works of infidels'. To call Darwin an atheist was going too far, but his lack of respect for religion gave Coleridge that impression.

For Coleridge 1796 was a critical year. Soon after meeting Darwin he started *The Watchman*; but it failed in May. In July he returned to Derby with his wife Sara. They stayed for five weeks with the recently widowed Mrs Elizabeth Evans of Darley, the sister of William Strutt. Coleridge was hoping to become tutor to her daughter. When that fell through, Darwin's friend Dr Peter Crompton offered Coleridge financial help (to the tune of £100 a year) to start a school in Derby. This was probably on Darwin's recommendation.

Darwin also tried to help Coleridge by offering him a job as a research assistant 'to read the books of all former philosophers' and summarize their findings – if we are to believe the shorthand notes of one of Coleridge's impromptu lectures.[57] So Derby did its best for Coleridge, and he enjoyed visits to Dovedale and Ilam with Mrs Evans, whom he later called 'the greatest WOMAN I have been fortunate enough to meet'.[58] But he left in August and went to live at Nether Stowey in Somerset in the autumn.

The next year, when John Thelwall was to lecture in Derby, Coleridge wrote, 'I shall be with you in spirit. Derby is no common place ...'.[59] This is the letter in which he calls Darwin 'the first *literary* character in Europe, and the most original-minded Man'.

Darwin began the studies for his books in 1770, after Polly's death. For twenty years he acquired scientific knowledge for a poem of epic length, and for *Zoonomia*. Coleridge adopted the same plan. He wrote to Joseph Cottle in April 1797: 'I should not think of devoting less than 20 years to an Epic Poem. Ten to collect materials and warm my mind with universal science ... the next five to the composition of the poem – and the five last to the correction of it'.[60] That this life-plan never came to fruition was probably due to Coleridge's opium addiction, and he may privately have looked back on Darwin as a Borgia who poisoned his rival.

[10]

For Erasmus the happiest event of 1796 was the marriage in April of his son Robert to Susannah Wedgwood, Josiah's eldest daughter, who was one year older than Robert and had known him since early childhood. She had often stayed at Derby with the Darwins, and was a favourite of Erasmus, who wrote to Robert a month before his marriage:

I am happy to hear you are so near the time of your marriage with a lady whom I have always much esteemed, as an accomplished lady, with a distinct understanding and an excellent heart; all which I was frequently witness to during her father's illness; whose loss still affects me.[61]

It is not often that a son marries the woman his father would have chosen; but in this as in so many matters Robert seems to have fallen in with his father's ideas. The conformity was probably subconscious, but no less significant for that.

By marrying Susannah Wedgwood, Robert also became much richer than his father. In her father's will[62] Susannah had been left £25,000, equivalent to nearly £2 million today. Robert learnt how to manage money from his brother Erasmus, and proved to be a superb financier. None of his children had to think of working for their living, as their grandfathers Erasmus and Josiah had so assiduously done.

In this same letter Erasmus also has news for Robert about his grandmother. 'It will give you pleasure to hear', he says, 'that your good grandmother is recovered, for the present at least, from an anasarca [dropsy], I suppose, of her lungs and limbs'. Erasmus had travelled to see his mother at Sleaford, where she was staying, with either her daughter Ann or her daughter-in-law Jane: 'she expected to die on the night I was there'. He gives Robert details of her treatment and finishes with a phrase already quoted: 'She is 93 and I hope will live to be 100, as a better mother never existed!' Either alone or with the family, Erasmus usually visited his mother each Christmas, and sometimes also at Easter or in the summer.

Things were changing at the family house in Full Street. The two girls Violetta and Emma were away at school in Ashbourne for much of the year. The most troublesome of the other four children was the wild boy Francis, now ten. In one alarming incident, Fig. 17, he and George Bilsborrow are amusing themselves by shooting sharp arrows at live pigs, when a mad dog appears. The archers climb convenient trees, while the unfortunate pigs are bitten by the dog and 'die of Hydrophobia'. After that, the dog bites the nearby horse and then 'is killed in Mr Upton's garden by the mob in pursuit'. Francis may have been improving on the truth here, but his wish to record the episode reveals the cast of his mind. Bringing up the children without discipline seems to have worked well for the girls, but not for Francis.

William Strutt was still Darwin's closest friend in Derby, and Strutt's inventiveness helped to enliven the meetings of the Derby Philosophical Society. His father Jedediah Strutt had become Darwin's next-door neighbour in 1795 when he moved into Exeter House. Both the Strutts were frequent patients.

The same can be said of Joseph Wright, who suffered attacks of asthma

FIG. 17 Another remembered episode in the life of the wild boy Francis Darwin, in 1796, when he was ten. He and George Bilsborrow are amusing themselves by tormenting pigs with bows and arrows. A mad dog appears, so they climb trees while the dog bites the pigs and a horse. As drawn by Francis's daughter Violetta about forty years later

in 1796. 'I consulted Dr Darwin in the last attack who has, I think with success, put me under a course of Foxglove for a dropsical habit, which he suspects is the cause of my difficulty in breathing'. Wright added: 'I can lie down ... have a better appetite and am certainly better in every respect'.[63]

Of Darwin's old friends, Edgeworth and Watt were now the closest. Several of Edgeworth's letters from Ireland in 1796 have survived, though Darwin's replies have not. On 27 February Edgeworth writes mainly about the Irish elections, in which he was a candidate. He also asks if Darwin has seen the sketches of Lady Hamilton in several different attitudes – 'one or two of them put me in mind of Mrs Darwin'.[64] On 11 April Edgeworth reports having met a man from New York who said Darwin was in the highest repute there, the poetry of The Botanic Garden being 'placed above that of any of our former English classics'.

Erasmus felt a special affinity with James Watt, and he is the only one in the Lunar circle to be addressed as 'my dear friend'. Of the three known letters to Watt in 1796, the most intimate is that written on 21 June, after hearing of the death of Watt's only surviving daughter Margaret, at Glasgow. 'Life is a forced state! I am surprized that we live, rather than that our friends die'. Erasmus had held this view for many years: long ago he had said that Polly 'ceased to live'. 'What is there in the world', he asks Watt, to make men of sixty 'wish to continue in it?', especially when the 'prospect of the public affairs of this nation' is so dismal:

> Activity of mind is the only circumstance which can prevent one from thinking over disagreable events, which already exist, or are likely soon to exist, in England as well as in the other countries devoted to this bloody war![65]

'Activity', he says, may not produce pleasure, 'but I think it always prevents or lessens present pain'. As for 'this bloody war', he would have been appalled to know that it would go on with only brief pauses for a further nineteen years. 'Where would be the harm of a speedy peace?' he might have said, echoing Beddoes.

Meanwhile Beddoes himself fired another shot in his pamphlet war, entitled *An Essay on the Public Merits of Mr Pitt*. This was more subtle than is usual with Beddoes because it offers ironical praise of Pitt. As it was so rich in irony, Darwin suggested that an inverted exclamation mark should be used to warn the casual reader of lurking irony.[66] Since one aim of irony is to give the discerning reader the pleasure of discerning it, Darwin's idea of labelling it may seem ironical. But if he had sprinkled *The Botanic Garden* with i signs, he might have escaped the sneers of many stupid critics over the years. Besides his barbed praise of Pitt, Beddoes also suggests additives to make food more nourishing: 'Could opium be used?', he asks. The idea of lacing bread and gruel with opium deserves an exclamation mark both ways up, the irony lying in Beddoes's unawareness of it.

[11]

Volume II of *Zoonomia* appeared in the summer of 1796, with the lightly revised second edition of Volume I to accompany it. Volume II is even heavier than Volume I, and extends to 772 pages, with 300,000 words: it is a work of reference rather than a readable book. Darwin begins with a catalogue of diseases, divided into Classes, Orders, Genera and Species, then gives details of each disease (sometimes with case histories) and his favoured treatment for it.

The format and scope of the catalogue are best shown by examples:

CLASS I: *Diseases of Irritation*

ORDO I: Increased irritation

GENUS I: With increased actions of the sanguiferous system

SPECIES

1. *Febris irritativa*	Irritative fever
2. *Ebrietas*	Drunkenness
3. *Haemorrhagia arteriosa*	Arterial haemorrhage
4. *Haemoptoe arteriosa*	Spitting of arterial blood
5. *Haemorrhagia narium*	Bleeding from the nose ...

CLASS III: *Diseases of Volition*

ORDO I. Increased volition

GENUS II: With increased actions of the organs of sense

SPECIES

1. *Mania mutabilis*	Mutable madness	
2. *Studium inane*	Reverie	
3. *Vigilia*	Watchfulness	
4. *Erotomania*	Sentimental love	
5. *Amor sui*	Vanity ...	[ii 3; ii 317]

And so it goes on, numbers 6 to 18 being desire of home, superstitious hope, pride of family, ambition, grief, irksomeness of life, loss of beauty, lust, anger, rage, and the triple fears of poverty, death and hell.

It is easy to take a superior modern attitude to Darwin's hard labour in organizing illnesses into genera and species. Yes, most of his treatments were ineffective, especially for diseases of irritation and sensation. But great intellectual energy went into the attempt. At the time of its publication, Volume II must have seemed like a revelation. Here was a life-raft, it seemed, for hard-pressed doctors thrashing around in an ocean of illness. Here were 474 diseases, all nicely classified, with specific treatments for each, sometimes with question marks to show when Darwin was unsure, even after a lifetime of medical practice. Today we may wonder why he continued with the practice of bleeding, but at least his use of opium was beneficial in relieving pain. On some subjects, like natural childbirth, he seems quite up-to-date:

As parturition is a natural, not a morbid process, no medicine should be given, where there is no appearance of disease. The absurd custom of giving a powerful opiate without indication to all women, as soon as they are delivered, is, I make no doubt, frequently attended with injurious, and sometimes with fatal consequences.   [ii 189]

There are some vivid descriptions of disease:

Scarlatina maligna. The malignant scarlet fever begins with inflamed tonsils; which are succeeded by dark drab-coloured sloughs three or five lines in diameter, flat, or beneath the surrounding surface; and which conceal beneath them spreading gangrenous ulcers...   [ii 245]

This is one of many diseases in which 'the patient generally dies in a few days'. So we cannot blame Darwin for trying everything:

> M.M. A vomit once. Wine. Beer. Cyder. Opium. Bark ... Broth. Custards. Milk. Jellies. Bread pudding. Chicken ...

Here M.M. stands for *methodus medendi*, or 'method of healing' (not *materia medica*). The treatment already sounds like the contents of the larder, but there is much more to come. Darwin suggests giving oxygen, passing electric shocks through the tonsils, and seeking a method of inoculation – 'no one could do an act more beneficial to society, or glorious to himself' (ii 246).

Darwin is at his best on the diseases of volition. He knows that bodily ailments are often of mental origin, and that many obsessions will have to be recognized as diseases before they can be cured. For example, *spes religiosa*, superstitious hope, is a 'maniacal hallucination' that in mild form produces merely 'an agreeable reverie', but when given public support has 'occasioned many enormities': 'What cruelties, murders, massacres, has not this insanity introduced into the world!' Then there is *orci timor*, the fear of hell:

> Many theatric preachers among the Methodists successfully inspire this terror, and live comfortably upon the folly of their hearers. In this kind of madness the poor patients frequently commit suicide; although they believe they run headlong into the hell which they dread! Such is the power of oratory, and such the debility of the human understanding!   [ii 379]

The next disease is quite different, and fashionable today – *satyriasis* or 'ungovernable desire of venereal indulgence'. Darwin's fourfold treatment has a unexpected end: 'M.M. Venesection. Cathartics. Torpentia. Marriage' (ii 380). Three pages later those who fear 'the supposed ill consequences of self pollution' suffer a similar fate: 'M.M.... Marry them ... a certain cure'.

Credulity is a deplorable disease, Darwin thinks, endemic in 'the bulk of mankind', who 'have thus been the dupes of priests and politicians in all countries and in all ages of the world' (ii 410). 'Credulity is made an indispensable virtue' by religious sects, and is best cured by increasing 'our knowledge of the laws of nature'.

Darwin's kindness to the mentally ill emerges in a case of hallucination:

> Miss G---- ... said, as I once sat by her, 'My head is fallen off, see it is rolled to that corner of the room, and the little black dog is nibbling the nose off'. On my walking to the place which she looked at, and returning, and assuring her that her nose was unhurt, she became pacified, though I was doubtful whether she attended to me.   [ii 361-2]

Another unrecognized disease is 'loss of beauty', often 'painfully felt by

Ladies'; some of the usual remedies, particularly cosmetics containing white lead, have 'destroyed the health of thousands'.

After discussing the diseases of Association, Darwin adds a ninety-page supplement on 'Sympathetic Theory of Fever', which was influential in its day. Two of his suggestions have since proved their worth. The first is blood transfusion, a revival of an old idea. The second, deriving from Brindley's experiences with mill-stones, is the idea of whirling patients in a centrifuge, or rotative couch, as Darwin calls it. Watt made a detailed engineering design to Darwin's specification, shown in Plate 13B. As W. J. White remarks in his history of the centrifuge in aerospace medicine, 'Darwin's analysis marked the beginning of the therapeutic use of centrifugation'.[67] It is a subject with far-reaching future applications in creating artificial gravity in space stations.

Volume II of *Zoonomia* ends with 118 pages of Materia Medica, defined as 'all substances which may contribute to the restoration of health' – and *may* is the right word. They fall into seven classes, of which the first, Nutrientia, is most important because it includes food. Digressing, Darwin notes that population is sparse 'where men lived solely by hunting' and that agriculture allows a great increase. 'But pasturage cannot exist without property both in the soil and the herds', and 'an inequality of the ranks of society must succeed', an inequality which he thinks is too great. To secure 'the greatest sum of human happiness', he says, 'there should be no slavery ... and no despotism'. As well as food, he includes oxygen and blood transfusion in the Nutrientia. His second class of restoratives, which 'increase the irritative motions', include opium, alcohol, love and joy. Those in the third class increase secretion, and range from ginger to hopeless distress; those in the fourth, which increase absorption, include acid of vitriol and electric sparks. And so on: the medicines are classified as thoroughly as the diseases.

Despite the fallacies, those few who have read Volume II will have found it impressive. Here is a complete conspectus of all the diseases of humankind, brought under control in an ingenious system. As Beddoes remarked, 'his analysis of morbid phenomena is one of the greatest exertions of the human understanding'.[68] Or, as William Stevens said of Darwin, 'Few men have so much exercised their Minds'.[69]

CHAPTER FOURTEEN

Confronting adversity
1797–1799

During 1797 Darwin was hard at work on his far-reaching book about plant life, *Phytologia*. The children all seemed to be prospering, and he hoped for a quiet and industrious year.

But the tide had turned, and this was to be the first of three years of mounting adversity. The dominant theme of 1797 was death, which made many unwelcome visits, beginning on 13 February when the aged Sir Robert Burdett died at Foremark.

More significant for Darwin was the death of Horace Walpole, on 2 March. He had continued to admire Darwin unreservedly and in the previous year had expressed a wish 'for a portrait of him as a man of great genius and a poet of the first order'.[1] Walpole was influential, and his departure can be seen as symbolic of the decline in Darwin's fame.

The next fatality was on 26 March, when Erasmus's old friend James Hutton died in Edinburgh at the age of seventy. Intellectually, Darwin was probably closer to Hutton than to any other of his friends. Their minds, untrammelled and imaginative, were attracted to the history of the Earth and of life. Though Hutton rejected biological evolution, he did describe natural selection in 1794: so these topics may have been discussed in their twenty-year exchange of letters, of which only two remain. The loss of Hutton would have been keenly felt by Darwin.

Death struck nearer home when his mother died at Sleaford on 26 April, aged ninety-four. Erasmus had visited her earlier in the month, and on 6 May he told Robert that 'she then complained that her eyes were become dim, and her recollection failed her'. She had passed her life, he says, 'with the greatest respectable character; and with as much happyness as falls to the share of most in this sublunary world'. She had seen all of her seven children grow up healthy and thriving – an unusual privilege in the eighteenth century.

As a postscript to this letter, Erasmus mentions that the engraver J. R. Smith has 'just sent a print of my head, well done I believe'. The first impression, costing half a guinea, would 'soon be sold'; the second would sell for five shillings. Embarrassed at this self-display, Erasmus adds, 'But the great honor of all is to have one's head upon a sign post – unless indeed upon Temple bar!'[2]

This letter was written on the day when Derby's most honoured son, Jedediah Strutt, died aged seventy. Darwin's neighbour and patient, he had been seriously ill for several months. As Arkwright had died five years before, it was the end of an era for Derby: the two founder-fathers of the Derbyshire cotton mills were gone.

On 13 June there was an uninvited visitor to Darwin's house; it was William Godwin, and by mischance Darwin was away. Godwin told Mary Wollstonecraft that

> Dr Darwin was gone to Shrewsbury, and not expected back till Wednesday night. At this moment I feel mortified at the recollection. We concluded that this was longer than we could with propriety wait for him. I believe we were wrong. So extraordinary a man, so truly a phenomenon as we should probably have found him, I think we ought not to have scrupled the sacrifice of 36 hours.[3]

So Godwin gives his impressions of Elizabeth instead. 'We paid our respects', he says, 'to his wife, who is still a fine woman, and cannot be more than fifty. She is perfectly unembarrassed, and tolerably well-bred'. Unabashed at his own condescension, Godwin goes on: 'she seemed ... to put an improper construction on our visit, said she supposed we were come to see the lions, and that Dr Darwin was the great lion of Derbyshire'. Elizabeth was well practised in dealing with uninvited visitors, and the serious-minded Godwin was evidently a victim of her 'sportive humour'.

Godwin was travelling with his friend Basil Montagu, and they went on from Derby to meet Robert Bage, whose novel *Hermsprong* had come out the previous year. Then they returned to London, where Godwin was soon to suffer anguish when Mary Wollstonecraft died after the birth of her baby, the future Mary Shelley. Darwin never did meet Godwin, although they were soon to be satirized together.

Another victim of 1797 was Darwin's friend and patient for thirty years, Joseph Wright. His usual summer bout of illness began in May with severe asthma, and he became weaker after taking to his bed. Darwin had no answer, and Wright died on 29 August, a few days before his sixty-third birthday.

Darwin was good at keeping friends over the years, and Wright was among them. Unfortunately no letters between them have survived. (The same applies for Bage, Boothby, Garbett and Whitehurst, who were all long-term friends.) I have earlier suggested that Darwin made quite frequent medical calls on Wright, but the link was more than merely medical. Joseph Farington wrote: 'Dr Darwin makes it a rule never to contradict his children.... Wright silently imitates Darwin in this respect'.[4] There is no confirmation that Wright visited the Darwins socially, but it does seem likely: after all, it was Wright who brought Erasmus and Elizabeth together.

The longest of all Darwin's friendships was with Richard Dixon, his childhood companion at Elston. They had kept in touch for sixty years when Dixon died in 1797.

No correspondence with Boulton, Watt or Keir has survived from 1797, but Edgeworth was still writing often. On 5 July he reports unrest in Ireland and the burning of houses. He also refers to the book he and his daughter Maria were writing, the much-praised *Practical Education*, based not on theory but on practical experience with sixteen children (so far).

On 11 September Edgeworth had an old and sad story to tell: 'My dear Doctor, I wish you could infuse a fresh portion of health into the constitution of my poor wife. – But I fear, alas! that is impossible....'[5] The dreaded consumption had seized Elizabeth Edgeworth as it had her sister Honora and then her step-daughter Honora. In his seventeen years of marriage to Elizabeth, Edgeworth 'never once saw her out of temper, and never received from her an unkind word, or an angry look'.[6] She died in November, aged forty-four.

Another wife who died in November was Erasmus junior's friend Eliza Hayley. Her husband, whom she had not seen during her nine years at Derby, wrote some memorial verses for her.

Darwin's sleeping Muse was not roused by any of these ten deaths. But he did write some smooth elegiac verses[7] for the poet William Mason, author of *The English Garden*, who died in April: Darwin was presumably responding to a request from one of Mason's friends.

Despite death's intrusions in 1797, Darwin was applying himself to life – the life of plants. In the previous year he had been asked to write on the subject[8] by Sir John Sinclair, the energetic President of the Board of Agriculture, who was himself producing a new type of survey, his *Statistical Account of Scotland* in twenty-one volumes. On 8 November Darwin wrote to Sinclair:

> I have employed the vacant hours which I could command, in writing a theory on vegetation, applied to agriculture and gardening. The work has proceeded but slowly, and it will yet be some months before I ... commit it to the press.[9]

He asks permission to dedicate the book to Sinclair: the dedication would say that the book 'was begun by his instigation and forwarded by his encouragement'. That Sinclair instigated *Phytologia* may be only a polite half-truth. Having dealt with animal life in *Zoonomia*, Darwin probably wanted to write about plant life, and Sinclair's request legitimized his wish. Publication of the book was to be delayed because Joseph Johnson was in prison in 1798, serving a six-month sentence for selling an allegedly seditious pamphlet written by Gilbert Wakefield, a classical scholar and unitarian preacher.

Johnson had at last brought out the book on female education in 1797. For Darwin this was a relic of the past, delayed in publication because it had to queue up behind *Zoonomia*.

[2]

Darwin was gradually reducing his medical commitments during the years 1797–9. The idea of making long journeys in an unheated boneshaking carriage during bad winter weather must have seemed less attractive now that he was over sixty-five. His national medical reputation was, however, at its highest in the afterglow of *Zoonomia*.

Patients often came to him from London, and one of these (probably about now) was Miss Feilding, who was a cousin of Lady Charlotte Finch, governess to the Royal Household. Miss Feilding stayed for some time at Darwin's house and emerged with her health restored.

King George III heard of Darwin's fame through Lady Charlotte and reacted positively:

'Why does not Dr Darwin come to London? He shall be my physician if he comes'; and he repeated this over and over again in his usual manner.[10]

The King had bitter memories of his treatment by physicians during his 'madness' in 1788–9. He particularly disliked the senior royal physician, Dr Richard Warren. Though he was useless during the King's illness, Warren now enjoyed an immense income. (Beddoes wickedly said that whenever Warren looked at his tongue in the mirror, he shifted a guinea from one pocket to another.[11]) Far worse than Warren was the 'mad-doctor' Francis Willis, who terrorized the King by frequent applications of the strait-jacket.[12] The King feared a recurrence of his illness. He would have been better off under Darwin's care, but neither Erasmus nor Elizabeth liked the idea of moving to London, so the King's plea was in vain.

In June 1797 Darwin received a visit from an unknown gentleman who had just arrived in Derby. 'I am come from London to consult you, as the greatest physician in the world, to hear from you if there is any hope in my case', he said. 'It is of the utmost importance for me to settle my worldly affairs immediately; therefore I trust that you will not deceive me, but tell me without hesitation your candid opinion'.[13] After examining him, Darwin had to say there was no hope; he could not expect to live more than a fortnight. The man seized Darwin's hand and said: 'Thank you, doctor, I thank you; my mind is satisfied; I now know there is no hope for me'. Darwin asked him: 'But as you come from London, why did you not consult Dr Warren, so celebrated a physician?' He replied: 'Alas! doctor, I *am* Dr Warren'. He died a week or two later.

Not all Darwin's patients were so dramatic, and with Tom Wedgwood it was back to square one. This time it was the turn of the worms again, according to Tom's self-diagnosis: Darwin half agreed in his letter of 7 February – 'the ascarides are a dreadful enemy'. A much longer letter from Darwin on 27 March shows him being tactful. Tom had pain in the temple, and Darwin hints that people can suffer pain without a cause, from 'torpid action (debility) of the part', in this case possibly a tooth, 'but this is not quite certain'.[14] He probably inserted the proviso in fear that Tom would have all his teeth extracted and then complain that the pain was worse. He was a difficult patient.

Although Darwin had reduced his medical travelling by 1798, he would still write lengthy letters to patients. One such letter, to Mrs Lucy Galton on 22 July, is full of Lunar-like banter. She had sent on to him a letter from Joseph Berington, a Catholic priest whose sister's linen returned from the wash with a strange smell. She (and later he) developed shivery fits, sweats, dry throat and burning stomach from contact with the linen. Darwin says 'Mr Berington's infected letter' should have been sprinkled with holy water, 'which must wash out all infection'. He suggests that Berington should 'exercise his apostolic powers, and exorcise the evil spirit'. After some more teasing, with classical, biblical and Napoleonic allusions, he promises to be serious. 'The power of imagination is well known to all', he says, 'but should be particularly well known to our ingenious catholic friend.... Do not the bones of Saints cure diseases? I believe those of the mind frequently, and sometimes of the body'.[15] There is more in this vein, and the sideswipes at Christianity are well integrated into the banter. Writing scientific treatises had not damaged his sense of humour.

Lucy Galton was still a frequent patient, and her daughter Mary Anne, the future Mrs SchimmelPenninck, was now old enough to be scandalized by Darwin's attitude to religion:

Dr. Darwin often used to say, 'Man is an eating animal, a drinking animal, and a sleeping animal, and one placed in a material world, which alone furnishes all the human animal can desire. He is gifted besides with knowing faculties, practically to explore and to apply the resources of this world to his use. These are realities. All else is nothing; conscience and sentiment are mere figments of the imagination. Man has but five gates of knowledge, the five senses; he can know nothing but through them; all else is a vain fancy, and as for the being of a God, the existence of a soul, or a world to come, who can know anything about them? Depend upon it, my dear madam, these are only the bugbears by which men of sense govern fools.'[16]

If she remembered this verbatim nearly sixty years later, he must have made an indelible impression on her.

In 1799 Darwin went on at least one medical journey, to treat Mary

Anne's father, Samuel Galton, at Bath. He charged Galton forty guineas.

Another sign of Darwin's prestige as a doctor was the publication (in 1799) of *Biographia Medica* by Benjamin Hutchinson, a collection of biographies of past doctors. The book is dedicated to Darwin as 'a man eminently distinguished in every department of science'.

[3]

Though still highly respected as a doctor, Darwin suffered three separate attacks during 1798, and one of these was an extensive criticism of his medical theory.

The author of the critique was Thomas Brown, a brilliant and precocious student who entered Edinburgh University at the age of fifteen to study law.[17] The first shot in his campaign was a long and polite letter to Darwin on 24 October 1796, when Brown was eighteen. He says that he read *Zoonomia* with great pleasure, but is surprised that 'no one as yet has answered'. Brown felt that the reasoning was sometimes 'more specious than solid'. Therefore 'I ... marked down my observations occasionally'. As they 'greatly swelled upon my hands', he says, 'I ... think of committing them to the press'.[18] Darwin must have read this escalating packet of trouble with growing horror. Still, he managed a courteous reply, saying he would be 'glad to read your manuscript, if it be not very voluminous', and would be 'ready to acknowledge any errors'. Had he known what was coming, he wouldn't have been glad at all.

A few weeks later Brown sent the manuscript to Darwin, who was dismayed at its length, probably about a thousand pages. Worse still, almost every page had plausible objections, sometimes easily answerable and sometimes liable to provoke interminable argument. Brown was already a master of polemical logic, and Darwin had met his match in disputation. He could not answer Brown fully without weeks of work, for which he had no time and not much inclination.

Darwin replied rather rudely on 2 December; how rudely we do not know, because Brown's biographer (David Welsh) politely withheld the letter from publication. However, Erasmus himself admitted to Robert that he had told Brown his book was 'impertinent garrulity, hard words'.[19] Brown replied to the rude letter on 5 December with his usual courtesy, saying he would not descend to asperity: 'the angry feelings I have never cultivated, as I do not think they add much to the dignity of our nature'. At this time Darwin did not realize how young Brown was: he would have been appalled to know he was being ticked off by an eighteen-year-old. After Brown's rebuke, Darwin made a politer reply on 20 December, in which he argues against some of Brown's speculations, for example that an idea cannot exist without sensation. Brown replied on 28 December, mainly to expound his ideas on ideas and their relation to sensation. Darwin wrote back on 12 January 1797 with a polite and spirited defence of his own metaphysical stance on the definition of sensation. Brown replied on 21 January, and there the correspondence ended. No agreement was likely on such abstract questions.

Brown's *Observations on the Zoonomia of Erasmus Darwin* was published about May 1798 and runs to 560 large pages. Brown severely criticizes Darwin's materialism, his evolutionary ideas, and his fourfold division of the sensorium. Darwin felt wounded by having his life's work torn apart by an unqualified boy – for it was not until 1798 that Brown changed from law to medicine. Erasmus told Robert that 'a Mr Brown has published I see 8 shillings worth against Zoonomia; part of which he sent me some time ago'.[20] Brown's attack, unwelcome though it was, enhanced *Zoonomia*'s fame: probably no other serious scientific book has evoked so solid a riposte so promptly. This was cold comfort for Darwin.

[4]

The second attack on Darwin in 1798 had an immediate effect: within a few weeks he lost part of his prestige as a poet and could no longer be regarded as pre-eminent.

The weapon was satire, the attack was government-inspired and the originator was George Canning, Under Secretary for Foreign Affairs in Pitt's government, and later Prime Minister. The war had been going very badly in 1797, with Napoleon Bonaparte conquering much of Europe and the British navy in mutiny. To help in maintaining morale, the *Anti-Jacobin* periodical was founded, with the aim of combating all ideas subversive of the established order. Canning controlled the magazine and he saw that Darwin's evolutionary ideas were deeply subversive of established religion because Darwin denied God the guiding role he was designed to fill. Canning also wished to attack Godwin, whose *Political Justice* was subversive of all government. So, with two collaborators, Hookham Frere and George Ellis, Canning set out to destroy Darwin's reputation with a parody, *The Loves of the Triangles*, written in Darwinian verse, and to damage Godwin by implying that he (under the name 'Higgins') was the author. The 294 lines of the parody[21] were published serially in three numbers of the *Anti-Jacobin* for 16 April, 23 April and 7 May 1798.

The Loves of the Triangles is as silly as its title suggests: a parabola, a hyperbola ('blue-eyed wanton') and an ellipse are made to sigh for the love

of a rectangle. The sillier the better, of course, for that implies that the
original was silly too. The serious criticism is reserved for the notes, where
Canning ridicules three of Darwin's ideas: that human beings have evolved
from lower forms of life; that electricity will have important practical
applications; and that the mountains are older than the Bible says (six
thousand years in the orthodox interpretation). As all three of Darwin's
ideas have proved valid, Canning's weapon was a boomerang which returned to discredit him many years after everyone had forgotten about it: so
Darwin has had the last laugh. But his laugh is hollow because the parody
did seriously damage his reputation at the time.

The damage was done by the digressions in the poem, which link Darwin
with the French Revolution. The most effective digression is at the very end,
where Pitt is guillotined:

> Down falls the impatient axe with deafening din;
> The liberated head rolls off below,
> And simpering Freedom hails the happy blow!

The adjectives sound Darwinian, and his sentiments are neatly perverted.

Later in the year Darwin was among the many 'Jacobins' caricatured in
Gillray's cartoon, 'The New Morality'. Fig. 18 shows the central section of
it. Darwin seems to be drawn as an ape with a basket on his head containing plants, on each of which grows a bonnet-rouge. The basket is labelled 'Zoonomia or Jacobin Plants'. This is quite a mild rebuke, but it shows
how the land lay. Darwin's plants also appear in a cartoon by Rowlandson
in 1799.[22]

[5]

The third attack on Darwin in 1798, and the most important in the long
run, was a little book called *Lyrical Ballads* by Wordsworth and Coleridge.
Both these young poets – Wordsworth was twenty-eight, Coleridge twenty-
six – had been much influenced by Darwin,[23] but were now in revolt
against his style and blazing a new trail for English poetry. Their experiment succeeded and the new trail became the main highway for the future,
leaving the Darwinian style beached like a whale on the sands of time.

In the Advertisement to *Lyrical Ballads* Wordsworth shoots straight at
Darwin when he refers to the 'gaudiness and inane phraseology of many
modern writers'. He may have been thinking of Darwin's clumsy couplet
about the sunflower, in which the phrase 'each gaudy band' occurs twice.

In the preface to the second edition Wordsworth says he wishes to 'write
about incidents and situations from common life' (not sylphs and gnomes)

FIG. 18 Central section of the cartoon 'The New Morality' by J. Gillray, for the
Anti-Jacobin Magazine, August 1798. Erasmus Darwin appears as an ape carrying
a basket of 'Jacobin Plants' on his head. Also satirized are Priestley, Wakefield,
Southey and Coleridge

'in the real language of men in a state of vivid sensation' (not in the un-
real glitter of Darwinian couplets). Wordsworth rejects poetic diction and
asserts that 'all good poetry is the spontaneous overflow of powerful feelings', in obvious contrast to the 'manufactured' Darwinian verse.

The success of *Lyrical Ballads* meant that Darwin would not remain a popular poet, except among older readers. Yet his influence on *Lyrical Ballads* is far stronger than that of any other author. Eleven of Wordsworth's nineteen poems have probable links with Darwin,[24] and Coleridge's 'Ancient Mariner' is deeply Darwinian.

Wordsworth had been attracted to Darwin because he supported the French Revolution, relished mountain scenery, and provided the authority of science (or so it seemed) for the ideas that plants experience emotions and that all nature, however humble, is to be valued.

When Volume I of *Zoonomia* appeared, Wordsworth was impressed by the chapters on sleep, dreams and reverie. Early in 1798 he became very keen to read it again and wrote to Joseph Cottle, probably on 28 February: 'I write merely to request (which I have very particular reasons for doing) that you would contrive to send me Dr Darwin's Zoonomia *by the first carrier*'.[25] Wordsworth received the two volumes about 13 March and kept them for two months. He wrote a number of the *Lyrical Ballads* during this time, and *Zoonomia* left its mark on nine of them.

The most obvious parallel, which Wordsworth acknowledged, is his poem 'Goody Blake and Harry Gill'. In *Zoonomia* Darwin tells the true story of a young farmer in Warwickshire who on a cold night watched for a thief who was stealing sticks from his hedge. It was an old woman, and he jumped out and caught her after she had gathered a bundle of sticks. Then, in Darwin's words,

> ... her load was left upon the ground, she kneeled upon her bottle of sticks, and raising her arms to heaven beneath the bright moon then at the full, spoke to the farmer already shivering with cold, 'Heaven grant, that thou never mayest know again the blessing to be warm'. He complained of cold all the next day.[26]

The resemblance to Wordsworth's poem is striking, to say the least:

> Her bundle from her lap let fall; / And kneeling on the sticks,... / She pray'd, her wither'd hand uprearing ... / (The moon was full and shining clearly) ... / 'O may he never more be warm!' ... / He went complaining all the morrow / That he was cold and very chill.[27]

The farmer took to his bed, Darwin tells us, dressed in a wealth of waistcoats. But all in vain. 'From this one insane idea ... fear of the cold air', he stayed in bed twenty years until he died.

A less obvious example is 'Tintern Abbey'. It is from the section 'Of Reverie' in *Zoonomia* that Wordsworth took his central idea of uniting animal pleasure in nature (the 'glad animal movements') with the tranquil recollection of images of natural objects, to create 'a sense sublime'.[28]

Coleridge was deeply impressed by his talk with Darwin, and I see the 'Ancient Mariner' as the outcome of that talk because the poem expresses the philosophy of universal sympathy and organic happiness formulated in

Phytologia. Darwin's philosophy of life has two facets, both stemming from his belief in evolution. First, because all life has a common microscopic ancestor, all animals are our cousins and we should treat them kindly; this precept extends to worms, insects and plants. The second facet stems from the apparently cruel struggle for existence in nature. Yes, it is 'the survival of the fittest' (to use a later term); but it is also, by and large, the survival of the happiest. Darwin believed that all creatures and plants enjoy life, with the most complex animals having the greatest capacity for enjoyment. When a creature dies, often because it is no longer capable of happiness, it gives pleasure to a myriad of smaller creatures, so that the sum of happiness is maintained, or increased.

In Coleridge's poem, written a year or so after he met Darwin, the mariner shoots an albatross, incurs a burden of guilt, and endures it in agony, relieved only when he watches the glowing microscopic creatures in the ship's wake at night. 'O happy living things', he says. He 'blesses them unawares', and the albatross falls from his neck.

Coleridge is asking us to have sympathy with all organic nature:

> He prayeth well, who loveth well
> Both man and bird and beast.

This is Darwin's philosophy with religious wrapping – we should love all God's creatures rather than all evolution's creatures.

The crucial episode of the luminous tracks may be drawn from a note of Darwin's:

> In some seas, as particularly about the coast of Malabar, as a ship floats along, it seems during the night to be surrounded with fire, and to leave a long tract of light behind it. Whenever the sea is gently agitated, it seems converted into little stars, every drop as it breaks emits light, like bodies electrified in the dark.[29]

Coleridge's word picture is more compelling but quite similar:

> Beyond the shadow of the ship,
>   I watched the water-snakes:
> They moved in tracks of shining white,
> And when they reared, the elfish light
>   Fell off in hoary flakes.[30]

(The luminous snaking wake of the ship is sometimes seen as a huge snake-like animal: there is no need to invent mythical monsters when the scientific facts suffice.)

Coleridge's 'Kubla Khan' is even more redolent of Darwin, whose poems abound in underground rivers, caverns, domes and blossomy lawns. And it is not just in poems: he was fascinated by the science of underground water flow, the life-blood of artesian wells. In *The Loves of the Plants* (III

85–130) he describes the 'spacious cavern' and 'massy dome' of Thor's cave near Wetton, and the 'extensive and romantic common' below, 'where the rivers Hamps and Manifold sink into the earth' and flow three miles underground:

> Where Hamps and Manifold, their cliffs among,
> Each in his flinty channel winds along.

From here it is not far to Coleridge's land of Xanadu,

> Where Alph, the sacred river, ran
> Through caverns measureless to man,

near a 'pleasure dome' and a 'romantic chasm'. The river Manifold bubbles up from the ground in boil-holes at Ilam, which Coleridge went to see during his summer visit to Derby in 1796. The boil-holes may be the real-life origin of the 'mighty fountain' that 'flung up momently the sacred river' in 'Kubla Khan'.

Dozens of other parallels with Darwin in 'Kubla Khan' have been noted.[31] The usurpers Wordsworth and Coleridge may have overthrown the old school of Darwin, but they had not yet escaped his grip.

[6]

Fortunately the attacks on Darwin's public image in 1798 were compensated by some good news in his private life. On 10 April he wrote to Robert:

> We are all excessively happy in hearing that Mrs R Darwin is safe in her bed; and congratulate you both on this addition to your family. I shall now begin to think myself beginning to grow old, having acquired the name of Grandfather....[32]

This first child of Robert and Susannah was a daughter Marianne. Two months later Erasmus refers to her as 'the little presbyterian'; so presumably he was surprised to hear that she was being brought up as a nonconformist rather than in the Church of England.

With fourteen children, of whom ten were still living, Erasmus must also have been quite surprised that he had not qualified as a grandfather until the age of sixty-six. This was a contrast with Elizabeth, who had become a grandmother six years before, at the age of forty-five.

Writing to Robert on 8 June, Erasmus gave him some disturbing news about his brother Erasmus junior, who had been in London for several weeks: 'his neglect of small businesses (as he thinks them, I suppose) is a constitutional disease'. He was nearly arrested for a small candle bill, 'which had been due 4 or 5 years', and a Derby tradesman 'has repeatedly complained ... that he owes Mr D. £70 and can not get him to settle his account'. His father concludes that this neglect arises '*from defect of voluntary power*. Whence he procrastinates for ever! But this must not be told of him, as it might injure him. And he is both a truly ingenious and a truly honest lawyer, a rare character!'[33]

This is the first sign of any deficiency in Erasmus junior's career as a lawyer. His father regarded his phobia for accounts as a trivial blemish on the image of an honest and ingenious lawyer. It seems unlikely that Erasmus ever discussed the problem with his son.

The younger children were less of a worry than their elder half-brother. Edward was now sixteen and had nearly reached his final height of six feet two inches. His father implies in letters that Edward was preparing to be a lawyer, but in fact he later pursued an Army career.

It was now seventeen years since Darwin had abandoned his botanic garden at Lichfield, which had been maintained by William Jackson,[34] his collaborator in the translations from Linnaeus. Jackson died in August 1798, aged sixty-three, and Darwin had to look for a new tenant – and to face the fact that the botanic garden would soon succumb to the invasion of wild nature.

His poem *The Botanic Garden* looked like lasting much longer, for Johnson was planning a new octavo edition. Cheaper but still beautifully printed, this was the fourth edition of Part I, and the fifth of Part II.

The first American edition of *The Botanic Garden* appeared in 1798, with some 200 lines of pleasant introductory verse by Elihu H. Smith, the young and energetic doctor who had proposed the publication of the poem in America.[35] Smith rejoices that 'knowledge and right' will triumph over ignorance: 'a proud column', he says, will 'bear inscribed, immortal, DARWIN's name'. Smith wrote to Darwin on 10 August, and Darwin replied; sadly, however, Smith never saw the letter because he became ill and died on 19 September, aged twenty-seven.

Darwin's other books had not been forgotten by publishers. *Female Education* was published in both Ireland and America in 1798. *Zoonomia* had already appeared in Ireland and America, and Johnson was planning a third English edition. And *Phytologia* was ready for the press by the end of the year.

Authors sometimes neglect their friends when tied to the treadmill of writing, and even Darwin seems to have done so. Edgeworth is the only one of his old friends from whom we have letters written during 1798. Edgeworth had soon decided to marry again, as he told Darwin in a letter on 21 May: 'I am going to be married to a lady of small fortune and large accomplishments ... liked by my family, loved by me'.[36] With Ireland on the brink of rebellion, Edgeworth wasted no time, and ten days later he married the lady, Miss Frances Beaufort. This fourth marriage was as happy as the second and third. As a bonus, Edgeworth was delighted to acquire a new friend and collaborator in his brother-in-law Francis Beaufort, an energetic young naval officer with a taste for science. Soon, Maria tells us,[37] Edgeworth became 'as much attached' to Francis Beaufort as he had ever been to Thomas Day (though she still calls Erasmus 'his most intimate friend'). This new friendship was to prove important when Beaufort later became Hydrographer to the Navy, and sent H.M.S. *Beagle* on its world voyage. Now recognized as the greatest of British hydrographers,[38] he also devised the Beaufort wind scale that is still in force today.

During 1798 Edgeworth became a member of the Irish Parliament and was surprised to find the Irish politicians 'very harmless creatures', though Darwin had predicted they would be savage. Inventive as ever, he offers Darwin the idea of warming hothouses by air pipes laid through dunghills, which he says will ensure a supply of air at 95° Fahrenheit. He also mentions a speaking machine just announced from France, which was not as good as Darwin's machine of 1771. Soon Edgeworth had other preoccupations, for in the autumn the French landed at Killala on the west coast, and Edgeworthstown was on their road to Dublin. But the invaders were defeated in a battle nearby, and the Edgeworth family escaped unscathed after a hazardous week.[39]

Edgeworth's adventures probably inspired a sprightly letter from Keir to Darwin at about this time. Keir imagines a French invasion of England: 'I suppose, like Archimedes when Syracuse was taken and soldiers rushed into his house, you will tell the French, *when* they come to Derby, not to disturb your meditations; and that you are just on the point of catching the *matter* of electricity by the tail, and the *matter* of heat by its whiskers.'[40]

Darwin's newer friendships with Beddoes and Tom Wedgwood were fading. Wedgwood had begun the final nomadic phase of his life, when he bought houses in the south of England in a vain search for a home where his perplexed mind might find peace. Darwin lost track of him during these wanderings.

As for Beddoes, he was fully occupied with his Pneumatic Institution, and Darwin was content to let him do his best, not wishing to involve himself any more in pneumatic medicine with its complex apparatus. Beddoes had taken on as an assistant a young Cornishman recommended by Tom Wedgwood and Gregory Watt. His name was Humphry Davy and he was nineteen. Within a year Davy vindicated Beddoes's faith in the medical use of gases by discovering the anaesthetic effects of nitrous oxide ('laughing gas'). But, amazing as it now seems, no one – not even Beddoes or Darwin – took notice of Davy's immediate suggestion that nitrous oxide could serve as an anaesthetic in medical operations.[41] Not until forty-five years later was nitrous oxide used as a dental anaesthetic, a role it filled for more than a century.

If some of his friendships were on the wane, Darwin was still attracting new disciples, such as Dr Robert Thornton, who was starting to publish his botanical illustrations gathered in *The Temple of Flora*, the finest of all books of botanical drawings. Thornton became a devout Darwinian and treated *The Botanic Garden* almost as a bible. Darwin returned the compliment by commending Thornton's plates as having 'no equal'.[42]

Darwin's public image was tarnished by the satires and other attacks: but he also had his champions. In the *Monthly Magazine* he was called 'superior perhaps to any other contemporary writer', while Polwhele spoke up for the pictures painted in *The Botanic Garden* as 'the most beautiful, in short, that were ever delineated by the poetic pencil'.[43] One of Darwin's American admirers, the chemist Samuel Mitchill, wrote a poem in Darwinian style about 'Septon', the essence of septicaemia and bitter enemy of oxygen.[44] There were generous biographical sketches of Darwin too, such as the nine-page notice in the book *Public Characters of 1798–1799*, which concludes:

> Our necessarily confined limits prevent us from paying a just homage to the character of this extraordinary man, who, as a poet, a physician, a philosopher, and a philanthropist, claims the admiration and gratitude of mankind.[45]

[7]

In 1799 there was still no end in sight to the war: Napoleon seemed to be invincible on land and more of a menace than ever. William Pitt brought in a temporary new financial measure called income tax. Erasmus was puzzled to know what income he should declare to the commissioners. He told Robert on 10 May: 'I kept no book, but believed my business to be £1000 a year, and deduct 200 for travelling expenses and chaise-hire, and 200 for a livery servant, four horses and a day laborer'.[46] His income would have been higher a few years earlier, but he had by now reduced his medical work-load. 'The income Commissioners gave me much trouble and calculation, but settled it at last nearly as I had estimated it',[47] he told Robert on 8 August.

His letters to Robert have a new theme: invitations for Susannah and the baby Marianne to visit Derby: 'we are all as much desirous to see Mrs R. W. Darwin as we used to be to see Miss Wedgwood – I don't know how to say any thing kinder or stronger'. This was written on 10 May 1799, and there may have been a visit soon after.

Two visitors who definitely came were Edgeworth and his daughter

Maria, probably in April or May. Maria was now thirty-one and about to become the most celebrated novelist of the day in England, after the success of *Castle Rackrent* the next year.[48] Maria liked Darwin very much and said he was 'not only a first-rate genius, but one of the most benevolent, as well as wittiest of men. He stuttered, but far from lessening the charm of his conversation ... the slowness with which his words came forth, added to the effect of his humour and shrewd good sense.'[49]

A new medical treatment finds its way into Erasmus's letter of 10 May: vaccination. 'The variolae vaccinae I have read about ... but as inoculation given in the best manner ... to children 3 or 4 years old, is in general so mild a disease ... the cow-pox cannot be required'.[50] This was Erasmus's first reaction. As soon as the favourable evidence accumulated, he became a strong advocate of vaccination.

The same letter also shows that *Phytologia* had reignited his enthusiasm for invention. He told Robert: 'My present hobby is a new drill plough for my book of agriculture, which is beginning to be printed, and is to be call'd *Phytologia*'. This drill plough is fully described in *Phytologia*, with detailed drawings. It seems ingenious and can deliver seed of any size from horse beans to wheat at any specified density per acre. He used a seed-box designed by Thomas Swanwick, a Derby schoolmaster, and on 13 October he commended Swanwick's invention in a letter to the Society of Arts.[51]

With little more to do on *Phytologia*, Erasmus was working on his second long poem, eventually published under the title *The Temple of Nature* four years later. He probably began it in 1798, because there are manuscript drafts of the poem[52] in exercise books of the same design as those used for *Phytologia*. I would guess that much of the poem was written in 1799, with some additions later.

[8]

Amidst the pleasantries of Erasmus's writing and his family life, a ghastly tragedy was lying in wait at the end of 1799.

Erasmus junior had caused his father concern in the previous year by his failure to settle accounts, as we have seen. In 1799 this 'defect of voluntary power' – code for laziness? – became even worse. In the summer the young Erasmus decided that he wished to retire from his legal business. He was not so young now: it was his fortieth birthday in September, and that may have triggered his decision. He had made enough money to be able to retire early in comfort, just as his grandfather had done at Elston in the 1720s.

The first mention of this news is in the letter to Robert from his father on

8 August: 'The Botanic Garden at Lichfield is now let by me to Mr Bond', he says, and continues:

> Erasmus talks of building a cottage, and going to live there, retiring from business! – all which I much disapprove – therefore you will please not to mention it, and I hope it will all fall through.[53]

This first hint that his son wished to retire was obviously a shock, and it is no surprise that Erasmus senior opposed the idea. His own life as a doctor had been one of ceaseless activity, and he feared his son would do nothing in retirement, merely wasting his life. His plan for a cottage at Lichfield did soon fall through. Presumably the hassle of organizing it seemed worse than settling accounts.

Early in November Erasmus junior travelled to Lincoln with his step-mother Elizabeth, and he reports the outcome in a jokey letter to Robert's wife Susannah on 15 November. He would be pleased 'to come and see you at Shrewsbury', but cannot say when. 'For lo! a wondrous Revolution has taken place in all my plans. I who have been building Cottages (in the Air) all my Life, am doomed to dwell in a large forlorn old Pile'. To explain this surprising news, he tells her that, while in Lincoln (and buoyed up by the bubbling Elizabeth),

> I agreed for the purchase of a farm about four miles North East of this place [Derby], whither I intend removing at Lady Day next, and where I hope to pass the remainder of my days. It is called the Priory and is I believe the original religious House.[54]

He then extols the virtues of the Priory, which 'adjoins a fine dry Common' and has 'some good Fish Ponds' in the garden. 'The Religious of former days knew how to select good Situations', he says, 'and took care that fasting should not be a severe Punishment'. He invites Robert and Susannah to visit him 'when I am got settled in my convent'. He adds that Elizabeth 'was delighted with her Journey to Lincoln, and boldly went to the top of the great Tower of the Cathedral'.

This is the letter of a man with a new lease of life. For the first time he had a life-plan he could look forward to with pleasure, instead of just grinding away for ever at legal documents. He told Polwhele he thought he would be happy 'in literary retirement'.[55]

His father's disapproval had now melted into grudging acceptance. In a letter to Robert on 23 November his father tells him that 'Erasmus has purchased a place 5 miles from Derby ... where he intends to live ... and to sleep away the remainder of his life!' Having shaken off his remaining doubts with this flip remark, Erasmus senior becomes more positive:

> Erasmus gave £3500 for the Priory, and it is thought a very cheap purchase, as it

had been long exposed to sale. It is a fine situation with 3 fish-ponds descending down a valley, with a view of the Derwent, and of Derby tower.[56]

But still the accursed accounts stood between Erasmus and a happy retirement. Over Christmas, perhaps imbued with a sense of centennial urgency – the 1800s would be his new life – he set to work on the accounts, at home. He lived in a house with a garden bordering the river, probably in the Morledge area of Derby near the present bus station, and close to the weir, which today has a white-water race more than a hundred yards wide.

The crisis came on 29 December. Charles Darwin in his *Life* of his grandfather says that, according to 'his confidential clerk',

> Mr Darwin had been working for two nights, and when urged in the evening of December 29th to take some rest and food, he answered with a most distressed expression, holding his head, 'I cannot, for I promised if I'm alive that the accounts should be sent in tomorrow'.[57]

What happened next is quite unknown: six weeks later, his father told Robert, 'I still can conjecture nothing of the final events'. And if he could not find out, at the time and on the spot, no one can.

Charles Darwin, accepting family tradition, says that his uncle 'seems to have rushed out of the house, and leaving his hat on the bank, to have thrown himself into the water'.[58] This leaves many doubts. Would he have 'rushed out' into pitch darkness down a long garden on a moonless night? If he was suicidal, would he have stopped to put on his hat and also, it seems, his coat and neckcloth? Did he 'throw himself', or accidentally fall? On the next day, 30 December, his father told Robert:

> I write in great anguish of mind to acquaint you with a dreadful event – your poor Brother Erasmus fell into the water last night at the bottom of his garden, and was drowned.[59]

The idea that Erasmus probably committed suicide was tacitly accepted by the family in later years. But I think it just as likely that he fell into the river by accident. If he had intended suicide when he went out, he would surely have left a note, for he was a literary and painstaking lawyer. So if it was suicide, it was unpremeditated, a sudden impulse on seeing the black water. But as the night was moonless and stormy, and he probably had no lantern, he could well have missed his footing and fallen in. This is more likely if he had been drinking alcohol: Anna Seward (admittedly not an entirely reliable source) says he was 'on the couch complaining of head-ach' before he went out into the garden. He may have gone out to 'clear his head' and was unsteady on his feet through lack of sleep or because he was not used to the drink. Or he could just have misjudged his position in the dark; or slipped on the muddy bank.

Once in the river he would not have survived long in the icy water. He could probably swim, but was unathletic and dressed in heavy clothes. He would soon have been swept over the weir, and injury would have been added to hypothermia.

The first written allegation of suicide is in Anna Seward's *Memoirs of the Life of Dr Darwin* four years later. But in her account of the tragedy, from second-hand sources, she falsely accused Erasmus senior of being indifferent to his son's death. After protests by Robert Darwin and Edgeworth[60] she was forced to publish a complete retraction in a number of magazines.[61] Her description of the events of the evening is therefore also suspect. What she says[62] is that at 7 pm Erasmus, complaining of headache, sent his 'partner' (possibly the confidential clerk mentioned earlier) on an errand. Soon after 8 pm the partner returned and found him gone. The servants had not seen him since he went outside 'about an hour before'. Anna says the partner ran out into the garden and found Erasmus's hat and neckcloth. The alarm was raised, and boats were sent out. Dr Darwin was summoned, and stayed on the bank a long time.

It was his son's clerk, Mr Parsons, who brought the news that his body had been found, probably the next day. Emma and Violetta were with their father at the time, and five years later Emma recalled the scene:

> My Papa immediately got up, but staggered so much that Violetta and I begged of him to sit down, which he did, and leaned his head upon his hand ... he was exceedingly agitated, and did not speak for many minutes ... he soon after said that this was the greatest shock he had felt since the death of his poor Charles.[63]

Anna Seward in her biography had dared 'to accuse my dear Papa of want of affection and feeling towards his son', Emma continues, whereas in fact 'he very frequently and *always with kindness* spoke of him'. 'I want to scratch a pen over all the lies, and send the book back to Miss Seward ... and to swear the truth of what I have said before both houses of Parliament'. Emma's indignant reaction confirms that her father felt the loss of his son very deeply. Four years later Robert said that his father had found it a constant exertion to obtain relief from the thought of his son's death. Indeed, although Erasmus lived on for over two years, his *joie de vivre* died on 29 December 1799.

The anguish over his son's death was sharpened by the feeling that he ought to have foreseen and prevented the tragedy. Whether accident or suicide, his death originated in distress about the overdue accounts, and his father was aware of this problem. He was supposed to be a doctor of great sympathy, insight and benevolence, yet he had failed to treat his own son for 'defect of voluntary power'. Of course there were mitigating factors: his son was forty and seemed well able to care for himself; and failing to keep accounts up to date appeared more like laziness than deep neurosis.

Erasmus senior had no premonition about the tragedy: earlier in the day he had written to Beddoes saying he was 'truly sorry to hear Mr T. Wedgwood is in so indifferent a state of health', and offering to let Tom stay for '2 or 3 days at my house' for treatment.[64]

After a suspected suicide it is usually easy to ferret out a source of stress. But Erasmus had no worry about debt or mismanagement: the accounts just needed updating. It is not a usual cause of suicide, though here it was a long-standing phobia. My own choice of verdict would be 'accidental death'; others may prefer 'found drowned', the likely coroner's verdict (though I have found no evidence of an inquest).

Whatever the verdict, this was a tragic end to a successful career, and a very sad end to the 1700s for the whole Darwin family.

CHAPTER FIFTEEN

Downhill
1800–1802

The death of his son was an enduring sorrow Erasmus could not escape. As executor, he had the 'laborious and painful' duty of working daily on the very accounts that had defeated his son, and to settle them as best he could.

In his first recorded letter of 1800, to Joseph Johnson on 10 January, he refers to 'my great affliction for the sudden death of my beloved eldest son, who used to call at your house'.[1]

James Watt sent 'a kind letter of condolence', and Erasmus replied on 21 January: 'My dear friend ... there are evils in mortal life which must be borne ...'. Though time and 'the sympathy of our friends' may help, he says, the grief remains: 'you know what it is to lament the loss of a beloved child!'[2]

The same sadness pervades his letters to Robert. 'The settling your poor Brother's affairs is a long and tedious process', he wrote on 8 February, 'He had settled with very few indeed for the last 10 years'.[3]

In the aftermath of this 'most calamitous event', as he calls it, Erasmus was not receiving much support from Elizabeth: 'Mrs Darwin bore this sad shock worse than I did, who have forced occupation, but I think she begins to be at times more cheerful'. This was her first taste of tragedy, and she may have felt she had contributed by encouraging her stepson to buy the Priory. Erasmus himself admitted that 'I am happyest when employ'd in medical business and from home'. The previously happy home was now a constant reminder of the tragedy: the cold silent killer still lurked at the end of the garden.

In his next letter, on 26 February, Erasmus sent Robert a proposed inscription for his brother's monument. After a small change suggested by Robert, the final version was:

To great abilities in his profession of the Law
He added the probity of ancient manners
with the elegance of modern ones.
Was strongly attach'd to his friends,
   cordially beloved by them,
   and most sincerely lamented.[4]

Ever a good lawyer, Erasmus had updated his will[5] and had left the
Priory at Breadsall to his father. What should be done with it? The answer
is in the letter to Robert on 26 February:

> As I grow old and shall perhaps in a year or two cease to practise physic, Mrs
> Darwin, as well as myself, think of laying out some money, perhaps 2 or 300£, on
> the house your poor Brother bought called the Priory, which I am to pay for at
> Lady Day. And we think to retire thither sometime – I wish he could have lived
> there with us![6]

Instead, 'Mrs D and myself intend to lie in Breadsal church by his side': they
were to do so.

On 20 March Erasmus confirms the plan for renovating the Priory.
Elizabeth 'dislikes town, and our young ladies also much wish it'. Because
of the alterations 'it may be another year or two before we go thither, if at
all during my life'.[7] Erasmus had lost his 'steady supply' of cheerfulness: he
felt his days were numbered and he had nothing to look forward to.

Settling the accounts was still proving difficult. There were some large
bad debts, on which Erasmus despaired of obtaining payment. 'I cannot
yet tell how your poor Brother's affairs will turn out', he told Robert on
20 March and again on 19 April. The outcome was important to Robert
because he had borrowed about £2000 from his father to help in building a
new house at Shrewsbury, on a hill overlooking the river. It was completed
in the spring of 1800. Robert would have felt obliged to repay some of the
money if the bad debts could not be recovered, and in April Erasmus asked
him to 'let me know what money you can without any inconvenience repay
me'.[8] This was because Erasmus found he had to return £1000 'which your
poor Brother had borrowed'. Robert offered to pay back £620, and on 2
June Erasmus told him, 'I shall want no more money'.[9] By then most of the
accounts had been settled, apart from 'the great account with Mr Pole',
which eventually went to arbitration, with Francis Mundy and Mr Balguy
as referees. Erasmus junior presumably kept no records of work for his step-
brother. After several meetings with the referees, agreement was reached in
December.[10] The amount involved seems to have been about £1700.

These financial dealings are tedious, but they dominated Erasmus's life.
Any leisure time was occupied in supervising the alterations at the Priory,
which 'makes me, I believe, think less of disagreable subjects'. It was not a
time for creative thought about life's origins and progress. His new poem
was probably put aside.

Elizabeth felt the need for escape during the year, and in June she took
her three daughters, Violetta, Emma and Harriot, to stay at Shrewsbury
with Robert and Susannah, whose new home and weedless garden were
much admired by the visitors. From Shrewsbury they went for about two
weeks' holiday to Barmouth on the Welsh coast. After returning to Derby

in July, they made another journey in August 'to Buxton, and to see the wonders of Derbyshire for 3 or 4 days, as Castleton Hole, and Chatsworth, and Matlock'.[11]

There was one positive development in 1800: the reappearance of the copying machine. In his letter of 8 February Erasmus tells Robert: 'The writing-machine shall be done; and when you come in Summer, you shall see this *plain* one and my fine mahogony one'.[12] Robert could then choose which he would like. The copying machine had been constructed when Robert was twelve: perhaps he had only just heard about it, and had asked if he could have one. But if Erasmus had had the mahogany one for twenty years, why did he never use it? And why did he use Watt's copying-press in 1786? Possibly he lent his machine to Erasmus junior, whose law business called for much copying, and it came back to him on his son's death.

On 20 July Erasmus says, 'The double-pen machine is not quite finished to my likeing, so that I think not to send it at present'.[13] He says he never sought a patent because he saw no advantage in it and 'have been careless of whom I shew'd it to. The machine you mention has been stole from it, I dare say.' Robert had probably seen one of M. I. Brunel's machines,[14] which were on sale in 1800. Erasmus says his machine can be made for '20 or 30 shillings'. On 12 September he tells Robert, 'I have this day sent you my double-pen machine, which performs very well indeed, I think better than my other more expensive one'.[15] He advises using 'thinnish ink', to be corked when not in use, and adds that Elizabeth sewed the lead weights in their linen covers.

The machine for Robert may not have been the same design as the one sent to Greville in 1779, because it was cheaper and more portable. Neither the mahogany nor the plain one exists today, as far as I know.

There is no sign that Darwin used the copying machine in 1800 for his own letters, which are quite numerous and seemingly all originals. Among them are two letters to Boulton, from 'your old and affectionate friend'. He probably wrote to Keir too, and to Edgeworth, from whom he received a letter in April.

In none of Darwin's known letters is there any mention of the war. But it was still going on, and would-be reformers were still being imprisoned. One of these was the high-minded Gilbert Wakefield, confined in Dorchester gaol for publishing a pamphlet critical of Bishop Watson. Wakefield read Darwin's *Botanic Garden* while in gaol and was greatly impressed: 'I have read his first volume ... with extraordinary delight and admiration'.[16] In August Wakefield sent Darwin a satire he had written and some comments on *The Botanic Garden*. Darwin replied on 19 August:

> I am much obliged to you for your severe and elegant satire, which you have so good cause to write, who so long have felt the persecution of these flagitious

times! When one considers the folly of one great part of mankind, and the villany of another great part of them, the whole race seems to sink into contempt.[17]

He invites Wakefield to visit him 'if you are ever released from the harpy-claws of power'. Soon after leaving prison, however, Wakefield died of typhus fever at the age of forty-five.

Another side-effect of the war was shortages of bread, and on 20 November Darwin wrote to Watt asking him to recommend a hand-cornmill, because 'I wish to grind my own corn'. James and Ann Watt had recently called at Full Street, and Darwin manages a weak joke about the shortness of their stay, saying he hopes 'Mrs Watt and yourself will some-time make a visit or a visitation, not a viz like your last'.[18]

Darwin still had a number of patients in 1800 and one of them was Georgiana, Duchess of Devonshire, who suffered from painful inflam-mation of the eyes. After she visited Beddoes in 1793, he told Darwin that her knowledge of modern chemistry was superior to what he would have supposed 'that any Duchess or any lady in England was possessed of'.[19] And indeed the two surviving letters from Darwin to the Duchess (in November) are highly scientific, being concerned with the 'Galvanic pile' or, strictly, 'the pile of Volta', since it was Volta who announced early in 1800 that he could produce a steady electric current, as we now call it. This epoch-making discovery, the basis for nearly all subsequent uses of electricity, was seized on by Darwin as a possible treatment for some eye problems.

Darwin tells the Duchess how to construct and use the pile:

> The Galvanic pillar may consist of about 30 or 40 half-crown pieces, as many pieces of Zinc of similar dimensions, and as many circular pieces of cloth, which must be wetted in salt and water. Two thick brass wires, about 2 ft long, com-municate from each extremity of the pillar to each temple. The temples must be moistened with brine.
>
> Plates of silver about the size of crown-pieces, and smooth on both sides, are rather better.[20]

The shock of the electricity makes a flash in the eyes, he says, and a hundred shocks a minute can be given. He offers to obtain the zinc plates 'if your Grace wishes to construct a pillar', and says 'I should be extreemly happy to show your Grace the application of Galvanism, the effects of which would surprise you, I am sure'. Though Darwin is already sceptical about the medical value of the treatment, he offers to send Mr Hadley to Chatsworth 'to galvanize your Grace's eye'.

Darwin was on good terms with the Duchess, and she asked him to comment on her poem 'Passage of Mount St. Gothard'. However, he de-clined her invitation for a social visit to Chatsworth. 'I am sure your Grace does me great honour, and I should be happy to see Mr Spencer, but it is so inconvenient to me to leave home.'[21] Darwin had come a long way in life: thirty or forty years earlier he would have jumped at the chance to treat any Duchess. Yet now he was responding discourteously to an invitation from the most famous and most charming Duchess of her day, whom he respected for her scientific and literary talents. It was a complete turn-around. Probably it was because he felt his horizons were drawing in. But it may be that Elizabeth was piqued at not being invited too. Why should the daughter of Earl Spencer ignore a daughter of the Earl of Portmore?

For Erasmus the most important event of 1800 was the publication of *Phytologia* in March. He would also have been pleased by the elegant new octavo edition of *The Botanic Garden* which had appeared not long before (although it was dated 1799).

[2]

The new plant that came out with the daffodils in 1800, *Phytologia; or the Philosophy of Agriculture and Gardening*, had 306 quarto leaves and a quarter of a million words.

This bulky volume is the best of Darwin's prose works: it is free of the basic fallacies that mar *Zoonomia* and is solidly grounded in the good earth; it has many new ideas and some major discoveries, notably the specification of photosynthesis and of plant nutrients. Darwin says that he hopes 'the modern improvements in chemistry' will enable him to develop 'a true theory of vegetation', and this he largely does.

Phytologia is in three parts. The first, on the 'physiology of vegetation', covers plant structure and functioning. Although we associate life with 'palpable warmth and visible motion', he says, the 'cold and motionless fibres of plants' are also alive: 'vegetables are in reality an inferior order of animals'. A bud torn from the branch of a tree 'will grow, and become a plant in every respect like its parent'. Thus 'every bud of a tree is an individual vegetable being', and a tree 'is a family or swarm of individual plants' (pp.1–2).

As the 'progeny of vegetables in buds, or bulbs ... exactly resemble their parents', there is no variety for evolution to work on. What is needed is sex:

From the sexual, or amatorial, generation of plants new varieties, or improvements, are frequently obtained; as many of the young plants from seeds are dissimilar to the parent, and some of them superior to the parent in the qualities we wish to possess.... Sexual reproduction is the chef d'œuvre, the master-piece of nature. [pp.115, 103]

Darwin notes how ingeniously plants disperse their seeds: some seeds have plumes to fly in the wind; some are sticky, ready to be carried by animals; and so on. Digressing into animal life, he suggests artificial insemination to breed 'new kinds of mules', using 'the method of Spallanzani, who diluted the seminal fluid of a dog with much warm water, and by injecting it fecundated a bitch, and produced puppies like the dog' (p.119).

Darwin explains that leaves are the lungs of plants and, like animal lungs, have a huge surface area for interaction with atmospheric gases. He believed plant leaves 'breathed' through minute pores (discovered thirty years later, and called stomata); in 1789 he had tested this idea by carefully covering the surfaces of several leaves with oil, which killed the leaves.

Darwin's worst mistake in his plant physiology is to take the analogy with animals too far by suggesting a circulation of sap in what he calls the 'aortal arteries and veins' of plants, and discussing the 'muscles, nerves and brain' of vegetables. Here he concentrates on insectivorous and sensitive plants: the Venus fly-trap closes when it feels an insect on it; a whole stem of mimosa collapses when one leaflet is cut with scissors. He concludes that each individual bud of a plant possesses muscles (used in the Venus fly-trap), nerves (to feel the insect) and brain (to direct the nerves and muscles). Thus he persuades himself that plants feel, 'though in a much inferior degree even than the cold-blooded animals' (p.133).

Darwin's sharpest insight in Part I is to recognize the vital role of sugar, and its conversion into starch (or vice versa). He knows sugar has food value, because

> the slaves in Jamaica grow fat in the sugar-harvest, though they endure at that time much more labour.... Great God of Justice! grant that it may soon be cultivated only by the hands of freedom ...   [p.77]

As a step towards this humane goal, he suggests growing sugar beet in Britain: 'In many plants sugar is found ready prepared ... thus in the beetroot, the crystals of it may be discerned by a microscope' (p.77).

Part II of *Phytologia* is on 'The economy of vegetation' and includes an impressive seventy-two-page chapter on 'Manures, or the food of plants', a great advance on any previous discussion of the subject. Darwin's success stems from his belief that plants are like animals and need food, which he then analyses. He recognizes carbonic gas (carbon dioxide) and water as providing their main food, in the presence of sunlight:

> This carbonic gas ... is the principal food of plants.... Next to carbonic acid the aqueous acid, if it may be so called, or water, seems to afford the principal food of vegetables ... when vegetable leaves are exposed to the sun's light, they seem to give up oxygen gas.   [pp.193, 194]

The main solid product of 'digestion' in plants, he says, is sugar (or starch), as shown by 'the great product of the sugar-cane, and of the maple-tree in America' (p.189). Darwin has here stated all the components in the process of photosynthesis that is the basis of plant life on Earth and may be summarized as:

carbon dioxide + water + light energy $\rightarrow$ sugar + oxygen,

in the presence of 'green matter'. Darwin was the first to 'put it all together', though not in this neat equation. Several parts of the process of photosynthesis had been discovered earlier, by Ingenhousz, Priestley and others,[22] who showed that plants absorb carbon dioxide and emit oxygen in sunlight. (It was forty years before chlorophyll was identified as the essential 'green matter'.)

Photosynthesis keeps plants going, but they need other items of diet too. Here Darwin is fifty years ahead of his rivals.

He begins with nitrogen: 'The azote, or nitrogen ... seems much to contribute to the food or sustenance of vegetables ... and is given out by their putrefaction ... forming volatile alkali [ammonia]' (p.195).

Darwin also somehow managed to discern the importance of nitrates: he suggests that 'the acid of nitre', from which nitrates form, 'probably may contribute much to promote vegetation' (p.232).

Darwin's next choice is phosphorus, which was not then known to be an element, although he thought it 'probably' was: 'Another material which exists, I believe, universally in vegetables, and has not yet been sufficiently attended to, is phosphorus' (p.207). Darwin's faith in phosphorus sprang from his observation of phosphorescence in all decaying matter, such as wood, putrescent veal or the heads of fish in the streets of Edinburgh, by which he could read his watch, as mentioned in chapter 1.

People like to attach names to discoveries, and this is a harmless foible if the names are correct. But Darwin's successes in specifying photosynthesis and the importance of nitrogen and phosphorus are usually ignored.[23]

Carbon is also on Darwin's essential menu for vegetables because they all feed on carbon dioxide, or carbonic gas as he calls it.

Calcium is another vital element, Darwin believes, and he suggests a search for calcium phosphate, hoping that we might 'discover a mountain of phosphate of lime in our own country'. This was a rational precognition of the widespread search for phosphates later in the century.

Nothing that can help the fertility of the soil should be wasted, Darwin insists: the Chinese say that 'a wise man saves even the parings of his nails and the clippings of his hair'. He proposes sewage farms: 'The manures of towns and cities ... should be ... carried out of towns ... for the purposes of agriculture' (p.242). Darwin's concern for manure reaches its logical conclusion in his injunction: 'Burn nothing which may nourish vegetables by its slow decomposition beneath the soil'. The needless burning of 'a hair or a straw', he says, 'should therefore give some compunctions to a mind of universal sympathy' (p.255).

Darwin's amazing insights into plant chemistry can perhaps best be called rational intuition. He did not give scientific demonstrations of their truth, but merely plausible reasons, like the glowing fish-heads. His insights were all confirmed as valid, but not for more than forty years. Long before that, *Phytologia* had been forgotten, having been displaced by Sir Humphry Davy's *Elements of Agricultural Chemistry*, published in 1813. Davy knew much more than Darwin about chemistry, but Davy's book seems outmoded when set beside Darwin's. I suspect that Davy never read *Phytologia*: had he done so, he would surely have seized on some of Darwin's ideas and tested them by chemical analysis.

The next topics in *Phytologia* are more practical: the draining, watering and aeration of soil. Darwin recommends the boring of artesian wells and also tells us how to find natural springs: for example, in places where mists begin earliest, or frosts melt earliest. For the drainage of valleys and marshes he offers his horizontal windmill (as already shown in Fig. 11), and an elaborate water pump of his own design, with two pages of explanation and an intricate drawing.[24] His drill-plough is also on offer, with ten detailed drawings and fourteen pages of instructions. With three such major inventions, the book is as notable for its mechanisms as for its theories.

Part II of *Phytologia* ends with a discussion of the diseases of plants and the ravages of insects, particularly the aphis. This he says could be destroyed 'by the propagation of its greatest enemy, the larva of the aphidivorous fly', thus using 'the natural means of devouring one insect by another' (p.356). Darwin is rightly recognized[25] in the western world as a pioneer in the biological control of insects, a technique now much favoured. (However, it had been used in China centuries earlier.[26])

Darwin doesn't stop at insects. What about biological control for rats and other species regarded as vermin?

> American ... water-rats ... are so liable to be affected with tape-worm as is supposed much to diminish their numbers.... Could some of these diseased American rats be imported into this country, and propagate their malady amongst the native rats of this climate?   [pp.583–4]

So Darwin was also a pioneer in germ warfare, or at least worm warfare. In the 1950s his idea was paralleled half-intentionally by myxomatosis in rabbits; and there have been other examples since.

Part III of *Phytologia*, on 'agriculture and horticulture', is a practical handbook of food production. Darwin devotes fifty pages to fruits, full of ripe wisdom about pruning, grafting, preservation, and so forth. He goes into great detail, and even bursts into verse:

Behead new-grafted trees in spring,
Ere the first cuckoo tries to sing;
But leave four swelling buds to grow
With wide-diverging arms below....   [p.429]

He is just as keen on seeds, and points out that land yields more food per acre under grain than under animal pasturage. But Darwin is not a vegetarian: he believes in eating both animal and vegetable food, because human teeth and intestines are structurally midway between 'those of the carnivorous and phytivorous animals'.

When he delves into root crops, Darwin comes up with a very radical specimen, an aerial potato from the odorous garden of a well-named military friend: 'I was this day shown by my friend Major Trowel of Derby a new variety of the potato in his excellent new-made garden, the soil of which consists of marl mixed with lime and stable-manure' (p.474). Apparently the ground was so rich that the potatoes burst out into the air on stalks.

Returning to earth, Darwin offers useful ideas on the bark, leaves and wood of trees. To grow trees straight, he says, you should plant them close: then their 'contest with each other for light and air propels them upwards'. And where should they be planted? 'In the present insane state of human society', he says, when 'war and its preparations employ the ingenuity and labour of almost all nations', farmland should be reserved for growing food. But 'all those unfertile mountains from the extremity of Cornwall to the extremity of Scotland, should be covered with extensive forests of such kinds of wood as experience has shewn them to be capable to sustain' (pp.527–8). On barren mountains 'pines, as Scotch fir', he says, might 'succeed astonishingly'. So Darwin specifies (a century early) the Forestry Commission's twentieth-century planting programme.

Finally, Darwin offers his philosophy of organic happiness. He first warns of the savagery of nature – vegetables being eaten by animals, and weak animals by stronger ones:

> Such is the condition of organic nature! whose first law might be expressed in the words, 'Eat or be eaten!' and which would seem to be one great slaughter-house, one universal scene of rapacity and injustice!   [p.556]

Among all this apparent misery can we 'find a benevolent idea to console us?' Yes: the more active animals have a greater capacity for pleasure, and these are the animals most likely to survive. So the evolutionary struggle for existence maximizes organic pleasure. Many geological strata, such as limestone and coal, are the remains of animal or vegetable life, and so the very mountains (or some of them) are 'monuments of the past felicity of organized Nature'. All life works all the time towards the triumph of pleasure. That is the 'consoling idea' of his philosophy of organic happiness.

Darwin was ahead of his time in his clear-sighted view of the struggle for existence. By the time Tennyson rephrased it as 'nature, red in tooth and claw', the idea was less unthinkable and awareness of it helped in the partial acceptance of evolution in the 1860s after the publication of the *Origin of Species*. Erasmus is still ahead of opinion today with organic happiness, which has not yet been adopted by either evolutionists or eco-warriors.

Although a better book, *Phytologia* did not have the success of *Zoonomia*. Darwin's time of fame was past; he was no longer among the glitterati. The book received little more notice than if it had been written by an unknown author. There was an Irish edition, a German translation, praise from Sir John Sinclair and a small clutch of favourable reviews. That was all. *Phytologia* has never had the credit it deserves for its advances in ideas about photosynthesis, plant nutrition and practical agriculture, not to mention the eco-philosophy of organic happiness proceeding from 'a mind of universal sympathy'.

[3]

After these scientific insights it is a comedown to return to daily life in 1801. The financial problems were almost settled, and Erasmus told Robert on 11 January that 'I shall be able by Lady Day to pay off the 2000£ still owing on a mortgage of the priory, and the whole of your poor brother's debts besides'.[27] However, he was still not sure 'what overplus there may be in the end', because of the accounts still unpaid.

In this letter Erasmus gives Robert some practical advice on travelling. 'I am sorry you complain of the irksomeness of travelling. You should have a light sulky with a prong occasionally to let down behind in going *up* steep hills and also a chain for a wheel ... and you will be perfectly safe.' Robert was also complaining of rheumatic pains, and Erasmus says these are often caused by 'sitting always on the same side of the fire, which makes one part tenderer than the other'. Robert was thirty-four, but here gives the impression of still being daddy's boy.

Erasmus himself was still busy in his profession. On the same day, 11 January, he also wrote a detailed six-page medical letter[28] to John Waldie (1781–1862), whose father suffered from a gravelly complaint rather like Boulton's.

On 15 January Erasmus reports the death of his nephew Thomas Hall, the son of his eldest sister Elizabeth, who had herself died in the previous year, at the age of seventy-four, after twenty-five years as a widow. She was six years older than Erasmus, and they were never close after her marriage, for which he wrote his 'Epithalamium'.

These deaths in the family may have provoked Erasmus into wishful thinking about his own age: 'I mistook a year in my age, I believe – as I now think I was only 68 on the 23rd of December last',[29] he told Robert. In fact he was sixty-nine in December 1800. He had regarded 23 December as his birthday ever since the calendar change in 1752, when eleven days were 'lost'.

Early in March 1801 Erasmus became seriously ill, probably suffering from pleurisy or pneumonia. He gives some details in a letter to Robert dated 18 March and written by a scribe: 'As the pulse is so regular, I don't think there is any water in the Chest, and as it is so slow I do not think there is any abscess, but that it is simply a continuance of inflammation'.[30] His self-treatment is to lose blood 'once in 3 or 4 days' and to take '20 drops twice a day' of the tincture of foxglove.

Erasmus gradually recovered and was able to write a letter himself on 1 April. He can now climb stairs very slowly, but his pulse keeps missing a beat – 'every other, or every third, or every fourth', he says. 'I suppose I am like all corpulent old people, *thick-winded* – in part owing perhaps to the *growing up* of some air-vessels, or pulmonary arterial branches?'[31] On 6 May he says: 'I am I think perfectly recover'd, but am like other corpulent old men soon fatigued with walking, especially up hill or up stairs'.[32] Meanwhile the alterations at the Priory continued, and Erasmus held to his intention of moving there in 1802.

During the summer there are no further letters to Robert that have survived, but there is a brisk and efficient letter to William Strutt on 6 August:

Dear Sir,
1. I wish on Sunday morn. to see the grand effects of your electric apparatus.
2. To learn if positive electricity exists *in* glass or *on* it.
3. If glass or sealing wax can be electrised by pressure only? ...
5. A Galvanic *pile* with finely powdered fresh charcoal instead of water ...[33]

And there is much more. He seems to be in better form, and about to start a research programme into the fundamentals of electricity. What is more, it was carried through: the results appear in Note XII of *The Temple of Nature*. So this Note cannot have been written until 1801, even if the others are earlier. Most of the verse for *The Temple of Nature* was, I believe, written in 1799, possibly with some revision in 1801.

Darwin did not take much notice of the world at large in 1801. But he would have registered Pitt's resignation, Nelson's victory at Copenhagen, and perhaps the publication of Southey's *Thalaba*. His own literary reputation was still under attack: in an anonymous poem called *The Millennium* he is ridiculed for suggesting that 'plants may hate, desire, and love', and then condemned for chronicling the 'loose amours' of 'vegetable whores'. Coleridge wrote a short poem in similar vein, published by the *Morning Chronicle* in June.[34]

Darwin himself had a substantial book published in 1801: it was the third edition of *Zoonomia*, in four octavo volumes totalling 2086 pages. There are three interesting additions to the chapter on evolution. In a new section about vegetables, Darwin suggests that changes have arisen 'by their perpetual contest for light and air above ground, and for food or moisture beneath the soil'.[35] For example, plants too slender to rise by their own strength become climbers, adhering to stronger trees. This is as close as can be to 'the survival of the fittest' without using those words.

Darwin also comments on extinctions in species, not mentioned in the first edition:

> This idea is shown to our senses by contemplating the petrifactions of shells, and of vegetables, which may be said, like busts and medals, to record the history of remote times. Of the myriads of belemnites, cornua ammonis, and numerous other petrified shells, which are found in the masses of limestone which have been produced by them, none now are ever found in our seas.[36]

The third addition is a new theory of heredity, which seems like a precognition of modern views, if his 'fibrils or molecules' (really 'small particles') are read as DNA molecules. 'Collected separately by appropriated glands of the male or female', he says, these 'molecules' when mixed generate the new embryon, 'resembling in some parts the form of the father, and in other parts the form of the mother, according to the quantity or activity of the fibrils or molecules at the time of their conjunction'.[37]

[4]

The first news from 1802 is an advertisement in the *Derby Mercury* on 14 January: 'To be let and entered upon 5th April next. A large excellent DWELLING with a Brewhouse and all other convenient offices, a five-stalled stable, lounge, pleasure and kitchen gardens, the house pleasantly set at the lower end of Full Street, Derby.' Four acres of ground across the river were also available, if required. So the move to Breadsall Priory was to be made as planned.

Erasmus was now seventy, but there was no falling off in his mental agility and flair for innovation. He had at first been cautious about the new technique of vaccination for smallpox introduced by Edward Jenner a few years before. Now, convinced by the results, he was enthusiastic. With his usual insight he foresaw the situation that prevails today, as appears from a letter to Jenner on 24 February 1802: 'Your discovery of preventing the dreadful havoc made among mankind by the smallpox ... may in time eradicate the smallpox from all civilized countries'.[38] He also thought of using religion in the service of preventive medicine: 'the vaccine disease is so favourable to young children that in a little time it may occur that the christening and vaccination of children may always be performed on the same day'.

Erasmus's last letter to Robert, on 22 March, was written from Yoxall Lodge in Needwood Forest, where he was treating Thomas Gisborne for a fever. He tells Robert: 'we go to reside at the Priory in a day or two, and have sold our house and orchard in Derby'.[39]

When they made the move to Breadsall Priory (Plate 13A), the new rural surroundings seem to have pleased everyone.

But after two weeks the euphoria turned to alarm, because Erasmus became ill, as Robert Darwin told Edgeworth in a letter on 1 May:

> On the 10 of April, he was attacked with a severe cold fit of fever, followed with a proportionate hot fit, and with feelings and symptoms that threatened an inflammation of the lungs, from which he had suffered so much last spring. In this state, he was bled twice during that day, and lost 25 ounces of blood; the pulse became soft and slow, he got well in two days and remained so, to all appearance.[40]

Elizabeth's foster-mother Mrs Susan Mainwaring arrived to stay with the Darwins a few days later, and Robert's letter continues:

> On Saturday, the 17th, walking in his garden with Mrs Darwin and Mrs Mainwaring, a lady of his own age, the conversation turned on the extent of his alterations, when Mrs M remarked that he would not finish in less than ten years. 'Mrs Mainwaring, ten years is a long time for me to look forward. Five years since, I thought, perhaps, my chance of life better than yours; it is now otherwise.' Mrs Darwin expressed some surprise, to hear him speak in this manner, and complimented him on his good colour, his spirits etc. 'I am always flushed in this manner just before I become ill.'

Erasmus remained well during the evening of the 17th.

He was occupied in writing a long letter to Edgeworth:

> We have all been now removed from Derby about a fortnight, to the Priory, and all of us like our change of situation. We have a pleasant house, a good garden, ponds full of fish, and a pleasing valley somewhat like Shenstone's – deep, umbrageous, and with a talkative stream running down it. Our house is near the top of the valley, well screened by hills from the east, and north, and open to the south, where, at four miles distance, we see Derby tower.
>
> Four or more strong springs rise near the house, and have formed the valley, which, like that of Petrarch, may be called *Val chiusa*, as it begins, or is shut, at the situation of the house. I hope you like the description, and hope farther, that yourself and any part of your family will sometime do us the pleasure of a visit.[41]

But it was not to be. The next morning, Sunday 18 April 1802, Erasmus died before finishing the letter.

The letter was sent to Edgeworth, with a note by Mrs Mainwaring: 'Sir – this family is in the greatest affliction. I am truly grieved to inform you of the death of the invaluable Dr Darwin.' Mrs Mainwaring says he 'got up apparently in health; about eight o'clock he rang the library bell. The servant, who went, said, he appeared fainting. He revived again – Mrs Darwin was immediately called. The Doctor spoke often, but soon appeared fainting; and died about nine o'clock.'[42]

Apparently he had slept well that night until past 7 o'clock, but, soon after he got up,

> he was seized with a violent shivering fit, and went into the kitchen to warm himself; he returned to his study, lay on the sofa, became faint and cold, and was moved into an arm-chair, where without pain or emotion of any kind he expired a little before nine o'clock.[43]

This is Charles Darwin's account, based largely on his father's letter to Edgeworth. Charles visited Elizabeth at the Priory many years later: she 'showed me the sofa and chair, still preserved in the same place, where he had lain and expired'.

The post-mortem, by Dr Francis Fox and Henry Hadley, did not reveal any obvious cause of death, the heart being in good condition. However 'there was found a considerable degree of adhesion of the Lungs on the right side to the pleura', though 'the substance of the Lungs was perfectly free from inflammation or any other disease'.[44] Robert, after seeing the post-mortem report, told Edgeworth that the 'cold fever fit ... seems to have been the immediate cause of his death'. He adds that Erasmus 'sometimes supposed there was local disease about the heart (angina pectoris), but this idea seems to have been unfounded, and he had himself, latterly, rather given up the opinion'.[45]

In view of Erasmus's illnesses in the previous week and in the previous year, a lung infection seems the most likely cause of death.[46]

Erasmus was buried in the twelfth-century Breadsall Church, and the memorial inscription reads:

Of the rare union of Talents
which so eminently distinguished him
as a Physician, a Poet and Philosopher,
his writings remain
a public and unfading testimony.
His Widow
has erected this monument
in memory of
the zealous benevolence of his disposition,

the active humanity of his conduct,
and the many private virtues
which adorned his character.[47]

[5]

Erasmus's friendships were all intact when he died, and James Watt's last letter to him was by a poignant chance written on 19 April, the day after his death. Watt asks about an estate at Ashbourne that he was interested in acquiring. He also says that 'our friend Mr Boulton' has suffered illness 'brought on by his unreasonable activity'.[48] Boulton was now seventy-three and, in Watt's opinion, should have subsided into inactivity.

Watt was deeply upset at losing Darwin, his counsellor and medical adviser for so many years: 'He was almost my most ancient acquaintance and friend in England, I having been intimate with him for 34 years, and on many occasions much indebted to his good offices'.[49] Watt's letter to Robert Darwin on 24 April is full of kindness, and includes a sincere tribute: 'For my part, it will be my pride, while I live, that I have enjoyed the friendship of such a man'.[50] On 5 May Watt wrote to Beddoes: 'Permit me to condole with you on the loss of our valued friend Dr Darwin; the news was a great shock to me.... He will be long and sincerely lamented by all who knew him!!!'[51] (Watt was normally parsimonious with exclamation marks.)

The tributes from Watt and others were only one side of the coin: on the other side the vultures moved in to pick his bones, and several quite baseless slanders had to be refuted by Robert Darwin and Edgeworth.

The most important obituary was that in the *Monthly Magazine* for June 1802, entitled 'Biographical Memoirs of the late Dr Darwin' and running to seven pages of small print.[52] The author, possibly the editor Richard Phillips, who disliked Darwin, promises to describe the life of 'this far-celebrated man' without fear, favour or affection; and he keeps his promise. Darwin, he tells us, had 'two natural daughters'; was in youth 'fond of sacrificing to both Bacchus and Venus'; ate 'a large quantity of food'; and had a stomach that 'possessed a strong power of digestion'. This is all snide but not untrue, and the comments on Darwin's books are generous and perceptive. There is half a page on *Zoonomia*, 'unquestionably a noble effort of human labour or of human wit'. More surprising are two laudatory pages about *Phytologia*: 'As a philosophical agricultor Dr Darwin must ever be entitled to the highest consideration', the author rightly says. He does not like *The Botanic Garden* and quotes Darwin himself as telling a friend that he did not aim 'to touch the heart'. However, the obituarist praises Darwin's technical skill:

No man, perhaps, was ever happier in the selection and composition of his epithets, had a more imperial command of words, or could elucidate with such accuracy and elegance the most complex and intricate machinery.

Finally we are told that 'there are reasons for suspecting that Dr Darwin was not a believer in Divine Revelation', because 'a few days before his death ... the Doctor was observed to speak with a considerable degree of sedateness on the subject' to a friend, and added, 'let us not hear anything about hell'. His evolutionary philosophy was of this world.

Four slanders mar this biography. First, Darwin is said to have 'frequently walked with his tongue hanging out of his mouth': even Anna Seward was indignant at this 'idiot-seeming indelicacy', and expressed 'her entire disbelief of its truth'.[53] The second slander, which upset his family most, is that Darwin was irascible and that his death was brought on by 'a violent fit of passion'. This was immediately refuted by Dewhurst Bilsborrow, who refers to Darwin's 'mild and good humoured benevolence' and says, 'I have the *concurrent testimony*' of the servants and others that '*not a single angry word passed on that day*'.[54] Edgeworth also wrote in, with a longer view:

> I have known him intimately during thirty-six years, and in that period have witnessed innumerable instances of his benevolence and good humour, and but very few of that hastiness of temper which so often accompanies good-nature. Five or six times in my life I have seen him angry ... but then the motive never was personal. When Dr Darwin beheld any example of inhumanity or injustice, he never could restrain his indignation.[55]

Edgeworth goes on to refute the third slander, that Darwin wrote merely for money. The fourth slander is that flattery was the 'most successful means of gaining his notice and favour': on the contrary, he seemed almost immune to either fame or flattery. 'Throughout his letters I have been struck with his indifference to fame', Charles Darwin remarked.[56]

The most widely-read obituary was that in the *Gentleman's Magazine*. This was quite friendly, and ends: 'They who had the happiness of his acquaintance and friendship will deplore his loss, as they can scarcely hope to find such an assemblage of talents and virtues again united in the same individual'.[57]

The best of the obituarists was Erasmus's oldest Lunar friend, the judicious James Keir. After the remarks about his sympathy and benevolence (quoted in chapter 3), Keir discusses Erasmus's independence and originality:

> Your father did indeed retain more of his original character than almost any man I have known, excepting perhaps Mr Day. Indeed the originality of character in both was too strong to give way to the example of others.... He always paid little regard to authority, and he very quickly perceived the analogies on which a new theory could be founded. This penetration or sagacity by which he was able to

discover very remote causes and distant effects, was the characteristic of his understanding.... If to this quality you add an uncommon activity of mind and facility of exertion, which required the constant exercise of some curious investigation, you will have I believe his principal intellectual features.[58]

Keir also sees Darwin's books as 'a more faithful monument and more true mirror of his mind than can be said of those of most authors', because he wrote not for gain or fame, but solely from 'ardent love of the subjects'. Keir understates Darwin's 'uncommon activity of mind'. Between 1783 and 1803 Darwin produced books running to more than a million words, most of them closely argued and embodying new discoveries or original ideas. This is equivalent to a book of more than 50,000 words every year for twenty years, even though he was busy as a doctor during much of this time. His literary output is almost as amazing as his scientific insight.

CHAPTER SIXTEEN

A pageant of life
1803–1832

Darwin's best poem was yet to come. *The Temple of Nature* was not published until 1803. The verse is as skilful as ever, and this time he has a real story to tell – the pageant of life from its origins to its present diversity. And that story is now seen as correct in its essentials. It is an extraordinary achievement, for the scenario that Darwin calmly presents was not to be scientifically established for a further hundred years, and then only after long argument. He believed that life originated as microscopic specks in primeval seas and gradually evolved under environmental pressures, and without assistance from any deity, through fishes and amphibians to the land-based forms now seen on Earth.

Darwin's chosen title for the poem was *The Origin of Society*, and this appears as the running head at the top of every even-numbered page, and in the subtitles; for example, page 1 reads, 'ORIGIN OF SOCIETY. CANTO I. PRODUCTION OF LIFE'. *The Temple of Nature* appears as the title only once – on the title page, with *The Origin of Society* in smaller type as an alternative. Before publication[1] the poem was announced as *The Origin of Society*; but Joseph Johnson was cautious after his imprisonment and felt that people would not like being portrayed as descendants of a microscopic speck. So the neutral title was added before the book was published in April 1803. To avoid confusion, I shall continue to use *The Temple of Nature* while keeping in mind Darwin's own wish.

He says in the preface that he aims 'simply to amuse' by presenting the 'operations of Nature' as he believes they occurred. He distances himself from the action by first calling on the Muse to say how organic forms arose. In response she visits the Temple of Nature and passes on the request to Urania, Priestess of Nature and Hierophant of the Eleusynian mysteries. Once again the dominant figures in the poem are female. After 222 lines of build-up, Urania begins the lecture written for her by Darwin. She calls Nature the child of 'God the First cause', but that is the only act of God in the poem.

In a few quick couplets Urania runs through the formation of the Earth and the evolution of microscopic life:

Ere Time began, from flaming Chaos hurl'd
Rose the bright spheres, which form the circling world;
Earths from each sun with quick explosions burst,
And second planets issued from the first.
Then, whilst the sea at their coeval birth,
Surge over surge, involv'd the shoreless earth,
Nurs'd by warm sun-beams in primeval caves,
Organic Life began beneath the waves.   [I 227–34]

This new life was microscopic:

Hence without parent by spontaneous birth
Rise the first specks of animated earth;
From Nature's womb the plant or insect swims,
And buds or breathes, with microscopic limbs.   [I 247–50]

This is in line with the orthodox modern view that life arose spon-
taneously on Earth, through amino-acids formed from simple organic
molecules in the atmosphere or oceans with the help of solar ultra-violet
radiation, lightning or thermal vents. Darwin's belief in spontaneous generation was based on the results of many experiments, all of which must
have suffered from contamination, unlikely though that seemed at the time.
So Darwin arrived at the right starting point for evolution via a fallacious
belief.

He summarizes evolution in three close-packed couplets:

First forms minute, unseen by spheric glass,
Move on the mud, or pierce the watery mass;
These, as successive generations bloom,
New powers acquire, and larger limbs assume;
Whence countless groups of vegetation spring,
And breathing realms of fin, and feet, and wing.   [I 297–302]

In life's early stages, he says, there were 'vast shoals' of tiny creatures
with shells, which on their death formed the strata of coral, chalk and limestone, and helped to create land. This offered new opportunities:

After islands or continents were raised above the primeval ocean, great
numbers of the most simple animals would attempt to seek food at the edges or
shores of the new land, and might thence gradually become amphibious ...
                                                                   [I 327 note]

Or, to put it in verse, the host of sea creatures

Leaves the cold caverns of the deep, and creeps
On shelving shores, or climbs on rocky steeps.
As in dry air the sea-born stranger roves,
Each muscle quickens, and each sense improves;
Cold gills aquatic form respiring lungs,
And sounds aerial flow from slimy tongues.   [I 329–34]

In support of his ideas, Darwin has a long note on 'Amphibious animals', such as the diodon and lamprey, with both gills and lungs, and points out how the evolutionary progress from water to land is paralleled by the growth of the human embryo:

> Thus in the womb the nascent infant laves
> Its natant form in the circumfluent waves,   [I 389–90]

and then 'bursts his way' into the light of day, 'tries his tender lungs' and becomes 'a dry inhabitant of air'.

Canto II is entitled 'Reproduction of Life'. Darwin believes that asexual reproduction came first:

> The Reproductions of the living Ens
> From sires to sons, unknown to sex, commence....
> Unknown to sex the pregnant oyster swells,
> And coral-insects build their radiate shells....
> Birth after birth the line unchanging runs,
> And fathers live transmitted in their sons.   [II 63–4, 89–90, 107–8]

The male bias here is curious: Darwin even refers to 'parturient Sires'. Whether regarded as male or female, asexual clones receive the thumbs-down from Darwin because they sink under inherited disease:

> The feeble births acquired diseases chase,
> Till Death extinguish the degenerate race.   [II 165–6]

The remedy is sex, which combats inherited disease, adds to organic happiness and improves the species by introducing variety. Sexual rivalry may provoke battles among males in some species; on the other hand, there may be married bliss, and Darwin amuses himself by describing Love's flower-decked car, with lions, tigers, 'herds domestic', birds, fishes, insects and plants all following behind it, to 'swell the triumph of despotic Love'.

Canto III on the 'Progress of the Mind' balances the physicality of Canto II. Urania tells her audience of nymphs, virgins and naiads how human powers of reason developed. Most animals, she says, have weapons or armour, citing bulls, stags, boars, eagles, electric eels and snakes. Only humans rely on hand, eye and brain:

> Proud Man alone in wailing weakness born,
> No horns protect him, and no plumes adorn....   [III 117–8]

The forms learnt by touch in infancy are reinforced by the eye,

> Symbol of solid forms is colour'd light,
> And the mute language of the touch is sight.   [III 143–4]

This leads on to Darwin's theory of ideal beauty from 'the nice curves

which swell the female breast' and to an erotic tale of Eros wooing Dione –
one of four scenes portrayed by Fuseli.

Then Darwin explains how he thinks the mind develops and can grasp
art and science. This theory is too complex to expound here and deserves
fuller study. One of the keys to mental advance, he believes, is 'the fine
power of Imitation': we imitate what we see or hear, or what others have
done. Sometimes a creative artist or scientist produces something original
out of these imitations. By imitation too we gradually learn speech and
language, through which we express thoughts and weave them into a
culture by memory. Darwin praises reason, basis of 'all human science
worth the name', but warns that our vaunted wisdom is not so different
from the instinctive wisdom of the wasp, bee or spider, which links 'the
reasoning reptile to mankind'.

Darwin was all in favour of sympathy and benevolence. 'The seraph,
Sympathy', he says, 'charms the world with universal love', and the Temple
of Nature has this motto:

> IN LIFE'S DISASTROUS SCENES TO OTHERS DO,
> WHAT YOU WOULD WISH BY OTHERS DONE TO YOU.   [III 487–8]

This precept, 'if sincerely obeyed by all nations, would a thousand-fold
multiply the present happiness of mankind', he says.

In Canto IV, 'Of Good and Evil', Darwin begins with the web of
slaughter in the struggle for existence. He ranges from a wolf to a seed, and
implicates the females from the start:

> The wolf, escorted by his milk-drawn dam,
> Unknown to mercy, tears the guiltless lamb;
> The towering eagle, darting from above,
> Unfeeling rends the inoffensive dove;
> The lamb and dove on living nature feed,
> Crop the young herb, or crush the embryon seed.   [IV 17–22]

The owl kills small creatures, which themselves prey on others; insects like
the gadfly and ichneumon fly lay eggs in animals or other insects. Even the
plants are at war:

> Yes! smiling Flora drives her armèd car
> Through the thick ranks of vegetable war;
> Herb, shrub, and tree, with strong emotions rise
> For light and air, and battle in the skies;
> Whose roots diverging with opposing toil
> Contend below for moisture and for soil.   [IV 41–6]

It is just as bad at sea, where the shark 'darts on the scaly brood that swims
below'. All in all,

Air, earth, and ocean, to astonish'd day
One scene of blood, one mighty tomb display!
From Hunger's arm the shafts of Death are hurl'd,
And one great Slaughter-house the warring world!   [IV 63–6]

The roster of evils continues with a depressing list of human ills, from the 'iron hand' of Slavery and the pains of Disease to writhing Mania, ragged Avarice, earthquake, pestilence, hunger and 'the curst spells of Supersitition', which fetter 'the tortured mind' (IV 84–5).

Is there nothing but woe, then? On the contrary, Urania replies, good and evil are nicely balanced. Human beings enjoy the pleasure of consciousness, the delights of natural scenery, the warmth of sunshine, the fragrance of flowers, the taste of fruits, the charms of music, painting and all the imaginative arts; and above all they may 'drink the raptures of delirious love'. There are also the satisfactions of philanthropy, the triumphs of science, and the heroic endeavours of those who fight against the suppression of knowledge by governments:

Oh save, oh save, in this eventful hour
The tree of knowledge from the axe of power....   [IV 283–4]

As knowledge grows and science advances, Darwin foresees tower blocks, piped water and traffic jams:

Bid raised in air the ponderous structure stand,
Or pour obedient rivers through the land;
With cars unnumber'd crowd the living streets ...   [IV 315–17]

Then he returns to nature and points to the perils of overpopulation:

Each pregnant Oak ten thousand acorns forms
Profusely scatter'd by autumnal storms....
The countless Aphides, prolific tribe,
With greedy trunks the honey'd sap imbibe....
– All these, increasing by successive birth,
Would each o'erpeople ocean, air, and earth.   [IV 347–8, 351–2, 367–8]

The process applies with humans as well as aphides:

So human progenies, if unrestrain'd,
By climate friended, and by food sustain'd,
O'er seas and soils, prolific hordes! would spread
Erelong, and deluge their terraqueous bed;
But war, and pestilence, disease, and dearth,
Sweep the superfluous myriads from the earth.   [IV 369–74]

Here Darwin has probably been influenced by T. R. Malthus's *Essay on the Principle of Population*, published in 1798, which may have shown him more clearly how overpopulation actuates the 'survival of the fittest'.

Darwin is pleased that 'every pore of Nature teems with life', because all life contributes to the sum total of organic happiness: 'when a Monarch or a mushroom dies', he says, alchemic powers soon take over and new life burgeons. So, even when 'earthquakes swallow half a realm alive', we should not grieve too much, because 'the wrecks of Death' are only a change in form. Long ago Pythagoras saw how 'restless atoms pass from life to life' and proposed his 'moral plan'

> That man should ever be the friend of man;
> Should eye with tenderness all living forms,
> His brother-emmets, and his sister-worms.   [IV 426–8]

Finally Darwin salutes the mountains of limestone as the remains of creatures that once enjoyed 'the Bliss of Being':

> Thus the tall mountains, that emboss the lands,
> Huge isles of rock, and continents of sands,
> Whose dim extent eludes the inquiring sight,
> ARE MIGHTY MONUMENTS OF PAST DELIGHT.   [IV 447–50]

He is keen to propagate the gospel of organic happiness:

> Shout round the globe, how Reproduction strives
> With vanquish'd Death – and Happiness survives;
> How Life increasing peoples every clime,
> And young renascent Nature conquers Time.   [IV 451–4]

There is no more to be said. The astonished nymphs and naiads troop silently into the Temple for a ceremonial finale.

[2]

The Additional Notes to *The Temple of Nature* are a book in themselves – 120 pages of essays on a wide variety of topics. Darwin is forever pressing against the frontiers of knowledge, and sometimes he steps over the boundary of the known.

In the first essay, on spontaneous vitality, he describes the many experiments that have led him to believe in it, and he again commends 'microscopic researches' as likely to reveal 'a new world'.

He has ten pages of advice about the other extremity of life, old age and death. Much of this is valid today because we have still not 'well ascertained' the 'immediate cause of the infirmities of age'.

It is no surprise to find a note on Reproduction and the advantages of sex. As a follow-on, Darwin discusses hereditary diseases and says 'it is often hazardous to marry an heiress, as she is not unfrequently the last of a diseased family'. This warning about heiresses was repeated in a weaker form by Darwin's grandson Francis Galton in his book *Hereditary Genius*,[2] and it is ironic that Galton fails to note how his grandfather had forestalled him.

The longest essay propounds an electromagnetic theory of chemistry. Darwin suggests that 'electric and magnetic attractions and repulsions' control chemical reactions on an atomic scale, and 'may be applied to explain the invisible attractions and repulsions of the minute particles of bodies in chemical combinations and decompositions' (p.75). In this extraordinary discourse Darwin proves himself a pioneer of modern electrochemistry.

Three of the essays delve into psychology, and E. S. Reed[3] calls Darwin 'the most important European psychologist' of his time. One of his many ideas (discussed by Logan) is that 'the excitation of the nerves of vision by light and colours' creates four sources of pleasure: novelty, repetition, colour melody and association.

The theory and structure of language elicit an impressive essay starting from the premise that words are the symbols of ideas, and proceeding to complex languages. This leads on to his thorough analysis of articulate sound, which is the basis for the speaking machine.

These essay-notes are more mature and better organized than those in *The Botanic Garden*, and focus on subjects of prime interest to Darwin in his last years – chemical affinity, spontaneous vitality, ageing, language and taste. He also relaxes with chatty notes on volcanoes, mosquitoes and Egyptian hieroglyphics.

Apart from the multi-page Additional Notes, there are 153 shorter footnotes covering every subject under the sun and a few beyond it. For example, Darwin imagines that all the suns and their planets 'may again sink into one central chaos; and may again by explosions produce a new world'.[4] Or, in fashionable jargon, 'the universe is swallowed by a black hole and then regurgitated': this has become a popular speculation in recent years.

With *The Temple of Nature* Darwin rounds off his life's work. Most of his time had been devoted to the science of life, first as a doctor, then as a botanist and theoretical biologist. Now he had united animal biology and botany with his concept of evolution. It was rejected at the time, but 'what he dared to think, others ... could think after him'.[5]

[3]

The Botanic Garden had been immensely popular but *The Temple of Nature* fell flat. In the intervening ten years the world had been turned upside down. The bright hope of the early French Revolution was gone. Instead Napoleon was poised to invade England in 1803: Martello Towers were needed, not Temples of Nature. Worse still, Darwin's evolutionary theme was thought to be an insult to both Christianity and human dignity, as well as seeming wildly improbable to most readers. They were much happier with Paley's *Natural Theology* (1802), which was seen as the Church's riposte to *Zoonomia*, and refuted Darwin's speculations with the certainties of theo-zoology. Paley had no doubts: 'Design must have had a designer. That designer must have been a person. That person is GOD.'[6] 'And who was GOD's designer?' Darwin might wickedly have asked if he had not been dead.

His own book had mixed reviews. His verse still commanded respect: indeed Anna Seward remarked in 1803 that 'one half' of the 'world of letters' regarded him 'as infinitely the first genius of the age, both as to poetic system, and execution'. The *Monthly Magazine* was friendly: 'the lamp of Darwin's genius burns brightly to the last'. The *Monthly Review* praised the 'splendour of his verse'.[7] The ideas, not the verses, were the target for abuse. The *Anti-Jacobin Review* condemned Darwin for his 'total denial of any interference of a Deity', and the *Critical Review* attacked him for trying 'to substitute the religion of nature for the religion of the Bible'. The *Gentleman's Magazine* called his poem 'glaringly atheistical', while the reviewer in *The British Critic* was so upset that he gave up: 'We are full of horror and will write no more'.[8]

Internationally, too, Darwin was slapped down. In America Joseph Priestley wrote a scathing review. The idea of evolution from microscopic creatures was, he thought, ridiculous. Priestley was appalled at God being made redundant in his role as species-creator: 'if there be any such thing as *atheism*, this is certainly it'.[9] Darwin was also condemned for his evolutionary ideas in that ragbag of German romantic agony *The Night Watches of Bonaventura* (1804) and in Washington Irving's *History of New York* (1809).[10]

A persistent critic of Darwin's evolutionary ideas was Coleridge, who was angry that Darwin had cast off the Creator like worn-out clothes, and distressed at the thought of humankind evolving by blind chance and natural forces. In a letter to Wordsworth in 1815, Coleridge condemns Darwin's belief in 'Man's having progressed from an Ouran Outang state – so contrary to all History, to all Religion, nay, to all Possibility'. Instead he prefers to believe 'the History I find in my Bible ... that Man first appeared with all his faculties perfect and in full growth'. Can anyone believe, he asks, 'that a male and female ounce [leopard] ... would have produced, in course of generations, a cat, or a cat a lion? This is Darwinizing with a vengeance.'[11]

More recently, historians of ideas have been fascinated by Darwin's use of the Orphic and Eleusinian mysteries;[12] and his evolutionary ideas in *The Temple of Nature* have at last been effectively presented to biologists by Richard Keynes.[13]

[4]

The published *Temple of Nature* narrates evolutionary development from microbes to humankind, as Darwin believed it happened. But manuscripts of earlier versions of the poem show that it started off as something quite different, and there are several changes of title too.

One early notebook is confidently entitled 'The Progress of Society: a poem in five cantos'.[14] These cantos were to cover the five Ages of Hunting, Pasturage, Agriculture, Commerce and Philosophy. There were to be many mythological digressions, as in *The Botanic Garden*, and these included a visit to the 'Shrine of the Goddess', where the 'Priestess or Hierophant' was in command.

This early version of the poem was Utopian and unrealistic, a tale of continual progress from rude human beginnings to the golden 'Age of Philosophy', when 'Virtue's soft forms our glowing hearts engage' and 'Liberty returns'; when, in short, life is wonderful.

In two other manuscript notebooks[15] Darwin changes the title to 'The Temple of Nature, or the Progress of Society: a poem in five cantos'. In both notebooks the first line of the poem is: 'Four past eventful ages, Muse! recite'; and there are many pages of verse on the 'five Ages' theme.

Darwin's early version is obviously modelled on Richard Payne Knight's poem *The Progress of Civil Society* (1796),[16] which has six sections on hunting; pasturage; agriculture; arts, manufactures and commerce; climate and soil; government and conquest.

After he had written hundreds of lines (or perhaps thousands) on this theme, Darwin scrapped his original plan in favour of the realistic scenario of the poem as it was published.

This was an interesting and ruthless decision, for he was throwing away a great deal of what he had written. One reason for the decision would have been the embarrassing similarity to Knight's poem. A second was dissatisfaction with the painting of pretty mythological pictures instead of facing up to the real world. In *The Botanic Garden* Darwin had supplied a model for the Romantic poets when he commented obliquely on the world via the behaviour of Greek gods and goddesses: Keats's *Hyperion* (1820) can be seen as the last poem in this genre. Darwin himself had now already decided to abandon it and to write a poem that would combine the two sides of his life, poetic feeling and scientific realism.

As 'The Temple of Nature' was one of the titles in his notebooks, it seems likely that he submitted the poem to Johnson as 'The Origin of Society; or The Temple of Nature', and that Johnson made a last-minute interchange.

[5]

Although Erasmus had enjoyed life at the Priory for only a few weeks, he had seen enough to know that the move was a success for Elizabeth. She continued to live there for thirty years, and the house became known as 'Happiness Hall' to her Galton grandchildren because they enjoyed their visits so much, thanks to her warm-heartedness.[17]

But that lay ahead. At the time of her husband's death she was fifty-four, and their children, aged between eleven and twenty, needed her guidance in the next few years. Although Elizabeth and Erasmus were as capable and healthy a pair of parents as could be imagined, only two of their seven children were to have good lives. The other five died before their mother.

The eldest, Edward, tall and probably burly, had been working as a clerk in the office of the attorney Nathaniel Edwards, who had taken over many of the clients of his former partner Erasmus junior. It seems that a legal career did not suit Edward. He became a cavalry officer and retired early to live at Mackworth, near Derby. In his forties he was a martyr to dropsy and could not walk. He weighed over twenty-five stone and was unable to get out of his carriage when he visited the Priory. He died at the age of forty-seven in 1829.

The healthiest and most talented of the children was the eldest daughter Violetta, who lived to be ninety. In 1807 she married Samuel Galton's son Tertius, and they had seven children. The eldest of these, Elizabeth Anne (Mrs Wheler), lived to the age of ninety-eight. The second, Lucy, married James Moilliet, son of Keir's daughter Amelia, so that the Moilliets are a triply Lunar family, descended from Darwin, Galton and Keir. Violetta had three sons, Darwin, Erasmus and Francis Galton, all of whom lived to be eighty-nine or more. The youngest, Francis, had much in common with his grandfather Erasmus Darwin.

The third child of Elizabeth and Erasmus was Emma, the daughter who was so indignant about Anna Seward's slanders against her father. Her niece Elizabeth Wheler said 'she was very beautiful, agreeable and amiable, and most kind-hearted'.[18] About 1811 she took over a small charity school started by her younger sister Harriot. Emma's health was poor and she never married, continuing to live at the Priory with her mother. She died in 1818 at the age of thirty-four after a long and painful illness.

The fourth of their children was Francis, the pigsticking young tearaway, who became a doctor. He was enterprising and energetic but had none of his father's intellectual insight. Nor did he look like Erasmus, having an aquiline face. However, he was tall like his brothers, about six feet two inches. In 1808, after a year at Emmanuel College, Cambridge, Francis embarked on an adventurous two-year journey via Spain to Greece and Turkey. He started out with four companions, all of whom died en route. In his Travels[19] he tells the story as if it were quite normal to spend a small fortune on almost suicidal voyages and expeditions, interrupted by fatal and near-fatal illnesses, in a war zone where every ship sighted was a threat. On returning, Francis began practice as a doctor in Lichfield. He married in 1815 and had ten children. He was knighted in 1820, possibly by mistake or possibly because he resuscitated the Prince Regent after he had passed out during a drinking bout. Francis loved country life and gave up his practice in 1822 to live for twenty-five years at Sydnope Hall in a remote area north of Matlock where he kept 'wild pigs in the woods and tame snakes in the house'.[20]

The fifth child, John, went to Repton school and St John's College, Cambridge, and chose the Church as his profession. He was ordained at York and became rector of Elston in 1815. He also became a heavy drinker, and 'drank himself to death with gin and other spirits ... in the meanest public houses in Derby', according to Maria Edgeworth.[21] 'His bill for spirits the last year of his existence was above £200'. He died in 1818 at the age of thirty-one.

The sixth child, Henry, had of course died as a baby.

The youngest of the children was the beautiful Harriot, who started an infants' school for poor children in Derby before she was twenty. In 1811, when she was twenty-one, she married Captain Thomas Maling, 'a large handsome sea officer'. Maria Edgeworth, who met her in 1819, says Harriot 'has a sweet voice and excellent things to say with it. She appears to have a large portion of her father's genius and her mother's strength of character.'[22] Harriot travelled widely with her husband and died of dysentery at Valparaiso in 1825 when she was thirty-five.

Elizabeth also outlived two of the three children of her first marriage. Her son Sacheverel continued to live at Radburn Hall and in 1807 changed his surname to Chandos-Pole by royal charter[23] after proving his descent from a sister of the warrior knight Sir John Chandos, who died in 1370. This long ancestry did not help Sacheverel to a long life: he died in 1813, aged forty-four. His wife and three of his children survived him. Elizabeth's eldest daughter Mrs Elizabeth Bromley had seven daughters, one of whom became the second wife of Thomas Maling, by then an Admiral. Mrs Bromley died in 1821 aged fifty. Elizabeth's second daughter Millicent was happily married to John Gisborne. After giving birth to eleven children she lost the use of her limbs, but she recovered six years later and lived to be eighty-three.[24]

Elizabeth herself retained her humour and energy to the end. She took delight in gardening at the Priory and in welcoming family and friends to stay. She died peacefully on 5 February 1832, aged eighty-four. She had been sitting in a chair when she complained of uneasiness, went to bed, and expired.[25] At her death she had had eleven children, forty-one grand-children and twenty-eight great-grandchildren. Three of the children and fifty-seven of the others survived her.

All Erasmus's older relatives were to die within fifteen years. His brother John, the conscientious clergyman, died in 1805, aged seventy-four, and his sister Ann in 1813, aged eighty-five. The longest-lived of his brothers was the eldest, Robert the naturalist, who died at Elston in 1816 at the age of ninety-two.

This reverse pattern of age also applied with Erasmus's younger friends. Tom Wedgwood succumbed to his debilities in 1805 at the age of thirty-four. In 1808 Tom's medical adviser Dr Beddoes died aged forty-eight, with his left lung collapsed (perhaps from too much inhaling of noxious 'medicinal' gases?). And in 1809 Anna Seward made the fifty-yard journey from the Bishop's Palace to the Cathedral for the last time. She was sixty-six.

Darwin's old Lunar friends obeyed his jokey precept and 'lasted well'. His 'most antient' friend in Birmingham, Matthew Boulton, died in 1809 at the age of eighty-one, honoured as 'the father of Birmingham'. Edge-worth died in 1817 at seventy-three, the father of twenty-two children and hundreds of inventions, including what are called 'macadamized' roads. James Watt remained in top form mentally: Maria Edgeworth met him just before his death and called him 'the best Encyclopaedia extant'.[26] He died in 1819, aged eighty-three, full of honours and recognized as the greatest of British engineers. Finally, the earliest of all Darwin's Lunar friends, James Keir, died in 1820 aged eighty-five.

Some of the younger generation were also 'lasting well'. Susanna and Mary Parker ran their school jointly until 1809, when Susanna retired after her marriage to Henry Hadley, the Derby surgeon who had attended Erasmus in his last illness (and had earlier tumbled down the stairs at Full Street). In 1818 the Hadleys were living in Queen Street, Derby, with their two children, Henry and Eliza. Susanna was also the much-loved foster mother of her husband's niece, later Elizabeth Greaves, who said 'What I owe to her no tongue can tell'.[27] The school at Ashbourne was run by Mary Parker until 1827, when she retired at the age of fifty-three. Susanna and Mary seem to have fulfilled their father's prediction that 'they may be happier than my other girls'. They were friendly with their half-sister

Violetta Galton: Susanna was visiting the Galtons when her husband died in 1830. Susanna's mother, Mary Day, continued to live in Birmingham and died in 1820.

Meanwhile a new Darwinian patriarchy was arising at Shrewsbury. As the years passed, Robert Darwin (Plate 12B) became a commanding figure in the town. He was extremely successful in his medical practice: between 1810 and 1820 his income from medical fees averaged £3025 a year.[28] Robert was about six feet two inches tall, and gave up weighing himself when he reached twenty-four stone. He needed a heavy coachman to test the floor-boards for him before he went into a new patient's house. Robert and his wife Susannah had two sons and four daughters, all long-lived. Susannah herself died in 1817, aged fifty-two, probably of peritonitis.

Robert sought respect and respectability, and wished to avoid any public notice or controversy. He even tried to buy up all the copies of his spirited pamphlet against Withering. Capable but not original, very astute with money but not intellectual, Robert adopted many of his father's ideas and practices. He abstained from alcohol. He was keen on the psychological treatment of patients. He was sceptical of religion, and an (undeclared) un-believer, according to his son Charles.[29] Robert was aware of the fracas with Canon Seward over '*E conchis omnia*', because Anna had made sure it was well known in Lichfield. In his twenties Robert declared himself a believer in evolution by having a bookplate made with the dreaded motto on it (Fig. 19).

ROBERT. WARING. DARWIN.
MD. F.R.S.
SHREWSBURY.

FIG. 19 Robert Darwin's bookplate, used mainly in the 1790s. Like his father's (Fig. 7), it carries the provocative evolutionary motto *E conchis omnia*

He had watched with horror the controversy caused by his father's evolutionary ideas, and kept quiet on the subject ever after. But did he still believe in evolution? My answer is 'yes', because Robert was a man who stuck to his views of life without any change. He never became religious, he never took to alcohol. He was constant, consistent and conservative. Though he ceased to use a bookplate after about ten years, that doesn't imply any change of views – only that he had used up all the labels and didn't bother to organize new ones.

So I would conclude that Robert never abandoned his belief in evolution and that he deserves much credit for bringing up his son Charles in an evolution-friendly atmosphere. By being a silent evolutionist rather than a hell-fire Victorian father, Robert greatly helped Charles to bring himself to believe in evolution in defiance of orthodox scientific thinking. Not that they ever discussed evolution: Robert was a formidable figure, psychologically as well as physically, and his children stood in awe of him. Charles had the utmost respect for his father: 'his reverence for him was boundless, and most touching',[30] according to Charles's son Francis.

In his youth Charles disappointed his father. Of his years at Shrewsbury School Charles said: 'The school as a means of education to me was simply a blank'.[31] In 1825, when he was sixteen, Robert sent him to Edinburgh to learn medicine, just as Robert's father had once sent him. Charles found the course distasteful and left Edinburgh after two years. He went on to Cambridge University, with the idea of becoming a country clergyman like his great-uncle John. Though professing to have wasted his time at Cambridge, Charles obtained a good pass degree in 1831 and became skilled as a naturalist and geologist.

At this time Edgeworth's close friend and collaborator Francis Beaufort had been Hydrographer to the Navy for two years and was energetically organizing a much-needed project for updating charts world-wide. Beaufort was about to send H.M.S. *Beagle* on a round-the-world survey voyage, under the command of Robert FitzRoy. When Charles was suggested as a candidate for the post of naturalist on the voyage, Beaufort at once recommended him to FitzRoy as 'a Mr Darwin grandson of the well known philosopher and poet'.[32] Charles was keen to accept. At first Robert said no, but was persuaded to change his mind. So Charles sailed away on the *Beagle* to begin his illustrious career. The date was 27 December 1831.

[6]

Erasmus was still influential as 'a well known philosopher and poet' long after his death. *The Botanic Garden* remained popular, going through seven editions and being translated into French, Portuguese and Italian. A volume of selections, *Beauties of the Botanic Garden*, appeared in 1805, followed by his collected poetical works (that is, *The Botanic Garden* and *The Temple of Nature*) in 1806, to be republished in 1824–5. There were further editions and translations of *Zoonomia*, as already mentioned, and Darwin's medical reputation remained very high. His granddaughter Elizabeth Wheler remembered family consultations with doctors in the 1820s: 'When they heard that my mother was daughter to Dr Erasmus Darwin it was with difficulty my father could make them take a fee. Sir Astley Cooper almost embraced my Mother, he was so pleased to see a daughter of Dr Darwin.'[33]

The young poets influenced by Darwin in the 1790s grew older and prosier: they turned against him without ever quite throwing him off. Coleridge was haunted by Darwin's evolutionism, which he continually opposed. Coleridge became well known as a critic; yet his much-admired theory of 'dramatic illusion' was almost identical to Darwin's 'theatric reverie' as defined in *Zoonomia*.[34]

Some vestiges of Wordsworth's allegiance also remained, and he never forgot Darwin's picture of Cambyses's army being buried in sand,

> ... awhile the living hill
> Heaved with convulsive throes – and all was still.

Wordsworth echoed these lines in his poem 'To Enterprise' (1821):

> An Army now, and now a living hill
> That a brief while heaves with convulsive throes –
> Then all is still.[35]

Darwin's successor as a popular poet was Walter Scott, with his *Lay of the Last Minstrel* (1805). Scott took little notice of Darwin, but he was generous in judging fellow-poets: he spoke kindly of 'the Darwinian style' in 1796 and later praised 'the march of Cambyses'.[36]

Many other poets of Wordsworth's generation (or earlier) were influenced by Darwin, including Cowper, Campbell, Crabbe and even Goethe. About twenty of them are discussed briefly in my book *Erasmus Darwin and the Romantic Poets*.

Among the Romantic poets of the younger generation Darwin had a strong hold over Keats and Shelley but was little heeded by the others.

John Keats had a life curiously similar to Darwin's in that each qualified in medicine and then turned to poetry in the last quarter of his life (though Darwin's life was much longer, of course). Reacting against medical horrors, Darwin and Keats both liked to write about 'Nature's gentle doings' and about gods and goddesses exempt from illness. Keats was very good at hiding his debts to others, and there are not many echoes of Darwin to be heard. There are about thirty 'possibles', chiefly in the *Odes* and *The Eve of St Agnes*.[37] Their affinity emerges most clearly from their similar vocabularies. Numerical analysis shows that many words used by Darwin far more often than by most other poets are also overused by Keats: examples are *beauty*, *blush*, *crystal*, *tiptoe* and *vermeil*.[38]

Percy Bysshe Shelley was the most scientific of the Romantic poets, and was deeply influenced by Darwin. Indeed, my own interest in Darwin began when I noticed his influence while writing a book on Shelley[39] in the late 1950s. Darwin helped to inspire Shelley with a faith in science and technology that rivalled Darwin's own. He led Shelley towards a scientific style for nature poetry, towards the idea of the unity of the human and natural spheres, and towards the empathy with nature apparent in 'The Sensitive Plant'. There are many obvious verbal echoes of Darwin in Shelley's major poems, particularly *Queen Mab*, *Prometheus Unbound*, *Adonais*, the 'Ode to the West Wind' and 'The Cloud'; I have given these before[40] and shall not repeat them. A less obvious parallel is provided by the second stanza of Shelley's 'Skylark', where he likens the (dark) skylark to a 'cloud of fire' springing 'higher and still higher'. This seems to derive from Darwin's description of a hot-air balloon.[41]

Among the other poets of the younger generation, interest in Darwin was patchy. Lord Byron almost ignored him despite several personal and family links.[42] John Clare admired Darwin's poems.[43] Darwin also had some influence on the early poems of Leigh Hunt, Felicia Hemans, T. L. Peacock, Eleanor Porden and even Alexander Pushkin.[44]

The best known instance of Darwin's hold over the younger Romantics is his vital role in the birth of Mary Shelley's *Frankenstein*. The preface to the first edition in 1818 begins: 'The event on which this fiction is founded has been supposed, by Dr Darwin, and some of the physiological writers of Germany, as not of impossible occurrence'.

The book originated in conversations between Shelley and Byron in Switzerland in the summer of 1816, when Mary was eighteen. In the preface to the 1831 edition she says that, in discussing 'the nature of the principle of life', they 'talked of the experiments of Dr Darwin', who (they said) 'preserved a piece of vermicelli in a glass case till by some extraordinary means it began to move with voluntary motion'. Darwin did no such thing; but in the note on spontaneous generation in *The Temple of Nature*[45] he described *vorticellae*, microscopic animals which after being dried up for several months, leaving them apparently dead, can be revived by putting them in water. Perhaps Shelley mentioned *vorticellae* and Mary misheard it as *vermicelli*; perhaps Shelley himself made the mistake; another possibility is a memory of Edgeworth's wooden robot that 'came to life' in response to changes in humidity. Whatever the explanation,

Frankenstein was born in confusion (or interdisciplinary serendipity?).

Brian Aldiss[46] sees Darwin as the chief father-figure of science fiction. The technically-futuristic science fiction, like that of Jules Verne, is foreshadowed by Darwin's technological prophecies in *The Botanic Garden*. And *Frankenstein*, the seminal work in the more humanistic vein, owes its origin to his biological speculations.

So, despite having been put down by the Establishment for his obnoxious evolutionary views, Darwin remained influential for two or three decades after his death through his firm grip on Wordsworth, Coleridge and Shelley, his looser hold on Blake, Keats and a dozen others, and his long-term inspiration in science fiction. His labours in botany were recognized when the genus of plants *Darwinia*[47] was named after him in 1811; and he was commemorated in two busts by William Coffee.[48] Above all, Darwin lived on through his medical fame.

CHAPTER SEVENTEEN

Legacies
1833–1998

Belief in evolution, passed on to his son Robert and reincarnated in his grandson Charles, can be seen as the finest of Erasmus's legacies. 'Reincarnated' may seem too strong a word, but I use it because I see such similarity of mind between Charles and his grandfather.

It is true that their outward lives were very different. Whereas Erasmus never left Britain, Charles was a world traveller in his twenties, returning in 1836 after the voyage of the *Beagle*. Then in 1839 Charles married his cousin Emma Wedgwood, repeating the scenario of his father's marriage. (Each married, about a month before his thirtieth birthday, a childhood friend who was one year older than himself, and whose father was named Josiah Wedgwood.)

In 1842 Charles Darwin (Plate 12C) went to live at Down House in Kent. There he worked and thought for forty years, a semi-invalid devotedly attended by Emma and surrounded by a growing family. It was a quiet life, almost static; in contrast, Erasmus had to earn his living by driving round the countryside to see patients. But these were the outward shows, dictated by circumstance. Inwardly the two had much in common.

The mental affinity between Charles Darwin and his grandfather emerges most clearly from their books. The first similarity is that for both of them the scientific book was their favoured vehicle of expression: Erasmus published more than a million words in eleven volumes; Charles more than two million in twenty-three volumes. For both, these books are 'a faithful monument and true mirror' of their minds.

And all of Charles's books, except the earliest ones about the voyage of the *Beagle*, have parallels with Erasmus's.

The most striking similarity between them arises with the four volumes of Charles's treatise on *Cirripedia*, the product of eight years' work dissecting and classifying barnacles. The parallel is with the four volumes of Erasmus's *System of Vegetables* and *Families of Plants*, the product of eight years' work translating Linnaeus's plant classifications. Charles was doing original research, whereas Erasmus was only translating. Still it is

extraordinary that they both spent so many years on a scientific classification project resulting in four published volumes.

Erasmus's writings on evolution have an obvious parallel in Charles's
three books about evolution.[1]

Both Darwins were fascinated by the fertilization processes in plants –
'nothing in my life has ever interested me more', Charles said.[2] This is the
obsessive theme of *The Loves of the Plants*, and of three books by Charles,
Contrivances by which Orchids are Fertilized, *Cross and Self Fertilization
in the Vegetable Kingdom* and *Different Forms of Flowers on Plants*.

Both seized on signs of sensibility in plants. 'He could not help personify-
ing natural things', and 'it has always pleased me to exalt plants in the scale
of organized beings',[3] are quotations that would do for either. Actually,
both refer to Charles, and he wrote books on *Insectivorous Plants*, *Climbing Plants* and *Power of Movement in Plants*. These are the very types of
plant seen by Erasmus as supporting his idea of vegetable sensibility, in *The
Botanic Garden* and *Phytologia*.

Erasmus's many geological notes and verses, and his liking for the 'living
rocks of worm-built coral', find parallels in Charles's books on *Coral Reefs*
and *Volcanic Islands*. Erasmus's note on 'External Signs of Passions'[4] foreshadows Charles's book on *Expression of the Emotions*.... Even Erasmus's
wish that we should 'eye with tenderness' our 'sister-worms' was fulfilled
by Charles's sympathetic book about the activities of worms.[5]

Both of them were admired as scientific authors. Although Charles did
not have Erasmus's talent as a poet, some of his prose was reckoned poetic.
Bishop Wilberforce in his adverse review of the *Origin of Species* praised
Charles's 'perspicuous language', sparkling 'with the colours of fancy and
the lights of imagination'.[6]

The similarities in their books are evidence of the same cast of mind.[7]
Like Erasmus, Charles had a talent for making friends, as shown by his
vast correspondence, scheduled to fill thirty volumes. Both were family
men: Erasmus had twelve legitimate children, Charles had ten children.
Charles was hard-working but Erasmus worked even harder, with his
punishing medical practice and his long closely-argued books. Sometimes
Erasmus stepped out of the web of rational argument to propose a biological speculation, like evolution. Rational argument was the backbone of
Charles's books. Yet he too was willing to make his grand speculation
about evolution by natural selection: he could not answer the objections
and 'maintained his faith in his position regardless of the valid arguments
that could be brought against it'.[8] The family faith in evolution sustained
him.

[2]

The similarity between the writings of Erasmus and of his grandson Charles may suggest that Charles derived his ideas directly from Erasmus. But that is not so. The story is more complex.

Soon after beginning his abortive medical course at Edinburgh, Charles was treated to a tirade in favour of evolution from Dr Robert Grant:

> I listened in silent astonishment, and as far as I can judge, without any effect on my mind. I had previously read the *Zoonomia* of my grandfather in which similar views are maintained, but without producing any effect on me. Nevertheless it is probable that the hearing rather early in life such views maintained and praised may have favoured my upholding them under a different form in my *Origin of Species*. At this time I admired greatly the *Zoonomia*....[9]

A book whose evolutionary theories he 'admired greatly' at the age of seventeen might well influence him when he began redeveloping such theories himself twelve years later. Though he was not conscious of it, his mind was prepared.

Charles was right to say that reading *Zoonomia* had no immediate effect. Otherwise he would have become an evolutionist twelve years earlier. As it was, he seems while aboard the *Beagle* to have accepted the special creation of species.[10] Although his grandfather and father were both evolutionists, Charles had not yet arrived at evolution – an ironic situation in view of future events. It was not until after he read Malthus in 1838 that Charles hit upon 'a theory by which to work' and began to formulate his own evolutionary ideas. He knew it would be unwise to publish these views, and he spent twenty years gathering evidence before being persuaded into publication in 1858, and more fully in 1859.

As we have seen, Erasmus had also waited about twenty years before publishing his views in *Zoonomia* because his earlier attempt at coded publication via the motto *E conchis omnia* had been so quickly scuttled by Canon Seward. Unfortunately for Erasmus, the long war against the French had started in 1793, just before *Zoonomia* came out. Even in peacetime he would have been condemned for subverting human dignity and for depriving God of his function as creator of species. As it was wartime, he was also guilty of undermining national morale. To suggest that the British were descended from monkeys (or, worse, microscopic specks) was almost treason. He utterly failed to convince the world about evolution.

He was in good company: evolution was later advocated[11] in vain by Prichard (1813), Wells (1818), Lawrence (1819), Matthew (1831) and Chambers (1844). The paper by Charles Darwin and Wallace presented at the Linnean Society in 1858 had no better success.

It was Charles's book *On the Origin of Species by Means of Natural Selection* ..., published in November 1859, that made the world take notice, and eventually persuaded more and more people that evolution by natural selection was the key to understanding the past and present pageant of life.

There are no overt references to Erasmus in the *Origin of Species* but many subconscious echoes. To give one example, Erasmus notes that in some species the males 'combat each other' for 'exclusive possession of the females', with the outcome

> that the strongest and most active animal should propagate the species, which should thence become improved.[12]

Charles, who marked this passage in his copy of *Zoonomia*, says that sexual selection depends 'on a struggle between the males for possession of the females', with the outcome that

> generally, the most vigorous males, those which are best fitted for their places in nature, will leave most progeny.[13]

Other examples are the many stylistic similarities, the treatment of organic happiness, and the title and final sentences of the *Origin*.[14]

As well as these echoes there are ironies when Erasmus comes closer than Charles to modern views. Erasmus's time scale of 'millions of ages' had to be much compressed by Charles to meet the mistaken arguments of Victorian physicists. And on the inheritance of acquired characters Erasmus was less committed than Charles. Erasmus cautiously suggested that 'many of these acquired forms or propensities are transmitted to their posterity'.[15] Charles wrote, 'Perhaps the correct way of viewing the whole subject, would be, to look at the inheritance of every character whatever as the rule, and non-inheritance as the anomaly'.[16]

It is curious too that *The Loves of the Plants* had the answer to one of Charles's chief evolutionary problems – geographical dispersal, especially through seeds carried by ocean currents. 'Until I tried, with Mr Berkeley's aid, a few experiments', Charles remarks, 'it was not even known how far seeds could resist the injurious action of sea-water'.[17] This is not so, for Erasmus in his note on *Cassia*[18] gave details of seeds carried from America to Norway and still capable of germination. Besides *Cassia* he mentions 'the fruit of the anacardium, cashew-nut; of cucurbita lagenaria, bottle-gourd; of the mimosa scandens, cocoons; of the piscidia erythrina, logwood tree; and cocoa-nuts', and several seeds carried from the West Indies to Scotland and Ireland.

At this point I feel obliged to escape from the flood of wet seeds to declare my own attitudes towards Charles and Erasmus. Charles Darwin is for me a shining example to all subsequent scientists: through steady work and rational thought over many years, he came to a logical conclusion and changed humankind's view of itself. I and many others can empathize with Charles, follow every step in his progress and see nothing there that we could not have done or thought of ourselves. He was not even particularly efficient, as is shown by his lapse over the seeds and by his failure to seize on the idea of evolution when he read *Zoonomia*: but such deficiencies are human and endearing. He was fallible, and yet he succeeded. In contrast, Erasmus sparkles with illuminating insights that I cannot explain: how could he have produced the scenario of evolutionary development a hundred years early? In short, I look at Erasmus with wonder and at Charles with fellow feeling.

When he wrote the *Origin of Species*, Charles was not conscious of any debts to Erasmus. That state of innocence was to end in 1860 when Bishop Wilberforce's sardonic review[19] appeared. He pointedly remarked that 'if we go back two generations we find the ingenious grandsire of the author of the *Origin of Species* speculating on the same subject, and almost in the same manner'. Erasmus had been ridiculed in Canning's notes to 'The Loves of the Triangles', and Wilberforce quotes a whole page from Canning's diatribe, confident that it will be just as lethal to Charles.

Faced with this attack, Charles had to take a stance. At first he decided to disown Erasmus by insisting on the differences between them. This was not altogether fair and, as Charles was an honourable man, I think he eventually became uneasy about it and wanted to make amends.

I can see no other reason for his startling decision in 1879, at the age of seventy, to write a biography of his grandfather. It was a brave and enterprising act: he had spent thirty-seven years at Down on scientific work and had written nothing like it before; he felt completely at sea, and feared he would make a fool of himself. But he persevered, wrote to his cousins for family stories, and produced an admirable book that I have often quoted from.

Then diffidence set in, and he allowed the biography to appear in a book with the title page, 'Erasmus Darwin, by Ernst Krause', followed in smaller type by 'with a preliminary notice by Charles Darwin'. This 'preliminary notice' runs to 127 pages and is much more important than the 86-page essay which it prefaces. This injustice was repaired in the second edition, in 1887, after Charles's death, where the title page reads, 'The Life of Erasmus Darwin, by Charles Darwin'. Still, it is the first edition that has been reprinted, so Krause is usually given as the author, and the book is omitted from many lists of Charles Darwin's publications, such as that in the standard facsimile of the *Origin*.[20]

This is strange enough, but it is even stranger that the book as Charles wrote it has never been published, because he let it be censored by his daughter Henrietta who disliked the free-thinking Erasmus. She did not wish to damage the Darwin family image by allowing her father to praise him, and she removed most of the comments favourable to Erasmus. Consequently, the published version is very different in tone from the first set of proofs, giving a false impression of her father's views. She also rearranged the text, with no concern for chronology.

Henrietta's censorship may seem surprising, as Charles stated that he himself, his elder brother Erasmus, and their revered father were all unbelievers,[21] and thus more deplorable than his grandfather. By a curious logic, this proved that old Erasmus was even more wicked, because he had such a bad hereditary influence.

Charles meekly accepted Henrietta's cuts. He wrote to his cousin Francis Galton on 14 November 1879: 'I am *extremely* glad that you approve the little life of our grandfather, for I have been repenting that I ever undertook it as work quite beyond my tether. The first set of proof-sheets was a good deal fuller, but I followed my family's advice and struck out much.'[22] About one-eighth was cut.

Charles intended the book to end with a generous tribute to Erasmus, which I quote from the proofs, in fairness to Charles:

> His energy was unbounded. In his day he was esteemed a great poet. As a physician, he was eminent in the noble art of alleviating human suffering. He was in advance of his time in urging sanitary arrangements and in inculcating temperance. He was opposed to any restraint of the insane, excepting as far as was absolutely necessary. He strongly advised a tender system of education. With his prophetic spirit, he anticipated many new and now admitted scientific truths, as well as some mechanical inventions. He seems to have been the first man who urged the use of phosphate of lime in agriculture, which has proved of great importance to the country. He was highly benevolent and retained the friendship of many distinguished men during his whole life. He strongly insisted on humanity to the lower animals. He earnestly admired philanthropy, and abhorred slavery. But he was unorthodox; and as soon as the grave closed over him he was grossly calumniated. Such was the state of Christian feeling in this country at the beginning of the present century; we may at least hope that nothing of the kind now prevails.[23]

His hope was vain. Henrietta disapproved, and Charles's tribute remained unpublished for nearly a hundred years.

[3]

The living legacy of Erasmus in 1833 included five of his children: Robert Darwin; Susanna Hadley and Mary Parker; Violetta Galton and Francis Darwin.

Robert was of course still at Shrewsbury, and still in medical practice. In 1846 Charles remembered him saying, 'This day, sixty years ago, I received my first fee in Shrewsbury'.[24] Robert died in 1848, aged eighty-two, before his son became famous.

Susanna Hadley and Mary Parker both often visited their half-sister Violetta, and when Susanna died in 1856, at the age of eighty-three, Violetta's daughter Elizabeth Wheler said 'it was a great grief to my mother and all the family'.[25] Mary Parker, 'who was much respected by the Darwin family', died at Ashbourne in 1859 when she was eighty-five.

Sir Francis Darwin also died in 1859, at Breadsall Priory, where he had been living since 1846. The high-spirited Violetta Galton lived on at Leamington until 1874: five of her children survived into the twentieth century.

In 1878 Erasmus emerged life-like from his grave, according to Elizabeth Wheler: 'Last year some alterations were made in Breadsall Church, and the Darwin Coffins were exposed. My grandfather's Coffin had burst open and his remains were visible and in perfect preservation. He was dressed in a purple velvet dressing gown and his features unchanged.'[26] After enjoying this brief view of Earth and air, he was decently reburied.

Violetta's son Francis Galton had different features, being more aquiline. But he inherited the inventiveness and wide interests of Erasmus, who would have been pleased by three of Galton's practical innovations: the idea of identification by fingerprints; his pioneering in anthropometry, with many applications, such as 'identikit' pictures; and his work in meteorology that led to weather maps and the founding of the Meteorological Office. Galton's advocacy of eugenics might not have appealed to Erasmus, who would by then have seen that many of the well-born children of his second marriage had not succeeded in life.

Galton was interested in his grandfather's work (even if he did not read it all), and in 1886 he took the trouble to arrange for a bust of Erasmus to be placed in Lichfield Cathedral with a double-edged inscription:

> A skilful observer of Nature, vivid in imagination, indefatigable in research, original and far-sighted in his views. His speculations were mainly directed to problems which were afterwards more successfully solved by his grandson Charles Darwin, an inheritor of many of his characteristics.

The hereditary influence of Erasmus seems to have continued in the next generation, distributed among three sons of Charles. The best known of these is Sir George Darwin, often called 'the father of geophysics', and his researches into tides and the evolution of the Earth-Moon system are still relevant today.[27] The second, Sir Francis Darwin, was an eminent botanist who also wrote stylish essays and verse. Sir Horace Darwin, the third, became an engineer and founded the Cambridge Scientific Instrument

Company. All three appear in person in Gwen Raverat's delightful book of reminiscences, *Period Piece*.

[4]

Many of Erasmus's scientific ideas and mechanical inventions were re-discovered or reinvented by others. Sometimes the later inventors were in-debted to him; more often, not. Any topic discussed in *The Botanic Garden* may have come to the notice of budding scientists or inventors, for there were thousands of copies in the libraries of affluent Victorian households. For example, the inventor of the aeroplane, Sir George Cayley, quoted Darwin's verse in one of his papers on aerial navigation.[28] On the other hand, when a canal lift like Darwin's was built in 1875, his influence was nil, since his design was buried in the Commonplace Book, where few would have seen it. The effect of his biological ideas was equally hit-or-miss. Lamarck's evolutionary theories in his *Philosophie Zoologique* (1809) were almost certainly influenced by *Zoonomia*; but sewage farms emerged without a whiff of help from Darwin's proposal in *Phytologia*.

Darwin's fame as a poet faded quite slowly, because literary reputations are passed down from teacher to pupil. Charles Darwin said, 'I have myself met with old men who spoke with a degree of enthusiasm about his poetry, quite incomprehensible at the present day'.[29]

That some Victorians still thought Darwin important as a poet is shown by G. L. Craik's popular two-volume *History of English Literature*, of which the third edition was published in 1866. Craik gives Byron three pages, Shakespeare nine, Milton twelve and Darwin eighteen. For him Darwin is among 'the great poets of the era'; and 'no writer has surpassed him in the luminous representation of visible objects in verse'. But Craik also attacks him: 'Every line is as elaborately polished and sharpened as a lancet.... Nothing is done in passion and power'.[30] Darwin was on the way out.

By 1900 he had sunk into limbo, and could be ridiculed without being read. For example, E. V. Lucas, writing a chapter about Darwin in 1907, says 'his methods I intend to display by a burlesque'. He then quotes all 284 lines of *The Loves of the Triangles* and none of Darwin's own.[31]

The sniping from literati was as nothing beside the fire and fury of the militant suffragettes who, it is believed, burnt down Breadsall Church[32] in June 1914 – a poor reward for Darwin's efforts on behalf of women. Apparently his tomb was incinerated. So, if he really was a live look-alike seventy years after his death, he went through the tidy sequence of burial, re-creation, reburial and cremation.

Darwin's reputation showed no sign of rising like a phoenix from the ashes. Instead he became a target for the arrows of error.[33] Some of the error-mongers derided his verse after misquoting it; some just ignored his evolutionary ideas; some dismissed *Zoonomia* and *Phytologia* as poems – a mistake that has persisted.[34]

There were a few brighter moments in the early twentieth century. Detailed analyses of Darwin's poems in German by Brandl and Eckhardt[35] appeared between 1902 and 1909. Livingston Lowes revealed his influence on Coleridge in *The Road to Xanadu* (1927). Hesketh Pearson's biography *Doctor Darwin* (1930) was amusing and widely read, but largely ignored his achievements. A more sympathetic portrait emerged from Alfred Noyes's long poem *The Torchbearers* (1922–30). J. V. Logan's study of *The Poetry and Aesthetics of Erasmus Darwin* (1936) is still the best commentary on his aesthetics and psychology. Logan also appreciates the comic intent of his poems, particularly *The Loves of the Plants*, 'the fine flowering of Darwin's bent to write light and humorous verse'.[36]

Erasmus Darwin began to attract more interest in the 1950s, with papers by Eric Robinson and Nora Barlow,[37] and C. D. Darlington's book *Darwin's Place in History*. Also there were books from literary critics and historians, and a new Russian edition of *The Temple of Nature*.[38] In 1963 R. E. Schofield's *Lunar Society* appeared, and a short book of mine on Darwin.

In the 1970s Erasmus's own writings came back into print,[39] and there were two literary books about him by Donald Hassler.[40] In 1986 the 'Erasmus Darwin Walk' round Lichfield was set up by John Sanders. Soon after came my *Erasmus Darwin and the Romantic Poets* (1986) and Maureen McNeil's *Under the Banner of Science: Erasmus Darwin and his Age* (1989). A concordance to *The Botanic Garden*[41] appeared in 1994, and in 1995, thanks largely to Gordon Cook and Denis Gibbs, the Erasmus Darwin Foundation was created. In cooperation with the Dean and Chapter of Lichfield Cathedral, the Foundation secured funds to restore Darwin's house at Lichfield as a museum and study centre, to open in 1999.

[5]

I have come to know Erasmus Darwin much better after going through all the new documentation and writing this book.

I am more amazed than ever that, in the midst of a busy life as a doctor, he could produce such a stream of perceptive scientific ideas that were often correct. Scientists today find it hard to produce one or two. His mechanical ingenuity and foresight amaze me too: inventing the technique used for steering modern cars is extraordinary; his speaking machine and copying machine, though both lost, were apparently never improved upon (except by new technology, as in tape-players and photocopiers). I wonder at the insight into human nature and talent for friendship that enabled him to recruit the Lunar Society members and, when they met, to keep them alert and happy with social banter.

At the other extreme – solitary, serious study – there are his weighty tomes *Zoonomia* and *Phytologia* that are difficult to read because they are so closely argued (sometimes, of course, from false starts). Also in the totally serious vein are his translations from Linnaeus.

Another transmutation takes us from this heavy prose to the light verse of *The Botanic Garden*, written with a delicate touch and technical skill that gave him pre-eminence among the English poets of the 1790s. At the same time Darwin was an Enlightenment man, 'overall the leading *philosophe* of late eighteenth-century England',[42] an enthusiast for science and invention and for the Industrial Revolution. He was the poet laureate of the new manufacturing technology. Yet his gift for verse and six-year primacy as a poet are only half the story. The other half is his pervasive influence over the Romantic poets. For them *The Botanic Garden* was an inspiration, and a treasure chest of appealing images.[43]

Then in *The Temple of Nature* Darwin went beyond Romanticism to re-engage with the real world, and shot far ahead of his time by describing the evolution of life from microscopic creatures in primeval seas through fishes and amphibians to land animals and our very selves.

After all this high endeavour, it seems bathos to mention his professional success as the leading medical man of the 1790s. Yet this was the talent that absorbed most of his time and energy. And in the day-to-day grind, his scientific insight was sometimes obscured by the fog of current practices. Still, he was famous for curing the sick, even if it was mainly due to keen observation, skill in psychology and common sense. Perhaps I have been too severe over Darwin's medical performance. So here, in reparation, is the short story of a satisfied patient, the antiquarian Samuel Pipe Wolferstan: Darwin's simple prescription of a milk and vegetable diet, with daily exercise on horseback, restored him from debility to perfect health,[44] and he outlived Darwin by eighteen years.

The effective use of so many talents was a talent in itself, as his grand-daughter Violetta Darwin remarked:

> I know nothing more wonderful than the *variety* of his genius. Many would have been bewildered by such a compound gift, and in trying everything would have done nothing, but he made his mark in all that he undertook, and his great closely-printed Quartos show an almost superhuman energy, written as they were during such a medical career; and he combined with all this learning and labour an uncommon fund of wit and a great fondness and aptitude for society.[45]

These social virtues impressed people who never knew about his other talents, as Keir indicates: 'I think all those who knew him will allow that sympathy and benevolence were the most striking features'.[46] As Anna Seward said, he always cheerfully gave his medical advice to the poor but never took fees. What he earned instead was 'the admiration and gratitude of mankind'[47] – or at least of his patients and readers, his friends and above all his families, for he was successful too as a husband and a father.

This is how he was seen. What of his inner feelings? The newly discovered manuscripts show that he was very sensitive and much subject to the overflow of powerful feelings. He needed to keep the lid on these emotions. But they erupted on stressful occasions, as in the touching elegiac tributes to his first wife Polly, the poem in memory of his son Charles, his anger at Withering's attacks on his sons, his passionate courtship of Elizabeth Pole and the protracted mourning for his son Erasmus. He would not talk about such events: as Robert remarked, 'he never would allow any common acquaintance to converse with him upon any subject that he felt poignantly'.[48] The outpourings of feeling were sometimes only momentary, as in the sarcasm noted by Anna Seward or in anger at a badly behaving patient. But he became angry with himself when he let his emotions become public. As his grandson Charles remarked, he 'wished to conceal his own feelings, and perhaps did so too effectually'.[49] He probably always lived with the fear that his feelings would break out inappropriately.

Another sign of this inner conflict is his stammer, and his success in speaking through it. His son Robert thought that his greatest talent was in conversation, especially in explaining abstruse subjects. Coleridge called him 'wonderfully entertaining and instructive' as a talker. It is as if the stammer forced him never to waste words on trivialities, and always to be witty, informative or amiably sociable. It had some advantages in drawing attention to him when young and in enabling him to hide those momentary floods of feeling – 'it gives me time for reflection'. His stammer would have been less pronounced in a friendly and relaxed atmosphere, and perhaps that is why he always wore his winning social smile.

When all is said, it is the depth and variety of his achievements that distinguish Erasmus Darwin. Twenty years ago I listed many of the subjects in which he made pioneering contributions. As this list provides a useful record, I have updated it here in a note.[50]

Endowed with supreme talents in many branches of human culture, Darwin succeeded in using his gifts effectively for the benefit of patients, family and friends, and, via his books, of society at large. He achieved more in a wider range of subjects than anyone in his own time or in succeeding generations. Such diversity of genius may never be seen again.

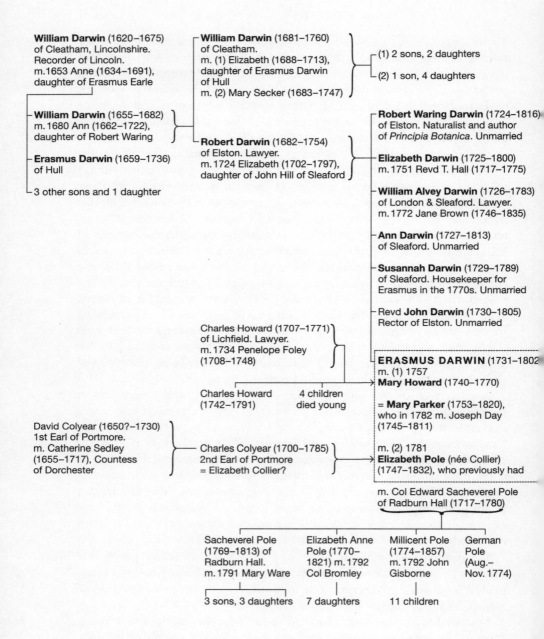

William Darwin (1620–1675) of Cleatham, Lincolnshire. Recorder of Lincoln. m.1653 Anne (1634–1691), daughter of Erasmus Earle

William Darwin (1655–1682) m.1680 Ann (1662–1722), daughter of Robert Waring

Erasmus Darwin (1659–1736) of Hull

3 other sons and 1 daughter

William Darwin (1681–1760) of Cleatham. m. (1) Elizabeth (1688–1713), daughter of Erasmus Darwin of Hull m. (2) Mary Secker (1683–1747)

(1) 2 sons, 2 daughters

(2) 1 son, 4 daughters

Robert Darwin (1682–1754) of Elston. Lawyer. m.1724 Elizabeth (1702–1797), daughter of John Hill of Sleaford

Robert Waring Darwin (1724–1816) of Elston. Naturalist and author of *Principia Botanica*. Unmarried

Elizabeth Darwin (1725–1800) m.1751 Revd T. Hall (1717–1775)

William Alvey Darwin (1726–1783) of London & Sleaford. Lawyer. m.1772 Jane Brown (1746–1835)

Ann Darwin (1727–1813) of Sleaford. Unmarried

Susannah Darwin (1729–1789) of Sleaford. Housekeeper for Erasmus in the 1770s. Unmarried

Revd **John Darwin** (1730–1805) Rector of Elston. Unmarried

Charles Howard (1707–1771) of Lichfield. Lawyer. m.1734 Penelope Foley (1708–1748)

Charles Howard (1742–1791)

4 children died young

ERASMUS DARWIN (1731–1802 m. (1) 1757 **Mary Howard** (1740–1770)

= **Mary Parker** (1753–1820), who in 1782 m. Joseph Day (1745–1811)

David Colyear (1650?–1730) 1st Earl of Portmore. m. Catherine Sedley (1655–1717), Countess of Dorchester

Charles Colyear (1700–1785) 2nd Earl of Portmore = Elizabeth Collier?

m. (2) 1781 **Elizabeth Pole** (née Collier) (1747–1832), who previously had

m. Col Edward Sacheverel Pole of Radburn Hall (1717–1780)

Sacheverel Pole (1769–1813) of Radburn Hall. m.1791 Mary Ware

Elizabeth Anne Pole (1770–1821) m.1792 Col Bromley

Millicent Pole (1774–1857) m.1792 John Gisborne

German Pole (Aug.– Nov. 1774)

3 sons, 3 daughters

7 daughters

11 children

Five generations of the Darwin family, centred on Erasmus

— 3 sons, 2 daughters

— 3 sons, 3 daughters

Charles Darwin (1758–1778)
Medical student. Unmarried

Erasmus Darwin (1759–1799)
Lawyer. Unmarried

Elizabeth Darwin (1763–1764)

Robert Waring Darwin (1766–1848)
of Shrewsbury. Doctor.
m. 1796 Susannah Wedgwood
(1765–1817)

William Alvey Darwin (1767–1767)

Susanna Parker (1772–1856)
Schoolteacher. m. 1809
Henry Hadley (1762–1830)

Mary Parker (1774–1859) of
Ashbourne. Schoolteacher. Unmarried

Edward Darwin (1782–1829) of
Mackworth. Army officer. Unmarried

Frances Anne Violetta Darwin
(1783–1874) m. 1807 Samuel
Tertius Galton (1783–1844)

Emma Georgina Elizabeth Darwin
(1784–1818). Unmarried

Sir **Francis Sacheverel Darwin**
(1786–1859). Doctor and traveller.
m. 1815 Jane Ryle (1794–1866)

Revd **John Darwin** (1787–1818)
Rector of Elston. Unmarried

Henry Darwin (1789–1790)

Harriot Darwin (1790–1825)
m. 1811 Capt T. Maling

Marianne Darwin (1798–1858)
m. 1824 Henry Parker

Caroline Darwin (1800–1888)
m. 1837 Josiah Wedgwood III
(1795–1880)

Susan Elizabeth Darwin
(1803–1866). Unmarried

Erasmus Alvey Darwin
(1804–1881). Unmarried

Charles Robert Darwin
(1809–1882)
m. 1839 Emma Wedgwood
(1808–1896)

Emily Catherine Darwin
(1810–1866) m. 1863
Charles Langton

Henry Hadley. Surgeon

Eliza Hadley. Unmarried

Elizabeth Anne Galton
(1808–1906) m. E. Wheler

Lucy Harriot Galton
(1809–1848) m. J. Moilliet

4 daughters (Millicent,
Emma, and 2 died as babies)

Darwin Galton (1814–1903)

Erasmus Galton (1815–1909)

Sir **Francis Galton** (1822–1911)

3 sons (Reginald, Edward, John)

7 daughters (Mary, Emma,
Frances, Georgina, Violetta,
Ann, Millicent)

References

The place of publication of books is London, unless otherwise stated.

The following abbreviations are used in these references:

Bebbington: P. S. Bebbington's thesis, 'Samuel Garbett' (1938). Birmingham
   Central Library No.488968.
Bedini: S. A. Bedini, *Thomas Jefferson and his Copying Machines*. Charlottesville,
   Virginia: University Press of Virginia, 1984.
Coleridge, *Letters*: S. T. Coleridge, *Collected Letters* (ed. E. L. Griggs). 6 vols,
   Oxford: Oxford University Press, 1956–71.
Commonplace Book: Erasmus Darwin's manuscript Commonplace Book, kept
   at the Darwin Museum, Down House, Kent. Available as a microfilm at
   Cambridge University Library and Derby Local Studies Library.
Craven, *Derby*: M. Craven, *Derby: an Illustrated History*. Derby: Breedon Books,
   1988.
Craven, *Whitehurst*: M. Craven, *John Whitehurst of Derby*. Ashbourne: Mayfield
   Books, 1996.
DAR: signifies manuscripts in the Darwin Archive at Cambridge University
   Library. The most important group for Erasmus Darwin is DAR 227.
C. Darwin, *Autobiog.*: Charles Darwin, *Autobiography* (ed. N. Barlow). Collins,
   1958.
C. Darwin, *Life*: Charles Darwin, *The Life of Erasmus Darwin*, with an essay on
   his scientific works by Ernst Krause. Murray, 2nd ed., 1887. (1st ed., 1879, gives
   Krause as first author.) Passages cited from the proofs but deleted from the
   published version are given as: 'C. Darwin, *Life*, p.5 (deleted)'. (For the proofs,
   see DAR 210.11.45.)
DNB: *Dictionary of National Biography*.
Dr. of Rev.: D. King-Hele, *Doctor of Revolution*. Faber, 1977.
Ec. Veg.: E. Darwin, *The Economy of Vegetation* (see Appendix 1).
Edgeworth: R. L. and Maria Edgeworth, *Memoirs of R. L. Edgeworth*. 2 vols,
   Hunter, 1820. (Reprinted, Irish University Press, Shannon, Ireland, 1969.)
E.D. & Romantic Poets: D. King-Hele, *Erasmus Darwin and the Romantic Poets*.
   Macmillan, 1986.
Elegy: *An Elegy on the Much-lamented Death of a most Ingenious Young
   Gentleman*. Robinson, 1778.
Essential Writings: *The Essential Writings of Erasmus Darwin* (ed. D. King-Hele).
   MacGibbon & Kee, 1968.
Fam. Plants: *The Families of Plants* (1787) (see Appendix 1).

Gent. Mag.: *Gentleman's Magazine.*

Gignilliat: G. W. Gignilliat, *The Author of Sandford and Merton.* New York: Columbia University Press, 1932.

Godwin and Mary: *Godwin and Mary* (ed. R. M. Wardle). Constable, 1967.

Goodwin: A. Goodwin, *The Friends of Liberty.* Hutchinson, 1979.

Hayter: A. Hayter, *Opium and the Romantic Imagination.* Faber, 1968.

Letters: *The Letters of Erasmus Darwin* (ed. D. King-Hele). Cambridge: Cambridge University Press, 1981.

Lich. Rec. Off.: Lichfield Record Office.

Logan: J. V. Logan, *The Poetry and Aesthetics of Erasmus Darwin.* Princeton, N.J.: Princeton University Press, 1936.

Lov. Pl.: E. Darwin, *The Loves of the Plants* (3rd ed., 1791) (see Appendix 1).

Manley: G. Manley, 'Central England temperatures: monthly means 1659 to 1973'. *Q. J. Roy. Met. Soc.* 100, 389–405 (1974).

Meteyard: E. Meteyard, *The Life of Josiah Wedgwood.* 2 vols, Hurst & Blackett, 1865–6. (Reprinted, Josiah Wedgwood & Sons, Barlaston, 1980.)

Moilliet: J. K. Moilliet (ed.), *Life and Correspondence of James Keir.* Privately printed, 1868.

Moilliet and Smith: J. L. Moilliet and B. M. D. Smith, *'A Mighty Chemist': James Keir.* Privately printed, 1983.

Muirhead: J. P. Muirhead, *The Origin and Progress of the Mechanical Inventions of James Watt.* 3 vols, Murray, 1854.

Nicolson, *Wright*: B. Nicolson, *Joseph Wright of Derby, Painter of Light.* 2 vols, Routledge, 1968.

Origin of Species: C. Darwin, *On the Origin of Species by Means of Natural Selection.* 1st ed., Murray, 1859; facsimile reprint, Harvard University Press, 1964.

Pearson: K. Pearson, *The Life, Letters and Labours of Francis Galton.* 4 vols, Cambridge: Cambridge University Press, 1914–30.

Phil. Trans.: *Philosophical Transactions of the Royal Society of London* (1666 to present).

Phytologia: E. Darwin, *Phytologia* (1800) (see Appendix 1).

Priestley: *A Scientific Autobiography of Joseph Priestley* (ed. R. E. Schofield). Cambridge, Mass: M.I.T. Press, 1970.

Pus and Mucus: C. Darwin, *Experiments establishing a Criterion between Mucaginous and Purulent Matter.* Cadell, 1780.

SchimmelPenninck: *Life of Mary Anne SchimmelPenninck* (ed. C. C. Hankin). 2 vols, Longman, 1858.

Schofield: R. E. Schofield, *The Lunar Society of Birmingham.* Oxford: Oxford University Press, 1963.

Scott: R. F. Scott, *Admissions to the College of St John the Evangelist in the University of Cambridge*, Part III. Cambridge: Deighton Bell, 1903.

Seward: Anna Seward, *Memoirs of the Life of Dr Darwin.* Johnson, 1804.

Seward, *Letters*: *The Letters of Anna Seward.* 6 vols, Edinburgh: Constable, 1811.

Seward, *Poetical Works*: *Poetical Works of Anna Seward* (ed. W. Scott). 3 vols, Edinburgh: Ballantyne, 1810.

Stevens, *Journal*: *The Journal of the Rev. W. B. Stevens* (ed. G. Galbraith). Oxford: Clarendon Press, 1965.

Stock: J. E. Stock, *Memoirs of the Life of Thomas Beddoes.* Murray, 1811.

Syst. Veg.: *A System of Vegetables* (1783) (see Appendix 1).

Tem. Nat.: E. Darwin, *The Temple of Nature* (1803) (see Appendix 1).

UCL: University College London Library.

Walpole: *The Letters of Horace Walpole* (ed. P. Toynbee, Oxford, 1905). (The later 48-volume edition by W. S. Lewis is not used because of a misprint in a vital sentence.)

Watt papers: James Watt Papers at Birmingham Central Library.

Wedgwood: *Letters of Josiah Wedgwood* (ed. K. E. Farrer). 3 vols, Manchester: E. J. Morton, 1974. (My quotations from Wedgwood's letters are from the MSS at Keele University Library. But I refer to the published version because it is more accessible, gives all the MS reference numbers and differs only trivially from the MSS.)

Wheler: Elizabeth Anne Wheler, 'Memorials of my Life'. (Typescript owned by the late Dr J. L. Moilliet.)

Zoonomia: E. Darwin, *Zoonomia* (1796) (see Appendix 1).

The following styles of numeration are used:

    for volume and page numbers in multi-volume books: ii 439–56

      (or Vol.I, p.xcii, if page numbers are small roman);

    for volume and page numbers in periodicals: 23, 246–51;

    for canto and line numbers in Darwin's poems: III 47–53.

CHAPTER 1 (pages 1–24)

1 R. Thoroton, *Antiquities of Nottinghamshire* (1790 edition) i 350; R. Brooke, *Battle of Stoke Field* (Liverpool, 1825) and ... *Fields of Battle ...* (Liverpool, 1857; repr. 1975); C. Brown, *History of Newark* (1904) i 168–71; D. Smurthwaite, *Battlefields of Britain* (1993), pp.121–2.

2 R. B. Freeman, *Darwin Pedigrees* (1984); C. Darwin, *Life*, pp.1–2; Pearson, Vol.I, Pedigree A.

3 Royal Society MS Journal Book.

4 *Phil. Trans.* 30, 963–8 (1719).

5 S. R. Howe, T. Sharpe and H. S. Torrens, *Ichthyosaurs: a History ...* (Cardiff, 1981).

6 Lincoln's Inn *Black Books* (1899) iii 256–7.

7 W. Moore, *The Gentlemen's Society at Spalding* (1851); S. Piggott, *William Stukeley* (1985), ch.3.

8 *Nottinghamshire County Records of 18th century* (Nottingham, 1946), p.118.

9 *Letters*, p.8.

10 C. Darwin, *Life*, p.4.

11 E. D. Barlow, *The Listener*, 23 August 1956, pp.265–7.

12 Pearson, Vol.I, Plates III–XX.

13 C. Darwin, *Life*, p.53 (deleted). Also DAR 227.5:12.

14 C. Darwin, *Life*, p.6.

15 Commonplace Book, after p.174.

16 C. Darwin, *Life*, p.6.

17 C. V. Kendall and M. P. Jackson, 'A History of the Free Grammar School, Chesterfield' (1965). Typescript at Derbyshire County Library, Matlock.

18 UCL Pearson papers 577, p.9.

19 Ibid., pp.42–3.

20 Ibid., pp.39–41.

21 The first citation in the *OED* is dated 1771.

22 DAR 218: D3.

23 UCL Pearson papers 578, p.34.

24 DAR 227.3:1.

25 DAR 227.1:1; also *Letters*, p.3.

26 Nottinghamshire Archives D.D.A. 62/4.

27 UCL Pearson papers 577, p.5. Also *Letters*, pp.4–8.

28 DAR 227.8:120.

29 Scott, p.132.

30 DAR 227.8:120, and Scott, pp.459–60.

31 C. Darwin, *Life*, p.12.

32 T. Newte, *Tour in England ...* (1788), p.4.

33 S. Ayling, *George the Third* (1972), p.25.

34 From *Luctus ...*; also *European Mag.* 27, 75–6 (1795).

35 *London Mag.* 20, 325 (1751).

36 W. H. Gurney Salter, *History of the Gurney System ...* (Oxford, 1925).

37 UCL Pearson papers 577, p.57.

38 Ibid., p.32.

39 Wellcome Institute Library, London, WMS 2043.

40 DAR 227.8:120. His son said Erasmus 'kept 12 terms' at Cambridge, but this seems to be wrong.

41 E. Heberden, *William Heberden* (1989), ch.2 & 3.

42 From MS in St John's College Library, Cambridge.

43 UCL Pearson papers 577, p.44.

44 For Johnson, Sayle, etc. see Scott, pp.579, 588, 603–4.

45 MS in private hands.

46 Volume of Anatomy Students' Class Lists, 1720–74, Ref. Da 50, Edinburgh University Library.

47 Moilliet and Smith, p.5.

48 DAR 227.6:76.

49 Ibid.

50 *Letters*, pp.8–9.

51 See *Fragments from Reimarus*, ed. C. Voysey (1879).

52 *Letters*, p.56.

53 UCL Pearson papers 577, p.30.

54 *Monthly Mag.* 13, 458 (1802).

55 *Zoonomia* i 473.

56 *Phytologia*, p.208.

57 *European Mag.* 27, 75 (1795): *Medical Register for 1779*, p.130.

58 DAR 227.1:2.

59 DAR 227.8:120.

60 DAR 227.1:2.

61 DAR 227.1:4.

62 R. Porter, in *Sexual Underworlds of the Enlightenment* (Manchester, 1987), p.212.

63 See R. Porter, *English Society in the Eighteenth Century* (1982) and R. Porter, *The Greatest Benefit to Mankind* (1997), ch.X, for surveys of the era and its medicine.

CHAPTER 2 (pages 25–40)

1 For Lichfield history, see *Victoria County History of Staffordshire*, Vol.14 (1990) and H. Clayton, *Coaching City* (1971). For turnpikes, see E. Pawson, *Transport and Economy* (1977).

2 See D. D. Gibbs, *Brit. Med. Journ.* 25 January 1969, 1, 242–5.

3 For Lady Gresley, see F. Madan, *The Gresleys of Drakelow* (1898). For T. Seward see *DNB* and

F. Swinnerton, *A Galaxy of Fathers* (1966), pp.35–47. For Anna Seward, see M. Ashmun, *The Singing Swan* (1931) and J. Brewer, *Pleasures of the Imagination* (1997), ch.15.

4 Seward, pp.8–9.

5 Stebbing Shaw, *The History and Antiquities of Staffordshire* (1798) i 409.

6 See M. W. Greenslade, *The Staffordshire Historians* (1982), pp.84–97.

7 Commonplace Book, after p.174.
8 See R. Porter, *England Society in the Eighteenth Century* (1982), p.13; J. Burnett, *A History of the Cost of Living* (1969); M. J. Daunton, *Progress and Poverty* (1995), pp.443–7.
9 DAR 227.5:12 (Robert's notebook).
10 *Phil. Trans.* 50, 240–54 (1757).
11 H. Eeles, *Philosophical Essays* (1771), p.115.
12 Seward, p.10.
13 DAR 227.1:14.
14 Marriage Register, at Lich. Rec. Off.
15 *Letters*, pp.12–14.
16 A. L. Reade, *Johnsonian Gleanings*, Vol.III, p.175 (1922); T. Newton, *Works* i 22–3 (1782).
17 See DAR 227.9:5–15. Also Lichfield Rec. Off. D/C/7.
18 Pearson, Vol.I, Pedigree E.
19 Lich. Rec. Off. D15/8/3/2.
20 Seward, pp.14–15.
21 DAR 227.1:16.
22 DAR 227.1:17.
23 *European Mag.* 1, 288 (1782).
24 Seward, *Poetical Works*, Vol.I, p.lxviii.

25 *A Collection of Poems* ii 296, 301 (1748).
26 Seward, *Letters* ii 312.
27 See A. Geikie, *John Michell* (1918); C. L. Hardin, *Annals of Science* 22, 27–47 (1966).
28 *Phytologia*, p.383.
29 Schofield, p.24, and E. Wright, 'Benjamin Franklin, the British Statesman' (Ameri. Phil. Soc., 1981).
30 See Craven, *Whitehurst*, and C. Hutton's memoir in *The Works of John Whitehurst* (1792), pp.6–20.
31 For Garbett, see Bebbington; and A. & N. Clow, *The Chemical Revolution* (1952), pp.133–42.
32 For Bage, see *The Life of William Hutton* (ed. L. Jewitt) (1872), esp. pp.171–2; P. Faulkner, *Robert Bage* (1979); *Godwin and Mary*, pp.99–101.
33 For Baskerville, see *DNB* and J. H. Benton, *John Baskerville* (1914).
34 H. Bode, *James Brindley* (1973).
35 Stringer Collection, Bodleian Library.
36 J. Gould, *Trans. South Staffs. Arch. Hist. Soc.* 23, 111 (1983).

CHAPTER 3 (pages 41–53)

1 Seward, p.2.
2 DAR 227.5:12.
3 Ibid.
4 DAR 227.6:76.
5 Seward, pp.5–6.
6 C. Darwin, *Life*, p.40.
7 *Zoonomia* ii 505.
8 Edgeworth, *Memoirs* (3rd ed., 1844), p.299.
9 Coleridge, *Letters* i 179.
10 Seward, pp.2–3.
11 C. Darwin, *Life*, p.40.
12 Ibid., p.42.
13 Coleridge, *Letters* i 177.
14 *Phil. Trans.* 51, 526–9 (1760).

15 R. Sorrenson, *Notes Rec. R. Soc.* 50, 29–46 (1996).
16 Royal Society Certificate, 1761.
17 See *DNB* for Hadley and Ross.
18 Bulloch's Roll, Royal Society Library.
19 Schofield, p.28.
20 Lich. Rec. Off. D15/8/3/2 and D15/8/4/4.
21 *Aris's Birmingham Gazette*, 25 October 1762.
22 Lich. Rec. Off. D25/1/1 ff.19–20.
23 DAR 227.7:13.
24 Seward, p.4.
25 *Letters*, p.16.

26 *Letters*, p.58.
27 Seward, *Poetical Works*, Vol.I, p.cxiii.
28 Seward, pp.64–5. See also DAR 227.7:44.
29 D. Defoe, *Tour of Great Britain* (3rd ed., 1742) iii 67.
30 A. & N. Clow, *The Chemical Revolution* (1952), p.133.
31 Schofield, p.28.
32 *Letters*, p.15.
33 Ibid., pp.16–17.
34 Ibid., pp.27–29.
35 Ibid., p.30.

36 See S. T. McCloy, *French Inventions of the Eighteenth Century* (1952), pp.37–40; and K. T. Rowland, *Eighteenth-Century Inventions* (1974), pp.27–8.
37 See L. T. C. Rolt, *Horseless Carriage* (1950), ch.1.
38 *Letters*, p.18.
39 J. Gould, *Trans. South Staffs. Arch. Hist. Soc.* 23, 109–17 (1983).
40 *Letters*, pp.18–22.
41 Minutes at Lich. Rec. Off.
42 DAR 227.9:21.

CHAPTER 4 (pages 54–81)

1 For Wedgwood, see Meteyard; and R. Reilly, *Josiah Wedgwood* (1992).
2 For Turner, see *DNB*.
3 For Bentley, see *Thomas Bentley* (Guildford, 1927), and Meteyard.
4 Wedgwood i 19–24.
5 C. Hadfield, *Canals of the West Midlands* (3rd ed., 1985) p.19.
6 DAR 227.3:4.
7 DAR 227.3:5.
8 DAR 227.3:3.
9 DAR 227.3:6, 7, 8, 11.
10 UCL Galton papers 10. The first draft was about 9 pages, the second about 30: see UCL Galton papers 39G.
11 UCL Galton papers 190A.
12 UCL Galton papers 10.
13 Wedgwood iii 273–312.
14 Ibid. i 58.
15 DAR 227.3:14, 15.
16 DAR 227.3:17; Wedgwood iii 266.
17 Wedgwood i 68.
18 *Monthly Review* 33, 468–73 (December 1765).
19 DAR 227.3:20.
20 DAR 227.1:19.
21 Edgeworth i 185. For Small, see G. Hull, *J. R. Soc. Medicine* 90, 102–5 (1997).

22 T. Jefferson, *Autobiography* (1914), pp.5–6.
23 *Letters*, p.39.
24 For Ash, see *DNB*.
25 *Annales de la Soc. J. J. Rousseau*, Tome 6, p.43 (1910).
26 C. Darwin, *Life*, pp.28–9. See also UCL Pearson papers 577, p.92.
27 H. Pearson, *Doctor Darwin* (1930), p.39. For Edgeworth, see D. Clarke, *The Ingenious Mr Edgeworth* (1965), and M. Butler, *Maria Edgeworth* (1972).
28 *Letters*, pp.36–7.
29 From MS at Royal Society of Arts (Guard Book A).
30 See *Observations on Ackermann's Patent Movable Axles* (Ackermann, 1819); and E. Tompkins, *History of the Pneumatic Tyre* (1981), p.67 and Fig. 11.1.
31 *Letters*, p.37.
32 R. Strauss, *Carriages and Coaches* (1912), p.26.
33 Edgeworth i 162–4.
34 Ibid. i 165–7.
35 Seward, p.17.
36 *Letters*, p.40.
37 Schofield, p.48.
38 DAR 218:B5. See also DAR 218:B1.

39 *Letters*, p.34.
40 Ibid., p.38.
41 Muirhead i 4.
42 Ibid., Vol.I, p.cxx.
43 *Letters*, p.46.
44 Ibid., pp.46–7.
45 *Partners in Science* (ed. E. Robinson and D. McKie) (1970), p.13.
46 See *Letters*, p.200, and Muirhead ii 279.
47 E. Robinson, *Trans. Newcomen Soc.* 35, 153–77 (1963).
48 Moilliet, p.8.
49 *Letters*, p.48.
50 Muirhead i 32.
51 *Letters*, p.53.
52 *Bisset's Poetic Survey* (1800), p.12.
53 Moilliet, p.49.
54 C. Darwin, *Life*, p.41.
55 *Aris's Birmingham Gazette*, 29 September 1766.
56 J. Boswell, *The Life of Samuel Johnson*, March 1776.
57 Ibid., 16 September 1777.
58 Seward, pp.75–6.
59 *Pus and Mucus*, p.127.
60 Ibid., pp.127–8.
61 See Scott, p.589.
62 DAR 227.7:5.
63 DAR 227.7:7. For Jauncey, see Scott, pp.636–7.
64 DAR 227.7:9.
65 Ibid. A facsimile of Charles's letter appears in *Notes Rec. R. Soc.* 49, 235 (1995).
66 Seward, p.63–4. Anna is wrong about the dates of the tour.
67 C. Darwin, *Life*, p.81.
68 DAR 227.7:5.
69 DAR 227.7:164.
70 DAR 227.7.165.
71 DAR 227.7.167.
72 Ibid. For Garbett's family, see Bebbington (Appendix).
73 *Letters*, pp.41–2.
74 See Craven, *Whitehurst*, ch.6.
75 See Meteyard i 492 and ii 77–81.
76 DAR 227.1:20.
77 *Letters*, p.43.
78 See Meteyard i 500–2.
79 For the Tissingtons, see *Letters*, pp.44–5.
80 For Day, see Seward pp.17–55; Gignilliat; and P. Rowland, *Thomas Day* (1996).
81 Edgeworth i 197.
82 Ibid. i 183.
83 F. W. Gibbs, *Joseph Priestley* (1965). R. E. Schofield, *The Enlightenment of Joseph Priestley* (1997).
84 Priestley, p.61.
85 DAR 227.1:22.
86 Wedgwood i 207.
87 DAR 227.1:23.
88 DAR 227.1:25. For the history of horizontal windmills, see R. L. Hills, *Power from Wind* (1994), ch.2, and R. Wailes, *Trans. Newcomen Soc.* 40, 125–45 (1958).
89 *Letters*, p.51.
90 Wedgwood i 209.

CHAPTER 5 (pages 82–105)

1 DAR 227.5:12.
2 M. A. Hopkins, *Dr Johnson's Lichfield* (1956), p.96.
3 Ibid.
4 Above 64° each day. *Gent. Mag.* 39, 349 (1769).
5 *Letters*, pp.51–2.
6 DAR 227.2:7.
7 See Nicolson, *Wright*.
8 Typescript at National Gallery.
9 DAR 210.29.
10 D. Fraser, 'Wright and the Lunar Society', in J. Egerton, *Wright of Derby* (Tate Gallery, 1990).

11 Ibid.
12 See Nicolson, *Wright* i 104–5; and *Letters*, p.69.
13 J. Wright MS Account Book, p.34. National Portrait Gallery, Heinz Library.
14 J. Egerton, *Wright of Derby* (Tate Gallery, 1990), p.79.
15 *Letters*, p.54.
16 DAR 227.1:28.
17 Wedgwood i 327–38; Reilly, *Wedgwood* (1992), pp.111–12.
18 Wedgwood i 324.
19 *Letters*, p.56.
20 For Clive, see Scott, p.583.
21 For Gifford, see *DNB*, and *Gent. Mag.* 77, 477–8 (1807).
22 DAR 227.1:27.
23 B. Schonland, *The Flight of Thunderbolts* (2nd ed., 1964), pp.28, 33.
24 From MS in grangerized copy of Stebbing Shaw's *Staffordshire*, at William Salt Library, Stafford. Revised version published in *Gent. Mag.* 54, 87 (1784).
25 Seward, *Letters* vi 136–7.
26 DAR 218:B4.
27 DAR 227.7:160.
28 Seward, pp.12–14.
29 DAR 227.1:29.
30 C. Darwin, *Life*, p.76.
31 DAR 227.2:7.
32 Ibid.
33 C. Darwin, *Life*, p.76.
34 DAR 227.8:5. Reproduced in *Notes Rec. R. Soc.* 49, 239 (1995).
35 *Pus and Mucus*, pp.130–1.
36 Seward, p.13.
37 DAR 227.1:142.
38 C. Darwin, *Autobiog.*, p.224.
39 G. C. Cook, *Notes Rec. R. Soc.* 50, 60 (1996).
40 *Zoonomia* i 353. See also *Zoonomia* ii 40 and ii 495–6.
41 G. C. Cook, *Notes Rec. R. Soc.* 50, 62 (1996).
42 C. Darwin, *Life*, p.6.
43 DAR 227.5:12.
44 Ibid.
45 Seward, p.21.
46 J. Egerton, *Wright of Derby* (Tate Gallery, 1990), p.221.
47 M. Keynes, *Notes Rec. R. Soc.*, 48, 69–84 (1994). Nicolson, *Wright* i 193.
48 Nicolson, *Wright* i 53–4.
49 Seward, p.36.
50 See Edgeworth i 207–9.
51 Schofield, p.56.
52 DAR 227.1:30.
53 DAR 227.1:32.
54 Wedgwood i 387–8.
55 DAR 227.1:31.
56 DAR 227.1:32.
57 Ibid.
58 DAR 227.1:35.
59 DAR 227.1:34.
60 DAR 227.1.36.
61 *Tem. Nat.* Add. Note XV, pp.107–20.
62 See J. Voskuil, *Trans. Newcomen Soc.* 26, 259–267 (1949).
63 From MS at Down House, reproduced in *Essential Writings*, Fig. 10.
64 *Letters*, p.63.
65 *Letters*, p.64.
66 DAR 227.7:17.
67 DAR 227.9:24.
68 C. Darwin to J. Hooker, 10 January 1864. DAR 115:226. For Francis Boott, see *DNB*.
69 From parish registers at Derbyshire Record Office, Matlock.
70 The MS of her book is in the Botany Library of the Natural History Museum.
71 J. Hooker to C. Darwin, 23 November 1864. DAR 101.254.7.

CHAPTER 6 (pages 106–120)

1 See DAR 210.14:13 and C. Darwin, *Life*, p.88.
2 Seward, *Poetical Works*, Vol.I, p.xxii; and *Selections from the Letters of Robert Southey* (1856) iv 334.
3 See memorial in Lichfield Cathedral, south transept. Also M. Ashmun, *The Singing Swan* (1931), pp.178–87 & 239–42.
4 DAR 227.3:24.
5 Account book, p.8. Nottinghamshire Archives DD.3B 2/1.
6 DAR 227.9:5 & 227.9:9.
7 Account book, p.5.
8 A. Chatwin, 'Bushbury': typescript at Wolverhampton Library.
9 Wedgwood ii 66, 73.
10 DAR 227.1:37.
11 Wedgwood ii 92–5.
12 Ibid. ii 105.
13 DAR 227.1:40.
14 Wedgwood ii 109–17.
15 Ibid. ii 121–2.
16 DAR 227.7:16.
17 DAR 227.1:42.
18 Wedgwood ii 100–1.
19 DAR 227.1:39.
20 Moilliet, p.50.
21 *Letters*, p.63.
22 Account book, p.18.
23 Lich. Rec. Off. D15/8/3/2.
24 DAR 218:D7.
25 Wedgwood ii 124. See also R. L. Edgeworth, *Roads and Carriages* (1813), pp.140–1.
26 UCL Pearson papers 577, p.52. Dated 24 July 1772.
27 See M. Butler, *Maria Edgeworth* (1972), pp.43–5.
28 Gignilliat, pp.77–8.
29 *Letters*, p.67.
30 *Phil. Trans.* **64**, 344–9 (1774).
31 DAR 227.8:8.
32 See *Burlington Mag.* **110**, 659–66 (1968).
33 B. Boothby, *Sorrows Sacred to the Memory of Penelope* (1796), p.71.
34 J. Cradock, *Memoirs* (1828) iv 198.
35 DAR 227.2:17.
36 For Hutton, see D. R. Dean, *James Hutton and the History of Geology* (1992).
37 J. Jones, H. S. Torrens and E. Robinson, *Annals of Science* **51**, 637–53 (1994).

CHAPTER 7 (pages 121–140)

1 DAR 227.7:19.
2 DAR 227.7:21.
3 Muirhead ii 81–2.
4 Ibid.
5 J. Dos Passos, *Jefferson* (1955), p.287.
6 Muirhead, Vol.I, p.clviii.
7 Royal Society Archives: Letters and Papers, Decade VII, No.2.
8 Muirhead, Vol.I, pp.clvi–clvii.
9 *Papers of Thomas Jefferson* (1950) i 165.
10 See Schofield, pp.141–2.
11 *Letters*, pp.71–2.
12 See Craven, *Whitehurst*, ch.7.
13 *Letters*, p.68.
14 *Letters*, p.74.
15 See W. Blunt, *The Compleat Naturalist* (1971).
16 See D. E. Allen, *The Naturalist in Britain* (1976), ch.2.
17 *Letters*, p.76.
18 *Letters*, p.77.
19 UCL Pearson papers 577, p.12.
20 UCL Galton papers 35.
21 Pearson i 17–21.
22 See J. Pilkington, *Derbyshire* (1789), ii 114–17.
23 *Letters*, p.340.
24 Nicolson, *Wright* i 37.
25 UCL Pearson papers 577, p.14.

26 C. Darwin, *Life*, p.83.
27 Wright painted W. A. Darwin in 1776: see Nicholson, *Wright* ii 108 (Plate 176).
28 DAR 227.7:23.
29 *Pus and Mucus*, pp.128–31.
30 Ibid.
31 DAR 227.5:12.
32 *Elegy*, p.24.
33 Boswell, *Life of Johnson*, March 1776.
34 H. S. Torrens, *Newsletter Geol. Curators Gp.*, No.1, pp.5–10 (1974); A. L. Reade, *Johnsonian Gleanings*, Part VIII, pp.122–58 (1937).
35 See Wedgwood ii 192.
36 Wedgwood ii 281.
37 T. Bentley, *Journal of a Visit to Paris* (1977), p.59.
38 D. Clarke, *The Ingenious Mr Edgeworth* (1965), p.85.
39 F. Mundy, *Needwood Forest* (Lichfield, 1776), p.4.
40 Ibid., pp.45–6.
41 Seward, *Letters* iii 154.
42 See *Notes and Queries*, 13 February 1875, pp.122–4.
43 DAR 227.2:9.
44 Commonplace Book, p.8.
45 *Zoonomia* i 352; Commonplace Book, p.27.
46 See M. Rowbottom & C. Susskind, *Electricity and Medicine* (1984), ch.2.
47 Commonplace Book, p.51.
48 Ibid., p.51.
49 Ibid., p.65.
50 Seward, pp.125–6.
51 Ibid., p.126.
52 Ibid., pp.126–7.
53 UCL Pearson papers 577, p.19.
54 Commonplace Book, pp.58–9.
55 See D. Tew, *Canal Inclines and Lifts* (1984), and *Dr. of Rev.*, p.332, note 31.
56 Commonplace Book, p.33.
57 C. Hart, *Aero J. R. Aero. Soc.* (January 1985), p.17.
58 See C. Hart, *The Prehistory of Flight* (1985), ch.3.
59 Commonplace Book, p.38.
60 C. Hart, *Aero J. R. Aero. Soc.* (January 1985), p.20.
61 Commonplace Book, pp.56–7.
62 Hayter, pp.101–3.
63 Seward, p.104.
64 Ibid., pp.104–5.
65 Ibid., p.107; UCL Pearson papers 577, p.76.
66 Ibid., pp.105–6; *Letters*, pp.86–7.

CHAPTER 8 (pages 141–169)

1 Schofield, p.143.
2 *Letters*, p.83.
3 Ibid., p.82.
4 Ibid., p.84.
5 See *DNB* for Duncan.
6 *Pus and Mucus*, p.132.
7 *Zoonomia* i 322.
8 *Pus and Mucus*, p.132. See also C. Darwin, *Life*, pp.80–3.
9 DAR 227.1:46.
10 *Letters*, p.89.
11 Janet Browne, *Charles Darwin Voyaging* (1994), p.41.
12 *Elegy*, p.4.
13 Ibid., pp.8–9.
14 Ibid., p.22.
15 C. Darwin, *Life*, p.82.
16 Seward, pp.108–15.
17 DAR 227.3:27.
18 Commonplace Book, p.66.
19 Ibid., p.51.
20 *Phil. Trans.* 68, 86–96 (1778).
21 Commonplace Book, p.85.
22 S. P. Thompson, *J. Soc. Telegraph. Eng.* 17, 576 (1888); Schofield, p.166.

23 A. Bennet, *New Experiments in Electricity* (1789), p.81.

24 Craven, *Whitehurst*, pp.29–31.

25 Commonplace Book, p.45.

26 See *Dr. of Rev.*, p.119 for illustration.

27 Seward, pp.128–9.

28 *Gent. Mag.* 53, 428 (1783).

29 Seward, pp.130–1.

30 Edgeworth ii 267.

31 Commonplace Book, p.72. See also L. Schiebinger, in *Science and Sensibility* (1991), p.132.

32 C. E. Stringer, ... *Lichfield* (1819), p.126.

33 Seward, pp.98–9.

34 *Letters*, pp.94–5, where there is more about Greville.

35 British Library Add. MS 42071 ff.48–52.

36 *Letters*, pp.94–5.

37 *Letters*, p.96.

38 Excerpts in *Letters*, pp.97–8.

39 See Bedini, pp.36–9 for details, including a drawing.

40 See L. T. C. Rolt, *James Watt* (1962), p.100; J. P. Muirhead, *James Watt* (1858), pp.273–9; and J. H. Andrew, *Trans. Newcomen Soc.* 53, 1–15 (1981).

41 DAR 227.3:29. Watt writes bigrapher as 'biagrapher' and hollow as 'holland'.

42 Bedini, ch.III.

43 Ibid., pp.9–10. See also W. B. Proudfoot, *The Origin of Stencil Duplicating* (1972) and M. H. Adler, *The Writing Machine* (1973).

44 Seward, p.117.

45 Based on Bodleian Library MS Eng. poet d.10 fol.82; and *Gent. Mag.* 55, 641 (1785).

46 *Letters*, pp.91–3.

47 C. Darwin, *Life*, p.26 (deleted).

48 DAR 227.1:51.

49 DAR 227.1:52.

50 Edgeworth i 363.

51 DAR 227.1:53.

52 DAR 227.1:54.

53 Commonplace Book, p.87.

54 Schofield, p.74. See also Meteyard ii 29–30 and 447.

55 Wedgwood ii 542–3.

56 DAR 227.1:56.

57 Wedgwood ii 541–2.

58 DAR 227.1:56.

59 Commonplace Book, p.89.

60 Edgeworth i 364–5.

61 Commonplace Book, pp.83, 103.

62 Ibid., p.82.

63 Ibid., pp.80, 84.

64 DAR 227.1:60

65 Wedgwood ii 443.

66 See R. Reilly & G. Savage, *Wedgwood: the Portrait Medallions* (1973).

67 Edgeworth ii 268.

68 Nichols, *Illustrations of the Literary History of the 18th Century* (1818–48) vii 216.

69 *A Concordance to Erasmus Darwin's poem 'The Botanic Garden'* (Wellcome Inst. Hist. Med., 1994).

70 A. Seward, *Elegy on Captain Cook* (1780), p.10.

71 J. Boswell, *Life of Johnson*, 25 June 1784.

72 A. Seward, *Elegy on Captain Cook* (1780), p.5.

73 Wedgwood ii 573–4.

74 *Letters*, pp.100–2.

75 Seward, pp.138–45.

76 UCL Pearson papers 577, p.23.

77 Ibid., pp.50–1.

78 Ibid., p.21.

79 Ibid., p.75.

80 Ibid., p.82.

81 Ibid., pp.85–6.

82 DAR 227.1:61.

83 See *Cicero, the Letters to his Friends* (1927) i 268–77.

CHAPTER 9 (pages 170–191)

1 Seward, pp.148–9.
2 Ibid., p.150.
3 Ibid., p.151.
4 UCL Pearson papers 577, p.79.
5 Ibid., p.77.
6 Ibid., p.87.
7 Ibid., p.88.
8 Parish Register: at Derbyshire Record Office, Matlock.
9 H. Clayton, *Coaching City* (1971), p.10.
10 M Craven & M. Stanley, *The Derbyshire Country House* (1991), pp.167–9. Radburne Hall is not open to the public.
11 Nicolson, *Wright*, Plates 88, 92 & 93.
12 DAR 227.1:62.
13 Edgeworth i 188, 381.
14 *Letters*, p.107.
15 Nicolson, *Wright* i 26 and Plates 4 & 5.
16 Seward, pp.104–5.
17 Seward, *Letters* i 33.
18 *Letters*, p.121.
19 Muirhead ii 123.
20 *Letters*, p.104.
21 See *Dr. of Rev.*, pp.141–3.
22 J. P. Muirhead, *The Life of James Watt* (1858), pp.392–5.
23 Birmingham Central Library, Boulton & Watt papers 308/83.
24 DAR 227.5:12.
25 *Godwin and Mary*, p.101.
26 See Bebbington, Part I.
27 See Manley, pp.394–8.
28 *Letters*, p.107.
29 Quotations from *Letters*, pp.109–14.
30 Quotations from *Letters*, pp.116–23.
31 See *Monthly Review* 68, 433–5 (1783).
32 *Syst. Veg.*, pp.i–ii.
33 Ibid., pp.ii–iv.
34 From *Fam. Plants*, p.xvii (where the wording is better).
35 *Syst. Veg.*, p.xi.
36 *Monthly Review* 72, 401–10; 73, 1–13 (1785).
37 A list is given in *Notes Rec. R. Soc.* 42, 178 (1988).
38 Commonplace Book, p.110.
39 *Letters*, pp.120–1.
40 Priestley, p.206; and DAR 227.1:67.
41 DAR 227.1:67.
42 DAR 227.1:68.
43 DAR 227.3:31 (draft).
44 See B. Tattersall, *Stubbs and Wedgwood* (1974), pp.23, 54–7.
45 DAR 227.1:68.
46 DAR 227.1:69.
47 Commonplace Book, p.113.
48 DAR 227.1:70.
49 From MS at Down House.
50 T. S. Whalley, *Journals and Correspondence* (1863) i 381.
51 *Letters*, p.127.
52 Ibid.
53 *Letters*, p.128.
54 Commonplace Book, pp.107–9 & 114.
55 For details, see L. T. C. Rolt, *The Aeronauts* (1966).
56 *Lov. Pl.* II 25–8, 31–2, 47–54.
57 *Ec. Veg.* I 289–96.
58 See J. E. Hodgson, *History of Aeronautics in Great Britain* (1924).
59 DAR 227.5:12.
60 *Letters*, p.128.
61 E. Robinson, *Annals of Science* 9, 360–1 (1953).
62 *Letters*, p.129.
63 F. Galton, *Memories of my Life* (1908), p.10.
64 DAR 227.1:71.
65 Manley, p.398.
66 Ibid., p.395; and B. Franklin, *Writings* (ed. A. H. Smyth, 1906) ix 217.
67 *Phil. Trans.* 74, 201–32 (1784).
68 Royal Society Archives: Letters and papers, Decade VIII, No.102.

69 C. Sheffield, *Erasmus Magister* (Ace Books, New York, 1982).

70 *Weekly Entertainer*, 29 September 1783, p.303.

71 *Letters*, p.128.

CHAPTER 10 (pages 192–221)

1 M. Craven, *The Derby Town House* (1987), pp.44–7.
2 1.3°C for Dec.–Feb. Manley, pp.394–8.
3 Craven, *Derby*, p.79.
4 Ibid., p.80.
5 See S. Glover, *History and Gazeteer of the County of Derby* (1829–33) ii 422; also D. Defoe, *Tour of Great Britain* (3rd ed., 1742) iii 67.
6 See R. S. Fitton and A. P. Wadsworth, *The Strutts and the Arkwrights* (1958).
7 See R. S. Fitton, *The Arkwrights* (1989).
8 See W. Bemrose, *Bow, Chelsea and Derby Porcelain* (1898); and J. Twitchett, *Derby Porcelain* (1980).
9 Such as Speed's map of 1610.
10 *Phil. Trans.* 75, 1–7 (1785).
11 Ibid.
12 See C. Darwin, *Life*, p.122.
13 See L. T. C. Rolt, *The Aeronauts* (1966), pp.61–2.
14 DAR 227.1:73.
15 *Letters*, p.134.
16 J. Kington, *Weather of the 1780s* (1988).
17 DAR 227.1:72.
18 From MS at Down House.
19 Derby Local Studies Library, 8672.
20 Ibid., BA 106 MSS/9230.
21 Ibid., BA 106 MSS/9229.
22 Ibid., 4181. See also S. Bagshaw, *History ... of Derbyshire* (Sheffield, 1846), p.77.
23 See C. L. Hacker, 'William Strutt', *J. Derbys. Arch. Nat. Hist. Soc.* 80, 49–70 (1960).
24 For a full list of members, see R. P. Sturges, *Midland History* 4, 212–29 (1979).
25 For further details of the Society, see E. Robinson, *Annals of Science* 9, 359–67 (1954).
26 C. Darwin, *Life*, p.54.
27 Craven, *Derby*, pp.111–12.
28 *Letters*, p.131.
29 Seward, p.5.
30 Edgeworth ii 82.
31 C. Darwin, *Life*, pp.64–5.
32 See G. P. Tyson, *Joseph Johnson* (1979).
33 *Letters*, p.139.
34 *Letters*, p.134.
35 Gignilliat, pp.239–40.
36 DAR 227.1:72.
37 DAR 227.1:75.
38 DAR 227.1:77.
39 DAR 227.1:78.
40 DAR 227.1:76.
41 Seward, *Letters* i 14–15.
42 *Letters*, p.141.
43 *Lov. Pl.* II 101–4.
44 F. D. Klingender, *Art and the Industrial Revolution* (1972), p.36.
45 *Poetry of the Anti-Jacobin* (ed. L. Rice-Oxley) (1924), p.95.
46 *Lov. Pl.* II 87 note.
47 *Letters*, p.141. See also Schofield, pp.349–55.
48 Schofield, p.350.
49 DAR 227.1:81.
50 *Medical Transactions* 3, 285 (1785).
51 From MS 'Withering Letters' at Royal Society of Medicine.
52 Ibid.
53 *Letters*, p.145.
54 *Lov. Pl.* I 175–80.
55 From MS owned by Mrs V. Kindersley.
56 DAR 227.1:79.
57 *Letters*, p.142.

58 *Letters*, p.144.
59 See *Letters*, pp.125–6, for further details.
60 DAR 218:E1–19.
61 DAR 227.1:83.
62 Edgeworth ii 83.
63 Polwhele, *Traditions and Recollections* (1826) i 87.
64 DAR 227.1:50.
65 DAR 227.5:12.
66 DAR 227.5:7.
67 G. C. Peachey, *William and John Hunter* (1924), p.90.
68 J. Gray, *History of the Royal Medical Society* (1952), Appendix II.
69 DAR 227.5:7 & 12. *Life and Letters of C. Darwin* (ed. F. Darwin, 1887) i 8. For Crompton, see *Letters*, p.267.
70 DAR 227.1:80.
71 Seward, *Letters* i 34.
72 C. Darwin, *Autobiog.*, pp.28–9.
73 DAR 227.7:14.
74 C. Darwin, *Life*, p.85.
75 DAR 227.5:140.
76 *Phil. Trans.* 76, 313–48 (1786).
77 C. Darwin, *Life*, p.84.
78 *Letters*, p.67.
79 See Schofield, pp.270–4.
80 *Letters*, p.164.

81 C. Darwin, *Life*, p.36.
82 The drawings are reproduced in *Letters*, pp.146–71.
83 *Letters*, pp.146–59.
84 *Letters*, pp.161–2.
85 Commonplace Book, p.45.
86 Ibid., p.157.
87 See *New Scientist*, 23 November 1996, p.41; 21 December 1996, p.20; 30 August 1997, p.13.
88 *Fam. Pl.*, p.8.
89 C. Darwin, *Life*, p.87 (deleted).
90 C. Darwin, *Life*, p.5.
91 R. W. Darwin, *Principia Botanica*, 3rd ed. (1810), dedication.
92 DAR 227.8:109. For a portrait of Robert, see Pearson i 16–17.
93 *Letters*, p.167.
94 DAR 227.1:91.
95 DAR 218:E10–11.
96 DAR 218:E17.
97 For Beddoes, see D. A. Stansfield, *Thomas Beddoes* (1984) and R. Porter, *Doctor of Society* (1992).
98 J. Nichols, *Literary Anecdotes* 9, 380 (1815).
99 Commonplace Book, p.89.
100 *Letters*, pp.166–7.
101 See W. Herschel, *Phil. Trans.* 77, 231 (1787); P. Moore, *Phil. Trans.* A 285, 481 (1977).

CHAPTER 11 (pages 222–251)

1 Moilliet, pp.78–81.
2 DAR 227.1:98.
3 T. Quayle, *Poetic Diction* (1924), p.51.
4 See *E. D. & Romantic Poets*.
5 DAR 227.1:98.
6 DAR 227.6:27.
7 DAR 227.1:98.
8 DAR 227.1:104.
9 DAR 227.1:107.
10 DAR 218:E23.
11 DAR 218:E22.
12 DAR 227.1:109. A translation of

Fourcroy came out in 1788: see W. A. Smeaton, *Fourcroy* (1962).
13 MS 'Withering Letters' at Royal Society of Medicine.
14 *Letters*, pp.182–3.
15 *Letters*, p.187.
16 See E. Posner, *Hist. Med.* 6, 51–7 (1975).
17 See D. S. L. Cardwell, *From Watt to Clausius* (1971), ch.2; and R. Fox, *The Caloric Theory of Gases* (1971), pp.54–60.
18 *Phil. Trans.* 78, 43–52 (1788).

19 See *Phil. Trans.* 52, 547–54 (1762); or *Phil. Trans. Abridged*, Vol.XI, p.633.

20 See *OED*, 'devaporate'. Darwin also coins 'precipitate'.

21 For air, pressure is proportional to absolute temperature to the power 3.5.

22 See *Essential Writings*, note 46 (p.203).

23 *Lov. Pl.*, p.99.

24 *Letters*, pp.177–9 (includes drawings).

25 Moilliet and Smith, p.31.

26 See *Zoonomia* ii 452–3.

27 *The Works of John Whitehurst* (ed. C. Hutton, 1792), pp.17–19. *Ec. Veg.* II 17, note.

28 SchimmelPenninck i 151–3.

29 *Letters*, p.181. There were now two new Lunar members, Jonathan Stokes and R. A. Johnson: see Schofield, pp.223–9.

30 DAR 227.1:97.

31 DAR 227.1:103.

32 DAR 227.3:36.

33 DAR 227.1:105.

34 DAR 227.1:96.

35 *Ec. Veg.* II 315–16. For a wider view, see H. Thomas, *The Slave Trade* (1997).

36 DAR 227.1:110.

37 DAR 227.1:112.

38 *The Correspondence of Charles Darwin* viii 491 (1993).

39 *Lov. Pl.*, p.182.

40 See Hayter, pp.101–3.

41 See *E. D. & Romantic Poets*, pp.111, 196, 240, 81–2.

42 See ibid., pp.65, 90, 195, 240.

43 See ibid., p.218.

44 *Critical Review* 68, 379 (1789).

45 Walpole xiv 124, 125, 126.

46 DAR 218:B10.

47 SchimmelPenninck i 243.

48 *Crit. Rev.* 68, 381 (1789); *Monthly Rev.* 80, 337 (1789); *New Ann. Reg.*, 1789, p.276.

49 *Analytical Review* 4, 29–36 (1789).

50 Seward, pp.174, 296, 361.

51 See *Poems of W. B. Stevens* (ed. G. Galbraith, 1971).

52 *E. D. & Romantic Poets*, pp.64–8.

53 Ibid., pp.89–119.

54 D. V. Erdman (ed.), *The Illuminated Blake* (1974), pp.33–4.

55 See *E. D. & Romantic Poets*, ch.3.

56 Logan, pp.111–30.

57 D. Hassler, *Erasmus Darwin* (1973); and *The Comedian as the Letter D* (1973).

58 M. McNeil, *Under the Banner of Science* (1987), ch.1.

59 J. Browne, *Isis* 80, 593–621 (1989).

60 J. Bose, *The Nervous Mechanism of Plants* (1926); S. N. Basu, *Jagadis Chandra Bose* (1920).

61 See P. Tompkins and C. Bird, *The Secret Life of Plants* (1974); P. Simons, *The Action Plant* (1992); the film 'Microcosmos' (1997); and *New Scientist*, 26 September 1998, p.24.

62 I. Fleming, *Moonraker* (1959), p.112.

63 *Letters*, p.185; Wedgwood iii 77.

64 DAR 227.1:112 and 113.

65 DAR 227.1:113.

66 E. Dowden, *The French Revolution and English Literature* (1897), p.20. See also P. Rowland, *Thomas Day* (1996), pp.360–4.

67 DAR 227.1:119.

68 See D. R. Dean, *James Hutton* (1992), p.52.

69 *Ec. Veg.* II 315–16 note.

70 *European Mag.* 16, 462 (1789). Also in 3rd and later editions of *Ec. Veg.*

71 J. Thomson, *Liberty* (1736), lines 701–16.

72 Wedgwood iii 84–5.

73 Wedgwood iii 92–3.

74 DAR 227.1:117.

75 Wedgwood iii 101.

76 See W. Mankowitz, *The Portland Vase* (1952), pp.58–9. For 44 interpretations, see *J. Glass Studies* 32, 172–6 (1990).

77 DAR 227.1:120.
78 *Letters*, pp.185, 187.
79 *Ec. Veg.* I 281–8.
80 *Letters*, p.196.
81 Watt papers LB/2.
82 J. Pilkington, *Derbyshire* (1789) i 263, 275.
83 *Letters*, p.181.
84 *Letters*, p.192.
85 Moilliet, pp.110–11.
86 *Lov. Pl.*, pp.41–2.
87 *Lyrical Ballads*, 1800 preface.
88 *Lov. Pl.*, p.47.

89 S. T. Coleridge, *Shakespearean Criticism* (ed. T. M. Raysor, 1930) i 129.
90 DAR 227.1:119.
91 Watt papers LB/2.
92 *Letters*, p.200.
93 *Letters*, pp.201–2.
94 *Letters*, p.204.
95 *Letters*, p.206.
96 DAR 227.1:129.
97 Wheler i 14.
98 DAR 227.1:129.
99 DAR 227.1:132.

CHAPTER 12 (pages 252–280)

1 DAR 227.3:39.
2 DAR 227.1:137.
3 DAR 227.3:39.
4 See R. R. Easson and R. N. Essick, *William Blake: Book Illustrator* (1979) ii 87–91.
5 See J. Frazier, *The Ecologist* 4, 176–80 (1974).
6 DAR 227.1.135.
7 DAR 227.1:134.
8 B. Boothby, *Sonnets sacred to the Memory of Penelope* (1796), p.10.
9 Lich. Rec. Off. D15/8/3/2.
10 Seward. p.395.
11 DAR 227.6:33.
12 Moilliet and Smith, p.41.
13 See R. B. Rose, *Past and Present* 18, 68–88 (1960), Schofield, pp.357–62, and V. Bird, *The Priestley Riots and the Lunar Society* (1994).
14 Goodwin, pp.180–2.
15 Priestley, p.200.
16 DAR 227.1:138.
17 DAR 227.3:39.
18 Birmingham Central Library MS 486802.
19 *Letters*, pp.215–17.
20 Broadsheet dated 10 October 1791 at Derby Library.
21 Lines 5–11, 13–16, 25–40, 51–5, and 57–8 are largely Anna's.

22 *Gent. Mag.* 53, 428 (1783).
23 Seward, *Letters* ii 313.
24 See *E. D. & Romantic Poets*, pp.212, 246–7.
25 Walpole xv 110.
26 Seward, p.193.
27 SchimmelPenninck i 151–3.
28 W. Hayley, *Life of Cowper* (1803) ii 58. The idea is still alive: see *Iceberg Utilization* (ed. A. Husseiny, 1980), pp.624–7.
29 Seward, pp.211–12. Cowper: Camb. Univ. Lib., Shelfmark Syn.4.79.13.
30 G. H. Darwin, papers in *Phil. Trans.* 1879–82 and *The Tides* (1901), ch.16.
31 D. Hassler, *Erasmus Darwin* (1973), pp.30–4, analyses these verses.
32 *Iliad*, Book 14.
33 Cowper: Camb. Univ. Lib., Shelfmark Syn.4.79.13.
34 William Salt Library, Stafford, MS HM 37/54.
35 J. Michell, *Phil. Trans.* 74, 35–57 (1784). See also *Q. J. Roy. Ast. Soc.* 30, 117 (1989).
36 *Analytical Review* 15, 287–93 (1793).
37 Both poems are prefixed to later editions of *The Botanic Garden*.

38 DAR 227.3:40.

39 *Letters*, p.222.

40 *Critical Review* 6 (NS), 162–7 (1792).

41 *New Annual Register*, 1792, p.295.

42 L. T. C. Rolt, *Thomas Telford* (1958), p.29.

43 Walpole xv 41.

44 Seward, pp.178 & 355.

45 L. T. C. Rolt, *Thomas Telford* (1958), p.29.

46 *The Fenwick Notes of William Wordsworth* (1993), p.170.

47 Coleridge, *Letters* i 216, i 305–6.

48 *A Concordance to 'The Botanic Garden'* (Wellcome Inst. Hist. Med., 1994).

49 *E. D. & Romantic Poets*, p.65.

50 C. Darwin, *Life*, pp.111–12.

51 H. S. Torrens, in *British Association Lectures 1993* (Geological Society, 1994: ISBN 1897799020), pp.4–8. See also E. W. Owen, *Trek of the Oil Finders* (1975), ch.1.

52 See D. King-Hele, *Q. J. Roy. Ast. Soc.* 26, 237–61 (1985).

53 Ibid.

54 Ibid.

55 See J. T. Wilson, *IGY, the Year of the New Moons* (1961), p.28.

56 See D. King-Hele, *The Observatory* 95, 1–12 (1975).

57 *Lov. Pl.* IV 45 note. Third and later editions.

58 DAR 227.1:142.

59 DAR 227.1:143.

60 *Life and Letters of Maria Edgeworth* (ed. A. J. C. Hare, 1894) i 21.

61 DAR 227.1:144.

62 J. Davy, *Life of Sir Humphry Davy* (1836) i 61.

63 *Letters*, p.223.

64 See DAR 227.6:35 for further details.

65 DAR 227.6:36.

66 C. A. Lubbock, *The Herschel Chronicle* (1933), p.237.

67 R. P. Sturges, *Midland History* 4, 224 (1979).

68 *Derby Mercury*, 9 August 1792.

69 DAR 227.1:146.

70 *The Life of John Gisborne* (1852).

71 *Letters*, p.325.

72 DAR 227.1:145.

73 E. Fearn, *Derbys. Arch. J.* 88, 47–59 (1968).

74 See *DNB*, and J. C. Marshman, *Carey, Marshman and Ward* (1859).

75 Printed in *Politics for the People*. No.XI, 21 December 1793.

76 Goodwin, p.253.

77 See Goodwin, pp.287–90.

78 For Muir and Palmer, see *DNB*.

79 *State Trials*, Vol.XXII, p.1008 (1817). See also *The Farington Diary* (ed. J. Greig, 1922) i 27.

80 Stevens, *Journal*, p.69.

81 *Letters*, p.228.

82 C. Wordsworth, *Social Life at the English Universities* (1874), p.588.

83 Seward, *Letters* iii 215.

84 C. Darwin, *Life*, p.64, and DAR 210.14:16 and 23.

85 Derby Local Studies Library MS 11172.

86 See Nicolson, *Wright* i 18–21.

87 Ibid. i 20.

88 D. Stansfield, *Thomas Beddoes* (1984), p.78.

89 *Letters*, p.228.

90 DAR 227.1:147.

91 *Letters*, p.224. For Smith, see M. Walker, *James Edward Smith* (1988).

92 *Letters*, pp.231–2.

93 Stevens, *Journal*, p.65. M. Keynes, *Notes Rec. R. Soc.* 48, 69–84 (1994).

94 *Letters*, p.227.

95 DAR 227.1:149.

96 *Letters*, p.238.

CHAPTER 13 (pages 281–308)

1 See DAR 227.1:151; UCL Pearson papers 576; and R. C. Smith, *Derbyshire Miscellany* 4, 17–23 (1967).
2 DAR 227.1:153.
3 See D. Gardiner, *English Girlhood at School* (1929), pp.347–56; B. Simon, *Studies in the History of Education* (1960), pp.50–6; J. Kamm, *Hope Deferred* (1965), passim.
4 Stevens, *Journal*, pp.126–8.
5 *Letters*, pp.263–5.
6 See *Letters*, pp.240–9.
7 *Letters*, p.250.
8 Watt papers LB/2.
9 *Letters*, pp.251–2.
10 *Letters*, pp.258–60, with drawing of the apparatus.
11 *Letters*, pp.260–1.
12 For the Pigot family, see *E. D. & Romantic Poets*, pp.253–4.
13 See *Letters*, pp.266–9.
14 See *Letters*, pp.241–2.
15 See *Letters*, pp.255–7.
16 See Hayter, pp.101–3. Also R. Reilly, *Wedgwood* (1989) ii 17.
17 DAR 227.5:140.
18 DAR 227.1:152.
19 DAR 227.1:154.
20 G. Peacock, *Life of Thomas Young* (1855), p.49.
21 See *Letters*, pp.271–3.
22 See *Letters*, pp.262–3.
23 DAR 218:B15.
24 See R. Porter, 'Erasmus Darwin: doctor of evolution', in *History, Humanity and Evolution* (ed. J. Moore, 1989), pp.39–69.
25 *Zoonomia*, Vol.II, page v (the definition is shorter in Vol.II).
26 See E. S. Reed, *From Soul to Mind* (1997), ch.3; and *E. D. & Romantic Poets*, pp.71–8 and 128–32.
27 See G. H. Lewes, *History of Philosophy* (3rd ed., 1867) ii 364; T. Brown, *Observations on the 'Zoonomia'* (1798), pp.294–302.
28 *Tem. Nat.*, Add. Note VIII.
29 *Tem. Nat.*, Add. Note I, p.11.
30 Cornwall Record Office, Truro, DG 41/4.
31 See *Brunonianism in Britain and Europe. Medical History*, supplement No.8. Wellcome Inst. Hist. Med. (1988).
32 Stock, p.133.
33 See Goodwin, ch.8.
34 See E. Robinson, *Cambridge Hist. J.* 11, 349–55 (1955).
35 See Goodwin, ch.9.
36 G. M. Trevelyan, *History of England* (1945 edition), p.567.
37 DAR 227.1:155.
38 *Letters*, pp.279–81.
39 DAR 227.1:156.
40 Fitzwilliam Museum Library Collection of Mrs Hayley's correspondence.
41 Stock, p.102.
42 *Letters*, p.261.
43 *Letters*, pp.284–5.
44 *Letters*, pp.288–9.
45 *Letters*, pp.275–8.
46 Derby Local Studies Library, Book 8962.
47 *Monthly Magazine*, 1, 54 (1796).
48 *Staffordshire Advertiser*, 28 November 1795.
49 See H. F. Osborn, *From the Greeks to Darwin*, 2nd ed. (New York, 1929); and C. Zirkle, *Proc. Amer. Phil. Soc.* 84, 71–123 (1941).
50 See E. Mayr, *One Long Argument* (1991). For discussion of Erasmus's ideas on evolution, see J. Harrison, *J. Hist. Ideas* 32, 247–64 (1971).
51 DAR 227.1:143.
52 DAR 227.1:154.
53 *Tem. Nat.*, Add. Note VIII.
54 N. Eldredge and S. J. Gould, in *Models in Paleobiology* (San Francisco, 1972), pp.82–115.
55 Coleridge, *Letters* i 177.
56 Ibid. i 178–9.

57 See *E. D. & Romantic Poets*, pp.127–8.
58 Coleridge, *Letters* i 305–6.
59 Ibid.
60 Ibid. i 320–1.
61 DAR 227.1:158.
62 DAR 227.9:28.
63 Derby Local Studies Library Book 8962 (11 April 1796).
64 DAR 218:B18.

65 Watt papers W/9.
66 Stock, p.119.
67 W. J. White, *The Centrifuge in Aerospace Medicine* (Douglas Aircraft Co., 1964), ch.1. See also B. Cohen, *Human Neurobiol.* 3, 121–8 (1984).
68 Stock, p.133.
69 Stevens, *Journal*, p.126.

CHAPTER 14 (pages 309–328)

1 *The Farington Diary* (ed. J. Greig, 1922) i 153. For Walpole, see T. Mowl, *Horace Walpole* (1996).
2 DAR 227.1:159 (misdated 1801 in *Letters*).
3 *Godwin and Mary*, p.99.
4 Nicolson, *Wright* i 5.
5 DAR 218:B23.
6 Edgeworth ii 179.
7 Seward, pp.398–9.
8 DAR 227.2:20.
9 *Letters*, p.306.
10 C. Darwin, *Life*, p.69.
11 R. Porter, *Doctor of Society* (1992), ch.8.
12 See I. Macalpine and R. Hunter, *George III and the Mad-Business* (1969), ch.3.
13 C. Darwin, *Life*, pp.105–6.
14 *Letters*, pp.303–4.
15 *Letters*, pp.309–10.
16 SchimmelPenninck i 241–2.
17 For Brown, see D. Welsh, *Life and Writings of Thomas Brown* (1825).
18 Ibid., pp.42–61. Also *Letters*, pp.298–303.
19 DAR 227.1:161 and *Letters*, pp.298–303.
20 DAR 227.1:161.
21 Reprinted in *Poetry of the Anti-Jacobin* (ed. C. Edmunds, 1854); or, ed. L. Rice-Oxley, 1924. Four of the best lines are quoted in ch.11.
22 See M. D. George, *Catalogue of Political and Personal Satires*,

Vol.VII (1941), pp.469, 528.
23 See *E. D. & Romantic Poets*, ch.3–5.
24 See ibid., pp.71–9.
25 *Letters of William and Dorothy Wordsworth* (2nd ed., 1967) i 199.
26 *Zoonomia* ii 359.
27 'Goody Blake', lines 94–5, 97, (75), 100, 105–6.
28 See *E. D. & Romantic Poets*, pp.76–9.
29 *Ec. Veg.*, Note IX.
30 'Ancient Mariner', lines 272–6. See *E. D. & Romantic Poets*, pp.103–10.
31 Ibid., pp.111–19 and note 51.
32 DAR 227.1:160.
33 DAR 227.1:161.
34 See *Gardener's Magazine* 14, 345–6 (1838).
35 See *The Diary of Elihu H. Smith* (ed. J. E. Cronin, 1973).
36 DAR 218:B24.
37 See Edgeworth ii 261.
38 See A. Friendly, *Beaufort of the Admiralty* (1977).
39 See Edgeworth ii 209–38.
40 Moilliet, p.145.
41 See F. F. Cartwright, *The English Pioneers of Anaesthesia* (1952), p.79.
42 See C. Bush, *18th Cent. Stud.* 7, 295–320 (1974); *Temple of Flora* (Collins, 1972), p.4; *Phytologia*, p.578.

43 *Monthly Mag.* 6, 325 (1798); and R. Polwhele, *The Unsex'd Females* (1798), p.4.
44 See C. R. Hall, *A Scientist in the Early Republic: S. L. Mitchill* (1934), ch.4.
45 *Public Characters of 1798–1799* (4th ed., 1803), p.118.
46 DAR 227.1:162.
47 DAR 227.1:163.
48 See M. Butler, *Maria Edgeworth* (1972), p.1.
49 Ibid., p.32.
50 DAR 227.1:162.
51 *Letters*, pp.316–17.
52 DAR 227.2:21–5.
53 DAR 227.1:163.

54 DAR 227.7:33.
55 R. Polwhele, *Traditions and Recollections* (1826) ii 529.
56 DAR 227.1:164.
57 C. Darwin, *Life*, p.75 (deleted).
58 Ibid.
59 DAR 227.1:165.
60 See C. Darwin, *Life*, pp.70–7; also DAR 227.4:10–17 and DAR 227.6: 122–8.
61 E.g. *Monthly Mag.* 17, 378 (1804); *Edinburgh Rev.*, April 1804, pp.236–7.
62 Seward, pp.404–10.
63 DAR 227.6:122.
64 *Letters*, p.319.

CHAPTER 15 (pages 329–345)

1 *Letters*, pp.320–1.
2 Watt papers 6/24.
3 DAR 227.1:166.
4 DAR 227.1:167.
5 DAR 227.9:37.
6 DAR 227.1:167.
7 DAR 227.1:168.
8 DAR 227.1:169.
9 DAR 227.1:170.
10 DAR 227.1:175.
11 DAR 227.1:173.
12 DAR 227.1:166.
13 DAR 227.1:172.
14 See Bedini, pp.36–8.
15 DAR 227.1:174.
16 G. Wakefield, *Memoirs* (1804) ii 229, 289–95.
17 *Letters*, p.323.
18 Watt papers 6/24.
19 Stock, p.100. See also B. Masters, *Georgiana* (1981) and A. Foreman, *Georgiana* (1998).
20 *Letters*, p.325.
21 *Letters*, p.326.
22 See, e.g., F. W. Gibbs, *Joseph Priestley* (1965), ch.9.
23 An honourable exception is John Russell's *History of Agricultural*

Science in Great Britain (1966).
24 See *Essential Writings*, Fig. 15.
25 See e.g. R. Carson, *Silent Spring* (Penguin, 1965), p.252.
26 C. Ronan, *Cambridge Illustrated History of World Science* (1983), p.181.
27 DAR 227.1:178.
28 Univ. of California, Los Angeles, Library: MS 169/I:38. For the Waldie family, see *DNB*.
29 DAR 227.1:179.
30 DAR 227.6:61.
31 DAR 227.1:180.
32 *Letters*, p.333.
33 *Letters*, p.335.
34 See *E. D. & Romantic Poets*, p.120.
35 *Zoonomia* (3rd ed., 1801) ii 243.
36 Ibid. ii 244.
37 Ibid. ii 295.
38 *Letters*, p.336.
39 DAR 227.1:182.
40 DAR 218:C1.
41 *Letters*, p.338.
42 Edgeworth ii 264–5.
43 C. Darwin, *Life*, p.126.
44 DAR 227.8:15.
45 DAR 218:C1.

46 G. C. Cook and D. King-Hele, *Notes Rec. R. Soc.* 52, 261–5 (1998).

47 C. Darwin, *Life*, p.127. For Erasmus's will, see UCL Pearson papers 576.

48 Watt papers LB/3.

49 Ibid.

50 Muirhead ii 279.

51 Watt papers LB/3.

52 *Monthly Mag.* 13, 457–63 (1802).

53 Seward, pp.424–5.

54 *Monthly Mag.* 13, 548–9 (1802).

55 Ibid. 14, 115–16 (1802).

56 C. Darwin, *Life*, p.68.

57 *Gent. Mag.* 72, 473–4 (1802).

58 DAR 227.6:76.

CHAPTER 16 (pages 346–362)

1 See *Monthly Mag.* 14, 433 (December 1802).

2 *Tem. Nat.* Add. Notes, p.45; F. Galton, *Hereditary Genius* (Watts, 1950), pp.124–33.

3 E. S. Reed, *From Soul to Mind* (1997), p.xi; and Logan, pp.67–77.

4 *Tem. Nat.* IV 453, note.

5 J. D. Bernal, *Science in History* (1969), p.639.

6 W. Paley, *Natural Theology* (6th ed., 1803), p.473.

7 Seward, *Letters* vi 73; *Monthly Mag.* 15, 632–6 (1803); *Monthly Rev.* 43, 113–27 (1804).

8 See N. Garfinkle, *J. Hist. Ideas* 16, 386 (1955); *Gent. Mag.* 79, 120 (1809); *British Critic* 23, 174 (1804).

9 J. Priestley, *Trans. Amer. Phil. Soc.* 6 (1), 119–29 (1804).

10 See *E. D. & Romantic Poets*, p.141.

11 See ibid., pp.140–5, for these citations.

12 See E. Sewell, *The Orphic Voice* (1960), and I. Primer, *J. Hist. Ideas* 25, 58–76 (1964).

13 See R. D. Keynes, *J. Molec. Evol.* 40, 3–6 (1995) and *J. Theor. Biol.* 187, 461–71 (1997).

14 DAR 227.2:22. For Darwin's idea of progress, see M. Ruse, *Monad to Man* (1996), pp.59–64.

15 DAR 227.2:23 & 24. Also UCL Galton papers 11.

16 See F. J. Messman, *Richard Payne Knight* (1974), and *The Arrogant Connoisseur* (ed. M. Clarke and N. Penny, 1982). Also A. Ballantyne, *Architecture, Landscape and Liberty* (1997), pp.201–2.

17 Wheler i 16.

18 Ibid. i 45. See also M. Edgeworth, *Letters from England* (1971), pp.29, 154.

19 F. S. Darwin, *Travels in Spain and the East* (1927).

20 Pearson i 23.

21 M. Edgeworth, *Letters from England* (1971), p.154.

22 Ibid., p.155.

23 British Library Add. MS 6671.

24 *Life of John Gisborne* (1852), p.30.

25 Ibid., p.209.

26 M. Edgeworth, *Letters from England* (1971), p.176.

27 DAR 210.14:13.

28 DAR 227.5:140.

29 C. Darwin, *Autobiog.*, p.87.

30 *Charles Darwin* (ed. F. Darwin, 1902), p.3.

31 C. Darwin, *Autobiog.*, p.27.

32 Janet Browne, *Charles Darwin: Voyaging* (1994), p.158.

33 Wheler i 62.

34 *E. D. & Romantic Poets*, pp.128–32.

35 *Ec. Veg.* II 497–8; 'To Enterprise', lines 114–16.

36 *Letters of Sir Walter Scott* (1932) i 62.

37 *E. D. & Romantic Poets*, pp.229–47.

38 Ibid., pp.247-50.
39 D. King-Hele, *Shelley: his Thought and Work* (3rd ed., 1984).
40 *E. D. & Romantic Poets*, ch.8.
41 *Ec. Veg.* IV 144-6, 151.
42 *E. D. & Romantic Poets*, pp.253-9.
43 Ibid., pp.265-7.
44 Ibid., pp.260-4, 267-9.
45 *Tem. Nat.*, Add. Note I, p.7. See also *Tem. Nat.* I 290.
46 B. W. Aldiss, *Billion-Year Spree* (1973), ch.1.

47 The genus *Darwinia*, akin to the myrtle, was named in his honour by E. Rudge. It includes about 35 species, mostly in Australia: see F. Bodkin, *Encyclopaedia Botanica* (1986), pp.323-6.
48 See Plate 1 and M. Keynes, *Notes Rec. R. Soc.* 48, 69-84 (1994). One of the busts dates from 1804: see *Monthly Mag.* 18, 557 (1805). For Coffee, see B. R. Bricknell, *William John Coffee* (1998).

CHAPTER 17 (pages 363-373)

1 *Zoonomia, Phytologia* and *The Temple of Nature*; the *Origin of Species, Descent of Man ...* and *Variations of Animals ...*
2 *More Letters of Charles Darwin* (1903) ii 419.
3 *Life and Letters of Charles Darwin* (ed. F. Darwin, 1887) i 117; C. Darwin, *Autobiog.*, p.135.
4 *Tem. Nat.* III 342 note.
5 C. Darwin, *Formation of Vegetable Mould through the Action of Worms* (1880).
6 S. Wilberforce, *Quarterly Rev.* 108, 226 (1860).
7 See also H. E. Gruber, *Darwin on Man* (1981), ch.3.
8 P. J. Vorzimmer, *Charles Darwin: the Years of Controversy* (1972), p.xv.
9 C. Darwin, *Autobiog.*, p.49.
10 See R. D. Keynes, *J. Theoret. Biol.* 187, 461-71 (1997).
11 See C. D. Darlington, *Darwin's Place in History* (1959) and D. King-Hele, *Erasmus Darwin* (1963), ch.5.
12 *Zoonomia* i 507.
13 *Origin of Species*, p.88.
14 See *Dr. of Rev.*, p.311-13; *Origin of Species*, pp.79 and 490.
15 *Zoonomia* i 506.
16 *Origin of Species*, p.13. Unchanged in later editions.

17 Ibid., p.358.
18 *Lov. Pl.*, pp.124-5.
19 S. Wilberforce, *Quarterly Rev.* 108, 225-64 (1860).
20 *Origin of Species* (1964 facsimile edition), pp.491-4.
21 C. Darwin, *Autobiog.*, p.87.
22 Pearson ii 194.
23 C. Darwin, *Life*, p.124 (deleted). DAR 210.11:45. Previously printed in *Dr. of Rev.*, pp.314-15.
24 C. Darwin, *Life*, p.86 (deleted).
25 Wheler ii 430.
26 DAR 210.14:16.
27 See D. E. Cartwright, *Tides: a Scientific History* (1999), pp.147-50.
28 See J. L. Pritchard, *Sir George Cayley* (1961), pp.93, 233.
29 C. Darwin, *Life*, p.92.
30 G. L. Craik, *History of English Literature* (1866) ii 382-97.
31 E. V. Lucas, *A Swan and her Friends* (1907).
32 J. C. Cox, *Derby Archeol. J.*, 37, 91-6 (1915). Wargrave Church in Berkshire, where Thomas Day was buried, was also burnt down in 1914.
33 See *Dr. of Rev.*, p.318.
34 See ibid., p.319; I draw a veil over later errors.
35 See ibid., p.338, note 20.

36 Logan, p.99.
37 E. Robinson, *Annals of Science* 9,
   359–67 (1953); 10, 314–20 (1954).
   N. Barlow, *Notes Rec. R. Soc.* 14,
   85–98 (1959).
38 For details, see *Dr. of Rev.*,
   pp.319–20.
39 See Appendix 1.
40 See Appendix 2.
41 See Appendix 2.
42 R. Porter, *The Enlightenment*
   (1990), p.23.
43 See B. Blackstone, *The Consecrated
   Urn* (1959), and Hayter, p.101.
44 *Gent. Mag.* 90 (2), 277 (1820).
45 DAR 210.14:22.
46 DAR 227.6:76.
47 *Public Characters of 1798–99* (4th
   ed., 1803), p.118.
48 C. Darwin, *Life*, p.76.
49 Ibid.
50 In alphabetical order, the subjects are: adiabatic expansion, aesthetics,
   afforestation, air travel, animal camouflage, artesian wells, artificial bird,
   aurorae, balloon flying, biological adaptation, biological pest control, canal
   lifts, carriage springs, carriage steering, cataract surgery, centrifugation,
   climate control, clouds, cold and warm fronts, compressed-air actuators,
   copying machines, cosmology, educational reform, electrical machines,
   electrochemistry, electrotherapy, evolution, exercise for children, feminism,
   fertilizers, formation of coal, geological strata, hereditary diseases, hydrogen
   engine, ideal gas law, individuality of buds, language, liberation of slaves,
   limestone deposits, manures, mental illness, microscopy, mimicry, moon's
   origin, nerve impulses, night airglow, ocular spectra, oil drilling, oil lamps,
   organic happiness, origin of life, outer atmosphere, oxygenation of blood,
   phosphorus, photosynthesis, plant nutrients, Portland Vase, psychology, rocket
   motors, rotary pumps, science fiction, secular morality, seed-drills, sewage
   farms, sexual reproduction, speaking machines, squinting, steam carriages,
   steam turbines, stomata of leaves, struggle for existence, submarines, survival
   of the fittest, telescopes, temperance, travel of seeds, treatment of dropsy,
   ventilation, water as H_2O, water closets, water machines, weather maps, wind-
   gauges, windmills, winds, word coining. (The pages where these subjects are
   mentioned can be found in the index.)

APPENDIX I

Erasmus Darwin's Writings

A CHIEF PUBLICATIONS

1 Poem on the death of Prince Frederick. In *Academiae Cantabrigiensis Luctus in obitum Frederici celsissimi Walliae Principis*. Cambridge: Bentham, 1751. Republished in *European Magazine* 27, 75–6 (1795).

2 'Remarks on the Opinion of Henry Eeles, Esq., concerning the Ascent of Vapour'. *Philosophical Transactions of the Royal Society* 50, 240–54 (1757).

3 'An uncommon Case of an Haemoptysis'. *Phil. Trans.* 51, 526–9 (1760).

4 [Anonymous] *A View of the Advantages of Inland Navigations; with a Plan of a Navigable Canal* ... [pamphlet] (sold by Becket and De Hondt) (1765).

5 'Experiments on Animal Fluids in the exhausted Receiver'. *Phil. Trans.* 64, 344–9 (1774).

6 'A New Case in Squinting'. *Phil. Trans.* 68, 86–96 (1778).

7 [Anonymous] *An Elegy on the much-lamented Death of a most ingenious young Gentleman* ... London: G. Robinson, 1778.

8 *A System of Vegetables* ... translated from the thirteenth edition of the 'Systema Vegetabilium' of ... Linneus ... by a Botanical Society at Lichfield. 2 vols. Lichfield: J. Jackson, for Leigh and Sotheby, London, 1783.

9 'An Account of an artificial Spring of Water'. *Phil. Trans.* 75, 1–7 (1785).

10 'An Account of the successful use of Foxglove in some Dropsies, and in the pulmonary Consumption'. *Medical Transactions* 3, 255–86 (1785).

11 *The Families of Plants* ... translated from the last edition of the 'Genera Plantarum' ... by a Botanical Society at Lichfield. 2 vols. Lichfield: J. Jackson, for J. Johnson, London; T. Byrne, Dublin; and J. Balfour, Edinburgh, 1787.

12 'Frigorific Experiments on the mechanical Expansion of Air'. *Phil. Trans.* 78, 43–52 (1788).

13 'Of the Medicinal Waters of Buxton and Matlock', in J. Pilkington's *A View of the present State of Derbyshire* (Derby: Drewry, 1789), pp.256–75.

14 [Anonymous] *The Botanic Garden; a Poem, in Two Parts.* [quarto]
Part I, *The Economy of Vegetation*. London, J. Johnson, 1791 [actually 1792].
Part II, *The Loves of the Plants*. Lichfield: J. Jackson, for J. Johnson, London, 1789.
Later English editions [the last three are octavo]:
Part I. 2nd edition, 1791. 3rd, 1795. 4th, 1799. 5th, 1806. 6th, 1824.
Part II. 2nd, 1790. 3rd, 1791. 4th, 1794. 5th 1799. 6th, 1806. 7th, 1824.
Irish edition: Dublin: Moore; Part I, 1793; Part II, 1796.
American editions: New York: Swords, 1798. 2nd ed., Swords, 1807. Abridged version, 1805.

Translations. Part I: Portuguese, by V. F. N. da Cunha; Lisbon, 1803–4. Part II:
French, by J. P. E. Deleuze; Paris, 1800. Italian, by G. Gherardini; Pirotta,
Milan, 1805; Naples, 1817; 2nd ed., Milan, 1818.

The Beauties of the Botanic Garden. [selections] London: Cadell, 1805. New
York: Longworth, 1805.

Facsimile reprints by Scolar Press, Menston, 1973; by Scholarly Press, MI, 1977;
by Garland, New York, 1979; and by Woodstock Books, 1991 (Part II only).

15 *Zoonomia; or, The Laws of Organic Life.*

Part I. London: J. Johnson, 1794.

Parts II and III. London: J. Johnson, 1796. With 2nd ed. of Part I, corrected.
2 vols.

Third edition: London: J. Johnson, 1801. 4 vols.

Irish editions: Dublin: P. Byrne, 1794–6 (2 vols); Dugdale, 1800 (2 vols);
Gilbert and Hodges, 1803.

American editions: Part I. New York: Swords, 1796. Parts II and III.
Philadelphia, Dobson, 1797 (2 vols). Later editions: Boston, Carlisle, 1803
(2 vols); Boston, 1806 (ed. S. L. Mitchill); Boston, Thomas and Andrews,
1809; 4th ed., Philadelphia, E. Earle, 1818.

Translations. German, by J. D. Brandis: Hannover, 1795–9 (5 vols). Pesth,
1801, 1805. Italian, by G. Rasori; Milan, Pirotta, 1803–5 (6 vols).
Portuguese, by H. X. Baeta, 1806 [Summary of Pts I & II; Part III in full].
French, by J. F. Klyskens; Ghent, 1810 (4 vols).

Facsimile reprints by A. M. S. Press, New York, 1974; and by Scholarly Press,
MI, 1977.

16 *A Plan for the Conduct of Female Education in Boarding Schools.* Derby:
J. Drewry, for J. Johnson, London, 1797.

Irish edition: Dublin, Chambers, 1798.

American edition: Philadelphia, Ormrod, 1798.

Facsimile reprints by Johnson Reprint Corp., New York, 1968; and by
Routledge, 1996, in *History of British Educational Theory*, vol. 5.

17 *Phytologia: or the Philosophy of Agriculture and Gardening.* London:
J. Johnson, 1800.

Irish edition: Dublin, Byrne, 1800.

German translation, by E. B. G. Hebenstreit. Leipzig, 1801 (2 vols).

18 *The Temple of Nature; or, The Origin of Society.* London, J. Johnson, 1803.
2nd ed., 1806 [as part of *Poetical Works*]. 3rd ed., London, Jones, 1825.

American editions: New York, Swords, 1804; Baltimore, Bonsal & Niles,
1804.

German edition: Brunswick, L. Lucius, 1808. Russian translation, by N. A.
Kholodkovskii, 1911, in Journ. Min. National Education; in book form,
Moscow, Acad. Sci., 1954; 2nd ed., 1960.

Facsimile reprints by Scolar Press, Menston, 1973; and by Scholarly Press, MI,
1977.

B OTHER PRINTED SOURCES

1 *Essential Writings of Erasmus Darwin* (ed. D. King-Hele) (McGibbon & Kee,
1968) has selections from his books and papers.

2 *The Letters of Erasmus Darwin* (ed. D. King-Hele) (Cambridge: Cambridge University Press, 1981) prints the 272 letters known at that time, with notes.

3 The paper about the mortality of horned cattle was printed in the Derby *Weekly Entertainer* for 29 September 1783, pp.301–3.

4 Some of Darwin's shorter poems have appeared in print:

(a) The poem on Gurney's shorthand was printed in the *London Magazine* 20, 325 (1751) and in the third edition of T. Gurney's *Brachygraphy* (1752).

(b) Five poems written as letters appear in *The Letters of Erasmus Darwin*: the 'Platonic Epistle to a married Lady' (96 lines); the Tea-Vase poem (36 lines); the 'Speech of a Wood-Nymph' (16 lines); a Christmas letter-in-verse in 1749 (48 lines); and the poem to Anna Seward's cat (16 lines). *Letters*, pp.91–3; 86–7; 77; 4–5; and 101–2 respectively.

(c) Six poems, including the epitaph to Small and the 'Dread Dream' poem, are printed in Anna Seward's *Memoirs*.

(d) The 'Address to the Swilcar Oak' was published at the end of F. N. C. Mundy's poem *Needwood Forest* (1776).

(e) The 'Ode to the river Derwent' is in *Gent. Mag.* 55, 641 (1785); and 'Idyllium, a Prison' in *Monthly Mag.* 1, 54 (1796).

(f) Typescript copies of some early poems and those to Elizabeth Pole are in University College London Library, Pearson papers 577.

C MANUSCRIPTS

Nearly all the known manuscript letters, and other autograph papers, are to be found at the thirty Libraries and Archives listed in *The Letters of Erasmus Darwin*, pp. xv–xvi. For the Commonplace Book, see page 377.

More recently, 196 letters have become available at Cambridge University Library: 174 of these are catalogued in DAR 227, and 22 in DAR 218. The James Watt papers, transferred in 1995 from Doldowlod to Birmingham Central Library, include twenty-seven letters from Darwin to Watt: six of them did not appear in the *Letters*. To these should be added one letter at Nottinghamshire Archives, one at the Sutro Library, San Francisco, one at the Library of the University of California, Los Angeles, as well as an unknown number in private hands.

The largest collection of 'other autograph papers' is at Cambridge University Library and includes the twenty-five-page guide to shorthand and the early drafts of *The Temple of Nature*. The manuscripts of the canal pamphlet are at University College London Library. There are good numbers of relevant non-autograph manuscripts at most of the thirty Libraries and Archives already mentioned, at Lichfield Record Office and Derby Local Studies Library, and privately owned, by the late Miss Susan Darwin and Mrs Vivien Kindersley, notably the satirical poem 'To Peter Pindar' (1785?).

APPENDIX 2

Selected Books and Papers

I have consulted about three thousand books and a thousand papers with information relevant to Erasmus Darwin: some are cited among the numbered references on pages 379–99, those most often used being listed on pages 377–9. As an addition to that list, here is a further small selection of books and papers related to Erasmus Darwin. The many authors omitted should not fret: they are in good company.

The place of publication is London, unless otherwise stated. If a title is not self-explanatory, I have added a comment.

M. Ashmun, *The Singing Swan*, New York: Greenwood Press, 1968. (First pub. 1931.) Life of Anna Seward.

B. Blackstone, *The Consecrated Urn*. Longman, 1959. Darwin's influence on Keats and others.

E. Blackwell, 'The Life, Times and Work of Erasmus Darwin'. MA thesis, University College London, 1949.

J. Bowlby, *Charles Darwin: a biography*. Hutchinson, 1990.

J. Browne, 'Botany for gentlemen: Erasmus Darwin and *The Loves of the Plants*'. *Isis* 80, 593–621 (1989).

D. Clarke, *The Ingenious Mr Edgeworth*. Oldbourne, 1965.

H. Clayton, *Coaching City*. Bala: Dragon Books, 1971. Portrait of Georgian Lichfield.

A. Coddington, 'Erasmus Darwin the Whole Man, and his concept of love'. PhD thesis, Rutgers University, N.J., 1986.

A Concordance to Erasmus Darwin's poem 'The Botanic Garden' (ed. D. King-Hele). Wellcome Inst. Hist. Medicine, 1994.

C. D. Darlington, *Darwin's Place in History*. Oxford: Blackwell, 1959. On proponents of evolution from 1790 to 1860.

E. Fearn, 'The Derbyshire Reform Societies, 1791–1793'. *Derbys. Archaeolog. J.* 88, 47–59 (1968).

R. B. Freeman, *Darwin Pedigrees*. Printed for the author, 1984.

H. E. Gruber, *Darwin on Man*. Chicago: University of Chicago Press, 2nd ed., 1981.

J. Harrison, 'Erasmus Darwin's view of evolution'. *J. Hist. Ideas* 32, 247–64 (1971).

D. M. Hassler, *The Comedian as the Letter D: Erasmus Darwin's Comic Materialism*. The Hague: Nijhoff, 1973.

D. M. Hassler, *Erasmus Darwin*. New York: Twayne, 1973. Darwin as a literary figure.

M. A. Hopkins, *Dr Johnson's Lichfield*. Owen, 1956.

W. P. Jones, *The Rhetoric of Science*. Routledge, 1966. On eighteenth-century poets who wrote about science.

M. Keynes, 'Portraits of Dr Erasmus Darwin, by Joseph Wright, James Rawlinson and William Coffee'. *Notes Rec. Roy. Soc.* **48**, 69–84 (1994).

R. D. Keynes, 'Erasmus Darwin's *Temple of Nature*'. *J. Molecular Evolution* **40**, 3–6 (1995).

D. King-Hele, 'Erasmus Darwin, the Lunaticks and evolution'. *Notes Rec. Roy. Soc.* **52**, 153–80 (1998).

F. D. Klingender, *Art and the Industrial Revolution*. Paladin, 1972. (First pub. 1947.) Much about Wright and Darwin.

J. L. Lowes, *The Road to Xanadu*. New York: Vintage Books, 1959. (First pub. 1927.) Revealed Coleridge's debt to Darwin.

M. McNeil, *Under the Banner of Science: Erasmus Darwin and his Age*. Manchester: Manchester University Press, 1987.

A. Noyes, *The Torch-Bearers*, Vol.II. Edinburgh: Blackwood, 1925. Erasmus's evolutionary ideas expressed in verse.

H. Pearson, *Doctor Darwin*. Dent, 1930; Penguin, 1943. Entertaining picture of Darwin and his friends.

R. Porter, *English Society in the Eighteenth Century*. Allen Lane, 1982. Often refers to Darwin.

R. Porter, *Doctor of Society: Thomas Beddoes and the Sick-Trade in late Enlightenment England*. Routledge, 1992.

R. Porter, *The Greatest Benefit to Mankind*. HarperCollins, 1997. Chapter X is on Enlightenment medicine.

N. Priestland, *Erasmus Darwin: philosopher, scientist, physician and poet*. Nottingham: Ashbracken, 1990. A pleasant introduction (seventy-one pages).

E. S. Reed, *From Soul to Mind: the emergence of psychology from Erasmus Darwin to William James*. New Haven: Yale University Press, 1997. Sees Darwin as a pioneer of psychology.

R. Reilly, *Josiah Wedgwood*. Macmillan, 1992.

E. Robinson, 'The Derby Philosophical Society'. *Annals of Science* **9**, 359–67 (1953).

E. Robinson, 'The Lunar Society: its membership and organization'. *Trans. Newcomen Soc.* **35**, 153–77 (1963).

L. T. C. Rolt, *James Watt*. Batsford, 1962.

P. Rowland, *The Life and Times of Thomas Day*. Lewiston, N.Y.: Mellen, 1996. The best book on Day.

R. E. Schofield, *The Enlightenment of Joseph Priestley*. University Park, PA: Pennsylvania State University Press, 1997. On Priestley up to the age of forty.

The Scottish Enlightenment (ed. D. Daiches, P. Jones and J. Jones). Edinburgh: Saltire Society, 1996. (First pub. 1986.)

E. Sewell, *The Orphic Voice*. New Haven: Yale University Press, 1960. Discussion of *The Temple of Nature*.

C. Sheffield, *Erasmus Magister: an historical fantasy*. New York: Ace Books, 1982. Detective stories with a Sherlock-Holmes Erasmus as hero.

R. P. Sturges, 'The membership of the Derby Philosophical Society, 1783–1802'. *Midland History* **4**, 212–29 (1979).

B. and H. Wedgwood, *The Wedgwood Circle, 1730–1897*. Cassell, 1980.

A. Wolf, *A History of Science, Technology and Philosophy in the Eighteenth Century*. Allen & Unwin, 2nd ed., 1952. (First pub. 1938.)

APPENDIX 3

Acknowledgments

I am most grateful to George Pember Darwin for his many donations of family papers to the Cambridge University Library, and to Patrick Zutshi, Keeper of Manuscripts at the Library, for enticing me into examining the latest addition, seven large boxes filled with thousands of papers (DAR 227). These manuscripts are the very essence of my biography.

Subsequently, Rosemary Thomas read the first draft of the book in manuscript, and her many suggestions for changes in substance and style have led to a much better book.

Valerie McMillan was responsible for transforming the manuscript into the disc from which the book was printed. This called for skill and accuracy, and much patience too, when the stylistic and editorial amendments grew excessive.

Giles de la Mare has played an essential role as publisher, and also through his continual encouragement and detailed editorial critique.

Another source of encouragement for me has been the recent upsurge of interest in Erasmus Darwin that has led to his house at Lichfield being restored and now being about to open as a museum and study centre. I thank all those who have contributed to this project, and particularly the members of the Erasmus Darwin Foundation: what seemed a mere dream five years ago has become reality.

I am grateful to the many people who have helped me with the biographical research or with the quest for manuscripts and illustrations. To Gordon Cook and Denis Gibbs, the initiators of the Erasmus Darwin Foundation, for their continual support. To Maxwell Craven for making available his unique knowledge of Derby past and present. And to many others who made important contributions: Erasmus Barlow, Janet Browne, Bill Bynum, (George) Erasmus Darwin, the late Susan Darwin, Sheila Dean, Nick Gill, Stuart Harris, Adrian Henstock, Milo Keynes, Richard Keynes, Vivien Kindersley, Lynn Miller, Keith Moore, Peter Rowland, John Sanders, Hugh Torrens, Arnott Wilson, and numerous librarians and archivists. I thank all of them for their help.

I have been fortunate in being able to benefit from the unique facilities of the Cambridge University Library, where the new manuscripts reside and much of my research was done.

Finally, I would salute the efforts of all the authors, past and present, whose writings have proved so crucial to my story, as the references show. Foremost among these are Anna Seward and Charles Darwin.

For permission to quote from manuscripts I thank:

Mr George Pember Darwin and the Syndics of Cambridge University Library
English Heritage (Down House)
University College London
Birmingham Central Library
Lichfield Record Office
Derby Local Studies Library
The Royal Society
The Trustees of the Wedgwood Museum, Barlaston
The Royal Society for the Encouragement of Arts, Manufactures and Commerce
The late Miss Susan Darwin
Mrs Vivien Kindersley
William Salt Library, Stafford
Nottinghamshire Archives
The Royal Society of Medicine
The Master and Fellows of St John's College, Cambridge
The Cornwall Record Office
The Syndics of the Fitzwilliam Museum, Cambridge

The illustrations specified are reproduced by courtesy of:

Professor Horace Barlow (Plate 12C)
Birmingham City Archives (Plate 11B)
The British Library (Plate 9)
The Syndics of Cambridge University Library (Plate 4C)
The late Major J. W. Chandos-Pole (Plate 10A)
The Master and Fellows of Darwin College, Cambridge, and the Darwin Family
    Portraits Trust (Plates 2A, 2B, 4A)
The Darwin Family Portraits Trust (Plate 16)
The late Sir Robin Darwin (Plate 1)
English Heritage (Down House), (Plates 7C, 15; Figs 8, 9, 10)
The Institution of Mechanical Engineers (Plate 5C)
Mrs Valerie McMillan (Plate 7A)
The late Dr John Moilliet (Plates 5D, 8B, 12A)
The National Gallery, London (Plate 6B)
John Smith and Co., Derby (Plate 5A)
Dr Rosemary Thomas (Plate 3B)
The Trustees of the Wedgwood Museum, Barlaston (Plates 5B, 7B, 12B)
The Wellcome Trust (Fig. 2)

Index

Figures in **bold type** indicate leading references on a subject. Books and poems (other than Erasmus Darwin's) are indexed under their authors' names. Dates of birth and death (if known) are given for Darwin's contemporaries and a few others. For most Darwin family members, their relationship to Erasmus is given in brackets, their dates being in the family tree on pages 374–5.